THE CITY IN ROMAN AND BYZANTINE EGYPT

THE CITY
IN ROMAN AND
BYZANTINE EGYPT

Richard Alston

London and New York

First published 2002
by Routledge
11 New Fetter Lane, London EC4P 4EE

Simultaneously published in the USA and Canada
by Routledge
29 West 35th Street, New York, NY 10001

Routledge is an imprint of the Taylor & Francis Group

Typeset in Garamond by
Keystroke, Jacaranda Lodge, Wolverhampton
Printed and bound in Great Britain by
The University Press, Cambridge, United Kingdom

British Library Cataloguing in Publication Data
A catalogue record for this book is available from the British Library

Library of Congress Cataloging in Publication Data
Alston, Richard, 1965–
The City in Roman and Byzantine Egypt / Richard Alston.
p. cm.
Includes bibliographical references and index.
1. Cities and towns, Ancient—Egypt.
2. Cities and towns, Ancient—Rome. I. Title.
HT114 .A53 2001
307.76′0932—dc21
2001019245

ISBN 0-415-23701-7

CONTENTS

LIST OF ILLUSTRATIONS

Plate

Figures

LIST OF TABLES

PREFACE

This book has been a long time in gestation. After I finished my doctoral thesis on the Roman army in Egypt in September 1990, I obtained a one-year post at Manchester University. The thesis had been in many ways disappointing. I had hoped that it would allow me to write about cultural change in the early Roman empire and, as it turned out, my main conclusion, and one which others had already reached for other provinces, was that the army was not central to the complex processes of cultural change in the Roman empire. It seemed to me that the interaction between Rome and the province was more fundamental than I had imagined. As the hoped-for permanent post at Manchester evaporated into the general political and financial crisis gripping British academia, I applied to the British Academy and they were generous enough to fund me to work on a project on urbanization and acculturation in Roman Egypt, for which I thank the academy. In three years at King's College London, I laid the foundations for this book.

In 1998, now at Royal Holloway, I was given a sabbatical during which the idea of the book took shape and I started to draft the various chapters. For various reasons, explained in the second chapter, it seemed to me best to avoid any attempt at cataloguing the urban phenomena of Roman and Byzantine Egypt. The result is a discursive analysis which makes no claim to completeness. Even given the size of this book, I have touched on many issues that could not be fully explored and I am sure that I have missed scholarly problems through both ignorance and oversight. Those attempting to use this as a work of reference may find themselves disappointed. Many texts are not discussed, many sites ignored. There is no attempt here to reread any papyrus and I may have missed significant rereadings though I have made every effort to check readings in the standard reference works. This is primarily a historical analysis rather than an archaeological or papyrological study.

I have incurred many debts over the last years. I thank my colleagues at King's College, especially Jane and Dominic, at Royal Holloway, and at University College London, especially John North, Tim Cornell (before and after he departed for Manchester) and Lin Foxhall (who similarly has been a source of support in her new incarnation at Leicester). The staff of the Institute of Classical Studies and Royal Holloway libraries have been unfailingly helpful. Ray Laurence provided much moral support and guided me to particular bodies of comparative literature. Kate Gilliver was a continual source of support (in spite of being profoundly unconvinced by my approach) and has read through and commented on the majority of the manuscript. Charlotte Roueché, Judith Herrin and Averil Cameron encouraged me to look to later periods. Chris Carey has been a tremendous support and has shown a startling faith in me throughout my time at Royal Holloway. Effie Spentzou read a couple of sections when I despaired of making any sense and encouraged me to think critically about my discipline. My brother, Dr Robert Alston, contributed his statistical knowledge and computing skills at various points with great perception and diverted attention from his many projects. He also spent a great deal of time listening to what I needed and interpreting to the numerically illiterate his methods and results, and this in spite of the fact that all in the family mock his arithmetic at every possible opportunity. My greatest debt, though, remains to my children, Sam and Joshua, who enrich my life in countless ways, and to Sara. Sara has also lived with this book for years and read every word. Unfailingly supportive and ever ready to listen to me ramble, it was Sara who brought me to London nearly fifteen years ago and introduced me to the ways of this particular city. Her urban experience informs this book as much as my own.

It was in the spring of 1998 that my mother was diagnosed with cancer. Within ten months, the cancer killed her. Significant parts of this book were drafted at her bedside as she slept, or on the long train journeys to be with her. This book is dedicated to Joan Margaret Alston whose life and memory is a blessing to us.

Acknowledgements

Figure 5.5 is reproduced by kind permission of the Trustees of the British Museum and is © Excavations at el-Ashmunein IV: Hermopolis Magna: Buildings of the Roman Period. 1991. The Trustees of the British Museum, published by British Museum Press.

Plate 3.1 is reproduced by kind permission of the Trustees of the Kelsey Museum, University of Michigan.

Abbreviations

The abbreviations used follow the conventions laid down in John F. Oates, Roger S. Bagnall, William H. Willis, and K.A. Worp (1985) *Checklist of Editions of Greek Papyri and Ostraca* (*BASP* Suppl., 4), Atlanta, or in *L'Année Philologique*.

A note on transliteration and names

In most cases, I have avoided Anglicizing or Latinizing names and have retained Greek versions. I have, however, standardized spellings. When a place or person is generally familiar in a Latin or English form, I have opted for that form. I have also opted to use the Greek suffix 'eion' to represent 'place of' or 'temple of', so that Sarapeion is the temple of Sarapis and Iseion the temple of Isis.

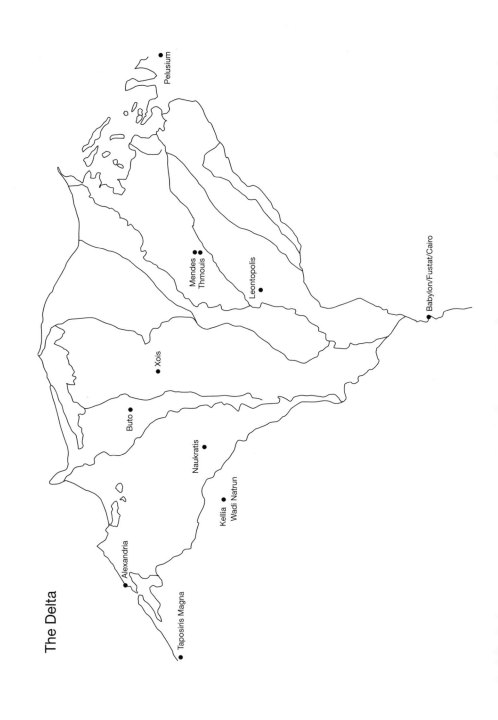

The Delta

Pelusium

Mendes
Thmouis

Leontopolis

Babylon/Fustat/Cairo

Xois

Buto

Naukratis

Kellia
Wadi Natrun

Alexandria

Taposiris Magna

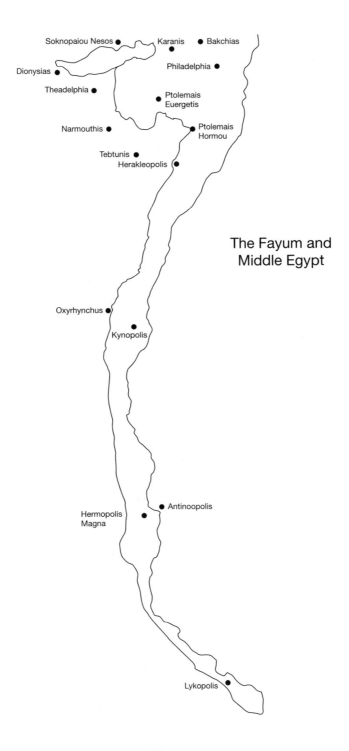

The Fayum and Middle Egypt

Upper Egypt

Aphrodito

Antaiopolis

Panopolis

Qena

Dendera
Koptos

Diospolis Parva

Apollonospolis
Parva

Medinet Habu
Jeme

Karnak

Luxor

Thebes

Southern
Upper Egypt

Latopolis

Hierakonopolis

Apollonospolis Magna
(Edfu)

Kom
Ombo

Syene
(Aswan)

1

INTRODUCTION

This book traces the history of the city in Roman Egypt from the Roman conquest until the fall of the Byzantine empire in the East in the mid-seventh century. During this time Egypt's distinctive urban forms first took on the trappings of the Classical or Roman city and then became Christian. Such transformations can be seen as part of the dynamic that shaped the Roman empire and, as a result, have been extensively studied. Roman Egypt, however, presents us with an opportunity to write a rather different type of urban history than that of other provinces, a history which in many ways bears a closer relationship to that of modern cities. The archaeological record for Egypt is far poorer than that for many other provinces, but Egypt is rich in texts, both literary and documentary, and although the documentary record is often frustratingly partial in that the excavated and published papyri which provide us with the texts have an uneven chronological and topographical distribution, they allow us to begin to reconstruct the social lives of Egyptians to an extent undreamed of elsewhere. We are not, therefore, limited to a history of the public faces of cities, their monuments, their inscriptions, the writings of their elites, but can begin to understand what the transformations of the city meant for ordinary people and to uncover the forces that shaped the everyday lives of residents of the cities of Roman and Byzantine Egypt.

My history starts in 30 BC, an important moment in the political history of Egypt, with the annexation of Egypt by Octavian, who was about to become Augustus. It is not, of course, an end or a beginning for urbanism within Egypt, which has a history stretching back millennia before the Roman conquest, and most of the cities with which I concern myself were ancient, established settlements in 30 BC. Nor did 30 BC mark a significant assault on Egypt's traditions. Egypt had been subjected to Persian rule for long periods after 525 BC and Greek rule since Alexander's conquest, with perhaps the latter period leaving a deeper mark on traditional culture. Nevertheless, the Roman annexation did not just mean a new foreign ruler, but brought sweeping changes to Egyptian society. The Romans established a hierarchy of settlements within the province. At the top of the hierarchy were 'Greek' cities such as Alexandria. On the next rung were the *metropoleis* of the *chora*. These were the local capitals of administrative regions known as nomes. The nomes themselves had their origins in Pharaonic administration and many of the *metropoleis* appear to have acted as nome capitals before the Roman annexation. Nevertheless, the Romans enhanced their status in relation to the third level of settlements, the villages. This settlement hierarchy corresponded to a system of social orders that appears to have been entirely new. Alexandrians, citizens of the 'Greek' cities, and Romans were at the top of the social pyramid and the rest were classified as Egyptians. The Egyptians were divided into two groups, the metropolites and the villagers, and the metropolites were further subdivided into 'those from the gymnasium' and the others. These distinctions were marked by the poll tax, which was levied at differential rates on the adult male population. Although there are complications (such as the exemption of certain priests of the traditional Egyptian temples), the Alexandrians and Romans were exempted from poll tax, the metropolites paid the tax at a reduced rate, and the villagers paid the full levy. This tax was essentially new and marked the imposition of a new political and fiscal system on Egypt. Since the new status groups had differing tax liabilities, the Romans introduced procedures for ascertaining status. Boys who reached fourteen applied for metropolite and gymnasial status and underwent a status-examination known as an *epikrisis*. The form of the examination differed slightly from place to place and between those from the gymnasium and ordinary metropolites, but the documentation submitted established status by descent in both male and female lines.

This is an unconventional urban history and one which looks to methodologies and ways of thinking that may be foreign to many ancient historians. My reading has taken me far from Egypt (and indeed ancient history) into social theory, modern history, human geography and developmental economics, and although I have only skimmed the surface of these intricate and separate disciplines, I hope that those who work in those fields will find something of interest here as well. I have tried to be explicit about where my ideas have come from and to question my assumptions about urban life. The result is that many sections of this book are discursive and follow my search for inspiration away from the strict confines of my subject. I tend to the belief that history should be self-critical and explore as fully as possible the interaction of the historian's assumptions and epistemology with the primary material and thereby allow the reader to question the author and to take a critical approach. I seek to be honest and explicit about my sources of understanding, though, inevitably, others will see further into the weaknesses of my approach than I possibly can. Such candour though, has increased the scale of this book, and that is a matter of some shame. Even so, I am sure that this exploration will disappoint some because of its incomplete nature. Indeed, it was never meant to be a complete history of all the urban settlements of Egypt in this period. There are many cities I do not discuss and I am sure I will have missed or misread important texts and failed to read literary sources or archaeological reports which might have significantly altered this book. There are no new readings of papyri here and I have relied on the published versions of texts without seeking out, as I know a good historian would, photographs of originals in order to check readings. My lack of skill and the sheer number of texts compel this methodological weakness. Nevertheless, I do not believe that my interpretations depend on particular readings of single texts but on a great mass of data, and so I hope that any errors are minor.

This book operates with rather loose chronological descriptions. After some thought, I have chosen to maintain these rather than opt for the altogether artificial precision of centuries. The Roman period covers the years 30 BC– c. AD 200, the late Roman period from c. AD 200 to c. 350 and the Byzantine period from c. 350 to c. 640. This history does not, however, follow a chronological pattern but is constructed around the spatial divisions of the city. There are adequate reasons for doing this which will be explained in the rather long chapter that follows. In each of the subsequent chapters, I take a space, the house, the street, the city and the region, and explore change over time in that space; and, I hope, gradually, perhaps too gradually, a complete picture of the diverse and multifaceted cities of Roman and Byzantine Egypt dimly emerges.

2

CITIES AND SPACE

Introduction: cities, countryside and culture

The ancient city, by which I mean the cities of Greece and the Roman empire, provides English with whole series of value-laden terms, normally carrying positive connotations: 'politic', 'politics', 'urbane', 'civil', 'civilization' and 'citizen'. Obviously, there is something of the medieval and the modern city within these words; they are not completely divorced from their more recent associations, but their Latin and Greek etymologies carry with them a hint of the Classical and the prioritization of the urban in that culture. The link between civilization and Classical or other urbanisms is deeply rooted within Western culture and so pervasive that many writers have been encouraged to subvert contemporary political and urban cultures by comparison with alternative rural worlds. Pastoral, resting on an evaluation of an often fictionalized, mythologized, past ruralism, habitually expresses a disquiet about contemporary life, a disquiet which normally centres on the city (Williams 1973). Cities can provide examples of all human virtues and vices and this behavioural richness makes cities both attractive and dangerous, generating in the literature of many periods an ambivalent view of urbanism, so that the city is often depicted as dysfunctional or terroristic or authoritarian, representing in different ways concerns about the uncontrollability of urban masses and the criminality of putative underworlds. In English literature, the pastoral tradition can be pushed back with reasonable confidence to the seventeenth century, though there are echoes of the distinctive themes of pastoral even earlier. Yet it was the industrial revolution, the economic backbone of modernism, which produced an urban civilization and those showing disquiet about this process almost inevitably turned to pastoral. Pastoral is, however, a modern reinvention of a Classical tradition stretching back at least to Theocritus in the third century BC. The pastoral of antiquity is no more of an unvarnished portrait of contemporary rural life than modern pastoral. It is the poetic equivalent of the monkish flight to the desert to escape the concerns of the world; the sophisticated writers of Greece and Rome, like their modern counterparts, found their sanctuary in imagined rural landscapes.

The Classical world was, like the modern world, 'a world of cities' (Finley 1977; Tomlinson 1992: xi; Owens 1991: 1–3), though the phrase has become a cliché, at once meaningful and meaningless. Whereas modern civilization may be described as urban because of the concentration of population in urban settlements, only a minority (estimates vary wildly) of the ancient population lived in cities. In terms of population, the ancient world was a world of villages, small towns and isolated farms. Yet these rural areas, it is argued, were bound to the city through political, economic, cultural and social networks of varying levels of intensity. It is these networks which make the 'world of cities' a meaningful cliché. The culture of antiquity is topographically concentrated in the city and this concentration allowed poets and others to express their uncertainties and discomfort through pastoral.

The cultural centrality of the ancient city in modern and at least some ancient perceptions of Classical civilization raises certain difficulties for the historian of urbanism. The study of ancient urbanism is not a separate field, a subdiscipline, within that broadly and poorly defined area of study that we now call Classics, but is the mainstay of the discipline. So closely is Classics associated with the city that its chronological parameters are set by the history of urban settlements. Classics begins with Homer, the proto-history of the Greek *poleis*, and concludes with the decline of urbanism in the West at some point just before or after the fifth-century barbarian invasions and in the East either just before or after the seventh-century Arab invasions. Indeed, the fierce contestation of urban history in the late antique period is partly a result of the academic boundary wars fought within and between disciplines. The reception of the ancient city is, therefore, inevitably caught up with the reception and use of Classics in the modern age and reactions to the ancient city parallel reactions to Classical culture.

Viewing the ancient past

Most of this chapter is concerned with a search for a theory, a way of seeing and making sense of the city. In so doing, I consider, among other things, the place and function of history, the status of historical facts and the nature of academic discourse. I regard this as a key chapter since I hope that this theoretical perspective works to enrich and make sense of the diverse and complex material presented in the later chapters. Nevertheless, many would question the need to devote so many pages to this theorizing. Richard Evans's (1997: 253) attack on aspects of post-modernism concludes by arguing that if one is only 'very scrupulous and careful and self-critical', one can 'find out how it [the past] happened and reach some tenable, though always less than final conclusions about what it all meant'. In Evans's view, there is no need for theory, just good scholarly research. Such an approach has much to recommend it and has been and probably still is the dominant theoretical approach to understanding the past, ancient, medieval or modern, and it is far from self-evident why, given our ability to respond to many aspects of Classical culture (such as the pastoral) and the professional immersion of ancient historians in their sources, the revised positivist empiricism of Evans, with its emphasis on a careful, self-critical empathy, should not work.

There has been a tension in Classical scholarship between those who perceived a considerable distance between themselves and the Classical world and those for whom antiquity spoke directly to their contemporary concerns. The Renaissance saw a widespread desire to emulate the achievements of antiquity on the part of politicians, scholars and artists (Momigliano 1947), and popes like Julius II and Alexander VI (with his Classically named son) could dream of emulating their namesakes. The distance between the contemporary and the past was, for them, slight. That distance became greater in the seventeenth and eighteenth centuries and it is these centuries that see the rise of the Classical scholar whose *raison d'être* was to guide people across the cultural gulf that separated them from antiquity. The Grand Tour brought prosperous aristocrats from northern Europe to Italy to experience the Classical past and by the eighteenth century, the first modern excavations at Pompeii and Herculaneum provided a secondary focus to Rome.[1] But although the tourists could familiarize themselves with Rome through the literary sources, the material culture and especially the remains of Pompeii and Herculaneum presented rather different problems. Such monuments needed reconstruction and evaluation to make them comprehensible and this needed expertise. The first scholars were antiquaries, more intent on accumulating information than on imaginative reconstructions of the past, though, since only the simplest of reconstructions are technical, reconstruction merged into interpretation (Momigliano 1950; Beard and Henderson 1995: 1–6).

Potts (1994: 36–7) argues that Winckelmann, whose systematic history of Classical art (1764) effectively founded modern art history, found a way of writing the general history of a period by deploying the concept of the *zeitgeist*, an energy infusing an age, and thereby took a major step in conceptualizing and differentiating the history of the Classical world. This differentiation of antique and modern became more marked in the reception of Greek antiquity. The politics of the Balkans had meant that Greece was effectively out of bounds to the Grand Tourist, but an easing of the political situation and, perhaps, a renewed emphasis on Greek culture drew North Europeans to Greece. Greece had some of the exoticism of the Orient and carried with it the promise of spiritual, sexual, physical and intellectual danger. The liberal thinkers of the eighteenth and nineteenth centuries could experience antiquity, run naked across beaches and dabble in the politics of revolution in the comparative safety of a distant land, but the 'otherness' of Greece, with its promise of a personal fulfilment denied to so many western and northern Europeans, contributed to the popularity of Classical culture and the turning of Greece into a different space, and the enacting of (wild) fantasies within Greece fundamentally altered the contemporary response to antiquity. Stuart and Revett's visit to Greece caused an architectural sensation in late eighteenth-century England. The taste and elegance of 'authentic' Classical architecture was transmitted to England and Classicism became the mark of the distinction of a patron and his house (Jenkyns 1980: 1–11). Classicism was a badge of status and learning but it also functioned a little like pastoral, and although Lord Byron's antics may have been romantic, they were consistent with the Romantic rejection of much of the modern.

Inevitably, some, such as Ruskin, stepped away from the Classical ideal, searching for some inspiration in later, more devotional architecture and art. Utilitarians questioned the purpose of Classics. New scientific discoveries threatened the hegemony of Classical science. New geographic discoveries broadened geographical perspectives. Most importantly, Christianity, the dominant moral and intellectual force in the West, could not easily be reconciled with Classicism, in spite of the best efforts of Victorian editors (Jenkyns 1980: 67–73; 148–54; Dover 1976).[2] The attack on the supremacy of Latin and Greek was underway in pre-revolutionary America as early as 1768. Nevertheless, the Classical world proved an extraordinarily flexible and powerful paradigm, providing inspiration for political revolutionaries in America and France (Rheinhold 1984: 36–7; 97–104; Richard 1994) and fuel for conservatives who sought to resist or abhor democratic movements (Cromer 1910: 8–9) or the rise of new social groups (see Ste Croix 1981: 41–2; Badian 1972; Brunt 1965; Jenkyns 1980: 48), or feared the erosion of the civilized in Africa or even in the darker corners of the inner cities (Haverfield 1916; Patlagean 1976; Said 1993).[3]

From the early nineteenth century to the present day, Classics has had to compete and justify itself in a world self-consciously different from the Classical past by arguing either that we are very similar to the ancients and thus we are studying ourselves in a rather peculiar context (Livingstone 1916), or that they differed from us in certain respects and by studying the similarities and differences we can understand our culture better (Cromer 1910; Bryce 1914), or that we are very different from them but studying their culture helps us reflect on our culture (Fustel de Coulanges 1980 [1864]; Murray 1990), or that we are very different from the ancients but they are part of our heritage, the roots from which our civilization is sprung, and thus we should study the heritage that is Classics (Beard and Henderson 1995; Grant 1991; Griffin 1986; Mackail 1925: 3–4; 219). For many, antiquity, in spite of the manifest differences, continued and continues to speak directly to modern sensibilities and to have a particular and peculiar resonance and value in our culture (Rheinhold 1984: 36–7).[4]

A good test-case of the uneasy parallelisms between contemporary nineteenth- and early twentieth-century life and Classical culture is imperialism. Few saw the British and Roman empires as equivalents (Haverfield 1916) and it was generally accepted that there were crucial differences.[5] Yet, Cromer was able to write

The world has not so very much changed in 2,000 years. Whenever, for instance, I read the graphic account in the Acts of the Apostles of how the Chief Captain, after he had scourged St Paul, was afraid when his very intelligent subordinate whispered to him that his victim was a citizen of Rome, I think I see before me the anxious governor of some Egyptian province in pre-reforming days.

(Cromer 1910: 3)

Francis Haverfield, who has some claim to be the first modern professor of ancient history in Britain and who was responsible for the modernization of British ancient history and a revolution in Romano-British studies (Freeman 1997; MacDonald 1924), produced a very influential account of the relationship between modern and ancient imperialism. Haverfield was keenly aware of the differences between Rome and Britain and yet the paradigm of the British empire was always present, informing his analysis. He saw in the administrators of Rome parallels with the cultured men sent out from his university to administer the empire (Haverfield 1912: 10–12; 1923: 23; 1916). Haverfield's (1916) claim that ancient history ended in 1815 (a rather unusual date to choose) reflects a conception of his distance from the Classical past, yet the relationship between present and past remained close. Many who have followed, British, French and Italian, have used the paradigms of the European colonial empires, sometimes consciously, and much of the current debate on Roman imperialism is infused with the ideologies of colonialism and post-colonialism (Alston 1996; Freeman 1996; 1997; Mattingly 1996; 1997b; Hingley 1996). Most scholars are aware of differences of varying degrees of importance between ancient and modern and much energy is spent on elucidating these differences, yet that distance seems bridgeable without great difficulty. The texts are not approached as if they come from some radically different culture but as if there is a transposability between modern and ancient experience.

This sense of a shared experience has much in common with contemporary historical methodologies which, both in Britain and on the continent, were hostile to theoretical discussions. Historians collected empirical data, assessed that data and turned it into narrative using a methodology little more complex than common sense and instinct (Elton 1967). There was no perceived need to develop a body of theory to overcome the differences between the past and the present. There was, however, another tradition, particularly prominent in German Classics. Fustel de Coulanges, first published in 1864, wrote

We shall attempt to set in a clear light the radical and essential differences which at all times distinguished . . . ancient peoples from modern societies. In our system of education, we live from infancy in the midst of the Greeks and Romans and become accustomed continually to compare them with ourselves, to judge their history by our own, and to explain our revolutions by theirs. What we have received from them leads us to believe that we resemble them. We have some difficulty in considering them as foreign nations, it is almost always ourselves that we see in them. Hence spring many errors.

(Fustel de Coulanges 1980: 3)

This thesis argued for the radical difference of ancient and modern societies and that understanding of an ancient society required reconstructing that society from its most fundamental elements (in this case family and religious groups). Fustel's work influenced the development of social sciences, through Durkheim and others, and the emerging grand theorists, such as Max Weber (who wrote extensively on the ancient city) and Marx.

Despite the immense importance of these theories in the history of the twentieth century, both were for a long time largely ignored by historians and Classicists within the empiricist tradition. One need not doubt the political motivation behind such hostility, but there was also a professional pride. Crude attempts to simplify the complexities that historians revelled in and doctrinaire Marxist interpretations certainly weakened interest in general theory. I suspect also that many Classicists were simply not interested in the kinds of issues that were central to much sociological thought. In the 1960s, social theory came back into vogue, partly because of a perceived need for self-justification in an increasingly technologically advanced environment and partly in response to the institutional and academic threat posed by sociology. E.H. Carr's (1961) hugely influential *What is History?* attacked the empiricist tradition and argued that all history is history of society (sociology) and that historians ought to consider 'society' more directly. Carr's plea was for an expansion of the historiography of the middle years of the twentieth century away from narrowly political concerns to encompass the holistic ideas of certain nineteenth-century historical thinkers, ideas which were central to contemporary politics. In ancient history, Carr's message was taken up by Moses Finley.

Finley's originality lay in his mastery of rhetoric, a combative (even exhilarating) style, and an intellectual range far broader than was common among Anglo-American Classicists (Finley 1981: ix–xxvi). He revived Weber and the sociological approach (though Momigliano, his contemporary, was also interested in such theories). Instead of using empiricist 'common sense' approaches which tended to interpret ancient evidence through modernizing eyes, he provided a methodology by which ancient historians could reconstruct ancient society from theoretical principles (Finley 1985a; 1985b). In so doing, he encouraged historians to look at the ancient world as a system, a holistic approach which was, of course, common to much of sociology and economic theory, and was able to reduce the complexity of ancient society and the multifaceted source material to produce a comprehensible model for the workings of ancient society. For Finley (1977), the ancient world exhibited certain characteristics which differentiated antiquity from both earlier and especially later historical periods and Finley emphasized aspects of ancient

9

societies which (he claimed) changed but little: the ideology or cultural values of the elite, technology, slavery, the concentration of political authority in the hands of an urban elite. Such elements formed a substructure and the great political dramas of conventional ancient history were relegated to the superstructure, relatively irrelevant in determining the nature of ancient society. The emphasis on structures, especially underlying structures, placed Finley in opposition to the empiricist tradition. The piling up of facts was of no purpose unless it elucidated the structures of society and writers had to engage with these essential problems. Finley (in common with many others) argued that empiricist writers carry their socio-economic assumptions across from the modern world to the ancient. His assault on Peter Fraser's (1972) magisterial empiricist volumes on Ptolemaic Alexandria argued that after several hundred pages, the reader still had little idea about the economic and social life of Ptolemaic Alexandria (Finley 1985b: 47–66, esp. 61–6), the fundamentals of a proper understanding of the city.

Finley's own consideration of ancient society revived and refurbished Weber's idea of a consumer city (Finley 1977; 1985a: 123–49) an idea based on several fundamental assumptions, crudely summarized below:

- The city (the location of political and cultural life), not their country estates, was the main home of the political and economic elite.
- The ancient city was mainly run by a group of rich, landed aristocrats rather than by industrial or commercial concerns, either individual or collective.
- Urban populations either were mainly composed of aristocrats and their households or were supported by supplying the needs of those households.
- Trade and industry were minor factors in the ancient economy.

Finley's ancient city differed radically in economy, politics and culture from the modern city. It was a distinct and historically unique social formation. Far from operating like a medieval or modern city, it was radically different from its more modern ancestors.

Ancient historians have adopted three positions on Finley: he is right, he is mostly right but we need to make some adjustment, or he is completely wrong. Attention has been focused on his model of the economic role of the city, and the debate has been vigorous, but has not been broadened to consider the implications of Finley for our general understanding of the culture of the city.[6] Changes in urban form and architectural style can be dismissed as irrelevant to these debates, representing shifts in fashion (the superstructures of society), not in the substructures or essential ideology, but although one might agree that ancient cities showed certain common characteristics, it is a radical step to ignore the manifold differences between ancient cities in the period from the foundation of the Greek *poleis* to the fall of Rome or to reduce the manifest diversity of urban forms to a single model. Such reductionism responds to the teleological needs of Finley's historical theory, which was to set the ancient world in the context of the stages of world history. The function of the typology is not to explain what life was like and how life was shaped in ancient cities but to compare those ancient cities with medieval and modern cities and to understand further the dynamics of human development. Finley's reductionist method is deployed to certain very specific and limited purposes in the elucidation of his historical theory. Yet for those interested in the 'changes in fashion', in historical developments within the Classical period, or who reject the Finleyite theory, his method offers little, beyond a warning about using overly modernizing vocabulary and encouragement to think about the basic material and intellectual structures of ancient society (Alston 1997c). As, for complex reasons to be discussed below, the teleological assumptions with which Finley engaged have become less popular (and are certainly not a main theme of this analysis), so the debates about the consumer city have become marginal.

Although Finley's methodology has been taken up by many others of various ideological persuasions (Marxists, neo-Marxists, Weberians, etc.) his closest ideological alignment appears to be with the *Annales* school, developed mainly in French historiography. The emphasis placed by Braudel (1972; 1981; 1982; 1984) and his followers on the continuities of 'deep structures', the rhythms of economic and cultural interaction across the Mediterranean, changing and developing only slowly, is essentially similar to the structural stability of Finley's model.[7] Although one might not agree with Finley's theory, the suggestion that the rhythms of change in antiquity were dependent on deep-set and fundamental structures, obviously reflected in our sources but never discussed or really perceived by the ancients themselves, further devalues the empathetic approach, because empathy with any individual or group of individuals does not bring social understanding since they themselves only had a partial under-standing of their society. Whatever the ultimate judgement, those who argue for a theorized approach would seem to have a case that needs considering.

It seems to me that, attractive though the positivist, empiricist approach may be, the distance between ourselves and antiquity is great and that although in imagination that distance can be crossed and antiquity does, for me at least, have a different resonance than the ancient cultures of China or Meso-America, I cannot simply read all the information available concerning the cities of Egypt and dream my way back to them, as perhaps Cromer could; but also, even if I could, I have no faith in my imagination not to transpose many of my modern preconceptions to antiquity. Second, it is obvious to me that many do not share my perceptions of the modern world, that there is no single, obvious, shared understanding of the workings of the world, that my view of the modern world is not necessarily inherently the right view, and that complex theories are necessary to make sense of the culture we live in. Sociology did not develop to make sense of the past, but of the present, about which we are infinitely better informed and in which we live. Since I do not think that positivist empiricism is enough to understand the modern world, then it follows that we need theory to understand other worlds.

11

In what follows, I am not looking necessarily for a single holistic grand scheme which will explain everything (which would make life simpler), though such theories will be discussed, but for guidance in how to write about the ancient city: whether I should concentrate on architectural design, the urban morphology (the layout of the city), economic structures, administrative systems, or individual experiences (so far as these can be reconstructed). Many writers have derived meaning from the diversity and confusion of cities but have used a bewildering variety of approaches, and this is a profoundly contested area. Nevertheless, even with its twists and turns, this primrose path on which I embark does, I believe, lead not to an everlasting bonfire, but to a coherent and defensible approach.

Writing the city: ancient cities, modern geographies

It is startlingly obvious that when ancient writers wrote 'urbs' or πόλις they meant something rather different from our conception of 'city'. Nevertheless, this difference requires elaboration: how is the ancient city different? Even the busiest of tourist sites, such as Pompeii, is a very different experience from the modern city. The technology of urbanism has been transformed. Most of our cities are filled with the smog of cars and lorries and the streets have been reshaped to provide them with access and to increase the rapidity with which they can cross urban space. Cars render the environment hostile, often marginalizing the pedestrians and certainly confining them to narrow strips alongside the main thoroughfares. Yet, they allow an ease of movement into and through the city, not just for individuals but also for businesses and other institutions. The commercial framework of modern cities is dependent on the internal combustion engine, and the urban form and experience is shaped by that dependency. There are other obvious differences: language, religion, public authority, the distribution of 'essential facilities' (power, water), the layout of houses, the relationships of buildings to streets, the sources of entertainment, etc. Nevertheless, we can, as visitors to the site, imagine Pompeii as a city. We see pavements and traces of traffic. We see shops and streets. We see houses and municipal buildings. We can see the bustle of the ancient city. Whether our imaginations produce an accurate image of that city is another question, but the city is comprehensible in our terms as a human settlement. It is not the difference that is so seductive about Pompeii, and many other Classical sites, but its familiar morphology so that we can understand it (rightly or wrongly) as a city. As with the textual experience of ancient society, the 'Pompeii experience' seduces even the most wary. There are differences which can be glossed, ignored not translated, but the process of transposition into our world seems transparent: the stones show us, perhaps through a clouded glass, the nature of the ancient city; we need only to bare our sensitivities to understand. In so doing, the difference of ancient urbanism is elided, an elision that makes the ancient city useful to modern polemicists of various persuasions.[8]

12

One of the most interesting and complex examples of this reuse of the Classical tradition is Lewis Mumford's (1991 [1961]) magnificent polemical account of urbanism through the ages. For Mumford, an understanding of the processes and morphologies of historical urbanisms frees us from the limitations imposed by current urban morphologies, shifting our focus from the de-humanizing characteristics of modern urbanism by embracing the human scale of some ancient cities. The relationship of history and architecture is complex for Mumford in that he had a deep regard for the historically specific within urbanism and the linkage between social and cultural forms and urban morphology,[9] yet the premise of his work is essentially that urban forms are ahistorical in that they can be transposed to a modern context. For Mumford, the ideal of urbanism was reached in Classical Greece (somewhat modified by an acceptance that standards of sanitation were not high), a view many would still broadly accept (Murray 1990). This idealization of Greek (or more specifically Athenian) urbanism rests on a view that Athens represented an integration of citizen and city: the city was the citizens and represented them. It was a city on a human scale which celebrated the community, a triumph of urbanism that was represented in the cultural efflorescence of Classical Athens. Rome (Mumford 1991: 248–77), by contrast, was not the city of culture embodied by Athens, instead it was a necropolis: a city of death. The vastness of Rome overwhelmed the individual and the values of Classical urbanism which were replaced by materialism. 'Rome', writes Mumford (1991 [1961]: 275), 'remains, in its vastness and confusion, the complete embodiment of purposeless materialism': a soulless urban disaster with poor sanitation, high mortality and weak social and political control.

Other treatments of Rome have also approached the subject with a modern eye. Scobie (1986) treated Rome as a nightmare city of slums and smells, thieves and dangerous bustle. In an earlier generation, Carcopino (1941: 13–64) sang of monumental Rome's brilliance (with obvious contemporary reference points), which he contrasted with the more difficult problems of private housing, street order and sanitation, which the Roman authorities tackled boldly, if not always with great success. With Mumford, Carcopino and Scobie, there is an acknowledgement of difference, yet an acceptance that we can reconstruct the ancient experience of the city and transpose modern ways of understanding the environment onto the ancient city. The contrast drawn between public monumentality and private squalor is a kind of back-street versus front-street dichotomy beloved of historians of modern urbanism (Stambaugh 1988: 51). This is not necessarily wrong, though it is not a feature of Strabo's description of the city (V 3.7–8) and Ammianus' much later description of the glories of Rome (XIV 6 12–25) contrasts rather the vacuity and moral laxity of the Roman aristocracy with the glories of the city, though it does mention the poverty and debauchery of the lower orders (XIV 6 25).[10]

Haverfield (1910) was characteristically more cautious and more interesting than many in his discussion of ancient town planning. He spoke to the Town

Planning Conference in October 1910, as town planning was emerging as a serious issue, and although his talk takes a cautious line on the utility of modern town planners looking for inspiration to their Roman predecessors, he suggests that the Romans' systematic approach to urban development was of great value, a ringing endorsement of the town planners' objective of large-scale design. Three years later, Haverfield's argument was more complex. In a survey of ancient urban morphology, Haverfield (1913: 14–47) argued that town planning improved the lot of the inhabitants of the city but was also the mark of civilization: orthogonal streets were symbolic of ordered societies, though the logic of this escapes me.

The assumption of the transparency of the ancient urban experience and the transposition of ancient and modern urbanism often goes almost unnoticed. Favro's (1995) attempt to bring to life the monuments of Augustan Rome by imagining two walks through the city, one during the late Republic and the other by the same man in the latter years of the reign of Augustus, tries to interpret the urban experience and give meaning to the urban form. Her method is more courageous and open, but essentially similar to that of many others. There is no attempt to reconstruct the mentality of those walking through the city or to consider how that might be shaped by the political and moral concerns of the antique mind, rather than the aesthetic and historical knowledge of the modern viewer.

The late twentieth-century fascination with the manipulation of images and representation of status (so prominent in Western political life) has its counterpart in the study of the ancient city. Most obviously, this has been reflected in an increased interest in the way that emperors manipulated their public images through art and architecture (Zanker 1988; Elsner and Masters 1994; Boatwright 1987; Darwall-Smith 1996; Wallace-Hadrill 1993; Patterson 1992a). The large-scale construction projects that the emperors undertook and the ways in which they actively sought to manipulate their public images offer parallels with modern states and, most resonantly, with fascist building projects in the 1930s (Quartermaine 1995). Historians, with the help of those trained in art history, have become expert in extracting meaning from pictorial and especially architectural icons and turning the art and architecture of the period into a meaningful discourse. Monuments have become artefacts to be 'read', translated from the fragments of archaeology that survive, as Classicists have for centuries struggled to knit together their damaged and fragmentary manuscripts to recreate the literature of the ancients. This historiographical development, the political dominance of image-makers in Western politics, and post-structuralist concerns with spatiality and 'image' (and especially the fluidity of meanings within imagery) make a fascinating conjunction.

As political historians (defined rather broadly) have looked to public monuments, so social historians have been drawn to the houses of the ancients, and here Pompeii has figured significantly in discussions (Dwyer 1991; Laurence and Wallace-Hadrill 1997; Wallace-Hadrill 1994; 1988; Allison 1997a; 1997b; Knights 1994). The very completeness of the city (though, as most admit, an illusory completeness) encourages hopes of a partial reconstruction of how the Romans lived in their houses and used their buildings as backdrops to social interaction (Wallace-Hadrill 1994). For the Roman aristocratic house, perhaps more than houses in some other cultures, was the stage for much of the drama of Roman society. The *atrium* is seen as a zone of interaction where the Roman elite met its clients (Wallace-Hadrill 1988, though see Allison 1997a), reinforced social relationships and played out the minor dramas of social interaction that laid the scenes for the greater dramas to be enacted in the formally public spaces of the city (Laurence 1994: 122–32). The house has been brought to the forefront of Roman social relations, providing a spatial context into which our texts can be placed, read and understood (see chapter 3 for an extended discussion of these themes). This does not mean to say that there are no disagreements. The Roman house is a contested space. There are disagreements as to methods of interpretation, whether we should use texts and how we should use them, the roles of decoration, of artefacts found within the house, and of architecture in determining social interaction, the transferability of architectural and sociological perceptions from house to house, from site to site, and the population and function of space within the house (see the essays in Laurence and Wallace-Hadrill 1997). But the importance of the house is accepted and this perception is shared not just by those working on domestic architecture: the house seems an ideal example of social history in action.

Classicists' interest in the house has much in common with developments in other disciplines. As a casual visitor, I have enjoyed the delights of Dutch, Danish, Scottish and various English houses preserved in museums. Such collections are not just for students of architecture, or the slightly crazed historian, but were filled with tourists and local residents out on Sunday jaunts. Some of these museums recreate a whole site, with all its multifarious activities, while others collect a hotch-potch of houses from different regions, of different architectural styles and different functions: houses which could never be side by side in 'reality', forming a conglomeration that has no 'natural' rationale. Yet, as at Pompeii, the visitors who flock to these museums (unless one wishes to insinuate that such activity fills a temporal rather than a cultural need) must come because they can or believe they can derive some understanding of these buildings and the people who lived in them. Almost more than any other artefact, houses have a resonance for moderns that seems to allow us a window into the past.

In the hands of professionals, especially when armed with additional knowledge and material drawn from the culture external to the house, the house can be packed with meaning and the greatest descriptions become hymns to the house, replaying and reflecting the cultural values of the occupants. Clive Knights, writing on the Roman house, breaks away from historical methodologies since

authentic understanding . . . is never a matter of historical reconstruction, fact upon fact, event after event, piecing together information; it is matter of revelation by interpretation . . . The Pompeian
house . . . is an embodiment of Roman culture; it is a conglomeration
of symbols arranged in a way that testifies to a sense of belonging. Its
symbolic organization is rooted with a great degree of complexity to
its wider field of reference, the city . . ., the Empire, and on to the
cosmos.

(Knights 1994: 114)

The cosmos infuses Knights's Pompeian house. The gods appear not only in the
religious contexts such as the domestic altar and family and household
celebrations, but permeate every aspect of life, every corner of the Roman
consciousness in an 'unrelenting manner'. The entry through the long, dark
fauces into the *atrium*, which was lit from the *tablinum* and through the
impluviate roof, was a ritualized crossing of boundaries, a penetration of the
domestic world in which light and dark, order and chaos were contrasted and
ritualized through Janus, god of entrances, and Vesta, goddess of the hearth
and symbol of the *familia*. The *familia* past and present is represented through
the family deities, the *lares*, with their connection to the underworld, the world
of the dead that is ever-present. Still further Knights's house resonates, since
the regular pattern of *fauces*, *atrium*, *tablinum*, *peristyle*, speaks to him of the order
of the planned Roman city, laid out in accordance with the demands of the gods
as reflected in the plans of the surveyors. The wall-paintings reflect the world
of myth with impossible vistas, stocked with the legendary and the divine, but
also the external world, with landscapes realistic and mythic. At the centre
stands the *pater*, the man of the house. Knights's house is a world in itself.

The poetry of architecture appears more famously in Bourdieu (1977: 90–1)
and, even in translation, is moving and evocative, capturing the reader through
its plain and descriptive language:

> The interior of the Kabyle house, rectangular in shape, is divided into
> two parts by a low wall: the larger of these two parts, slightly higher
> than the other, is reserved for human use; the other side, occupied by
> the animals, has a loft above it. A door with two wings gives access to
> both rooms. In the upper part is the hearth and, facing the door, the
> weaving loom.

Off our guard and seduced by the plainness of speaking, by the shortness of
sentences, we are not ready for the declaration of meaning:

> The lower, dark, nocturnal part of the house, the place of damp, green
> or raw objects – water jars set on the benches on either side of the
> entrance to the stable or against the 'wall of darkness', wood, green

fodder – the place too of natural beings – oxen and cows, donkeys and mules – and natural activities – sleep, sex, birth – and also of death, is opposed to the high, light-filled, noble place of humans and in particular of the guest, fire and fire-made objects, the lamp, kitchen utensils, the rifle – the attribute of the manly point of honour (*nif*) which protects female honour (*hurma*) – the loom, the symbol of all protection, the place also of the two specifically cultural activities performed within the house, cooking and weaving.

And so we are subjected to a monster, rolling sentence, disorientating us, confusing us with clause on clause and drawing us in and, almost before we know it, we are experiencing Bourdieu's Kabyle house. This is perhaps meant to reconstruct the voyage of discovery as we enter an unfamiliar environment. We first notice simple things, the major architectural features, the walls the internal arrangement of light and dark, the fire grabbing attention with its perpetual motion and promise. Then, we begin to see other things: the association of the dark side with water, with the 'earthier' elements of life. But Bourdieu continues his description with further dichotomies. Fertility heads to the dark end of the house, as does sickness. The guest sits next to the loom. Male and female are differentiated and the house is set in a wider context: representing polarities of inside and outside, male and female, sun and moon. Boundaries of gender and cosmology, humanity and (re)production are all represented in the house.

Let us add a third description, this time autobiographical, from an industrial town in northern England.

The house stood on a cobbled street on which there were a few cars, mostly old saloon cars, rather battered and some obviously incapable of movement. Children played on the street, normally at the end furthest from a tarmacked road. The tarmac designated the space of cars, dangerous space which the little children were forbidden to enter, though they sometimes did. The small end-of-row terrace house was in the best position on the street with only one shared side, but was otherwise identical to its neighbours. It had two entrances: the rear was from a cobbled alley, through a tall, wooden gate which led into a back-yard with various outbuildings, including a disused lavatory and a coal bunker (also disused). Access from the yard to the house was through a painted, wooden, unnumbered door. This was the family entrance. At the front of the house, was a small iron ornamental gate, about three feet high and a wall of similar height, enough to keep out small children and deter dogs. The door, set to the right of the house (the neighbour being to the left), was numbered and had a letter-box. It was painted and wooden, heavier and better-made than its rear partner. The door gave entrance onto a narrow passageway, the 'hall'. To the left was the 'sitting-room' in which the furniture was of good quality, the floor was carpeted and fabric curtains stood by a large window which looked out onto the street. There were trinkets on shelves, mementoes of holidays, photographs. The gas fire in the grate filled the space that had been occupied by the coal fire of which there was now little obvious reminder. There was no table in the room. We return to the passage. At the end of the passage was a door leading to a large room. As one entered that room, one met a staircase to the left, very dark, narrow, steep and uneven, leading up to bedrooms and the bathroom. The room itself was very plainly furnished: an old table and chairs and a rather battered sofa. Along the back wall was a series of cupboards made of very cheap wood, painted. There was a sink and a cooker (gas). Next to the cooker was the door leading to the backyard. This was the family room, the room of eating and living, where the children played and where the woman of the house cooked and washed and worked. Upstairs, one emerged from the boxed-in staircase to an even darker hall. To the right was a tiny bathroom. There were two further bedrooms, filled by their small beds and a litter of each child's possessions: individual space. To the left, was the 'master-bedroom' but here it was a misnomer. Positioned above the sitting-room, this was also a room of softness, decorated in an obviously feminized style.

One of the fundamental divisions was between adults and children. Adults talked, children played. Adults went into the sitting-room, children, with their messy habits, were confined to the backroom. Adults shared bedrooms, children were separate (usually from birth). The house was a different environment for them. The dark stairs, for instance, were a lot less dark once you could reach the light-switch. Children were sent out to the street and played in safe areas, learning social roles, and how to play football on cobbles. Boys roamed further as they grew older (though girls became increasingly restricted), reaching public spaces such as parks and school yards, spaces in which they were often transgressing and from which they were frequently chased. Individuality grows in these hinterlands as status is created apart from and unseen by family. Often men excluded themselves from the house: they worked, went to sporting events, social clubs, including the Church and/or the public house, leaving the house as the realm of the woman, the housewife.

One of the problems of such descriptions is their truthfulness. This can be defined on a number of levels: is this description literally true? If we entered a house, would we see the things described, laid out before us? There is little point in taking a view on this. The thickness of the description adds weight to convictions of truth. Each detail reinforces the authority of the author. I need only say that the house I depict is based on childhood memories. The descriptions simplify and more details could be added, colours, sounds, smells, minute descriptions of artefacts. I could add yellows and browns and greens but it would not necessarily be based on a firmer recollection and perhaps every little detail becomes less firm in the memory, more likely to be invented. The second issue is that of representative truth. 'A Roman House', 'A Berber House', 'The Northern English Terrace-House', make implicit or explicit claims to essentiality. To what extent do we devalue and simplify the range of typologies, of decoration, of meanings, built into the houses? My house sat on the corner of a particular street and was a particular house, and yet the description carries an implied assumption that houses of this type were similar. Yet I have been in houses, similar in architectural style, which were arranged differently and lived in architecturally very different working-class housing in other urban areas of England. We must also wonder of what our houses are representative. The terrace-house reflected the social status of the family in the many and subtle variations within the broad and conscious class descriptors that operated at the time. Like insects under the hand of the entomologist, the species and type can be classified, recorded, preserved and filed away, but the joy of entomology lies in the almost infinite variety of the types.

The family occupying my corner house have moved. The street, last time I visited, was denuded of children. The population had changed. No longer white, working-class families, but a mixture of immigrant communities (mainly Asian), and old and unemployed white families. Racism was a problem. Spatial arrangements had also changed. Fewer houses appeared to have the strong dichotomies between private and display rooms. Internal walls have sometimes disappeared. Functions of rooms have changed. Cultural values have altered, perhaps quite radically where houses are occupied by immigrant Asian or student populations. But this sense of change is not new. It was a feature of the street two decades ago. As children, my parents' generation had a different experience of street and home life than my generation, and my grandfather's tales sound very different from my father's, and one or two generations before my grandparents, such houses did not exist. Houses give a sense of materiality and permanence when, in a larger time-scale, all is in flux.

We are used to a rhetoric of change in the modern world. It is a feature of modernity. Yet change was also a feature of Roman housing (as the excavations at Pompeii are starting to demonstrate (Wallace-Hadrill 1997)) and of Romano-Egyptian housing (see chapter 3). The literature of the late Republic and early Empire abounds with complaints about change (nearly all change in the eyes of the conservative Roman literati was regarded as bad). Vitruvius (*De Arch.* VII 3–4) complained of new-fangled painting styles while Velleius Paterculus (II 14) tells us of the old-fashioned virtue of Livius Drusus, who told an architect who wanted to provide him with privacy that his house was to be open to the sight of all, a demonstration not just of showmanship and the wealth of the house-owner, but also of his openness to scrutiny. Cicero (*De Oratore* III 33 133), again setting the story in the past, talks of those who sat giving advice in their *atria* as well as in the public spaces of the city. There is a prevalent tendency to mythologize and idealize the social relations of the past and this included those embodied in the house so that even the simplest of houses carried an imprint of the past within contemporary architectural practice and social ideology. We thus experience a trick of time, making fools of us by turning the anthropologist into a historian and architecture into myth or rhetoric.

The most serious problem lies in the truth of our representations of social relationships. We are interested not just in the walls and their decor, the easily describable decorations and furnishings, the patterns of light and darkness, or even the customary activities of the individuals, but in the lives of those who inhabit the house and their experience of so doing. How would those who lived in these houses react to their descriptions? One may, in the case of the Berber and Roman house doubt whether the descriptions could have been understood by those who lived in them. By writing about their houses, we impose other ways of thinking on the structures. It is not pleasant to be analysed and judged, reduced by the anthropological panopticon, but certainly, in modern Western society, that is our lot. We are numbered and counted, followed on our demographic and economic maps and charts, assessed individually at examinations, in our work and in countless activities. In academic life, we are continually monitored and watched and read and reviewed as we go through the process of publication, teaching and 'professional development', and we all know the system is imperfect. I am not reducible, I might proclaim, to a lecturer, B grade, ancient history (though, of course, I am). Structuralism is a very particular form of reductionism which turns life into networks of polarities, and, distinctively, into walls of words. Reading structuralist analysis one is continually reminded that the technique stems from linguistics and the oppositions of formal linguistic analysis in which words are so often defined negatively. Such formal patterning does not correspond to life as it is lived. We may, if lucky, on presenting observations of their houses to the observed be told that we are right, but my experience of talking to general audiences about houses is that they quibble: they are uncomfortable with the radical reductionism of the above accounts. Most people seem to believe their house is arranged by rational, functional requirements. They do not see how much is culturally peculiar since these peculiarities have been naturalized. When faced with this question, I have often been tempted to suggest more rational, functional arrangements of sleeping space (not difficult to devise) than those normally adopted in modern British houses, but the space in front of houses offers less explosive territory, especially when American suburban democracy is compared with the crenallation of many British front walls. Nevertheless, non-academics often have an instinctive feel for social organization which deserves to be taken seriously. If, living in houses, we are unaware of the meanings of the spatial relationships, may we not wonder whether the so-very-clever outsiders have invented a spatial discourse rather than laying bare spatial relations? How does that spatial discourse distort the experience of living in those spaces?

Let us return to Bourdieu's description. This is a work of literature. The factual is presented anonymously. There are no identifying features. It is any Kabyle house. We enter. The short sentences give way to the long. The formal introduction gives way to the detailed display of erudition. We are swept up with the description's complexity, its cadences and its beauty. It has meaning for us and is evocative. By the end, we have been seduced. But it is so quick. The space of a few seconds displays to us the full meaning of the house, and we don't even know its name. This is not a meaningful relationship, it is the briefest of brief encounters. Compare this with what must be the real relationship with a space so complex. To understand it, we must live with it. Perhaps we need to grow in a similar space or even in that space. The space is revealed slowly. We come to understand what this represents. We come to feel what we should do in such a place. We become attuned to its cadences of light and dark, its rhythms of life. It moves, in English, from being our house, to become our home. We invest it with our experience. We associate it with our memories. Yet the anthropologist can describe all this in less than a page of text.

There can be no complete history. A complete history of a life would take a lifetime to write and another to read and still the ramifications of the life would elude us. The complete history of a moment requires too many perspectives to make it comprehensible. We must reduce in writing. The problem with the analyses is not that they do not describe everything, but they miss out something that is important to our understanding. They miss out the lived-in quality of the buildings and, one may suspect, the inhabitants' feelings for those buildings. The historian and geographer must accept the partiality of their role as recorder of the spatial environment, but we must also consider what purpose that leaves us? The above analysis has not shown that space is an unimportant factor in society, only that it is difficult to write about.

Hillier and Hanson (1984: 2) write that space is a symbolic code, like a language, but the study of space, like linguistics, struggles to find a mode of expression, to free itself from the code in which it was constructed. People, they argue, are good at thinking in symbols but very bad at talking about them. Yet this raises a further issue. If one can talk about a symbol and deconstruct that symbol adequately, why bother mystifying the process by constructing symbols? What is the function of a symbolic pattern other than to suggest but not to state clearly? Buildings are flexible and although people impose social codes on their buildings and invest them with meaning, it is the flexibility of those codes which makes them so useful. People adapt their domestic space (Rapoport 1969). Economic circumstances impose a flexibility on buildings. Houses which were built in the nineteenth century as large town houses, suitable for a large middle-class family and their servants, became too big to be comfortably occupied by the smaller middle-class households of the twentieth century. But the buildings were not torn down. They were transformed into independent units, sometimes with remarkably few architectural changes (Lawrence 1990). With these changes, the population of the house was also transformed. No longer are such properties the dwellings of families, but they are now occupied by young couples or single people, often comparatively briefly. Again, the arrival of immigrant communities in many British inner cities, especially Asian communities, has transformed the public culture of many areas, but their impact on the domestic architecture of these areas seems negligible. They simply occupied the old working-class housing. Users of buildings and, indeed, many artefacts, will alter the functions for which the artefacts were designed, finding new uses for old objects (Wilk 1990). This capacity for reinvention warns against any literalness or dogmatism in our interpretation of architecture.

What is true for domestic architecture is no less true for the public space of the city. Public monuments may be somewhat easier to understand than domestic buildings since, in some cases at least, the buildings are intended to have a clearly comprehensible message. The building code had, therefore, to be clarified and made obvious: the buildings had to speak and we can, therefore, attempt to reconstruct that message with some confidence. An obvious example is the Forum of Augustus in Rome (Zanker 1988: 108; 113–14; 129; 194–5; 210–15; Wallace-Hadrill 1993: 56–8), and here we have not just the architectural evidence, the surviving fragments of inscriptions, but also contemporary or almost contemporary textual material (Ovid, *Fasti* V 551–66; Suetonius, *Div. Aug.* 29; 31). The Forum encased a temple to Mars Ultor, a temple that had been promised in the earliest days of Augustus' power and which dominated one end of the Forum. The temple was decorated with the name of the emperor and contained statues and images of the gods who were associated with his family: Venus, Mars, Divus Julius, Romulus. Down the flanks of the forum stood statuary that displayed the history of Rome. There were statues to Aeneas and Romulus, founders of the Roman people and city as well as the Augustan family, and then the legendary kings of the first 'Roman' settlement in Italy (which pre-dated Rome itself), the important members of the Julian family, and the so-called *summi viri*: men who had made the greatest contribution to Roman history, normally defined as those who had been involved in conquest (Dudley 1967: 125–7). For those unable to recognize the depicted figures, brief notes were inscribed by each statue giving their place in Rome's glorious history. It became, then, a historical extravaganza where one might walk in Rome's past and be taught of Rome's glory (fittingly, a military glory) while overlooked by the founders of the people and city. The culmination was a statue and inscription voted by the senate and probably placed centrally within the Forum to Augustus himself, *Pater Patriae* (Father of his Country), refounder of the city and one of the greatest of Roman conquerors. Enemies in politics and civil wars stood next to each other and Rome appears as a state harmoniously driving towards world conquest. As such, it was not only representative of history, but also of geography (Nicolet 1991). For here, the empire was displayed and the empire had become the world, or nearly so, as far as the Romans knew.

This is a complex which is not difficult to 'read', especially since we have similar textual versions of Roman history (Virgil, *Aeneid* VII 788–883). It is, of course, an architectural discourse that is meant to be read and the juxtaposition of text and monument within the Forum make that reading seem crashingly obvious. We can imagine the effect of the monument at its height. The tall, dominating temple looming over those assembled (often for important state occasions), reminding the assembled of their insignificance in comparison with the gods, yet also investing the cityscape and the human with the divine presence: here were gods who had walked among men. The statues of the flanks of the Forum, of the great men of Rome, may be seen as heroized by their presence in the forum, and as legend and history are intermingled, the remote past is blended with figures well known from recent history or even those whom they had seen. Thus, the division between the human and the divine was eroded. All, however, culminated with Augustus, who is associated with the glories of Rome's history and with Rome's divine origins. This man (who was confidently expected to become divine on his death) was depicted between divine and human in his lifetime.

The creation of Augustan monumentality within Rome was a counterpart to the way in which the calendar was reshaped to proclaim the virtues and achievements of the imperial house (Ehrenberg and Jones 1949: 44–54; Suetonius, *Nero*, 55; Nock 1952; *RMR* 117; Laurence and Smith 1995–6). August came into being. Festivals of imperial birthdays and remembrances of imperial victories or other significant events reshaped the temporal frame and, most spectacularly, Augustus declared the past over with his celebration of the advent of a new golden age in the Saecular Games of AD 17, a golden age which was continually replayed in monuments such as the Ara Pacis. Here is an equivalent to the reinvention of history practised by Marxist totalitarian regimes, airbrushing undesirables from the photographs, causing unpleasant facts and people to be made to disappear and rendered insignificant. Roman thought, like Marxism, was historical (Edwards 1996). It looked to the past to understand the process of the present. Reshaping history changed the meaning of the present and monuments quickly assimilated themselves to history. Historians, especially historians of antiquity, are always in danger of conflating chronology. Yet the temporal rhythms of life are different from those of history. We live sequentially, gradually changing, developing and ageing, but we also live cyclically, repeating patterns of life from year to year, from season to season and from day to day. In this cyclical movement, the repeated experience of a building renders it less modern, less grating: the lived experience of a city naturalizes monuments. Thus monuments constructed by Augustus in the old Roman Forum, which mimicked the monuments constructed to celebrate the victories of the Republican past, may have been rapidly assimilated into Roman consciousness (Zanker 1988: 79–82). Those who recited the histories of monuments, turning monuments back into language, may have noted their 'newness', but the monuments were already locating Augustus in history, encouraging the process that leads to me teaching and writing about him two millennia later. Zanker (1988: 85–102; 110) writes of Augustus needing to develop didactic imagery, imagery that could be read and understood and used to impose the meanings of the new regime.

Of course, guaranteeing that the audience reaches the correct reading is rather more difficult and history, especially modern history, is littered with people's palaces which inspire the hatred of the people (Romania) and squares, designed to demonstrate that the state was at one with the people, that have been filled with revolutionaries. As ancient historians, we have comparatively few architectural appreciations and those that we do have are often untrustworthy. For instance, Ovid's Mars (*Fasti* V 551–66) visits the temple of Mars Ultor in the Forum of Augustus and is made to marvel at how he is made greater by his association with the emperor. In an age when the literature was self-reflexive and riddled with irony (and perhaps nowhere more so than in Ovid), our reading of Ovid's reading of Mars' reading of Augustus' Forum is nothing if not variegated in tone (see also Edwards 1996: 23–5; 40–1).

Nevertheless, most monuments are not obviously didactic and the viewer may be unable to turn such complex structures into discourse. The process of architectural creation is not normally straightforwardly propagandistic: meanings are too complexly interwoven with the symbols to produce simple political slogans. Architects reflect their culture and the values of those who commission the work, but, as with poetry, the lines of thought are blurred, because of the complexity of the symbolic media.[11] Yet, we must remember that these are symbols and as such represent more than the 'surface' message. A myth resonates with more meaning than the anthropologist can deconstruct. In addition, as soon as one introduces the metaphor of reading (arguably inappropriate for architectural history), one immediately faces the issues of authorial intent and readers' divergent interpretations, since there is very frequently a difference between the cognitive (read) understanding of a monument and its architectural (authorial) intention or function.

This difficulty in understanding cityscapes is not limited to archaeologists and ancient historians. Cities are bewildering in their complexity, which is, of course, partly a function of their size. Strangers become lost in the different regions and disorientated by their unfamiliarity. Those who live in a city gain a feel for its geography, though even their understanding is limited. I escorted a visitor through South London and we travelled through the city on public transport. She became visibly nervous when we entered Brixton, an area with a large Afro-Caribbean population and which has had more than its share of social and economic problems. But Brixton was familiar territory. I passed through that area most nights and sometimes was there very late. It was not a place in which one felt particularly safe, but one learnt, somehow, not to look for trouble and I never felt under threat. Like other vibrant modern inner city areas, it was subject to certain tensions but was no different from many other areas. Yet the place we had passed through ten minutes previously, full of tower blocks and alleys, fast-moving traffic, and without people was, for me, truly terrifying. The robbing of European tourists who wander from the safe areas in certain American cities also demonstrates these difficulties of interpretation and, of course, Europeans in America may find the spatial arrangements relatively familiar. In Old Cairo or in Naples or in many non-European cities, the tourist may be more confused by unfamiliar spatial arrangements.

This confusion, given the broad morphological similarities of many modern cities, is rather disturbing. Visitors seek visual clues to understand a site and its social rules from the architecture, while planners seek to determine patterns of social interaction through architecture. Both groups often fail spectacularly. Planners have designed spaces which they thought, presumably, would work; spaces in which a community could grow and prosper. When British high-rise social housing developments were seen to be a disaster, low-rise estates followed, but the social problems, the crime and the alienation, were not solved. The planners' difficulties stem from the fact that the construction of environments is a mental process. Cityscapes which fail their communities become imbued with negative meanings: the spaces become hostile, controlled by others or uncontrolled, spaces we cannot understand or belong in, depersonalized and alienated from the 'community'. Yet although such cognitive cityscapes are not obviously determined by architecture, it seems obvious that buildings influence cognition.

Hillier and Hanson (1984) offer an alternative and radical approach to this methodological cul-de-sac. Whereas post-structuralist geographers emphasize cognition as crucial to the understanding of the world, Hillier and Hanson take exactly the opposite line (pp. 7–9). Space, they argue (pp. 22–3), is produced by society but also determines society and the intellectual and interpretative frameworks that form the essence of society. Since they are both produced by the same creative force, any theory of social space must avoid at all costs a separation between spatial pattern and social interpretation. There is no theoretical distinction between perspectives of the social subject ('the reader', to adopt earlier terminology) and the (authorial) design of the spatial object. One can thus read a society directly from its spatial patterns without recourse to cognitive approaches. Hillier and Hanson strive for 'a method of describing space in such a way as to make the social origins and consequences a part of that description' since 'the fundamental proposition is not that there is a relationship between settlement forms and social forces but that there is a relationship between the generation of settlement forms and social forces' (p. 82). This seems theoretically unproblematic, though historically astonishing. By developing a formal system of spatial description, they create mathematical models which allow them to generate and describe complex spatial relationships. This formal 'language' provides them with a means of describing and therefore predicting societal integration. When this is applied to modern estates, it shows that instead of helping the formation of communities by bringing people together, the structure of estates often divides people into small groups and clusters of houses with very limited integration with their neighbours. This is clearly an important theoretical development and their formal language of space offers a way of thinking about spatial relations in a much more ordered manner.

Nevertheless, the difficulties are clear. The theory does not account for agency or for history. Let us take Hillier and Hanson's example of two neighbouring, contrasting areas of housing, one being an established street system and the other being a new estate. In the old street system, interaction was nine times greater than in the new estate, measured by number of encounters. Meeting neighbours was, therefore, far more problematic on the new estate than in the established street system. Yet, several factors are not assessed. There is the almost purely spatial issue of transport: the private car isolates individuals from the environment. There is an issue of the age profile of the inhabitants: children and their carers and the aged are more likely to spend time in social interaction on the streets. There is the issue of the desire to meet neighbours which may be shaped by many different social factors, and one should consider the quality and type of interaction with neighbours. Finally, there is the issue of history. Relationships are often built slowly. Populations that grow up together are more likely to have a stronger sense of community than those of new settlements planted on the area without pre-existing social ties. Further, even within established communities factors extraneous to the architecture can influence social interaction. For instance, the increased prevalence of illegal drug use, especially of heroin or certain forms of cocaine, dramatically increases levels of criminality and violence, destroying communities. Other factors, such as economic exploitation, racial tensions or family structures, may also play a part. Hillier and Hanson's premise relates to the generative forces of social space and society and one would, therefore, expect a closer correlation between spatial and societal patterns when spatial patterns were not externally imposed by planners, in something akin to the organic and unplanned development of many medieval villages, yet even in this situation, non-spatial factors, such as political, economic and cultural change, may have a significant impact on society without necessarily affecting the architectural environment. Hillier and Hanson, then, help us to understand social space, but their attempt to turn the inter-relationship of built space and social form into a statement of 'lawful relations' (p. 20) seems unlikely to succeed.

The conjunction of social and spatial formation has been at the heart of human geography almost since its beginnings as an academic discipline. The attack on positivist empiricism in geography and the subsequent debates and flirtations with social theory, especially Marxism, mirror developments in other disciplines.[12] Although Marxist thought, perhaps particularly attractive to a discipline with a strong materialistic bias, has been influential, many practitioners of human geography have turned instead to pioneering cognitive approaches to their topic which may be classed as part of the post-modernist movement.[13] In so doing, they have created a distinctive way of thinking and writing about geography. Drawing on many sources of inspiration, but especially Foucault and Said, post-modernists argue that ideological relations are constructed within even the most simple and seemingly objective representations of the environment. For instance, cartography's claim to represent the reality of the world has been subjected to sustained assault. It is not that maps are wrong in that they show features which are not present, but that they select environmental features and lay particular stress on them. Maps of Europe produced by the Nazis prior to 1938 showed Germany, but also substantial 'German' minorities in other European countries in such a way as to make the case for the annexation of the Sudetenland (Harley 1988). Similarly, projections of the world which emphasize the prominence of Europe and North America were and are standard and can be seen as reflecting economic and ideological relations. All cartographers must choose what to include and what to omit and make value judgements. Buildings might be included in maps but their environmental impact, noise, smell, traffic, etc., is not normally part of cartographic convention. Wood (1993; cf. Harley 1992) argues that behind even the most seemingly neutral map, e.g. maps composed of satellite images of the world, lies editorial, ideologically driven intervention.[14] The ideologically neutral map does not exist.

In itself, this perception seems uncontroversial and not to represent a serious methodological problem. After all, historians are continually made aware that each generation writes its own history, shaping that history around the issues it finds interesting or important. To return to our descriptions of houses: these strip away much and are clearly incomplete (there is no description of construction techniques for example), but this does not mean that they do not aid our understanding. Yet, the post-modernist critique runs deeper. Foucault's discussion of the social and medical sciences showed how the discourse that arose in the eighteenth and nineteenth centuries concerning social and medical issues legitimated and brought power to the medical and social-care professions. The reification of social relationships that came as part of the discourse was at least in part responsible for the gradual construction of many of the institutions of social control that supervised the newly defined 'deviances'. Such institutions and their supporting professions and discourses created 'technologies of power' that allowed the study of social relationships and the manipulation of society and individuals by the empowered. This self-justificatory and self-reproducing discourse, which is the basis of much modern social science, undermines confidence in the ideological purity (the objectivity) of modern academic disciplines. This is a prominent problem in geography, which as a modern discipline has a very particular relationship with colonialism since it both legitimated European colonialism and contributed significantly to the colonialist venture (Godlewska and Smith 1994). The integration of academic discourse, as exemplified by Said's critique of Orientalism (1978; 1993), and imperialist government, with its potentially transforming effect on local societies, places geographical discourse within the sphere of politics (Mitchell 1988; Myers 1994), a reversal of the modernist tendency to portray academic disciplines as by definition apolitical. Such moral and political issues have led some to reject the old ways of approaching geography by disassociating themselves from the 'positivist objectivism' of traditional methodology and to search for a more politically aware approach.

This is not a problem that is particular to geography. History, archaeology, anthropology (especially), linguistics, biology, and no doubt many other disciplines were involved in the creation of an academic and intellectual environment that justified imperial expansion and racism and provided the colonial powers with the ideology and information necessary for the colonial project. The argument is, however, more complex than simply deploring the past sins of intellectual investigators in order to attack the intellectual basis of their inquiry. The situation of authors (political, social and intellectual) influences the way in which they construct their images of the object studied. It follows that others, situated differently within the nexus of social relations, will have different conceptions of the same object, and the reason a particular interpretation becomes important has only a remote relationship with any objective 'truth-value', but everything to do with the way in which a particular discourse is empowered within societies. Since such discourses have real political consequences (or at least seem to), then the responsible academic faces substantial problems in peddling his or her particular interpretation as 'the truth', especially once aware that this can only be a relative truth. Post-structuralist, historicist and literary critiques of the social technologies that shape our ways of seeing and understanding have undermined belief in academic objectivity.

The academic deconstruction of theories of knowledge has been remarkably successful in raising problems about accepted methodologies, but many practitioners have chosen to ignore the critique, not necessarily because writers are unaware of the problems facing their literary and intellectual endeavours, but because the deconstruction of the traditional frameworks of knowledge has not produced generally accepted new theoretical bases for understanding the world. More commonly, perhaps (outside the rather insular field of ancient history), intellectual energy has moved from the development of grand theories (like Marxism) which might explain world history and develop universal laws of social development (Benko 1997). The rise of non-Marxist feminism as well as leftist inclusivist movements, such as those associated with 'political correctness', has changed the nature of radical thinking. Critical attention has turned to the small scale, to subversions of particular institutions and modes of thought, and to community action. Small-scale direct action and single-issue politics have become the backbone of the radical agenda. The age of revolution has been replaced by an age of adjustment. Instead of academics dealing with big theoretical issues, with grand theory, a greater emphasis has been placed on small groups and individuals and the study of their roles in shaping society. Nevertheless, even though this escapes from the potentially dehumanizing classifications by gender, race, class, etc., the concentration on small groups does not solve the problem of academic power, of reshaping agendas and issues through representation, since although the statements of subjects concerning their environment and political relations are given great weight by many writers and oral testimony has been seen as one way of capturing the sentiments of those who otherwise have no say in the formation of academic and indeed popular discourse, such testimony is often radically reshaped in subsequent presentations. Writers have moved closer to their objects of study, but even in studies of the micro-relationship of society, they worry about their role in shaping and reformulating the experiences of those they study.

The sense of doubt (sometimes called the crisis of modernity) that has afflicted many of the social sciences has also led to a retreat from the object of study. The accuracy of representation and the ideological implications of representation have driven theorists and critics away from a study of what is represented to a study of the representation. Barnes and Duncan (1992b) argue that this is inevitable since rhetoric is central to writing and that writing always builds on pre-existing literary models. This reworking of genre means that style must always intervene. Even if a researcher could magically obtain and understand an absolute truth, this truth could not be transmitted without the use of obfuscating rhetoric. Social contexts, institutional settings, political status of the author and historical context all infiltrate texts. 'Writing is constitutive, not simply reflective; new worlds are made out of old texts, and old worlds are the basis of new texts' (Barnes and Duncan 1992b: 3). Such intertextuality extends beyond the text to the experience of the landscape. Simon Schama (1995) has shown how at various times landscape features were invested with broad social meanings, from the nationalism of German forests to the individualistic wilderness of America's West. In Georgian England, the tree became a symbol of family and society, the oak emerging as a sign of British greatness (Daniels 1988), while Palladian architecture tamed and civilized the landscape in ways unseen since the Classical period (Cosgrove 1988). This understanding of landscape is shaped by cultural discourse and thus the mental image of the landscape is formed through text. Such infiltration of text into understanding of geography is central to Said's analysis of Orientalism through which a vast region was studied, understood and governed. The discourse shapes perception. Cosgrove and Domosh (1993: 35–6) reject the idea that this theoretical perception entails a 'crisis of representation' since it only becomes a crisis 'if we somehow think that we are conveying some independent truth about the world, that we are relaying an authentic representation'.

Consciousness of the social and literary construction of knowledge has led to an epistemological crisis. Barnes and Duncan (1992b) argue that 'in this world of one text careering into another, we cannot appeal to any epistemological bedrocks in privileging one text over another'. Cosgrove and Domosh (1993: 36) claim that '[d]ebates over interpretations are not about which is the most "truthful" or "authentic" but instead are part of a social and political struggle for the production of meaning'. They maintain that it is possible to write without asserting value and authority as author and that the 'stories' of geography should be seen as part of the moral and political discourse and evaluated as such. 'Truth' is marginal and although Cosgrove and Domosh allow that texts should be relatively truthful, the connection with truth or, as Barnes and Duncan have it, the 'epistemological bedrock', seems distinctly immaterial. We are, to over-extend the metaphor, either walking on air or in the middle of a severe earthquake. The post-modern reaction is to stick to the small and trace its cultural ramifications and relations, to explicate while avoiding broad generalization. It becomes an individual narrative, a kind of academic poetics with only a hazy relationship to reality, in which the writer's motive is often to display wit (Benko 1997; Barnes and Duncan 1992b). A post-modernist approach, emphasizing individual experience, is (hopelessly) fragmented. As Dear (1997) points out, such fragmentation tends to withdraw meaning: the images become all that matters.

Such theorizing relates closely to the phenomenological approach of Bachelard and others. Bachelard's (1994) analysis of the poetics of space is an essay more on poetics than on space. He finds that his discourse about space (p. 14) very quickly becomes personalized and that, for instance, his attempts to describe his home quickly become divorced from material reality and come to refer to his archetypal home while the reader is drawn not into Bachelard's home, but the reader's 'home', being the building that is his or her single, emotional, archetypal home. There is a free-flowing association in Bachelard's writing which invests his conception of space and operates at a non-logical level. For Bachelard, space has a poetry because it engages in an extra-verbal communication beyond its formal grammar and syntax. The house exists within an individual experience that is almost impossible to recapture in language except as poetic traces and thus lies beyond normal scientific experience: its materiality is inaccessible. Bachelard (1994: xxii) asserts that *logos* 'is everything specifically human in man' (an almost biblical representation of the primacy of language) and the 'house is our corner of the world . . . a real cosmos in every sense of the word'. The experience is all and is ultimately untransmittable.

Such radical individualism is, I believe, ultimately untenable. In spite of post-modern critiques, there is a materiality about landscape which is difficult to escape. Although 'a landscape is a cultural image' (Daniels and Cosgrove 1988: 1), it differs from a painting, a text or a cinematic image in that people live in landscapes in ways more intimate and pervasive than their inhabiting of 'art'. Barnes and Duncan (1992a: 252) reckon it 'intriguing and disturbing' that signs are generally understood, acted upon and recognized outside academia. The application of critical theory drawn from the problematics of literary interpretation to understanding the landscape is in itself subject to historicist analysis which suggests that the metaphor of reading the landscape is a (post-)modern 'understanding' (Daniels and Cosgrove 1993; Stock 1993). Ley (1989) has argued that twenty years of the drive towards the great god of theory in geographic analysis has produced no new meaning and direction for the discipline and wonders whether the aesthetic brilliance of theoretical analysis, the scholarly emphasis upon individual brilliance and artistic skill, and society's lauding of individualism have turned theory into an intellectual game with little or no relationship to social realism. People function in the sea of post-modern confusion where there is no reality, without seemingly being too bothered, though (as argued above) they are occasionally confused. Maps help people get from one part of a city to another. Bachelard's worries about the cosmological implications of his wardrobe are not generally shared. The evaporation of the 'epistemological bedrock' is capable of a *reductio ad absurdum*. There may be many different cognitive worlds but these are not so radically different as to impede function, and the experience of urban living suggests that although there are different social experiences of any particular urban settlement, people within the urban culture develop a functional urban literacy. Although we should not reduce the complexity of the urban experience, we can understand cityscapes.

Given the limitations on difference, we should be able to write meaningfully about cities, capturing that complexity. This, however, remains puzzlingly problematic. Wood's (1993) analysis of maps offers a metaphor. Wood points out repeatedly that maps are social constructs, ways of seeing the world that privilege certain values and interpretations of the environment. Maps edit, distort and omit, but although cartographers are intellectually aware of this, the map is still represented as ideologically neutral and is remarkably difficult to deconstruct. Unlike most works of literature, the map elides the voice of the author, so that the author becomes anonymous or is swallowed by the bureaucracy of a governmental agency. Conventions of depiction, rigorous training and induction into a tradition serve to hide the assumptions of the author, as anyone who has been trained to any level in an academic discipline knows. With maps, where authors claim to be institutions not individuals and conventions dominate, we see a layering of authorial invention from those who thought of the map, who invented the symbols and conventions, who surveyed the area, who decided what was to be surveyed or what was to be included, who drew the map, who designed its legends, to those who printed it. Few maps speak with one voice. The 'author' is multilayered and multivocal and, like choirs performing the same piece of music, each rendition of their work is subtly different (Wood 1993: 70–6). So, I would argue, with cities, their differences are part of the multilayering of the site. Since a city's environment is composed of symbols and mental structures and architecture and these vary from building to building and from individual to individual, it is this conglomeration of forms and meanings that renders cities so difficult to understand, and yet in the way that Wood can begin to deconstruct maps, so we should be able to analyse cities.

There are various ways in which the authorial cacophony of cityscapes can be rendered comprehensible (though all these have significant disadvantages and I will return to the post-modern critique in the last pages of this chapter), such as drowning out all but one voice or fragmenting the city into individual units, but my emphasis on the authored cityscape points towards production and away from cognitive readings of the city. Harvey (1990) (developing and explaining a fundamental element of Marx's thinking) points out that modern capitalism tends to hide forces of production. Thus, an item on sale in a modern retail outlet does not display the hours of labour and the effort and the investment that produced it: its price is a function of demand related to supply. So, with the environment, the forces that produced a particular spatial arrangement are often not openly displayed and yet those forces must have existed: we do not know why a building was put in a certain place, but there must have been a negotiation that put it there. Although innumerable accounts of cities and landscapes historicize the environment, turning the cityscape into a palimpsest in which the history of the site can be read by the discerning, such exegeses are not part of normal social interaction. Buildings tend to form part of the established 'natural' landscape soon after construction and we do not normally relate to them through consideration of their socio-political origins. The arrival of the railways in the nineteenth century and the redevelopment of dockland areas in certain British and American cities had serious effects on the economic and social structures of the communities concerned, but in viewing these communities after the changes we see not the spatial transition but the resultant pattern.

Buildings are erected through a series of separate decisions by various individuals often acting in official capacities, and the spaces produced are modified by the actions of other individuals acting on that space. These individual decisions are not random: it is simply improbable that all across the East of the Roman empire councillors decided to erect colonnades along the main thoroughfares of their cities without there being some social or political force that encouraged them so to do. People respond to social forces, and although responses may be varied, perhaps even almost down to the individual level, the forces are not so varied and thus form a possible subject for analysis. This perception has led Harvey and Scott (1989) to argue for a return to grand theory in the study of the workings of capitalism on the landscape in order to establish a comprehensible narrative of the cityscape. Benko (1997) and Soja (1989) also argue for a geography that exposes the manipulations of capitalism. Soja (1989: 81) argues that he has 'opened the possibility of a complex socio-spatial dialectic operating within the economic base, in contrast with the prevailing materialist formulation which regards the organisation of spatial relations only as a cultural expression confined to the superstructural realm'. By so doing, he offers a way of viewing spatial relations through a pattern of economic exploitation expressed in rather unconventional Marxist terms. Benko (1997) is more hostile to post-modern cognition-led approaches to geography, arguing that the disavowal of holistic theories of the world and its systems combined with a critique of knowledge led to a refusal to examine the broad constraining and constructing forces of society, such as capitalism, so that social investigation has become a study of language rather than things.[15]

Behind such Marxist-influenced analyses stands the French philosopher and revolutionary Lefebvre. Lefebvre's (1991 (French edn 1974)) assault on the issue of space seeks to rethink some of the Marxist and Marxist-influenced conceptions of capitalism through consideration of spatiality. Lefebvre (1991) was not particularly interested in urban space *per se*. He claimed that capitalism had become a global system, as our politicians continually remind us, and dedicated his work to expanding on the implications of that expansion. Lefebvre recognized that spatial forms were endlessly overlapping and that space was produced and lived in at many interconnected levels: the house, the estate, the city, the region, the nation, the globe. This interconnection renders capitalism a cosmology since capitalism was manifest within all levels of spatial relations and these spatial relations were also generative of capitalism, a theory that links neatly with Hillier and Hanson's perception of space and society as co-creations. The implications of this are broad, but the perception is not confined to Lefebvre. Heidegger, for instance, saw space as part of ontology, the study of being. He argued from a semantic link between the German *bauen*, to build, and *sein*, to be. The creation of a building brings into being not just the building, but the locale (or environment) of the building. It creates an inside and an outside, but a building is always more than a mental structure: it has materiality. To be is to dwell in space and this is related to the construction of dwellings (Heidegger 1993: 347–63).

Pearson and Richards (1994), summarizing earlier work, argue that there was a crucial evolutionary stage in human existence in which humans went from being hunter-gatherers to being domestic, a stage which required a change in mental constructions so that the architectural environment was opposed to the natural landscape. Of course, one may push the boundaries of this spatial awareness further back in human development; many hunter-gatherer groups in various species have a range across which they travel, which is limited either by environmental factors or by the activities of other similar groups. This may be considered a home (though not a house) and one may wonder whether this necessitated the beginnings of a complex spatial awareness, territoriality and society. Nevertheless, the construction of a house (though I see little reason why a cave could not perform this function) is a fundamental development since it concentrates the conception of 'inside', limiting the range of home, and therefore allows an association and concentration of values that define humanity (culture) as opposed to nature.[16] It is, I think, significant, that so many simple houses which doubled as shelter for the 'domesticated' (a strange word) animals divide off the animal from the human.

As buildings became better, they acquired an ability to withstand the passage of time that allowed the investment of culture in the building to be chrono-logically sustained. The building can even outlast a generation or the powers of memory. In such cases, the building becomes history. It transcends the passage of time and, of course, death. Culture can then be preserved over generations. The nature of time changes and history can begin. This, of course, can be quite problematic for a society. Hodder (1994) argues that in the Neolithic period, the association of the head of the household with the culture of the house was so great that in some communities the house was burnt on the death of the significant household member.[17] Probably some memorial was then erected so that the memory of the house/dweller would be preserved. New houses were constructed on neighbouring plots and the continuity of house-life and human-life was maintained. The structural similarities between tombs and houses in many Neolithic communities become more comprehensible from this perspective. Tombs were like houses in that they were monuments of humanity and culture: houses and tombs defeated death by providing for the humanity (culture) of the dead in the next life. For communities that resumed a semi-nomadic existence, the house became a more malleable symbol of culture and probably less suitable for the community's need to preserve its social order. In such cases, the tomb could provide a symbol of cultural identity and this explains what seems to be an extraordinary investment in tombs at sites where there is little evidence of a similar investment in housing (Hodder 1992: 45–80).

Buildings, then, are potentially representative of our culture and humanity and can become part of a cosmology. The orientation of Neolithic houses in the Orkneys, for instance, seems to be related to the movement of the sun, though it seems unlikely that this is a functionalist arrangement. Whitelaw (1994) finds that cosmological factors are important in the layout both of individual areas and shelters but also of the settlements of semi-nomadic groups such as the !Kung. In larger communities, such cosmologies can be traced in public space: the centrality of temple or church, orientations towards the east or to Mecca. Even in very complex settlements, such as the English industrial town, the pattern of finely graded housing, of areas of working-class, middle-class and upper-middle-class occupation, the divisions between retail zones in the centre of the town and industrial concerns, and the further integration of the community through a transport network, suggests an awareness of place in the world, of belonging, of being and that the integration of cosmology and buildings has been maintained.[18]

Heidegger's view of the social meaning of building, shared to a certain extent by archaeologists and geographers, suggests that at some level, house, city, nation, world, spatiality is identifiable with culture and identity.[19] The multilayering of spatial perspectives represents a multilayering of identity (being) which must in itself vary between cultural groups. Thus any attempt to write about urban spatiality must tackle this layering of space and identity and represent the patterns of spatiality at levels from the house, to the district, to the city, to the world.

We are, then, looking at a system for understanding our place in the world and interpreting that system is obviously contentious. For Lefebvre, this world system was the product of a fundamental change in capitalism at the end of the nineteenth century when capitalism 'went global'. Space was the creation of the capitalistic system, and this included mountains and deserts named, mapped and known through capitalistic exploration (cf. Said 1978; Pratt 1992).

Lefebvre's crucial insight was, however, that capitalist spatial patterns also created or formed the locus of the capitalistic system. In his view, capitalism is all-pervasive, determining the way we live, the way houses are built, the way cities run, urban–rural interaction, and international and interregional relations, but also the spatial patterns produced by capitalism allow capitalism's continuation and only by disrupting those spatial relations will capitalism be ended. Lefebvre characterizes the spaces of capitalism as dehumanizing, deploring mass-produced boxes which emphasize verticality, the superhuman scales of piazzas and tower blocks (Le Corbusier 1970), whereas revolutionary space will be humanized and reject the overarching values of the capitalistic system. This has some similarities with Harvey's (uncontroversial?) claim (Harvey 1990: 418–19) that 'each social formation constructs objective conceptions, of space and time sufficient unto its needs and purposes of material and social reproduction and organizes its material practices in accordance with those conceptions', but differs in that Lefebvre's claim that there is a single capitalist system which operates differently in different parts of the globe implies just one social formation. Lefebvre grounds his system by continually emphasizing the production of space and asking why that space was produced, by whom and for whom. For Lefebvre, space is lived: it has smells, sounds and physicality. He has no truck with those who would turn spatial relations into a pattern of words, a discourse, which he regards as a form of linguistics: a code of codes serving to demonstrate nothing but linguistic aptitude (cf. Dear 1997), since space has a materiality that derives from its status as a product and is therefore more than mere words. It follows from this that space cannot be 'read' for it is not a discourse and individual interpretations of particular spaces, unless set within an appropriate analytical context, are of limited use.

Such Marxist-influenced analyses of social space offer a narrative of historical development and class struggle within the workings of a capitalistic system that turns the city (or any space) into a battleground in which the struggles of the various interest groups are represented. Such an analysis does not need to concentrate on the individual or the fragmented city, but can progress through consideration of the workings of social forces. Nevertheless, Marxist-influenced narratives suffer from the problems that affect Marxist thought generally, though at varying levels of influence: notions of historical inevitability, the identification of sub- and superstructural cultural elements, the over-reification of a capitalistic system, and the suppression of individual agency in the face of historical systems. These problems are not new to Marxist thought and were already evident as Marx and Engels worked on the formulation of Marxism's basic texts. Some of the problems arise from an overly rigid application and theoretical development of Marxism, especially in the hands of Soviet and structuralist Marxists. Such approaches have been criticized as 'economism' by more flexible scholars (arguably including both Marx and Engels themselves), of whom Gramsci is one of the more interesting and influential. Faced with the rise of the intellectual challenge of fascism and the rather painful and obvious failure of the radical politics so prominent in Italy prior to 1922 to produce a revolution, as well as the theoretical and practical problems raised by revolution in Russia and the rise of the Soviet state, Gramsci started to rethink 'the philosophy of praxis', as he called Marxism. As he was a practical politician, Gramsci's theories were firmly set in an understanding of Italian history and contemporary politics. He worried about the role of intellectuals and the rise of the 'modern Prince', rethinking Machiavelli's importance to political thought. He rejected (Gramsci 1971: 168) the 'predetermined teleology' of 'economism' and argued that the tendency of 'economism' to see all political struggles as representations of class conflicts was a peculiarly mechanical interpretation, while at the same time attacking those intellectuals who saw all struggle as 'conjunctural', representing temporary alliances of social forces (1971: 177–8). Gramsci retained many of the fundamentals of Marxism. He accepted that there was an economic substructure that exercised a formative role over the political and cultural superstructure of society and that the development of that substructure was manifested in the political development of society. The manner in which this was manifested is not, however, quite so clear or straightforward and he also accepts that superstructural elements can influence the economic substructure. In his essay on the modern prince (1971: 125–47), he seems to come perilously close to suggesting that the political power of the 'great man' lay in capturing the spirit of the age and in manipulating the political forces to make use of the historical dynamism of class struggle, in the same way Machiavelli's ideal prince (although not within Machiavelli's discourse, which is criticized precisely because it abstracts all economics from political debate) was attuned to the economic forces of the age in allying with the progressive bourgeois against feudal lords, though Gramsci seems to believe that modern politics is more naturally a matter of party than individuals. Gramsci's analysis allows for political initiative and ascribes a crucial role to intellectuals (given such a wide definition that it might be better to render it as 'ideology' rather than referring to a particular social group) in shaping political debate and events, though ideology or the intellectual group is in itself subject to the workings of the substructure in its formation (Gramsci 1971: 3–23; 191). Gramsci opens a distance between the working of politics and culture, which influences and reflects on the substructure, and the economic determinism of class struggle. This leads to substantial analytical problems. Gramsci (1971: 202–4) suggests that political activists were continually being distracted from the interest of their social class, leading to movements in which class relations were confused and explains this with the rather cumbersome notion of two consciousnesses in the proletarian, a practical consciousness reflecting class status (Marxist) and a theoretical consciousness representing cultural and intellectual background (historical). Political consciousness, Gramsci (1971: 333) argues, only came about when these 'hegemonies' were aligned. Gramsci's analysis embeds theory in practical politics. In so doing, he faces the unpredictability of political life and, while accepting the broad basis of Marxist thought, postulates a dualism between what one might call substructural and superstructural ideological elements that allows limited individual freedom and political unpredictability.

Thompson (1978), in a detailed attack on Althusser, struggles with many of the same issues, again from the perspective of political engagement and as a working historian. Thompson's main point is that Althusser's Marxism is overly philosophical, excluding the practical workings of society from his theorizing. Thompson grapples with the teleological features of Marxism and the problematics of human agency within the theory. Marxism *helps* Thompson to explain history, *helps* him to understand historical events, but history does not in itself confirm Marxist theory or follow a course predictable from Marxist theory (p. 238), partly because historical agents (individuals) act unpredictably. This unpredictability stems from the fact either that individual human agents do not allow themselves to become assimilated to social structures or that such structures fail to assimilate individual human agents (pp. 347–8). Unlike Gramsci, Thompson does not elaborate on the 'unstructured' elements of the human personality. However, as with Gramsci, there is little sense of the relative importance of these elements, though Gramsci's Marxism suggests that economic elements will tend to determine.

Lefebvre transcends some of these difficulties since his emphasis on an all-embracing spatiality of capitalism suggests such a powerful force that the individual is rendered insignificant. Similarly, the intellectual juggernauts of modernism, social scientific thought and Orientalism (as described by Said and Foucault), sweep through societies, crushing individualism and leaving little room for resistance. Neither Said nor Foucault give much significance to the role of individuals in shaping discourse. Nevertheless, although modern capitalism has unleashed tremendous political and economic forces, the modern seems to most of these authors to assimilate imperfectly, allowing loci of resistance to develop, and although one must acknowledge the importance and power of the economic in modern society and indeed in all other societies, it seems to me that the distance opened up by Gramsci's notion of two hegemonic consciousnesses and Thompson's imperfect assimilation is sufficient to undermine notions that the economic determines social structure (even for the modern world), the basic tenet of Marxist thinking.

The collapse of Marxism as an analytical system seems to have led to an abandonment of grand theories and a return to theories of accidental development, radical individualism and local historical study (Harvey 1990; Benko 1997) in which meaning is subsumed by ironic observation of the accidents of fate, but such analyses tend to ignore and thereby naturalize the global workings of the capitalist system and other extralocal historical influences. The reversion to an ironic trope in writing marks a distancing of historians and geographers from global politics and, in some ways, a retreat of understanding in the face of our increased knowledge of the immense variety of human responses to the modern world, such as the reinvention of ethnicity

37

in American cities or the development of a geography of sexual orientation.[20] How can theory make sense of post-modern diversity in an increasingly economically uniform world?

Faced with the problems of general theories which seem not to work and theories of individual agency which would tend to dissolve society into an anarchic competition, which again does not seem to reflect the significant levels of social and ideological cohesion demonstrated in modern societies, social scientists have looked for a middle course: a theory that would retain social structures as a formative and limiting factor on social behaviour while allowing for individual agency. Here lies the importance of Giddens's theory of structuration (Giddens 1979; 1984).

All social structures must work at the level of the individual since although social force may be applied to achieve a certain social conformity, this is not an obvious factor in most societies (though there are limiting cases to which I shall return). Social structures are, however, generally not material. Even such a seemingly material institution as money is, in itself, not 'real', since the concept of exchanging a small round piece of metal or a piece of paper or adjusting some digits held electronically for some goods or services depends on a shared series of assumptions of value: if large numbers of people stopped believing in money, money would cease to exist. Society exists largely as a mental structure: it is not natural. That social structure must come into being by a process of education and socialization, as Bourdieu (1977; 1990) argues. The sharing of those mental structures produces society and individuals may exercise choice over or even modify those mental structures in so far as they are not constrained by social forces which police these structures. For example, I may choose not to believe in money or private property, but that choice carries certain implications which may be extremely inconvenient and may lead ultimately to me being subjected to certain physical constraints. This may seem to offer a considerable dynamic to social analysis and, indeed, analysis of social action may have to depend on an evaluation of each actor's motivation in accepting or rejecting elements of the social structure, although the freedom of action may be significantly limited. The socialization process not only shapes awareness of social convention but also influences intellectual processes. If our categories of social thought are tied to our social structure through such social phenomena as language, the room for radical rejection of social values seems limited. For instance, if we categorize people by 'man', 'woman', 'boy', 'girl' our thought transmits particular notions of gender and age which have implications for discussions of sexuality, family and other matters. A society that emphasizes skin colour would probably produce individuals who find it very difficult to think about society in ways that reject those social constructions. Bourdieu (1977) outlines this process of indoctrination and suggests its pervasive influence. Structuration theory faces similar problems to Marxism in that its workings depend to a certain extent on the level of social integration, i.e. the extent to which social values are internalized by the social actors. If one holds that such internalization is weak, then individual agents will have comparatively greater importance in historical explanations and social change may be bewilderingly rapid and varied, but if one holds that internalization is strong, then social structures will suppress individual agency and social change would stem from extra-societal factors, such as environmental change or interaction with other social formations (Geertz 1973: 142–89). Yet, even in the most stable social systems, patterns of generational change with often related adjustments of relative economic standing and processes of interaction between social formations (for very few historical societies have ever existed in isolation) introduce a dynamic in the replication of social structures.

Harvey and Scott (1989) argue that the interest shown in human agency over the last twenty years has produced nothing but 'inchoate swirls of human agency'. On the other hand, systemic analyses of modern and pre-modern societies such as structuralism and Marxism either ignore historical change or fail to explain the immense variety of societal responses to historical developments. It seems to me that Gramsci, Thompson and Giddens tread that difficult middle course in allowing individual agency while accepting that individuals influence and are influenced by internalized social ideologies. Such theories can be linked to the critiques of knowledge of Foucault and others, which stress the political and social embeddedness of knowledge (our understanding of the world is influenced by our social structure and influences that social structure), and maintain a dynamic view of society derived from broadly theoretical analyses of historic societies.

The dynamic elements within these theories might be expected to appeal to a historian. If a society at any given moment is in flux as social actors manipulate socio-intellectual structures and are influenced by forces external to their traditional socio-intellectual structures and the level of internalization of socio-intellectual structures is variable, then history is central to our understanding of societies. Also, although static description of societies may be analytically useful in providing a chronological starting point, most societies, and certainly ancient societies, would always be undergoing limited and probably disputed change. Explaining what is must always involve explaining what was. The dynamism and fluidity of society have, however, a logic in that although societies are untidy and disordered and disputed, the coherence of social forces and social structures means that they are hardly ever anarchic.[21] The historian's task is to capture society's dynamism, its variety and its cohesion.

I started this chapter by noting the revival of a Classical poetic form in the early modern period and have traced the interplay of Classicism and modernism and the varying construction of the Classical heritage in the nineteenth and twentieth centuries. The engagement with the Classical heritage has informed modern urbanisms, imperialisms and our world views in such a way that Classics remains a living heritage. For me, studying ancient urbanism has resonances for my understanding of modern society, as all human history should in some way connect with our experience of being human to make the study of history worthwhile. Paradoxically, it is those resonances, those common-sense inter-pretations of the past that drive me towards the support of theoretical perspectives to construct a better, more plausible rhetoric. I have become suspicious of those resonances, of how one understands societies, ancient and modern, and feel that my instinct for the past and present is no longer a safe guide. As Gregory (1994: 86) points out, in his long and sometimes strangely moving discussion of theory in modern human geography, 'theory is a sort of moving self-reflexivity . . . , always incomplete and constantly responding to the problems and predicaments of human existence and human practice'. I have looked explicitly to theory and to comparative approaches throughout this book to bolster and inform interpretations and to ground my understanding of human society.

Traditionally method (as opposed to theory) was about writing the author out of history and obtaining something close to objectivity through self-criticism. Facing a history still overwhelmingly culled from what modern historians would call secondary sources, the writings of ancients living often many years after the events described, ancient historians have developed a comparatively sophisticated awareness of the perspectives of their 'primary' material which is often applied to the writings of moderns as well. Nevertheless, ancient historians have tended to regard grand theory of the type debated in this chapter as a potential distortion in which the concerns of the modern are transposed onto antiquity, preferring instead a modified positivism which has largely allowed a self-aware common-sense approach to the writing of the self into history. Much post-modern theory has centred on this issue of the subjective observer within academic discourse, but instead of looking at how this observer attains objectivity, the theory has attempted to put the individual back at the centre of narratives. This emphasis on the individual works in two directions. It represents a refusal to accept determinism, whether Marxist economism, fascist or geographical. Even if human beings are continually faced by social, political, environmental and economic powers that suppress their freedoms and force their decisions, there is a recognition of a human choice somewhere in the historic pattern. Second, post-modernism erodes the objectivity of the writer in crucial ways. Much of the energy of this development has come from groups who claim to represent the interests of those disempowered by previous narratives, the colonized, those classed as social deviants, and feminists. Overwhelmingly, it is argued, it was a white, male, middle-class, educated eye that read, understood, classified and exercised power through the 'objective' academic discourses of the post-Enlightenment period. Cosgrove and Domosh (1993: 27) argue that 'the writing of our geographies is a process of creating and inscribing meanings'. Scientific, positivist geography suppresses other voices and emphasizes single views of the world. Objectivism, they argue, is associated with masculinity while female readings may generate 'ambiguous, enclosing, containing interpretations, resolving contradictions in an embrace of oppositions'. Rose (1993: 10–39) argues similarly that the white bourgeois heterosexual male has a distinctive view of the world and has constructed a particular social-scientific masculinity that asserts its power to construct an objective view of the world. Fundamental to the

> construction and possession of other imaginary bodies is the masculinist denial of the male body; others are trapped in their brutal materiality by the rational minds of white men. This erasure of his own specificity allows the master subject to assume he can see everything.
>
> (Rose 1993: 39)

The feminist critique blends with the postcolonial reassessment of objectivity, as presented by Said (1978; 1993), Pratt (1992) and Mitchell (1988), in which the objectivity of modern viewers was a way of producing power relations.[22] Even such post-modern accounts have been criticized as being Eurocentric and monotonal in not recognizing the variety of European responses or of local reactions to and assimilations of colonial discourse (Crush 1994; Gregory 1994: 175–8; Driver 1992; Slater 1992).[23]

As a white, European, male, bourgeois academic, I find it very tempting to dismiss the arguments. The realities of historical research and writing are such that traditional positivist historical discourse would appear to have considerable truth-value and I would find it difficult to argue that historical knowledge and understanding have not progressed over the last century (Evans 1997; Elton 1967). The 'science-model' of historical writing is persuasive and if truth-value is abandoned as a means of evaluating historical texts and we are forced to rely solely on political or moral utility, we face academic schizophrenia, an inability to judge truth in a world of different voices. Nevertheless, the post-modern argument has considerable moral and epistemological force. The process of classification, study, reorganization and control that came with empire saw an imposition of European ideology and structures on colonized populations. The colonized were made 'readable' and controllable by the enforcement of European discipline (Myers 1994; Mitchell 1988). This classifactory system is an exercise of power as it is to call me a white, bourgeois male: it enforces a series of stereotypes and devalues political or rhetorical responses. We ought to consider other perspectives. The world must have looked very different to those subject to the power of the colonizers. What did they think when their towns, laws, political life and economic organization were rationalized and civilized? The genteel women of the British middle class of the nineteenth century, confined to a feminine world of houses while their men engaged in a masculine world of work and affairs, may have differed greatly from their husbands in their world view (Davidoff et al. 1977; Tosh 1991). The travellers of Britain, moving from site to site, often harassed and marginalized, experience a different geography from the settled population (Sibley 1992). One cannot argue that views different from those that hold intellectual hegemony are insignificant. Such views contribute to the experience of urban life and are in themselves socially and politically significant. Any attempt to reconstruct what it was like to live in the city, the society of the city (which I have argued was an ideological discourse), and why the experience of the ancient city had a certain distinctive shape, renders the perspectives (arguably the cities) of those marginalized by the dominant discourses important, and how does one choose the single discourse that animates and correctly interprets the city? Objectivity is, as is admitted by all, impossible and 'partial objectivity' or 'attempted objectivity', although recognizing the imperfections of the world, is a poor excuse for a philosophical position. How then does one stop the inchoate whirl that Marxists claim threatens to overwhelm analytical insight and avoid the abyss of relativism into which history disappears? On what epistemological bedrock can we found our new historiographic Jerusalem?

We could do worse than follow Gregory's (1994: 416) humanistic response. After more than 400 pages of theoretical discussion he concludes with his manifesto for cultural geography:

> The task of a critical human geography – of a geographical imagination – is, I suggest . . . [to construct a geography] that recognises the corporeality of the vision and reaches out from one body to another, not in a mood of arrogance, aggression and conquest but in a spirit of humility, understanding and care. This is not an individualism; neither is it a corporatism. If it dispenses with the privileges traditionally accorded to 'History', it nonetheless requires scrupulous attention to the junctures and fissures between many different histories: a multilayered dialogue between past and present conducted as a history of the present.

Gregory's manifesto is for a cultural geography that treads lightly through people's lives and perceptions and tries to incorporate those lives and perceptions within understandings of geography. Gregory suggests what is I think a modified investigative individualism that recognizes the importance of social forces (of History perhaps) in shaping histories. This acceptance of the value of divergent understandings importantly modifies the Gramscian stance taken earlier in the chapter. The Marxist-informed history is not the only history that we can write and is not the only history that informs and shapes the city. Inevitably, there are many histories and responses to the social forces that create the city, but probably not an infinite variety. Societies impose normative values and frameworks so that, in spite of the variety of experience, there were probably broadly shared understandings of the city which were shaped by social, political, economic and cultural forces.

Finally, we must return to the issues of objectivity and truth. I think the problem for historians can be solved by separating these two concepts and undermining the concept of the truth. If objectivity is impossible, so is arriving at a single, objective truth. The values of other stories must be allowed. In what follows, however, I hope that the mass of historical data assembled will persuade the reader that my way of viewing ancient society, and implicitly modern society, is in a limited sense true. Its truth is limited by the incompleteness of the narrative, the partiality of the narrator, the imperfections of the text in presenting the narrator's thought, and the imperfections of the evidence (ignoring plain errors). Nevertheless, a mass of evidence is deployed to convince the reader of the validity of my understanding, of the values and concepts articulated within this book, and that my way of looking at the world should at least be taken seriously. I claim neither objectivity, nor that mine is the only possible interpretation, but I do want to persuade the reader either to adopt my views or to think about the conclusions that I have come to from my reading of ancient documents and a comparative reading of modern texts. Ultimately, I think that the particular ideology of the interpreter of the past, informed by extensive readings, can and should be communicated because, in the last instance, I believe that the Gramscian notion of intellectual hegemonies does apply and that hegemonies can thus be changed. Although I do not claim to have uncovered the truth with anything approaching objectivity, I do claim an informed reading of the world and, like all informed readings, that should be of interest.

Instead of being a prologue to what will happen, a search for method, this chapter has been about a search for theory, a way of seeing the world, of which the rest of the book is merely a worked example.

3

HOUSES

Our investigation of the spatiality of the Romano-Egyptian city starts at the level of the house. Houses have a special place in many cultures and the study of housing frequently captures imaginations, offering, it seems, an insight into how individuals conduct their lives in other societies. As we saw in the last chapter, Bachelard (1994) turned the house into a cosmological image, a representation of the divine order, refracted through history and experience. His lead has been taken by others (Knights 1994; see pp. 15–21), though normally in less florid terms. Living in houses is, of course, an almost universal facet of humanity; even nomadic groups have settlements and individuals adopt specific shelters within those settlements and such structures are, broadly, recognizable cross-culturally as 'houses', structures which I argued in the last chapter were primary containers of culture (see pp. 33–4). Many houses would seem to operate both as a generative factor in constructing social ideologies and as a construct of those ideologies and thus reflect both the similarities and strangeness of other cultures, their very familiarity perhaps making us more sensitive to cultural variance. Thus, I think, we may be more comfortable in understanding and unfolding the implications of their familiar and unfamiliar elements and both more sensitive to the nuances of different spatial arrangements and somewhat surer in our interpretation than we might be if starting with the broader spaces of the city, or the region, or the province. The house is a starting point for those we study. It is a home: the most intimate of spatial forms and where humans begin to learn about the society and culture into which they have been born. For us, so often the home is the base for the rest of our lives, which we leave to compete in the world and to which we return for security. It forms the solid base around which our lives are constructed. Of course, this is my cultural prejudice and there is no guarantee that Romano-Egyptians shared my perception and emphasis on the home. Nevertheless, the possibility of the centrality of the home to the social formation of the individual and to his or her education ('education' in its broadest sense) means that starting with the smallest spatial unit in the city seems appropriate.

Methodology: sources and approaches

The sources available for reconstructing the houses of Roman Egypt and, more importantly, how people used those houses, are uniquely rich and problematic. The papyri are our main source for the communities of Roman and late Roman Egypt and the range of documentary evidence they provide is without parallel. Historians argue whether the many thousands of inscriptions from the provinces of the Roman empire reflect the lives of 'ordinary' people, or at least the lives of those 'ordinary' people sufficiently wealthy to purchase stone monuments, but the traces of lives in the papyri, although again probably not encompassing the full socio-economic range of ancient communities, indisputably bring the lower classes to the attention of the historian. Moreover, the texts are far more varied than the epigraphic evidence, since we have far more than the tombstones and the official decrees that comprise the majority of our epigraphic record; we have the tax documents, the contracts, the letters, the receipts, and the legal documentation of the population. This is, of course, the attraction of the papyrological material for the social historian, but, frustratingly, this material is fragmentary, a fragmentation that operates at various levels. The documents themselves are often in a dreadful state and papyrologists spend weeks, months and sometimes years patching the documents together, attempting to improve readings, and assessing the nature of the gaps. The record is also patchy: some sites produce very many papyri, others have produced none. Even within sites, the chronological distribution of the documents and, indeed, the types of documents, are certainly not random, though the effect of processes of preservation and recovery on the surviving record cannot easily be reconstructed. Finally, the biographical traces in this documentation are mere fragments. There are very few people from Roman and Byzantine Egypt about whom one could construct a plausible biography without the aid of the techniques of historical fiction. Archives commence and end without any obvious rationale. People drift in and out of even the most tightly organized archives and the archives themselves tend to reflect particular aspects of people's lives: some archives concentrate on legal and financial matters, while others consist of private letters, attesting friendships, social lives and everyday business. Normally, only selected aspects of lives are preserved and the very incompleteness of the record, which is certainly not random, discourages generalization. Moreover, most individuals are attested by only a single reference, without historical or social context and very often without even a clear location. Without context, the little histories on the papyri become anecdotes whose meaning is almost infinitely negotiable.

Let us take some examples. *P. Oxy.* I 91, *P. Oxy.* II 281 and *P. Oxy.* I 95 are framed together in the archives at Royal Holloway and Bedford New College. These three texts come from the Grenfell and Hunt excavations at Oxyrhynchus and were presented to Holloway College by Arthur Hunt in 1900. *P. Oxy.* I 91 is a receipt for payment made for the services of a female slave who had been acting as wet nurse and nanny for a certain Helena. The payment was made to the slave's male owner. This document does not stand alone. Various fragments of other texts were glued to it in antiquity, though little sense can be made of these scraps. *P. Oxy.* II 281 is a complaint from a woman about her husband who, having been taken into her house when he was penniless at or before their marriage, first took to abusing her and then ran off with her dowry which she was now seeking to reclaim. *P. Oxy.* I 95 is a contract for the sale of a female slave, Dioskorous, from a Graeco-Egyptian to a Roman. Hunt can hardly have selected these three texts at random: all three might be expected to have been of particular interest to the female students of Holloway College. Yet although we could list other documents of similar type and reconstruct the legal framework in which these women operated or, indeed, were subjected to male authority, the texts themselves float free of context. We know virtually nothing about the social reality of the people involved, their social relationships, their feelings. We do not know whether Dioskorous was bought for her sexual attractiveness or her potential as a worker. We do not know whether the infant Helena ever went back to visit her wet nurse or what the husband might have claimed in his defence. Together, the texts tell a different story than if they were apart, a story of slavery, of economic exploitation and domestic strife, but their togetherness is a modern association, an early reaction to feminism and women's education, a gesture to the still unborn women's history. Apart, they tell three different, unrelated and partial stories, free of social and physical context. Apart, they are anecdotes, difficult to interpret. Oxyrhynchus, as Fikhman (1976) entitled his book, is for us a 'city of papyrus', a world of documentary anecdotes floating free from the materiality and historicity of the ancient city.

Papyrology has emerged as a subdiscipline within Classics, a discourse separate from the mainstream where even the abbreviations and numbering of the documents can seem cabbalistic to outsiders.[1] Primarily, papyri are interpreted within the context of the history of the documentary form. This is in some ways unavoidable and epistemologically the safest route. The problem facing those who wish to reconstruct a social world using these documents is that so much of that world has to be generated from the papyri themselves. Historians can be relatively confident about changes in the papyrological record, but less sure as to whether these reflect real social changes. The sheer weight of documentation is also intimidating for those brought up in 'mainstream' ancient history where the sources are exiguous and generalizations fundamental to the writing of history. For the historian of Graeco-Roman Egypt, there is always a temptation to the let the texts speak and to adopt a minimalistic approach to the organization of the material. Thus, the papyri can overwhelm the narrative, turning social history into papyrological history. The papyri are remarkably resilient and inimicable to attempts to make them into the building blocks of histories. It is this problem which van Minnen (1994) has recently attempted to address in a methodological and programmatic paper. He aims to encourage papyrologists to examine their material in the context of other archaeological artefacts and, as a test case, recombines the archaeological and papyrological material from a house in Karanis, a large and uniquely well-attested village on the north-east fringe of the Fayum.

Most papyri come to us without archaeological context. Some come from known sites, but others appear on the antiquities market having been illegally excavated and, for obvious reasons, neither the antiquities' merchant nor the purchaser were very inquisitive as to the exact provenance of the papyri. The site of Karanis is an exception. The systematic, if rapid, excavation of the site has for half a century provided us with the only large collection of Egyptian papyri which had anything approaching adequate archaeological documentation.[2] The arid conditions which preserved the papyri also preserved other organic matter and so the archaeological record of Karanis is astonishingly rich. The cloth, the wood, the basketwork, the remains of the flora and fauna as well as the more durable material culture, stone, brick, pottery, lay all about when the excavators started their operations. The clearing and recording of the site was a mammoth task and the intimidating scale of the surviving record has, I think, prevented much attempt at a synthetic account of the site. Scholars, as van Minnen complains, have worked on the papyri, or the various types of artefact (pottery, lamps, statues, buildings), but have not put the material together. Van Minnen sought to rectify this omission.

Van Minnen's account raises certain methodological problems, especially in regard to the deposition of the remains (see Maehler 1983 and below), but the approach opens possibilities. Literary fragments, tax registers and family archives can be brought together with the surviving material remains and the results are potentially evocative, exciting even, leaving open the possibility of a total history of the inhabitants of the house. But, in some ways, van Minnen's published study does not live up to this promise. In part, this may be a matter of scale. Van Minnen's study is a first programmatic attempt and, of necessity, such a study must be incomplete. To develop a picture of the community and the place of individuals within that community, one needs to look at more than one house and van Minnen's programme is for a rolling series of studies of individuals, families and houses in context. Nevertheless, the problem with the micrology of Karanis is, I suspect, rather more deep-set than van Minnen allows. Even when the available, imperfect, fragments of evidence are compiled and edited, we are still left with a notable absence. We are still looking for ghosts and although we may know the name of the occupant of a house, that he was a scribe, that he lived with children and that he may have read Greek literature, we are still a long way from a biography. The fundamental problem behind van Minnen's analysis and I suspect why there have not been more micro-studies of Karanis or of other Greek and Roman settlements in Egypt is that simply amassing the material and connecting the papyrological and archaeological remains (even allowing for the substantial methodological difficulties that thereby arise) does not, in fact, provide us with a way of understanding these houses and their pattern of occupation. The crucial interpretative context does not emerge straightforwardly from the material. We look at photographs of a wooden peg in house C45 and the rope that is tied round it and wonder at its seemingly miraculous state of preservation, but we cannot give it meaning (plate 3.1). A rope, on a peg, on the wall of a house has no significance for us. It must, however, have had a meaning for whoever put it there, whoever went to the trouble of banging the peg into the wall, whoever decided it would be a good place to put the rope.

In the last chapter, I argued that it was the mental constructions of the environment that animated human geography and also crucially disrupted positivistic readings of the environment. This was the problem geographers faced and it is also the problem with which architects, anthropologists and archaeologists must grapple. Bourdieu's (1977: 90–1) description of the Kabyle house again sets us underway (see pp. 16–17). Bourdieu's reading is cultural. Each space is invested with meaning, compare Bachelard (1994), Knights (1994) or, Girouard (1978), but that meaning is not automatically readable from the archaeological record.[3] If we were to enter the ruins of an English working-class terrace-house, I do not think that we could easily reconstruct the complexities of social relations and negotiations that shaped the lived environment of the house. Yet that material should be there, and we should be able to make something of it. The architectural space and the distribution of artefacts are culturally created, representations and results of what went on in the house. Hillier and Hanson's (1984: 82) programmatic statement that the social forces that shape and form society are the very forces that shape and form social space must also apply to the distribution of artefacts within the architectural space. The problem the historian faces is that the artefacts and the architectural space do not speak to us. Those spaces were understood by those who lived in them because of a shared culture, a shared set of beliefs and understandings, shared ways of looking at space, and, most important, the years of experience. Bourdieu's description of the Kabyle house was the result of a deployment of ethnographic and architectural information. It is impossible to imagine an archaeologist, faced with a scatter of material remains in what is often a fairly simple structure, being able to produce a description of a house approaching this complexity without ethnographic material.[4]

The most successful studies of ancient housing have been conducted on Campanian examples, on the houses destroyed by the volcanic eruptions of AD 79 (Wallace-Hadrill 1988; 1994; 1997; Laurence and Wallace-Hadrill 1997; Dwyer 1991; Allison 1997b). The reason for this is not just the remarkable preservation of many of the ancient sites, but also that we can bring to bear knowledge gleaned from ancient texts. Thus, studies draw on discrete types of material which are used to generate a picture of the social use of housing. Methodological purists have objected to this policy since the process may privilege textual material and the archaeological material may be used to support broad historical conclusions derived from that textual material, as certainly has been the case in the past. It is only by treating the archaeological

Plate 3.1 A section of the northern wall of C45K, showing a wall peg with rope attached (Kelsey Museum Archives: 5.2684; photographer: G. R. Swain.)

material separately, as a coherent body of evidence according to its own rules, they argue, that we can come to understand the ancient site. After all, the texts are about Roman houses and the archaeology is Campanian (Allison 1997a; 1997b with further bibliography; Grahame 1997; 1998). There is force in this argument, but the alternative of rejecting the insights offered by textual material and of turning to models drawn from anthropology to understand the spatiality of houses seems even less attractive (Nevett 1997). Better studies have taken this criticism seriously, but have attempted to use the texts as a way into the archaeology, as a key to unlocking some of the secrets of the houses and also as a point of departure from which the varied archaeological record can be assessed.

With Egypt, the situation is rather different since there is not the same geographical distance between the textual and the archaeological material. We can link texts to sites and be reasonably confident that some of the often simple surviving descriptions of houses can be associated with house-types identified in the archaeological record. The problems we face are more closely connected with the nature of the record. The archaeological record is very uneven and all the surviving examples of Roman period housing come from village sites, mainly Karanis. More seriously, the ancient literary record for Rome explicitly deals with spatiality and spatial issues, by locating activities, by describing events such as the morning *salutatio*, and by discussing transgressions of spatial rules, but the papyri do not have discursive treatments of spatial issues. It is, as a result, far more difficult to reconstruct individual perceptions of spatiality in Egypt than in Rome. Although there are grounds for optimism (the ideologies that informed spatiality must be reflected in the papyrological texts, as they are reflected in the archaeological record, and we are comparatively well informed about Romano-Egyptian society), the reader should be aware of the limits of our knowledge.

Bourdieu's description brings us to a further theoretical problem which, I think, must inform our expectations of what we can achieve in the study of the house. In some cultures, the house can be seen as the primary *locus* of culture. Bourdieu calls this the *habitus* and it is convenient to adopt his terminology. The *habitus* is a 'structuring structure', a place where the values of the culture are learned and reproduced, transmitting that culture and being a central part of it (Bourdieu 1977; 1990; cf. Giddens 1979; 1984 and also p. 38 above; Donley-Reid 1990). The house is where children typically watch their mothers and fathers, and other family members and learn the patterns of interaction, of language, of non-verbal communication. They learn discipline and about power and, indeed, love. Bourdieu's description portrays a place of socialization. Patterns of house occupancy and the necessity of negotiation between occupants have often been thought to have a socializing effect on young adults, part of the process of settling down and becoming responsible citizens. House ownership and occupancy can be correlated with civil and political rights in many historical societies. Yet, this process was not confined to the house. Children quickly observe that male and female patterns of activity can be very different and their relationship with houses is thus altered. In some cultures, males and females, young and old, occupy different houses and thus social divisions and oppositions are made explicit. In many cultures social roles are played out and learnt in public space. The Roman aristocrat greeted his clients in his house, welcoming them to his *atrium*, but then he went out, to the Forum, the theatre, the baths, and there he met others, dispensed favours (if powerful) and greeted friends. The social theatricals of the Roman aristocrat may have been extreme, but lesser dramas are enacted in other social contexts. We need to learn complex social rules to function in society, but these rules are not difficult to learn as we observe them being enacted and enforced every day. As Bourdieu showed for the Kabyle, space, time, gender and the cosmos all conform to an order, an order that holds societies together, and he was able to transcribe much of that order into the spatial patterns of the house. It seems to me unlikely that such transcriptions could be completed for houses in all cultures (nor does Bourdieu make this claim). The house is an important *locus*, but there are other important *loci* which contribute to socialization. For instance, in societies which have a close correlation between gender and spatial divisions, socialization for males especially may take place in 'public space'. In societies in which there is a powerful street culture, early twentieth-century British working-class areas, many Islamic cities and some American inner-city residential areas, the street may be a more important area of social activity than the house.

A second problem derives from the theoretical emphasis on production of space for which I argued in the last chapter. Social space within a house is produced by the interaction of the individuals inhabiting that house, but, as argued in the last chapter, those individuals are not completely free agents, nor can one argue that those agents always produce the physical space of the house. The homogeneities of architectural design and patterns of usage within particular societies are such that they could hardly be produced by the workings of individual agency. Social, economic and cultural pressures shape domestic space, perhaps making it necessary for house owners to have a room for display, to exclude non-familial males from houses, or to have space to conduct certain crucial economic activities, and these pressures do not necessarily spring from within the house-community itself. Nevertheless, the architect does not impose meaning on the residents. Those who occupy a house may live in an entirely different fashion than the architect intended and this becomes particularly clear if one considers houses in many modern inner cities which might have been occupied by residents of different ethnicity and class, different types of household, or by groups who for particular reasons chose to reshape the functions of the various rooms (Lawrence 1990; Wilk 1990; Rapoport 1969; though cf. Kus and Raharijana 1990). To understand the house, we must engage in a dialogue between forces internal and external to the house.[5] The house cannot be isolated from social forces and practices in the wider social and spatial environment.

Such an approach makes it easier to explain change. To jump ahead a little, the houses of Roman and Byzantine Egypt change over this period and this can be attributed to forces external to the house-community. Such developments have serious implications. To return to Bourdieu (and Giddens), the process of maintaining a social structure is continual; the mental construct that is social structure is continually being recreated and enacted. This social structure is represented spatially but also reinforced and naturalized by that spatiality. The very same factors that reproduce social structure, reproduce spatiality. So what happens when the *physical* environment is changed? This is a common problem: immigrant communities, for instance, are faced with a new and different physical environment. Those who wish to preserve their cultural identity might simply enforce their mental spatial patterns on the new physical environment, so that although the physical spaces are retained, the new occupants impose a pattern of usage and a spatial ideology derived from their homelands. Yet, even in an extreme case, such as a large-scale enforced immigration, it seems likely that the spatial practices of the host society would influence the immigrant group, if only through the interplay of public, local and domestic spatial practice. Such locational shifts must influence the *habitus*, the *loci* of acculturation and socialization within a society, but since social values are transcribed in spatial structures, then although one may reinscribe those same social values, it is likely that the social values themselves will change. Immigrant communities are, however, something of a special case. In a society with a relatively stable population, an observable change in domestic architecture would seem to suggest a society in flux and probably undergoing wholesale cultural change.

The discussion below is organized both chronologically and thematically. First, the analysis is devoted to establishing the physical forms of Romano-Egyptian houses, using both papyrological and archaeological material. In the second section, I will turn to peopling the houses, establishing the cultural uses of domestic space. Both these sections are limited to the Roman and late Roman period to *c*. AD 300. The remaining period will be considered separately in the third and fourth sections. This division is artificial and is imposed by changes in the nature of the evidence. In spite of the artificial nature of the division and the evident and expected continuities from the earlier period, I argue below that the houses of the fifth and sixth centuries were significantly different from those three centuries earlier.

Domestic architecture

Archaeology and Karanis

The vast majority of our examples of Romano-Egyptian domestic architecture come from the University of Michigan excavations at Karanis, supplemented by a brief season at Soknopaiou Nesos, where houses of a very similar type were uncovered (Boak 1935). The excavations were never completely published. Preliminary reports appeared during or soon after the excavations and there has been a trickle of final reports since then, including a report on the topography of the site (Husselman 1979; Boak and Peterson 1931; Boak 1933; Harden 1936; Wilson 1953; Haatvedt and Peterson 1964; Shier 1978; Johnson 1981; Gazda 1978; 1983). The excavators were engaged in rescue archaeology and, therefore, undertook a large-scale operation, attempting to clear the majority of the site.[6] The state of preservation of the remains was so good and so much was found that it seems that the level of record-keeping fell somewhat below modern standards. Nevertheless, the available published documentation and the photographic archives (held by the Kelsey Museum) are extraordinary and provide a rich insight into village life in the Roman Fayum. Here, one can only outline the complexity and diversity of the available material.

The street system of Karanis was complex.[7] There were a number of 'main' thoroughfares (e.g. CS100; CS210; CS52; CS95), several metres wide and comparatively unobstructed, a series of narrower streets (e.g. CS150; CS120; CS23; CS46), and a number of passageways and alleys. Some of the latter (e.g. CS105; CS125; CS35) gave access to single houses and must, *de facto*, have been privatized. Houses had entrances onto all types of streets.

The houses themselves were made of Nile mudbrick, often interspersed with wooden beams. They were multi-storey, with commonly two or three floors, and often seem to have had access to the roof. Most of the houses were terraced, sharing sometimes three walls with neighbours. The walls were punctuated with doorways and a few narrow windows, sometimes barred and shuttered. In spite of these breaks, the walls give an impression to a modern eye of a certain uniformity, even a facelessness, in the architecture. The entranceways were often protected by windbreaks which probably prevented sand or dirt entering houses. Behind the windbreaks stood wooden doors, mostly single leaf but some double doors. Some of these could be locked either through the use of simple keys or through bolts.

Most of the plans are of ground floors only, though some of the houses were preserved to more than one storey and several contained basements. Nevertheless, one can gain some impression of their size from the publications, though my measurements are approximate (Alston 1997a). The 106 houses measured had a mean area of 75.2 m² and a median area of 70 m², though such averages conceal a range of house sizes from over 200 m² to under 30 m².[8] These averages compare with average ground plan areas from Priene of 207 m², Kassope 210 m², Abdera *c.* 161 m², Dura Europos[9] 256 m², Olynthus 289 m², Pompeii 271 m², and Herculaneum 241 m² (Hoepfner and Schwandner 1986; Wallace-Hadrill 1994: 76; Alston 1997a).

The plans of the houses were often complex. As far as one can tell, nearly all the houses had access to an open courtyard. Here, there is evidence for cooking and food preparation, agricultural work and animal husbandry and it was probably the major work area of the house. Some of the floors were paved; others were just beaten earth. The yard appears normally to have been towards one side of a building, though there is a possible exception in which the yard may have been a central court (Husselman 1979: 49–54).[10] Apart from the presence of the yard, there was no obvious uniformity in ground plan. Although the available published plans (Husselman 1979) make formal analysis of the access patterns difficult, I provide a few examples, together with access diagrams from several randomly selected British houses.[11]

The British middle-class houses show similar patterns of access with complex clustered plans. The rooms are grouped around common passageways. In all the examples given, a more private upstairs is distinguishable from the more public downstairs by the limitation of points of access to those upstairs rooms, making

Figure 3.1 Map 11: Karanis (after Husselman 1979)

Key:

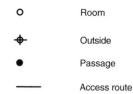

House C45: A complex clustered plan

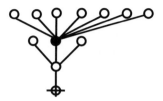

House C203: A simple linear plan

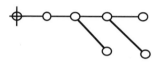

House C63: A complex plan combining linear and clustered elements

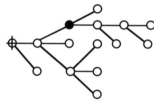

House C118: A complex linear plan

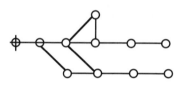

House C127: A simple clustered plan

House C404: A complex linear plan with limited clustered elements

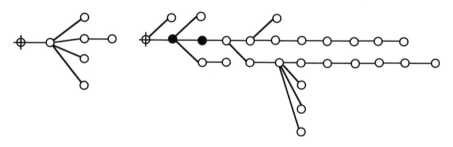

Figure 3.2 Selected houses from Karanis: schematic access plans

the privacy of upstairs far easier to preserve than the downstairs with its complex patterns of access.[12] With the block of flats, the pattern is very clear: a communal passage and stairwell give access to fourteen separate flats, all comprised of a series of rooms clustered round a central passage. The pattern obviously allows control of access and the privacy of each flat. The terraced house seems to be a rather simpler version of middle-class housing, with a distinction between the bedrooms upstairs and the more public downstairs in the layout, though it has a stronger linear element.

Key:

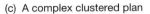

○   Room

⊕   Outside

●   Passage

——— Access route

(c) A complex clustered plan

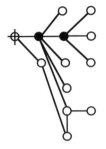

Three middle class houses

(a) A complex clustered plan

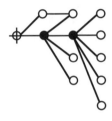

A terraced house: a largely linear approach to a clustered element

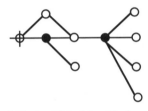

(b) A complex clustered plan

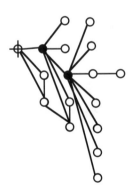

A block of flats (simplified): a simple clustered plan

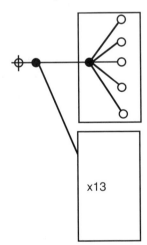

x13

Figure 3.3 Modern British housing

The diversity of the Egyptian examples is striking when compared with the relative homogeneity of the British comparisons. We are, of course, hampered by the relative lack of information concerning upper storeys, though the plans published by Husselman (1979) suggest that access within the upper storeys was organized on a linear rather than a clustered basis. The linearity of several of the Egyptian examples carries obvious implications: use of a room at the end of the access plan requires use of all intervening rooms and, correspondingly, access to the deeper rooms in the houses could be controlled at any one of the access points between the outside and that room. We do, however, have examples of some clustered layouts, C45, C127 (cf. C50, C86), a pattern also shown by a rather difficult house (and therefore not planned here), C78 (Map 12). This house consists of a complex series of rooms which connected to a central corridor, off which there were eight similarly sized cell-like rooms. C73/117 (Map 11), set centrally within a block, also has seven rooms (possibly originally eight) either side of a central corridor with two larger rooms at the end of the corridor. The relationship of this sequence of rooms with houses C114 and structure C92 seems obscure. These houses had easily separable units and we shall meet this type of arrangement again in the much later houses of Byzantine Alexandria.

The decor of the houses is problematic. Karanis was abandoned over centuries and the 'Pompeii premise' in which a site is found in working order, simply abandoned by its people, a kind of archaeological *Mary Celeste*, does not apply (and most now doubt whether it applies even to Pompeii, see Allison 1997a; Schiffer 1985). Houses will have been stripped of valuables, probably by the diminishing population, or looted in the centuries of decline, and one must presume that anything of value would have been reused. The material remains

Figure 3.4 House C78

do not suggest a particularly prosperous community in the second and early third centuries, though the glass from the site, mostly of fourth-century date, is notable both for its quantity and quality. Nevertheless, in all periods, members of the community were able to invest surplus wealth in their houses, in terracotta, bronze and stone figurines, wooden furniture, some reasonable quality textiles, and wall paintings (Gazda 1978; 1983; Husselman 1979: 35–6; pl. 98; 102). Many of the houses had rooms with niches (Husselman 1979: 47–8; pls 24–6; 69–74; 96; 101). Some of these were unadorned and may have been used as cupboards and general storage areas. Others had elaborate framing stone carving and decorations within the niches, usually of a religious nature. These shrines and the figurines would seem to reflect a vibrant domestic religion.

The Fayum (and perhaps especially Karanis) was a heavily Hellenized area of Egypt and this might suggest that the housing here would be rather different from that in other areas of Egypt. We have, however, no 'control group' with which to compare the Karanis houses.[13] Nevertheless, it is extremely difficult to detect any specifically Greek or Roman influence in the domestic architecture and there seems little reason to believe that the domestic architecture of the village was atypical.

Domestic Architecture in the Papyri[14]

Houses appear in several different contexts within the papyri but mostly in documentation relating to property transfer (wills, sales, rentals, mortgages), taxation documents (such as the census and lists of residence), documents relating to legal disputes, the process of building, and in topographical descriptions. These provide a significant body of data from all periods from the first to the seventh century and from both urban and rural sites. There are differences in the type of evidence available in the different periods: Byzantine descriptions of houses tended to be more elaborate than those from the Roman period (certainly after the early first century AD). Yet, even in the Byzantine period, many of the descriptions of houses lack detail. The purpose of the descriptions was normally to identify the house or the part of the house under discussion and to preserve legal rights. Thus, in most cases, only major architectural features are mentioned. The most commonly mentioned features include the number of storeys, the αὐλή (aule: yard), any πύργοι (purgoi: towers),[15] wells, the αἴθριον (aithrion: court), the πύλον (pylon: gatehouse), the συμπόσιον (symposion: dining room) and sometimes outbuildings, such as dovecotes or stables. Descriptions also mention a specific house-type, the οἰκία διπυργία (two-towered house), which must reflect a prominent and specific architectural feature, and the rights of access which, if the narrowness of some of the alleys in Karanis are representative, must have been important to preserve. Houses were further identified by the neighbours, normally assuming a close orientation to the cardinal points of the compass and describing all four neighbouring plots (one of which would be the street), and houses in cities were normally further located by street or district.

The number of storeys typically varied between one and four, though there is one case of a seven-storey house (*P. Oxy.* XXXIV 2719). It seems very likely that the average house in city and village was of two storeys (Husson 1983a: 257–67). Forty-seven per cent of village houses and 40 per cent of urban housing whose number of storeys is attested (n = 109) were of two storeys. Twenty-five per cent of attested village housing was of three or more storeys while 42 per cent of urban housing comprised more than two storeys, a difference that is statistically significant.

One could add figures derived from house descriptions which mention a room being on a particular storey without specifying the height of the house. This increases the number of cases but seemingly does not significantly alter the pattern of attestations.[16]

The αὐλή was a court or yard (Husson 1983a: 45–55). These are frequently attested in the papyrological material in both urban and rural contexts. Many houses had this kind of yard and the frequency of their attestation encourages identification with the workyards attested at Karanis. These yards could contain πίργοι (towers) or wells (*BGU* XI 2033; *P. Bub.* 1; *P. Oxy.* II 243; LII 3691; *P. Vind. Tandem* 27). The πίργοι were agricultural buildings used mainly for storage and were probably free-standing. Αὖλαι could be sold separately from the house (*P. Oxy.* III 505; XIV 1696; 1697) and individuals could own more than one αὐλή (*P. Mich.* VI 428). A peripheral location for αὖλαι (as suggested in the Karanis excavations) suggests that such yards could be exchanged between neighbouring properties.[17]

The αὐλή is to be distinguished from the αἴθριον, clearly also a courtyard (Husson 1983a: 29–36). Houses could have both an αὐλή and an αἴθριον, but it is not unusual for there to be no mention of an αὐλή in descriptions of houses with αἴθρια. Αἴθρια are not evenly distributed between cities and villages. Of the located occurrences in the papyri, 78 (61 per cent) come from probable urban contexts while only 49 can probably be connected to villages, 28 of those attestations relating to houses at Tebtunis in the Fayum.[18] The relative paucity of village examples and the clear differentiation between αὐλή and αἴθριον suggests that the αἴθριον courtyard should be typologically distinct.

Table 3.1 Number of houses by storey: firm attestations[a]

Settlement type	Number of houses by storey						
	1	2	3	4	5	6	7
Villages	20	33	18	—	—	—	—
Cities	7	15	10	5	—	—	1

[a] Data derived from Husson 1983a: 257–67, excluding *P. Berol. Bork.*, since that text seems only to mention the number of storeys in cases where the houses were other than two storey, and a computer search, with additions from *SB* XX.

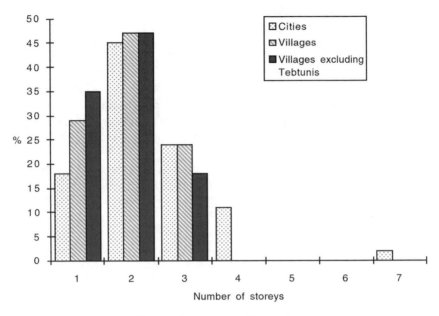

Figure 3.5 Percentages of houses by storey and by settlement type

Unfortunately, such distinctions are not obvious at Karanis, though there may be unrecognized examples and it seems possible that we have an example at house 3 in Kellis (see pp. 105–7). There are no examples of the sale of αἴθρια separate from that of a house, which suggests that the αἴθριον was an integral feature.

Such a courtyard might be pictured in a unique but puzzling plan from Oxyrhynchus (*P. Oxy.* XXIV 2406). This house plan depicts a gatehouse, a central courtyard which contained an οβολισκος (meaning uncertain) and what appears to be stairs. Behind this courtyard, and separate from the gatehouse, stood the house itself. The courtyard is, frustratingly, labelled ατρειον, a word derived from the Latin *atrium*. Although *atrium* and αἴθριον have the same root, the words are not interchangeable (Chantraine 1964; Boëthius and Ward Perkins 1970; McKay 1975). This papyrus represents our one attestation of the word from Egypt in a domestic context (Husson 1976). The Roman *atrium* house is a distinctive type, as mainly represented at Pompeii, and the house depicted on the plan is clearly not an *atrium* house as we would normally understand it. It seems most likely that the architect, perhaps to add to his prestige, used the Latin rather than the more normal Greek word which, I would suggest, was αἴθριον. The house depicted did not have an obvious αὐλή and it would seem likely that in such circumstances an αἴθριον would fulfil some of the functions of an αὐλή.[19] An αἴθριον could contain domestic equipment (*P. Oxy.* XII 1488). Although clearly a distinction operated in architectural terminology and presumably in perceptions of houses, we should not exaggerate the difference between an αἴθριον house and other houses. A small αἴθριον house may have little if any more space than a house without an αἴθριον but with an αὐλή.

Gatehouses, πύλα, are commonly attested in the papyrological evidence (Husson 1983a: 243–6). Many of the pylons attested were not domestic and the word was used of entrances to gymnasia (*P. Köln* I 52; *P. Oxy.* I 55 = *W. Chr.* 196 = *Sel. Pap.* II 307), and granaries (*P. Mich.* II 121 r. iii 5), as well as the more well-known usage in relation to temples and city gates (e.g. *P. Oxy.* XLIII 3094; *SB* X 10299 = *Stud. Pal. Pap.* XX 68 = *Stud. Pal. Pap.* V 127).[20] The domestic gatehouse is sometimes called the πρόπυλον (*P. Mich.* V 288; 307; *P. Oxy* II 243 = *M. Chr.* 182), though it is unclear whether this differed in any way from the πύλον. In some cases, a πύλον contained or was closely associated with a ταμεῖον (a treasury or a strongroom) (*P. Mich.* V 295; 298 = *PSI* VIII 913 [*BL* III, 115]). Θύρα (Husson 1983a: 93–107; 1983b) was the normal word used for doorway, and it seems probable that the πύλον was architecturally distinctive, perhaps even a separate structure from the main house. There is little evidence for the appearance of such structures, though the evidence of rooms in πύλα suggests that they could be substantial. We need not assume that all gatehouses domestic and public conformed to a similar pattern since the same word could presumably have been used to describe gatehouses in traditional Egyptian or Classical styles, but it is certainly attractive to look for parallels to the domestic πύλα in the traditional, monumental, trapezoidal gatehouses of Egyptian temples.

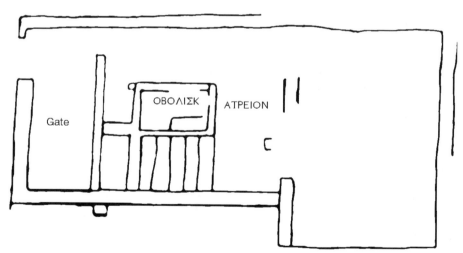

Figure 3.6 P. Oxy. XXIV 2406

The οἰκία διπυργία (the two-towered house) also appears to have been a distinctive house-type. These houses were unevenly distributed between urban and rural sites, with nine of the twelve provenanced references relating to urban contexts. Of the three village examples, two related to families of considerable wealth (*P. Oxy.* XIV 1703 *BL* VIII, 249; *PSI* X 1159). It seems very likely that the οἰκία διπυργία was a particularly high-status residence (Alston and Alston 1997; Husson 1983a: 251–2; Nowicka 1973; Rostem 1962). The appearance of the house is again uncertain but it seems likely that the towers were integral and prominent features of the houses. Some clue may come from the hieroglyphic determinative for a large house which features two prominent towers attached to the frontage (Parlebas 1977; Davis 1929).

There is a single reference to a three-towered house (οἰκία τριπυργία) (*P. Oxy.* LXIV 4438 of AD 252). This house was bought by the wife of a former magistrate of Oxyrhynchus from a gymnasiarch of the city who was the son of a former magistrate. It was a well-equipped house and clearly a residence fitting for members of the elite.

Although towers in yards were probably used for storage and possibly also as granaries, providing an alternative to the 'bin' granaries discovered at Karanis (e.g. House C123), towers on the front of houses probably functioned differently. In the heat of summer, the higher one rose off the street, the further away one was from the dust and the more chance one had of catching a breeze.[21]

Many other features of houses make fleeting appearances in the papyri. For instance, some houses had an ἐξέδρα (*exedra*), a room which was probably distinguished by being open to the street and might have been used as a shop, a storeroom or a hall (Husson 1983a: 73–7). In the later period, such rooms could be on upper storeys and perhaps a translation as 'balcony' or 'veranda' would be more appropriate (*P. Erl.* I 73; *P. Flor.* I 13; *SB* VI 9462).[22]

We have an attestation of the construction of a private bath house in AD 186 belonging to a Serenos which had at least five chambers (Husson 1983a: 58–60; *P. Oxy.* XVII 2145). Another probably second-century bath house belonging to Arrius Apollinarius was taken into public ownership and was used as a public bath house by the early third century (*P. Oxy.* XLIV 3173; 3176; L 3566; Krüger 1989) while the Tiberii Iulii Theones, an elite family based in Oxyrhynchus, had a private bath house by the mid-second century (*P. Theones* 15). This conspicuous expenditure is probably mirrored by a third-century stone house

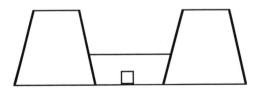

Figure 3.7 Determinative of a large house: οἰκία διπυργία (?)

(presumably built to contrast with the predominant mud-brick) which is by far the most expensive house attested in the papyrological record (*P. Oxy.* XIV 1634). The house was not, however, unique (*P. Oxy.* III 489 [AD 117]; Nowicka 1969: 32). These attestations suggest that some at least were willing to invest large sums of money in their houses (see also pp. 102–4).

The papyrological material suggests that there was a vast range of housing in Roman Egypt and that houses were typologically variegated. Houses ranged from the small residences attested at Karanis to large and luxurious houses in cities hinted at in the papyri.

A crude assessment (crude because it cannot distinguish between typology and size) of this range can be made from the evidence of house prices.[23] We have insufficient prices with which to draw firm conclusions, but the evidence does allow us to distinguish certain patterns that may reflect the 'real' housing stock of Roman Egypt.[24] First, median prices of houses by settlement type in each century show a considerable difference between urban and rural housing. Although this may be explained in various ways, analysis of the individual prices in figure 3.9 shows that houses of most price levels could be found in the various types of settlement. This suggests that factors such as higher land prices in cities than villages are unlikely to be significant. The gap between urban and rural prices is likely to reflect architectural differences in the housing stock (cf. Husson 1976).

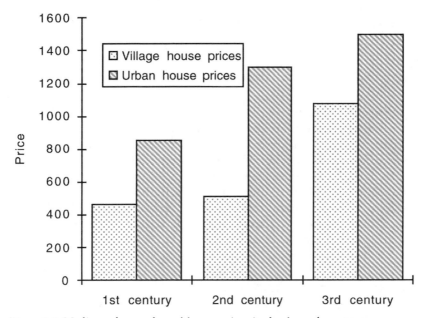

Figure 3.8 Median urban and rural house prices in drachmas by century

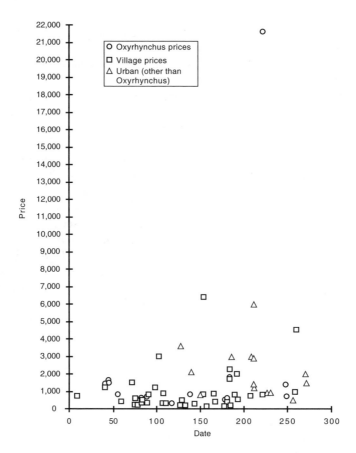

Figure 3.9 Dated house prices (in drachmas) from Roman Egypt by settlement type

A second observation rests on considerably weaker grounds. Figure 3.9 shows that prices in the first century of our era were comparatively tightly bunched. From the early second century and increasingly towards the end of that century, however, prices show a considerably greater range. This process is represented in figures 3.10–3.11, which show the difference between mean and median prices of houses over the first three centuries. With little significant difference in the first century, medians and means had moved far apart by the third centuries. The data set is so flimsy that a single price, such as the stone house valued at 21,600 drachmas in 224 (*P. Oxy.* XIV 1634), or minor changes in method can have a significant effect on the statistical measures.[25] Nevertheless, taking a slightly larger data set, as in figure 3.10.2, does not substantially alter the picture. Nevertheless, the patterns of figure 3.9 and the further analysis of changes in house prices in figures 3.10–3.11 are, in my view, significant. The statistics reflect a change in the housing market: more comparatively expensive

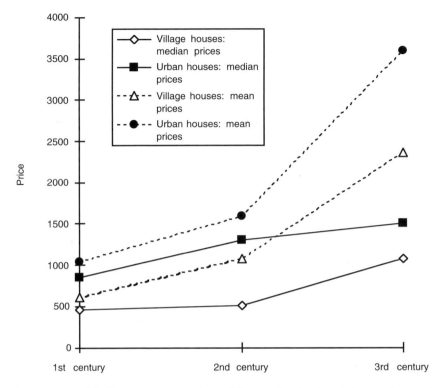

Figure 3.10.1 Median and mean prices of houses (in drachmas) by settlement by century

houses were being sold in the second and third centuries, which in turn suggests significant investment in housing and the development of a more conspicuous and luxurious house-type.[26]

Conclusions

The pattern that emerges from the surviving papyrological and archaeological material from Egypt is diverse. The houses of Karanis show considerable typological variation and it is likely that there were other variants that have not been identified in the archaeological record. Judging from the patterns of attestation of architectural features and the differentials in house prices, urban housing was more diverse than village housing. Although most house-types could be found in both urban and village contexts, the substantial difference between urban and village housing lay in the relative distribution of the various house-types. The αἴθριον house-type, with its central courtyard (Nowicka 1969: 122, for an early example), was probably a lighter and better ventilated

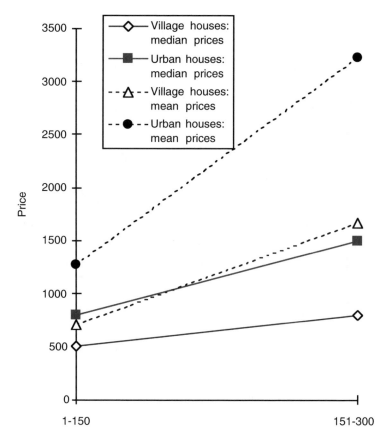

Figure 3.10.2 Median and mean prices of houses (in drachmas) by settlement by 150-year period

house than many of those at Karanis and conformed to a fairly common Mediterranean pattern of gatehouse (or fore-house), court, and house (or back-house) (see also pp. 100–1), the environmental advantages of which are, I think, sufficient explanation for its popularity (Toulan 1980). The central courtyard may have performed some of the functions of the abundantly attested αὐλή, or workyard, but the αὐλή appears to have been architecturally marginal and hence probably provided less light and ventilation for the house. The Karanis houses, with their small, high windows and external courts, must have been hotter and darker than the predominantly urban αἴθριον houses (Stead 1980). The gate-houses and οἰκία διπύργια (if I am correct in associating the towers with the facade of the house) laid emphasis on the front of the house. These arrangements may have presented an imposing facade to the street, marking very clearly the boundary between the street and the house.[27] Even the comparatively plain

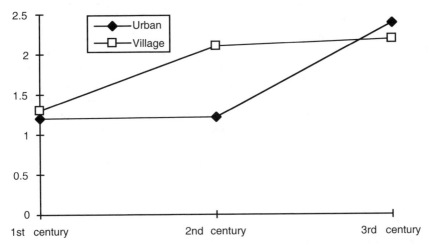

Figure 3.11 Ratio of median to mean prices by century and by settlement

houses at Karanis seem to turn a rather severe face on the outsider. High, barred and shuttered windows and locked and bolted doors faced any visitors. Architecturally, the division between house and street seems emphasized.

The houses at Karanis were multi-room dwellings and, in some cases, had intricate plans. Many of the Karanis houses were equipped with niches, some of which had a religious purpose, but, apart from these, the decor of most of the Karanis houses appears to have been simple. We have no parallel archaeological evidence for urban housing, though there is every reason to believe that the houses of Karanis were replicated in the cities of Egypt. Nevertheless, cities appear to have had more traditional, large Egyptian-style housing and there is limited evidence for more Graeco-Roman features, such as bath-houses. While the average urban house in the third century fetched less than twice the price of its first-century equivalent, the average price of urban houses more than tripled in that period. This suggests architectural development and perhaps the introduction of a new house-type.[28]

Living in houses: reconstructing the community of an urban house

Egyptians, Greeks and Romans all operated a system of partible inheritance. A person's property would be divided, in roughly equal proportions, between his or her surviving children (Pestman 1961; Zingale 1991; 1997; Montevecchi 1935; 1973: 207; Amelotti 1966). In Egyptian custom, it seems that the eldest son tended to receive twice as much as his siblings, though there was no other gender differentiation in the distribution of property (Hobson 1983). The use of wills gave the deceased the potential to manage that property transfer and divide the estate logically, rather than relying on lawyers or the legatees reaching some agreement, though many wills simply state the proportion of the estate to go to each of the legatees. Some property divisions made some effort to preserve the integrity of separate property units (*P. Tebt.* II 382; *P. Strasb.* IV 284 [though this is lacunose]). Thus, the will of Taarpaesis alias Isidora daughter of Apollonios (*P. Köln* II 100), dated to AD 133, divided her property between her three children. Her son received a house, with αἴθριον and αὐλή, in Oxyrhynchus, another house and various patches of land at Phoboos and Ophis in the Oxyrhynchite. His sisters received jointly half a house in Oxyrhynchus and a quarter of a house in Phoboos. A division of property at Bakchias dating to AD 72 (*P. Mich.* III 186; 187) divides fractions of property between two heirs, one getting a slightly larger fraction (quarter of a house), the other gaining a thirty-sixth of three properties. Nevertheless, other divisions split each of the various properties owned by the testator (e.g. *P. Tebt.* II 319 = *Sel. Pap.* I 53; *CPR* I 11) or even used a combination of the above measures (*BGU* I 241 *BL* I, 30–2; *BGU* I 234 *BL* I, 28–9; *P. Mich.* V 322; 326; *SB* XX 14285) and in many cases only one substantial item of property was bequeathed and the heirs had little choice but to divide it (*P. Ryl.* II 157 = *Sel. Pap.* I 52; *P. Lond.* II, p. 187, 293 *BL* I, 261–2; *SB* X 10572; *SB* VIII 9824; XII 10788). For instance, in 118, a house, αὐλή and four palm trees were divided unequally between four people, 40 per cent to one person, 40 per cent to two, and the final 20 per cent to a fourth party (*P. Oxy.* III 503). Property was divided in virtually every conceivable way. The inevitable result of this was that individuals came to own small fractions of property, both in land and in houses.

The division that took place through posthumous transmission of property could be rationalized through subsequent concentration of property through inheritance, sale and purchase, or rentals, and many of the house-sale documents deal with only a fraction of the house.[29] It is not, however, clear whether sales of fractions of houses were normally or even often used to concentrate ownership of divided houses in the hands of a single individual. Individuals sold fractions of houses while retaining a fraction of the same house (e.g. *P. Fay. Towns* 31 = *M. Chr.* 201; *P. Corn.* 12). The fragmentary nature of many of our documents means that relationships between purchaser and vendor and between the contracting parties and the neighbours can be assessed only in a comparatively small number of cases. From 105 cases, 64 (61 per cent) sales showed no prior relationship between the purchaser, the vendor or the neighbours. In 19 cases (18 per cent) the sale was within a family, though in 22 cases (21 per cent), the sale involved people who were related to the owners of or themselves owned neighbouring properties. This pattern is further complicated as it is far from easy to establish connections between cousins since although patronymics and metronymics form a normal part of nomenclature, papponymics, though used, are far less frequently given. One must assume, therefore, that a considerable number of prior relationships are not attested in the documentation. Also, since sale documents normally include the descriptions of neighbouring plots in order to identify the plot under discussion, there was no need to state the names of those holding the remaining portions of the house. There was some consolidation of ownership within a single house (e.g. *P. Lond.* III, p. 151, 1158, though see *P. Lond.* III, p. 152, 1298) but multiple ownership of a house does not seem to have been regarded as particularly problematic. Nevertheless, there is a distinct pattern of topographical concentration in the ownership of domestic property since houses or fractions of houses were often bought by neighbours.[30]

How the fragmentation of the house worked in practice is unclear. Although the fraction of the property to be sold was stated in the surviving contracts, there was, normally, no further description of the division of the house. Some houses appear to have been divided (*P. Mich.* X 584; *SB* XVI 12391 = *P. Oxy.* II 331; *SB* X 10572; *CPR* I 11; *P. Cair. Isid.* 105; cf. *P. Gen.* I 11 = *P. Abinnaeus* 62 of the fourth century) so that there was either a notional or architectural separation between the various parts of the houses. However, most houses with multiple owners were held 'in common and undivided' (e.g. *PSI* VIII 910; XIII 1320; *P. Mich.* V 276; *SB* VIII 9824; XII 10788). Ownership and residence are, of course, not necessarily related and many of the practical problems would disappear if one were to assume that shared ownership was often merely a financial relationship, the house, or fractions of it, being rented out to the residents.

Tax collectors and officials were interested in both ownership and residence since information on the former was important in property disputes and levying taxes on property and on the latter for levying poll tax. A number of surviving registers record residence of males of fourteen years or over.[31] These registers were organized topographically, listing the men by household (since households would presumably pay taxes together) and by the fraction of house occupied, and show that households could occupy only a fraction of a house, the remaining fraction presumably being occupied by another household. The modern Western equation of a single household to a house does not apply to Roman Egypt as the modern equation of a single owner for a single house has been shown not to apply.

This is foreign to the ideology of modern, Western house occupation, though not unusual as a practice. Students, young adults, single, poor individuals, and, in some cases, destitute families will share domestic space with those unrelated to them, especially in areas of high housing costs, and the practice was common in many historical societies. Yet, we still have to construct an artificial terminology to describe the resulting relationships. Some of the terminology used here was developed by the Cambridge Group for the History of Population and Social Structure to describe the residential patterns found in past societies. I shall use 'relatives' to refer to those descended from a single common progenitor or who have been joined by marriage to the descendants of that progenitor and 'family' for the co-resident group of relatives. I shall use 'household' to refer to a co-residential unit which acts together legally and financially. Such households are normally constructed around a single family. I shall use 'houseful' to describe the residents of a single house.

It is possible to use the registers of men by household and house to estimate both the average size of households and of housefuls. We cannot reliably estimate the size of individual households but we can calculate the likely overall population of an attested area of a community from the number of men attested.[32] Estimating the number of households formed and houses occupied by this population is considerably more problematic. Men will not have been evenly distributed throughout the various households of a community and so some households will have had no male members liable for the poll tax. Households and housefuls without resident poll tax payers would not be entered on the registers, but some allowance has to be made for these invisible housefuls and households in our calculations. This is not easily done since it depends not only on demographics but on the rate of remarriage after the death of a husband and the social acceptability of a woman having no husband or adult male within her household or house. A study of Bagnall and Frier's (1994: 179–312) catalogue of census declarations suggests that 11.5–14 per cent of all groups which submit a single census declaration had no male members of an age to pay poll tax.[33] It is simply unclear to me whether the group that submitted the census report and thus forms the basis of Bagnall and Frier's analysis was the houseful or the household, though clearly it was not the family. It seems that the legal duty to submit the census return fell in the first instance to the house owner, though some census declarations were submitted by individuals who did not own the house or any portion of the house in which they resided. The census declared itself to be 'by house', but although census returns also frequently mention other properties owned by the declarant, it is unclear how the legal duty to declare occupants would be apportioned in houses with multiple owners. In practical terms, it seems to me very likely that the census declarations were not rigorous in their definition of household and that both housefuls and households were declared (Bagnall and Frier 1994: 11–14).[34] Since housefuls were significantly larger than households, the proportion of housefuls without adult males will have been lower than the proportion of households, but it is impossible to assess whether the 11.5–14 per cent reflects the proportion of housefuls or households lacking adult males. As a result, since there is no better alternative, the same adjustment has been applied to both.

For all texts (table 3.2), the adjusted average number of occupants per house (houseful) is 7.61–7.78 and the number of people per household is 5.40–5.52. The ratio of number of occupants per house to household size is 1.41. Most of the tax registers used to arrive at these figures come from the village of Philadelphia and only two texts probably have an urban provenance. The sample provided is too small to treat as significant but the urban ratio of number of occupants per house to household size is also 1.41, though simply compiling the figures from second-century Ptolemais Euergetis and third-century Oxyrhynchus is questionable (see below). The urban texts can be supplemented by a late third- or early fourth-century text from Hermopolis (*SB* XVIII 13146). This is an incomplete register of males occupying ten houses.[35] The official

Table 3.2 House occupancy and household size

Document	Provenance	Date (AD)	No. of Households	No. of Houses	No. of Men	People/ Household	People/ House	People/ Household (adj.)	People/ House (adj.)
P. Lond. II 257, p.19	Philadelphia	c.95	111	74.4	216	6.03	9	4.97–5.08	7.41–7.57
P. Lond. II 258, p.28	Philadelphia	c.95	61	48.1	174	8.84	11.21	7.27–7.44	9.23–9.44
P. Lond. II 259, p.36	Philadelphia	c.95	15	13.3	26	5.37	6.06	4.42–4.52	4.99–5.10
P. Lond. III 901, p.23	Fayum	I/II	13	6	21	5.01	10.85	4.12–4.21	8.93–9.13
BGU II 493, 494, 497, 498, 503, 504	Ptolemais Euergetis?	II	14	6.5	25	5.53	11.92	4.56–4.66	10.76–11.00
P. Oxy. XLVI 3300	Oxyrhynchus	c. 270	12	12	16	4.13	4.13	3.40–3.48	3.40–3.48
All			226	160.3	478	6.56	9.24	5.40–5.52	7.61–7.78

appears to have been working with a list of house owners to which he then added the names of those resident. It is not clear whether the house owners were also resident. Only five of the houses had complete entries and 29 men were registered. This suggests a resident population of about 84, or 16–17 people per house, which seems extremely high, though the sample is, of course, very small.

The figures are quite startling, demonstrating that a significant number of houses were occupied by more than one household. The Philadelphia texts suggest that about 36 per cent of houses had multi-household occupancy. The ratio of houseful to household size is also high, but neither measure is unparalleled. Helin (1972) shows that the ratio of houseful to household size in Liège in 1801 was 1.45 and that 36 per cent of houses were shared. In pre-industrial England the houseful to household ratio was much smaller, 1.22 (Wall 1972). In addition, comparative figures from nineteenth-century Preston show that 10 per cent of houses were shared (Anderson 1972), which compares with eighteenth-century North America with about 21 per cent of houses shared (Greven 1972). The Egyptian statistics are, therefore, towards the upper end of the historical range.

A more serious discrepancy emerges with Bagnall and Frier's (1994: 68) calculation from the census returns that urban registering units ('census unit') were normally comprised of 5.31 people, while rural 'census units' had 4.58. A separate series of returns, though possibly not a representative sample (see below), from Ptolemais in Upper Egypt, dating to the census of AD 89, gives 4.3 persons per 'census unit'. My corresponding figures are given in table 3.3.

The discrepancy between my figures and those produced by Bagnall and Frier for urban households and housefuls does not seem significant, but my figures for village population suggest a much denser concentration of people in houses and households. My figures also suggest that village housefuls and households were larger than their urban equivalents. Bagnall and Frier (1994: 66–70), however, to add further complexities, not only demonstrate that urban 'census units' were larger than village 'census units', but that urban families were on average smaller than rural families (4.04 persons/family : 4.46 persons/family).[36] The discrepancy between family and 'census unit' sizes is a function of the numbers of slaves and lodgers in urban 'census units'. Bagnall and Frier demonstrate the complex and somewhat contradictory patterns of 'household'

Table 3.3 Number of people per houseful, household and census unit by site

Data Source	Urban Sites	Village Sites
Bagnall and Frier 1994: Census Unit	5.31	4.58
Bagnall, Frier and Rutherford 1997:		
Ptolemais Census Unit (AD 89)	4.3	—
Alston: Households	4.02–4.11	5.58–5.70
Alston: Housefuls	5.66–5.78	7.86–8.04

formation, but nowhere in this analysis is there a simple resolution of the contradiction between their figures and those arrived at in the above analysis.

The surviving village texts analysed above almost certainly all come from the same survey of Philadelphia in the first century and this, I believe, is sufficient to explain the discrepancy. The village texts have a geographical and chrono-logical homogeneity foreign to Bagnall and Frier's corpus of census documents, which draws evidence from nearly three centuries and from various types of settlement. This has clear methodological implications. My conclusions about village households and housefuls are strictly relevant to a single village in a single period. The extremely small urban samples come from two cities in different periods and show worryingly different patterns, especially when compared with the third tiny sample from Hermopolis. Clearly, combining that evidence, as in the final line of table 3.2, hides wide variations in patterns of occupancy and is methodologically questionable. The quantity of available surviving evidence means that Bagnall and Frier make a similarly questionable but methodologically necessary assumption that demographic patterns in Roman Egypt were essentially stable, prone to only short-term fluctuations insufficient to distort the overall picture, though they discuss, without reaching a firm conclusion, the possibility of a significant demographic change after the Antonine plague of c. AD 166 (Bagnall and Frier 1994: 173–8). If the figures for 'household' size are broken down by date from the census data presented by Bagnall and Frier, we get figure 3.12.[37] The surviving numbers of certainly complete and firmly dated returns are such that the figures are not meaningful: the urban averages for the first century, 103, 145, 159 and 173, rest on only five returns. The urban means fluctuate wildly while village means show more stability.[38]

The families attested at Ptolemais in AD 89 (Bagnall et al. 1997) represent a significant sample for which the mean household size is 4.3. The problem with this list is that it represents a sorted compilation probably by the status of the adult male declarant which may favour nuclear families and certainly favours younger adult males. The logic behind the compilation cannot be established and since the sample is unlikely to be representative, it has not been incorporated into the above statistics.

These data do not contradict the possibility (and we can be no stronger than this) that there were fluctuations over time as well as between urban and rural sites in the size of 'households' as registered in the papyrological material. Variations in household size have been noted in other societies, though the comparative data are mixed. Herlihy (1973) points to dramatic changes in household size in Verona between 1409 and 1502 with household size rising from 3.68 in 1409 and 1425 to 5.2 in 1456 and 5.89 in 1502. Once these findings are analysed by district, average household size rose across the ten districts of Verona by between 5 per cent and 83 per cent. Average household size in these ten districts varied between 2.89 persons and 5.53 in 1425 and 5.17 and 9.77 in 1502 (cf. Herlihy 1970). Servants were counted as a part of the

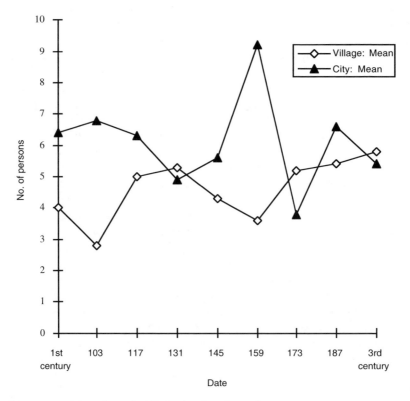

Figure 3.12 Mean 'household' size by date from the census returns

household and a large proportion of the increase seems to have been due to an increased use of servants, though family size does also seem to have increased marginally over this period. Herlihy (1985: 69–70) shows that there were significant variations in household size among the peasants of the eighth century according to the wealth of the particular household and argues (1985: 144–56) that in fifteenth-century Tuscany there were two identifiable and separate patterns of household formation with the top 25 per cent of households tending to differ in structure. Japanese figures also show regional variation (Nakane 1972) and change in household size, with a decline of sometimes more than 40 per cent in household size between data collected for 1671–1700 and 1851–70 (Hayami and Uchida 1972). Greven's (1972) study of eighteenth-century Massachusetts shows that houseful sizes fell by about 5 per cent in 26 years but figures for household size for England show a fairly constant mean household size of about 4.75 people from 1650 to 1801 (Laslett 1972). It seems possible that household size is comparatively stable in societies where the household is predominantly formed on the basis of the nuclear or conjugal family, whereas household and houseful sizes vary considerably over time in societies with more complex family structures. Although it cannot be demonstrated, I suspect that families with complex structures could react to demographic or economic changes by varying their household or houseful size whereas control of family size (within a conjugal family) was more problematic.[39] We might, therefore, expect dramatic variation in household and houseful size in relation to economic and (especially?) demographic pressures. Certainly, fourteenth- and fifteenth-century Italy was subject to startling demographic shifts (Herlihy 1967; 1970; 1973), but it is probable that the demography of Roman Egypt was similarly unstable (Rathbone 1990; Alston, forthcoming). Such demographic instability, which would be 'ironed out' by Bagnall and Frier's methodology,[40] should, if the above argument is correct, produce variations in household size by date and by location within Roman Egypt.

We cannot then take the figures in table 3.2 as being representative of the general situation in Egypt in the Roman period.[41] Nevertheless, table 3.2 does demonstrate that in certain communities, in certain periods, many households shared houses and the census records and the pattern of house sales seem to prove that this was a general situation in the first three centuries AD.

The nature of the communities that lived in these complex groups and divided houses is not clear. The partition of property between heirs did not necessarily lead to the formation of separate households and one of the most frequently attested households in the census data is the *frérèche*: the household composed of brothers, sometimes with their wives and children. Nevertheless, some families took a different route and families seem to have split into separate households while probably remaining within the same house. For instance, in the longest of the Philadelphia registers (*P. Lond.* II, pp. 36–42, 257), we see, for instance, that Anoubion, son of Apollonios and Tanom, and his brother Dios were registered as having separate households while living in adjacent portions of a house or houses. Sarapis son of Nekepheris and Thaisous and his brother Petesouchos had a similar arrangement. Peteamounis son of Petermouthis and Thermouth(arion) and his brother Maron also appear to have separate neighbouring households in fractions of one or more houses. The half brothers Dikranes and Ptollis, sons of Petesouchos, grandsons of Dikranes, formed separate neighbouring households, each having two sons. The five sons of Panegb( ) and Tasoouk( ) registered as separate households in spite of the fact that they inhabited fractions of a house or houses next to each other. Other relationships are not clear within the record. Dios son of Atomneos and his brother Pachnoub(is) of Atomneos lived in a fraction of a house next to two brothers Pepi of Atomneos and Pachnoub(is) of Atomneos. The two sets of brothers, however, had different mothers and grandfathers. It defies logic, however, to assume that these families were not somehow related, especially as these names are comparatively uncommon. Nevertheless, there is no obvious relationship between many neighbouring households in the text and the pattern of ownership observable from the house sale documents, in which often apparently unrelated owners share ownership of a single house, was probably reflected in house occupancy patterns. Some housefuls were families, others were not.[42]

The Egyptian pattern is not, in this respect, particularly unusual and in many societies the house is not equated with an integral and autonomous social unit, as is very obvious in societies which have separate male and female houses.[43] In many traditional African societies, the compound is a more meaningful socio-spatial unit than the houses within that compound and Hobson (1985a) tentatively suggested that the same might be true for Philadelphia. This suggestion is worth exploring since it would suggest that the significant social unit was not necessarily the house or the family, but a larger group (clan?) which would tend to co-reside in a number of separate houses. In such circumstances, reconstructing the population in any individual house would be of only minor sociological significance compared with the society of the clan (Rapoport 1981).

Hobson's study was based on a close reading of *P. Lond.* II, pp. 36–42, 257.[44] As Hobson noticed, the distribution of male names across that document is uneven. We would expect similar names within a particular household given the Egyptian patterns of nomenclature. For instance, Petesouchos, a very common Fayumic name, appears eight or nine times in 110 households, but appears in eight of the first 56 households and has one dubious attestation in the remaining 54 households. Onnophris makes six appearances, all between the tenth and the 64th household. Panom( ) and Panomgeus appear seven times, six of those occasions being between the 68th and the 91st household. Orsenouphis appears in seven households, six of which are between the 62nd and the 97th households. Names based on the root 'Samb' are attested eight times, seven of which are between household 30 and 83. Statistical analysis of this pattern is made more complex by the known and observable tendency of relations to have neighbouring houses, which tends to produce a 'tight cluster' of similar names. Names will not, therefore, be distributed randomly across the village. However, if we wish to know whether there was 'loose clustering', that is whether names tended to group together across, say, fifteen to thirty households, then we must discount the evidence of the 'tight clusters'. Once this is done, the apparent 'loose clusters' disappear. Relatives may live close together but we do not see 'clan' compounds controlling significant sectors of the village.[45]

Two other texts can be analysed in the same way, though these texts have rather different format and purposes from the London papyrus. *P. Oslo.* III 111 from AD 235 details the ownership and (some of?) the residents of just over fifty houses in the Hermaion district of Oxyrhynchus. The text is somewhat lacunose and the layout of the district not easy to reconstruct, but for the purpose of analysis I have numbered each house in the order of its appearance in the text. We see some clustering of individually owned property. Aurelia Apollonia, for instance, owned houses 7, 8 and 9. Such contiguous concentration is, however, unusual. Didymus, a former magistrate of the city, or his freed owned houses 10, 18, 20, 48 and 49. Soter alias Soterianus owned houses 3, 4, and 13. Theon alias Zoilos, a former gymnasiarch, owned houses 10, 30, 52 and 54 while also owning plots at 37 and 41. Alexander Serenus owned properties 14, 16, 17 and 36. Nepos son of Dionysios owned houses 23, 28 and 29, and Athenaios alias Herakleides owned houses 51 and 57.

The other text is *P. Berol. Bork.*, an early fourth-century topographical survey from Panopolis. This text identifies houses and other buildings normally by a single male resident (or owner), his heirs, or sometimes by a female who is described by reference to her male relatives. The task of identifying the men is complicated since the compilers often omitted patronymics, which is rather unusual in Egyptian documents. There is some clustering of houses. Bassos owned neighbouring houses. Five houses later, we have an entry for the house of Pachoumios and the next house was ascribed to the sons of Pachoumios, though not necessarily the same man. Three houses further on, we reach two properties connected with Apollonidos. A little further in the tour of the city and we come to an empty plot owned by Alexander, who was also associated with the house two plots away. Next to Alexander's house was an empty plot partly belonging to the priest Ploutogenes, whose house was separated from the plot by that of Serenos, the builder. Five plots later, we come to two houses (?) associated with Denarius. His neighbour, Plotinus, had two properties separated by a single plot. Nine plots later, there were two houses associated with the sons of Ploutogenes (almost certainly not the same man as above). From this point, it becomes much more difficult to identify both the male associated with the house and any clustering of such association. Approximately ninety and ninety-five entries later, we meet two houses of Nikostratos. Considerably further on, we reach the following sequence: the house of Kolanthos (*musikos*), the house of Agathos (goldsmith), the house of Agathos (youth), the house of Asklas son of Agathos Da[imonos] and the house of Kolanthos (former *kosmetes* (a magistrate) of the city). It seems possible that some of these men were related. A little later and we come to the house of Onnophris, carpenter, whose workshop was divided from his house by a single plot. The pattern continues.

The three texts show a topographical concentration of ownership, a pattern suggested by the house sale documents, though the properties were not necessarily contiguous. The process of concentration of property through purchase and inheritance and dispersal of property at death might work to concentrate kin in a particular area. Nevertheless, kin do not appear to monopolize an area and where kin inhabit a number of topographically related houses, others, not obviously of the same group, can reside among them.

A further reason to reject compounds lies in the architecture. Houses are significant architectural and spatial units within communities and I shall argue below that this reflects the importance of the 'houseful' as a social unit. If the compound was a significant social unit, we might expect to see some architectural evidence of compounds or some reflection of kin- or clan-based divisions within the papyrological record.[46] With the exception of priestly residences within the temple complex, which are a completely different case, compounds have not been detected in the archaeological record for Roman or for pre-Roman Egypt.[47] Although important boundaries in space, such as gang territories in cities, may have no obvious physical manifestation detectable to the archaeologist, one would expect more obvious markers of compounds, perhaps in the arrangement of houses or in the identification of houses by compound names, than we see in the Egyptian material. The traditional African compound or the Serbian *zadruga* (Hammel 1972) do not appear to have been features of Egyptian spatial arrangements. Nevertheless, Hobson's suggestion and our exploration of the possibilities draw attention to the way in which social relations spill out beyond the boundary of the house. Many topographically close houses would contain households which were socially related. The house community sits in a network of social relationships which spread across the street and possibly further. Whereas in some cultures the community of the house is comparatively isolated, situated among neighbours with whom social relationships are weak, the Egyptian house appears more integrated. Nevertheless, Egyptian housefuls and families were complex and confusing social institutions and to investigate further we must return to architecture.

We have already seen that a number of architectural features of Egyptian housing tend to emphasize the frontage of the house, marking a break between inside and outside. Even where these architectural features do not clearly exist, houses seem to present a rather defensive front to the street.[48] The locking of doors and barring of windows (though small high windows are of some environmental benefit) have symbolic as well as practical implications. Also, the boundary between public and private space is clearly acknowledged in the texts (though there was encroachment on public space from Karanis, especially with the construction of windbreaks to protect doorways). The legal right of access to the public street was rigorously defended and this seems to show an emphasis on the outside–inside division. Such boundary marking is often associated with divisions between public and private.[49]

Wallace-Hadrill's (1988) already classic analysis of the Roman house presents us with a graduated distinction between public and private. The visitor comes from the public street through the *fauces* to the *atrium*, a room traditionally used for reception (McKay 1975: 34). The visitor could see beyond the *atrium*, through the *tablinium* to the *peristylum*, a garden area around which the household could relax and entertain their guests, and perhaps also examine any art works, fountains or other decorative elements included in the garden. Perhaps off this area would be a *triclinium*, a dining area, where the household would host quite small and discrete dinner parties. Off the atrium and perhaps beyond the *peristylum* there were other rooms, *cubicula*, of more uncertain function but perhaps often used as bedrooms. Such rooms had rather broad entrances, often without obvious barriers, though they probably provided a measure of privacy (Riggsby 1997). Thus, we have the basic layout of the Roman house. One of its most notable features is that it was so open and it is so difficult to perceive what we would call private rooms (Riggsby 1997; Dunbabin 1996). The Roman elite house was the setting for significant social interaction between household members and outsiders (Treggiari 1998; 1999) and was so designed to allow a physical representation of gradations of intimacy between the householders and outsiders. As a result, few spaces were truly public (all were clearly demarcated as being within the house) or private (most spaces seem to have been accessible to outsiders). Although the architectural design does not determine usage, and usage of space within the house was extremely flexible and probably changed dramatically in the course of a day (George 1997a; Allison 1997a), the design-function of the house is a significant reflection of social expectations.

In the medieval English noble house, the pattern was slightly different (Girouard 1978: 30–64). As in the Roman house, the medieval noble entertained and was on display in his residence: it was part of his duty and a way of asserting his status and cementing social relations. Initially, then, the lord and lady would meet and dine with his loyal retainers, very often nearly all men, in the great hall which formed the centrepiece of the early medieval aristocratic house. Social distinctions were retained and made explicit through seating plans, formality of meals (even though many must have been drunken and riotous), and through subtle (the location of the salt) and less subtle (the use of a dais) social and spatial markers. Such distinctions became increasingly formal to the point that the lord retreated from the great hall to the great chamber for all but the most populist of public events and continued to retreat over the centuries to the privy chamber and to a suite of rooms beyond the privy chamber. This centuries-long retreat was a response to economic, technological and social development. The lord had become less of a military figure (or at least any military role was now undertaken away from the house) and more of a political manager (though clearly lords had a military capacity into the seventeenth century). The retreat was not a futile drive towards privacy, but an attempt to control and to grade access to the lord from the general access area of the great hall to the privileged arena of the great chamber and the privy chamber. The lord remained a public figure and the concentration of power on the individual meant that, wherever his location, individuals would seek to gain access.

Greek houses tended to have a rather different arrangement with respect to visitors, though there was no standard 'Greek house plan' and some of the late luxurious Hellenistic houses of Delos and Ephesus (Chamonard 1922; Bruneau and Ducat 1983; Bruneau 1970; Strocka 1977; Nevett 1995; 1999; Trümper 1998) seem worlds apart from the rather smaller residences at Olynthos and Priene (8.8 m × 23.5 m at Priene, 17 m × 17 m at Olynthos). The excavated houses at Olynthos were 'παστάς houses', so called from the corridor or παστάς (*pastas*) which ran between the central court and the main house (οἶκος). Entry points varied, but normally entry was into a central court, often through double doors, and there is considerable evidence of carts being brought into the court

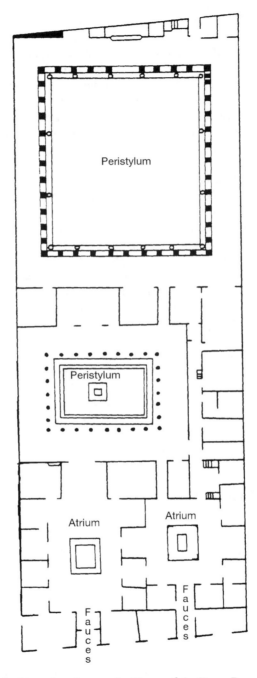

Figure 3.13 A double atrium house: the House of the Faun, Pompeii

(Robinson and Graham 1938: 75; 78–80), suggesting that they were used for agricultural labour. Off this court, sometimes so separated that it could be entered without approaching the οἶκος, but often more integrated into the house, was the ἀνδρών. This room is recognizable because of the raised floor and the higher standard of decor and was used as a banqueting room for the male-only social dinners. More elaborate houses provided the ἀνδρών with an anteroom, of uncertain purpose (Robinson and Graham 1938; Robinson 1946; Pesando 1989). Houses at Priene show significant variations from the Olynthos houses but these are variations around a common set of structures. Entrance to the Priene houses was typically down a long corridor or passageway which gave entry to the central court. At one end of the court was the οἶκος and παστάς and the παστάς normally gave entry to an ἀνδρών. Another set of buildings stood at the opposite end of the court to the οἶκος (Wiegand and Schrader 1904; Hoepfner and Schwandner 1986: 143–85). This arrangement allows for male visitors to the house, but the areas open to access for those visitors are somewhat restricted. This has been seen as marking a fundamental difference between Roman and Greek domestic architecture for, as Wallace-Hadrill (1988) writes, '[t]he Greek house is concerned with creating a world of privacy, of excluding the inquisitive passer-by. The Roman house invites him and puts its occupants on conspicuous show.' Jameson (cf. Nevett 1994; 1995; 1999) argues similarly that

> the Classical Greek house shows a common, underlying conception even though the actual working out may vary considerably, from town to town, from house to house. The house is a closed unit, immediately adjacent to the street but with its interior invisible from it
>
> (Jameson 1990: 97)

and goes on to argue that this separation was symbolic of the closed nuclear family.

The Egyptian house would seem to correspond more to the Greek than the Roman model. The forbidding gates seem to shut out outsiders and there is little evidence for reception rooms in the archaeological material. The papyrological material is a little more complex. A number of dinner invitations have survived, normally inviting individuals to celebrations the next day (Montserrat 1990; 1992; Koenen 1967; Skeat 1975; Vandoni 1964; Youtie 1948; Milne 1925). These invitations relate to coming-of-age ceremonies, marriages, crownings (as magistrates?) and birthdays, and there is one possible invitation to a *kline* of Anoubis (a funerary feast?). Most, however, are invitations to the *kline* of Sarapis, which appears to be a feast in honour of that god. The meal is held in various locations: in the birth house (λόχιον: a building attached to a temple, probably the Sarapeion) (*P. Oxy.* I 181[50]; *P. Col. Youtie* I 51), at the Sarapeion (*P. Oxy.* I 110; XXXI 2592; XXXVI 2791; LII 3693; *PSI* XV 1543; *SB* XVIII 13875), in the house of the Sarapeion (*P. Oxy.* XIV 1755; *P. Col. Youtie*

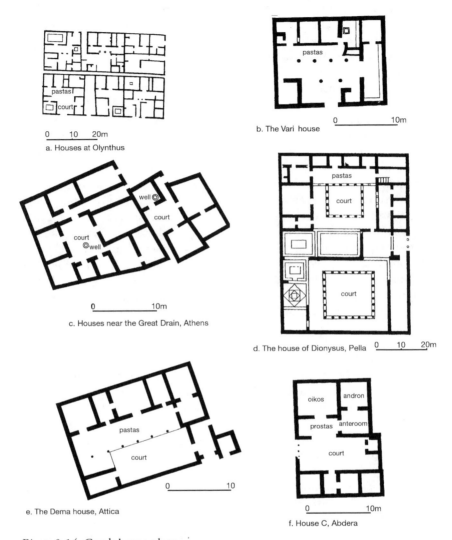

Figure 3.14 Greek house plans

I 52; *SB* XX 14503), the Claudian (?) Sarapeion (*P. Oxy.* III 523), at the Ischyrion (?) (*P. Oxy.* III 524), in the Thoereion (*P. Oxy.* XII 1484; *P. Köln* I 57), the Demetrion (*P. Oxy.* XII 1485), in the Sebasteion (temple to the emperors) (*P. Oxy.* XXXIII 2678), in the house of Horus (?) (*P. Köln* VI 280), in a building connected with Aphrodite (*Archiv* 21 (1971), 46), in the gymnasium (*P. Oxy.* XVII 2147), in the temple of Hadrian (*SB* XVI 12596), in the house of the centurion (*P. Fay. Towns* 132), in a guest chamber (ξενία) (*P. Oxy.* IV 747), in 'the house' (*P. Oxy.* I 111; *SB* V 7745; *P. Fouad* I 76), in his/her (private) house

(P. Oxy. VI 926; XII 1579; XXXVI 2792; P. Oslo. III 157; P. Fuad I Univ. 7; P. Yale I 85; SB XIV 11944; XVI 12511), and at an unspecified location (P. Oxy. VI 927; IX 1214; XII 1486; 1487; 1580). Over half of all dinner invitations are to dine in temples or public buildings (21). Some of the invitations are, however, unclear. Five have either unspecified locations or the locations are lost in lacunae. Three others invite the recipient to dine in 'the house', which one would not hesitate to associate with private houses but for the invitations to 'the house of the Sarapeion'. Whatever the case, 25–46 per cent of the extant dinner invitations are to private houses.

In the Greek house, at a place like Olynthos, the dinner would presumably have been in the ἀνδρών and would have been limited, presumably, to males. Female participation in dinner parties may have been possible when sanctioned by religious practice, but it seems more likely that if females feasted, they were separated from the males. The location of the ἀνδρών suggests that some thought it desirable to separate respectable women from male diners (Jameson 1990; Nevett 1994; Walker 1983). In Roman culture, women participated in private dinner parties and this was seen as one of the major differences between Greek and Roman social life (Vitruvius, de Arch. VI 4). The elder Agrippina famously refused to eat even an apple at the table of the emperor Tiberius for fear of poison (Suet. Tib. 53.1), while less tense dinners appear to have been moments for flirtation and perhaps covert assignations (Yardley 1991).[51] Such dinners may have been variously located around the palatial villas occupied by the Roman elite, though purpose-built dining areas, often arranged to take maximum advantage of views, were a feature of many houses (Clarke 1991; Bergmann 1991; Scott 1997; Foss 1997; Ellis 1988; 1991; 1997; Slater 1992; Dunbabin 1996). In the late Roman period, the dining room appears to have been a major feature of great houses, perhaps the main arena for the display of wealth and power (D'Arms 1991; Rossiter 1991) famously satirized in the Cena Trimalchionis of Petronius' Satyricon. These were central features of houses and there was no obvious concern to limit diners' access to the rest of the house. Although there may have been occasions when men and women were entertained separately (Livia and Augustus held separate feasts for the men and women of Rome at times of public celebration (Dio LV 2) and accounts of dinners normally concentrate on the male participants), women may have been guests at most parties (Clement of Alexandria, Paed. II 33).

The precise location of the parties attested in our dinner invitations is uncertain. We have no archaeologically attested dining halls associated with private houses, but the papyri refer to συμπόσια (dining-rooms), the rental or sale of which are frequently attested, and an open space, such as an αὐλή or αἴθριον, could be adapted for many purposes.[52] The συμπόσια were probably secure since they could be used for storage: one letter asks for the retrieval of a cushion (conceivably part of the furnishings) from a συμπόσιον (P. Oxy. VIII 1159), while another asks for baskets to be brought from the συμπόσιον (P. Oxy. XXXVI 2784). Nearly all our texts associate συμπόσια with particular houses.

Triclinium (the Latin equivalent of συμπόσιον) is used occasionally, though often for the fittings of the συμπόσιον rather than for the room itself (Husson 1983a: 267–71; *P. Oxy.* X 1277; *BL* IX, 184; *BL* VIII, 243). A first-century house sale from Tebtunis (*P. Mich.* V 295) locates a *triclinium* in the gatehouse. A rental agreement describes 'two rooms which are συμπόσια' (*P. Oxy.* VIII 1129 = *Sel. Pap.* I 46), which might suggest that the difference between a συμπόσιον and other rooms lay not in the architecture but with the decor. Most texts, however, treat the συμπόσια as if they were architecturally separable features of houses and their rental or sale separate from that of the attached house indicates a certain architectural disconnection. For instance, a mortgage of a house seems specifically to exclude the συμπόσιον from the security offered (*P. Oxy.* LXI 4120). The evidence for συμπόσια in gatehouses also indicates that such rooms could be used without necessarily breaching the privacy of the rest of the house. The rental documents cover usage over considerable periods and it may be that those leasing the property were interested in commercial exploitation, perhaps sub-leasing for much shorter periods to others (Husson 1983a: 267–71). This may parallel the arrangement of the various temple dining areas which were probably within the temple enclosure but separate from the temple courts (*SB* VIII 10167).

The location of entertainment facilities seems similar to Classical Greek practice, though the purpose of the arrangement does not seem to have been to seclude the women of the house. Although Romano-Egyptian dinner parties were normally held by men, some of our invitations were issued by women (*P. Oxy.* XII 1579; *P. Col. Youtie* I 52). The invitations do not give the names of those invited and we cannot be confident that guests were not divided by gender on arrival, but it seems likely that parties were attended by both men and women. A specifically male dining area, the ἀνδρών is infrequently attested in the papyri from Roman and Byzantine Egypt (Husson 1983a: 37) and a fourth-century house from Hermopolis (*P. Lond.* 978) appears to have had multiple ἀνδρῶνες. The attestations tend, however, to be quite late and it seems very likely that there was no difference between this room and the συμπόσιον.

The earliest attestation of a seemingly private συμπόσιον dates to the reign of either Trajan or Hadrian (Husson 1983a: 267–71; *SB* X 10278; cf *P. Fam. Tebt.* 31; *P. Corn.* 50) and the term continued to be used into the post-Byzantine period. Many of the references to such rooms in fact come from later in our period, especially the fifth and sixth centuries, partly because of the frequent mention of συμπόσια in the property dealings of Patermouthis and relatives at Syene (see below).[53] It may be that such private rooms became increasingly popular in the later period. Texts from sixth-century Syene locate συμπόσια on the second floor of a gatehouse (*P. Lond.* V 1722 = *Sel. Pap.* I 30; 1723; 1733; *P. Münch* I 9; 11; 12). A seventh-century συμπόσιον at Apollonospolis Magna was similarly above the gatehouse (*SB* VI 8988). These later rooms seem to have been small suites, often with access to a terrace or roof or to a cellar. The word crossed into Coptic and was used of rooms in the seventh- and eighth-century town of Jeme (see below). The verbal usage and the archaeological evidence make it very unlikely that these were specialized dining-rooms and they are translated simply as 'room' (Schiller 1953; Till 1939). The Greek documents in the Patermouthis archive deploy a considerable range of architectural terms but sixth-century Syene was a bilingual society and it would be surprising if a technical term had different meanings in Greek and Coptic. It seems very likely that the function of the room had changed somewhat by the later period, though the process by which the term lost its original meaning is unclear.

Pharaonic Egyptian attitudes to domestic space differ from those in the Classical texts. Egyptian literature portrays the house as a place of peace and rest, an escape from the hurly-burly of public life where both men and women could relax (Parlebas 1977). It was a place of safety for the entire family. Tomb paintings clearly show the transaction of business in private houses and some house models also place considerable economic activity in a domestic setting. The status of those entering the house is, though, often uncertain and a wealthy Egyptian was likely to have had many visitors when dealing with household business: many of those depicted may have been members of an extended household, the servants, slaves and managers of the main family. Some texts suggest that entry into the house of another was generally held to have been for some nefarious purpose (though going over the back wall using a ladder was hardly conventional) (Manniche 1987: 20). The house was also a place where status was displayed. It was quite common for Egyptian houses of the pre-Ptolemaic period to have the name of the occupant, especially if the occupant was of high status, inscribed above the doorway (Anus and Sa'ad 1971), marking out his ownership. The doorway may have been a place of cultic activity, as it is in many cultures. According to Plutarch (*Moralia* 353D = *De Iside et Osiride* 7), on 9 Thoth (an Egyptian month) most Egyptians gathered outside their houses and ate fish. The priests marked their superior status (and that of their houses) by burning the fish rather than eating it.

Some of these attitudes may have continued into the Roman period. *P. Berol. Bork.*, discussed above, associates each house with a single, named, (normally) male individual. A roughly contemporary register of guards of the nightwatch at Oxyrhynchus (*P. Oxy.* I 43v) also associates named individuals with specific buildings, near which the guards were stationed. Letters were often addressed to houses named after their residents, though the resident was not always the intended recipient of the letter (Llewelyn 1994a; 1994b).[54] Similarly, it is likely that houses continued to be regarded as a place of safety, a private place of retreat for the family, in spite of the evidence for entertainment of guests in houses. The emphasis on gates and the securing of the house from the street is, of course, a common feature of traditional Egyptian architecture. Entrance to the temple complexes was often restricted by huge walls and funnelled through various gateways. Even once the temple had been reached, the visitor passed through the temple pylons into ever more holy space and at each level there was the possibility of excluding the visitor. A similar emphasis on gateways to the house suggests that entry was important, that the division between the street and the house was obvious. The division between public and private seems strongly marked in both the archaeological record and the papyri. House sales carefully define access to public space (Taubenschlag 1927; cf. Pestman 1985) and many contracts of all kinds note that they were signed in the street, in the public sphere, rather than in the house, the temple, or the market.[55]

Yet, looked at broadly, this Romano-Egyptian pattern of spatial use is somewhat paradoxical and unnerving. Duncan (1981) schematically classifies cultures and their practices with regard to housing. The scheme is simple and logical and seems to apply to many modern and historical societies. Cultures that place a high value on patrilineal descent, on preserving the male line, will tend to police female contact with non-familial males. As a result, women will tend to be secluded in the house, which becomes a container of women. Men, on the other hand, will not spend time in this female space and will seek to exert status in the male sphere, 'public space'. They will use ties outside the home, especially relatives (reinforced by the ties of patrilineal descent), perhaps social clubs, as groups within which to assert status and through which to compete with other similar groups for status. In so competing, economic surpluses will be spent in this sphere (the society wedding, the generous donation to the political group), but also asserted through the group and its hierarchies. Wealth will be displayed and spent communally. The society will emphasize the collective. By contrast, other societies emphasize the individual. In such cases, status will not depend on family or descent and there will be little or no pressure to seclude women. Social activities will tend to be privatized: status is asserted within the home and through the display of domestic wealth. Inevitably, women will come into contact there with outsiders. The extended family will be less important than the nuclear. Such an approach to social analysis is not meant to describe specific societies but produce descripta which allow societies to be classified and conceptualized. One might call the one type of societies traditional or collective, and the other the capitalistic or individualistic. Duncan reflects a tradition that goes back to Weber, if not before, in seeing individualism and collectivism as a basic socio-cultural dichotomy. I would, however, argue that these models do not apply to Roman Egypt, and possibly not to Roman society either.

Romano-Egyptian houses seem to reflect status, yet the house does not appear to have been a major centre of social activity. Rather, the emphasis on boundaries and the absence of obvious internal display in much of the housing of the Roman period suggests that the house tended to be a place of seclusion. There also appears to have been an emphasis on extended families, as we shall see in a moment, and various groups within the city which could become foci for the assertion of collective status: guilds, temple associations, gymnasial group, etc. Egyptian society was generally patrilocal. Descent was also important in achieving status, especially in the Roman period, when not just priestly status but also entry to metropolite, gymnasial and, later, Antinoopolite status (see

p. 2 for these groups) depended on descent.[56] Nevertheless, there is little evidence to suggest the seclusion of women. Indeed, the evidence rather suggests that women entered the public sphere openly and regularly. Second, and more problematically, many houses were not family citadels from which the external could be excluded: the external was there, sharing facilities, living alongside the nuclear or patrilineal unit. Furthermore, control of a woman's body must have been made more difficult by the relative absence of sexual taboos. Roman Egypt was one of the few cultures where sibling marriage was encouraged outside very select groups, such as royal families.

The Weberian argument is that societies will *tend* to show more elements of one social type than the other but that all the various elements are likely to be present in a particular society: it is the *significance* of those elements which is crucial. Nevertheless, and although Duncan's characterizations of societies are familiar to moderns, Egyptian society does not fit the model and I suspect that this discordance is caused by distinctively different conceptions of 'family' (Saller 1997).[57] In spite of the fundamental problems, Duncan's work usefully illustrates how conceptions of social identity, masculinity and femininity, family patterns, and use of houses are closely interrelated.

Women inside and outside houses

Since status in Pharaonic and Roman Egypt was inherited, one might expect there to have been a great concern to restrict male access to females in order to limit illegitimacy. Confining women to the domestic setting was an effective way of achieving this, but when we examine attitudes towards the female body, female sexuality and access to public space where women could, presumably, encounter possible sexual partners, we find no evidence for strict control. Indeed, women seem to have enjoyed comparative freedom and traditional attitudes towards the display of the female body and possibly also sexual activity seem to have been surprisingly unrestricted (Feucht 1997).

The social and economic role of women in Roman Egypt was restricted. Women could own property and land, but their active participation in economic production was probably largely confined to the domestic context (Hobson 1983; 1984b). Whereas in the Pharaonic period, there is some evidence for women being actively involved in farming and in craft production (Feucht 1997), there is little similar material from Roman Egypt. Farmers and craftsmen, as far as they are attested in our documentation, were male (though see Alcock 2000 for a possible exception). The extensive accounts of the Appianus estate from the third-century Fayum, for instance, have not produced a single case of a female being employed either permanently or casually for agricultural labour (Rathbone 1991: 164). Women could, however, take active economic roles. Dowries were overwhelmingly in cash or jewellery (Rowlandson 1996: 152–71), with the result that women who controlled their own dowries had considerable capital and were involved in loaning that capital (though some loans may have been disguised dowries, see Gagos et al. 1992; Whitehorne 1984; *P. Oxy.* II 267 = M. *Chr.* 281 *BL* VI, 96, VII, 129). Women could also act as agents (though not in law) for their menfolk when their men were away and numerous letters instruct women to perform economic tasks (Beaucamp 1993). Tax collectors seem to have often taken for granted the ability of women to act as representatives of their men, to the point of offering violence if the women failed to produce the demanded taxes. A series of letters to Pompeius, a veteran of Graeco-Egyptian origin, offers an insight into the kind of roles women could play. Charitous wrote to Pompeius about some administrative problem he had. She went to see a certain Zoilas, who then visited the office of the Royal Scribe (the senior scribe and record-keeper of the nome) and failed to find Pompeius' name on the register. Other business was to be communicated to Pompeius when Zoilas visited him (*SB* VI 9120). Heraklous wrote to Pompeius about problems she was having with a certain Sarapous. Sarapous kept confronting Heraklous in her house and Heraklous was starting to fear for her safety. Pompeius was summoned to deal with the problem (*SB* VI 9121). Herennia wrote to Pompeius about certain transactions including various measures of cloth and lentils (*SB* VI 9122). Herennia also wrote to Pompeius about taxes which were being levied by the temple of Souchos on all inhabitants of the Arsinoite which she had put off paying on the grounds that Pompeius was about to arrive (*P. Merton* II 63). These women acted without or on behalf of Pompeius and, though they clearly deferred to him, their freedom of action and ability to negotiate with men is notable.

Such economic activities need not have taken women outside the home and the limited economic roles played by women seem to suggest that some restrictions operated: there were predominantly male spheres of activity. However, there is no evidence that women showed any reluctance to leave the domestic setting or that there was any attempt to restrict women's movements. Greek writers were surprised at the freedoms afforded to Egyptian women, especially that women were allowed to visit the market. Similarly, Philo of Alexandria thought it necessary to explain that Jewish women were restricted in their movements (Alston 1997b; Philo, *In Flaccum* 89; *Spec. Leg.* III 169–74; see below), which seems reasonable circumstantial evidence that Greek and Egyptian women were not similarly confined.[58]

When women did venture out, it seems that some did so in style. Dowries make frequent mention of jewellery, and mummy portraits and other funeral monuments depict women wearing often elaborate jewellery.[59] Walker and Bierbrier (1997) use the jewellery and hairstyles to date the mummy portraits by comparison with dated examples from Graeco-Roman portraiture and in so doing demonstrate that not only were Egyptian women adorning themselves with elaborate jewellery, but they were also following the fashions of Rome. Jewellery was a means of displaying wealth and status and this explains why the woman were shown with their jewellery on funerary monuments. These women were on display, fulfilling a public role.

Attitudes towards sex and marriage were complex and very difficult to determine. The authorities took a certain interest in marriages since they related to status and would affect the distribution of property on death, but marriages did not have to be registered. They were matters of private law (Allam 1990). Nevertheless, marriages appear to have been major economic transactions, not to be entered into lightly, and most of the documentation generated by marriages relates to property transactions: normally the dowry and any testamentary bequests of property to be enacted before the death of the parents (which appears to have been a way of providing the couple with a certain amount of land and providing the husband with some guarantee that his spouse would inherit her share of the family property). This economic transaction was also sometimes celebrated as a major rite of passage. One couple who were unable to attend the wedding of a friend's son because of illness and legal business were asked to help with supplying flowers. They refused payment and sent apologies since they could only find 1,000 roses, but substituted 2,000 narcissi (in addition to the 2,000 already requested) for the missing roses (*P. Oxy.* XLVI 3313).[60] Dinners were held to celebrate marriages (Perpillou-Thomas 1993: 15–19; esp. n. 34). Yet, Allam (1981) concludes that such festivities were probably the exception.

Legally, there were two forms of marriage, a marriage with an unwritten contract and a marriage with a written contract. 'Uncontracted marriages' could change to 'contracted marriages' with the birth of children. A couple could, therefore, have a sexual relationship before the marriage was properly contracted. It is impossible to know what social constraints operated on such relationships. For instance, did the couple drift into a relationship, cohabit and then negotiate for a settlement, or did they 'marry' (commit themselves, possibly publicly, to a long-term partnership) before the start of a sexual relationship on the understanding that a settlement would later be reached? Both patterns seem implausible given the economic implications of marriage. Loans to the prospective husband may have been important here in establishing intent and seem to have operated as a preliminary investment in the relationship by the bride's parents, to be formalized later through the dowry (Gagos et al. 1992). This is surely the correct interpretation of the rather complex dealings of the weaver Tryphon in first-century Oxyrhynchus, who contracted a loan with his pregnant cohabitee (the relationship presumably predating the loan), who may also have been the nursemaid of his daughter (*P. Oxy.* II 267). The birth of a child signified the success of the relationship and this seems to have been the trigger to move to a properly contracted marriage.[61] In many ancient legal systems marriages were formed essentially by cohabitation with the intent to be married and divorce was separation or the ending of that intent to be married. Such informality reflects the non-sacramental nature of marriage in the ancient world and in most circumstances, the state did not become involved in these private matters. However, legal informality does not necessarily reflect social informality and long betrothals, complex negotiations over the giving of dowries, and social and sometimes religious ceremonies marked the importance of the transition from the unmarried to the married state in many societies. In Roman Egypt, however, that transition seems somewhat blurred.[62]

Attitudes towards sex are even more difficult to determine. The relevant material is exiguous and difficult to interpret. In the Pharaonic period, severe penalties for adultery coexisted with a revealing code of female dress and freedom of movement. Most authorities seem to view Pharaonic and Ptolemaic women as comparatively powerful (Feucht 1997; Eyre 1984; Lesko 1994; Pomeroy 1984; Pestman 1961). Male sexuality was also controlled within marriage and spouses were expected to be sexually exclusive. In the Roman period, clothing appears to have been more encompassing. Women wore clothes which covered their bodies from neck to ankle (Schneider 1982), but the use of jewellery shows that bodies were used for display and it seems probable that women were meant to appear sexually attractive.[63] One might expect that the appearance of women in the social world and their contacts with non-familial males would produce a certain amount of extra-marital sexual activity. Here, again, the evidence is mixed. Illegitimacy is often attested. Men and women appear in the texts either designated as being 'without father' or carrying a metronymic and no patronymic. Youtie (1975) has argued that the rates of illegitimacy are low compared with modern and early modern Europe and America and has suggested that problems of status (that is, mother and father were of such different status groups that they could not contract a marriage) might account for some of the illegitimacy. Nevertheless, Christian and pre-Christian attitudes to marriage and divorce are so different that comparison of illegitimacy rates seems inappropriate. It was far easier both to form and to break legitimate relationships and there was less social pressure to discourage acknowledgement of children.[64] The illegitimacy rates seem to me to be significant and the absence of obvious social stigma suggests that extra-marital sexual activity may not have been limited to prostitutes and their clients.

Nevertheless, there is surprisingly little evidence of adultery or of sexual crime.[65] Montserrat (1996a: 102–5; cf. Whitehorne 1979) failed to find a single solid case of adultery (though he did find several possible attestations).[66] Beaucamp (1992: 71–4) found more evidence of breaches of sexual *mores* in the later period, but some of these are certainly rendered dubious by their context. In the sixth century, the village of Aphrodito complained about Kollouthos, a powerful local official who, among other misdemeanours (such as being a pagan), violated virgins, and similar charges were laid against the pagarch Menas (*P. Cair. Masp.* I 67004; 67002). An insulting letter of the Christian period suggests that the recipient's daughters had had intimate relations with a soldier and were not entirely respectable (*P. Green.* I 53 = W. *Chr.* 131; *BL* III, 70, VI, 446). Such invectives are hardly trustworthy. More spectacular is the case of Aurelia Attiaena who petitioned a tribune in the fourth or fifth century. Attiaena had been seized by Paul who carried her off to his house and there they became married, a female child being born, at which point, they moved back to Attiaena's house.[67] Fatherhood did not, however, reform Paul and he left with some of Attiaena's property to live with another woman. He was taken back through the offices of certain priests and offered security for his good behaviour but abused Attiaena's property and absconded with the property of soldiers who had been billeted on Attiaena. The soldiers took their revenge on their host. She then sued for divorce but was again kidnapped and returned to Paul's house where the other woman was still living. The chronology is a little confused but she both returned to her house and became pregnant, whereupon Paul returned to his other woman and issued threats against her. Attiaena asked for the two ounces of gold that had been pledged for his good behaviour and for action to be taken against him (*P. Oxy.* L 3581). Attiaena was an orphan and seems to have had no male support within her household or from relatives against Paul and Paul's ability to deploy the resources of the Church in his cause, rather than the Church coming to the defence of the unprotected female, seems somewhat surprising.[68] Nevertheless, Attiaena's petition, while not quite unparalleled (*P. Oxy.* XVI 1837; II 281 = M. *Chr.* 66; *P. Cair. Masp.* I 67005), is extraordinary and Beaucamp (1992: 73) concludes that 'le nombre d'actes de violence sexuelle mentionnés dans les sources papyrologiques est faible'. Arnaoutoglou (1995) points out that there is not a single case of a man citing female misbehaviour as the reason for divorce, though women cite male misbehaviour in order to encourage officials to act more vehemently in recovering their property. Sexual relationships reach our sources mainly through property transactions and one might conclude either that the sexual aspects of encounters were too important and personal to be shared with the community or that the community was deeply unsympathetic to both men and women wronged in cases of adultery and sexual violence. It seems extremely unlikely that women were so closely and successfully supervised that illicit contacts were as uncommon as our sources would seem to suggest and such illicit sexual contacts may be implied in cases of the tearing of clothes that appear in more general petitions. Certainly, cases of desertion suggest that some men at least gained illicit but consensual access to 'respectable' women.

There must have been many single women. Divorce was common and, given the rate of mortality, so was widowhood. In Egyptian law, as in Roman law, divorce was also easy: either party was free to break the relationship, at which point the woman was entitled to the return of her dowry (el-Mosallamy 1997). The financial and practical constraints that have acted to discourage women from divorcing their husbands in many historical societies were also largely absent. Since Egyptian society was patrilocal, a woman normally lost her entitlement to reside in the matrimonial home on divorce, though provision might be made for continued residence if she was widowed. Of course, the situation was rather different if the woman owned the home or the couple shared ownership (Barker 1997). Patterns of inheritance and partition of ownership of houses worked in the woman's favour since it is likely that many women will have had at least share of a house to which they could retreat. A woman who became single for whatever reason was not obligated to reside with an adult male, which strongly suggests that a woman was regarded as physically, emotionally and legally capable.[69] In such circumstances, a comparatively relaxed attitude to female sexual activity outside marriage and to female activity in the public sphere was probably necessary.[70]

We have, then, a complex pattern of social relationships. The house was a place of security for women and women were expected to centre their activities on the household. Nevertheless, any constraint was either light or limited and women displayed their finery in public and probably would meet non-familial men regularly. This was a patriarchal society and men took leading public roles in all areas. Women were, however, regarded as capable of taking a public role and dealing with necessary household business in the wider community. Many women will have had a 'public persona' and were not merely known to those of the house.

Men, families and houses

We have already seen that there is some evidence for the identification of individuals and houses and that, therefore, houses were markers of status. In this section, I shall explore that relationship a little further by looking at patterns of residence. These are illuminated by a group of documents known as *epikrisis* returns: applications to be registered in a particular status group normally submitted for boys who are about to be fourteen. We have returns for prospective priests, metropolites, members of the gymnasial group, Romans and Alexandrians, and each group had its own procedure, though individual entries often have variations from those norms (Nelson 1979). The gymnasial applications are most useful for this investigation. Those who were submitted for *epikrisis* for membership of the gymnasium had to show that they were descended from men of gymnasial status on both sides of the family. Unlike the metropolite returns where the examining official was only interested in the status of parents and sometimes grandparents, second-century texts demonstrate that a boy's descent had to be traced back to a registration of gymnasial membership in *c.* AD 70 in order to achieve entry to the gymnasial class. In some cases, individuals traced descent back to an initial registration, probably at the formation of the gymnasial group, in the reign of Augustus (Bowman and Rathbone 1992; Nelson 1979: 26–35). Each generation was not only identified, but their district of residence within the city at the time of registration was stated. We can thus trace the pattern of movement of a small number of families across the city over an extended period. Most of the documents are, however, incomplete and the patrilineal residence pattern is far better attested than the matrilineal.[71]

These returns show two surprising characteristics. First, although some families stayed in the same district for generations, others moved across the city. We only have the district of residence at the moment of registration and there was no requirement on those registered to remain in that district, so that several shifts of residence may be lost in the period between the registration of each male child. Second, families showed a clear tendency to return to their original districts of residence. Secondary movements across the city were, therefore, not random. It seems likely that the family returned to reside in an original family house. Such a close association between a particular family and a house might help explain the more complex 'household' formations observable in the census returns since although practical reasons may have encouraged the development of complex households, they may reflect a reluctance to move away from a house that had come to have a particular emotional hold. Even if the younger generation of a family moved, it seems likely that that generation would inherit property in the old area and such an economic tie must have encouraged the tendency to return and must also have maintained a connection between the old house and the new family. The direct motivation for the return cannot be established, yet the pattern of movement suggests strong ties in the descent group over three or four generations.[72]

One should not over-emphasize this emotional connection. The active housing market we observe in the papyri surely could not have existed if each generation felt morally obliged to hold onto the houses of the previous generation, and we have plenty of evidence of 'maternal' and 'paternal' houses or fractions thereof being sold (Montevecchi 1941). It seems to me very unlikely that all houses carried the same emotional investment and it may be that the conservatism was peculiar to certain social groups. Nevertheless, although the particular regulations governing membership of the gymnasial group were clearly imposed by the Roman authorities and the concern with descent in this case stemmed from Roman ideas, descent appears to have been an important element in the construction of an individual's identity both during and before the Roman period. Egyptian nomenclature was extremely conservative, names passing from generation to generation, and hereditary groups were a familiar form of social organization to the Egyptians. Families which broke up and formed separate co-residential families retained strong bonds and we must add to our list of significant social units the separately residing extended family, an extended family that was a satellite of a main family residence. It seems possible that those social bonds were focused in a particular residence.

No family can be an island. The community of the house sits at the centre of a series of different social networks which stretch beyond the houseful to non-residential family, to neighbours with whom there were kin or other ties, and social bonds stretched beyond, as we shall see in the next chapter, to various community organizations which, to a greater or lesser extent, integrated the community of the house into the wider urban society. Women, those important bearers of the reproductive potential of a family, do not seem to have been restricted in their movements; another case of the family escaping from the house. Also, at dinner parties and perhaps other occasions, the community was invited to the house, though it is likely that access to the house was limited at these celebrations. In all these areas, the boundary between inside and outside, between the community of the house and the rest of the world, was permeated. Yet, the architectural boundary of the house was significant and in at least some cases was marked by gates, locks, bars and towers.[73] What was being protected behind these fortified walls when so much seemed to pass through them? What did the house mean to Romano-Egyptians?

One of the most notable architectural features of the Karanis houses is their niche-shrines (see Trümper 1998: 68–76 for Greek parallels). These were sometimes simply built from the mud-brick, but there were also elaborately carved stone shrines. Painting was common, though only traces survived when the site was excavated. These were one of the few ornamental features in houses notable for their general lack of ostentation. We have already mentioned the festival celebrated at the door on 9 Thoth which again marked out the house and presumably brought the houseful together. There is limited evidence for household cultic activities centring on doorways from earlier periods and doorways appear to have been elaborately decorated in contrast to the generally rather plain exterior of Pharaonic houses (Davis 1929; Anus and Sa'ad 1971; Tietze 1985; Kemp 1989: 151–3; 294–307).[74] The identification of houses with individuals shows that the house was a significant locus of status and the significance of the house community was expressed both architecturally and, probably, religiously.

In many cultures house and family can become synonymous and in such circumstances it is quite easy to identify the function of household cult. Household religious activities in Judaism, the marking of the threshold and the celebration of *shabbat* (the sabbath), emphasize the unity of the family and in many modern Jewish families it is an occasion when the whole family sits and prays together, affirming its unity. In aristocratic Roman houses such activities were dominated by the ancestral cult of the owning family and it, together with other manifestations of household cult, formed a way in which the *familia* was given a centrality. Nevertheless, Foss (1997) suggests that the distribution of shrines throughout larger Roman houses reflects divisions within the household and in spatial usage. We have similar evidence for sub-groups within houses in Roman Egypt and we must wonder at the function of the attested religious activities: did they reinforce the coherence of families or of the houseful or of the different communities within the house?

The Karanis material shows that most houses were architectural units. Although the houses were divided into many small rooms, their layout was such that those using the house would need to have access to most of the rooms. If the Philadelphia figures are even approximately correct, in some villages, and possibly in cities as well, a third of houses were shared between different households and families, yet the architectural design of houses was not conducive to occupation by separate communities. The division of the houses into rooms would allow the separation of various household functions or limited separation of various households or other groups (conjugal groups, children, etc.) and a compromise position between integration and separation of households in a houseful is possible, even likely, though we do not have the ethnographic information that would allow any hypothesis to be confirmed. If the house was a place of escape and rest, then the preservation of that sense of safety must have depended on the ability of the various groups within the house to integrate and recognize their shared interest. This process of integration may allow the development of quasi-familial relations between the various houseful members. This is, I think, a rather startling possibility since the papyrological record suggests that a great deal of emphasis was placed on the family as it was crucial for the inheritance of status and property. This legal centrality of the family was, however, somewhat eroded by social practice. The pressure to ensure legitimate heirs did not, for instance, lead to men imposing radical constraints on the social activity of women. In any case, there would have been substantial problems in secluding women if, as seems likely, non-familial males frequently resided with families, and the incorporation of different families in housefuls undermines any exclusive emphasis on families. Second, non-legal documentation has a considerably less restrictive view of family than legal texts. The letters frequently make use of familial designations, often as marks of respect. Thus, a younger man writing to an older might address him as 'father' and the use of sibling designations was extremely common, though not, seemingly, automatic. This, of course, is deeply frustrating for historians and papyrologists attempting to reconstruct families since 'siblings' especially might be 'fictive family' and there is often little way of distinguishing biological and fictive relations from the non-legal documentation. References in letters to a 'sister' are particularly difficult to understand since the writer may be referring to a sister, a wife, or (given the Egyptian custom of sibling marriage) both. Contemporaries were aware that it could cause problems and phrases such as 'with the same father and mother' and 'with the same father and from the same womb' are common. We cannot know whether familial designations were formulaic (as they are in many modern societies) or reflected a close social tie; once more we are hampered by a lack of ethnographic data. The use of such designations in many societies does not suggest that individuals are in doubt as to their biological relatives and one cannot believe that the Egyptians would be confused on this point. Yet, Egyptian seems to have lacked many of the familial designations, such as 'cousin', that many societies have used extensively and sometimes in similar ways to the Egyptian use of 'brother', 'sister', 'father', and probably 'mother' (Cerny 1957; Depla 1994). This does not mean that relationships outside the nuclear family were regarded as unimportant. Saller (1997) argues convincingly that the elaborate vocabulary used in Latin to describe various relations and a legal obsession with grades of relatedness do not mean that fine degrees of kinship were observed socially and I argue that the extended family (co-resident or separately resident) was extremely important. I would expect, though I cannot prove it, that members of the extended family would be addressed using nuclear family designations. Rather than showing an absence of feeling, the lack of gradations in familial designations made it more difficult to differentiate socially between family, extended family and non-kin. In legal texts, when it mattered, Greek or Latin vocabulary was used or relatives could be described through cumbersome use of multiple close-family designations (the wife of the son of my father's brother, etc.). I suggest that this was an erosion of the social exclusivity of the nuclear family: the use of nuclear family designations often could, in fact, reflect significant quasi-familial relationships. As the house has proved to be permeable, not an isolated fortress protecting and imprisoning, so the family seems also permeable, just one element in a network of overlapping powerful social relationships. The nuclear family was special, but other bonds, to the extended family, to the co-residents were also important.

To modern eyes, the traditional Romano-Egyptian house was a rather strange place and the pattern of social and familial relations within and outside the house was complex. The normal English terminology of family has been stretched to describe the various social ties we have been exploring. It is not so much that the social relations described are unfamiliar, but the emphasis that seems to have been placed on these relationships was so much greater than is normal for the societies with which I am most familiar. The peculiarity of Egyptian families in this period has, however, long been known and I now turn to the best-known of those peculiarities, brother–sister marriage, as an epilogue to this section.

Brother–sister marriage

There has been no satisfactory explanation for the popularity of brother–sister marriage in Roman Egypt and I have no startling solution to the problem to offer here. Recent scholarship has explored the demographic implications of extensive sibling marriage and improved our understanding of the prevalence of the custom. In many ways, however, the problem has become more intractable. Among certain social groups, in certain regions, sibling marriage appears to have been favoured above other possible marriage options (Scheidel 1995; 1996: 9–51; Bagnall and Frier 1994: 127–33), so that sibling marriage cannot be dismissed as of marginal demographic and social importance. However, the Ptolemaic census returns emphasize the peculiar social and geographical circumstances of the phenomenon since, in contrast to Middle Egypt where sibling marriages account for about 20 per cent of all marriages, they attest not a single certain example of sibling marriage (Bagnall et al. 1997). By contrast, Western societies are far more aware of the variety of sexual practice and that sexuality and sexualization are social practices. What is possible or approved of in one society is unthinkable in another. Attitudes to female sexuality and the age of commencement of female sexual activity vary dramatically by culture, class and period. The prevalence of homosexuality and paedophilia in Classical Athens and ancient Greece have proved problematic for many hellenophiles over the last three centuries (Dover 1976) and now paedophilia and incest in modern Western societies have become issues of social and political concern, almost amounting to a moral panic. From a situation where it was believed that such activities were the perversities of a tiny minority of socially and possibly mentally dysfunctional individuals, the publicity given to various dramatic cases has encouraged those subjected to such violent and exploitative sexual assaults to seek help and exposed something of the extent of such covert activities. Such sexual assaults are often interpreted as expressions of power, of an ability to violate, in which the role of sexual attraction to pre-pubescents and adolescents and within families is questionable, though feminist and other critiques of sexuality have drawn attention to the exercise of social power and status in many sexual contexts, the more extreme cases being sexual harassment and rape. In any case, a biological mechanism that would prevent sexual attraction between close kin seems less likely than it did a generation ago. The problem seems so much less extraordinary than it did when Hopkins (1980a) employed anthropological, biological and sociological techniques in an attempt to resolve the issue. We are so much more aware of the vagaries of sexual activity that, I would argue, we can substantially shift the focus of debate from explaining how Romano-Egyptians could enter upon sexual relationships with their siblings to why most societies condition most siblings not to find each other sexually attractive.

Sibling marriage reinforces a family's hold on property and prevents the division of estates between children. It has the value of convenience and the parties are known to each other. Outsiders do not have to be brought in, with the potential disruption that would follow, and women do not have to be sent to other families, with the potential dangers that entails.[75] The main disadvantage, apart from its genetic implications,[76] is that marriage tradition-ally offered a way of forging new social links or reinforcing social links with those marginal to the nuclear family. Shaw (1992) argues that brother–sister marriage in Egypt was a Ptolemaic innovation that arose principally from a reluctance of the early Greek settlers to intermarry with the surround-ing Egyptian population. This is theoretically plausible: sibling marriage can be a way of marking a family as special and distinct from the rest of the population. Incestuous gods and royals are commonly attested and in these cases a separation of the incestuous family from the rest of society is clearly signalled.[77] Historically, the theory is problematic. There is little evidence that the Greek settlers were particularly reluctant to intermarry with Egyptians and, even if they were, Greeks do not seem to have settled in isolated farmsteads but in organized settlements, so that there would be possible Greek partners. Also, the Greek diaspora in the fourth and third centuries BC did not just reach Egypt, but spread to Syria and elsewhere, though sibling marriage is not attested in these areas. Shaw's explanation only works if there are no examples of sibling marriage from the pre-Ptolemaic period, and although there is no firm evidence for sibling marriage, the evidence for endogamy is such that it remains a possibility (Cerny 1954).

Nevertheless, incest is about the special status of family. It marks the relationship between particular people as being different. It upsets us because it violates the family and the trust that should exist between parents and children and between siblings. The psychological trauma of incest is, therefore, immense. It shakes the foundations of social identity because these are built on or around our families. Incest was used by royals to enforce a family identity and to strengthen the bonds in a family, but if the incest taboo is also a reflection of our psychological investment in family, our belief that those links are special, inviolable, not to be sullied by sex, then the absence of that taboo may reflect a relative underinvestment in family. Can it be a coincidence that many ancient royal families have histories of recriminations and bloodshed that would be completely implausible if placed in any other social context? The relative absence of emotional investment in sibling relationships suggests that the nuclear family was simply not so important to the Romano-Egyptians.

Much of the argument over the last pages has been speculative and I make no apology for that. To understand the social meaning of the house, we have to understand what went on inside and the social and cultural values of the people who occupied the house. Yet this was a private world and much that went on simply cannot be reconstructed with any certainty. We can, however, begin the process of uncovering and unwrapping those layers of individual and social identity, the social bonds and practices, and the symbolism that centred on the traditional Egyptian house.

Changing houses, changing cultures: ethnic identity and cultural change

In the previous section of this chapter, I tended to search for a norm within Egyptian society. Nevertheless, we have some evidence for considerable architectural and social diversity. This evidence is drawn from two areas: the Jewish house in first-century AD Alexandria, for which we rely on the writings of Philo, and the seeming emergence of more 'Romanized' houses during the first centuries AD in Oxyrhynchus and elsewhere. We do not, however, have any evidence for the most serious possible divergence: regional variation within Egypt, an issue to which I will return in discussing late Roman and Byzantine houses.

The Jewish house in first-century AD Alexandria

The history of the Jewish community in first-century AD Alexandria is transmitted to us mainly through the writings of Philo, a Jewish philosopher and theologian resident in that city.[78] Philo came from the highest echelon of Jewish society. Philo's brother had risen to prominence as a wealthy financier in Alexandria and had powerful political connections, while his nephew, Tiberius Julius Alexander, rose to dizzy heights, becoming prefect of Egypt under Nero (Turner 1954; Barzano 1988), from which post he played a central role in the conspiracy that launched Vespasian on his successful bid for the throne. Subsequently, he was probably something of an *éminence grise* of the new Flavian regime and perhaps even prefect of the praetorian guard. Philo was also politically prominent, though his political career seems to have been local: he was chosen by his co-religionists to participate in an embassy to the emperor Gaius to beg for the restoration of the historic rights of the Jewish community, an event memorably recounted in his *Legatio ad Gaium*.

Philo's immense surviving literary work is, however, concerned with biblical theology rather than history or politics. His concerns are traditional and addressed to primarily Jewish themes. His intellectual landscape is dominated by the Bible. Nevertheless, Philo wrote exclusively in Greek and was heavily influenced by Greek philosophy (Mondésert 1999; Runia 1990). He is in himself a testament to the blending of Hellenistic and Jewish culture in Alexandria. This combination of Greek and biblical concerns, together with certain theological ideas, meant that Philo was extensively mined by the Church Fathers, especially his compatriot Clement of Alexandria, and it is probably the use to which his work was put in the Christian tradition that accounts for his survival. Scholars are deeply divided as to the extent to which Philo reflects contemporary 'mainstream' Jewish thought of the Rabbinic tradition. Since the Rabbinic tradition has come to dominate modern Judaism, this is an important theological debate, though for me the debate is only significant for evaluating the historicity of the society described by Philo: was it contemporary Alexandrian society, an image of 'biblical society', or a concoction of biblical, Palestinian Rabbinic and Alexandrian Jewish worlds? Opinions are deeply divided and the issue of language is central to the debate (Goodenough 1962: 9–11; Sly 1996: 62). Philo used a Greek version of the Bible that differs in significant respects from the Hebrew and the surviving later Greek recensions. He viewed the Greek translation as divinely inspired and therefore of no less value than the Hebrew original. His reliance on the Greek is so different from modern scholarly methodology that many have been convinced that Philo cannot have known Hebrew. This leaves, however, a substantial problem in that Philo uses Hebraic etymologies as part of his philosophical method. It has, therefore, been suggested that he had access to a now lost tradition of theological writings that translated Hebraic etymologies into Greek (Runia 1990). Yet, others have argued that Philo shows some knowledge of contemporary developments in Palestinian Judaism and such a sophisticated approach to the interpretation of Hebraic texts that he must have had some Hebrew (Belkin 1940: 29–48). This complex debate has reached no firm conclusion. For my part, the evidence of interaction between Palestine and Alexandria and the familiarity of Alexandrians with Hebrew and Aramaic (the contemporary language of Palestine) seem to make it extremely likely that Philo had some of these languages, even if Greek was his first language and his literary language of choice (Alston 1997b).

Philo's reliance on Greek and his philosophical technique raises issues about his religious identity and that of his intended audience. On the former issue, there appears to be a consensus: Philo was a devout Jew (Birnbaum 1996; Mendelson 1986; Goodenough 1962: 75–90). The latter poses more problems. The biblical exegeses seem to have been written for those who already had a detailed knowledge of and interest in the Bible and one would presume that his intended audience was Hellenophone Jewish. Yet, there was a tradition of philosophical speculation in Alexandria and of Greek interest in both Judaism and the religion and culture of Egypt. Philo could have been read by Greek literati seeking to expand their knowledge of this old body of religious and philosophical thought and this would explain why, from time to time, Philo tells his audience details about Jewish life in Alexandria that his Jewish audience must surely have known and where the comparison is, implicitly, with gentile behaviour.[79] It seems best to view Philo's audience as a mix of Jews and sympathetic Greeks. This mix of sources and audience makes the historical evaluation of Philo problematic since it is likely that biblical and post-biblical Rabbinic *topoi* are blended with contemporary exempla.

Philo's concern with the Jewish house is primarily moral and the architectural descriptions provided are sparse, though probably accurate. The sequence of space from the street appears to have been the gatehouse, the entrance to the court, the court and the θάλαμος (*thalamos*: the marriage chamber or the domestic quarters). This sequence was probably indistinguishable from that of the non-Jewish house.[80] In the early first century, the Jewish community was heavily assimilated and dispersed across the city (Alston 1997b; Balconi 1985; Schubart 1913). Rather than develop a specifically Jewish architecture (whatever that would have been), the community is more likely to have adopted and adapted local domestic architecture. Unfortunately, that domestic architecture is not directly attested in the archaeological material and perhaps our only archaeological clue which might add some detail to Philo's description comes from the tombs that encircled the city, some of which have been explored. The major feature of these grand tombs (mostly Ptolemaic) is a central hall, often with supporting columns, off which there was a series of passages and rooms in which the bodies were deposited (Breccia 1922; Arafa 1995). The tombs were adorned by both elaborate architectural features, often derived from Classical models, and painting, often with Egyptian motifs.[81] Of the other literary evidence, only Caesar's description of the towers of Alexandrian buildings (*De Bell. Alex.* I 18) offers further detail, though the passage suggests that Alexandrian domestic architecture may have been very similar to that discussed in the previous section.

Philo's description, however, is valuable not for its architectural detail but as evidence for the use and symbolism of the house in contemporary Jewish society. He describes the pattern of female use of space, claiming that married or mature women were normally confined to the courtyard, taking the entrance to the court (from the gate) as their boundary, while the unmarried were more strictly confined to the θάλαμος or the μεσαύλον (*mesaulon*: inner court), where they would be hidden from the gaze of all but the closest male relatives (Philo, *In Flaccum* 89; *De Specialibus Legibus* III 169).[82] Men were confined to the πύλον, where there was an ἀνδρών (*Legum Allegoriarum* III 40). Philo portrays a segregated house which sat within a wider gendering of space. Thus, men may visit the courthouse, the markets, the senate house and public meetings while women are 'suited' to the indoor life (*De Specialibus Legibus* III 169). Men should manage the affairs of the city while women should manage the household (*De Specialibus Legibus* III 170).

This picture is idealized.[83] Most of our other data on Jewish housing come from Palestine, where separate male and female quarters may have been a feature of some Judaean houses. Even here, though, the seclusion of women was dependent on the social and financial status of the family (Archer 1990: 102, 114–17) and may have been an ideal more honoured in the breach than the observance. The Rabbinic presumption of female guilt if a woman was taken from the market and raped should be tempered by the abundant anecdotal Rabbinic evidence for completely respectable women frequenting markets (Ilan 1995: 128–34). One would presume that similar laxity was common in Alexandria and what Philo's family could afford to do (or Philo wanted to present them as doing) may not have been possible or desirable for other less wealthy or less devout Jews. Even Philo's descriptions of behaviour depart from the absolutism of the ideal. He states that women were not allowed to intervene in conflicts even in defence of their husbands, since even worse problems might arise if the women became involved in street disturbances (*De Specialibus Legibus* III 171–2). This picture of reclusive Jewish womanhood sallying out to brawl in the street is somewhat jarring. He also allows his women to travel to the temple (not obviously chaperoned). When undertaking such journeys, the woman should avoid the busiest times, pass through quiet streets and not enter the markets (*De Specialibus Legibus* III 170).[84]

The Philonic house was more than a container of women. It was a place of rest and withdrawal. This sense of retreat allowed Philo to use the house as a powerful, resonant symbol: the house became a metaphor for the soul (*Legum Allegoriarum* III 40; 238–9; *Quaestiones in Genesim* IV 15). The private workings of the soul stood apart from public view. Inner peace could be found in a world of bustle and business. In *Quaestiones in Genesim* IV 15, Philo extended the spatial metaphor of the soul so that the inner part became the female, irrational element while the outer was male and therefore rational. In this Philo may be adapting an established tradition that saw the house as a symbol of the female body.[85] In this context, we can understand Philo's shock and indignation when the prefect Flaccus responded to the rioting of AD 38 by sending the soldiers to search the Jews' houses for weapons, thereby exposing the women of the household to outsiders (*In Flaccum* 89). Jewishness, as conceived by Philo, was caught up with the house. It was an image of his ethnicity and culture, an image that defined his very soul.

One cannot, of course, always live within the soul and the irrational 'female' elements might escape male control and enter the public arena. Philo himself was not restricted to his house. He seems to have enjoyed the entertainments offered in the city and uses imagery drawn from athletics and the theatre (see notably *De Ebrietate* 177; *De Agricultura* 35). The anti-semitic atmosphere of the early decades of the first century (see pp. 219–35; Alston 1997b) may have had an effect on the patterns of Jewish social activity, encouraging Jews to restrict their activities to Jewish or domestic contexts, and it would be natural to assume that the riots of AD 38 would engender a reluctance to enter that hostile space. The relationship of Jewish women to public space must also have been rendered more complex. If Jewish women had regularly transgressed the Philonic boundaries before AD 38, after that date the boundary must have become more significant since the hostility of the street had become more explicit. The pressure to remain secluded and protected must have increased. For these reasons, the Jewish woman's and the Jewish man's experiences of the house and, therefore, all their spatial experiences must have been profoundly different from those of their Graeco-Egyptian neighbours in spite of the probability that their houses were architecturally similar.

The rise of the 'Roman' house

The evidence for the rise of a new house-type in the cities of Middle Egypt is slight. The most likely explanation for the changes in house prices analysed above is architectural innovation. There is a little evidence for the elaboration of domestic architecture in this period in addition to that cited previously. We know of various private bath houses in Oxyrhynchus of the second and third centuries and the stone house of Aurelia Isidora (see p. 64). There is evidence of more luxurious housing in Alexandria and its suburbs from the third century. Excavations at Kom el-Dikke uncovered fragments of luxurious housing largely destroyed by later fourth- and sixth-century developments. Enough survived of one house to reconstruct what Rodziewicz (1984: 35) calls 'une villa romaine ancienne' with what may have been a peristyle court, as was common in Greek-influenced houses across the Mediterranean. Fragments of another Roman house, known as the 'maison aux oiseaux', of the first century AD have been uncovered. The house was named after one of a number of small mosaics discovered underneath later developments (Rodziewicz 1984: 44–51) and the architectural fragments preserved suggest it had a peristyle court (Majcherek 1999). Elements of what appears to be a private bath house were also discovered. Such small bath houses can be paralleled at Edfu and at Karanis (Rodziewicz 1984: 53; Bruyère et al. 1937: 65–74; el-Nassery et al. 1976).[86]

The case for interpreting this material as evidence for a significant development in housing is considerably strengthened by comparison with other provinces, especially Africa. Urban houses in Africa in the second century show a considerable development from the first century AD (Lloyd 1979: 53–9; 89–101; 140–8; Blanchard-Lemée 1975: 107–29; 153; Kendrick 1986). Therbert (1987) argues that the domestic architecture of elite African houses evolved significantly towards the dominant Mediterranean type: elaborate houses centred on one or more colonnaded gardens off which there were elaborate dining facilities and considerable evidence of luxury (mosaics, wall-paintings, Classical statuary, etc.). I have found no close parallels for this in the Egyptian archaeological material of the first three centuries AD, though there is more evidence of such developments from the fourth century onwards (see below). It would be attractive to relate the emergence of more luxurious housing in the second century to the contemporary rapid development of more Romanized civic centres (see pp. 235–45). Ostentatious housing would, then, be a 'private' response to the increased Romanization of civic culture, though it is less clear whether such changes would represent an 'internalization' of the values of Roman culture. The problem is exacerbated since there is no clear architectural definition of 'the Roman house' after the *atrium* house, which is traditionally regarded as a distinctively Roman style, became less popular in the late first century AD.[87] The Roman elite appears to have placed more emphasis on their rural residences and to have developed more architecturally elaborate villas which contained many elements associated with Greek architectural forms (Bodel 1997; Clarke 1991; Leach 1997; Eck 1997; Brothers 1996; Brödner 1989; George 1997b: 31–5). In towns, a form known as axial peristyle becomes common across the Mediterranean (Meyer 1999). Elsewhere, 'villas', which appear across the empire in the first and second centuries AD, show extreme regional and typological variations so that historians wonder whether 'villa' is a meaningful designation and doubt whether the provincial forms have much similarity to any 'Roman' styles (Percival 1976; 1996; Smith 1997; van Aken 1949; Balty 1989). Nevertheless, the dramatic nature of the developments and their chronological coincidence with Roman conquest are difficult to explain except as part of a cultural and economic shift that historians have traditionally associated with Romanization.[88]

It is, of course, common for there to be a disparity between the culture that produced a particular architectural style and the culture of those who 'consume' those houses. Immigrant communities, for instance, used local architectural forms. The reverse of this pattern is also true. European colonialists imposed European house-types without necessarily altering local patterns of behaviour. More spectacularly, the Prince Regent's construction of a Moghul Palace at Brighton did not mean that he was an Eastern potentate, however much he might have wished to be. The implications of this are broad: a Roman did not need to live in a house displaying distinctive 'Roman' architectural elements and those who lived in 'Roman' house-types need not be Roman. Therbert (1987) argues that moves towards a more homogeneous domestic architecture of elite houses reflects increasing cultural homogeneity. I would suggest that it reflects a desire on the part of the elite to associate with Mediterranean elite culture, which may, ultimately, not be a different position.[89] In spite of the obvious methodological problems (we have seen throughout this chapter the difficulties of understanding how people lived in and regarded their houses simply from the architectural form, and the house was, after all, only one of many potential loci of identity available), the suggestion that some at least may have wished to be seen as assimilated to more general Mediterranean cultural values is indicative of mentalities, whether or not those people actually adopted more Mediterranean *mores* or remained true to traditional Egyptian modes of behaviour.

The Late Roman and Byzantine house: continuities and change

In this chapter the break between Roman and the Late Roman and Byzantine periods relates as much to a change in the nature of the available evidence as to any putative social change and the transition in the nature of the evidence is gradual. Much of the discussion of first- to third-century housing above depends on the architectural and other details preserved in property transactions and taxation registers from the villages and cities of Middle Egypt. Unfortunately, family structures and patterns of house occupancy are much less clear for the later period, partly as a matter of chance and partly because of changes in the workings of the bureaucracy. There are also fewer house sales, though the practice clearly continued, and, in any case, it is far more difficult to compare prices in the later period than in the earlier. Much of our papyrological data comes from a single archive, the Patermouthis archive, and this gives us a picture of housing at Syene (modern Aswan). In addition to this archive, we have financial and administrative records relating to buildings at a large residence near Oxyrhynchus owned by the Apion family. There is also a range of isolated documents from elsewhere in Egypt (rentals, sales and property divisions) with which we can supplement the main archives. The archaeological evidence is, however, better than that for the earlier period.[90] Excavations in Alexandria have explored a number of houses of the fifth to the seventh century. Excavations on Elephantine (the island off Aswan) uncovered houses in the courtyard of the temple of Chnum, probably occupied from the sixth to the ninth or tenth centuries. Other Late Roman and early Arabic period housing has been uncovered at the town of Jeme, West Thebes, though the excavation here was somewhat below modern standards. The houses of Jeme continued to be occupied long after the Arab conquest. Those excavating the site at Abu Mina have uncovered two town houses of the sixth century which seem to have continued in use until the widespread destruction at the site in the early seventh century, probably related to the Persian invasions. A large villa-like structure of the fourth century has been found at Marea while a block of fourth-century houses has been excavated at Kellis in the Western Desert. Most of these houses were occupied towards or beyond the end of the period and I shall start at the top of the social scale and work towards an understanding of the poorer housing of the sixth century and later. But first I turn to the fourth-century material, starting with the extraordinary site of Kellis.

Kellis[91]

Kellis is a village at the Dakleh oasis in the Western Desert. The archaeological study of the site was part of wider cultural and anthropological study of the Oasis as a whole in an attempt to understand the history and ecology of an area which is becoming increasingly developed. The site is still under investigation and any remarks are preliminary, but there is enough published papyrological and archaeological material to allow detailed analysis.

The site has been comparatively well-publicized because of the nature of the papyrological finds. The courtyard of one of the excavated houses was littered with hundreds of fragments of papyrus and wooden boards. Some of this material was the normal run of domestic and administrative business similar to fourth-century material from other areas of Egypt, though the topographical and chronological compactness of the documents allows papyrologists to piece together rather more of the political and social lives of the inhabitants of the house and its neighbours than is possible for most other communities. Some of the material is extraordinary in that it contains literary and documentary evidence of a heretical fourth-century group known as the Manichees who had vaguely messianic, dualistic views of the universe and who were hunted down during the fourth century (Gardner and Lieu 1996). This raises the possibility that the community in the three excavated houses might have been rather unusual, though the documentary material, while suggesting that the site was far from 'normal', does not suggest that these people were very different socially or economically from the valley population. It seems a reasonable assumption that the architecture of the houses was relatively normal.

A single block of three houses has been excavated (figure 3.15), all the material in which appears to be of the fourth century. Initially, the houses were roughly rectangular and of roughly equal size. At some point, House 2 expanded by taking some of the space of House 1, through which an entrance was constructed. The houses had different layouts. House 3 was the most elaborate. It had an entrance hall which gave access to a passageway. The passageway led to two halls, the furthest away being the work yard at the back of the house. This had animal pens and evidence of food preparation. It was an αὐλή. The nearer hall was an inner court (possibly an αἴθριον) (6) around which most of the other rooms were clustered. The majority of the written material was found here, though only a small number of coins. The inner court gave access to eight rooms, including the staircase, though only six of those rooms had direct access to the court. The pattern of coin loss in the rooms was irregular with three rooms having fifty or more losses while two rooms (3 and 5) had fewer than five coins discovered in them, which suggests that the rooms had rather different functions.

Figure 3.15 Houses from Kellis (after Hope 1987)

Houses 1 and 2 were rather more simply constructed and the finds less extraordinary. Both houses had an extensive work yard, though no internal court. House 1 has a clustered plan, the rooms being built off a central corridor. House 2 is more difficult to characterize.

Although the houses look different from those at Karanis, the papyrological material is very similar. Architecturally, the use of space seems more expansive and none of these houses had prominent gatehouses, though access was not particularly easy. *P. Kellis* 21 reports an assault which started with the assailant bringing an axe to break into the house. A property division from AD 335 (probably for a different house) divides a house between five siblings. A gatehouse containing a room is mentioned, as is a granary, neither of which are obvious in the excavated houses (*P. Kellis* 13). Single rooms in houses were also rented out (*P. Kellis* 32; 33).

The residents of Houses 2 and 3 appear to have had close social connections. In AD 333 a certain Pausanias, a magistrate of the local city of Mothis, gifted land to Aurelius Psais son of Pamour (*P. Kellis* 38a). The family of Pamour occupied House 3. The plot appears to have been an undeveloped area that lay to the north of House 3 and next to an unidentified structure which the papyrus describes, somewhat implausibly, as a camel shed. A Pausanias also appears in letters found in House 2. Gena, a carpenter, wrote to Pausanias to say that he would be delayed and that Timotheus should be sent in his place. Pausanias was addressed as 'lord' and displayed 'nobility' (*P. Kellis* 5). A Pausanias wrote to his lord and brother Gena about some grain to be exchanged for pigs by Timotheus (*P. Kellis* 6; cf. *P. Kellis* 63). Aurelius Gena appears in a petition found in House 3 complaining that he and his fellow *komarch* (chief official in the village), also called Gena, had been attacked by a former urban magistrate, Harpokration, and his henchmen. The son of Harpokration, Timotheus, came and stole pigs (*P. Kellis* 23). Thirty-three villagers, including three church officials, petitioned on behalf of an Aurelius Gena in another text found in House 3 (*P. Kellis* 24). A letter with Manichaean elements found in House 3 greets the sons of the lord, Pausanias and Pisistratos, both good Greek names (*P. Kellis* 63). The connection between the houses is also shown by the development of House 2 into space which must have been originally part of House 1, a development which would have been rather difficult if the houses had different owners.[92] Local, powerful magnates, such as Harpokration and Pausanias, clearly exercised considerable influence within the village, perhaps developing little blocks of influence such as we see elsewhere, and this may account for the obvious community of the three houses.

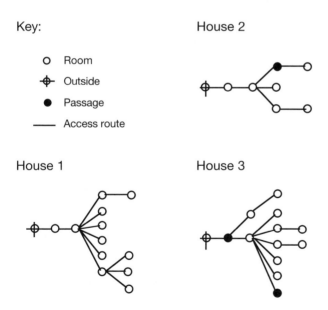

Figure 3.16 Houses from Kellis: access plans

Marea and the 'villas' of Alexandria

The site of Marea (modern Al Mina) sits on the southern side of the Lake Mareotis, opposite Alexandria. It was a port through which the agricultural produce of the hinterland was transported to Alexandria. The site was further developed in the later period after the increased importance of the shrine of St Menas brought the lucrative pilgrim-trade through the port. The town had a large church, dock facilities and a number of shops along a colonnaded street (el-Fakhrani 1983). Several houses have been discovered here, though there is little published evidence. One of the more important structures is a large villa complex about 2.5 km from the town. The villa was built on the site of a small Ptolemaic settlement but was developed as a villa in the late fourth or fifth century. It covered 1,500 m^2 and had two peristyle courts. It had an agricultural function and contained a winery, cisterns and a well.[93] Rodziewicz (1988) suggests that the villa was rebuilt in the sixth century and its facilities were improved. A 'chapel' was added in this rebuilding. The villa looks to have been an estate house which was largely self-contained and which provided for the needs of its workforce and owners. It was probably a rather smaller version of the later palace of the Apions.

El-Fakhrani (1983) identified what appears to be a different villa on the edge of the town. This villa also had a winery and was constructed around a large peristyle court.

The Palace of the Apions

The Apions were a powerful family of the fifth and sixth centuries (see pp. 313–16) and an archive relating to the running of their estate was published mainly in *P. Oxy.* VI and XVI, though documents have made their way into other collections. The family's lands appear to have been concentrated around Oxyrhynchus, but they also had lands in the Fayum and Herakleopolite and are likely to have had properties which are not attested in the archive. They were sufficiently powerful and prominent to have political careers in Constantinople and may even have married into the imperial family (Hardy 1931; Gascou 1985: 61–75).

The archive is mostly concerned with the administration of the Apions' lands but some of the documents deal with the maintenance of their house. The house was in the προαστίον (suburbs), though is also described as being 'outside the gate', as are some (tenant?) farmers (*P. Oxy.* XVI 1913; *P. Princ.* III 158) and was probably a residential and administrative centre as well as a working farm.[94] It is normally only attested in relation to the costs of maintenance and, therefore, the baths are the best-known element of the building. The Apions employed doormen and a manager for the baths, which were probably elaborate and well furnished. Mats bought from a local monastery were used in the bath house (*P. Oxy.* XVI 2015; I 148 *BL* VII 128 = *P. Klein. Format* = *Stud. Pal. Pap.* III 282) and water was probably piped in (we have two receipts for the lead used in soldering: *P. Oxy.* VI 915; 1002 = *P. Turner* 52; cf. *PSI* VIII 955). Few other features of the house are attested.[95] An account of wine distributed from various cellars to units of farms mentions a cellar in the πρόθυρα of the house, probably the front gatehouse (*P. Oxy.* XVI 2044). A rather strange text of the seventh century lists property in the hands of Onnophris *symmachos* (soldier-guard) at the προαστίον (*P. Oxy.* XVI 1925). The list of property includes from the *triclinium* (the dining room) a large couch, a shield, two icons (one of St Kollouthos and the other of the Virgin Mary), another couch, various doors (probably quite valuable property given the shortage of wood in Egypt), couches, balustrades; and from the bath house, lion-headed taps and other material. It looks as if the house was being stripped but the context is uncertain.

The house of the Apions would appear to have been a palatial suburban villa, probably very similar to the large elite residences uncovered elsewhere, the most famous probably being Piazza Armerina in Sicily, though one assumes that the Apions had not attained that level of luxury. The house was equipped with a dining-room and elaborate bath house and may have been architecturally complex.

Houses at Abu Mina

Abu Mina was developed in the Christian period as a healing shrine to St Menas, an extremely popular saint who had been buried at a spot chosen when the camels carrying him refused to move on. Menas is often depicted with two recalcitrant camels. The shrine on the edge of the desert developed rapidly and acquired a bath house, a large church, market facilities and houses (Grossmann 1982; 1989; Grossmann et al. 1994; Grossmann and Kosciuk 1991; 1992; Grossmann et al. 1997). The best-excavated house is the so-called 'ostraca house' in which a large dump of Arabic ostraka was found. The excavated house was comparatively large (21 m × 14 m) (Grossmann 1995). The main entrance appears to have opened onto an adapted peristyle court which gave access to two symmetrical areas, one of which was further divided into two rooms. The back row of pillars marked off a cross corridor which led to three back rooms. This arrangement is very similar to the Classical Greek παστάς houses found at Olynthos (see also Jones 1973). The simple and Classical design of the house was disrupted by later developments. Walls were used to partition the house, perhaps creating three or more separate residences. The house was probably destroyed in the early seventh century when much of Abu Mina was burnt by the Persians and the dump of Arab ostraka could post-date the house.[96] The house is probably of the sixth century, though it is not easy to date. We have, therefore, at the end of the Byzantine period in Egypt a house which in style looks back to Greek precursors built nearly a millennium earlier.

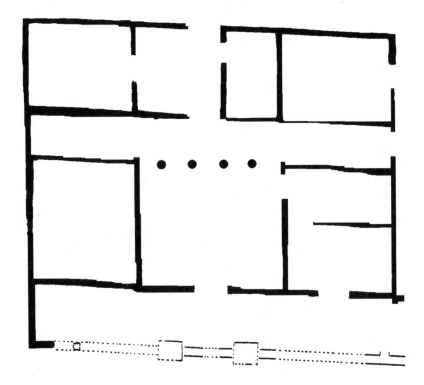

Figure 3.17 The ostraka house (after Grossmann 1995)

Houses at Marina el-Alamein

On the border between Egypt and Libya, it is difficult to know whether Alamein will have conformed to Libyan or Egyptian architectural styles. The site appears to have flourished from the Roman to the Byzantine period. The excavated houses have little dating material, but appear to be late and show no traces of Arab-period occupation. As with the ostraka house at Abu Mena, the house shows similarities with the παστάς houses of Classical Greece, especially in the use of columns within the courtyard (Marina el Alamein 1991; Medeksza 1998).

Houses in the Patermouthis archive and other papyrological attestations[97]

Husson (1981; 1990) argues that the Patermouthis archive shows continuity of architectural style from the first century AD. The texts detail transfers of property by Patermouthis and his family over more than half a century. The long descriptions of houses in the archive are peppered with terminology familiar from earlier centuries. The αἴθριον, the αὐλή, the πύλον and the συμπόσιον feature in the houses. The house described in *P. Lond.* V 1722 (Porten 1996: D22) of 530 had a new πύλον which had two συμπόσια on the second floor and a third on the third floor. *P. Lond.* V 1723 (Porten 1996: D30) of 577 is a rental agreement in which each floor of the house is described in some detail, though the lacunae render the text difficult to understand. *P. Lond.* V 1724 of 578–82 (Porten 1996: D32) concerns a house with a πύλον, an αἴθριον and a παραδρόμιδος (*paradromidos*: hall). *P. Münch.* 9 (Porten 1996: D40) of 585 concerns the sale of half a συμπόσιον and a room on the fourth floor of a house. *P. Münch.* 11 (Porten 1996: D45) of 586 concerns the sale of half a house with a πρόθυρον (fore-gate?), πύλον and αἴθριον. *P. Münch.* 12 of 591 (Porten 1996: D46) concerns the sale of half of what appears to be the same house. *P. Münch.* 13 of 594 (Porten 1996: D47) concerns the sale of half an αὐλή. *P. Lond.* V 1733 (Porten 1996: D49) of 594 concerns half a συμπόσιον on the second floor and a connected 'roof-room' (?), all in a house with a πρόθυρον, an αἴθριον and a παραδρόμιδος. The same property appears in *P. Münch.* 8 (to be taken with *P. Lond.* V 1857; Porten 1996: D23) of *c.* 540.

Patermouthis was a soldier serving in the local military unit. His economic status, however, is uncertain. We do not know whether Patermouthis survived on his military earnings (whatever they might have been in this period) or had some other means of support. The family's property seems quite elaborate. The main house seems to have had a gatehouse. The αἴθριον probably stood between the gatehouse and the rest of the house, as seems to have been traditional, but the other features are difficult to locate. The shift in the meaning of συμπόσιον means that it is difficult to know whether there were rooms for entertaining within the house (see pp. 83–5). If συμπόσιον is to be taken as a suite (perhaps 'apartment' would be a better term), it would suggest that the house could easily be divided into different residential units. There is a strong possibility of multi-family occupancy and the detail with which rooms are described perhaps suggests a rather more formal division of space than is apparent in earlier documentation. Again, houses are associated with individuals, possibly even deceased individuals, suggesting that the house was still a mark of status. There may have been changes in how the house was regarded and in its layout, but the Patermouthis archive does not make those changes obvious.

Texts from elsewhere in Egypt suggest a similar pattern. Aurelia Ptolemais from Ptolemais Euergetis sold a city house in 309 which had both αἴθριον and αὐλή (*SB* XVI 12289). A house in Aphrodito sold in 613–40 had an enclosed αἴθριον, three ἀνδρεώνες (male dining-rooms), two together and one seemingly in an upper chamber, a gatehouse and an ἐξέδρα (*SB* XVIII 13320 = *P. Mich.* XIII 665). A sixth-century text from the Apion estate (*BGU* I 305) attests the renting-out of a house with an αἴθριον in Ptolemais Euergetis which belonged to the estate. A rental agreement from Hermopolis (*SB* XVIII 13620) from the end of the fifth or the first decades of the sixth century concerns a house with an αὐλή and a well. We also see rental and sale of συμπόσια separately from the rest of the house (*P. Bodl.* I 45; *P. Rendel Harris* II 238). An αἴθριον appears with two συμπόσια in a lease from Oxyrhynchus dating to AD 430 (*P. Oxy.* XVI 1957)[98] and the rental of single rooms within houses is common (*P. Bodl.* I 36 of 542 or 547; *P. Oxy.* XVI 1961 of AD 487).[99]

Terminological and architectural continuities may, however, mask elaboration. The texts themselves often detail relations between the various rooms, though not with any great clarity. Hall structures (ἐξέδραι) are more commonly attested and give the impression of greater architectural complexity in the various houses. Multiple dining-rooms within the same house again suggest architectural elaboration, though in this context we have no clue as to what a dining-room would have looked like or whether such rooms were defined by their fittings or fixed architectural features. Nevertheless, one would hardly wish to draw an analogy with the highly decorated facilities of various late Roman villas (Van Aken 1949; Ellis 1988; 1997; Scott 1997; Dunbabin 1996), even if some houses were more elaborate than their second-century predecessors. We have an inventory of domestic equipment drawn up by the headman of the village of Spania listing the property of his house in an appeal for compensation following some criminal activity. As headman, one might have expected that he would have had one of the more elaborate houses in the village. His property included a large amount of grain, wine, meat, safflower, agricultural equipment, cloth, iron and alabaster fittings (presumably decorative), mattresses or couch or bed coverings, beds, a rug, glassware, clothing, a gold crown and a gold 'finger'. It is possible that some of these were fittings for a dining-room, though it is more likely that the mattresses and coverings were for beds. Apart from the grain (perhaps due in tax) and the gold, there is little sign of wealth and the house seems rather plainly furnished (*P. Oxy.* XVI 2058; *BL* VIII 253).

Houses at Kom el-Dikke, Alexandria[100]

Excavations in central Alexandria at the mound known as Kom el-Dikke have uncovered a number of comparatively well-preserved late Roman houses. The standards of the excavation and their state of preservation mean that these are the best archaeological examples of late houses. The block of houses was of fourth- to seventh-century date, though some were only occupied towards the end of the period. The houses seem to have been built after the whole area was reshaped by the construction of a large, probably fourth-century, bath house across the street, and a theatre complex (possibly an odeion) and related facilities. Although seemingly simple structures, the houses themselves pose significant problems of interpretation.

The best preserved of these houses is House D (Rodziewicz 1984: 66–127). There is a rather confusing series of structures at the entrance of uncertain relationship to the house proper, but the plan of the rest of the house is relatively clear. House D consisted of a corridor or court 15.5 m long, off which there were ten rooms. Rooms D2, 3, 4, 7 and 6 lay to the south and rooms D14, 13, 12,

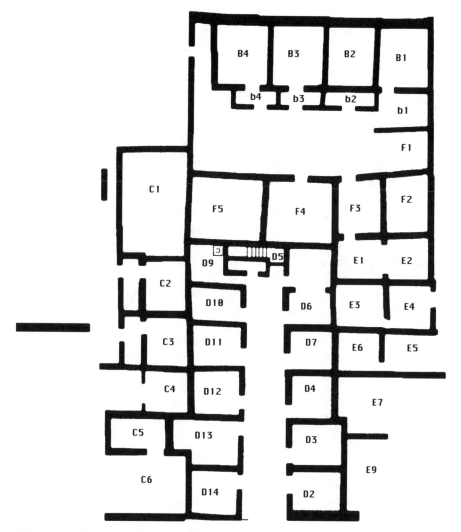

Figure 3.18 Houses at Kom el-Dikke (after Rodziewicz 1984)

11 and 10 to the north of the corridor-court. At the end of the corridor was a set of steps leading to an upper storey and a passage which led to D9, the latrine, a facility which appears to have been constructed from space that had belonged to D10. Apart from D10 and D6, which had been formed by the amalgamation of two earlier rooms, the rooms are very similar in size, as shown by table 3.4.

The regularity of the rooms and their almost square shape give the house a cellular appearance which makes it look as if it was a single design: possibly an institutional construction to house equals, soldiers or monks or perhaps guests

Table 3.4 Size of rooms of House D, Kom el-Dikke

Room	Proportions (m)	Area (m²)	Room	Proportions (m)	Area (m²)
D2	3.4 × 3.1	10.54	D10	2.1 × 3.4	7.14
D3	3.4 × 2.9	9.86	D11	2.7 × 3.3	8.91
D4	2.95 × 2.9	8.56	D12	3.2 × 2.85	9.12
D7	2.7 × 2.9	7.83	D13	3.1 × 3	9.3
D6	5.15 × 2.9	14.94	D14	2.9 × 3.1	8.99

at an inn. But the history of the house is more complex. The first rooms to be built were D2 and D3. D4, D6 and D7 followed sometime afterwards. The rooms of the north range were an entirely separate project. At some later point, the latrine was added and the stairs constructed. Rodziewicz (1984) interprets the house as a single entity, the unity of the house deriving from the corridor-court, the communal latrine and the stairs, all of which are late features in the house's evolution. Several rooms showed evidence for the manufacture of cheap jewellery. Fragments of glass, crystal and ivory were found. The best evidence, however, is from the corridor-court, which Rodziewicz divides into three zones. The zone near the entrance was for eating. Here, there are a number of stones arranged around the external walls of D13 and D14 which may have been used as seats. The central zone was for prayer since a rather battered fresco of an enthroned Madonna and Child, a very popular Egyptian motif, was discovered together with two lamp brackets on either side of the fresco. The Christianity of these late Roman Alexandrians was clearly displayed. The third zone, deepest into the house, was for ablutions. The waste from the latrine would have been removed manually. The seeming illogicality of this could be explained by postulating either a desire for privacy (not a common feature of earlier Roman toilet arrangements) or, more practically, that any breeze ventilating the house would have carried noxious smells through the rest of the house if the latrine had been positioned nearer the entrance.

Some of the rooms were crudely decorated with graffiti and most walls were plastered or washed and the plaster incised. Security also seems to have been a concern in that many of the doors appear to have been lockable.

The other units in the block are even more problematic. Houses B and F are built around a shared court which had communal facilities. The rooms are slightly more irregular but the houses still have a cellular structure. Rooms B1, B2, B3 and B4 each have an anteroom, but the walls of the anterooms do not line up exactly with the walls of the main room, and this seems to be primary evidence for the unity of House B. Rooms C1, C2 (in which considerable amounts of ivory were discovered), C3 and C4 appear to have had a similar arrangement. Rodziewicz suggests that House C may in fact have been two separate houses with entrance from a narrow alley. House F was constructed in three phases. Too little survives of the houses south of House D to make much sense of the general arrangement.

Several of the houses, not just House D, contained fragments of metal or worked bone. The bone pins and other small *objets d'art* were generally shaped on Dionysiac or Aphrodisian themes. This mildly licentious, pagan material develops themes common from popular culture of previous centuries and suggests that the seemingly devout inhabitants of the houses did not find any moral, cultural or religious message in the deployment of such traditional themes. E. Rodziewicz (1978) suggests that 'more respectable' themes for Christian and possibly Islamic customers became more popular over time with facial and floral imagery being used, but the tentative chronological sequencing appears to depend solely on stylistic criteria rather than stratified finds.

We have, therefore, a small number of houses, occupied from the fourth to the late seventh century and developed over that period. The occupants show signs of being devoted Christians, but some at least produced jewellery and personal ornaments that deployed traditional pagan motifs as well as more abstract patterns. Further interpretation of the nature of the occupation of the site is considerably more hazardous.

M. Rodziewicz (1988) tells us that the first thought of the excavators as they uncovered the houses at Kom el-Dikke was that they had found a monastery. The cellular rooms and the Madonna and Child fresco reinforced this view. Gradually, however, the chronology of the development was established and the evidence of jewellery production (though many monks did support themselves through craft production) was amassed which persuaded the excavators that they had a domestic residence. A similar cellular development at Taposiris Magna, which had always been interpreted as a fort or monastery, in spite of the fact that there was no explicit Christian material, could now be interpreted as domestic. The initial rejected interpretation has considerable appeal. The structures do not conform to our view of domestic architecture: they look as if they were constructed by an institution according to an established scheme. The closest ancient parallel is clearly late military and monastic accommodation and it is generally accepted that the monks borrowed their architecture from the military. There was some discussion at the Late Roman Seminar in Oxford as to whether these buildings were in fact workshops which could, similarly, be built institutionally to allow each craftsman access to the street and a set amount of space. Again, I think this idea must be rejected since the evidence of communal living seems too strong and, in any case, I have no strong parallel for the identification.[101] The identification of these structures as houses seems to me inescapable.

Yet, the spaces remain difficult to understand. House D is given unity by the communal facilities in the hall, but the excavators were less keen to see the similar courts around which other houses or rooms were constructed as providing unity, though they also had communal facilities (though a rather more crude provision). The evidence that some of the rooms could be secured from the hall suggests a strong division between the rooms and the hall. I think it improbable that this dichotomy was between private and public space. The hall space is too enclosed to be thought of as a street or alley, fundamentally public space. Rather, the division seems to be between the communal space of the hall and the more private space of the rooms.[102] The cellular construction seems to me to be the most efficient means of constructing separate units, as with monastic cells and late Roman military accommodation, and it is not apparent that the community inhabiting House D would have had communal use of the various cells, though the actual pattern of accommodation cannot be established.

Multi-household occupancy of a single house is, of course, nothing new and the sharing of facilities would presumably have created social bonds between the various occupants of the house. Intimate daily contact can hardly have been avoided. Even the design can be paralleled from Karanis (see p. 57). Nevertheless, this form contrasts starkly with the linearity of most of the Karanis houses. The design at Kom el-Dikke would seem to maximize private space.

The houses in the courtyard of the temple of Chnum, Elephantine

Excavations led by the German Archaeological Institute in Cairo on Elephantine uncovered a number of late Roman and early Arabic structures in the courtyard of the temple of Chnum, the main temple on the island. These structures were poorly preserved, normally only a few courses surviving above ground level. The excavation has produced little or no evidence of the decoration of the structures but the archaeologists have been able to establish the ground plans and the sequence of development at the site. The chronology established by Grossmann (1980) has been corrected by Gempeler's (1992: 45–51) study of the ceramics.

The first period of construction in the temple courtyard was in the mid-fifth century. This was the so-called military phase of construction. This period saw the construction of probably just over forty units within the courtyard. The units around the courtyard wall were approximately 4 m × 5 m, while the thirteen central units were approximately 5 m × 6 m. The ground floor of each was divided into two unequal rooms: a small entrance room which was largely occupied by a staircase to an upper storey and a slightly larger back room. Nothing of the upper storeys survived. There were two further phases of construction during which the regularities of the earlier plan were disturbed. Several units remained more or less untouched, but some were extended into the courtyard while others were demolished to extend the courtyard. The state of preservation means that it is more difficult to be certain about the locations of entrances to rooms and houses in some cases. The basic pattern, however, seems similar to the earlier military phase with several floor plans consisting of two rooms, one of which was dominated by the staircase. Where the walls survive to a sufficient height, niches have been found, probably for cupboards.

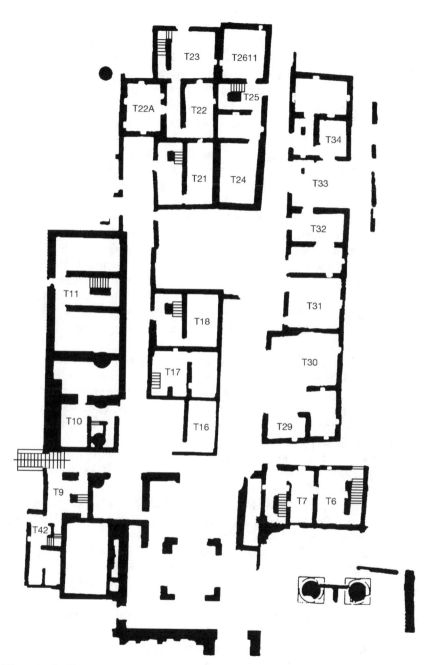

Figure 3.19 Houses at the temple of Chnum (after Grossmann 1980)

Gempeler (1992) dates the 'military phase' of construction to *c.* 425–50. The 'civilianizing' of the area is dated 500–30 and a third phase of construction developed some of the units in 550–75. The houses continued to be occupied after the Arab conquest and possibly as late as the late eighth century.

The identification of the initial building phase as military rests on historical rather than purely archaeological data. There was a military unit stationed on the island from the fifth century and the development of a fort in the temple courtyard can be paralleled at the legionary fort at Luxor, constructed around the courtyard of the temple *c.* AD 300 (el-Saghir et al. 1986). Yet, the 'civilianization' of the fort in the early sixth century does not seem to be related to an ending of the military presence on Elephantine. *P. Münch.* 2 attests a unit of soldiers of the camp on Elephantine as late as 578 and it would be perverse to suggest that the unit moved to a different location. The fort at Nessana in Arabia also has a small number of cellular rooms, which are normally interpreted as accommodation for the soldiers, but, like Patermouthis, the soldiers owned property in the town, where they may normally have resided (*P. Nessana* 21; 22).[103] The analogy with Nessana would seem to suggest either that the houses in the temple courtyard at Elephantine were military and continued to be military until the unit was disbanded in the seventh century, or that it was always a civilian development.[104] Rodziewicz's (1988) suggestion that domestic, monastic and military architecture were very similar seems equally as true here as in Alexandria.

Although this erodes the differences between military and civilian domestic architecture and allows similar interpretations to be developed for both types of architecture, it becomes more difficult to be confident as to the rationale behind the developments. The structures in the temple courtyard went through a quasi-evolutionary process in which new structures were developed from the old, though the basic framework of the old structures was preserved in the new. We cannot know the extent to which the new structures were determined by the ideology of the old, which is particularly important if we see the initial phases as military. Of course, unlike evolutionary processes, the builders did have the option of demolition and a revolutionary departure from previous architectural modes, but such developments would be quite radical. Any interpretation must be cautious, but the similarities in the cellular structure to the houses at Kom el-Dikke suggest a similar interpretation: that the units were designed to provide a maximum of separable space. The pattern is perhaps even clearer. The space between the cells is more clearly communal, but also could hardly be described as public, the alley being surrounded by the cells and presumably only used for access to the cells. The absence of available open space would also make the annexation of the alley-space attractive for cooking and other household activities. The cells themselves are more clearly self-contained, separate units and of a size which would seem to make them feasible containers of households.

The Houses of Jeme (Medinet Habu)

Medinet Habu, known as Jeme in the later period, was the site of a huge temple enclosure on the west bank of the Nile opposite modern Luxor. The enclosure encircles the mortuary temple of Ramesses III and it is this which has attracted archaeological interest and is a minor part of the tourist itinerary. The site was practically abandoned during the Saitic period (c. 664–525 BC), but was probably reoccupied in the Roman period. The rubble from this later occupation fills the temple enclosure and much of this had probably been sifted through by the *fellahin* before a team from the Oriental Institute in Chicago arrived, primarily to record the Pharaonic remains. Unlike many earlier excavators, however, the team broke off from their main project to record and excavate some of these later houses, partly in the hope of finding papyri in the remains.[105]

Most of the structures were domestic, though there were four churches associated with the town (Wilfong 1989). Two distinct archaeological levels were identified: a lower late Roman or Byzantine level dated from the numismatic evidence to the third, fourth and fifth centuries, and an upper Byzantine and Islamic level dating from the sixth century onwards (Nelson and Hölscher 1931: 50–1). The town was probably abandoned in the early ninth century (Wilfong 1989; Hölscher 1932: 46). The houses sit in a maze of narrow streets and alleys, ranging from 1.8 m to 1.1 m wide. The houses themselves were extremely small, the published examples having ground plans of about 36 m², but the houses were multi-storey with evidence of two or three floors in most cases. All houses seem to have had access to a courtyard, sometimes seemingly shared with other houses. Entrance to the houses was often through the court, though in some cases the court was enclosed and entrance was through a subterranean passageway into the court. At the entrance to the house stood two earthenware jars, a common feature in many hot climates since the porous jars cooled and moistened the air entering the house (Stead 1980). Lintels were often decorated with crosses. The ground floor was divided into two rooms, plus a staircase, and appears to have been very poorly lit and ventilated. Any decoration within the houses had been lost.

The houses differ somewhat from the houses at Karanis and the later excavated examples from Elephantine and Alexandria and the rather cursory publication of the remains adds further to the difficulties in understanding the site. The narrow streets and alleys and the difficulties in gaining access to the houses suggest that houses were not primarily places for the assertion of social status. The crosses on the lintels signified that the residents were Christian, but in this period they may also have had an apotropaic quality, keeping away demons and the evil eye. Some at least of the courtyards appear to have been communal, though the houses appear to have been more private. The narrow alleys and streets may also have been more communal than public, not truly open to strangers. Even though the architecture differs somewhat from that at Kom el-Dikke and in the courtyard of the temple of Chnum, the spatial patterns do show similarities.

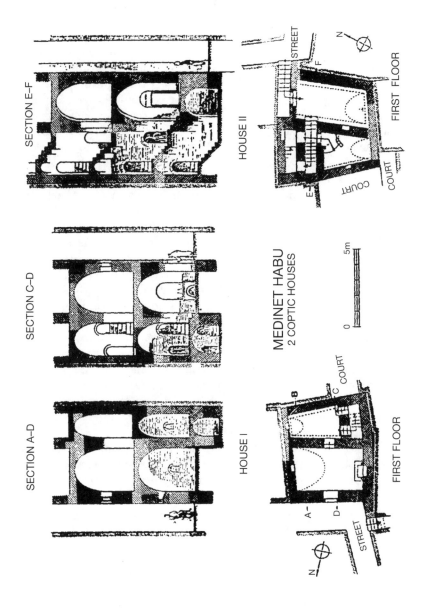

Figure 3.20 Houses at Jeme (after Nelson and Hölscher 1931)

Interpreting the late Roman and Byzantine house

The late Roman, Byzantine and early Islamic houses discussed in this section exhibit considerable variety, but also elements of continuity with housing of earlier periods. It seems very unlikely that the increased complexity and variety of domestic architecture is merely a feature of the greater topographical diversity of the sites examined in the second half of this chapter. Although we cannot be certain that the houses of Jeme do not correspond to a local architectural style that had been in use since the building of Medinet Habu, we do have considerable evidence for similarities in domestic architecture from sites as geographically diverse as Syene, as attested in the Patermouthis archive, and Alexandria, as described by Philo and possibly by Caesar.[106] Also, the cellular architecture attested in the environs of Alexandria finds some echo at Karanis and at Elephantine as well as in monastic and military contexts. Similarly, it seems very unlikely that the Apions were the only family to build themselves a suburban villa. We can reasonably consider the variety of architectural forms as a significant reflection of the diversity of domestic architecture within communities, not just as evidence of regional variations.

It has been a major tenet of this analysis that domestic architecture reflects social ideology as well as contributing to that ideology. It is, however, problematic to move from the materiality of architectural form to the more elusive area of ideology. Some conclusions seem so obvious that they are in danger of being banal. For instance, the different traditions observable in the housing of this period reflect both cultural and economic diversity. The residence of the Apions appears to find its organizational and architectural precursors in the palatial villas attested across the Mediterranean region in the late Roman period. We have several examples of villa-type structures from the countryside around Alexandria, houses built on a predominantly Classical model. The peristyle house at Abu Mina shows that similar Classical styles were adopted in less grand urban housing and the continued functioning of these houses into the late sixth and probably early seventh century suggests the continued health of the Romanized elite of the province (*contra* Ellis 1988; see also Hodges 1998 and Small and Buck 1994: 76–7 for earlier changes in the West). Nevertheless, there is considerable evidence of the continuity of Egyptian traditions. The vocabulary of the Patermouthis archive can be paralleled in earlier centuries, even though the meanings of some of the words may have changed somewhat. Finally, we have the tiny structures from Jeme and the cellular houses from Alexandria and Elephantine, the cultural precursors of which are far more difficult to find.

To make sense of these developments, however, we need to venture into more speculative territory. There is, I think, enough evidence to suggest a limited reorientation of spatiality in Egyptian houses in this period and that this is a response to more general changes in cultural values that were sweeping the Mediterranean. Rodziewicz (1988) has pointed to the blurring of military, monastic and domestic architecture.[107] In itself, this should not be a surprise. The army was an obvious institution from which coenobitic monks could draw architectural inspiration and Pachomius, the founder of coenobitic monasticism in Egypt, had apparently served in the Roman army. Yet, it is not clear why these forms should influence domestic architecture, which had, after all, rather different functions. The monk's relationship to his cell was very particular. The cell was a place of private contemplation. From as early as Athanasius' attempts to bring order to the variegated efflorescence of contemporary monasticism (Brakke 1995), it was the discipline of the cell which was presented as the proper environment for communing with the divine. The pilgrims came to the cell, met the holy man and were sometimes entertained by him, but the cell marked his individuality and his direct relationship with God (Athanasius, *Life of St Antony* 85). The monk needed to be solitary and to have private space. Perhaps it is not too far-fetched to see in the development of these cellular houses a similar function: a desire to define in space oneself or one's household.

Clearly, the same legal structures applied in the late antique period as earlier and houses continued to be divided at death. Rentals and sales of fractions of houses continued and even the tiny houses of Jeme could be divided between different occupants. Yet, the Byzantine documents are often much more specific than their Roman equivalents. Although this may partly be a matter of style, it also suggests a desire to define space more exactly and divide the house, a process which would be so much easier if the house had a cellular structure.

Such a process seems to coexist with some blurring of the boundary between public and private. This is easy to see in the great houses, which are estate centres, domestic residences and farms. In other places, better-attested residences of great families seem to have had audience chambers, bath houses, dining suites, and sometimes some structures with religious functions. It is difficult to decide to what extent it is legitimate to extend the rather sparse description of the Apion residence to fit this Mediterranean model, but there can be little doubt that their residence was both a public and a private building, a symbol of the power of the family and its local dominance.[108] But the blurring of boundaries can also be seen in the Alexandrian houses where the courts are so difficult to classify and understand, and in the narrow alleys at Jeme, and perhaps also in the courtyard of the temple of Chnum where the exact status of space cannot be defined. Modern Western ideas of public and private seem somehow inappropriate and a more graded vocabulary is necessary, even though, and this must be remembered, we know so little of how these spaces were used. Such alterations in spatialities can be seen as part of what could be thought of as an erosion of traditional Classical urban forms (Pentz 1992; Kennedy 1985a; Bouras 1981; Claude 1969). We can read out from the house to the city and changes therein, but we can also read inwards to the individuals who live in the house and are shaped by and shape its structures. What we may be seeing reflected in the domestic architecture of the late period is a change in individual social roles, a realignment of the individual and the social structures that integrated that individual into society. It is very tempting to see in this desire to define separate space, and in the complexities of the relationship between public and private, a turning away from the public and its institutions which can be seen in part as the rise of an individualism, identified by many cultural historians as an important feature of the late antique period (Brown 1971; 1988: 320–1; Haldon 1990: 381–4; 399–402; Markus 1990: 139–55).

Such a complex realignment of social forces should, however, make us suspicious of overarching historical interpretations and bring us back to the theoretical conclusions of the previous chapter. Here, in the houses of Egypt, we should search for the forces that produced space and for how that space and those forces might have been experienced, and it is the very heterogeneity of Byzantine housing that is so evocative and useful. Haldon's (1990) discussion of the seventh century portrays it as a century of transition between what we would call late antiquity and the Middle Ages. He sees the realignment of Byzantine culture as a response to the catastrophic military defeats of the mid-seventh century that forced a re-evaluation of all political and cultural structures, resulting in a religious conservatism and the emergence of radically new forms of social and political organization. A turning inwards was a response to a crisis, both political and spiritual, as God's chosen people found themselves on the losing side in a major war. Brown (1988: 320–1) sees this same sense of spiritual crisis alive in the late fourth and early fifth centuries in the writings of John Chrysostom, who encouraged a turning away from the pleasures of the city and the world of pagan entertainments, and a concentration on the inner life, a structural shift similar to that accomplished by the monastic movement. Markus (1990) discusses the same phenomenon in the religious thinkers of the West. This is clearly an important strain in Christian thought, and writers who brought the ascetic tradition into mainstream Christianity tended to emphasize the opposition between the individual Christian and the traditions of the pagan city. But Markus argues that this was but a moment in the thought of the West, if a crucial one, and that the fifth century saw a change in the relationship between Christian thought and the space of the city. This Christianization of urban space coexisted with two related phenomena in the West: the development of martyr cults and the rise of the aristocratic bishop. It was natural for bishops such as Ambrose, Gregory of Tours and Sidonius Apollinaris (Van Dam 1985; 1993; Harries 1994; MacLynn 1994) to use their power to build up the role of the bishop as the aristocratic leader of the community, to create citizens in Christ and to celebrate those local communities through local martyrs, real or invented. Thus in Gaul at least, the individualism at the heart of asceticism was tamed and brought within the community in the fifth century.

The Gallic model, however, cannot easily be applied to other areas, even within the West. The barbarian invasions of the fifth century posed a far more considerable threat to the traditional aristocracy and to the cities of Gaul than anything that occurred in the East. The religious leaders of the East were faced with a different kind of environment. The cities were vibrant. The Classical culture and political power of the aristocracy were not challenged by incoming barbarians. The ascetics remained but one of the cultural forces at work. Bluntly, the cultural process outlined by Markus that brought the ascetics within the Gallic city and brought asceticism to the forefront of political and social thought in the Christian literature of the period, thus eroding the division between the city and the desert (arguable already less distinct in Western monasticism), need not work in any other province (nor does Markus make any such claim). The ideology of individualistic ascetics was important and continued to be important in the East, as the popularity of the ascetic tradition attests, and it is to be assumed that this tradition influenced Egyptian culture. Nevertheless, the issue is not whether it was influential, but whether it came to dominate views of the individual and his or her social role. Again, we are pushed beyond the boundaries of the house to look at how the community of the house was integrated into the wider urban culture. What kind of social mechanisms applied in late antique Egypt? What did it mean to live in a city and to be an individual urban Egyptian?

Much of this discussion must be deferred to later chapters, but in the tiny houses and narrow alleys of Jeme, the remodelled forecourt of the temple of Chnum, and the network of rooms and houses in Kom el-Dikke the relationship between the street and house, between public and private, clearly does not conform to Classical and earlier norms. Status continues to be marked in these houses. The houses of Jeme have crosses on the lintels and the icons are placed centrally within House D marking the residence firmly as being occupied by Christians. Disappointingly, we cannot with confidence reconstruct the ties within the house, the links to non-resident kin, or the relationships with and beyond to the neighbours and the wider community for this period. Nevertheless, the pattern of domestic organization appears both to be different and to be within a Christian culture, and it is extremely tempting to unite those two observations.[109]

The social construction of the individuals and the households at Jeme, Elephantine and Kom el-Dikke (all very late sites) need of course not be replicated elsewhere. The houses of the Apions, the houses of the Patermouthis archive and the excavated examples from the Delta all show rather different patterns of cultural formation with perhaps more traditional Egyptian influence observable through the Patermouthis archive and Hellenic-Roman element in the villas around Alexandria, the houses at Abu Mina and the palace of the Apions. Yet, even in the Apions' palace, a local saint appears on an icon within the house, and Christianity influenced the formalities of the documentation of the Patermouthis archive so profoundly that it is difficult not to assume that it was a central element of the culture of Patermouthis, Kako and family. The new culture was felt, though we can only guess at its influence.

It is the diversity of architectural form that is so noticeable in the late antique period and we must produce a complex response to such material. It is inconceivable that the relationship of the Apions to the culture of the city was the same as that of Patermouthis or of the residents of Kom el-Dikke, though they must have shared some common cultural experiences and values. There is no reason to believe that they viewed themselves or thought of their place in the cosmos in similar ways. Indeed, there is every reason to believe that they viewed the world very differently. Christianity was an extremely successful ideology, though one in which there were major doctrinal disputes, but one cannot assume that the fascination with Christian doctrine and history at the centre of the literary tradition underplays other social forces within the cities. In Gramscian terms, Christianity was the hegemonic ideology, but it did not supplant all other ideological forces.

Conclusions

I started this chapter with some brief methodological and theoretical observations. After such a long chapter and a detailed survey of very specific evidence, it is appropriate to return to those observations. I noted the difficulty inherent in understanding spatialities without ethnographic information and that the analyses of houses advanced by anthropologists cannot easily be replicated for the ancient world. I also noted how positivistic approaches, simply assembling the evidence, can only produce a limited insight: the evidence itself does not speak. The example used was the rope on the peg in House C45 (plate 3.1). It would be a tremendous rhetorical *coup* if I could now give voice to that rope and give it meaning, but I cannot. This analysis has its limitations. In spite of the mass of evidence cited, much of the argument above is speculative and not everything is explained.

We have seen cultural diversity in the housing. We have seen variations in patterns of house usage and architecture and household formation over time between settlements of different types. We have also seen that there was considerable variety within settlements. Such complexity carries implications. Most modern theoretical models propose that architecture and social values are involved in a dialectic to produce social space. Thus, the values of the occupants interact with the architecture and it is not necessarily the case that the architecture and occupants share values. In a very stable society, it seems to me to be possible that the model of Hillier and Hanson, that architectural space and society are simultaneously generated (see pp. 25–6), may apply, that those designing and constructing the houses share the values of those who were to occupy them, and that those values were unchanging, but such organic development seems to me to be implausible for most complex societies. In any case, reading the architectural form, in our present state of knowledge, is only one method of interpreting space. The social values with which space is invested by particular individuals are very difficult, though not impossible, to derive from the architectural form itself. Once we start trying to understand what values the Egyptian population may have invested in their homes, we become aware of just how varied Egyptian domestic arrangements were and how they differed from those of the modern world.[110] The traditional Egyptian town-house, with its towers and gates, was a complex and probably crowded place. The community of the house was defended and had a certain unity, but was not isolationist. The residents had strong social ties to non-resident family members, possibly also to neighbours and to non-family co-residents. The house was identified with individuals: it was a mark of their status, a valued place that seemed to have a significant hold over the families (resident and non-resident) associated with it. It was a central, perhaps *the* central place for its residents. It was home. In many cultures, the home is a way of representing, of monu-mentalizing the family (however that is defined), and the specific spatial and concrete house is comparatively unimportant. Moving house is a traumatic experience for many families but it is not unthinkable since the family, with all its associations with 'home', is not thereby dispersed. Both home and family have an existence which is independent of a particular pile of bricks. I think it likely that the particular pile of bricks had more significant associations for Romano-Egyptians. The rather peculiar patterns of household formation and relationships within the nuclear family suggest to me that the space held more of the emotional weight that other cultures invest in the people or in particular artefacts within the house. Although it was possible for Egyptians to change residence, I would suggest it was less easy for them to establish separate homes.

Such emotional investment in architecture means that it is more appropriate to treat the house as a significant locus of acculturation or *habitus*, following Bourdieu, as discussed at the start of this chapter. Any changes in that locus would, therefore, become very important in evaluating the social and cultural history of the province. Variety in architectural organization is also culturally significant. We are here caught in a theoretical bind, since if ideology is the major factor in the formation of social space, as I have consistently argued, then changes in physical space are thereby devalued. Philo's description of the Jewish house, for instance, seems to suggest that the distinctive spatiality of that house was almost entirely a function of the differences between Jewish and non-Jewish ideologies. One would certainly not want to establish a straightforward correlation between architecture and culture. Nevertheless, there is a dialectic in operation and when we seem to see architectural change in combination with circumstantial evidence for the arrival of new ideologies, such as Graeco-Roman culture or Christianity, I think there is an overwhelming case for treating the new architectural forms as evidence of cultural change. We should not be crude or over-confident in our use of this perception. There were continuities in architectural form, as there were continuities in ideology and social organization across the period of study. It is patently foolish to discuss change in complex societies in absolutist terms: there will always be elements of continuity. The imposition of twentieth-century capitalism has caused dramatic social changes across the world, but it would be extreme to argue that there are no continuities with earlier forms of social and cultural organization. In spite of these doubts, the cultural significance of the house in the Roman period means that the changes we can detect probably reflect deep-seated cultural shifts in Egyptian society which transformed the ways in which Egyptians related to the society outside the house and to the social construction of individuals and households. At its deepest level, Egypt was changing.

4

STREETS, DISTRICTS AND NEIGHBOURHOODS

Introduction: unitary cities and neighbourhoods

The *polis*, the city of Classical Greece, is often presented as an ideal. Mumford (1991 [1961]: 142–200), Kitto (1951: 64–79; 109–35), Murray (1980; cf. Tomlinson 1992; Hölscher 1991) and countless others have idealized Greek urbanism, by which is normally meant the rather peculiar form it took in Athens. The *polis* is depicted as a political entity which closely bound together its inhabitants, turning isolated individuals into something more, citizens, who enjoyed membership of a community and a sense of belonging to the city so that Athens became the Athenians and the Athenians were Athens. The drama for which Athens is renowned celebrated this sense of identity, bringing the people together to worship the divine and to experience a common culture. Philhellene commentators eulogize the unitary Athenian community (perhaps surprisingly given the spectacular and violent crises that gripped the Athenian state in the late fifth century), discovering in it lessons for modern urbanism. The tradition reaches down through the influential Mumford (1991 [1961]) and Hall (1998), and Kitto's purple praise is reprinted in a recent textbook of readings on the city (LeGates and Stout 1996: 31–6). The *polis* is read as a pre-industrial ideal, a mythic city, united, though perhaps sometimes quarrelsome. Kitto (1951: 129) compares the *polis* to an extended and all-encompassing family, bound together by fictive ties of blood, a family which forged an intensity of creation.

A similar, if more generalized, romanticization of the pre-industrial town was a feature of the nineteenth and twentieth centuries, probably in response to a feeling that traditional ties of community had been eroded by the industrial *megalopoleis* (so deplored by Mumford and other theorists). This social tension between the world of paternalism and that of the new commercialism and industrialism is dramatized in countless Victorian and Edwardian novels. More pertinently, this dislocation of traditional society in the face of unbridled capitalism inspired the various socialist thinkers, from Marx and Engels to the Fabians, and may, perhaps, be seen at the heart of 'modernism', as urban an intellectual movement as one could imagine. Such dislocation remains a major

128

theme in political thought and, in spite of a brief period of triumphant *laissez faire* economics and the politics of unrestricted capitalism, the renewal of community, specifically targeted at the problems of urban alienation and poverty, remains a dominant political discourse of both left and right.

As is characteristic of social panic, the perceived decline in community is represented as modern, a feature of the current generation, as part of the 'crisis of modernism' so prevalent in the writings of the post-modernist movement (Gregory 1994: 245–6). Dislocation has become a predominant trope of writing about and 'reading' the city, with all the sense of multiple and negotiable interpretations that 'reading' implies.[1] The Victorians found that the new industrial cities could not be repaired by the old individualistic paternalism they thought had dominated previous approaches to urban deprivation and so turned to new municipalities to control the problem and ensure solutions while glorifying the more manageable communities of past times. Arguably, however, the image of an urban community bound together by benevolent patrons (now associated with Victorian paternalism in popular discourse), helping their lessers through communal or individual acts of charity, was already a myth by the sixteenth century when the poor were increasingly marginalized and demonized through a series of poor laws (Slack 1988). Nevertheless, the myth of the unitary city found validity in the Classical heritage, not so much in Rome, so often seen as the necropolis, the city of death and disorder, uncontrollable by its elites and suffering from political unrest and crime, an early 'industrial' metropolis (Mumford 1991 [1961]: 239–81; Favro 1995: 24–41; Nippel 1995; Scobie 1986; Laurence 1997; Yavetz 1958), as in the smaller cities, Pompeii and Herculaneum especially (Le Corbusier 1970; 1971; Haverfield 1910, cf. 1913).[2] By contrast, the city of the future, as in the 'gated cities', in the urban networks of Los Angeles (especially) (Davis 1992), and in Ridley Scott's *Bladerunner* (see Shurmer-Smith and Hannam 1994; Harvey 1990), with heavily policed, socially exclusive zones, attracts intense opprobrium.

The city as unitary community is a deeply embedded and highly valued ideal in conservative Western thought and I think we could, without too much fear of stereotyping, label it the traditional Western model. Others may wish to label it the Classical model, but, for rather obvious reasons, I think this would lead to confusion. Such cities display their hierarchies and identity through public space and monuments that tend to assert an ideological unity. In chapter 5, I shall examine how the public space of the city came to reflect the dominant cultural values of the period and that is a story that could be told through a single narrative, the city's narrative. In this chapter, however, I consider fragments of that city, the neighbourhoods. Powerful neighbourhoods are often seen as inimicable to the ordered city of the traditional Western type, but it will, I hope, become clear in the course of this chapter that the dichotomy is unreal and that the interrelationship between city and neighbourhoods and between houses and neighbourhoods is multi-faceted: I undermine the implied contrast between the utopian unitary community and the dystopic fragmented city.

The next four sections will consider the primary evidence for the neighbourhoods of the cities of Roman and Byzantine Egypt, their history, purpose, size, character and function. The results of these investigations are, frankly, confusing, and the final two sections attempt to clarify some of the issues raised by considering the Egyptian material in the light of comparative evidence of the nature of neighbourhoods and of the social and political significance of neighbourhoods. In so doing, I face a terminological problem. Many (all?) cities show some notable topographical variety so that observers become aware of differences between places within the city. A variety of words are commonly used to describe these locations, but here I shall refer to them as districts. Some of the topographical divisions of the city had administrative functions and I refer to these as administrative districts. I shall reserve the word 'neighbourhood' to describe the area occupied by a single socially significant community or to which a socially unitary character is ascribed. This last term is clarified in the penultimate section.

Districts in the city

The internal topographical divisions of the Ptolemaic city are mysterious.[3] *P. Turner* 18, a demotic text of 350–275 BC, mentions the gods of a Greek district and thereby suggests ethnic zoning. Ptolemaic settlers were organized into ethnic *politeumata* which appear to have had a certain measure of self-government (Thompson Crawford 1984). Roman-period administrative districts identified by names such as the Lycians' Camp or Cavalry Camp or by ethnic group (see below) might be taken as signifying an original topographically concentrated ethnic settlement, but the use of ethnic labels by the Ptolemaic bureaucracy was far from straightforward (Clarysse 1985b; 1992; 1995; Quaegebeur 1992; Goudriaan 1988; Bilde et al. 1992; Peremans 1970; vant Dack 1992; Bagnall 1988b) and firmly attested cases of ethnic differentiation tend, excepting the possible, probably exceptional and fiercely debated issue of the Jewish communities, to be quite early in the Ptolemaic period.

The information for the Roman period is far better, mainly because of the systematic use of administrative districts (ἄμφοδα). There were essentially two systems operating. In certain cities, notably Thmouis and Mendes, Apollonospolis Magna and Memphis, the administrative districts were numbered. There were at least twenty *amphoda* in Thmouis, some of which were divided into further numbered districts (the highest number being three). There were nine *amphoda* in Mendes.[4] Apollonospolis Magna had at least five: there are two references to the fifth *amphodon* (*O. Cairo* 70; 96) and numerous references to the fourth.[5] Panopolis had at least two *amphoda* (*P. Coll. Youtie* II 71; 73; *P. Panop.* 11 = *SB* XII 10978; *P. Panop.* 12 = *SB* XII 10979; *P. Panop.* 27 = *SB* XII 11220). The highest numbered *amphodon* attested at Memphis is also the fifth (*P. Münch.* III 71; *P. Vind. Sijp.* 24).[6] Antinoopolis, built in the AD 130s and with a rather different constitution from the other cities of the *chora*, had numbered quarters (four being the highest attested) which were further divided into blocks (πλινθεῖα) (thirteen being the highest number attested) (Calderini 1935–66: s.v. Antinoopolis). Other *amphoda*, at Hermopolis Magna, Oxyrhynchus, Ptolemais Euergetis, Thebes and Herakleopolis, were named. Alexandria had a system of numbered (or lettered) quarters, though named quarters also developed. The enumeration of administrative districts might be thought more suitable for 'planned cities' with regular morphologies than cities with old, established and irregular topographical distinctions. Antinoopolis was a planned city with an orthogonal street grid. Thmouis also had a regular street plan and was founded or refounded during the Ptolemaic period (Hansen et al. 1967; Hansen 1965; Naville 1892–3; 1894; Wilson 1982), though there is no evidence that nearby Mendes (1.5 km to the north) was similarly replanned. Alexandria, laid out by Alexander the Great but largely built under the Ptolemies, again conformed to the norms of Greek urban design and had a regular plan.[7] Ptolemais Euergetis and Oxyrhynchus do not seem to have had regular urban morphologies, judging from rather scanty evidence (*P. Oslo* III 111; *P. Oxy.* I 43v), but it would be rash to place much confidence in the emerging correlation. The evidence of amphodal organizations in the cities of Roman Egypt is such that we are forced to concentrate on Hermopolis Magna, Thebes, and especially Oxyrhynchus and Ptolemais Euergetis.

Hermopolis Magna was divided into four districts, Polis East, Polis West, Phrourion East and Phrourion West. The archaeology of Hermopolis is sufficiently clear that we can observe topographical boundaries running across the city north–south and east–west which, in spite of the fact that there was no firm evidence, seem likely to be associated with the amphodal division (see figure 5.6). The north of the site is dominated by a temple either constructed or substantially remodelled in the early Ptolemaic period by Philip Arrhidaios and dedicated to the baboon god, Thoth (later associated with Hermes). *BGU* III 1002 = *P. Lugd. Bat.* XVII 9 of 55 BC describes the temple enclosure as the Phrourion of Great Hermes, now the Phrourion of the King, suggesting perhaps some restoration work or a dedication within the complex. Roeder (1959) uncovered parts of a main east–west road running across the site. The temple area was to the north of this road and separated from the road by a huge wall, 637.5 m long (Roeder 1959: 26). A further wall of the enclosure ran north for about 600 m (Spencer 1989: 13).[8] The width of the foundations of the wall (20 m) suggests it was massive (Spencer et al. 1984: 30). This wall was cut down in places, probably during the Roman period, to make space for and give access to buildings north of the line of the enclosure wall (Bailey 1991: 15; Spencer et al. 1984: 45), but it may have been that much of the wall was left standing. In any case, the line of the wall remained significant within the topography of the city. The British Museum excavations have confirmed (though, in fact, there was little doubt) that this was the road mentioned in *Stud. Pal. Pap.* V = *CPH* 127v = *Stud. Pal. Pap.* XX 68 = *SB* X 10299, a famous papyrus dealing with the costs of repairs to the buildings and *stoai* along the road (known as Antinoe Street). The road ended in the Gates of the Sun and Moon, clearly the main east and west entrances to the city, and which were possibly named in imitation of the gates at Alexandria (cf *P. Oxy.* XXXIV 2719).

The *Dromos* of Hermes provided an equally obvious north–south line across the city. The road was 4.21 m wide in parts and along the road pedestals were found on which it seems large statues of the baboon god Thoth would have been placed. It was a processional way leading to the south of the city from the sacred enclosure. In the third century AD, the meeting of Antinoe Street and the *Dromos* of Hermes was marked by four columns (*tetrastylon*) erected in AD 176–9 (Bailey 1991: 29), one of three *tetrastyla* along Antinoe Street. The *Dromos* dated back to at least 1402–1364 BC and may have served as a market street (see p. 208).

Hermopolis was divided into quarters (in both senses of the word) by the intersection of these two roads. The resultant *amphoda* were very large. Polis West had about 2,317 houses and another unnamed *amphodon* had about 1,917 houses (*Stud. Pal. Pap.* V = *CPH* 101; see also pp. 331–3). The size of the *amphoda* limited their usefulness as topographical indicators and street names were frequently used to increase the precision of descriptions of location, though these street names were not legally required.[9] There is a little evidence that the *amphoda* were further divided for administrative purposes as well. *P. Ryl.* II 102 is a dossier of documents relating to status. Column ii, which appears to be an *epikrisis* document (see p. 000), mentions a registration in the ninth year of the emperor Domitian, in Phrourion West, '4th am( )'. Later in the same text, there is a reference to a registration in the ninth year of Antoninus Pius in Phrourion West in the '15th am( )'. Another gymnasial registration document (*P. Lond.* III, p. 127, 955 = W. *Chr.* 425 = *Sel. Pap.* II 320 BL I, 281 of AD 261) also has a numeral (24) and an abbreviation which may relate to Phrourion West. Either the *amphoda* were further subdivided or the numbers refer to some clerical system which allowed the retrieval of the original documents.

The administrative divisions of Thebes were no less complex. Thebes had been the capital of Egypt and was perhaps Egypt's most important religious site throughout the Pharaonic period. The archaeological record for pre-Roman Thebes is extraordinary, though Roman Thebes, which was a shadow of its former glory, is something of a mystery (Montserrat and Meskell 1997; Vandorpe 1995; Bataille 1951; Otto 1952; el-Saghir et al. 1986; Kees 1934; Golvin 1981; Varaille 1943; Lauffray et al. 1971; Lauffray 1971; Chevrier 1939). We have, however, a large number of documents from Thebes, the most useful for our purposes being receipts for the poll tax which was levied at lower rates on metropolites than on villagers (see p. 2).

In addition, there are many receipts for unspecified payments and for payments of taxes other than the poll tax. These include districts such as West Agora, East Agora (*O. Bodl.* II 1812), Agora 1 (*O. Theb.* 125), Agora 3 (or g( )) (*O. Bodl.* II 1629; 1630; 1631; 1632; *WO* 1474; *O. Wilbour* 43; *O. Tait Ashm.* I

Table 4.1 Poll-tax rates by district in Thebes and surrounding communities

The metropolis	16 drachmae: *O. Leid.* 43
Ag(orai)	12 drachmae: *O. Rom.* II 117
South and West	4 drachmae: *WO* 422 10 drachmae: *WO* 429 12 drachmae: *WO* 388; 389; 465 16 drachmae: *WO* 466; 480 17 drachmae: *WO* 463 20 drachmae: *WO* 431; 437; 441; 22 drachmae: *O. Bodl.* II 501 24 drachmae: *WO* 419; 431; 432; 434; 438;450; 452; 461; 472; *O. Tait* I: *O. Petrie* 84; 86.
Charakos	7 drachmae, 3 obols: *WO* 457 8 drachmae: *O. Meyer* 27 10 drachmae: *WO* 411; 424; 436; 453; 462; 469; 474; 475; 481; 492; *O. Leid.* 83 12 drachmae (including the bath tax): *WO* 530; *O. Tait* I: *O. Petrie* 103; *O. Theb.* 81
Opheion	7 drachmae, 3 obols: *WO* 454 10 drachmae: *WO* 446; 575 20 drachmae: *PSI* VIII 993
North Agora or Agora 2	8 drachmae: *O. Leid.* 95 10 drachmae: *O. Leid.* 79; 98; *O. Theb.* 45; 49; *O. Bodl.* II 10.
Memnonia	8 drachmae: *O. Tait* I: *O. Camb. Univ. Libr.* 31 16 drachmae: *O. Tait* I: *O. Petrie* 81; *O. Theb.* 36; 97 20 drachmae: *O. Tait* I: *O. Petrie* 87; *O. Theb.* 35; *O. Bodl.* II 510 24 drachmae: *O. Theb.* 32; 37; (with bath tax) *O. Theb.* 53
Pakerk	4 drachmae: *O. Meyer* 25 8 drachmae: *O. Meyer* 23; 24
Photr( )	24 drachmae: *O. Theb.* 33

69), Agorai (*WO* 1301; 1457; *O. Leiden* 81; *O. Tait* I: *O. Camb. Univ. Libr.* 68; *PSI* III 277; *O. Wilbour* 62; *O. Rom.* II 134; 173; 179; 180; 197; 206; *O. Tait* I: *O. Queens Univ. Belfast* 12; 14), 4 markets south (?) (*O. Thebes* 42), South Agora (*O. Rom.* II 83; 98), Charax 2 and 3 (*O. Bodl.* II 1633; 1636), the island (*WO* 923; *O. Tait* I: *O. Ashm.* 62; 64; *O. Rom.* II 175; 184; 195; 196; 200; 212; *O. Tait. Ashm.* I 62; 64), North and West (*O. Leid.* 47), Kerameion (*O. Wilbour* 62; *O. Rom.* II 231), and Parembole (the camp) (*O. Rom.* II 225).

Some of these districts were not recognized urban quarters, though the partial payment of poll tax and payments of poll tax for more than one year confuses matters. Probably urban districts include Charakos, North Agora or Agora 2, whereas Memnonia and South and West appear to have been rural districts. It is a little surprising that South and West was classed as a rural district since its very name suggests an urban context. North and West, again 'obviously' urban, may also have been rural. Thebes operated two systems for identifying the various markets, either by number of point of the compass, which leads to a certain confusion as whether Aγ B is the North Agora (which was certainly a term used) or Agora 2. Since we have reasonable evidence for Agora 1 and 3, and a suggestion of an Agora 4, the presence of an Agora 2 would be a reasonable supposition. Palme (1989) suggests persuasively that a reform c. AD 130 replaced designation by compass point with numbered markets. This, however, still leaves us with the attestation of the Agorai district for which there is no obvious or tidy explanation.

Kerameion or Ta Kerameia (the potters' quarter, perhaps El Medamud, north of Karnak (Vandorpe 1995)) and Opheios (Ipj or Aphis identified with modern Luxor (Vandorpe 1995)) should perhaps be associated with communities captured during Cornelius Gallus' campaign in Upper Egypt in 30–29 BC (*OGIS* 654 = *I. Philae* II 128 = *ILS* 8995) and which Gallus represented as separate from Diospolis Magna (Thebes). Nowadays tourists visit a dispersed landscape of monuments. On the east bank, El Medamud, Luxor and Karnak, perhaps the Charakos of the receipts (Otto 1952: 43, *contra* Wilcken 1899: 713), and on the west bank Medinet Habu, the Memnonion, the Ramasseum and Deir el Bahari were all probably occupied into the Roman period (Chevrier 1939; Lauffray 1971; Varaille 1943: pls. xcvi, xcix; Hölscher 1932: 40–4; Lichtheim 1955; Wilfong 1989; 1990; Laskowska-Kusztal 1984; Latjar 1991; Wagner 1971; Kákosky 1989). Strabo (XVII 1. 46), who visited in the company of Aelius Gallus, another of Augustus' prefects, describes Thebes as a number of associated villages rather than a city and I suspect that, very much as today, the Theban landscape was dominated by ancient religious architecture and a number of comparatively small, loosely related settlements.[10] The inclusion of these communities within the Roman city may have been fairly arbitrary.

The best-attested systems of amphodal divisions are those of Oxyrhynchus and Ptolemais Euergetis. The *amphoda* and the patterns of attestations are listed in tables 4.2 and 4.3

Tables 4.2 and 4.3 attest the local within the urban frame, but although the names of these districts (sometimes theophoric, sometimes derived from trades, sometimes from major public buildings, sometimes from ethnics, but often obscure) are evocative, we must exercise caution. After all, we would be surprised if all those living on Edinburgh Drive, London, were Scottish or if the residents of twenty-first-century Harlem spoke Dutch, and although one might be charmed by finding the eponymous trees in Acacia Gardens, Hazel Grove and Beechwood Avenue, we would not necessarily expect them or that

Table 4.2 The *amphoda* of Ptolemais Euergetis

District	No. of attestations by century[a]							
	I	II	III	IV	V	VI	VII	VIII
Alopolion		2	1		1–3	1–3		
Ammoniou		5						
Apolloniou Hierakiou	1	13	6	1				
Apolloniou Paremboles	1	12	8	1				
Arabon	2–3	6–7	1		1			
Bithunon Allon Topon	1	21	5	3				
Bithunon Isionos (Topon)	2	15–16	5–6	2		2	3–4	0–1
Boubasteiou		4	1	1				
Boutaphiou		9–10	1–2					
Gymnasiou		17–18	8–9	2		1		
Dionysiou Topon	1	23–24	4–5	1		[1]		
Helleniou	[1]	11	2					
Hermouthiakes		14	4	1		0–1	0–1	
Therapeias	2	21–22	3–4	1				
Thesmophoriou		13–14	5–6					
Hieras Pyles		13–15	6–8	1				
Isiou Dromou		8	1					
Kilikon	1	12–13	2–3					
Kopronos		1						
Linupheion		14	3					
Lykion	0–1	6–7	1			1		
Lysaniou Topon		9	1					
Makedonon	2	21–22	4–5	1	0–1			
Mendesiou		1						
Moereos	2	31–2	13–14	2	2	1	1	
Plateias		7						
Sekneptuneiou	2–3	5–8	2–4					
Syriakes	2	20	5	1				
Tameion = Katotero	4	42	6				1	
Phanesiou	1–2	6–7						
Phremei	2–4	43–46	3–4	5				
Chenoboskion Heteron	2	8	1			[0–1]	[0–1]	
Chenoboskion Proton		9		1		[0–1]	[0–1]	
Horionos Hierakiou		14						
Hagiou Apollo Omou				1				
Hagiou Bictoros						0–1	9–10	
Hagiou Dorotheou				1				
Hagiou Dorotheou Omou				1				
Hagia Thekles						1	1	
Hagiou Theodorou						0–6	1–7	1
Hagiou Theodorou Omou				1				
Hagiou Theotokou							3	
Hagiou Theotokou Omou				1				
Hagiou Leontiou				1				
Hagiou Marturon				2				
Hagiou Petrou				1				
Hagiou Sansneou						0–1	2–3	
Ale( )						4	1	

Table 4.2 (continued)

District	No. of attestations by century[a]							
	I	II	III	IV	V	VI	VII	VIII
Alupiou					1	1–2	3–4	
Aperotos						2	4–6	0–2
Apollo./Apolloniou							1	
Basil[ ]					1			
Georg.				1				
Gunaikou						1		
Ekklesias Kanon						3		
Heliou				1				
epoikou Theatrou				1				
Thebaion				1				
Theonos						1		
Hieron Signon				1				
Katotero = Tameion			1			2	7–8	0–1
Kleopatriou	[1	2	1]			2–8	1–8	0–1
Megales Ekklesias						0–8	5–16	0–3
Megales Ekklesias omou				1				
Mena				1				
Mikres Laures							0–1	0–1
Numphaiou						0–1	0–2	0–1
Olympiou Theatrou						0–1	1–2	
Paremboles						0–2	32–37	0–3
Paremboles ton andron				1				
Perseas						3	4	
Pioo( )				1				
Proklou						1		
Tetrapulou				2				
Tripylou						1	2	
Psapalliou						2	1	
Xerou Akanthiou					1			

[a] Documents dated to two centuries give rise to the ranges. Documents merely dated to the Byzantine period are ignored unless they are the only reference to the district, in which case they are given a date between the fourth and eighth centuries. In the later period, districts which appear to have some administrative function are included whether or not they are described as *amphoda*. Documents dated as Arab are assigned to the seventh or eighth centuries. Dubious attestations are bracketed.

'Gardens', 'Grove' and 'Avenue' be other than synonyms for 'street' (which is not to deny that Broadways are sometimes broad and Market Streets sometimes are the location of markets). Meaning and function cannot simply be assumed from names.

Table 4.3 The *amphoda* of Oxyrhynchus [a]

District	Number of attestations by century							
	I	II	III	IV	V	VI	VII	VIII
Akridos			1					
Anamphodarchon	2	1	2					
Ano Paremboles		5						
Borra Dromou		2–3	8–9					
Borra Krepidos		1	9	1				
Dekates		8	2–3	1–2				
Dromou Gymnasiou	4	4–5	8–9	6	1			
Dromou Thoeridos = Kmelos	6	11–12	13–14	4				
Dromou Sarapidos	2					4		
Hermaiou	7	7–8	12–13	1				
Herakleous Topon	2–3	0–3	3–5					
Heroiou		1	7					
Thermou Balaniou				1				
Thoereiou Thenepmoi	1	1			[1]			
Ibiotapheiou		1						
Ioudaikou	1	1						
Hippeon Paremboles	9	4–5	12–13	1	2			
Hippodromou	8	1	1					
Kretikou	1	5	8					
Lukion Paremboles	8	6–7	6–7					
Metroiou		2	3					
Murobalanou	1–2	1–4	11–13	2				
Nemesiou			3	1				
Notou Dromou	2	3	8					
Notou Krepidou	2	2–3	5–6					
Pammenous Paradeisou	2	10	19	1	5	2		
Plateias (Theatrou)	3	5	11	1				
Poimenikes	5	2–5	10–13			2		
[rumes Onnoph.]	2	0–1	0–1					
Temgenoutheos	10	2	10	1	[1]			
Chenoboskon	4	2–3	3					
Pses			1	1		1		
Abrahamiou Iatrou							1	
Hagias Euphemias						1		
Agoras Skuteon					1			
[Akakiou]						1		
Ano Achillidos						1		
Apolloniou				1				
Lauras Tou Xenodochiou							2–3	0–1
Kollo./Aollo								
oikias Ioannou					1			
Chalkes Thuras							1	

[a] The identification of Dromou Thoeridos with Kmelos comes from *P. Oxy.* III 478. Data in the table derived from Krüger (1990: 82–8) which replaces Rink (1924) with the additions of *P. Oxy.* LXIV 4440 (various); *P. Oxy. inv.* 91 B 173/c(b) (Anamphodarchon: Temgenouthis); *P. Oxy.* LV 3796, LXIV 4438, *SB* XX 14288 (Dromou Gymnasiou); *C. Pap. Gr.* II 1 26, *P. Oxy.* LXIII 4357; *SB* XX 14288 (Dromou Thoeridos); including *PSI* 67–9 which attest a laura Sarapidos; *P. Merton* II 76, *C. Pap. Gr.* II 1 44; *PSI* V 450 (Hermaiou); *P. Col.* VIII 231 and

Table 4.3 (continued)

C. Pap. Gr. II 1 82 (Hippeon Paremboles); *C. Pap. Gr.* II 1 15, 51, *SB* XX 14285 (Lukion Paremboles); *P. Oxy.* LXI 4120 (Kretikou); *P. Fouad* 30, *P. Oxy.* XVIII 2186, XXXVIII 2858, XL 2900, *PSI* V 457 (Metroiou); *P. Oxy.* LIV 3750; *C. Pap. Gr.* II 1. 71; 81 (Pammenous Paradeisou); *P. Oxy.* LXV 4479 (Plateias); *P. Heid.* IV 330, P. Oxy. LXV 4489 (Poimenikes); *P. Oxy.* XLIV 3183; *P. Oxy.* LXV 4478, and possibly *P. Oxy.* VII 1129 (Temgenoutheos); *P. Oxy.* LVIII 3916 (Chenoboskon) and possibly *PSI* III 175 (Thoeriou Thenepmoi) and excluding *P. Oxy.* XII 1550 (Dromou Gymnasiou); the speculative restoration of Sijpesteijn (1983) *PSI* VIII 871 (Hippeon Paremboles); *P. Oxy.* XL 2913, 2930, LI 3639 (Lukion Paremboles); *P. Oxy.* 3077 (Poimenikes); substituting *P. Oxy.* XL 2915 for 2925 (Murobalanou). See also the problematic districts in *P. Oxy.* LX 4079 and 4080.

Origins of the *amphoda*

Origins in Egypt

There is no evidence that there was a formal division in the Ptolemaic cities of the *chora*.[13] In the Roman period, '*amphodon*' (ἄμφοδον) is used as early as 13 BC (when the district was administered by an official), but the texts relate to Alexandria (*BGU* IV 1125 *BL* V, 15; IV 1179), whose urban administration was rather unusual (see p. 188).

P. Oxy. IV 711 from Oxyrhynchus, dating to 14 BC, is a more likely candidate for the first attestation of the amphodal system in the cities of the *chora*, though Whitehorne (1982, *contra* Bowman and Rathbone 1992: 122) would also associate this text with Alexandria. It refers to problems in the registration of ephebes επ[. . .]φ[..]ων in 14 BC and to an earlier registration in 25/24 BC. The text is lacunose but ἄμφοδων is an attractive restoration. The problems facing the official(s) writing the text are obscure, but they appear to have been engaged in a revision of ephebic lists drawn up in 25/24 BC (possibly by *amphodon*). The ephebate brought access to the gymnasium and 'those from the gymnasium' emerged as an urban elite in the Roman period, paralleling the curial and bouleutic orders (the town councillors and their families) of most Mediterranean cities. This appears to have been a central element of the Augustan administrative settlement of Egypt, paralleling the division of the population into various status groups paying poll tax at different rates (see p. 2), and it would be logical to see the formation of the Roman gymnasial group (though probably based on Ptolemaic gymnasial membership) as coinciding with or being introduced soon after the institution of the poll tax. The earliest clearly dated poll tax receipts date from 22/21 BC, but there are some from possibly 24/23 or even 28 BC and it is attractive to associate the revolt of Upper Egypt against Cornelius Gallus, the first prefect of Egypt, who was recalled to Rome by 26 BC, with rebellion against the imposition of a novel and severe form of tax (Rathbone 1993). Nevertheless, although the basic framework of what became the Roman administrative system was imposed on Egypt within the first years of Roman rule, it was clearly adjusted and refined over the following decades. For instance, it seems very unlikely that there was a general census of the population in the years 30–26 BC and the new poll tax, the lists of metropolites, and of those in the gymnasium must have depended on Ptolemaic systems of information-gathering. The Roman authorities eventually imposed a regular general census and the earliest dated census return is from AD 12 (*P. Mil.* I 13; Bagnall 1991). This census was initially on a seven-year cycle but, since the poll tax was not payable until a boy reached his fourteenth year, this was changed, possibly after AD 19.[14] Bagnall and Frier (1994: 5) and Rathbone (1993), for slightly different reasons, argue that the census was introduced *c.* 9–8 BC or 11–10 BC, but certainly not before those dates (see also Zucker 1961). The census post-dated the introduction of the poll tax by at least 15 years and did not reach its final form for at least another thirty years.

Similarly, the system of examination of gymnasial status changed in the first century AD. Our surviving documents are individual claims to status submitted normally as the boy approached his fourteenth birthday when he should enter the ephebate. These traced family records back to a general registration. In Oxyrhynchus, that registration appears to have been in 72/3, though it may have been in 63/4 at Hermopolis Magna and possibly 53/4 at Ptolemais Euergetis (*P. Amh.* II 75; *P. Ryl.* II 102: Nelson 1979: 27–35; *Stud. Pal. Pap.* IV, pp. 58–83; Montevecchi 1970; 1982).[15] The declarations listed the *amphodon* in which each male ascendant was registered from the applicant's generation. It seems that this was the minimum requirement and several lines are not traced back further (*P. Turner* 38; *P. Oxy.* XXII 2345). Other families traced descent back even further. The most popular initial citation was AD 4/5 (*P. Oxy.* II 257 = *W. Chr.* 147; X 1266; XII 1452; XVII 2186; XLVI 3276; 3283; *PSI* V 457; Zucker 1961), but also a registration in AD 56–9 was cited (*P. Mich.* XIV 676; *P. Oxy.* XLVI 3279). Although the later Neronian registration appears to have been by *amphodon*, only *P. Oxy.* II 257 = *W. Chr.* 147 (a first-century text) cites an *amphodon* of registration for the Augustan period, the relatively rarely attested Anamphodarchon. This is a rather puzzling omission if ephebes were registered by *amphodon* as early as 25/24 BC.

There is a similarly rather ragged pattern in the adoption of what became the standard word to designate a district, *amphodon*, a comparatively rare word in Classical Greek which is translated in the lexica as 'street'. In the early first century AD, in both Oxyrhynchus and Ptolemais Euergetis, the preferred word for 'district' was λαύρα, also meaning 'street' (Rink 1924: 8–9; Daris 1981).[16] Gradually, between AD 30 and 60, *amphodon* became the most popular word, though *amphodon* was in use earlier, especially in relation to Alexandria, and the problematic *P. Oxy.* II 257 = *W. Chr.* 147 refers to a registration in Anamphodarchon in AD 4/5. Nevertheless, it is tempting to associate the shift in usage between AD 30 and 60 with administrative changes, especially since administrators of the *amphoda* start to appear in the mid-first century AD. A text tentatively dated to *c.* 46 (because of its association with a similar text) seems to mention a former official of an *amphodon* (*P. Lond.* III, pp. 76–87, 604 b). More firmly dated attestations of *amphodarchoi* come from 62, 76/7 and 78/9 (*SB* XVIII 13324; *BGU* IX 2088; *P. Oxy*. XXXVI 2756) and these officials continue to be attested regularly in texts from throughout the later first and second centuries. Although one would not be surprised if evidence emerged that the *amphoda* were introduced as early as 25/24 BC, our current evidence suggests a post-Augustan date for their inception.[17]

Roman parallels

Amphoda were often mapped onto pre-existing, generally recognized topographical units, but the adoption of this system throughout Egypt suggests that it was imposed by the Roman authorities. Rome itself had several parallel administrative sub-units of the Roman citizenry and of the population of Rome: tribes, centuries (a timocratic division), *curiae* and *vici* (streets) (Staveley 1972; Taylor 1966). The closest parallels to the *amphoda* were the *curiae* and *vici*, both of which have long histories. There were thirty curiae in the city, each of which had an altar in the Temple of Vesta, the religious centre of the city (Dionysius of Halicarnassus, II 13–14; 20–3; 65; Staveley 1956). Although archaic and largely ceremonial institutions by the first century BC, the *curiae* and the curial assembly retained some religious functions and seem to have supervised adoptions, which perhaps suggests that they had some control over citizenship, the family or inheritance. They were also associated with the lictors who accompanied the consuls and who were responsible for the administration of corporal and capital punishments in the archaic system. These residual functions point to the antiquity of the curial system, a system which perhaps lost its relevance when Rome ceased to be the residence of a high proportion of the Roman citizenry. The *vici* were also apparently archaic divisions: Dionysius of Halicarnassus (IV 14) associates the creation of the *vici* with King Servius Tullius. Little else is known of them, though those in charge of the *vici* were probably responsible for the celebration of the cult of the crossroads (the *compitalia*), a festival which may no longer have been celebrated by the late Republic.

Attempts to organize and administer the lower classes of the city of Rome had a rather mixed history. In the late 60s and 50s BC, the aristocratic politician Clodius mobilized the lower orders in his campaign against the orator Cicero, whose account and perspective dominates our source material. Clodius' methods are somewhat obscure, but, in addition to what seems to have been a core of possibly paid supporters, he appears to have exploited various organizations that mobilized the lower classes, probably including *vici* and *collegia*. There is no precise definition of *collegium*, but *collegia* appear to have been associations formed around common elements such as religious worship, trade, neighbourhood, or even ethnicity. Their imperial manifestations seem to have had clear hierarchies, some funds, constitutions, formal meals, sometimes halls, and often connections with aristocratic patrons. Yet, as essentially organizations of non-aristocrats, they had the potential to give political voice to the concerns of the lower orders. Clodius' success in mobilizing the *collegia* may have created a potentially revolutionary situation of which the burning down of the Senate house in riots in 52 BC is the most potent symbol. Pompey and his troops intervened to quell these disturbances and Caesar later suppressed collegial organizations (Suet. *Div. Jul.* 42). Nevertheless, the potential of such local networks to mobilize the lower classes was administratively useful and Caesar himself used *vici* to register the population of the city in order to reduce and control eligibility for the corn dole.[18] Augustus revised Caesar's list, again registering the inhabitants by *vicus* (Suet. *Div. Aug.* 40. 2), though there may have been two lists of Rome's residents, a long list with up to 320,000 people and a short list with around 200,000, presumably the normal recipients of the grain dole.[19] Augustus continued Caesar's reforms of the urban administration of Rome in 7 BC by dividing the city into fourteen *regiones*, further subdivided into 265 *vici* (Suet. *Div. Aug.* 30; Pliny, *HN* III 66).[20] The *vici* were given magistrates, *vicomagistri*, selected from and by the inhabitants of each *vicus* and provided with a uniform and lictors, though the lictors may not have attended them each day. Apart from any administrative duties, such as maintaining residence registers and perhaps making provision for firefighting, the *magistri* had religious duties. Augustus revived the cult of the *Lares Compitales* (Spirits of the Crossroads), celebrated locally, and the *Ludi Compitales* (Suet. *Div. Aug.* 31; Dio LV 8). This cult became almost indistinguishable from that of the *Lares Augusti*, for which a central shrine was provided and at which, one presumes, the *vicomagistri* would jointly sacrifice. The imagery of the *Lares* was altered so that depictions of the two deities now showed them dancing round the Genius of Augustus. The imperial cult was, therefore, closely associated with the emerging refounded street administration of Rome and the new magistrates sometimes celebrated their entry into the Establishment by erecting lavish local shrines (Zanker 1988: 129–35; Robinson 1992: 11–13; Niebling 1956).

The system was exported to other communities, though the name of the district divisions varied. At Pompeii, for instance, the city had been divided into *vici* before the Augustan period (*CIL* IV 60; Castrén 1975: 80–2), but these were also reorganized in 7 BC (Laurence 1994: 40; Jongman 1988: 292–307; Mouritsen 1988: 67–8). Judging from the surviving Spanish charters, it seems very likely that the constitutions given to many first-century AD cities by the Roman authorities were very similar, probably adapted from a Caesarian or Augustan precursor (González 1986; Crawford 1995), and the *Lex municipii Malacitani* orders that *curiae* should be established within ninety days of the implementation of the city's new constitution (Spitzl 1984: 38). This curial organization is paralleled at Rome and at the Latin town of Lanuvium (Hardy 1912: 100; *CIL* XIV 2120). *Curiae* are also attested in Africa, though they may have differed somewhat from the Spanish and Latin institutions (Duncan-Jones 1974: 278–9).[21] In spite of the evident local variations, it appears that the introduction of neighbourhood administrative divisions was an important element in the imposition of Roman-style urban administration. The amphodal administration of the *metropoleis* of Egypt was, therefore, part of the Romanization of administration.

Topographical origins

While the administrative origins of the system were Roman, the divisions themselves pre-dated Roman rule in at least some cities. However, the nature of these pre-Roman divisions is not obvious and the names of the districts offer little guidance. To start with the *amphoda* of Ptolemais Euergetis, we have the districts of the salt-sellers, of the temple of Ammon, of the temple of Apollo the Hawk (Apollo being syncretized with Horus, the Egyptian hawk-god), the 'camp' of the temple of Apollo, of the Arabs, of the other places (altars?) of the Bithynians (?), of the temple of Bithynian Isis, of the temple of Boubastis, of the burial place of the cattle (Apis bulls or Hathor cows?), of the gymnasium, of the places (altars?) of Dionysios, of the Hellenion, of Hermouthiakes (perhaps associated with Hermes-Thoth), of the attendants (to the god or to the sick?), of the Thesmophorion, of the Holy Gates (of a temple or the city?), of the processional way of the temple of Isis, of the Cilicians, of a building associated with linen sale or production, of the Lycians, of the places (altars?) of Lysanios, of the Macedonians, of Mendesion (perhaps associated in some way with the city in the Delta or with the ram-god worshipped there), of Moeris (the Fayum lake), of the Square or Avenue, of the temple to Seknebtunis (the local crocodile god), of the Syrians, of the treasury (?), places of obscure meaning, of the first place of the gooseherds, of the other place of the gooseherds, of the temple of Horus the Hawk (perhaps to be associated with the temple of Apollo the Hawk). Oxyrhynchus produces a similarly heterogeneous list with districts of the hilltop, of the place of the upper amphodarchs (*vel sim.*), of the upper camp, of the north processional way (*dromos*), of the north quay, the tenth quarter, of the *dromos* of the gymnasium, of the *dromos* of the Thoereion, of the *dromos* of the Sarapeion, of the temple of Hermes, of the places (altars?) of Herakles, of the Heroon (possibly a Greek equivalent of an Egyptian god), of the warm baths, of the temple of Thoeris Thenepmoi, of the burial place of the Ibises, of the Jews, of the knights' camp, of the hippodrome, of the Cretan, of the camp of the Lycians, the temple of the Mother goddess (?), of the perfumed baths, of the temple of Nemesis, of the south *dromos*, of the garden of Pammenes, of the square or avenue (of the theatre), of the shepherds, of the street of Onnophris, of the Gateway of the Gods, and of Pses. The heterogeneity of these designations is striking. Several of the districts were named after temples or the roads leading from temples. The comparative absence of other forms of public buildings should not come as a surprise since Ptolemaic cities seem to have had few urban institutions other than those associated with the temples. A treasury at Ptolemais Euergetis, the hippodrome, various baths, and possibly the theatre at Oxyrhynchus and, of course, the gymnasia, are a slight collection of non-religious public buildings. Some of these 'temple' districts were not named after the temples themselves but after the processional ways. These were almost certainly the major thoroughfares of the city. Other topographical features include various 'camps'. It seems somewhat improbable that Oxyrhynchus had three fortified areas within the city, though we could compare these with the *phrouria* at Hermopolis and at Syene. Not only was the Oxyrhynchite an area in which the Ptolemies provided land for soldiers, but also some of the names of the camps (Lycians' and Knights') seem to carry further military associations. At Oxyrhynchus, the presumably riverine districts of North Quay and South Quay seem self-explanatory. Other districts are associated with trade groups. Gooseherders are prominent in both Oxyrhynchus and Ptolemais Euergetis, though it would be brave to relate this to their importance in the economy. The other trade groups attested seem less surprising. Ethnic groups also figure. Many of these (though not all) are (broadly speaking) Greek and one might speculate that these designations relate to Ptolemaic settlements.

The impression given by the list of names is of a variegated topography in the cities. There is no obvious dominant principle behind the distribution of names. Even the influence of temples and religious structures was somewhat diffused by the naming of *amphoda* after the *dromoi* associated with the temples rather than the temples themselves. Nor do these designations suggest that the city was a network of ethnic or trade enclaves. The *amphoda* may reflect an administrative topography, at least partly imposed by Rome, but the social and political topography of the city is not obvious from the names of the districts alone.

Administrative role of the *amphoda*

Egyptian cities were, for pre-industrial cities, quite big (see pp. 331–4) and this presented various administrative problems. Finding one's way across an Egyptian city, or indeed any other large pre-industrial city, especially if the city did not have a regular plan, was probably quite difficult (Llewelyn 1994a; 1994b; Ling 1990). The district designations allowed a greater level of precision in locating persons and property. They were used in this way in the early first century, especially in relation to property, which was often described by listing the neighbours. There was, presumably, no formal requirement to use such descriptions, any more than it was a legal requirement to say that a house was 'near the temple of Sarapis': it simply allowed any confusions and disputes to be cleared up more quickly.

The introduction of *amphoda* may have increased the formality of this usage. Documents used for property registration were sent to amphodarchs who maintained the registers. Registration of persons by *amphodon* was also underway by the mid-first century, if not earlier. Those applying to be registered as members of the gymnasium or of metropolite status had to give the district of registration of their male ancestors (only father and maternal grandfather in the case of metropolite status examinations), which was presumably to allow the checking of data in the city and gymnasial rolls.[22] It seems likely that the *amphodal* registers were also used in collecting tax. Registers from Philadelphia, Oxyrhynchus and Panopolis, and possibly Ptolemais Euergetis, appear to have been organized topographically to aid the tax man as he toured the city. In Egypt, the tax collectors were expected to go out and find the taxpayers (Hanson 1994). The register from Ptolemais Euergetis (*Stud. Pal. Pap.* IV, pp. 58–78 of AD 72/3) was organized by *amphodon*, though probably formed part of a much larger register that covered a significant proportion of the population of the city (see pp. 148–9). *P. Oslo.* III 111, dating from AD 235, lists houses and persons in a particular portion of the Hermaiou *amphodon*. It seems likely that a tax on houses at Hermopolis in the 270s was collected using a register of property by *amphodon*, though, I suppose, it is possible that the council simply appointed individuals to collect the levy from each quarter of the city without having any prior register (*Stud. Pal. Pap.* V = *CPH* 101). The early fourth-century topographical register of Panopolis (*P. Berol. Bork.*), however, does not appear to have been organized by *amphodon*.

In *c.* AD 200, Septimius Severus granted the *metropoleis* of Egypt full urban status, which meant that they developed town councils on the model of other Graeco-Roman cities. This led to a radical reform of the urban administration, one of the features of which was the introduction of tribal divisions. The city had a certain number of magisterial positions and these were to be rotated between members of the various tribes on an annual or part-annual basis. Tribal divisions were already in place in Alexandria (where they dated back to the Ptolemaic period, though they were probably either reformed or renamed in the first century AD: Montevecchi 1982), at Antinoopolis, and also, presumably, at Ptolemais. Tribal divisions were hereditary, though often had origins in topographical divisions, as in fifth-century BC Athens. The logic of the divisions at Alexandria and Ptolemais is lost in the beginnings of Ptolemaic history. Antinoopolis was also rather unusual in that the city was a new creation of the 130s and the population recruited from other areas, most notably from the Fayum. We have no idea how the various tribes were formed or whether the tribal divisions were in any way related to the topographical division of the city into blocks (Kühn 1913; Zahrnt 1988; Schubert 1990: 26–9; Alston 1995: 61–3; Johnson 1914). At Oxyrhynchus the tribes were numbered. There appear to have been six tribes in the early third century, expanded to twelve probably in 245–6 (Bowman 1971: 149–53; Wegener 1938; Lidov 1968). The tribes were not, however, an adequate replacement for the *amphoda*. As can be seen from tables 4.2 and 4.3, the early Roman *amphoda* continued to function in the third and fourth centuries as districts of registration for persons and property. In fact, the tribes appear to have been formed by unifying various *amphoda* and an archive of texts relating to the Oxyrhynchite corn dole dating to *c.* 268–71 (*P. Oxy.* XL 2892–2940) amply demonstrates that the numbered tribes had given way to tribes identified by one of the *amphoda* from which they had been constructed. Summary registers (*P. Oxy.* XL 2928; 2929) list twelve *amphoda* (presumably, in fact, tribes). Since there were somewhere between 23 and 28 *amphoda* in third-century Oxyrhynchus, each entry probably represented 2–3 *amphoda*. This tribal system continued in some form until at least the very late fourth century (W. *Chr.* 405 = *P. Flor.* I 39 *BL* VI, 38; *P. Oxy.* XL p. 7).[23]

The introduction of the tribal system saw a change in the titles of those administering the various districts. The amphodal registers were maintained in the first and second centuries by amphodarchs. In the third century, the *amphodogrammateus* (the scribe of the *amphodon*) replaced the amphodarch (though see *CPR* I 63 *BL* VIII, 97; 75; 88; 92 *BL* VIII, 98; *Stud. Pal. Pap.* XX 25; 29 *BL* VIII, 462; 47 for the survival of amphodarchies; Mertens 1958: 8–9). The *amphodogrammateus* appears to have been responsible both for the maintenance of amphodal records (declarations of birth, registrations of property, etc., were submitted to the *amphodogrammateus*) and also for nominations to compulsory public services or liturgies.[24] The lower echelons of Egyptian administration were run by pressed men, chosen more or less at random with the proviso that they had sufficient property to provide security for any service that had financial responsibilities. The introduction of the tribal system meant that urban public services (liturgies) were now provided by members of particular tribes, as were the magistracies. The *amphodogrammateus* is frequently attested in the period from AD 207 to 242/3 (*P. Amst.* I 49; *P. Oxy.* XVII 2131 = *Sel. Pap.* II 290; *P. Oxy.* LIX 3976; *P. Oxy.* I 81 *BL* I, 314, though see *P. Oxy.* VIII 1119 = W. *Chr.* 397 *BL* II.2, 98 (AD 253) and *SB* VI 9050 (98–117).

The *amphodogrammateus* was in turn replaced by the phularch, an office attested mainly from *c.* 245 to *c.* 277, though there are a number of later references (*P. Oxy.* XII 1535 *BL* IV, 62; XXXIII 2664 *BL* VIII, 260; *P. Col.* VIII 231; *P. Oxy.* XXXVI 2764; *P. Wisc.* I 2 *BL* VI 68; *P. Oxy.* XL (*passim*), though see *SB* IV 7375 (222–35); *SB* XVIII 13252 (369–70); *SB* XIV 11957 (420–50); Mertens 1958: 8–9; Parsons 1967). The phularch took responsibility for amphodal registers and supervised the nominations to liturgies. Village administration was also reformed *c.* 245 with the introduction of *dekaprotoi* and komarchs (Thomas 1975). The significance of these changes is not clear, however. Parsons (1967) argues that the change represents a downgrading of the office of *amphodogrammateus*, perhaps in response to difficulties in filling the post (Skeat and Wegener 1935 = *SB* V 7696), but the evidence is slight.

The abolition of the phularchy can be comparatively closely dated. Stray references from after the 270s show that the title continued to be used, but these probably refer to a leader of a tribal (in its modern sense) group rather than an urban administrator (Mertens 1958: 30–2). The phularch was replaced by the *sustates*. This official is attested from *c.* 286 (Mertens 1958: 30; van Minnen 1991; *P. Oxy.* L 3571; *PSI* III 164; *P. Laur.* IV 157; *P. Corn.* I 18; *P. Oxy.* XLIV 3183) until the late fourth or early fifth century (*P. Oxy.* LV 3796 (a restoration); W. *Chr.* 405 = *P. Flor.* I 39). The late third century appears to have been a period of considerable (but not exactly dramatic) change. Hyper-inflation made the old poll tax worthless and a new poll tax was introduced (Rathbone 1996; 1997). The first firmly attested payment of the new tax is from AD 296–7, a decade after the introduction of the *sustates* (*P. Oxy.* XXXIV 2717), and, given the frequency of attestation of payments until 319–20 (see the table published with *P. Oxy.* LV 3789 and further documents listed in *P. Oxy.* LXV 4490 (AD 299); cf. *P. Oxy.* LXV 4480 (AD 311), it seems unlikely that the tax was introduced much before AD 295. The period also sees the end of the established forms of both metropolite and gymnasial status applications. The last known old form of gymnasial status application is *P. Turner* 38 of AD 274/5 or 280/1 (Montevecchi 1975). The new form was considerably less formal: *P. Oxy.* LXV 4489 (AD 297) is an application to register a child in the class of the *dodekadrachmon* (payers of poll tax at 12 drachmas) and as one of those from the gymnasium. In contrast to earlier texts, only the parents' names are given (see also *P. Ups. Frid.* 6; *P. Oxy.* LIV 3754; *P. Col.* VIII 231). This declaration contains archaic elements since the poll tax was no longer charged at 12 drachmas on metropolites but at 1,200 or 1,600 drachmas (*P. Oxy.* LXV 4490), but such an anachronism is insufficient to suggest that the whole text refers to a system which no longer operated. The *sustates* continued to supervise liturgical nominations, maintain registers and deal with the poll tax throughout the fourth and possibly into the fifth century.

The next round of significant administrative change appears to have been in the early fourth century, when village administration was reformed *c.* 302–10 with the disappearance of the *dekaprotoi* and the (re)introduction of *sitologoi*. There appears to have been a thorough overhaul of urban administration in the early fourth century, with a host of new officials appearing (see pp. 277–81), but these reforms appear to have had no effect on the *sustates* or district administration.

The combining of various *amphoda* for certain administrative purposes did not lead to the abolition of the more minor *amphoda*. At least 22 of the first- and second-century *amphoda* of Oxyrhynchus are attested for the third century whereas 27 of the 32 first- and second-century *amphoda* of Ptolemais Euergetis are attested for the third and fourth centuries. Thus, the pre-AD 50 topographical divisions were preserved as administrative units into the fourth century. Nevertheless, the system did not continue unchanged into the fifth and sixth centuries, as can be seen from tables 4.2 and 4.3 (see also Fabbro 1982). Understanding the transition from the fourth-century system to that of the sixth century is made rather difficult because of a change in the nature of our available evidence, as shown in figure 4.1.

The pattern from Ptolemais Euergetis reflects the reduction in the number of published papyri from the various Fayum villages from the third century onwards, but numbers increase from a low in the fifth century with the publication of a number of papyri apparently from Ptolemais Euergetis itself. The Oxyrhynchite pattern similarly reflects the relative quantity of papyri from the first five centuries AD. Oxyrhynchus of the sixth and seventh centuries is

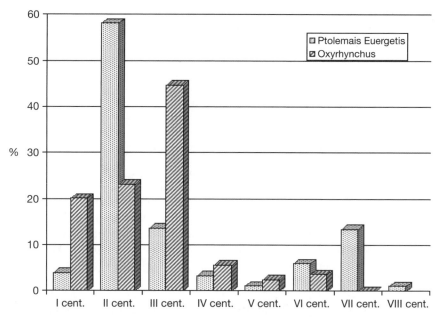

Figure 4.1 Attestations of *amphoda* at Ptolemais Euergetis and Oxyrhynchus by century.

Note: Based on middle figures of ranges derived from tables 4.2 and 4.3. 'Byzantine' documents are ignored.

mainly attested by the archives of the Apion estate (see also pp. 108–9) and although the estate archive has left us a huge number of documents, most of these detail the management of the land rather than the administration of the city. Our evidence of the fifth- and sixth-century city is slight compared with that for earlier periods.

A second problem relates to vocabulary. The designation of districts in the later period is irregular and uses a range of words, most of which could be translated as 'street'. Since streets existed within districts in the earlier period, in many cases it is difficult to know whether we are dealing with a street or an administrative district, though, of course, they could be coterminous. Nevertheless, Byzantine tax lists demonstrate that district divisions were not merely convenient topographical designations but continued to have an administrative purpose (see below). The sixth-century system was, however, different from that of two centuries earlier. Ptolemais Euergetis had forty-five new districts and probably nine of the old districts in the later period. Oxyrhynchus has at least seven new districts with three or four old districts attested. On the face of it, this amounts to a transformation of urban topography.

The transformation from the fourth to the sixth century is an administrative change. Precisely dating that change is difficult. It seems unlikely that the amphodal system was changed while the *sustates* continued to function, which pushes the change somewhat later than 416. The obvious change in urban administration in this period came at the end of the fifth or the start of the sixth century with the introduction of new officials such as the pagarch and the *pater poleos* (see pp. 309–11), and it may be that other forms of urban administration, such as liturgical service and tribal divisions, came to an end at the same time. Nevertheless, some form of topographical division for official purposes appears to have been reinvented.

Size and social nature of districts

The investigation of the administrative functions of the *amphoda* brings us little closer to the social importance of districts in the city. Such administrative divisions, however, provide a convenient jumping-off point for an investigation of social zones. First, however, one must investigate more mundane but central problems: we may know the names of the various divisions, their administrative purposes and their 'political' histories, but we also need to establish their social composition and their size.

Size of amphoda *and tribes*

It is a reasonable assumption that those creating the district divisions would have striven to divide the cities into roughly equal sectors, which, of course, would be much easier in a city with a regular plan, such as Thmouis or Antinoopolis. The urban plan of Apollonospolis Magna is not known, but *Archiv.* VI 427 = *P. Flor.* 333 + *P. Brem.* 21 of AD 116 gives the number of houses in ten urban areas of Apollonospolis as being 123, 126, 129, 130, 128, 129, 129, 132, 124, 123.[25] By comparison, the second or twentieth *amphodon* of Thmouis had 178 houses noted in a second-century register (*PSI* III 230 *BL* VIII, 395). Hermopolis Magna, however, had huge *amphoda*. *Stud. Pal. Pap.* V = *CPH* 101 lists revenues raised from a flat rate tax of 60 drachmas per house. Polis West produced 23 talents (138,000 drachmas) 1[. . .] drachmas while the second unspecified *amphodon* produced 19 talents (114,000 drachmas) 1[. . .] drachmas. This suggests that the two districts had at least 2,317 and 1,917 houses respectively. The difference is substantial, but the figures are of a similar order and both very different from those from Thmouis and Apollonospolis. Other figures are less easy to compare. *P. Oslo.* III 111, a survey of the northern sector of the Hermaiou *amphodon* of Oxyrhynchus, lists 57 plots, though not all those plots were occupied by houses. This could be expanded to 200–220 houses in the *amphodon*, though such an estimate rests on a number of extremely questionable assumptions. *Stud. Pal. Pap.* IV, pp. 58–83, is a fragment of a register of male inhabitants of Ptolemais Euergetis (Wessely 1902). The first extant entries are headed column 32 and the column contains a summary account which lists 385 men, 330 of whom paid poll tax at the metropolite rate, 3 at the village rate, 5 had died, and 47 were exempt. The rest of the text lists men in

Apolloniou Paremboles. A partial summary of this register in lines 561 following gives a total of 173 metropolites over fourteen years of age and fifteen tax-exempt Alexandrians. Four were abroad. This figure is substantially different from that for the unknown *amphodon*. For comparative purposes, we can use the calculations on pp. 70–3 to estimate the number of houses this population would occupy, bearing in mind the doubts expressed about such procedures. The unknown *amphodon* may have had about 130 houses while Apolloniou Paremboles may have had about 63 houses. This is a more substantial variation than we can see in other cities but, given the vagaries of method (and indeed of the primary evidence), there seems little reason to discount the material. There is no other evidence that would seem to allow us to estimate the size of *amphoda* and although there is, excluding the obviously unusually large *amphoda* of Hermopolis, a significant variation in the estimated sizes of the various districts, the figures are within a reasonable range of 63–220 houses, centring on 130 houses.[26] This is roughly comparable to the street community of modern Cairo studied by Fakhouri (1985), which had 191 families and a population of 1,221.[27]

Although assessing the absolute size of the various districts may be problematic, we gain some information on the relative sizes of the tribes of Oxyrhynchus and the Byzantine districts of Ptolemais Euergetis. The corn dole archive contains two summaries of those eligible for the dole at Oxyrhynchus by three named categories (*P. Oxy.* XL 2928; 2929), the information on which is combined in table 4.4 and analysed in figures 4.2 and 4.3.[28]

Figures 4.2 and 4.3 display the irregularities of the division of the receiving population between the various tribes, though there are limitations on these disparities. The size of the tribes, judging from the total number of men receiving the dole, varies by a factor of just under four, but more than half the

Table 4.4 Numbers receiving the corn dole

Tribe	3,000[a]	Remboi	Homologoi (100)	Total
Heroiou	21. [211]	93	4	308
Poimenikes	2.. [251]	11	3	265
Ippeon	107	24	6	137
Borra Dromou	169	132	14	315
Dromou Thoeridos	313	38	7	358
Borra Krepidos	28. [281]	103	6	390
Notou Krepidos	29. [291]	31	3	325
Hermaiou	183	24	12	219
Plateias	21. [211]	53	13	277
Kretikou	23. [231]	34	9	274
Pammenous	4.. [451]	34	11	496
Murobalanou	205	58	5	268
Total	2904	635	93	3632

[a] Restored figures in square brackets are calculated on the basis of 107 remaining from the incomplete list being distributed between the missing digits.

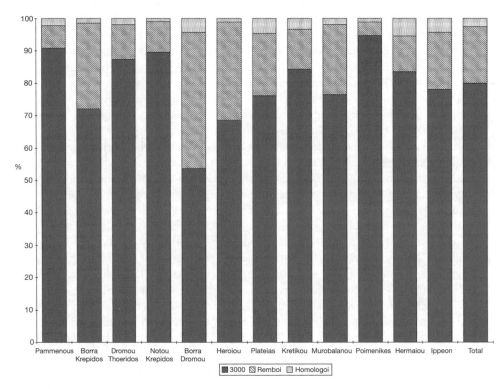

Figure 4.2 The corn dole archive: percentage of those in each receiving category by tribe

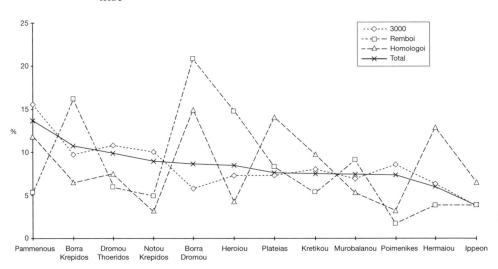

Figure 4.3 The corn dole archive: percentage of total registered population of each receiving category by tribe

150

tribes vary in the restricted range of 7.3–8.9 per cent of total recipients. The *homologoi* (the agreed) and the *remboi* (the remainder) exhibit startling variations which show a slight relationship with the changes in the larger category of the 3,000. There is, therefore, both an uneven distribution of men between tribes and an uneven distribution of men in the various categories within tribes.

It is difficult to move from the relative sizes of the various 'tribes' to the absolute populations of these areas. First, it seems very likely that only the members of the 3,000 were actually enrolled in the tribes, while the other groups were probably resident in the areas from which the tribes were drawn and were allowed to draw the corn dole either by agreement with their registered communities or perhaps because they had performed some service as residents (*P. Oxy.* XL, pp. 3–5). Since the *numerus clausus* of 3,000 had not been reached, it seems possible that all the male citizens who were eligible (that is over the age of 20) would have been registered for the dole, though there may have been significant numbers of adult male residents in the various districts who did not fall either into this category or into the other two known categories.[29]

Table 4.5 uses the corn dole figures to reconstruct the population of the various tribes (Bagnall and Frier 1994: 104). The figures are likely to underestimate the total. Although one may assume that those of the 3,000 started receiving the dole at 20, there was no fixed age at which men from other groups became eligible. Second, it is not clear to me whether the 3,000 will have included those eligible for the *gerousia*, the council of old men. The figures in table 4.5 assume that all men over 20 were included in the corn dole figures.[30]

The figures in table 4.5 are mostly about the 1,000 mark, already identified as a possibly significant population level. However, a tribe may represent as many as three *amphoda* and, if this is the case, the *amphoda* of Oxyrhynchus in the mid- to late third century seem rather small.

Table 4.5 Corn dole populations

Tribe	Number of men	Total population
Heroiou	308	1018
Poimenikes	265	876
Ippeon	137	452
Borra Dromou	315	1041
Dromou Thoeridos	358	1184
Borra Krepidos	390	1289
Notou Krepidos	325	1075
Hermaiou	219	724
Plateias	277	916
Kretikou	274	906
Pammenous	496	1640
Murobalanou	268	886
Total	3632	12008

The only possible comparable data come from *SB* I 5127 and 5128, two Byzantine tax lists from Ptolemais Euergetis which list payments by named districts. These figures present certain problems, as can be seen from figure 4.4.

SB I 5127 often lists more than one contribution from the same district (combined in figure 4.4) and the account would seem to be an 'in-progress' register. If we compare these figures with *SB* I 5128, we not only see that three districts not attested in *SB* I 5127 made significant contributions to the total money collected, but that the contributions in *SB* I 5128 do not appear to be in proportion to the contributions made by the same districts in *SB* I 5127. One could and perhaps should discount this material, but although they clearly do not *demonstrate* that the districts of fifth- to eighth-century Ptolemais Euergetis were irregular in size, I take these papyri as evidence *suggesting* such irregularities.

Although the administrative divisions of the cities were imposed by the Roman authorities, it seems that the mechanics of the system were left to local discretion. In some cases, instead of dividing cities into roughly equal blocks,

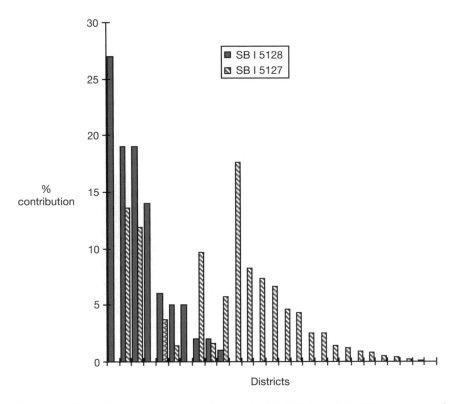

Figure 4.4 Contributions to the tax collected in *SB* I 5128 and 5127 in percent and by district

the authorities adopted pre-existing divisions which established notably unequal units. It seems reasonable to assume that these units were not merely administrative.

The social nature of districts

The above discussion builds up a strong *prima facie* case that the division of at least some of the cities into *amphoda* corresponded with divisions of the city detectable 'on the ground', that is either social or topographical divisions, or both. We should, however, remain cautious. At least one significant street in Ptolemais Euergetis did not become an *amphodon* in the early Roman period. The *laura Kleopatriou*, street of the Temple of Kleopatra, is attested relatively frequently in the first century (see n. 11). It was the site of a bank and also of a fountain and it survived as a significant topographical indicator into the Byzantine period, when it does appear to have been an administrative district, one of the few which preserved a pagan designation. If the *amphoda* were based on pre-existing community divisions, the correlation between communities and administrative districts may not have been perfect. Nevertheless, the fact that the new districts of the fifth century or later appear so often to have been constructed around churches, offering an analogy to the parish system, also encourages the view that the administrative districts were also significant social communities.

The number of references we have from the various districts of Ptolemais Euergetis and Oxyrhynchus is far too small to gain an adequate picture of the residents of a particular *amphodon*. This is particularly true in the case of Ptolemais Euergetis since most of the attestations relate to landholdings outside the city, noting only that a certain person is registered in a particular district. The material from Oxyrhynchus is a little more varied but still completely inadequate as a representative sample of the populations of districts over three centuries or more. It is difficult to believe that we know even the names of 1 per cent of the population of any of the districts over this period. Although probably valueless, table 4.6 summarizes any obvious characteristics of the better-attested *amphoda* of Oxyrhynchus.

This evidence is perhaps best employed in negative arguments. For instance, there is no evidence to suggest any notable division of areas between different ethnic groups. 'Greeks', as represented by the gymnasial group, appear to live in the same *amphoda* as 'Egyptians', as represented by the priests of the traditional temples. Second, there is no obvious evidence of craft or market zoning or that the gymnasial group sought to separate themselves from commercial sectors of the city. Some positive patterns do emerge. Priests appear more often in districts associated with temples, hardly a startling observation. More interestingly, the various weavers attested seem also to be close to the Sarapeion, with the exception of a weaver in the Hippodromou,[31] though attestations of weavers are concentrated in the first century AD and this may cause some distortion.

Table 4.6 Features of the main Roman-period *amphoda* of Oxyrhynchus

Amphodon	Characteristics
Anamphodarchon	Gymnasial residents
Ano Paremboles	Gymnasial residents
North Dromos	Gymnasial residents; craftsman resident
Borra Krepidos	Gymnasial residents; oil shop; Sebasteion.
Kretikou	Gymnasial residents; magistrate resident; probably identical with Ioudakes (P. Oxy. I 100).
Dekates	Fuller resident; hieroglyph-writers resident.
Dromou Gymnasiou	Gymnasial residents. Magistrates resident. Priests of the temples of Isis, Osiris, and Sarapis resident. Temple of Osiris and the Tameion nearby or in the district. Weavers resident.
Dromou Thoeridou (also called Kmelemou)	Temple of Cleopatra; magistrates resident and owning property here; weaver resident; Egyptian temple official resident, as is a hieroglyph writer.
Hermaiou	Priests of Thoeris, Isis and Sarapis resident; former magistrates resident. Bronze smithy; veteran resident; *amphodon* 'near' the temple of Sarapis.
Herakles topon	Gymnasial residents
Heroion	Gymnasial residents; pottery and associated buildings near a *stoa.*
Hippeon Parembole	Gymnasial residents; Kampos near the Temple of Serapis in this district; camel shed.
Hippodomou	Weavers resident; priest of Sarapis resident.
Lykion Paremboles	Gymnasial residents
Metroiou	Gymnasial residents
Murobalanou	Gymnasial residents; bread baker resident; priest of Isis at the temple of the siblings resident. District near the Temple of Serapis.
Nemesiou	Gymnasial residents; former magistrates own property here.
Notou Dromou	Priest of Sarapis resident.
Notou Krepidou	
Pammenous Paradeisou	Gymnasial residents; magistrates resident; near the gate; bronze smith resident
Plateias (theatrou)	Gymnasial residents; magistrate owns property here. A vegetable shop in Psou near this square.
Poimenikes	Pork butcher in district. Weavers resident. District near temple of Serapis and Temgenoutheos
Temgenoutheos	Residence of a priest of Athena; weavers resident; district near Poimenikes and the temple of Serapis.
Chenosbokon	Gymnasial residents; magistrates hold property here; bronze smith resident.

Another weak pattern lies in the distribution of the gymnasial and magisterial group, a group one might characterize as the elite of the Graeco-Roman city. They appear in seventeen of the districts listed above but do not appear in seven. This shows, probably conclusively, that the elite was not concentrated in a small area of the city, but neither are attestations of the elite evenly distributed. Although, clearly, this could just be a quirk of the published evidence, the form of the gymnasial *epikrisis* means that numbers of attestations are quite high and I suspect that the seeming absence of gymnasial residents from various *amphoda* is significant.

These emergent patterns can be treated with a little more confidence through comparison with the patterns of spatial distribution at early fourth-century Panopolis, as illuminated by *P. Berol. Bork.* Borkowski restored a text of about 630 lines and a related text of about 90 lines from various fragments, though this restoration is open to a certain amount of doubt. The fragments are topographic guides to the city listing the use of plots and, normally, a single male owner or resident. My brother and I (Alston and Alston 1997) analysed this text in a recent article. We fully accepted that the weaknesses in the data, being the gaps and the problems of restoration, raised fundamental problems and we chose, perhaps unjustifiably, to ignore the fact that we could not map the city. Nevertheless, my view was and is that, in general, it is better to try and use imperfect evidence than to strive for methodological purity, provided that one is explicit about problems. The result of my brother's statistical analysis was to show that no groups were tightly clustered within the text. However, it did show certain patterns summarized in table 4.7.

To start with those groups showing concentrations, the naval workers are the most strongly aggregated group. One presumes that they grouped around their place of work, the river. It is also no surprise that metal workers tended to congregate together. Such industrial production was potentially dangerous and produced a certain amount of pollution. They may have been encouraged by the urban authorities to concentrate their activities. Scribes and administrators (a fairly broad category) also seem to congregate. This is much less easy to explain and seems to have little obvious practical value. More significant is the non-random distribution of the elite and army officers (probably also members of the elite in the early fourth century). The particular measure used here identified the clustering of this group rather than its absence from large sections of the text. This means that the elite concentrated their residence in tight knots across the city, a pattern which would also fit the Oxyrhynchite evidence.

Other groups seem to be randomly distributed. Most trade and craft groups did not concentrate. Perhaps more surprisingly, there is no obvious concentration of religious structures or of priestly residences. It is, however, clear that large temple complexes in many Egyptian cities (see pp. 196–218) did represent significant concentrations of religious authority and a survey such as *P. Berol. Bork.* might ignore a huge complex or ascribe it to a single plot.

This material allows us to uncover something of the 'texture' of the urban community. A pedestrian crossing the city must have been aware that he or she was passing through areas of different character, either by the port, or in the area in which there were several metalworking establishments, or in an area of elite residence. There were also (as discussed below and in the next chapter) areas in which there were concentrations of civic buildings, of religious institutions, and

Table 4.7 Distribution of social groups in Panopolis from *P. Berol. Bork.*

A. Groups showing random distribution of members	1. Educationalists and educated workers[a].
	2. Educationalists, educated workers and administrators.
	3. Educationalists, educated workers and elite.[b]
	4. Educationalists, educated workers, elite and army officers.
	5. Educationalists and elite.
	6. Educated workers and scribes.
	7. Elite, army officers, chief priests and former chief priests and district scribes.
	8. Elite, priests, chief priests and former chief priests.
	9. Elite and goldsmiths.
	10. Religious buildings.
	11. Priests (excluding chief priests and former chief priests).
	12. Priests, including chief priest and former chief priests, and temple scribes.
	13. Priests, chief priests and former chief priests, religious buildings, and temple scribe.
	14. Priests and religious buildings.
	15. Goldsmiths.
	16. Construction workers, engineers, and architects.
	17. Cloth workers and cloth retailers.
	18. Food retailers.
	19. Food producers.
	20. Food retailers and producers.
B. Groups showing concentration of members[c]	1. Elite and army officers.
	2. Miscellaneous scribes (excluding linen-workers' scribe) and administrators.
	3. Naval workers.[d]
	4. Metal workers.

[a] Educated workers include doctors, lawyers and musicians.
[b] The elite are defined here as those who hold or have held magisterial offices and relatives of these men.
[c] These groups are those for which the real distribution was more strongly aggregated than 95 per cent of the randomized data. For groups 1–3, the pattern is strongest for the measure which identifies clustering. For the metal workers, the measure which identified absence from large sectors of the city provided the strongest pattern.
[d] Naval workers include shipwrights and sailors.

of commercial activity. There were visible districts, areas in which different types of activity would occur. The patterns displayed, even in this imperfect evidence, appear intricate. We do not seem to have large homogeneous districts which housed members of the elite or particular trade groups. Moreover, we do not see anything approaching an even distribution of elite or traders or religious institutions across large areas of the city. Those areas which show local homogeneity seem very small, and are perhaps better described not so much as a district or a zone, but as an enclave.

The uncertainties in the evidence and the complexities of the dimly perceived patterns undermine confidence. Nevertheless, this investigation begins to erode the idea that we have what one might call 'traditional' neighbourhoods within the Romano-Egyptian city; 'traditional' meaning not 'having its roots in the past' but what historians have traditionally thought of as neighbourhoods and social zones. Instead, I would like to substitute a far more complex understanding of the local geography of the city, and to gain perspective on this problem, I will break away from Roman and Byzantine Egypt to explore more fully how localities within cities elsewhere and in other times functioned. Before this, however, I turn to Alexandria, the history and organization of which was very different from that of the cities of the *chora*.

Districts in Alexandria

The history of Alexandria in the first century of Roman rule turns on issues relating to ethnic identity. Ancient polemics seeking historical justifications for first-century AD political positions discussed the supposed residential segregation of the Jews in the context of the riots in and after AD 38. It is appropriate to defer much of the discussion of those riots to chapter 5, and in this section I concentrate solely on the districts of the city.

Although Alexandria was on a thin and irregular spit of land between the sea and Lake Mareotis, it was a planned city and demonstrated the regular orthogonal arrangement common to such Graeco-Roman centres. The main east–west street divided the city into two unequal sections. This street ran from the Canopic gate (Strabo XVII 1 10) or the Gate of the Sun in the east to the Gate of the Moon in the west, though the gates may have been heavily remodelled and perhaps renamed by Hadrian or Antoninus Pius (Achilles Tatius V 1; John Malalas XI, p. 280; John of Nikiou, *Chronicle* 74; *P. Lond.* VI = *P. Jews* 1914). Strabo (XVII 1 8) also mentions a main north–south street, though there is considerable modern dispute as to its exact location. This provided a division of the city into four sections, but Philo (*In Flaccum* 55–6) describes the five μοῖραι (divisions) of the city, which were identified by the first five letters of the alphabet. There are two early attestations of officials of *amphoda* from Alexandria, both from the Augustan period, and it seems very likely that it was these districts that the officials were supervising (*BGU* IV 1125; 1179).[32] Given the shape of the city, it is very tempting to place two quarters north of the main east–west street and three to the south, but in fact we have very little information on the location of the five districts.

Most of our first-century information concerning districts of the city comes from Josephus (writing probably between AD 75 and *c.* 97) and Philo (writing in the early 40s AD), who debated with anti-semites as to whether the Jews were part of the main Greek city or an alien community. Although we do not

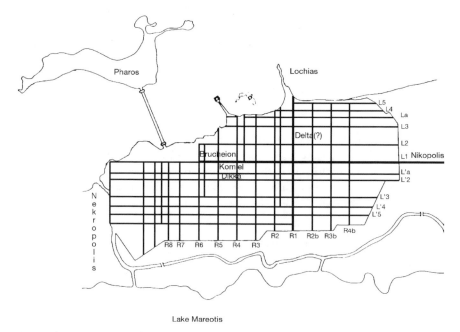

Figure 4.5 Street plan of Alexandria

have the other side of this polemic, the anti-semitic element, the argument of those opposing the Jews can easily be deduced. Philo (*In Flaccum* 55–7) tells us that the Jewish community in the city was spread unevenly across the five districts, but concentrated in two districts which could be called 'Jewish'. The rioters of AD 38 drove the Jews from four of the districts, restricting them to the Delta district. Jews caught in the 'wrong' sector were murdered: their bodies dragged along the paved streets marked with their blood the zone from which the Jews were excluded (Philo, *In Flaccum* 64–71). Delta was, however, too small to hold the Jews and the community spilled over the beaches and necropoleis of the city. Josephus, writing a generation after the riots (*Contra Ap.* II 33–4; cf. *BJ* II 495), also locates the Jewish community in the Delta quarter and accepts or seems to accept that the separation of the Jews was historic. The logic of Josephus' argument (*Contra Ap.* II 33–78) suggests that the anti-semites claimed that residential segregation paralleled constitutional separation and the riots restored the traditional spatial and legal divisions.[33] Philo (*In Flaccum* 55–6) denies that there was notable segregation prior to AD 38 and lays claim, if such segregation were to be enforced, to two-fifths of the city. This is a bold tactic, for it suggests that the Jews were just too populous to be regarded as alien and that they had never been treated as such. Josephus, however, attempts to subvert the link between spatial and political separation, arguing that the pleasant seaside location of Delta, not bordered by a noisy harbour, suggests that Alexander wished to favour the Jews.

The archaeological and papyrological evidence, such as it is, would tend to support Philo's view that the Jews were not concentrated (Balconi 1985; Schubart 1913). Jewish and Greek tombs were placed side by side and Jews can often only be identified in the papyrological record by nomenclature.[34] Nevertheless, the barbarities of AD 38 must have encouraged residential segregation. In anti-semitic rioting in AD 66, the comparative success of the Alexandrian Jews in holding off their enemies (until the legions intervened decisively against them) might suggest that the community was not as dispersed as it had been three decades earlier.[35]

Another of the identifiable quarters of the city was known as the Brucheion. This was the palace district of the city and, according to Strabo (XVII 1 8), comprised between a quarter and a third of the area of the city.[36] The palatial district appears to have been something of a maze of interconnected buildings developed through accretion to a central palace over the Ptolemaic period.[37] The complex extended from the harbour into the heart of the city and included the Museion and the *sema*. The Museion was the cultural centre of the Greek city, through which the Ptolemies had extended their patronage to so many Hellenophone scholars in the Hellenistic period that Alexandria had become probably the most important centre of Greek learning. The *sema* was the tomb of Alexander the Great, the eponymous founder of the city and, as the Ptolemies liked to think, the spiritual progenitor of the Ptolemaic and other Hellenistic dynasties. The Ptolemies themselves were interred with their founder. There was also a theatre and a temple to Poseidon. Antony constructed a retreat for himself on an artificial promontory, named the Timonion, after the legendary misanthrope Timon of Athens, where Antony mourned the shattering of his hopes at Actium and awaited his inevitable and final defeat at the hands of Octavian. Here also was a Caesareum, a temple to Caesar, though the identity of the Caesar to whom it was dedicated remains a matter of some scholarly contention (Fishwick 1987; Dio LI 15; John of Nikiou, *Chronicle* 63; Calderini 1935–66, 119; Philo, *Legatio ad Gaium* 151). The cursory description in Strabo only provides us with the 'highlights' of the district. He quotes from Homer's description of the palace of Odysseus to describe the area as being 'building on building', giving the impression of an almost unbroken series of royal enclosures. Clearly the domination of this portion of the city reflected the power and prestige of the Ptolemaic dynasty and although cultural institutions such as the Museion continued to flourish in the early Roman period, the area may have become something of a museum, in the modern sense.

The physical and economic geography of Alexandria meant that the Brucheion was always a prime area for development, being closely connected to the harbour district. The area was severely damaged in civil disturbances in *c.* AD 273 and several sources suggest that the area was still largely deserted a century later (Epiphanius, *De Mensuris et Ponderibus* 9 (*PG* 43, col. 249c–252a);

cf. Eusebius, *HE* VII 32 7–8; Amm. Marc. XXII 16 15). It seems unlikely, however, that Alexandria had an urban wasteland at its heart for long and John of Nikiou (*Chronicle* 63) states that the old Caesareum was rededicated as a church by Constantine, becoming the Church of St Michael, and one of the main churches of the city in the Byzantine period. The Caesareum was further developed by the patriarch John the Almoner in the seventh century when he built halls to accommodate the poor in the environs of the church (Ps.-Leontius, *Life of St John the Almoner* 27). There may also have been a monastery in this district by the early fifth century (Jerome, *Vita Hilarionis* 33 [Migne *PL* XXXIII p. 47]; Wipszycka 1994). By the seventh century, the area was known as the district of the Caesareum and it may have had a rather different shape to the old Brucheion.

It seems likely that the Brucheion was a topographically recognizable area rather than an administrative unit. There were other similarly identifiable areas within the city (Strabo XVII 1 10). Beyond the Brucheion, there were extensive harbour facilities and just beyond the walls to the west of the city was the necropolis. When Strabo visited, it was somewhat decrepit. He attributed its decline to the recent construction of an eastern suburb at Nikopolis or Juliopolis, a site developed to commemorate Octavian's final victory over Antony (Hanson 1980). In the south-west lay the temple of Sarapis, the major Egyptian temple of the city, which attracted considerable attention and patronage in the next centuries. The temple was visited by various emperors and seems to have been extensively redeveloped by Hadrian. After the destruction of the old pagan sanctuary and the site's occupation by monks (see p. 288; Calderini 1935–66: 140–7), the temple became an important Christian centre. There appears to have been another concentration of civic buildings in the centre of the city. There was the gymnasium, described by Strabo as the finest of the buildings, together with a temple to Pan located on a rock ridge. The hippodrome, the next building mentioned in Strabo's survey, may have been quite close to the edge of the city. Beyond the west gate lay Nikopolis, the location of the Roman garrison. This suburb had an amphitheatre and a stadium and was also the location of the main state granaries that held the grain to be transported to Rome (Hanson 1980; Rickman 1980: 121–2; *P. Gen. Lat.* 1 = *CPL* 106 = *ChLA* I 7 = *Doc. Eser. Rom.* 10 = *RMR* 58; 9; 10; 37; 68; *P. Lond.* VI 1914).

Other recognizable areas appear only briefly in the record. There was a district named after Hadrian (*P. Oxy.* VII 1045; *SB* V 7561) and there also appears to have been an area of the city known as Boukolou (Haas 1997: 270–2). The Boukoloi were associated with a pre-Alexandrian settlement on the site of the later city (Strabo XVII 1 6).

A Syriac *notitia* (included in the writings of the twelfth-century patriarch of Antioch Michael bar Elias) notes in addition to the five 'lettered' quarters, quarters of Hadrianos, Lochias, Antirhodos, the Refuge of the Sarapeum, the isle of Anotinos Pandotos,[38] Zephyrion, Canopos, New Canal, Nikopolis, Camp

Table 4.8 Districts in the *notitia* of Alexandria reported in Michael bar Elias (Fraser 1951)

Quarter	Temples	Courts	Houses	Baths	Taverns	Porticoes
A	308	1655	5058	108	237	112
B	110	1002	5990	145	107	—
Γ	855	955	2140	[ ]	205	78
Δ	800	1120	5515	118	178	98
E	405	1420	5593	[ ]	118	56
Totals	2478	6152	24296	371+	845	344
Totals given in text	2393	8102	47790	1561	935	456

of Manutius, and Bendideion. Fraser cautiously dates the original text between the reign of Hadrian and the consolidation of Christianity in Alexandria in the mid-fourth century since it does not mention any churches. Its reliability is perhaps more questionable than Fraser allowed, though the districts are all known from other sources.

The totals given in the text differ radically from the totals achieved by adding the individual entries (see table 4.8). Although this may show little more than very poor arithmetic, the number of houses in the five quarters, 24,296, is so different from the stated total of 47,790 that I am tempted to discount scribal error. Only in Gamma does the number of houses vary from the norm of 5,000–6,000 and this can be used to suggest seemingly realistic populations (using table 3.2) of 38,000–45,000 for the four 'normal' quarters, while that of Gamma may have stood at around 16,000. The totals suggest an urban population of about 187,000 or 368,000, both of which fall far below the frequently used estimate of 500,000 (Delia 1991). The text states that certain areas were not included within the calculation. Of those areas, the peninsula of Lochias, the islands of Pharos, Antirhodos and Anotinos Pandotos are likely to have been very small. The quarter of Hadrian is said to be immense but there is no evidence, as far as I am aware, which would allow estimations of the refuge of the Sarapeum (is this simply the area within the Serapeum compound?) or of the other quarters. The discrepancies between the listed buildings and the numbers given in the text are so substantial that it would be tempting to argue that our source has had access to a city total including the extraneous quarters and simply got confused, though one would have to assume that the total given for the temples was an error. Alternatively, one could argue that the listed additional quarters were suburban and would be excluded from any official count of the city's buildings and so the totals given in the text seem valueless.

Figure 4.6 demonstrates that the mixture of buildings that comprised each quarter (except Gamma) varied little. The number of temples seems high in relationship to the number of houses (either 1 temple : 10 houses or 1 : 20) and Gamma has an extraordinary 1 : 2.5 ratio of temples to houses. Clearly, such calculations could include wayside shrines, but such ratios strain credibility. The

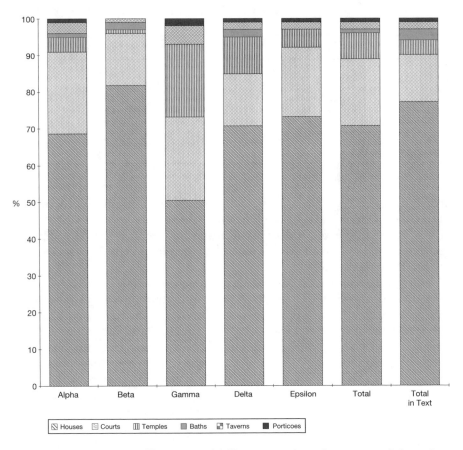

Figure 4.6 Percentage of buildings of different types in each quarter and throughout the city of Alexandria

number of baths also seems high at 1 : 40–50 houses, but the count presumably included a large number of small baths such as that discovered at Karanis (see pp. 112–16). The text appears to have been based on an original count, though it seems possible that at least some of the figures have been changed in transmission (there appears to have been some rounding of numbers), either through error or for rhetorical purposes. Nevertheless, I think the figures are likely to give a reasonably accurate impression of the mix of buildings within the five urban quarters.

The excavations at Kom el-Dikke (see p. 102) offer an archaeological insight into an Alexandrian district. The main excavation site is situated along the road traditionally numbered as R4, more or less in the centre of the city, and just to the south of the main east–west road (figure 4.5). The public buildings described below lie to the east of R4, opening onto an intermediate road between R4 and R5. To the west of R4 and thus behind these buildings lay the late Roman residential block extensively described in the previous chapter. The lowest excavated strata were of Roman date, though it seems almost inconceivable that the street was not extensively occupied in the Ptolemaic period. Only fragments of these early layers survive. The various scraps of mosaics and walls suggest it was a residential area of some opulence. The area was later redeveloped with the construction of a small theatre and a substantial set of public baths which seem to have filled most of the block.

The chronology of this development is complex (Kolataj 1992: 43–56). The stratigraphy of the bath house is more than a little confusing, partly because of the reuse of the site as a burial ground and then as a Napoleonic fort, but partly because a large explosion destroyed a substantial section of the bath house in the nineteenth century. A trial pit sunk next to the external wall of the baths to determine the stratigraphy exposed two major layers. Layer I contained a huge amount of pottery, mainly of fifth–seventh-century date and two coins, one of Constantius II (337–61) and the other of the late fourth century. The lowest part of this layer was an ash and slag fill. It looks very much as if layer I contains debris from the period of the use of the baths and that the lowest part of the layer was marked by a deliberate attempt to create a relatively even ground surface. Layer II appears to constitute the fill on the ruined houses beneath the bath complex. Pottery from this layer dated from the second to the fourth century but also contained a coin tentatively dated to 375–83. There is reasonably good numismatic evidence that the baths were substantially modified in the early fifth century and again in the early seventh century. The baths continued in use for only a short period after this last rebuilding. The ashes from the heating system contained a coin of Justinian in its lower layers and a coin of Phokas (602–8) in its upper layers, showing that the heating system was working in the first decade of the seventh century. In the fill above the ashes was late Roman pottery and Arabic material, strongly suggesting that the heating system fell into disrepair before the Arab invasion, possibly c. AD 618. There is some textual evidence for extensive repair work and refurbishment of bath houses in the mid-fifth century, notably on the baths of Trajan or Gratian and of Diocletian (Calderini 1935–66: 105; Theophanes Confessor, *Chronicle* AM 5945 (AD 452–3); AM 5949 (AD 456–7); AM 5957 (AD 464–5); AM 5959 (AD 466–7); AM 5961 AD 468–9).[39] Lukaszewicz (1990) argues that the discovery of a tiny fragment of a monumental inscription with the letters 'TA' pointed to the erection of the baths during the reign of a member of the house of Constantine, though a series of receipts for jars (of oil?) which were headed Δ Διοκληπανός suggests that the baths might be associated with the emperor Diocletian, though the exact resolution of the heading is obscure (Lukaszewicz 1984).

The baths were built on foundations of another larger public building of uncertain purpose (Kolataj 1992: 103–14). Not only were the foundations of this building probably more extensive than those of the later bath house, but, where they were reused, they do not seem to have been entirely appropriate for the later structures. Kolataj argues that the very scanty remains of this building suggest that it was never finished, perhaps never progressing beyond the foundations, concluding that the baths 'were an imperial foundation, initiated by Constantine the Great and executed by Gratian' (p. 198). This suggests that for almost a century, the northern part of this *insula* was little more than a building site. Kiss (1992b), who plausibly identifies the theatre as a bouleuterion (council-chamber), would like to date the construction of the theatre somewhat earlier than the 'completion' of the baths under Gratian on both stylistic and historical grounds, perhaps to the late third or early fourth century.

The scale of the development is impressive. A whole block of the city was transformed from residential use to be dominated by opulent public buildings. Considerable political and financial muscle must have stood behind the development and we should perhaps associate the appropriation of the land for public purposes with major political upheaval, maybe problems in the mid-third century or in the siege and capture of Alexandria by Diocletian in the first years of the fourth century (Boak and Youtie 1960: 17–20; Schwartz 1975; John Malalas XII p. 309), a destruction which probably then involved the emperor in the considerable expense of repairs and perhaps even re-establishing some of the institutions of the city (*Chronicon Pascale*, p. 514 (AD 302). If we assume that the building projects had imperial patronage (as had most major constructions of this period), the 'pause' in building postulated by Kolataj becomes even more historically problematic.

The early sixth century saw further development with the construction of what the archaeologists have termed lecture rooms, slightly to the north and west of the baths (Kiss 1992a). These were long, thin chambers with seats down either side with a curved closed end, also with banked seats. The chambers were designed to focus the attention of an audience, of possibly some eighty people, on a narrow central passage. These structures seem so suited to declamation that it would be almost perverse to look for an alternative use and it would be attractive to imagine the prestigious teachers of philosophy who continued to operate in Alexandria until the early seventh century at work in buildings of this nature (Sheppard forthcoming; Roueché 1990; Haas 1997: 187–9; Zacharias, *Life of Severus*).

The block to the west of R4 had a rather different history. In the Roman period, the block was occupied by housing, probably very similar to that across the street under the baths and theatre. These houses appear to have survived into the fourth century. The later constructions, as described in the previous chapter, may have been a little later, perhaps developing during the fifth century, but were certainly occupied in the sixth century and beyond (see figure 3.18).[40] Narrow passageways from R4, and possibly from other streets, gave access to a dense network of alleys and rooms or houses punctuated with what can only be described as semi-public yards. Some of these yards were decorated and perhaps even contained some furnishings of a rather simple nature. Access to the yards was probably controlled and was certainly controllable. There was an obvious dichotomy between the network of alleys and rooms and the street, even if that street was narrowed by encroachment (Majcherek 1995). This was clearly a neighbourhood or part of a neighbourhood. The alleys and yards provided a certain architectural focus for the rooms clustered around them, which suggests a level of communality. Many of the occupants also appear to have shared a trade. Extensive remains of jewellery working, sometimes in metal and sometimes in ivory, shows that the area had an unusual concentration of jewellers' workshops, though our evidence is nowhere near sufficient to argue that all or even most of the residents were supported by such craft activities.

Alexandria, then, presents us with a complex and changing picture, though one must remember that the above survey has pulled together material from nearly seven centuries. There is little evidence that the administrative districts had much social significance until the rioting of AD 38 concentrated the Jewish population in Delta. Similar outbreaks of ethnic hostility may have led to further concentrations of the Jewish population over the next decades, though the completeness of this residential segregation is unclear. The treatment of the Jews changed the nature of the Delta district and the creation of a Jewish 'ghetto' removed Jewish influence from other quarters and so affected the spatiality of the whole city. Other areas of the city had their distinctive characters and at least some of these can be traced in Strabo's account. At Kom el-Dikke we can observe a district development from what seems to have been a reasonably prosperous Roman residential district into an area dominated by public buildings behind which there was lower-class housing and craft production. Those living in these houses appear to have shared at least some facilities. Outsiders may have found it difficult to gain access to the area and there may have been some shared economic and political interests through craft activity. Much remains speculative, but here, in the sixth–eighth centuries, we seem to see something that looks like a socially significant local community.

What is a neighbourhood?

Although there is abundant evidence that there were differentiated districts within the various cities, the social significance of those districts has not emerged clearly. Nevertheless, this inconclusiveness is not surprising and reflects something of the nature of neighbourhoods as intermediary and shifting socio-spatial structures between the house and the city. By refining our conceptions of the various types of socio-spatial entity that could be called 'neighbourhood', the material in the previous sections can be placed in an interpretative context through which we can, perhaps, begin to understand what these districts meant to their residents.

Neighbourhoods have become a political issue in modern society since the decline of neighbourhoods is seen as being related to an absence of a strong community which would integrate and socialize individuals. Neighbourhood decline is associated with an increase in social alienation and related problems of criminality and aggressive individualism. In part, this results from a romanticization of village culture and much intellectual energy has been devoted to planning for village-like communities within urban contexts. Neighbourhoods are, however, primarily social and mental constructs, and although constructing an identifiable district may be comparatively easy, developing the associations that turn a district into a socially significant neighbourhood is more complicated. A development at East Kilbride, in the outskirts of Glasgow, attempted to foster community spirit by signposting. Each street within the estate was also given an estate plate, identifying it as part of 'The Murray'. When surveyed, the estate's residents were able to define objectively 'The Murray' on a map. Nevertheless, their subjective reality was that the 'The Murray' did not form their neighbourhood (Lee 1976). In an experiment conducted in Cambridge, individuals were asked to plot their movements and their conceptions of their neighbourhood. The experiment showed that although there was agreement on some boundaries, neighbours had significantly different views of the topography of their neighbourhood (Lee 1976).

Pratt (1998) observes that transportation difficulties and responsibility for child care often means that women are more closely bound to localities than men and have a different pattern of interaction within a neighbourhood. A neighbourhood which may be of little social significance for a man may be the arena in which his partner spends most of her life. Incomers may also find it difficult to gain access to neighbourhood communities or find the transition creates tensions with their previous expectations and experience. My family found moving from a socially and ethnically cosmopolitan area of south London to a rather more homogeneous area west of London something of a shock, while my parents had a similar experience in moving from industrial north–west England to rural Wales, finding themselves suddenly an ethnic minority. Whereas these disjunctures had relatively mild effects, black friends and students moving from cosmopolitan to almost uniformly white areas have sometimes found themselves isolated. The presence of a minority with a different experience of a district and who perhaps might find it difficult to integrate in a neighbourhood does not, of course, threaten the perception of neighbourhood or of neighbourhood community: it simply means that some residents might be excluded or feel excluded from the dominant social groups within a particular district. Yet, even outwardly cosmopolitan neighbourhoods may be only transient and shallow communities which obscure deeper divisions. For instance, a study of a highly cosmopolitan neighbourhood which might, one would think, not exclude any individual or group, suggests that there were many micro-divisions within the neighbourhood and that its cosmopolitanism merely concealed numerous social and ethnic divisions which operated at the level of the block or even between buildings (Pratt 1998). Residents may be particularly sensitive to micro-divisions in districts. Of course, districts do not have to be socially or ethnically uniform to be neighbourhoods. Any community must accommodate a certain range of individuals and many (all?) communities will have some form of social hierarchy. Yet, infinite divisions and gradations (class, ethnic, religious, etc.) may overwhelm those social forces which hold a community together.

Some post-modernist geographers emphasize the flexibility that comes with the multiplicity of axes of differentiation. As individual identity can be constructed around race, ethnicity, gender, sexuality, age, economic status, profession, religion, etc., so individuals' patterns of behaviour in a particular district may change. Moreover, such individuals may construct their neighbourhoods in diverse ways and around different local centres so that even those who live in neighbouring residences may have dissimilar views of the topographical extent and character of their neighbourhoods. This may mean that the character of districts is a matter of considerable tension (Nager 1997; Jacobs 1998). Attempts in Los Angeles to operate fine topographical divisions between and within districts nicely illustrate the political problems. In the modern city, such divisions can have considerable financial implications as people will pay more money for a house with the 'right' address and local tax differentials may mean that houses attached to wealthy areas may be charged considerably less than similar houses nearby in a poorer district. Similarly the secession of a wealthy district may lead to the association of social problems with the newly defined poorer district, the further development of social stigma, and a depression of economic status (Davis 1992). Thus, many have an interest in establishing and publicizing fine distinctions between neighbourhoods and although sociologists and geographers have often looked for rather broad descriptive categories for districts, a plethora of different categories can be used. A recent collection of terms for American urban residential areas came up with twenty-five different categories and I am sure that more could be invented (Davies and Herbert 1993: 60). Moreover, established residential areas can change quite rapidly, without a complete change in their population.

One of the facts of urban life is that people move about. A resident of a certain area may choose to engage in most of his or her social activity in another area. So, in addition to normally perceived divisions of class and ethnicity, one could have a gay geography, or a lawyers' geography, or an academics' geography of the city and, of course, there is no reason to assume that individuals belong to just one group. The mobility of the urban population may also mean that districts change character in the course of a day. The result of this is to fracture the experience of the urban environment so that patterns of differentiation are likely to be extremely complex.

It may be argued that these perceptions reflect the disparate nature of the post-industrial city. In the West, the 'post-industrial' economy has encouraged the decline of the 'company town'. Light industry and retail and service sectors typically require a different workforce, with a more varied skills base and, therefore, different levels of educational attainment. Generally, each firm requires far fewer workers. Even in traditional industries, multi-centre production and the computerization of production have both reduced the workforce of the traditional factory and dispersed that workforce over many production centres. Moreover, improvements in the transportation network have enabled a greater division between place of work and residence. This flexibility and mobility are not limited to economic matters. Telecommunications have brought services, entertainment and community to the home in ways unimaginable a hundred years ago. Patterns of intimacy have changed. Many in the industrial West communicate more often and more intimately with people living hundreds if not thousands of miles off than with those living yards away. We no longer depend on our neighbours for significant personal relationships, but can travel outside the local district. This freedom allows different social networks to be developed which have nothing to do with locality. Nevertheless, if residence is no longer so closely constrained by the location of work, then there is greater opportunity for people to make choices in their residential location so that areas may come to attract people of certain types. The post-industrial city, perhaps to a far greater extent than its industrial precursor, would seem to be a city of districts, some of which are of contested character, some of which are in flux, and those districts may be home to communities which experience similar change. For some, the residential neighbourhood may be a crucial part of their identity, while others may choose not to participate in local social networks or be excluded from those local networks and seek social networks centred away from their residence. This disparate experience of neighbourhoods appears to be a function of the particular conjunction of social and political forces in the post-modern city. It is not, therefore, an understanding that one would naturally transpose to our study of other social systems.

Nevertheless, the post-modern experience of neighbourhoods does, I think, suggest that neighbourhoods are socially negotiable, as well as reflecting the predominant social divisions within a particular society. Thus, one might expect not only that an ethnically divided society would have districts with distinct ethnic characters, but also that such divisions would be disputed. The division of a city into local communities would, therefore, be untidy and this expectation is confirmed by comparative historical studies. The cities of late medieval and early modern Italy, for instance, displayed their political division spectacularly in the urban landscape. Various noble lineages constructed towers, often very thin and extremely high, which acted as defensive installations in their constant feuding and vendettas (Lansing 1991). Yet the towers served more than just a practical purpose: their height led to their domination of the landscape, challenging the churches and perhaps other urban institutions for control of the skyline. Their frequency marked the division of the city into warring groups and was a potent symbol of the collective power of the aristocracy. They were symbols that more popular governments, acting against the feuds, literally cut down to size. Nevertheless, the relationship between the towers and the neighbourhoods in which they were situated was not simple.[41] A map of property owned by particular noble families near the Mercato Vecchio in Florence shows that even families such as the Medici did not have exclusive control of large blocks of property and that although there was an obvious, if small, concentration of Medici property, other noble families had houses between Medici residences. Noble families controlled numerous extremely small and disparate areas of the city. There also appear to have been at least two principles behind the creation of districts: aristocratic competition and a less hierarchical system of mutual aid between neighbours of similar social status. In Genoa, aristocratic extended families would share a tower and associated living quarters, whereas artisanal families lived in far smaller residential groups. Aristocratic women in Genoa tended to look to family members to provide them with legal support in their property dealings, while artisanal women looked to neighbours. 'Horizontal' social ties between neighbours appear to have been important for the lower classes.

Northern European medieval and early modern cities exhibited similar complexity. Although it is often assumed that medieval towns were dominated by powerful guilds, as represented in the elaborate guildhalls, and at least some medieval urban planners believed that this was the proper way of organizing the city, a survey of medieval German towns produced remarkably little evidence of the topographical concentration of specific trade groups (Denecke 1988). Langton (1975) argues that the presumed medieval model did not apply in seventeenth-century British towns either. Instead, there appears rather to have been limited zoning by wealth, perhaps suggesting an emergent class division within the cities. This pattern can certainly be seen in seventeenth-century London where the central and western districts of the city grew increasingly prosperous and benefited from investment in housing and the urban infrastructure, while the east progressively fell behind. Baigent's (1988) study of Bristol in the 1770s shows clearly that there was an uneven distribution of wealth in the city. The wealthiest suburbs were in the centre of the city (mainly occupied by traditional if prosperous artisans) and to the west, while the east was generally impoverished. Yet there was a substantial admixture in the various parishes. Social zoning was not absolute.

Pooley (1982) examines the problem of social zoning in nineteenth-century Liverpool. Since Liverpool grew rapidly in the nineteenth century and was at the forefront of the industrial revolution, it might be expected that it would show a high degree of residential segregation by class. There appears to have been very little class segregation by parish, but Pooley (1982) detected clusters of ethnic groups, social classes and particular trades by blocks and streets. It was in the later years of the nineteenth century and in the early twentieth century that the development of suburbs (and presumably transport networks) encouraged a middle-class flight from the urban centre, though enclaves of prosperity remained in grand Georgian terraces.[42] The relative absence of clearly defined class-based neighbourhoods appears to be a general characteristic of the early nineteenth-century city. Cannadine (1982) points out that the clarity with which nineteenth-century urban divisions were perceived by contemporaries and the difficulties facing modern historians in giving statistical weight to those perceptions parallel the clarity with which contemporaries viewed class differences and the infinite variegations with which the historian and sociologist are confronted. These cities present a parallel paradox to the post-modern cities since although all would accept that differentiated districts existed within cities, it is difficult to construct clear and agreed principles which differentiate those districts or to produce any agreement on the topographical boundaries and social significance of those districts.

These examples contrast starkly with the powerful neighbourhoods of many cities of the Near East. These cities sometimes give the impression of a series of boxes of ever-increasing size, starting with the family residence, the apartment block or house, the street, the quarter and the city. The quarters and the streets within them were often gated, creating private networks of communication and symbolizing a securing of the neighbourhood and its unity (Mitchell 1988: 56; Abu Lughod 1971: 64). Sixteenth-century Damascus had about seventy quarters in the city proper and thirty in a suburb, which compares to Aleppo with more than fifty. Some neighbourhoods had an ethnic basis. Jewish quarters were common in many cities and even these might be differentiated by type of Jew. Other quarters might have some pseudo-ethnic connections, perhaps with an associated rural area or with a particular religious or national origin (el-Messiri 1977; Lapidus 1984: 85–95). Late eighteenth-century Cairo was divided into fifty-three *harat* (quarters), each of which contained several *durub*, and each *darb* had about thirty houses (Abu Lughod 1971: 64). Fakhouri's (1985) study of a modern Cairene neighbourhood, the Darb el-Ahmar, shows that the alleys are playgrounds and courtyards, where the women sit, work and chat, while the children play. The men, however, occupy their own space, the corner coffee house. In spite of the rapid growth of Cairo during the twentieth century (from 1,071,000 in 1927 to 6,105,000 in 1985) and the quadrupling of population density, Darb el-Ahmar shows a high level of residential continuity, with two-thirds of male heads of households being born either in the district or in neighbouring districts, and most households have close family ties within the district. The *darb* and *harah* remain fundamental social organizations in Cairo, even though many of the gates have gone. The inhabitants may be socially and economically diverse, but the ties to the *darb* are so strong and fundamental that individuals are reluctant to abandon their local social networks. The community of the *darb* exercises a powerful normative influence. Its members are disciplined by the threat of exclusion from the social networks through which individuals function within Cairene society. These networks arbitrate disputes, arrange marriages, provide elementary social security, aid interactions with bureaucracy and the state, and form the core of much economic activity (Singerman 1995).

In spite of the complexity of neighbourhood formation observable in the historical and modern evidence, perhaps the most popular and familiar explanation for the formation of neighbourhoods suggests that neighbourhoods were typologically similar and 'natural' consequences of urban life. This model became influential through the work of the Chicago school and sociologists such as Gideon Sjoberg (1960) (to be discussed in the last section of this chapter). By contrast, the evidence presented in this section suggests that neighbourhoods are created by political processes and, since the process of politics so often entails compromise, debate, contentiousness and perhaps even policy reversals, neighbourhoods are often not clearly defined. Neighbourhoods need unifying features to give them an identity and those features may be ascribed (association with criminality, social deprivation or social exclusivity, etc.) or generated from within the community (through community organizations such as a mosque, church, coffee house, public house, school, etc.). We should expect to see an immense variety of processes at work which would result in many different types of neighbourhood. Moreover, it seems that establishing the existence of neighbourhoods and perhaps even their principle axes of differentiation from their surrounding neighbourhoods is insufficient to understand them; rather we need some measure of their social significance. To what extent was membership of a neighbourhood important to its residents? Here, again, we are faced with a variety of levels of significance, from the apparently powerful neighbourhoods of Cairo and similar cities to the virtual insignificance of neighbourhood in some modern, post-industrial contexts. The woman who commutes to work in the central business district of a city, who shops in its centralized retail districts, who socializes using the entertainment facilities variously located within the city, and who sleeps, washes, dresses, watches television and stores her personal possessions in her residence, may find neighbourhood something of an irrelevance in her everyday life. Whereas the gated quarter from which a woman may have strayed rarely and in which her friends and family and work were located, must have been very important in some pre-modern Near Eastern cities. This is not simply a modern or post-modern as against pre-modern dichotomy, as those who cannot find employment, insure their property, or get police protection or adequate social services because their residence is in the wrong district could affirm. We are thus left with a very loosely defined conception of neighbourhoods and an impression of the variety of historical experiences and sociological forms of these communities.

Conclusion I: neighbourhoods

Where does this leave the districts and neighbourhoods of the Romano-Egyptian cities of Egypt? The short answer is that I do not know. The imperfections of the evidence are such that we cannot reach anything but the simplest conclusions with confidence. I think, however, that we can, with a certain caution, progress a little further. There were topographically defined administrative units in the Roman and Byzantine city and district administration functioned into the sixth century and possibly beyond. The administrative structures of the mid-first century continued to operate, though modified at various times, until at least the end of the fourth century, after which a new system of administrative districts was introduced. Both systems were closely related to topographical divisions within the city.

It is difficult to know whether these districts had an ascribed social character or an internal community. There is some reason to believe that there was a measure of ethnic segregation in the cities of Roman Egypt. Although it does not appear that the Jews of Alexandria were particularly concentrated before AD 38 (the stories of looting of Jewish property, desecration of synagogues and enforced migration across the city make sense only if the Jewish community was comparatively dispersed prior to the riots), the difference between Josephus' rhetoric and that of Philo may reflect Josephus' experience of a topographically concentrated Jewish community. One would assume that the violence of AD 38 and later would have encouraged Jews to seek safety in numbers. There is good circumstantial evidence that the massacre of the Jews in Alexandria in 116–17 was replicated in other communities across Egypt (Alston 1995: 75–7), and there is a suspicion that anti-semitic texts and the letter of Claudius, which primarily concern Alexandria but were preserved on papyri found in the *chora*, reflect attitudes prevalent throughout Egypt (Hanson 1992).[43] The Jews, however, may be a special case. The Ptolemaic settlements of various ethnic groups in communities throughout Egypt may have founded ethnic neighbourhoods. However, these ethnic groups disappear from much of the papyrological and epigraphic record during the second century BC, and although ethnic divisions were recalled in the names of the *amphoda* of Roman Oxyrhynchus and Ptolemais Euergetis, they probably survived as traces of the past of the city.[44]

There is no other evidence to suggest that the administrative districts correlated with significant social divisions within the cities. The most obvious possible divisions in the cities of the Roman period were economic, ancestral and cultural (Greek–Egyptian). The nature of cultural divisions within Roman Egypt is problematic and it is enough here to note that the gymnasial group, probably the most 'Greek' in the population, did not dominate specific *amphoda*. The same may be said for ancestral divisions. We cannot see any real or fictive family ties holding *amphoda* together and the *amphoda* appear to have been too large to have been identified with a single family. Also, as we saw in the last chapter (pp. 92–3), families moved across the city. Our knowledge of trade and economic groups is even more scanty. Particular types of traders appear to have clustered together and we would certainly expect some concentration of retailing, as is displayed in many ancient cities, but the Panopolis material suggests that such clusters were small. The evidence appears overwhelming: if the *amphoda* of the Roman and late Roman periods were also neighbourhoods, then they were not of a socially uniform type. They were heterogeneous and this, of course, makes them more difficult to identify.

There are good grounds for exercising considerable caution here. Our evidence is scanty and drawn from seven centuries and one must assume that the situation changed over this period. In addition, our information about *amphoda* relates to their administrative functions while our primary interest is in neighbourhoods. There is no *prima facie* reason to believe that the *amphoda* would correspond to neighbourhoods, nor that there were neighbourhoods (as opposed to topographical or administrative districts) within the city at all. We are thus looking for traces of a social entity that may have had no parallel within the administrative systems of the city, and since the vast majority of our documentation is generated by that administration, those traces may be very faint. We might either over-interpret those traces or miss them altogether. What follows rests, therefore, on somewhat less than firm foundations.

The *amphoda* of Oxyrhynchus, Ptolemais Euergetis and probably Kynopolis appear to have been constructed around a single street or a defined and small topographical area within the city. It seems very likely that these *amphoda* would contain both the eponymous street and a network of other, less important streets. The streets were public space. House-sale contracts enshrine rights of access to the public space of the street. But 'public' is a flexible concept and may range from 'communal' (space controlled by a specific community within the city), to civic (belonging to the whole city), to completely free and unrestricted space (such as wasteland). The use of colonnades and orthogonally planned streets marks a claim to the street as civic space rather than as communal space. The rhetoric of the city dominates, but rhetoric can be ignored.

The presence of gatehouses and high house walls would not immediately suggest that streets were extensions of the private areas of houses. The distinction seems very marked and is further stressed by Philo. His discussion of the Jewish community leads us to believe that women, even married women, only ventured into the street at their peril (see pp. 100–1), even when in support of their spouse. But Philo represents the Jewish limitation on female access to the street as unusual and deserving of further elucidation. It is tempting to see in this a contrast with the behaviour of Alexandrian or Egyptian women more generally. Plutarch, *Moralia* 353D = *De Iside et Osiride* 7, tells us that on 9 Thoth the Egyptian population would eat fish in front of the αὔλειον. The αὔλειον was a court or doorway of a court and this may mean that fish was eaten in the gatehouse, but, in the Classical Greek Plutarch aspired to, αὔλειον means the outer door and hence places the fish-eating festival in the street. It was to the street that many would go to find witnesses for contracts, which suggests that it was comparatively easy to assemble a crowd. People could meet and argue, and violent altercations could occur on the street, but it is unclear whether the street context of such activity is the result of chance meetings or whether people spent much of their time on the street. When those determined on violence approached, they tended to bring with them an axe to break down a door (though an approach of an angry group might well encourage anyone sitting or standing in the street to scurry inside rapidly).

In some societies, religious ceremonies would bring people onto the street. In Rome, for instance, Augustus encouraged the development of the *Lares Compitalia*, which gave a religious aspect to the refounded *vici* with the *vicomagistri*. These shrines were quite prominent in Pompeii, which had a very similar pattern of district organization to that of Rome (Laurence 1994: 39–42). There is no very obvious parallel evidence from the *amphoda*, though the wholesale importation of Roman civic administration in the creation of the *metropoleis* would lead one to suspect that such shrines might have existed. There were, however, numerous shrines within the cities. Even if we ignore the extraordinary *c.* 2,400 'temples' of Alexandria (see above), *P. Berol. Bork.* lists eight 'temples' in the 411 plots of Panopolis registered, about one temple for every fifty houses, and these temples were fairly evenly distributed across the area of the city. The temples and shrines of Oxyrhynchus (Whitehorne 1995; see figure 5.5) were also dispersed, though with two main centres. Excavations at Hermopolis uncovered a small Domitianic temple of traditional Egyptian style in the south of the city whereas the main concentration of temples was to the north (Snape 1989). There is no evidence, as far as I know, that would allow us to establish how these temples functioned and for whom they catered. Dispersal in itself does not mean that the temples had a local catchment area and the temples may have been distributed across the city because of coincidences in the availability of land, money and the desire to invest in a new temple. Nevertheless, the proliferation of religious sites within the context of a city physically dominated by one or two major religious enclosures suggests that these shrines might not just have given identity to a district but also provided a focus for a neighbourhood.

Another obviously communal issue is the supply of water. Laurence (1994: 42–50), in showing that the water fountains of Pompeii were distributed throughout the city so that most people were within 80 m of a water supply, argued that the residential area that used a particular fountain might correspond to the localized neighbourhoods in the city of Pompeii and that 'This pattern of local divisions in the city would have been established by the manner in which the fountains were originally distributed by the designer' (p. 50). The location of fountains was not obviously related to any pre-existing neigh-bourhood division and Laurence's argument is that the location of these fountains either shaped or reshaped the neighbourhood geography of the city. The water supply within the cities of Egypt is little understood. Roeder's (1959: 28; 33; 123–5; Taf. 12) excavation of Hermopolis uncovered four water towers and numerous pipes, suggesting that a great deal of water was distributed around the city.[45] *P. Lond.* III, pp. 180–90, 1177 (= *W. Chr.* 193) of AD 113 from Ptolemais Euergetis gives details of the administration and finances of the water supply for that city. The text records a contract with four men to supply water. We have some details about the supply of water to a single water tower, that of Alsos. The tower was supplied with sixteen water-raising machines. Over 1,000 man-days of labour were paid for in a single month, 797 for day shifts and 306 for night shifts. Two machines were powered by oxen. There was at least one other water tower, that of Telesos. The water was supplied to baths, to the brewery in the temple of Serapis, to the synagogue and related institutions, and to three fountains (in the *dromos* (of the temple of Souchos?), the street of the temple of Kleopatra, and the street of the Macedonians). The supply of water seems mainly to have been paid for by contributions from the major officials of the city, the gymnasiarch, the *kosmetai* and the *exegetes*, but there were also contributions from those who used the water. The various fountains contributed 9 obols a day each. It is not obvious how this charge was collected. Only one of the named streets was recognized as being at the centre of an *amphodon* (Makedonon), though the street of the temple of Kleopatra was clearly topographically important and remained so into the Byzantine period. It seems unlikely that the fountains were particularly grand monuments: the difficulties of raising water to produce significant pressure would have complicated engineering. More likely, these fountains supplied drinking water to their districts. The collection of potable water and of water for other domestic purposes was a major task in most pre-industrial cities and it would seem possible that such facilities would form a focus for the people of a district.[46]

The relationship between neighbourhoods, temples and fountains, is, of course speculative. Better evidence for socially significant districts relates to very small-scale clusters of associated individuals, as is attested at Panopolis for certain trade groups and for members of the elite. One might, therefore, envisage social zoning at the level of the block. This pattern may be reflected in a complex archive of material from Karanis. Peter van Minnen's (1994; cf. Rowlandson 1998: 91; *P. Mich.* III 169; Strassi Zaccaria 1991) study of House B17 and its surroundings shows that this house was occupied by Sokrates son of Sarapion, who appears to have been an important figure within the village. Van Minnen plausibly connects this man (or his family) to a Sempronia Gemella who lived across a junction from him and who named her illegitimate twin sons Marcus Sempronius Sokrates and Marcus Sempronius Sarapion. This would suggest some connection between Gemella and Sokrates, though not necessarily that he was the father of the twins.[47] At such a local level, very small non-random distributions may have been significant. For instance, we see groupings of metal workers and naval workers at Panopolis but no evidence for large-scale concentrations of traders either in a 'business district' or in trade-specific districts. A number of first-century AD weavers operated in districts near the temple of Serapis in Oxyrhynchus, though it would be to push the evidence too far to suggest that the temple was at the centre of a weavers' district.[48] Nevertheless, the fact that one of the main markets of the city was situated on the *dromos* (Rea 1982) of the temple would encourage us to see the concentration as significant.

There is more evidence of institutions that may have formed a focus for neighbourhood feeling in the Byzantine period. Perhaps as many as nineteen of the new districts of Ptolemais Euergetis were named after Christian institutions. The prevalence of churches in Oxyrhynchus and Ptolemais Euergetis (see pp. 134–8) suggests, like the prevalence of temples, a religious topography of the city that could be mobilized to form neighbourhoods. One is on firmer ground with the archaeological remains. The intricate network of passages and rooms at Kom el-Dikke (see pp. 112–16) and the spread of material suggesting the production of jewellery or other precious trinkets gives some impression of a community, or at least a group of people with shared interests. The difficulties of differentiating public and private space at Kom el-Dikke also point to an intermediate space, a space to be filled by neighbours. A similar pattern might be suggested for the houses in the courtyard of the temple of Chnum (see pp. 116–18). Although here there is no difficulty in distinguishing between public and private in that the individual units seem to be more firmly separate houses, yet the alleys that give access to those houses do not appear to have been fully public. One can hardly imagine them as thoroughfares. Similarly, at Jeme (see pp. 119–20), the narrow alleys and the shared courtyards blur the boundaries between the public and the private, boundaries which one might assume were clear in law. The gradual encroachment of private dwellings or shops onto the public spaces of streets is a well-known phenomenon from early Byzantine urban sites elsewhere in the Roman empire (see below), and was probably a feature of Egyptian cities (Saradi 1998; Majcherek 1995). If the ordered, colonnaded thoroughfares of the Classical cities bespoke powerful urban administrations, so the intricacies of Kom el-Dikke, of the temple of Chnum and of Jeme represent communities knowable only to the insider, communities one might class as neighbourhoods. Here, of course, we are adrift from any positivistic mass of factual data, but the emergence of an Agora Skuteon at Oxyrhynchus, for example, suggests a concentration of cobblers, and seems slightly more plausible than gooseherders (Chenoboskion) and shepherds (Poimenikes) flocking together at Oxyrhynchus and Ptolemais Euergetis. Monasteries and churches may have created enclaves in which the devout resided and the impression often given is of cities surrounded by Christian institutions, which, given the somewhat fractious nature of early Christianity, may have not been completely integrated into the wider Christian community.

Yet this is only half the battle. We have identified a spectrum of different neighbourhood organizations and experiences of neighbourhood. None of the neighbourhoods identified appear to have the powerful presence of the gated neighbourhoods of some Near Eastern cities. In the Roman period, one can discern only small pockets of segregated communities and possibly the closest parallel would be the pattern of nineteenth-century Liverpool (Pooley 1982), where zoning was not observable at district level but could be seen at the level of the block. Nineteenth-century observers saw the city as socially divided and the attempts to evangelize the urban poor at the heart of the imperial metropolis imply a perception of major socio-spatial disjunctions within the metropolis. Would, then, the slight concentrations observable in fourth-century Panopolis be enough to give contemporaries the impression of social segregation within the city? As with class, people have a surprising sensitivity to minuscule gradations, sensitivities which often render crude bipartite or tripartite class analyses laughably unreal to those analysed. I don't think there is sufficient evidence to come to any conclusion about the Roman period, but there appears to be just enough to suggest that there were significant neighbourhoods in late Roman cities. The Byzantine period is more complex, but perhaps we should interpret our inevitably crude evidence as signifying powerful Byzantine neighbourhoods that significantly influence the social identities of their inhabitants.

Conclusion II: the unitary city?

One of the most influential studies of the development of neighbourhoods and districts is that of the sociologists of the so-called Chicago school (Burgess et al. 1925; see also Davies and Herbert 1993: 39–40), who regarded districts and neighbourhoods as evolving because of 'natural' social and economic processes, such as common desires for the more spacious environments of the outskirts or to restrict journey times to the central zone. These processes would initially and inevitably encourage development of workers' areas on the outskirts of the business district, which would eventually be overstepped by the 'flight to the suburbs', leaving a zone of poorer, less well-maintained housing, leading to a further decline in the status of an inner ring of housing which would, in turn, encourage the wealthier to head to suburban developments. Broadly, a city could be divided into concentric zones with a central business district, and then various grades of housing. In outline, the model is very simple, but the reality is more complex as factors such as ethnic groupings and communication corridors add layers of complexity. Nevertheless, such an evolutionary model can be used to explain geographical events, such as the gentrification of some urban districts as property prices in the suburbs soar and the young wealthy take advantage of cheap property and shorter journey times from the inner cities (Smith 1996). Although there are many problems with the Chicago model, as one might expect in a sociology now nearly eight decades old, its methodology and assumptions were influential, as can be seen in Gideon Sjoberg's (1960) work on the pre-industrial city. Sjoberg's analysis is essentialist, attempting to reduce the many and various pre-industrial urban phenomena to a series of general laws and a single morphological type. Sjoberg's city (Sjoberg 1960: 97–101) has a central religious institution or institutions which dominate economic functions, physically and institutionally, and form a focal point around which the elite cluster. Poorer groups are pushed to the outskirts of the city, which is further divided into ethnic or trade groups with rigorous segregation. This is a city of neighbourhoods dominated by a powerful central authority.

It is, of course, a truism and an article of faith of urban human geography that, as Herbert and Johnson (1976: 5) state, 'the urban landscape is a mirror reflecting the society which maintains it', but to reduce cities to broad morphological types, such as the pre-industrial city, the medieval city, the capitalist city and the post-modern city, stresses characteristics that various cities have in common (technologies for instance) at the expense of our lived experience of a multiplicity of different urban phenomena and the manifest differences between historical cities which should correspond to the same essential type. The approach also naturalizes the social processes that lead to the creation of cityscapes so that a city comes to be more a function of the particular economic world-system (capitalism, pre-capitalism, or whatever) than of any particular historical, political, geographic or social factors. The basic social assumption of the Chicago school was of class segregation onto which ethnic segregation was mapped as a further complicating factor and, since class was economically determined, so residence was a function of the economy. This ignores the value of other forces, e.g. history, family ties, patronal and political relations, which may influence patterns of residence and reduce the scope of human agency in shaping environments.[49] Harvey (1973: 137–40) argues that the Chicago model conceals the very 'unnatural' workings of the capitalist economy and that altering the ground-rules of that economy, by, for instance, radical rent reform, would reshape the distribution of population across a city. It is worth noting that the processes that have led to the development of large, economically distinct districts, as envisaged by the Chicago school, have often been administrative and political rather than purely economic. In many British and at least some American cities planned developments have had a major influence on residential patterns from the mid-nineteenth century. Various agencies were responsible for these projects, but whether it be state provision of social housing, which has arguably been one of the most significant factors in shaping the twentieth-century Western city, or industrial companies constructing housing for their workforce, or financial institutions sponsoring the development of 'suburban' housing, these projects have normally been aimed at specific social classes and thus have notably accentuated class residential segregation. In the United States, 'zoning regulations' and the politics of race have also significantly contributed to the social and economic differentiation of districts (Davis 1992).

Apart from the general theoretical problems, the major difficulty with Sjoberg's analysis is that it does not describe adequately some pre-industrial cities. The cities of Roman and Byzantine Egypt look somewhat different from the Sjoberg model and the spread of the elite across some medieval and some Roman towns appears to contradict its basic tenets. I know of no city of the Greek and Roman world which would show the type of radical division into neighbourhoods exhibited by some Near Eastern cities and which Sjoberg seems to take as axiomatic for the pre-industrial city (Hughes 1978; Jongman 1988: 289–311; Mouritsen 1988: 67–8; Wallace-Hadrill 1994: 77–8; Laurence 1994: 131–2; Alston and Alston 1997), and even in the Near Eastern cities, there are variations and exceptions: Cairo, for instance, does not appear to have displayed ethnic segregation (Goitein 1969; Lapidus 1969). The reductionist techniques of Sjoberg and the Chicago school, perhaps influenced by Weber, seem to place unwarranted emphasis on the economic structures of urbanism and although one would not deny the importance of economics in urban life, the direct link between economic structures and the patterns of district formation in pre-industrial cities is not obvious.[50] Rather, districts and neighbourhoods appear to be formed through the interaction of rather more complicated social forces. Communities need purpose to form; they do not just evolve.[51]

Timms (1976) argues that residential segregation allows groups to increase their visibility and to define their identity more clearly. Residential segregation (which could either be imposed on or emerge from within a community) is therefore a political process. Neighbourhoods are, then, a political statement of identity, and a way of defining particular groups. As Nager (1997: 709) writes, 'a place does not exist by itself. It is constantly reshaped in response to the changing social interrelations at all geographic locations.' Neighbourhoods are contested space and in contestation with the wider city. The existence of such contestation would seem to run counter to the ideal of the unitary city, suggesting a fragmented political structure and that individual identities of citizens would be formed through social interactions in differentiated districts rather than in the city as a whole. If a unitary city with weak neighbourhoods displays the power of the city (or rather those who control it), then the city of neighbourhoods may seem a city out of control (or rather out of central control) and thus perhaps more volatile. This is, however, a fundamentally Western dichotomy built on the experience of colonialism and although the workings of power in the city of neighbourhoods may be more diffuse, they are no less real than in the unitary city.

When Western travellers visited the cities of the East in the late nineteenth century, they were shaken. Mitchell argues that the visitors had to learn a whole new language of urbanism, but instead of that language 'speaking' to them, they found cities which had no message and no explicit grammar by which they could deconstruct the language.

> The separation of an observer from an object world was something a European experienced in terms of a code or plan. He expected there to be something that was somehow set apart from 'things themselves' as a guide, a sign, a map, a text, or as a set of constructions about how to proceed. But in the Middle Eastern city nothing stood apart that addressed itself in this way to the outsider, to the observing subject. There were no names to the streets and no street signs, no open spaces with imposing façades and no maps. The city refused to offer itself

in this way as a representation of something, because it had not been built as one.

(Mitchell 1988: 32)

Instead of being cities with obvious centres, built to reflect the control of some dominant cultural or political institution, these cities were multi-focal. Such a city is often labelled 'Islamic', but the label is unsatisfactory since it is closely related to Occidental preconceptions of the Orient so convincingly decon- structed by Said (1978; 1993). An Orient lacking in order and labyrinthine in construction corresponds to stereotypes of the 'Oriental' character of which nineteenth-century adventurers and imperialists were so fond. Yet, although many examples of this urban form can be derived from the Near Eastern Islamic societies, there is little that is distinctively Islamic about it. It would not be hard to find examples of similarly confused layouts from the cities of medieval Europe, for instance, where the Church and town authorities normally took little interest in town planning. Here, again, patchwork development took place, though it is difficult to assess the strength of neighbourhood organi- zations. One could also look to the early and unplanned industrial quarters of towns such as Salford (Engels 1971; Roberts 1971) for later examples of urban sprawl. Moreover, as Al Sayyad (1992), Kennedy (1985a) and others have shown, the Islamic conquerors of the seventh and later centuries were interested in fostering urban development in their newly acquired territories, probably for very similar reasons that Rome and the Hellenistic empires promoted urban growth (prestige and finance), and laid out new cities. Cairo, paradoxically the paradigm of an unplanned Islamic city for many early Orientalists, was initially, as it is now, a planned city (Al Sayyad 1992). Troops laid it out in a single day, according to legend. It was a rough square of 340 acres, 70 acres of which were palace and 70 acres were palatial gardens. The mosque was constructed opposite the palace across a square. The residential quarters were laid out by the military. Only after the tenth century did the city begin to lose its regularities and develop its flourishing commercial sector (Al Sayyad 1992). Fustat, which was eventually to merge with Cairo, seems to have been a much less rigorously planned settlement, showing the irregularities that were later to be seen as characteristic of Eastern cities. Yet, as Kennedy has shown for cities in Syria, the breakdown of the Classicism of urban plans may have pre-dated the Islamic conquest (Kennedy 1985a; 1985b; cf. Bouras 1981; Claude 1969; Pentz 1992). The differences between the multi-focal and the unitary cities encourage a series of dichotomous oppositions: Oriental : Occidental; Classical : Islamic; ordered : disordered; planned : evolutionary. Yet, these cities were not polar opposites. All cities are social products and even seemingly haphazard, patchwork development has a social rationale. David Ley argues that

The overriding commitment of spatial analysis in urban geography has been to uncover regularities in spatial relations and not to process studies. But this is to make the prior assumption that there is something in some way significant about spatial form in its own right. A recent critique by both humanistic and Marxian writers has commented that the urban form in itself is not as important a category as spatial analysts have claimed, for spatial form is not an end in itself, but an expression, a consequence of something else – the prevailing forces in society.

(Ley 1983: 7)

Thus, although there may be morphological similarities between Italian hill towns and the cities of medieval Egypt, at other levels there are profound differences. It is, of course, allowable to speak of an Islamic city to the extent that the social and cultural forces that moulded the cities of the Middle East and North Africa were themselves functions of Islamic politics and culture. Concerns about the status of and access to the women of the family, attitudes towards the family, and the relationship with the citywide political and social institutions, such as the mosque and the state, were clearly influenced by similar cultural values, but there can only be an Islamic city to the extent that there was a unitary Islamic society and political culture. Those structural and social relations may have some parallels with contemporary Western urbanism, but the social development of the Christian West notably diverged from that of the Islamic East. In Cairo, for instance, the political power of the mosque and its identification with the state was symbolized by the positioning of the mosque across the square from the palace, producing a monumental centre to the city of which any Classical potentate would have been proud. The state allowed and even manipulated the development of urban quarters, but did not seek to display or demonstrate its control (or did not have the power) to reshape radically the city and impose an orthogonal plan. Yet, the urban space of these cities was not 'organic': it was formed by political structures and the operation of power. It was these political and cultural structures that imposed and spread certain ideologies. Western perceptions of a seeming anarchy in street plan signifying an anarchic lifestyle could not be further from the truth. Many Islamic societies had powerful normative forces and rigorous control of domestic behaviour, as is reflected for mid-twentieth-century Cairo in the novels of Mahfouz. What was rather different was that those normative forces operating within these cities and quarters were largely beyond the control of the Western (or indeed any other) administrator.

Unsurprisingly, Western governments have tended to be rather hostile to cities of the multi-focal type. Colonial governments were conscious of their inability to exercise power in the various neighbourhoods and viewed this as a considerable weakness. The coffee houses and quarters, the society the government could not penetrate, could be used to foster active or passive resistance. This comes as no surprise if one accepts the above argument that the multi-focal city was also a product of political dispute.[52] Colonial governments, often under-resourced, found control of these local powers rather difficult. In 1840, Bowring (quoted in Mitchell 1988: 41) complained that it was impossible to enumerate the population since the Egyptians were unwilling to let civil servants into the harem.[53] Government could not control the traditional house and could not measure the Egyptian population. This provides a clear example of cultural resistance. Instead of being opposed by what they could recognize and treat as a clearly political organization, the British authorities met entrenched cultural values around which the Egyptians structured their resistance. The British were unwilling and perhaps unable to mobilize sufficient political and military force to overcome that opposition.

The colonial response to such resistance and the response of many other powerful states in different areas of the world was to disrupt pre-existing social networks by reorganizing the spatialities of communities. This is exactly what happened in modern Cairo, in Alexandria and in many other cities of the non-Western world, but it can also be seen at lower levels of society. For instance, the British pioneered the modern establishment of model villages in Egypt. New styles of houses were constructed and laid out 'scientifically' (however the Egyptian villagers chose to use them) and a clear hierarchy was established with four grades of houses. Such developments went hand in hand with the establishment of a local police force and army, the imposition of regulations affecting the freedoms of the peasantry, and the creation of a new education system (Mitchell 1988: 45).

Tensions between city and neighbourhood political organizations are common. Le Corbusier planned an entirely 'rational' new morphology for Algiers, replacing the alleys and courtyards of the medieval centre with avenues and squares and introducing an efficient modern transport system to bring the European workforce from their village to the city proper. New houses were to be built for the Algerians, boxes for living in, which ignored the various complexities of existing family structures. The plan was never put into effect and the French authorities had to fight the guerrillas of the independence movement in the maze of alleys and courtyards of the old city (Lamprakos 1992). In Zanzibar, the British similarly reshaped the old town and attempted to impose new administrative structures to bring order to the perceived chaos (Myers 1994). In Kathmandu, the populations of the 'village-like spatial segments' (known as *twa:*), there being networks of narrow streets centred on squares, formed the political organizations that lay behind the comparatively successful revolutionary movement of 1990. The physical structure of the areas prevents large numbers of troops being deployed quickly to suppress demonstrations and arrest political leaders (Routledge 1994). In mid-seventeenth-century Haarlem, the civic authorities acted first to lessen the influence of neighbourhood organizations (*gebuurten*) and then to close them down altogether, partly on the excuse that they held unruly gatherings (Dorren 1998). Hausmann's Paris cut through the old, riot-torn and revolutionary city with broad avenues and squares, convenient for cavalry and cannon, but which also gave the city a new monumental focus and structure, a process carried to its logical conclusion with Washington D.C. The first 'rationalization' of Cairo's street plan was conducted by the Napoleonic administrators, eager to be able to march their troops safely through the city (Abu Lughod 1971: 84).

Nevertheless, although in the West it has been traditional to see neighbourhoods as loci that could be mobilized against the central power in the city, they are not necessarily antipathetic to the ruling authorities. When the excavators at Kom el-Dikke first uncovered the residential quarter, the evidence of Christianity was so overwhelming that they believed they had uncovered a monastic institution and their reassessment of the site led Rodziewicz (1988) to question the identification of other 'monastic' sites in the region. The Christianity of the occupants was obvious and displayed. Neighbourhoods can be mobilized to impose cultural norms, as in the Islamic city, as well as to resist impositions. Thus a city with a morphology which seems multi-focal may still exhibit a high degree of cultural and religious uniformity and, indeed, neighbourhoods may be primary loci in which that citywide culture is imposed. We should remember that the modern interest in generating local communities within cities is a reaction against the perceived failure of existing social institutions to socialize populations: communities are perceived as a way of extending public control into these areas by consensus (perhaps after the failure of other methods) and are not a 'stepping-back' of the state to give power to the people. The city of neighbourhoods could be a culturally united city.

It is all too easy to forget that the city was a space through which people moved and this gives us an ability to explore and to develop different social roles. For instance, my wife's social roles and experiences of communities are far greater than mine, partly because of her physical mobility. She is part of the local neighbourhood, the community of the street, part of a community of mothers of young children based in the village, increasingly part of a church-based community operating through a nursery school, part of a school community in a different village, part of a second school community where she teaches, and part of two synagogue communities in different parts of London. This is, I suppose, part of the 'fracturing of the urban experience' (Westwood and Williams 1997) which Soja (1989) and Harvey (1991; 1990; cf. Harvey and Scott 1989) see as part of the 'flexible mode of accumulation' that characterizes late capitalism, but although economics are important, individuals' identities and the identities of communities may be shaped round a host of characteristics, so generating an incoherence in our reaction to place and in our construction of local communities.

Whatever the root cause of this modern incoherence, it seems possible that the experience of the city in the Roman and late Roman periods was also fractured.[54] The smallness of the enclaves that we can begin to identify as neighbourhoods, the fact that there do not appear to have been clearly defined boundaries between neighbourhoods, the accessibility of public space, the ability to join non-local groups, and, indeed, the negotiability of these small districts in what looks to have been a changing situation, all suggest that men were not restricted to their neighbourhoods in identity-formation. A man who lived in an elite enclave could visit other elite houses, attend other elite locales and define himself as a member of that elite in his public activities, or define himself otherwise. One would not want, I think, to read the extreme fluidity of boundaries in the modern city into the city of Roman and late Roman Egypt, but institutions that worked at a city level, either with small groups or with major sectors of the population, may have been important areas of socialization for men. The situation for women is less well attested, but although one presumes that access to many of these city institutions was limited, the absence of clear boundaries in the Roman and Late Roman period would seem to suggest that their access to public space, as opposed to domestic or communal space, was not notably restricted. In the Byzantine period, however, those boundaries appear to have become a little firmer, a little less incoherent, though perhaps still not approaching the embracing nature of the Cairene *darb*.

5

THE CITY

Introduction

The historiography of the Roman city in the provinces has tended to be reduced to simple dichotomous arguments over the extent to which native (colonized) populations adopted the imperial culture (Alston 1996), a discussion which draws much of its inspiration from the experience of nineteenth- and early twentieth-century European colonialism. Such debates presuppose that the dynamics of historical development were essentially ethnic. Thorough reassessment of the role of ethnicity in the Ptolemaic period (see pp. 157–9) suggests that although ethnic markers were used, they appear more as indicators of closeness to government than anything we would associate with ethnic identity. It was only with Augustus' settlement of 30 BC that a rigid and complex caste system was imposed. The Augustan settlement may not have reflected the complexity of late Ptolemaic society but the settlement and the ideology behind that settlement set in motion dramatic changes in the cities of the province.[1] The new cities of Roman Egypt developed slowly over the next centuries and this chapter traces and describes that development, topographically, architecturally, administratively and socially. In the fourth century, the cities took a new direction. Christianity, an extremely powerful ideological force, added a different dynamic to the political mix, changing some aspects of the cities, preserving others, dominating in some aspects of life, seemingly little affecting others. There are no revolutions in this chapter but that is not to say that all the change here was long-term, only observable in the long-view of the historian. At various points in this story the cities underwent comparatively sudden and dramatic changes and experienced considerable social and political turbulence. The political dynamics outlined in this chapter were, in my opinion, the fundamental sources of change which reshaped all levels of the spatial matrix in the Roman and Byzantine periods and deeply affected the everyday life of every inhabitant of the Egyptian city. There are several stories to be told here. One is of shifts in political power within the city. This is a story of political structures and administration (the mechanics of political power). Another is of the integration of the population into political structures and the relationship between administrative and political authority and cultural power. These are stories of structures, of gradual change so loved by many modern historiographers. But there are also stories of events which reshaped cities, of the minutiae of political struggles, of the threads of lives which went to make up the structural changes. Inevitably, this chapter faces the burden of description (often from complex and incomplete documentary and archaeological material), of multiple and contradictory narratives, and of an extended chronological range over which these various transformations are traced. Equally inevitably, the stories are simplified and condensed, though the overall structure remains fragmented. I hope, in the end, that the continuities and transformations of the city in Roman and Byzantine Egypt, their causes and effects, will emerge with something approaching clarity.

The forces that transformed the cities are best illuminated through an essentially chronological survey. This chapter is mostly organized by century. An exception to this is the discussion of administration, since the Augustan system survived, with modifications such as the introduction of councils, until the Diocletianic reforms.

The Augustan administrative system

The Augustan settlement

The Roman political settlement in Egypt was far from straightforward; indeed, one may even describe it as confused. It did, however, reflect certain fundamental elements of Roman political thinking. Throughout the period of expansionism, Roman politicians consistently preferred to deal with aristocratic elements in the subjugated areas. Monarchies and oligarchies received Roman support in return for political loyalty. After Cleopatra's prominent role in the civil war, a client monarchy in Egypt was not an option. Nevertheless, Rome still sought local allies. Throughout much of the East, Rome relied on a pre-existing Hellenized urban aristocracy, but in Egypt there were few of the familiar institutions of Greek civic government, no landed elite and no recognizable aristocracy. Instead, the Romans inherited a comparatively efficient royal bureaucracy and cities dominated by temples.

The Augustan settlement established (though I assume that this was presented as a restoration) a conventional hierarchical system, one plank of which was the elevation of Alexandria. Alexandria was the city of Alexander the Great, about whom many Romans had something of a fixation. His mausoleum, the *sema*, was near the centre of the city and Augustus was one of many who visited his remains. Also, Ptolemaic patronage of artists and intellectuals had made Alexandria the leading centre of Greek culture in the Hellenistic world, so, in spite of its reputation for violence, Alexandria was a city for which the Romans had a considerable respect, as was reflected in the extensive privileges granted to the city and the rigour with which its citizenship was policed

(*Gnomon of the Idios Logos* = *BGU* V 1210). Alexandrians were exempted from the poll tax imposed on the rest of Egypt (see p. 2). Applicants for Alexandrian citizenship were obliged (though presumably this was an old regulation) to demonstrate that both their parents were of Alexandrian status. The law appears to have been strictly enforced. This was reinforced by a ban on testamentary property transfers between Egyptians and Alexandrians, presumably so that illegitimate children could not be provided for by testament. Furthermore, Alexandrians appear to have been recruited into the most important Egyptian administrative positions, both in Alexandria itself and in the *chora* (see below). Pliny the Younger suggests that Alexandrian status was a necessary intermediate status for Egyptians before they could gain Roman citizenship, though this requirement is legally obscure and has given rise to a certain amount of debate as to the exact status of Egyptians in Roman law and there is some evidence that the requirement was often ignored.[2]

Another innovative feature of the Roman settlement was the creation of the *metropoleis* of the *chora*. Most of the cities already acted as local centres within the nomes of Egypt, a centrality most obviously expressed by the presence of a large temple. In the Ptolemaic period, residents of these cities do not appear to have had any special status and were probably administered through similar structures as the villagers. The Augustan settlement saw significant change. The poll tax was introduced and administered so that the metropolites were given a separate and privileged status in comparison with villagers (Rathbone 1993). Admission to metropolite status came to require that a candidate's father and maternal grandfather were both metropolites. Villagers and their descendants were excluded. In addition, village gymnasia appear to have been phased out during the Augustan period so that gymnasia became exclusively urban institutions (Bowman and Rathbone 1992). By AD 4–5, if not earlier, an urban gymnasial group had been formed and their membership registered (see pp. 138–9). 'Those from the gymnasium' became politically powerful. They could be treated as community spokesmen and provided officials for those urban administrative functions which were devolved to the cities. Although 'those from the gymnasium' did not receive any fiscal privileges, they were a hereditary elite within the metropolites. Thus an association between city and gymnasium developed which ensured a growing identification of the city with Greek culture.[3] Such changes were a radical departure from the administrative patterns of the Ptolemaic period and it is reasonable to regard the cities of the early Roman period as new municipalities on a Roman rather than a traditional Egyptian model (Bowman and Rathbone 1992).

Administrative officials

The new officers of the municipalities are abundantly attested in our documentation, partly because the holding of office was regarded as an honour and former officials cited the offices they had held almost as part of their nomenclature, and partly because these officials emerged as the most important individuals in the municipalities. Discovering the administrative functions of these offices is thereby complicated since the title might be used in documentation unrelated to the office-holder's official capacity. Also, officials and former officials were an administrative and political resource which could be deployed in different areas of the city administration.

Administratively, all the metropolitan offices were under the authority of the nome *strategos* in the pre-300 period. The relationship of these officers to the *strategos* was not, however, fixed. From AD 200, officials were appointed by the *boule*, though even before that date names seem to have emerged from meetings of city officials and been subject to ratification by the *strategos*. In this chapter, I will attempt to differentiate between those appointed via the *boule* and those appointed by the Roman provincial administration, by referring to the former as 'magistrates' and the latter as 'officials' or 'officers', though the distinction is somewhat artificial. The *metropoleis* had four major officers: the *exegetes*, the gymnasiarch, the *kosmetes* and the *agoranomos*.

Strabo (XVII 1 12) lists the officials of Alexandria. He starts with the *exegetes* ('who wears purple and has long-established honours and looks after the business of the city') and the *hypomnematographos* (the official recorder), the *archidikastes* (the chief judge), and finally the νυκτερινὸς στρατηγός (the night *strategos*). It is not clear what the superior level of bureaucracy was, but it seems likely that they answered to the prefect. Strabo does not mention the gymnasial officials (the gymnasiarch and the *kosmetes*) nor the other well-attested civic official, the *agoranomos*, though all these officials operated in Alexandria in the Augustan period.

The *exegetes* had a range of responsibilities (Kraut 1984) in the centuries prior to the foundation of the councils. They appointed legal representatives for those whose interests needed such protection, notably women and children (*BGU* XV 2462; *P. Brem.* I 76; *P. Merton 26; P. Mich.* V 232; *P. Mil. Vogl.* I 27; II 71; *P. Stras.* IV 284; *P. Tebt.* II 329; 465; *SB* V7558; *P. Diog.* 19; *P. Fam. Tebt.* 49; 50; *P. Oxy.* VI 888 = M. *Chr.* 329; 909; X 1269; XXXI 2584; *P. Ryl.* II 121; *PSI* X 1104; M. *Chr.* 323). This responsibility was probably delegated from the *strategos* and it may have been that the *exegetes* nominated guardians whose appointments were ratified by the *strategos* (*P. Oxy.* I 56 = M. *Chr.* 320). The *exegetai* supervised guardians' activities beyond the appointing process, perhaps being ultimately responsible for those entrusted to their care (*P. Heid.* IV 336; 337; *P. Harr.* I 71; *SB* XVI 12557). They also seem to have had some role in the registration of property transactions, or at least they were sometimes notified of such transactions (*P. Corn.* 16; *P. Ryl.* II 119; 120). Similarly, they sometimes supervised status examinations (*P. Grenf.* II 49; *P. Heid.* IV 304; 340; 341; 342; *P. Ryl.* II 101; *SB* V7333; XVIII 13243). This supervision of persons and property made the *exegetai* extremely powerful and more general problems were submitted to them (*P. Mert.* I 11; 13). Later, they appear to have assumed some financial responsibilities (*P. Oxy.* I 54; *P. Oslo* III 144; 158). This may explain why, when the contractor for the raising of water for the public baths resigned, responsibility returned to the *exegetes* (*P. Oxy.* XXXI 2569 (AD 265)). They also had a judicial role (*P. Ryl.* II 94; *BGU* II 388 = M. *Chr.* 91). Sometimes, they were involved in transactions involving large amounts of grain (*P. Merton* I 14; *P. Oxy.* I 88) and in the distribution of seed to public farmers (*P. Oslo* II 26; *P. Ryl.* II 149). They were probably the most important official within the city in the period before AD 200, though, after that date, the *prytanis*, the chair of the council, may have had higher status. The power of the *exegetai* was such that they were in a position to abuse their authority (*P. Fouad* 26). In a famous case from AD 192, a meeting of the officials of the city to appoint their successors was thrown into confusion when someone who had been volunteered to serve as *kosmetes* refused on the grounds of the expense of the office, but offered to take the senior office of *exegetes* instead, much to the irritation of the existing officials, who appear to have both refused his candidature for the senior office and accepted his withdrawal from the junior position (*P. Ryl.* II 77). As in other cases, the office became collegial, whatever its origins. In 294 (*P. Oxy.* VI 891) an *exegetes* was appointed for a few days, perhaps because of an emergency which had given rise to a vacancy in the magistracy, the expenses of his tenure being shared among the whole *koinos* (committee) of *exegetai*.[4] The *exegetai* may have also had an office in at least some cities since an unfortunately unprovenanced text from AD 200 (*P. Stras.* V 339) appears to be the accounts for their 'house', which apparently needed to be supplied with cake, clearly to boost morale after a hard day administering the city.

The *kosmetai* were gymnasial officials and in this capacity appear to have arranged and supervised various events within the gymnasium, such as the 'kosmetic' games (*P. Lond.* VI 1912 for the kosmetic games in Alexandria). The original office probably derived from Classical Athens where the official appears to have been in charge of ephebic military training, though for an institution central to ancient Athenian life, much remains uncertain about its operation (Pélékides 1962; Fisher 1998; Moretti 1977; Marrou 1948: 173–5). Although there was no military purpose in gymnasial training in Egypt in the Roman period (Kock 1948: 101; Nelson 1979: 58; Lesquier 1918: 155–63), the *kosmetes* retained responsibility for training ephebes. A long honorific list of ephebes at Antinoopolis is headed by the *kosmetes* (Rigsby 1978; *I. Portes* 9 = *SB* I 1481), as is a similar inscription from Leontopolis dated to AD 220 (*SEG* XL 1568). This role made them natural officials to supervise entry into the gymnasium through the *epikrisis* (*P. Mil. Congr.* XIV, p. 22; *P. Oxy.* III 477 = W. *Chr.* 144; XLIX 3463; *PSI* V 457; *SB* IV 7333; XIV 11387). Away from the gymnasium, they appear either as recorders or as supervisors of property transactions in association with the *exegetes*, though in the pre-200 period this appears to be a function that former officials performed (*P. Hamb.* I 14; 16; M. *Chr.* 215 = *BGU* I 112; *P. Laur.* III 86 (former *kosmetes*). At least one former *kosmetes* became a public banker (*P. Münch.* III 81; 101). It seems possible that the *kosmeteia* was not a collegial office in the first century AD, though this changed later

(*BGU* XI 2065; *P. Stras.* VIII 796; *P. Ryl.* II 77), as is clear from *P. Ant.* I 31 of AD 347, which is a reminder to Apollonios of Ammon that his month's term of service is approaching and a request that he look to the 'good management' of the city. After AD 200, *kosmetai* took a role in the taxation and management of rural areas and these magistrates or former *kosmetai* are attested in connection with seed and irrigation, as well as other forms of taxation (*P. Flor.* I 21; 6; *P. Cair. Isid.* 32; *P. Oxy.* XII 1458; *BGU* XIII 2279; *P. Oxy. Hell.* 24; *P. Princ.* III 126; *P. Ryl.* II 206b; *W. Chr.* 418). The power of the office was such that in 269 a *kosmetes* of Hermopolis was accused of using his influence tyrannically in a dispute over a private debt (*PSI* V 457). The office also appears to have been rather expensive (see below), perhaps because of the responsibility for laying on games, and it was to this office that the city council of Ptolemais Euergetis unsuccessfully attempted to conscript villagers in a famous case from the mid-third century (*P. Lond.* inv. 2565 = *SB* V 7696; Skeat and Wegener 1935; see p. 225).

The gymnasiarchy was a major office in some cities in the Ptolemaic period, though perhaps mainly in those cities with established 'Greek' constitutions, such as Ptolemais and Alexandria (Kortenbeutel 1937). The gymnasium required equipment, and games and festivals held within the gymnasium had to be paid for. In addition, the gymnasium contained baths, which needed maintenance and cleaning, and employed a paid attendant. In addition, oil was provided and water supplied and heated. The honour and expenses were shared among a college of gymnasiarchs and the number of gymnasiarchs per year varied considerably over time, possibly from two to twelve or even more (van Groningen 1924: 90–4). Yet, the gymnasiarchy remained a substantial honour and a second-century legal hearing established that a gymnasiarch-elect could bequeath his office to his heirs, who could sell it (*CPR* VII 4; Lewis 1983). A gymnasiarch's place in the community may be reflected by the record of an honorific decree, probably passed at Naukratis, issued by the magistrates, the *demos*, the Romans and Alexandrians, which provided for a statue for a gymnasiarch who had supplied the city with unguents, contributed to the funds for the shows and the baths, and taken on the management of the 'major baths' (*P. Oxy.* III 473; Lewis 1981). At Oxyrhynchus, the roster of market taxes for AD 143 suggests that the hieratic taxes from the market at the Sarapeion (one presumes it was the main market of the city) were under the control of the gymnasiarch, though the actual collection of the taxes appears to have been farmed (*SB* XVI 12695; Rea 1982; Bowman 1984).[5]

The *agoranomos* was also a survival from the Ptolemaic period, though in a rather altered form (Raschke 1974). This official would have been in charge of the market of the city, though direct involvement with the market is rarely attested. *Stud. Pal. Pap.* V 102 = *W. Chr.* 296, a lacunose third-century text from Hermopolis contains a report from an *agoranomos* to the council concerning income derived from the city market, specifically from the renting-out of stalls. It seems likely that the day-to-day management of the market would generate very little documentation. In the late Ptolemaic and early Roman period, *agoranomoi* appear to have controlled the city grain measure (*P. Oxy.* IV 836; *PSI* X 1099) and a document depository (the *agoranomeion*) and may have acted as public notaries. They were notified of important property transactions, such as the transfer of houses and the sale or manumission of slaves, and also supervised testamentary transactions (see, for instance, *BGU* I 193; *BGU* IV 1114; 1128; *P. Gen.* I 22; *P. Oxy.* I 48; 49; 50; II 263; 327; XIV 1706; XXXVIII 2843; 2856; LX 4058; *P. Turner* I 19; *SB* I 5616; XVI 12220; 12391 (slaves); *BGU* I 327 = M. *Chr.* 61; *P. Fouad* I 36; *P. Gen.* II 104; *P. Harr.* I 74; *P. Oxy.* III 482; XXXVI 2759 (testaments); *BGU* IV 1072 = M. *Chr.* 195; *P. Oxy.* IV 713 (dowries); *P. Oxy.* II 241; 243; 250; VIII 1105; XXIV 2720 (house sales). They were given probably professional assistance from scribes and others who dealt with the documentation and perhaps even provided technical help to traders. *Agoranomoi* frequently appear as witnesses to contracts (*CPR* I 53; 56; 57; 61–100; 202; VI 73; *P. Flor.* I 1; *P. Heid.* IV 301; *P. Oxy.* I 107; XXXVI 2777; *SB* VIII 9766). The city was rather over-provided with record offices. *P. Oxy.* II 238 mentions three separate depositories, the *agoranomeion*, the *mnemoneion* and the *grapheion* (the office of the scribe) (cf. *P. Oxy.* IX 1208; XII 1564; *P. Turner* I 26; *SB* IV 7379; VI 8971; XVI 12950), though it seems possible that the first two were combined. The *agoranomoi* appear to have worked as a college of at least two people in the Roman period (*SB* X 10299; V 7573). *P. Turner* I 19 gives the names of eight serving *agoranomoi* working at Oxyrhynchus in AD 119, while in AD 94 there were at least five operating in the same city (*P. Oxy.* I 73).

The *agoranomos* appears to have been the junior officer and the *exegetes* the senior (*P. Ryl.* II 77; Bowman and Rathbone 1992: n. 84). The gymnasiarch appears to have ranked higher than the *kosmetes*. Yet, it would, I think, be misleading to see the offices as a formal career structure through which an aspiring local politician would seek to pass, holding each office in turn. The qualification for office-holding appears to have been wealth not previous experience, and individuals could hold senior offices without necessarily having held the junior positions (see, for instance, *I. Portes* 75; *P. Grenf.* II 61; *P. Mil.* II 63; *P. Stras.* VI 555; W. *Chr.* 184; *P. Oxy.* III 507; XXXI 2588; XLII 3051; *PSI* IV 315). A third-century Hermopolite text throws some light on the status of the various magisterial positions. It lists guards assigned to the various magistrates in a procession. The *strategos* receives four, the gymnasiarch four, the *exegetes* two, the *agoranomos* one, the person in charge of the food supply and the chief priest of the emperors received two, the chief priest of Hadrian one, and the chief priest of Faustina was accompanied by one guard (*P. Amh.* II 124).[6] This would seem to suggest that the gymnasiarch was the senior official, though the guards were *palaestraphulakes*, guards of the gymnasium, which would imply that the event was connected to the gymnasium and, therefore, presided over by the gymnasiarch.

There were other officials, such as the chief priest, and the third century saw the emergence of conciliar magistrates (see below), including the *prytanis* (the chair of the council who appears to have taken an active role in leading the council and who became, consequently, effective head of the city administration) and the *hypomnematographos* (the council secretary). One of the lesser offices was that of the *eutheniarchos*, who was in charge of the provision of food for the city. The earliest dated appearance of the official is from AD 199 (*P. Oxy.* VI 908). In this contract, six former gymnasiarchs (one of whom appears to take a leading role acting through an agent) agreed to equip and supply mills to grind 20 *artabai* per day. This guaranteed production of 120 *artabai* per day and, therefore, 3,600 *artabai* per month. Since the third-century corn dole was distributed at one *artaba* per month, production was geared to feed 3,600 adult males (Alston and Alston 1997).

Although there may have been official sponsorship of mills prior to 199, there is no firm evidence for the earlier operation of official mills or of eutheniarchs (though see *P. Bas.* 13). Nevertheless, the food supply was an administrative issue much earlier. A text of AD 111 concerns the expenses faced by a former gymnasiarch 'for the *euthenia*' (the food supply) (*Stud. Pal. Pap.* XXII 94) whereas in 189 (*BGU* II 578) Diodotos, a former *agoranomos*, had the same responsibility (cf *SB* XVI 12139). Towards the end of the second century a *kosmetes* supervised the food supply (*P. Tebt.* II 397). In the mid-second century Tiberius Iulius Alexander erected a statue for Isis Plousia in Alexandria and detailed his career on the associated inscription (*I. Alex.* 32 = *SB* V 8911 = *IGRR* I 1044 = *OGIS* II 705). He had been a prefect of a cohort, *agoranomos* and in charge of the *euthenia* of B district of Alexandria. The division of responsibility for feeding the city by its constituent quarters is not attested elsewhere, but may be a function of the size of Alexandria. The earliest attestation of administrative concern for the *euthenia* I have found is also related to Alexandria and dated to the first half of the first century AD (*I. Portes* 32). It might be expected that Alexandria, given its size and rather peculiar role within the economy of Egypt, would have deployed administrative resources to ensure the food supply rather earlier than the cities of the *chora*, but these cities were not far behind. In the early 60s AD, a fragmentary letter to the *exegetes* from a member of the gymnasial group of Hermopolis Magna makes mention of some kind of dole for that group, though this may have been limited in both the number of recipients and the food supplied (*P. Heid.* IV 338; 339; 340; see also *SB* VIII 9699 for an early Hermopolite attestation in an account). The Alexandrian *euthenia* is better attested for the first two centuries AD. We know that it included wine as well as grain by 141–2 (*P. Diog.* 13; 14; *PSI* X 1123) and pork by 187–8 (*BGU* II 649 = W. *Chr.* 428). Antinoopolis was provided with a grain dole which was in operation by the late 160s (*P. Mich.* XII 629), but which was probably instituted with the foundation of the city. *Euthenia* also appears comparatively frequently in accounts, but it is normally impossible to ascertain for which city the goods were intended (see *BGU* I 81; *SB* VIII 9699; XVI 12515; *Stud. Pal. Pap.* XXII 110). It should not be assumed that this food was supplied *gratis* during the first two centuries AD, but the task of administering the food supply for the city was probably a considerable drain on the financial resources of the officials and magistrates (Carrié 1975; Fikhman 1975a).

Urban finances

The city had various sources of income, such as market taxes, which in second-century Oxyrhynchus brought the city about 3,000–3,800 drachmas per year (Rea 1982; *SB* XVI 12695), and rent from property or land owned by the city or land which had come into its possession, but the major source of revenue was undoubtedly the gymnasial and magisterial elite itself.[7] There were three main ways in which money could be extracted from them. In the third century, a fee was levied on those entering the council which Bowman estimates at 10,000 drachmas in the early third century (Bowman 1971: 26; 40–1). Officials and magistrates also paid a 'crowning fee'. They could also be asked for contributions to particular projects within the city on an *ad hoc* basis. After AD 200, the administration of this income and the various expenditures was through the council and issues would be discussed there, though it is less clear what policy-making fora there were in the earlier period. The various officers of the city shared a certain civic responsibility and acted either as a college of similar officers (such as the *kosmetai*) or even as a collective body of *archontes* (*P. Amh.* II 70; *P. Ryl* II 77; Bowman 1971: 15–16; Jones 1938; Jouguet 1917; *P. Aberd.* I 56; *P. Harr.* I 71; *P. Oxy.* VI 908; *P. Ryl.* II 86; *SB* V 7533; 7573; XVI 12345), especially in relation to central authorities, and one must presume that it was this body which both decided on and financed urban developments, perhaps in consultation with the *strategos*, or even with the prefect (*P. Oxy.* IV 705; XVII 2132; XLIII 3088; *P. Amh.* II 64). The everyday financial management of projects may have been delegated to a board of responsible officials (*P. Lond.* III, pp. 180–90, 1177; *P. Ryl.* II 86; *P. Oxy.* I 54; *SB* XIV 11959).

Large sums of money were expended in running the city. *P. Col. Youtie* I 28 *BL* VIII, 84, dating probably to AD 169, from Oxyrhynchus, is an unfortunately lacunose account of expenditure within the city. It includes a payment in relation to the baths of 3,000 drachmas, payments connected with the theatre of 5,000 and 3,400, and other payments (some of which may be connected with the theatre of 3,200+, 800, 4,000 and 1,000 drachmas. The total payments amount to at least 16,960 drachmas). A list of dates in column 2 of the account suggests the surviving portion dealt with a single month. If this is the case and if the period covered is an 'average' period (and these are two rather bold assumptions), then the city faced disbursements during the year of at least 200,000 drachmas. This was at a time when a Roman legionary soldier received 1,200 drachmas per annum. A lacunose list of persons may record those who had contributed. Officials or former officials are heavily represented, as shown in table 5.1.

Similar figures can be gleaned from *P. Oxy.* XVII 2128 = *Sel. Pap.* II 407, a second-century account relating mainly to building works. The water supervisors received 3,383 drachmas, 2 obols. There were also payments to the contractors for the doors of the Kapitoleion of 2,500 drachmas, for the gate of 2,000 drachmas, for the provision of glass of 3,500 drachmas, for bread of 7,651

Table 5.1 Persons mentioned in *P. Col. Youtie* I 28

Type of person	No. of persons
Non-office holders	6
Former *agoranomos* and gymnasiarch	1
Former *agoranomos*	2
Agoranomos	2
Gymnasiarch (or former gymnasiarch)	1
Exegetes	1
Kosmetes	1
Former chief priest	2
Manager	1
Holder or former holder of uncertain office	2

drachmas. The contractors of the Antonine baths received 2,000 drachmas, and the fifty nightwatchmen received 2,000 drachmas. The time period of the account is again uncertain, but it would seem likely that these were monthly or bimonthly payments, suggesting annual expenditure of 138,000 to 276,000 drachmas.

These accounts carry payments for running costs or small additions or improvements to existing buildings. If a city was engaged in a major construction project, expenses would rise and the magistrates were potentially faced with a huge bill. In 117, Vibius Maximus, the prefect, heard a case relating to the public finances of a city and the construction of the new baths (*P. Amh.* II 64). A certain Theon was asked to pay 50 talents (300,000 drachmas) and a female gymnasiarch had property distrained to the value of 20 talents (120,000 drachmas), recompense for which was to come from city funds, though the lawyers regarded this instruction with some amazement.[8] These payments were small fortunes and unsurprisingly there was pressure to reduce the expenditure of officials, especially the gymnasiarchs. Just two years earlier (*P. Amh.* II 70), the *archontes* (magistrates) of Hermopolis petitioned the prefect concerning the expenses of the gymnasiarchy and requested that these be lessened so that the gymnasiarch was only responsible for heating of the baths, the supply of water and expenses relating to the running of the gymnasium. Expenses of the water supply of the whole city were shared, as can be seen from *P. Oxy.* XVII 2128 = *Sel. Pap.* II 407, discussed above, and *P. Lond.* III, pp. 180–90, 1177, an early second-century account from Ptolemais Euergetis. This last provides considerable detail. The *kosmetes* paid 6,000 drachmas into the account in five payments, the exegetes 490 drachmas in two payments, and the gymnasiarch 2,080 drachmas in five payments. It looks as if the holders of these three positions were expected to contribute about 20,000 drachmas for the supply of water in the course of a year. In addition to these contributions, the city levied charges on the major users of the water, the Jewish community (presumably for the ritual baths), the bleachers, the baths of Severianus, the brewery of the temple and three fountains within the city.

Other texts attest fragments of urban expenditure. A first-century contract (AD 42) for the heating for the (baths of the) gymnasium for a year between the gymnasiarch elect and the contractors provided for payment of 2,000 drachmas (*P. Lond.* III, p. 104–5, 1166). A second-century account from Oxyrhynchus details expenditure for a single procession at the festival of the Nile amounting to about 130 drachmas for the priestly and 'religious' celebrants, but in addition to this there were payments to the mime (496 drachmas), the Homericist (448 drachmas), the musicians, the dancer, the *pankratistores* (fighters), 'competitors' and the boxer. Even if we assume that the rewards for these last only matched those of the Homericist and the mime, the celebrations must have cost about 3,600 drachmas. A couple of lines of the account dealing with income suggest contributions from the *exegetes* and the *kosmetes* of less than 55 drachmas each, though this raised the running total of income to 500 drachmas (*P. Oxy.* III 519 = W. *Chr.* 492 = *Sel. Pap.* II 402). An extremely lacunose second-century account from Oxyrhynchus (*P. Oxy.* XVII 2127) suggests that festivities in the theatre cost 6,000 drachmas, the procession of the *exegetes* (perhaps celebrating appointment) cost a further 6,000 drachmas (suspiciously rounded numbers), and 1,476 drachmas were spent on re-equipping the gymnasial baths. Aurelius Horion, an Alexandrian, petitioned the emperor to be allowed to establish a fund of 10,000 Attic drachmas (40,000 Egyptian drachmas) to provide prizes for the ephebic games to rival those on offer at Antinoopolis (*P. Oxy.* IV 705 = W. *Chr.* 153 = *CPJ* II 450).[9] An account submitted from the manager of the public and sacred treasury of the city to the board of *kosmetai* suggests payments for the hippodrome and for the guarding of the city of Hermopolis at some point in AD 195 amounting to two instalments of 5,600 drachmas (*P. Ryl.* II 86), whereas a third-century account of the expenses of a *kosmetes* suggests that the official may have been liable for 11,500 drachmas (*P. Princ.* II 71). Coincidentally, the man seeking to avoid the office of *kosmetes* and take the office of *exegetes* offered to pay 2 talents (12,000 drachmas) as a gesture of goodwill (*P. Ryl.* II 77). It may be that this was the 'crowning fee' for the *kosmetes*, though this is far more than the sum in *P. Oxy.* XLIV 3177 of AD 247, which is an agreement between the daughter of an *exegetes* and the *kosmetes* in charge of the treasury to meet her father's debt of 1,500 drachmas. Such sums pale into insignificance, however, when faced with the sums in *P. Wash. Univ.* I 4 (BL VIII, 508) of AD 198–9. This is a fragmentary notice of payments in relation to the office of *exegetes* and there may be two separate payments attested. The 'first' case involves payments made to absolve a debt. The nominated *exegetes* had died but his estate was obliged to meet the costs of his office. His wife, therefore, paid into the treasury 21 talents (126,000 drachmas).

These fragmentary accounts are obviously only partial descriptions of the expenditure of the gymnasial group and we are in no position to produce a definite estimate for the expense of the annual budget of a typical city. The extraordinary variety of sums paid seemingly as a matter of course by magistrates gives considerable pause for thought. Nevertheless, it seems likely that the running costs of the city were at least 250,000–400,000 drachmas per year in the late second century, without counting the expenses for the food supply or any major building works. About 1 per cent of this sum appears to have been extracted from market-taxes. If the higher figures for the expenses of officials are to be believed, and given that all the offices were collegial, the city must have extracted a very considerable income from the gymnasial office-holding class. It was their money that ran and built the city.

The 'long first century' of Roman rule: 30 BC–c. AD 96

The temple city

Every traveller, ancient or modern, to the sites of ancient Egypt is struck by the magnificence of the great urban temples of the Pharaonic and later periods. Their very scale lays a claim to centrality in the life of the city. Dorothy Thompson summarizes this for Ptolemaic Memphis:[10]

> The city was animated by the divine creative will, and the close connection between the god and his city is clear. In the eyes of the Egyptians who dwelled there, their city was inextricably linked with the cults that it honored; the city belonged to the primary order of things. . . . Memphis was a cult center, and as such was a well-established center long before the Macedonian conquest. As a city it was very old and the number of cults in the city commensurate with its very size . . . [T]he temples . . . were centers of production with their own workshops, storehouses and granaries. Indirectly, too, they had an economic role, making the city a magnet for priests, pilgrims and tourists who swelled the numbers while bringing revenue to the city.
>
> (Thompson 1988: 80)

Historically, the role of the temples had been of major importance in Egyptian political life. The Pharaoh was high priest and sometimes enjoyed quasi-divine status. The centrality of Pharaohs to the religious imagery of temples reflects the role of temples as a major arm of the state. The temples managed extensive resources to support their religious activities. The priests themselves, who were also part of 'secular' government (Kemp 1971), and the wealth of the temples reflected the prosperity of the Pharaoh (Janssen 1979).

Egyptian history of the post-Alexander period has been seen as a struggle between Greek and Egyptian elements. The temples have been represented as acting as foci of nationalistic resistance in this long ethnic conflict, though, nowadays, such simple interpretations are disparaged (Clarysse 1985b; 1992; 1995; Bagnall 1988b; Goudriaan 1988; Quaegebeur 1979; 1992; van Landuyt 1995; Thompson 1990; Otto 1905; Stead 1984). The temples, as centres of political authority, could be mobilized in times of political disturbance against the dominant power, but the use of religious rhetoric, and even of ethnic loyalties, in a rebellion does not necessarily mean that the primary motivation for a revolt was religious or ethnic: the close integration of political and religious power in antiquity means that any political revolt is likely to have some religious connotations. There is no evidence that the Ptolemies saw the temples as threatening their political authority, indeed rather the opposite. Ptolemaic ruler-cults came to share temples with traditional deities and introduced a Hellenizing element into traditional iconography and although the development of something which looks like a secular bureaucracy in the Ptolemaic period may also have altered the function of temples, perhaps distancing them a little from the ruling power (Huss 1992; Evans 1961; Whitehorne 1980–1), the archaeological evidence of temple-building and extension suggests that the temples enjoyed a period of greater prosperity under the Ptolemaic dynasty which, as in the Pharaonic period, should be taken as witnessing the power of the Egyptian state.

The incorporation of Egypt into the Roman empire in 30 BC changed the context of the relationship of the traditional temples and the state. Augustan poets attest strongly anti-Egyptian sentiments which focused on traditional deities and Augustus himself is recorded as echoing their views.[11] This overt hostility on the part of the Roman rulers contrasts dramatically with the attitude of all previous regimes, with the probable exception of the rule of Cambyses (525–521 BC) in the first Persian period, and this may have had immediate effects on the temples. For instance, Alexandria fell on 1 August 30 BC. Within days of this, Imouthes also called Petobastis, high priest at Memphis, died. His burial was delayed for seven years. His successor was not appointed for another two and a half years and although the next high priest, Psenamounis, came from a family that traditionally controlled the priesthood, he appears to have been the last of the family to hold this office. In addition, the office was combined with that of prophet of Caesar (Thompson 1990). Augustus' well-publicized refusal to visit the shrine of Apis signalled a divergence between Roman governmental interests and those of the traditional temples, a divergence which has been interpreted as leading to increased regulation, presumably aimed at depriving them of their assets and political authority, and to an inexorable decline in the traditional temples (Dio LI 16; Suet. Aug. 93; Whitehorne 1980–1; Evans 1961).

Yet, the various elements in the religious and political history of the period need to be teased apart. The Augustan rejection of Egyptian deities in 30 BC was designed for domestic consumption: Augustus would not be seduced by Egypt in the same way as his former illustrious enemy (Brenk 1992). Augustus played on this rejection to bolster his stance as a restorer of traditional values (Geraci 1983: 16–18; 127–8). There is, however, an argument for incompetence rather than malice in the administration of the traditional temples in the early Augustan period. The annexation and a rebellion of c. 28 BC may have disturbed the normal processes of Egyptian religious life. In fact, the Augustan period sees continued sponsorship of traditional Egyptian religion. In a Demotic text of 12 BC, also rendered in hieroglyphics (and with a summary in Greek), a grant of land to the temple of Isis Thermouthis at Dendera was recorded in a traditional manner. The *strategos*, a member of a local family which had controlled the Ptolemaic *strategia* of the region for generations, used a series of priestly and Ptolemaic courtly titles to describe his own position (Glare 1993: 84; Bowman and Rathbone 1992; Spiegelberg 1904: III 50044; *I. Portes* 24). The text gives no sign of Roman government beyond the fact that it is dated by the regnal year of Augustus. Two *stelai* from the Bucheum at Hermonthis in Upper Egypt show Augustus, in traditional Pharaonic garb and wearing the double crown of Egypt, sacrificing to Buchis, the bull-god, exactly as his predecessors were depicted. The first is dated to the first year of Augustus' reign (Mond and Myers 1934: II, *stele* 13; 14). In spite of Augustus' claim to worship gods not cattle (Dio LI 16), the priests perpetuated a fiction of Augustus as Pharaoh worshipping bovine deities. Similarly, in what may be the earliest papyrus of the Roman period in Egypt, dating to 30–29 BC, the lamplighters of the temple of Sarapis and of the temple of Thoeris swore an oath to Heliodoros son of Heliodoros and Heliodoros son of Ptolemaios, the ἐπὶ τῶν ἱερῶν (the officials over the temples) of the Oxyrhynchite and Kynopolite, that they would perform their lamplighting duties (*P. Oxy.* XII 1453). Nothing, apart from the name of the new king, suggests a break in the traditions of Egypt. Similarly, the Augustan period also saw the continued construction and extension or improvement of traditional temples. One of the most famous of the Augustan temples is that of Dendur, now in the Sackler wing of the New York Metropolitan Museum. The temple of Mandoulis from Talmis (Kalabsha), part of which is now in Berlin, but most of which was re-erected on higher ground following the flooding of Lake Nasser, was also an Augustan development. Both these temples were in Nubia and were part of Rome's efforts to extend her influence beyond Aswan, an imperialistic military endeavour which was expressed culturally in traditional Egyptian terms.

There was further extensive building in Upper Egypt under Augustus, especially at Elephantine (the temples of Satet and Khnum), Philae, Karnak and Kom Ombo (Vandorpe 1995; Grenier 1997; Gutbob 1995; Kaper 1998; see below). Elephantine and Syene were the traditional boundary between Nubia and Egypt.[12] Philae, just to the south of Elephantine, was an important diplomatic and trading post between Egypt and Nubia throughout the Roman and Byzantine periods. The Nubians who used the site preserved practices such as the use of Demotic in inscriptions, long after such traditions had declined elsewhere in Egypt (Zauzich 1983, but see also Quaegebeur 1981) and the temple continued to function long after the closure and Christianization of temples elsewhere within the Roman sphere (Procopius *De Bellis* I 19. 34–7; *Fontes Historiae Nubiorum* III 231; 232; 243; 245; 249–50; 252; 253; 256; 257; 260–3; 265–6; 272; 302; 306; 324; Bagnall 1993: 147; 251; Rémondon 1952).

The Outer Court of the Philae temple is possibly Augustan, while the West Colonnade is decorated by reliefs of Augustus and Tiberius. Both Tiberius and Augustus appear again on the first pylon the 'Birth-House' of Isis, and the temple of Isis. A sanctuary of Hathor within the complex was constructed under Augustus.

The temples of Chnum and Satet at Elephantine were developed from the Old Kingdom onwards and the temples appear to have been particularly prosperous during the Persian period and under the later Ptolemies (Junge 1987). The Augustan period saw the last major development of the temple of Chnum until its function changed in the late antique period. Terraces, which probably served as markets as well as providing an elaborate route from the temple of Chnum to a Nilometer, were constructed outside the temples (Jaritz 1980: 61). The route connected the main centres of cult and ceremony on the island (the temples and the Nilometer) and was probably used for processions. In the centre of the Chnum terrace was a small shrine-like construction, probably a podium from which announcements could be made and the market supervised. Elephantine, together with Syene, probably formed the administrative centre of the nome (*P. Paris* 17; *SB* V 7911).[13] The conservatism of these constructions is notable (Grenier 1997). Either the local authorities were showing their support for the regime by expending their resources on temple improvements and new temples, or the Roman authorities, in a manner which was traditional for the Romans, were seeking to gain the support of the local gods and population and demonstrate their own power by sponsoring construction at traditional temples. Whatever the case, the building programme in Upper Egypt was both a symbol of Roman power and of a desire to reach an accord between traditional religion and the new ruling power.

Egyptian temples, with their large staff and extensive resources, were very different from those of the Romans. Almost inevitably, as the Romans sought to clarify the complex land-tenure arrangements of the Ptolemaic period, temple property was classified as state land, probably its closest equivalent within the Roman legal system (Bowman and Rathbone 1992; Rathbone 1993; *P. Tebt.* II 302).[14] The temples were compensated either by a subvention or by leasing back some of their old land. Temples were major economic and political institutions over which the Romans sought a measure of control (*BGU* IV 1199), probably initially through the office of the prefect (Swarney 1970: 57–9). Most of the known regulatory framework appears to have been imposed in the early second century when the *idios logos* (a senior Roman official) relieved the prefect of some aspects of temple administration, such as levying fines following breaches of status and supervising temple activities (Swarney 1970: 83–97; 104; *P. Oxy.* XLIX 3470; 3471).[15] A system of status-examination for priests was either introduced or modified in the early second century (Nelson 1979: 60–2), and regular registration of temple personnel and property was also introduced (see the list in *P. Oxy.* XLIX 3473), though there are earlier registrations (*BGU* III 781).[16] Nevertheless, although the second-century reforms probably regularized supervision, the temples, as considerable sources of revenue (W. *Chr.* 92 = *BGU* I 1 = II 337; *BGU* I 25; 199; II 362 = W. *Chr.* 96 = *Sel. Pap.* II 340; *BGU* II 652; Evans 1961: 214; *P. Tebt.* II 291; 298), were too important not to be supervised in earlier periods and the Ptolemaic system of governmental control was probably carried over into the first century AD (*P. Grenf.* I 14; *P. Oxy* XII 1453; *P. Tebt.* I 5).

Many regulations for the management of temples are collected in the *Gnomon of the Idios Logos* (*BGU* V 1210; *P. Oxy.* XLII 3014). Chapter 71 ruled that priests must devote themselves exclusively to temple service, that they should not have long hair (traditionally priests were shaved), nor wear wool, even if they were excluded from divine processions. Chapter 73 forbade the second mortgaging of temple land. Chapter 74 established a fine of 300 drachmas for a *stolistes* (a grade of priest) who deserted his post. Chapter 75 established a fine of 200 drachmas for an ordinary priest who neglected duties and a similar fine for wearing wool, though a piper or *pastophoros* only had to pay 100 drachmas for the same offence, and chapter 76 established a fine of 1,000 drachmas for a long-haired, wool-wearing priest. Chapter 91 disallowed 'late-born' children (those whose fathers were over the age of 60 at the time of their birth) from officiating as priests, though such sons could be admitted into the priesthood (and presumably enjoy the revenues and status of office). Chapter 92 prevented children who had been exposed on dung heaps (the standard form of infanticide) and rescued by a priestly family from being made priests.[17]

One need not assume that this supervision was either hostile or unwelcome to the traditional priesthood. For moderns, one of the more controversial aspects of the administration of the temples is the sale of office (*BGU* V 1210, chapters 77, 78, 80; for examples of sales of offices see *P. Oxy.* LIX 3974; *P. Tebt.* II 294–7; *O. Theb.* D 122; 221; 235; *SB* XVI 12723). Yet, access to most priesthoods in antiquity was related to social and economic status and there is little to suggest that the procedures adopted in Egypt were injurious to Egyptian religious practice. Most of the rules within the *Gnomon* were, in fact, designed to ensure that the priests performed their duties and that the correct type of person entered the priesthood (Glare 1993: 37; 54–9). Accounts submitted to the *strategos* of the Polemon and Themistes district of the Arsinoite from the temple at Tebtunis in AD 107–8 note that fifty of the priests of the temple were ἀπολύσιμοι, free from poll tax (*P. Tebt.* II 298; Evans 1961: 249). Twice that number of the priests of Soknopaiou Nesos were ἀπολύσιμοι (Hobson 1984a). Priests also enjoyed exemption from compulsory public services (either manual labour, or administrative or financial duties) (*P. Bodl.* I 72; *SB* XX 15143; Gilliam 1947: 200). It seems very likely that the exemption from poll tax dates from the introduction of the tax and it is probable that the exemption from liturgy was also early. Such immunities increased the pressure to develop a regulatory structure to monitor entrants and the supervisory structures should not be seen as an attack on the privileges of the priests or of the traditional temples, but as an attempt to preserve and police that status.

Nevertheless, the Romans were probably responsible for a weakening of the power of traditional temples since Roman rule altered fundamentally the administrative and political context in which the temples operated. There was a transformation in the major local office, that of the *strategos*. In the late Ptolemaic and early Augustan period, the office appears to have been controlled by local, often priestly, families, but in the first century AD, the office appears to become the preserve of Alexandrians (Bastianini and Whitehorne 1987; Whitehorne 1981; 1988; Criscuolo 1985; Bastianini 1985; Bowman and Rathbone 1992; Glare 1993: 84; see also pp. 250–1). Effectively, this took a large measure of political control away from the old, locally based leading families and transferred it to the emerging Alexandrian elite. Moreover, the new metropolitan organization began to be more influential. This shift is particularly well illustrated by a sequence of inscriptions from Dendera, the first being the inscription of 12 BC already mentioned. The next one is from AD 1 and records that when Publius Octavius was prefect, M. Claudius Postumus *epistrategos*, and Tryphon *strategos*, those from the *metropolis* and nome dedicated the propylon to Isis, great goddess (*I. Portes* 25). Twenty-two years later, the next inscription (*I. Portes* 27) was 'for the emperor Tiberius Augustus, when Gaius Galerius was prefect, Q. Fresidius Pedo *epistrategos*, and Zoilos *strategos*, the building of the walls of the temple of Aphrodite and Isis, great goddesses, was finished . . .'. Then, sometime between AD 32 and 37, a further inscription (*I. Portes* 28) was erected for Emperor Tiberius Caesar, new Augustus, son of the deified Augustus, which recorded that 'when Aulus Avillus Flaccus was prefect, Aulus Folmius Crispus *epistrategos*, and Sarapion son of Trychambos *strategos*, those from the metropolis and the nome (dedicated) the *pronaos* to Aphrodite, great goddess, and her "temple-sharing" gods . . .'.[18] The final inscription in the sequence (*I. Portes* 30) dates from AD 42 and is 'For the *Pax* and *Concordia* of Tiberius Claudius Caesar Augustus Germanicus, in the presence of the gods (?), (dedicated) by Lucius Aimilius Rectus, prefect, and Tiberius Iulius Alexander, *epistrategos*, with Areios son of Areios being *strategos* . . .'.[19] Although the particular sequence at Dendera is unusually full, an inscription from Athribis (*CIG* III 4711) for Tiberius and his mother Iulia Augusta (better known as the empress Livia) and their house records the construction of a *pronaos* for Thriphis when C. Galerius was prefect. Throughout these late Augustan and Julio-Claudian inscriptions, the Roman authorities are fully represented, through the emperor, the prefect, the *epistrategos* and the *strategos*. No longer is the *strategos* a member of a leading local family. Also, in two of the Dendera inscriptions 'those from the metropolis and those from the nome' are designated as contributors. The urban–rural divide established through the Augustan poll tax is thus represented. As power within the city shifted, the traditional temples came under the control of the gymnasial elite, though this was not formalized before the formation of city councils in the third century. A set of accounts from Oxyrhynchus dating to AD 1 includes payments for sacrifices to the imperial cult, to the *pastophoroi* (a grade of Egyptian priests) and to the gymnasiarchs

(*P. Oxy.* VIII 1143). A long account of AD 117 concerning construction work at the temple of Artemis is described as being 'from the accounts of Herakleides alias Dareios former gymnasiarch and supervisor of the works on the temple of Artemis great goddess' (*SB* XIV 11958; cf. *P. Oxy.* XX 2272) and in 142, the repair of the temple of Eseph at Herakleopolis, probably the major temple of Herakleopolis (*SB* XIV 11959; Swiderek 1957–8; Vergote 1957–8), was supervised by a board of gymnasiarchs, *exegetai* and *kosmetai*. This new political culture removed the temples from the centre of political life in the cities and made them subservient to the gymnasia.

The rise of the gymnasial group did not immediately translate into an obvious decline in investment in traditional temples, though quantifying investment is obviously problematic. Grenier (1989) collects all the imperial temple inscriptions in hieroglyphs. One might expect the frequency of such inscriptions to correlate quite closely to periods of expansion in traditional temples.

On the face of it, tables 5.2.1–5.2.3 show a stark decline in temple-building over the first three centuries of Roman rule, with forty sites of building for the long first century, twenty-one for the short second century, and three for the third and early fourth centuries. Furthermore, Augustus and Tiberius are attested at twenty-one separate sites each. But to compare like with like, one needs to take account of the number of years in a particular reign (figure 5.1). The ratio of temple hieroglyphs to years of reign shows a marked preponderance of inscriptions under those emperors with very short reigns (Nerva, emperors of AD 69, Gaius). Next come Tiberius, Domitian, Titus, Antoninus Pius, Claudius with Augustus, Vespasian, and possibly Nero falling in the middle of the range. The emperors with the lowest ratios are Trajan, Commodus, Hadrian and Marcus Aurelius. The list therefore ends with four of the major second-century emperors, only Antoninus Pius standing in contrast to the decline in attestations.

The relationship between these epigraphic data and the prosperity of traditional temples is, however, extremely imperfect. Already in the Augustan period, extensions to traditional sanctuaries were being recorded by Greek inscriptions, such as that of the cattle-feeders at Soknopaiou Nesos (*I. Fay.* I 73 = *IGRR* I 1116), and the inscriptions from Dendera. The extensions of facilities at the temples at Karanis under Nero and Vespasian were similarly recorded in Greek (*I. Fay.* I 85 = *IGRR* I 1119; *I. Fay.* I 86 = *SB* VIII 9818; *I. Fay.* I 87 = *SB* VIII 10167 = *IGRR* I 1120), as was the repair work of AD 190 (*I. Fay.* I 89 = *SB* VIII 10169). Second, there is a bias in the evidence to the better-preserved and explored temples of Upper Egypt.[20] As the remaining and late sites of Middle and Lower Egypt receive more archaeological attention, it is likely that more traditional temples of the Roman period will be discovered and the map of hieroglyphic attestations of emperors will change. In Hermopolis, for instance, the British Museum team excavated a temple to the north of the site dedicated to Nehemet-'away, spouse of Thoth(-Hermes). The temple was built in traditional Egyptian style to a traditional deity. Although the excavators

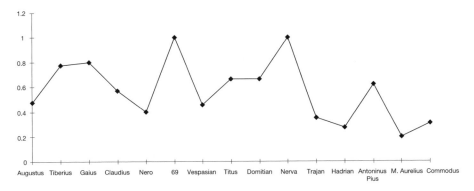

Figure 5.1 Ratio of the number of sites of temple hieroglyphs naming emperors (after
Grenier 1989) to length of reign

could not be sure whether an earlier temple had preceded the one uncovered,
the building (or renovation) was attributed to Domitian (Snape 1989; Bailey
et al. 1982: 5). In the south-west of the city, a temple to an unnamed deity
contained blocks carrying the cartouche of Ramesses II as well as a statue of the
same Pharaoh. The temple was renovated, though the style was not radically
altered, during the reign of Nero (Bailey 1991: 46–53; Roeder 1959: 27–8;
Bailey et al. 1982: 3–4). There was also a stray find of a block in the rubble of
a fifth-century AD pit with part of the cartouche of Domitian (Spencer et al.
1983: 9). Another block with a fragment of an imperial cartouche (possibly of
Hadrian) was discovered abandoned in the Coptic cathedral (Bailey et al. 1982:
4), while a more recent find has been attributed to Claudius (Baranski 1996).[21]
Thus, one comparatively fully excavated city increases Grenier's catalogue by
two probable temples with construction work under Domitian and Nero, and
also suggests that there may have been some traditional temple construction or
reconstruction under Claudius and Hadrian.

At Athribis in the Delta, an inscription dated to AD 22–3 noted the building
of a *pronaos* to Thriphis, great goddess, in honour of Tiberius and his whole
house (*CIG* III 4711). Clearly, this is a traditional deity. The fragmentary
inscription shows some sign of alteration during the reign of Hadrian or that
of Trajan (Michalowski 1962b).[22] We also know of five hieroglyph writers
at Oxyrhynchus in AD 108 (*P. Oxy.* VII 1029), though none of their work
has been preserved. We have evidence for the extensive rebuilding of the temple
of Eseph at Herakleopolis in AD 142 (*SB* XIV 11959), but again there is no
archaeological record of the construction. At Akoris, in Middle Egypt, there was
an enclosure built under Gaius for the temple of Souchos and Ammon (*I. Akoris*
2). There is no evidence of further building work in the epigraphy, though there
are several dedications from the second and early third centuries (*I. Akoris* 7; 8;
9; 10; 12) and the temple continued until at least AD 305 (which is the year of

Table 5.2.1 First-century imperial titles in hieroglyphics from temples (after Grenier 1989)

Temple	Augustus 30 BC–AD 14	Tiberius 14–37	Gaius 37–41	Claudius 41–54	Emperors Nero 54–68	Galba Otho 69	Vespasian 69–79	Titus 79–81	Domitian 81–96
Aswan (Isis)		*							
Aswan (Khnum)									*
Berenice	*	*							
Bigeh	*								
Koptos	*	*	*	*					
Dakke	*	*							
Dandur	*								
Debod	*	*							
Deir Chelouit									
Deir el Hagar						*	*	*	*
Deir el-Medina					*		*	*	
Dendera (Hathor)	*	*	*	*					
Dendera (Isis)	*								
Dendera (Propylon and other gates)	*	*			*				*
Douch									*
Edfu (Horus)		*							
Edfou (mammisis)		*							
Esna		*		*	*		*	*	*
Hou		*		*					
El-Kala	*								
Kalabshah	*								
Karnak (Khonsou)	*								
Karnak (Optet)	*	*							
Karnak (Osiris)		*							
Karnak (Ptah)		*							

Table 5.2.1 (continued)

Karnak (east sanctuary)						*
Kom Ombo	*	*		*	*	*
Kom er Resras						*
Luxor	*					
Medamoud	*				*	
Medinet Habu (gates)	*					*
Nag el-Hagar			*			*
Philae (Isis)	*					
Philae (south chapel)						*
Philae (Arsenouphis)	*					
Philae (Hathor)	*					
Philae (mammisis)	*			*		
Philae (gates and colonnades)	*	*	*			
Shenhour		*		*		
Tehneh			*			
Wannina	*		*			

Table 5.2.2 Second-century imperial titles in hieroglyphics from temples (after Grenier 1989)

Temples	Emperors					
	Nerva	Trajan	Hadrian	Antoninus Pius	Marcus Aurelius	Commodus
	96–8	98–117	117–38	138–61	161–80	180–92
Asfun el-Matana				*		*
Aswan (Isis)	*					
Deir Chelouit			*	*		
Dendera (mammisis)		*		*		
Dendera (gates)		*		*	*	
Douch			*			
Ermant				*		
Esna	*	*	*	*	*	*
Hou	*					
Kalabshah		*				
Kasr ez-Zayan				*		
Kom Ombo		*		*	*	*
Komir				*		
Medamoud		*		*		
Medinet Habu (gates)				*		
Medinet Habu				*		
Nadoura			*	*		
Philae (south chapel)			*			
Philae (Kiosk)		*				
Philae (gates and colonnades)			*	*	*	*
Tôd				*		

Table 5.2.3 Third- and fourth-century imperial titles in hieroglyphics from temples (after Grenier 1989)

Temples	Emperors						
	Septimius Severus	Caracalla	Macrinus and Diadumianus	Alexander Severus	Philip	Decius	Maximinus Daia
	193–211	211–17	217–8	222–35	244–9	249–51	305–13
Esna	*	*		*	*	*	
Kom Ombo			*				
Tahta							*

the last dated inscription) and possibly beyond (*I. Akoris* 36 cf. 30; 32; 34; 35; 39 and the undated 37; 38).

Even for Upper Egypt, the index is imperfect. At Aswan, for instance, there are remains of a temple erected by Ptolemy IV Philopater which appears to have been restored or enlarged by Tiberius, Claudius and Trajan. The last pagan inscription from the temple was of Valens, Valentinian and Gratian (Sayce 1886) suggesting continued usage until the end of the fourth century. There was also a temple with a *pronaos* erected under Domitian (Bresciani et al. 1978: 13; Jaritz 1975; Engelbach 1921; De Wit 1960). At Luxor, a small temple to Sarapis was built within the sacred enclosure of the temple of Amun and dedicated on 26 January 126, the birthday of Hadrian (Golvin et al. 1981). At Athribis (south of modern Sohag in Upper Egypt), the major temple, that of Ptolemy XIII Auletes, was expanded or renovated under Tiberius, Claudius and Trajan (Petrie 1908).

Figure 5.1 and tables 5.2.1–5.2.3 distort the geographical pattern of expenditure on the fabric of traditional temples, though they do not appear to misrepresent substantially the chronological patterns of temple-building. Perhaps the safest conclusion is negative. None of the evidence suggests that there was a notable decline in temple construction during the first 130 years of Roman rule in Egypt and only in the second century does a decline in epigraphic attestations of new buildings and restorations become notable.[23] Even so, it would be a mistake to paint these events in dramatic terms or to translate this pattern into an assumption of decline in the traditional temples or in traditional religious practice.

The temples and the economy: markets and guilds

There is a close association between markets and temples in early Roman Egypt (Otto 1905: 291–315; Smith 1971), though this does not apply in every case. At Karnak, the temple *dromos* led to a ramp on which there was a tribunal. This tribunal was oriented towards the quay (Lauffray 1971). It was here that an early Domitianic tariff list for the market was found (Wagner 1972 = *SB* XVIII 13315). At Syene (Aswan), the area in front of the main Ptolemaic temple was probably the location of the market and was adorned with statues of members of the imperial house (Sayce 1886; 1908). The main market at Oxyrhynchus was located at the Sarapeion, though there were other markets by the fourth century.[24] An Oxyrhynchite register of market taxes makes clear that the taxes charged on traders and their goods were hieratic (religious) (*SB* XVI 12695 = Rea 1982; *SB* XVIII 13631; *P. Köln* V 228; Krüger 1990: 101; *P. Oxy.* XIV 1639 *BL* VIII, 248). The main market at Hermopolis Magna, however, is known as the city or great market and is not obviously associated with a temple, though it is only attested from late texts (*P. Herm.* 24 *BL* IX, 107; *CPH* = *Stud. Pal. Pap.* V 127; 102). The location of the market at Ptolemais Euergetis is also unknown. Flinders Petrie's (1889: 59) excavations uncovered an area in front of the main temple of the city, presumably that of Souchos, which was not built over before the late antique period.[25] The area as described appears suitable for a market. There was also a bank near or in the *agora* (*BGU* III 702 = M. *Chr.* 333; *BGU* III 986). The principal city *agora* was, however, simply described as the Augustan *agora* by the late second century and contained a tribunal at which legal matters could be decided and from which official pronouncements could be made (*BGU* I 326 = M. *Chr.* 316 = *Sel. Pap.* I 85; *BGU* II 361 = M. *Chr.* 92).[26] There was another *agora* in the city in the early second century, the *agora himation*, where there was also a bank (*BGU* I 196 = M. *Chr.* 163; *BGU* II 415 = M. *Chr.* 178).

Banks seem to have a similar pattern of association with temples. At Oxyrhynchus, the best-attested banks were close to the Sarapeion, conveniently near the market (*SB* XVI 12700; *P. Oxy.* II 269 = *Sel. Pap.* I 69; *P. Oxy.* II 264; 267; IV 832; 835; VIII 1132; XXXIV 2722; *P. Turner* 17).[27] The banks in Ptolemais Euergetis were, however, more scattered. There was a bank at the Sebasteion (temple to the imperial house) in 147 (*BGU* I 88), and another near the temple of Athena, probably in the *stoa* outside the temple, in the mid-second century (*BGU* II 472; *P. Fay. Towns* 155; *CPR* I 231 *BL* I, 122; I 206 *BL* I, 121; *BGU* II 445; *P. Lond.* II, pp. 198, 320; pp. 199, 333 = M. *Chr.* 176; *SB* XVIII 13313).[28] There were banks in the street of the Kleopatreion (*BGU* II 445; *SB* IV 7465), at the temple of Bubastis (*P. Coll. Youtie* I 19), and near the temple of Tyche (*P. Hawara* 116), as well as banks associated with the *agorai* (*BGU* I 196 = M. *Chr.* 163; *BGU* II 415 = M. *Chr.* 178; *BGU* III 702 = M. *Chr.* 333; *BGU* III 986) and in other districts throughout the city (Calderini 1938).[29] At Hermopolis, one bank was situated on the *dromos* of Hermes, south of the main junction of the city (*P. Oxy.* XVII 2138). Public measures also seem to have been associated with temples. Temples sometimes appear to have had granaries, perhaps because measurements were made before depositing tax or payments made in kind (Clarysse 1985a).[30]

Temples were also associated with guilds. San Nicolo (1972: 20) saw no substantial difference between religious associations devoted to the worship of a particular deity (which are comparatively well attested during the Ptolemaic period) and the various trade guilds, which tend to be attested in documentation from the Roman period but which must have existed in the Ptolemaic era (van Minnen 1987). These religious σύνοδοι must have had more limited functions than trade groups, though, of course, the named religious function may conceal some other membership principle, such as membership of a trade group.

We have a number of guild constitutions from Tebtunis from the early first century (Boak 1937). *P. Mich.* V 243 of Tiberian date is a contract between Heron son of Orseus (president of the guild) and the other guild members. The contract lays down the rules. Each month the guild meets on the 12th day and each member pays 12 drachmas in dues. If anyone misbehaves at any of these meetings, the guild will impose a fine. If someone absents himself, the fine shall be 1 drachma for a village meeting and 4 drachmas if the meeting is in the city.

If someone marries, he must give 2 drachmas; for the birth of a son, 2 drachmas; for the birth of a daughter, 1 drachma; for the purchase of property, 4 drachmas; for the purchase of sheep, 4 drachmas; and for cattle, 1 drachma. If someone sees another member in trouble and does not come to his aid, the fine is 8 drachmas. If anyone pushes in front at a banquet, 3 obols becomes due. Intrigues against a fellow member or the corruption of his house produce a fine of 60 drachmas. If one member is imprisoned for a private debt, another is to stand security for 100 drachmas for 30 days. If one member dies, all are to shave their hair and come to the feast bringing 1 drachma and two loaves. Any with unshaven heads are fined 4 drachmas. Any who take no part in the funeral feast and offer no wreath are to be fined 4 drachmas. *P. Mich.* V 244 of AD 43 is remarkably similar. Here the fines for not attending the meetings are levied at 2 drachmas, 4 drachmas and 8 drachmas for a meeting in the metropolis. The whole of the guild stood security for a debtor for 100 drachmas for sixty days and they paid the poll tax of the guild president, who in return paid for the food and drink. *P. Mich.* V 245 of AD 47, again from Tebtunis, is the constituting text for the guild of salt-sellers. Prices were fixed and areas and communality of operation in cases of large orders agreed. Three rates of fines for missed meetings were imposed: 1 drachma, 2 drachmas and 8 drachmas. Other constitutions are more fragmentary (*P. Mich.* V 246; 247; 248). The guild of salt-sellers regulated their trade, as must many and perhaps all of the other trade guilds of the Roman period. They also allowed communal payment of taxes in order to gain licenses to trade. *P. Mich.* II 123 (a register of various contracts) attests two payments of 208 drachmas and one of 576 drachmas towards tax by the salt-merchants (r. VII 27; r. XXI 40; r. XXII 27). There were similar much smaller payments by the dyers and fullers (r. VI 16–18). A collection of registrations from Oxyrhynchus dating from the first to the fourth decades of the fourth century (*P. Oxy.* LI 3624–6; LIV 3731–73; *P. Harris* I 73; *P. Oxy.* I 85; II 202 cf *SB* XX 15134) seems mainly concerned with the regulation of prices. Not all guilds were trade guilds: some seem to have had primarily religious functions and others were guilds of farmers. In another of the contracts of *P. Mich* II 123, the president and scribe of the weavers of the small village of Kerkesoucha Oros pay for a prodigious amount of beer for the five others within his guild, suggesting that the activity at the monthly meeting was not purely economic. It is very likely that these meetings were held in temple dining rooms (see, for example, *I. Fay.* I 87 = *SB* VIII 10167 = *IGRR* I 1120; *P. Oxy.* VIII 1144; *PSI* XIII 1355 and pp. 81–3) and, since some of these social events took place in the metropolis, they were thereby integrated into the wider economic and social network of the nome.[31]

An example of the workings of a guild comes in *P. Tebt.* II 287 = *W. Chr.* 251 *BL* VII, 270 of AD 157–9, a report of a hearing before an unknown official concerning the tax to be levied on the fullers and dyers of the Arsinoite. The tax levels were fixed at 1,092 drachmas for the fullers and 1,088 for the dyers.[32] Some attempt had been made to increase the levy and this was resisted by the guild. The guild provided an institutional framework by which a more powerful group could organize and administer the guildsmen, but also a means by which powerless individuals could gain and express a certain social power (for parallels see Cracco Ruggini 1976; van Nijf 1997; Jones 1999; Patterson 1994). The guild was used to collect taxation but could also resist tax impositions. This double role explains official ambivalence to guilds and similar organizations. *Collegia* (plebeian clubs) were blamed for unrest in the late Roman Republic (Suet. *Div. Tul.* 42.3) and generated a nervousness verging on paranoia among the Roman ruling class.[33] Yet, in the imperial period, the *collegia* were integrated into the political structures of Roman cities, in both East and West.[34] Van Nijf (1997: 128) concludes from a detailed study of the epigraphic record from the East that 'It is obvious that they [the traders and craftsmen] used their honorific inscriptions not as public declarations of autonomy, separating themselves from the general populace, but rather as demonstrations of conformity, consciously adopting public models of euergetism.' In Egypt, this conformity was expressed under the auspices of traditional temples (Latjar 1991). One of the earliest Roman-period attestations of a trade guild records the building of a *peribolos* (encircling wall) by the cattle-feeders of Nilopolis, their wives and children, at the nearby village of Soknopaiou Nesos (*I. Fay.* I 73 = *IGRR* I 1116 = *OGIS* II 655; cf. *SB* XVI 12531 = *PSI* X 1149).

Some trade groups had an even closer relationship with traditional temples. Establishing the full range of temple activities and the typicality of activities attested in the documentary record is rather difficult. A long account from the temple at Soknopaiou Nesos lists payments made to the village scribe, for oil presses, to embalmers and vegetable sellers, for the beer tax, and to the fuller at Nilopolis (*Stud. Pal. Pap.* XXII 183; *P. Louvre* I 4 = *BGU* I 1 and II 337 = W. *Chr.* 92). It is not clear why these payments were made. Other payments are made to the nomarch for the tax on fishing boats and to the *dekania* of fishing boats (the organization that manned the fishing fleet). The fishing was conducted somehow under the authority of the temple. Fishermen also appear in a first-century registration document from Oxyrhynchus (*P. Oxy.* LXIV 4440). This text is a declaration of the sacred net-fishermen of Athena Thoeris, great goddess.[35] The fishermen are listed by district. These consist of Ploution, son of Hierax and Sarapous, and his brother Onnophris, living in the *amphodon* of Dromos Gymnasiou, Taroullas, son of Ptolemaios and Saraeus, and his cousin (?) Dionysos, son of Amois and Thermis, registered in the Dromos of Thoeris *amphodon*, Theon of Pausirion, living in Onnophris Street *amphodon*, Didymus, son of Theon and Heras, and his brother Sarapion living in the upper amphodarchy *amphodon*, Saras, son of Heraklas and Sinthonis, and his brother Patalis, living in the Cretan *amphodon*, Dionysios, living in the Plateia *amphodon*, and Doras living in Lykian Camp *amphodon*. Fishing among this particular group was a family business. Notably, the relatives registered are from the same generation: brothers and cousins, not fathers and sons, uncles and nephews.[36] Some fishermen, however, were not connected to temples. *P. Tebt.*

II 359 of 126 is a receipt for fishing-tax on the marshes at Tebtunis and Kerkesis. The tax was paid by the fisherman to the former manager of the tax (ἐπιτηρητής), without any mention of priestly or temple involvement (cf. *P. Tebt.* II 329).[37]

A long but fragmentary return of temple revenues from the temple of Soknebtunis at Tebtunis from AD 107–8 mentions income from the fishermen of Mouchis, income in corn, and, among various other payments, one for weavers, which may have been because priests collected the weavers' tax (*P. Tebt.* II 298 = *W. Chr.* 90 *BL* IX, 355). *P. Tebt.* II 305 is a receipt for a series of annual payments of weavers' tax for 135–7 paid to the managers of the hieratic tax at 'Tebtunis and neighbouring villages'. There are four further similar receipts from Tebtunis, dating from the middle decades of the second century (*P. Tebt.* II 601–4 = *SB* XII 10985–87). Another very fragmentary declaration of income and expenditure from 176–91 makes mention of payments for one or more weavers who used a particular type of loom (*P. Tebt.* II 598 = *SB* XVIII 13118). Thus, the priests of Soknebtunis appear to have been responsible for the collection of taxes on weaving at both Tebtunis and the surrounding villages. This is not quite as straightforward as it seems since most of our other information about weavers' and other trade taxes suggests that these were secular taxes (which compares rather well with the situation with fishermen). The editors suggest that the involvement of the temple resulted from a successful bid to farm the tax and that the tax was then sub-farmed to the managers operating in these texts, which would explain why other temples, such as that at Soknopaiou Nesos, were not so involved with weavers. Yet, this rather convoluted explanation is not appealing, partly because I find it difficult to see how the temple could bid for such a contract. Rather, I think it more likely that the temple was granted responsibility for the collection of this tax because of a prior relationship between the temple authorities and the weavers, very much in the same way as presidents of guilds were enabled to collect some taxes from guild members.[38] The second point of interest is the geographical spread of the tax concession. The temple at Tebtunis was particularly important within the southern Fayum (Anti 1930; Bagnani 1934). It was a centre of education in Demotic into the Roman period, keeping alive traditional Demotic literature (Tait 1992; *P. Tebt. Tait*) and it seems very likely that, like the temple at Narmouthis (Gallo 1992; Jouguet 1901; Vogliano 1936; 1937; 1938; 1939; 1942), it exercised some authority over the temples of neighbouring villages. Religion, politics, and trade have parallel structures.

We are dependent on scraps for the rest of our information. In AD 174 a priest of Tebtunis bought 20,000 stalks of papyrus from the lessees of the marsh of the Polemon district which he then had transported to Tebtunis. It looks as if he was going to make paper, though it is not clear whether this was a commercial operation or merely for the internal use of the temple (*P. Tebt.* II 308 = *W. Chr.* 319). An early third-century text implies a connection between a priestly tax and a tax on painters (*BGU* II 652) and as two other texts link taxes on fishermen and painters (*BGU* I 10; 277) and two more link a probably religious tax with painters (*BGU* I 25 = W. *Chr.* 270; *BGU* I 199 *BL* I, 26), some link between temples and portraiture seems likely. A late second-century contract from Herakleia in the southern Fayum between Pakysis son of Stotoetis, Stotoetis son of Stotoetis, Stotoetis son of Hereios, Hereios son of Stotoetis, Stotoetis son of Stotoetis, and Stotoetis son of Harpagathos (the leading priests of Soknopaios) and Ammonaphis concerns the rental of the oil mill of the temple for five years for 120 drachmas per year and certain small gifts (oil, eggs and chickens) to the contracting priests, a contract which would raise the eyebrows of most modern ethics committees (W. *Chr.* 323). Another interest of traditional temples was brewing beer. A second-century text from the Menelaite nome (*Archiv.* II (1903), p. 565 = *IGRR* I 1101) is a request for tax privileges for a brewery attached to a shrine of Aphrodite. There was a brewery at the temple of Sarapis in Ptolemais Euergetis which was charged 13 obols daily for the supply of water (*P. Lond.* III, pp. 180–90, 1177).[39]

Traditional temples were part of the state apparatus of control and taxation of trade during the Ptolemaic period. The licensing system operated. This was an effective way of levying taxation and also gave local individuals and institutions an interest in preventing black-marketeering, which otherwise would have been almost impossible to control. The temples were not exclusive centres of craft production or administration in their neighbourhoods. They maintained diverse interests and indeed those interests varied from temple to temple. Direct interests in craft production probably complemented their indirect role in the market through guilds. Given the diversity displayed in our existing evidence, it is difficult to know whether the far larger but poorly attested urban temples would have had a pattern of activity different from that of the village temples, but one presumes that their incomes and expenses will have been far greater.

Going to the temple: diners and worshippers

Four of the Tebtunis lists give the ages of guildsmen who, as contracting parties, were obliged to attended the monthly temple-dinners.[40] As is clear from figure 5.2, the age-profile is demographically improbable. Some attempt can be made to compensate for the paucity of data by 'smoothing' the statistics in figure 5.3.[41] Two other sets of figures are added. The second is the curve for the most plausible demographic model for Roman Egypt, and the third is data on the ages of priests from second-century Bakchias.[42]

Even allowing for the very small sample of the population which renders any conclusions provisional, figure 5.3 shows very peculiar patterns. First, it suggests that there were three points of entry to the priesthood. Priests seem to enter in their early twenties, in their early or mid-forties or in their sixties. As a result, the age-structure of the priests bears no resemblance to that of the general population. The age structure of the guildsmen does not show such

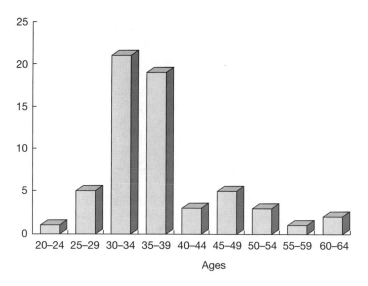

Figure 5.2 Ages of guildsmen in *P. Mich.* V 245, 246, 247, 248

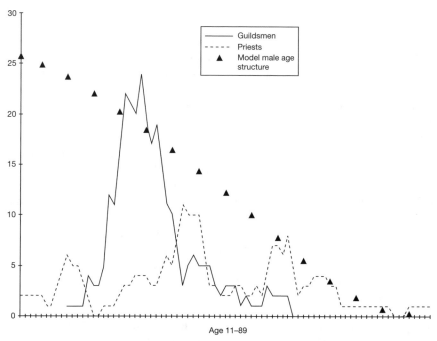

Figure 5.3 Rolling five-year cumulative figures for ages of guildsmen in *P. Mich.* V
245, 246, 247, 248, for ages of priests from *SB* VI 9319, 9320, 9321,
9338, and the model male age structure from Bagnall and Frier 1994: 100

213

clear patterns. Two features emerge: a bulge in the number of guildsmen older than age 29 and a decline far more abrupt than would be the case if it mirrored the model population.[43] It looks as if men tended not to be admitted to the guild until they had reached a certain age, probably normally in their late twenties or early thirties, and that men over a certain age, possibly in their fifties, tended to retire from guild membership. As with priests, entry was a matter of status and perhaps entry into guilds was a function of being the head of a working unit. This would provide an explanation for the rather peculiar pattern of relationships attested in the register of temple fishermen discussed above. A similar pattern can be seen in a register of five hieroglyph writers at Oxyrhynchus in AD 108. These were Teos and Onnophris, sons of Onnophris and Taseus, grandsons of Teos, and Asklas and Osmolchis, sons of Onnophris and Tesauris, grandsons of Osmolchis, all of whom lived in the same district of the city, and Ptolemaios son of Petosarapis, grandson of Petosarapis, who lived elsewhere in the city (*P. Oxy.* VII 1029). Instead of all the traders within the village or the nome gathering together, meals appear to be restricted to comparatively high-status individuals. Similarly, the priests themselves appear to have been age and status conscious, if the evidence from Bakchias may be extrapolated. Such material suggests a hierarchical community using the temples and thus that the social status of these prominent males was reinforced by what appears to have been the exclusion of others from important aspects of community life.

By contrast, 'private' dinner invitations do not suggest that the temple was 'off-limits' to those of comparatively low social status or to women. However, such an assertion must be qualified by an awareness of the poverty of our information. The invitations provide the name of the host, the nature of the occasion and the location of the dinner, but no guest list. A number of invitations are issued by women. Herais invited her guests to dine with her 'in the house' on the marriage of her children (*P. Oxy.* I 111; see p. 83 for the ambiguities of 'the house'). Dioskorous asked her guests to dine in the Sebasteion (temple for the Augusti) (*P. Oxy.* XXXIII 2678). Herais invited her guests 'into the house of the temple of Sarapis in the *kline*[44] of the lord Sarapis' (*P. Coll. Youtie* I 52).[45] Women were able to attend and participate in and probably lead meals and other festivities in temple dining rooms.[46]

The public could participate in temple ritual, especially in processions and specific festivals (Sadek 1987). *Stud. Pal. Pap.* XXII 183 and *BGU* I 1 = II 337 = *W. Chr.* 92 = *P. Louvre* I 4 list expenditure for 154 special festival days at the traditional temple at Soknopaiou Nesos. On three of the 154 days the priests were paid to robe statues, which perhaps suggests a greater public involvement, either by entry into the temple or by procession.[47] Many of the major traditional temples had associated *dromoi* or processional ways, often lined with statuary: sphinxes at Luxor, Karnak and Tebtunis, Thoth-baboons at Hermopolis, rams for temples of Amun (Thebes), hawks from Heliopolis, and many others elsewhere. *Komasteria* (procession houses in which processional participants were organized and perhaps robed) are attested in Ptolemais Euergetis, Panopolis, Apollonospolis–Heptakomias, and Hermopolis (Lukaszewicz 1986: 174) where the British Museum team excavated a building identified as the *komasterion* (Bailey 1986; 1991: 13–28; see also Roeder 1959: 102–5; for a village *komasterion* see *CPR* VI 72, for a Ptolemaic *komasterion*, *P. Tebt.* III 871). The *komasterion* of Hermopolis had external dimensions of 31.5 m by 40.66 m and the area of the hall was probably in excess of 950 m². It was a large, expensive, mid-second-century building and was potentially the starting point for long processions. The *komasterion* at Pesla in the Hermopolite was associated with Hermes–Thoth (*CPR* VI 72) while that at Apollonospolis–Heptakomias was associated with the *dromos* of Apollo and Aphrodite (*Archiv* VI, 427). At Koptos, all we know of the third-century *komasterion* was that it was near a bath house (*P. Got.* 7 *BL* V, 36). Less attractively, a first-century Hermopolite *komasterion* was near a dung heap (*SB* VIII 9699). Processions were built into the topography of the cities and it would be a safe assumption that the priests and others regularly made use of these facilities, thereby extending their religious authority beyond the sacred precincts and into the city as a whole. Such processions had a symbolic value, bringing the gods into the space of their city or village, breaking down the spatial boundary that the *pyla* marked. Potentially, processions were also events at which the community was on display, its relationship to the gods and internal relationships within the community re-enacted in a complex piece of urban theatre (Rogers 1991), but although the wildness of Egyptian festivals was a commonplace among Graeco-Roman writers, reconstruction of the passion of such activity is beyond us.[48]

Of the 154 days of festivals in the Soknopaiou Nesos accounts, many are for festivals specific to the cult. For instance, there are 19 days for the birth of Soknopaios, 9 days for the wedding of Isis Nephersis, 7 days for the installation of Soknopaios, 7 days for the founding of the precinct of Soknopaios, 7 days for the founding of the temple, 19 days for the birth of Nephersis, 7 days for Souchos, and 8 days for the founding of the shrine. Festivals specific to this temple occupied 83 days. One presumes that other cults will have had a similar number of days peculiar to the god, shrine, temple or sanctuary. In a village dominated by a single temple, this would probably only have a limited effect, but in Oxyrhynchus, for instance, the religious environment was much more diverse. According to Whitehorne's (1995) list of papyrological attestations, there were at least ten traditional temples in Oxyrhynchus and some of the temples to Hellenic gods mentioned in the papyri may also have been traditional.[49] If the temple at Soknopaios was typical, then with two large temples and, say, eight smaller traditional temples, there is a possibility that most days would see one or more traditional festival.[50] The intensity of religious activity within the city that this implies is in itself a justification for a professional priesthood and would suggest that, even if participation in a festival would not take all day, many festive days would not have affected everyday life for the majority of the inhabitants of the city.

Major public events were but one strand of the temples' religious activity. The temples were also the scene of personal devotions, mostly inevitably undocumented, though, at some sites, a large number of graffiti-like '*proskynema*' inscriptions acknowledged the writers' obeisance to the god. These are particularly notable at the temple of Mandoulis at Kalabsha where a large number of Roman soldiers scratched a permanent record of their presence onto the walls (Alston 1995: 163; 175–87) and at the temple of Pan in the Wadi Hammamat (*I. Pan*; cf. *I. Memnon.*). Both these were desert stations and reaching these places was perhaps regarded as an achievement, encouraging the visitors to mark their presence permanently. Although such records are not preserved for the major valley temples, some account of the religious practice of the population comes from personal letters. There are various types of personal letters from Egypt: some are more like business letters, short and to the point. Others are less formal. Many of these have a standard formulation, either opening or concluding the letter, which makes mention of prayers for the health of the recipient, and sometimes the recipient's family. Sometimes, this general statement is more specific, as in the letters of Sempronius.

> Sempronius to Satornila his mother and lady, very many greetings. Before everything, I pray that you are well, and at the same time I make *proskynema* everyday before the lord Sarapis . . .
> (*P. Mich.* XV 751 (trans. Rowlandson 1998: no. 108))

There are many more examples (cf. *P. Mich.* XV 752) and the following are selected randomly from a single volume of papyri.

> Isidora to Sarapias her daughter, many greetings. Before all else I pray your health and for that of all of yours and I make *proskynema* for you before the lord Sarapis and for all your children.
> (*P. Mich.* VIII 514)

> Ptolemaios to Tamustha, his mother, greetings. Before all I pray you are well and I make *proskynema* for you before the lord Sarapis.
> (*P. Mich.* VIII 517)

> Tabatheus to Claudius Tiberianus, her brother, many greetings. Before all else I pray that you are well and make *proskynema* for you before the lord Souchos.
> (*P. Mich.* VIII 473)

> Papirius Apollinarius to Claudius Tiberianus the most honoured, many greetings. Before all I pray that you are well. I also am well. I make *proskynema* for you each day before the lord Sarapis.
> (*P. Mich.* VIII 475)

This final formulation 'each day before the lord . . . ' also occurs in *P. Mich.* VIII 476, 477 and 478, and in the first of those the writer makes his devotions before 'Sarapis and the temple-sharing gods' (*sunnaoi theoi*).

One may compare this with letters from a soldier visiting Italy to his mother.

> Apollonarius to Taesis his mother, many greetings. First of all be in good health for me, as I am making *proskynema* on your behalf before all the gods. . . .
>
> (*P. Mich.* VIII 490)

> Apollonarius to Taesis his mother and lady, many greetings. First of all I pray that you are well. I, too, am well and I make *proskynema* on your behalf before the gods here in this place.
>
> (*P. Mich.* VIII 491)

Much later examples, and similarly vague, come from the archive of Paniskos.

> Paniskos to my wife Ploutogenia, mother of my daughter, very many greetings. First of all, I pray for your health each day before all the gods . . .
>
> (*P. Mich.* III 214)

> Paniskos to his wife and daughter, many greetings. First of all I pray before the lord god that I receive you back in good health together with my daughter . . .
>
> (*P. Mich.* III 216)

Less specific formulae tend to be used in the third and fourth centuries, a tendency which made it much easier for the form to survive into the Christian period (Tibiletti 1979: 107–25).

Letters from Alexandria very frequently make mention of obeisance before Sarapis, the main traditional god of the city. There is a temptation not to take these greetings seriously, as one might start letters 'Dear Mr. . . . .' when the contents of the letter make it clear that the person is anything but 'dear'. In some cases it is possible that the religious act may have been performed at a domestic shrine, before cheap terracottas of the gods (Dunand 1979), but the worship of the local deity places devotions in the context of public cult and one can assume, I think, that many of the acts of *proskynema* mentioned in the letters took place in the main traditional temple. This assumption is supported by two cases. The first is the mention of the *sunnaoi theoi*, gods whose statues or shrines would be inserted within the temple of the main god, which firmly locates this activity in a temple. The second is an occasion when the practice breaks down. Apollonarius writes of making *proskynema* 'before the gods here in this place'. The reference is geographically specific, though not specific about the cult.

Apollonarius was in Italy and faced with a plethora of competing gods and cults, without there necessarily being a dominant god. Coming as he does from Egypt, his confusion at trying to perform his duty by his family in the traditional fashion is clear.

The identification of cities with particular cults is very obvious. Most cities had theophoric names in both Greek and Egyptian. It was the temples that marked out the Egyptians in Classical ethnography and it was the temples and their different cults that identified the various cities. This was not just an outsider's view. Patterns of nomenclature across the various nomes of Egypt varied considerably, with 'Souchos-names' in the Arsinoite, 'Hermes-names' in the Hermopolite, 'Ammon-names' in the Thebaid and 'Lykos-names' in the Lykopolite. Such names identify local affiliations of individuals into the fourth century (see also *P. Berl. Bork.* and the 'Pan-names' in that text) and thus the local temple was part of the identity of the population (Hobson 1989).

Conclusion

The first century of Roman rule in Egypt saw a dramatic change in the administrative and political culture in which traditional temples operated. The temples were brought within the administrative structures of the newly Romanized state apparatus, probably to the detriment of at least some in the traditional priestly elite. The political power of the temple priesthoods was thereby reduced. This was not, however, a deliberate assault on traditional temples and it seems that the Roman authorities were generally supportive of the traditional priesthood. In many ways, the new rulers were represented traditionally to the people of Egypt through their support of or association with building projects in the traditional temples. At a more local level, the shift in political power only dented the influence of the temples, which continued to be the major topographical features of cities. The temples were in daily use by large numbers of people. The priests maintained a gruelling calendar of festivals which ensured that city life was regularly interrupted by processions and festivals. Markets appear to have been held close to temples and guilds met within the temples. Economic life centred on the temples. In spite of the evidence of guild membership lists, it was not just the powerful and male who had access to the temple and its facilities. The temple had a role in bringing together members of the community, male and female, in many and various celebrations. Whatever the changes in political structure, the temples were not eclipsed in the first century AD. They retained their position at the centre of the life of the city, providing many of the citizens with a shared political, religious and social identity.

Conflict in Alexandria

There were exceptions to the temple-cities of the first century, and even within the 'temple-cities' of the *chora*, there may have been individuals or groups who, for whatever reason, sought to stand apart from traditional temples. The most notable urban exceptions were probably the so-called Greek cities, places such as Ptolemais (Plaumann 1910), Naukratis, Paraetonium and Alexandria. Very little is known of the society and topography of Ptolemais or Naukratis, even though the latter has been the subject of extensive archaeological investigation (Petrie 1886; Gardner 1888; Hogarth 1898–9; 1905; Coulson and Leonard 1981; Coulson 1988; 1996), but Alexandria is one of the best-attested cities of the first century AD and indeed of the Roman and Byzantine periods in general.

The topography of Alexandria has already been briefly discussed (see pp. 157–65). In Strabo's account (XVII 1 6–10), the topographic heart of the city was the palace district, the Brucheion, with its close association with the harbours and elaborate palaces and temples which appear (XVII 1 8) to subvert the regular street structure and blend one building into the next, though the most glorious building was not a palace but the gymnasium (XVII 1 10). Strabo's emphasis compares interestingly to later writers such as Ammianus Marcellinus (XXII 16.12), Achilles Tatius (V 2), Aphthonius,[51] and the author of the *Expositio Totius Mundi et Gentium* (Simisatonius 1972: 35), who all lay stress on the Sarapeion (mentioned only in passing by Strabo).[52] It was to the Sarapeion that Vespasian retired in AD 69 to await news of his attempt on the throne and to which Caracalla retreated to commune with the god while his troops massacred the population of the city (Suet. *Vesp.* 7; Dio, LXXVIII 21–3; HA, *Anton. Caracalla* 6; Herodian IV 9; Alston 1995: 78; Lukaszewicz 1989).[53] Strabo did not suffer 'blindness' concerning Egyptian cult: he visited a number of religious sites and his *Geography* follows the normal pattern of Greek ethnography in identifying Egyptian cities primarily through their religious traditions. Rather, Strabo's reading of Alexandria was a historical interpretation which depicts Alexandria as the city of Alexander and the Ptolemies rather than that of Sarapis. The monuments of the Ptolemies were everywhere. On arrival, he was faced with the Pharos lighthouse, one of the wonders of the world. He saw the Timoneion, built by Antony as a retreat where he could mourn his defeat at Actium, and then the Kaisareion or Caesareum. This building has caused considerable controversy since it was obviously started by Cleopatra and there are several possible original deities, including her son Kaisarion, Julius Caesar, or possibly Mark Antony, though it became one of the earliest temples to the Augustan imperial cult (Fishwick 1987 [1995]; 1984 [1990]; Tkaczow 1993: 128–35; Fraser 1972: 24). The visitor's next encounter would be with the Brucheion itself and, somewhere buried within this area, the tomb of Alexander the Great.

Strabo is not quite unique in selecting the gymnasium as a key building, since Plutarch (*Life of Antony* 54–5), writing a century later, located the so-called Donations of Alexandria (a marvellous piece of political showmanship by which

Antony in the most public fashion tied himself and his fate to Egypt, to Cleopatra, and to his children by her) in the gymnasium.[54] Dio (XLIX 41), however, put the event 'in the *ekklesia*'. Alexandria did not possess the normal institutions of Greek government, a *boule* (council) or *ekklesia* (assembly), and so the location of Dio's version of the ceremony cannot easily be established. Strabo emphasizes the size of the gymnasium, but the more natural place for an assembly of the people was the theatre. Wherever the Donations took place, Strabo's preference for the gymnasium is presented as a response to the architecture: the gymnasium is not in his account associated with a specific historical event. Nevertheless, the gymnasium was not an ideologically neutral building. Claudius' letter to the Alexandrians confirms that those who had been educated in the gymnasium, the ephebes, were to hold Alexandrian citizenship (Bell 1924; *P. Lond.* VI 1912).[55] The formal legal requirements for Alexandrian citizenship were, however, related to birth (Delia 1991: 71–3). An Alexandrian had to be born to Alexandrian parents and then enrolled in a deme, and possibly in a tribe also, in the normal Greek fashion (Delia 1991: 41).[56] Nevertheless, Claudius' association of citizenship and gymnasium membership may not be an isolated association, if *P. Oxy.* IV 711 concerns Alexandrian status rather than the gymnasia of the *metropoleis* (see p. 138 and p. 390 n. 17; Whitehorne 1982; Bowman and Rathbone 1992; see also *PSI* X 1160), and may be paralleled at Athens (Schmalz 1996).

This association of the gymnasium and citizenship reverberates throughout the history of first- and early second-century Alexandria. From the reign of Gaius, and probably from earlier, ethnic conflict disfigured Alexandrian society. Jew and Greek fought in the streets, in literature and in the lawcourts, over what it was to be an Alexandrian. There were two very clear and contradictory answers to this question. To be an Alexandrian, one needed to have been registered in a deme (as outlined above) or to be an Alexandrian one needed to be born into one of the various communities within the city. It seems very likely that deme membership was associated with those who considered themselves Greek. The position of the other Alexandrian communities was rather more problematic. If Josephus' quotation is to be trusted, the Romans were aware of the problems. Josephus (*Ant.* XIX 281) quotes 'Claudius' edict' τοὺς ἐν ' Ἀλεξανδρεία ' Ἰουδαίους ' Ἀλεξανδρεῖς λεγομένους συγκατοικισθέντας τοῖς πρώτοις εὐθὺ καιροῖς ' Ἀλεξανδρεῦσι καί ἴσης πολιτείας παρὰ τῶν βασιλέων τετευχότας ('those Jews in Alexandria called Alexandrians were fellow-colonizers at the first with the Alexandrians and received equal rights from the kings').[57] There is an obvious struggle here with terminology to establish a dichotomy between the 'Jews called Alexandrians' and the 'Alexandrians', but although the terminology emphasizes difference, the groups are presented as of equivalent status (see Kasher 1985; Delia 1991: 8–27).

This would seem to be a fundamental problem, probably common to many of the cities of the Hellenistic East, most of which had multi-ethnic populations. Much modern scholarship has assumed that the problems in Alexandria stretched back into the early Ptolemaic period (Bell 1941; Turner 1954; Smallwood 1976: 224–50). There is, however, little evidence of anti-semitic activity prior to the Roman period, and certainly not on the scale of events in the AD 30s and later.[58] Although one might assume that low-level violence went largely unreported, this is something of a historical problem.[59] Recent writing on ethnicity and political conflict has divided into two starkly opposed camps (Glazer and Moynihan 1975; Parsons 1975; Østergård 1992; Hall 1997; Barth 1969). Some scholars prefer to see ethnic groups as having their origins deep in the constitution of human society and as being socially normal (Smith 1981; 1986; Bentley 1987), while others emphasize the specific contexts in which ethnicity becomes important in determining social relations and the varied ways in which ethnicity becomes manifest (Yinger 1986; Benbon 1988; Patterson 1975; Gellner 1983; Yelvington 1991). Whatever the ultimate origins of ethnic divisions, their mere presence in a society is not sufficient to explain why people decide that they are sufficiently important to be worth fighting and dying over. The anti-semitic rioting in the Roman period should be placed in a historical context which explains not only the specifics of the rioting in AD 38 and later, but also why there was seemingly an increased emphasis on ethnicity in the early Roman period, the most obvious development being the changed political structures that came with Roman rule.

The Augustan settlement made Alexandrian citizenship an important issue. The citizenship rolls became the responsibility of the prefect, who then appointed senior Roman officials to supervise the *epikriseis* which established status (Nelson 1979; Schubert 1990; Alston 1995: 216). It seems somewhat unlikely that this central control had a Ptolemaic precedent. Rather, Ptolemaic citizenship records were probably maintained within demes. In such circumstances, it is likely that 'undeserving' cases could sneak in and disputes arise as to the validity of citizenship claims. Membership of the gymnasium, which carried an implication of Greek identity and culture (and the gymnasium may itself have maintained lists of ephebes by year), probably became a rather convenient *prima facie* indicator of Alexandrian Greek identity and hence a relationship between gymnasial education (and thus Greek identity) and citizenship could be established.[60]

Even if the legal position was one of equality, the association of Greekness and the gymnasium with citizenship threw into doubt the place of the Jews within the city. In this light, the absence of the Jews from Strabo's Alexandria becomes significant, as is his emphasis on the Greek buildings and cultural heritage. The Jews were not merely secondary to the Greeks, but were relegated to invisibility in what was very largely a Greek city. Nor were the Jews part of Germanicus' Alexandria. Germanicus, effectively deputizing for the emperor, visited Alexandria in AD 19, in the perhaps mistaken belief that the city was part of his *provincia* in the East.[61] He arrived at a time when food was running short in the city. His response was to open the granaries to feed the Greeks.

Josephus tries to make the best of this in answering a jibe of the anti-semite Apion by arguing that it shows just how dreadful the situation had been, but this was hardly an adequate response. We do not have the text of Apion's polemic, but presumably he argued that by only feeding the Greeks Germanicus acknowledged that the city was Greek and that Jews did not enjoy full civic rights or equal status (Jos. *C. Ap.* II 63). Germanicus toured the city in Greek dress (the *chiton*) and without guards. He behaved not so much as the Roman conqueror inspecting the provinces, but as a compatriot, sharing the (Greek) culture of the city of Alexander, and the population appear to have responded with devotion (*P. Lond.* V 1912).[62]

One would, however, not wish to simplify either the cultural complexities of Alexandrian life in the early first century AD or the responses to that city. The predominant tendency of this period may have been to emphasize the Greekness of Alexandria and such approaches probably increased the level of ethnic differentiation within the city, but equating this with the racism and mono-cultural nationalism of the modern period would not be appropriate. Germanicus may have played the Greek in Alexandria, but when he went to Egypt, he also paid his respects to the sites of traditional Egyptian religion. Nor is it appropriate to equate his activities or those of other imperial figures (with the possible exception of Gaius) with the ideological anti-semitism of the Christian medieval West or of modern fascism. As Josephus and Philo make abundantly clear, the Roman emperors were continually reinforcing the Jews' rights to continue their long-established traditions of worship. Jewish and Egyptian traditions were valued, though not as valued as the Greek. Similarly, the carefully drawn boundaries between ethnic groups that we expect with ethnic conflict, especially when such ethnic boundaries are imposed or otherwise maintained by the state, appear to have been absent. Greeks, Jews and Egyptians may have differed in many ways, but they were still part of the same community (see n. 66). There is no better example of this than Philo himself, whose potent blend of Greek philosophy and Jewish theology attests a deep familiarity with both cultures.[63] Philo was happy to use theatrical imagery, for instance, even in his more erudite theological texts (Philo, *De Agricultura* 112–23; *De Ebrietate* 177). It seems likely that the traditions of cultural interchange and debate attested in Philo's work made the intellectual life of Alexandria particularly open to Christian influences and encouraged the early development of a theological school in the city. Yet, Philo in the *In Flaccum* also gives us the fullest and most sophisticated account of how this potentially creative atmosphere of cultural interchange soured and gave rise to violence in AD 38.

Philo's *In Flaccum* is a highly literary, carefully constructed description of the fall of Flaccus, prefect of Egypt.[64] It may be divided into three main sections. There is a long preliminary account which introduces the theme and seeks to break from traditions of diatribe by painting the early years of Flaccus' prefecture in comparatively glowing colours. It then has a long section (34–96) in which the persecution of the Jews is described in detail. Events then overtake

Flaccus and the rest of the work is devoted to his fall (111–90) and realization that he had sinned against God's chosen. The story of the fall of Flaccus, of his arrest, exile, loss of property, public humiliation, exclusion from public space, assault and murder, closely parallels the story of the persecution of the Jews, sharing the same narrative structure. The invitation to compare the fates of the Jews and Flaccus is explicit (*In Flaccum* 172–4) and this pattern of persecution, retribution and realization bears comparison to the narrative of *3 Maccabees* (see n. 58).

The immediate spark for the disturbances was the visit to the city of Agrippa, king of Judaea. Agrippa was received by the Jewish community and by Flaccus, but the latter was rather reluctant to have a man of such status in his province. The Greeks reacted badly to Agrippa's visit and staged a mock reception (presumably after Agrippa had left), acclaiming a local indigent, Karabas, king and leading him in triumph through the gymnasium. Flaccus made no effort to suppress the demonstration with its explicit hostility to the Jewish community and rebellious undertones (*In Flaccum* 36–40). Next, the Greeks of the gymnasium seized the theatre in a dawn raid. Again Flaccus did not act. The mob then demanded that the synagogues be brought under the authority of the Alexandrian people and statues of the emperors be placed within them (*In Flaccum* 41). Flaccus permitted this (*In Flaccum* 43, with comment 44–52). A few days later, Flaccus issued a proclamation condemning the Jews as 'foreigners' and withdrawing their civic rights (τίθησι πρόγραμμα δι' οὗ ξένους καὶ ἐπήλυδας ἡμᾶς ἀπεκάλει) (*In Flaccum* 54). The Greeks then drove the Jews from four of the quarters of the city, forcing them into the Delta quarter. Houses in other districts were attacked and looted, workshops burgled, and the property from them sold (*In Flaccum* 55–6). The Jews were now restricted to the Delta and access to civic facilities was prevented. One of those facilities was the market, which meant that food became difficult to obtain. Those venturing to the market or caught outside Delta were killed. Philo emphasizes the cruelty. Some Jews were burnt and their bodies left in the streets. Others were stabbed, beaten, stoned or trampled to death, and their bodies were dragged across the city so that their blood marked each street and their corpses disintegrated on the very fabric of the city (*In Flaccum* 64–71). The theatricality of the punishments is emphasized (*In Flaccum* 72).[65] Sympathizers received similar treatment, being beaten, tortured and crucified (*In Flaccum* 72).[66]

The topographical dynamic of these events, restricting the Jews' movements and excluding them from most of the city, changes somewhat in the next section. Flaccus ordered the arrest of the *gerousia*, the council of elders, which was appointed by Augustus (according to Philo) to govern the Jewish community within the city. These thirty-eight men were tied up, driven through the *agora* and thence into the theatre, where they were beaten so savagely that some died. In the Roman world, most corporal and capital punishments were inflicted in public, but there was a sliding scale of degradation by which certain privileges were granted to higher citizenship classes and Roman citizens enjoyed extensive protection from magisterial violence. Alexandrians were beaten in different ways from Egyptians, different implements being used, but in this case, the Jews were beaten as if they were Egyptians, the symbolism being all the more obvious since the beating was conducted in the theatre (*In Flaccum* 73–80). Next, soldiers were sent to search the Jews' houses, raiding the married quarters and dragging unmarried girls into the public eye, thereby violating what Philo represents as the traditional Jewish seclusion of women (see p. 101–2; *In Flaccum* 86–94). Women were seized, tortured and taken to the theatre to be humiliated (*In Flaccum* 95–6). And then Flaccus was arrested.

The topography of the city gives these horrendous events a certain structure, which in some ways differentiates them from later pogroms. This was not just a release of racist fervour; it had a ruthless logic which Philo is forced to face and reflect. The outbreak started in the gymnasium, that centre of Greekness within the city from which the Jews were excluded. The rioters were on secure ground and had not exerted their authority over the shared space of the city. But the seizure of the theatre was a major escalation. Here, they passed decrees as if they were a formally constituted *ekklesia* (assembly) and, astonishingly, Flaccus accepted those decrees. In so doing, he abrogated his authority to this Greek element and allowed them to take over the city. Their capture of public assets, such as the synagogues, was an inevitable consequence, and the installation of cult statues of the emperors a convenient pretext which associated the Roman state with their violence. The exclusion of the Jews from four of the five quarters of the city was also within the framework of an intelligent political debate. Those motivated solely by anti-semitism would have excluded the Jews entirely, as modern anti-semites and other racists have sought expulsion or complete destruction of their hated communities. This conflict concerned a restoration of a (fictional) historical order in which the Jewish colony was entirely separate from the Greek and restricted to Delta. That separation was policed violently. The killing and oppression of sympathizers in the non-Jewish community as well as terroristic tactics against those who dared cross the boundary are familiar from modern contexts. It is difficult to think of a more chilling way to mark the other districts as off-limits than through the progressive dismemberment of Jews in the streets.

The next stage was the exercise of power over the newly isolated community. Again this was exercised through the spatiality of the city. The attack on Jewish houses demonstrated that the power of Flaccus stretched even into the homes of Jews. Members of the *gerousia* were marched through the most public areas, paraded in front of a hostile crowd and humiliated, before some were killed. The beating of those in the *gerousia* demonstrated Greek and Roman control over the bodies of the men and the attack on the houses showed that this power could stretch to the bodies of women. Philo paints a picture of a community completely overpowered by a tyrannical prefect in league with a ferocious mob. No place and no body were safe, until the tables were turned and Flaccus found that no place was safe for him and his life was subject to the whim of the emperor.

Philo's is not the only tale to be told here. Deep within Philo's narrative is the story of Flaccus' attempts to run Alexandria. This is a difficult tale and one in which the sources are problematic, though the context in which Flaccus and other governors had to operate in Alexandria is quite well known. Even though Rome had elevated the status of Alexandria, relations between the Roman authorities and the Alexandrian population do not seem to have run smoothly in the first century AD. The Alexandrian population had a reputation for volatility which went back to their often strained relationship with their Ptolemaic rulers. Strabo (XVII 1.53) tells us of clashes between the prefect Petronius and stone-throwing Alexandrian mobs. Dio Chrysostom, *Oratio* 32, probably discussing events of *c.* AD 69, regards the freedom with which the Alexandrians expressed their discontent as being outrageous but customary for that city (Jones 1973). During his stay in the city Vespasian clashed with the urban population, possibly over taxes (Suet. *Vesp.* 19.2). In addition, we have the outbreaks of violence against Jews in 38–41, in 66, and in 117–18 (Alston 1995: 74–7).

This hostility between the Roman authorities and the Alexandrians generated its own genre of protest literature, the martyr act. These are collectively known as *Acta Alexandrinorum*, several of which are conveniently collected by Musurillo (1954; 1961). Although these were concerned with Alexandrian issues, their preservation in the papyrological record demonstrates that they were being read in the Fayum and the Oxyrhynchite. All the surviving accounts are fragmentary and although many are framed as verbatim accounts of hearings, all appear to have a strong fictional element. Distinguishing between the fiction and any kernel of historical truth enclosed is thankless and, in this regard, they have much in common with Christian martyr acts. One of the more obviously novelistic (Musurillo 1954: II = *P. Oxy.* VIII 1089) has three Alexandrians, Dionysios, Isidoros (of whom more below), and a certain Aphrodisia, who appears to accompany Isidoros, meeting Flaccus at the Sarapeion (perhaps secretly).[67] Isidoros is there pounced on by an unidentified old man who proceeds to dispense advice, mainly that Isidoros should seek a reconciliation with Flaccus. Flaccus himself appears suddenly and the papyrus becomes extremely lacunose. A large sum of money is mentioned (5 talents), perhaps a bribe, and 'doing harm to Isidoros and Lampo'. The story appears to be of a sordid conspiracy which does not reflect well on Flaccus. A more blackly amusing tale (Musurillo 1954: IV = W. *Chr.* 14 + *P. Lond.* inv. 2785) again involves Isidoros, this time with Lampo. They are answering accusations before Claudius who, since they have been responsible for the deaths of a certain Theon and a Naevius (though it is not clear how), warns them not to attack his friends. In one version, Isidoros takes offence at this and Claudius responds 'Are you the son of an actress, Isidoros', which suggests that his mother was a prostitute.

Isidoros replies in kind: 'I am not the son of a slave or of an actress but am the gymnasiarch of the glorious city of Alexandria. You are the rejected son of Salome, the Jewess.' Claudius' response to this undiplomatic exchange was to execute both Alexandrians. In another version, Isidoros responded to Claudius' advice to avoid attacks on his friends by launching on 'My lord Caesar, what [do you wish with Agrip]pa, that three-obol Jew?'. One presumes that this would have the same result as in the other version. These extraordinary exchanges are paralleled in a text with a late second-century dramatic date, which again appears to have two versions. In one a certain Appian denounces the emperor for profiteering in corn, while in the other Appian first accuses the emperor of being a tyrant and is led off to execution. He makes something of a scene, which allegedly causes a protest, and he is brought back before the emperor, whom he then calls a 'bandit-chief' (Musurillo 1954: XI = *P. Oxy.* I 33; *P. Yale inv.* 1536).

The source of this discontent with Rome is not clear, though the anti-Roman sentiments expressed are sometimes combined with anti-semitism.[68] Potentially, this might explain the upsurge of anti-semitic violence in the Roman period since if the Jews could be shown to have been closely identified with Roman rule, the assault on the Jews could be seen as a nationalistic attack on the Romans. The philo-semitic policy allegedly adopted by the Roman authorities does, however, appear to be something of a myth (though of course myths gain currency), and we have seen that the Romans identified with the Greek community of the city. My objections to this theory are more fundamental. One is an argument from silence. One would have expected that Philo and Josephus would have placed enormous stress on any identification of Roman and Jewish interests in the attacks on the Jews. Instead, they appear to be on the defensive. Certainly Philo, our only insight into the political thought of the Alexandrian Jewish community, though generous in his praise of certain Roman leaders (and we must be aware that Rome's treason laws did not encourage free debate on political issues), has a mixed attitude towards Roman political institutions (Alston 1997b; Barraclough 1984). Second, even weak governors may have regarded the Greek community's attacks on the Jews with great suspicion if they were simply covert attacks on Rome. Flaccus may have misjudged the situation, but Tiberius Julius Alexander, educated in Alexandria and with strong connections with the Jewish community, would hardly have been misled, even in AD 66 (see below), if anti-semitic activity was really anti-Roman. There does not appear to be a strong enough causal connection between anti-semitism and anti-Romanism to allow them to be seen as equivalent. Rather, we could see these hatreds as two separate strands in Alexandria's political debate which naturally came together in the somewhat overdramatic *Acta Alexandrinorum*.

One of the requests of the Alexandrians was to be given a greater level of civic independence through the reinstitution of a city council. This request was made in the embassy that visited Claudius on his accession and in the aftermath of the rioting in Alexandria (*P. Lond.* V 1912; cf. *PSI* X 1160). Claudius, in time-honoured bureaucratic fashion, sidestepped the issue by telling the Alexandrians that he would investigate. Presumably the investigation came to the conclusion that this was not desirable, though it may be that the vacuum at the heart of Alexandrian politics was the root cause of the violence. Whatever the ultimate cause of Alexandrian discontent, Flaccus was not the only governor to have significant problems keeping the city quiet.

Most of our information about Flaccus comes from Philo, who tells us that Flaccus commenced his prefecture by gaining a detailed understanding of Egyptian affairs, managing the finances of the province with energy, and drilling the soldiers. In order to secure the *chora*, he organized a sweep through the country which collected in any weapons held; a process of disarming that is attested in other provinces (Brunt 1975), but which cannot have been popular with the provincials. Philo's portrayal conforms to a stereotype of Roman provincial governors as represented most famously by Corbulo (Tacitus, *Ann.* XI 18–20; XIII 8–9; 34–41), Galba (Suet. *Galba*; Tacitus, *Hist.* I 5–49), and, to an extent, by Piso, Germanicus' enemy. These governors reinforced what they saw as traditional Roman virtues, such as discipline, and often engaged in the brutal drilling of troops. The edict of Tiberius Julius Alexander, issued in AD 68, makes mention of Flaccus in a long and complex section involving the exemption of some land from taxation (Chalon 1964; *OGIS* 669; Smallwood 1967: no. 391 (4)). Flaccus appears to have interpreted the law rather strictly (possibly abolishing a pre-existing exemption) and contrary to the more relaxed view that Claudius and later prefects took. The result was that later tax farmers could cite prefectural authority to tax certain exempt lands. A generation after Flaccus' prefecture, Tiberius Julius Alexander was attempting (as others had) to sort out the administrative muddle. Philo (*In Flaccum* 4) emphasizes Flaccus' air of dignity and his pride, but his regime appears marked by an authoritarian style.

The list of Flaccus' achievements in the first section of the *In Flaccum* includes a claim that Flaccus dissolved the clubs and guilds (ἑταιρείας καί συνόδους), which met for seemingly religious purposes but which were engaged in disorder (*In Flaccum* 4). This decision returned to haunt Flaccus. The date of the imposition of the ban is uncertain but crucial. Philo places the ban in the early years of Flaccus' governship, when Flaccus was a good governor. The transformation in the nature of his rule came with the deaths of Tiberius and Macro (his patron and the praetorian prefect). These deaths left him in need of political allies, especially since he had shown some animosity to the family of the new emperor, Gaius. Philo suggests that he turned to the Alexandrians for political support and specifically to three popular leaders, Dionysios, Lampo and Isidoros, all of whom appear in the *Acta Alexandrinorum* (*In Flaccum* 20), and whom Philo represents as demagogues who stirred up the populace against the Jews. This narrative makes perfect political sense, but the fact that there are two stories behind Flaccus' arrest and trial leads to doubts. The first and major narrative gives credit for saving the Jews to God and King Agrippa (*In Flaccum* 102–4;

116–24), but the minor narrative sees Flaccus summoned to Rome to face accusations levied by 'the most hateful men, Isidoros and Lampo' (*In Flaccum* 125). Lampo's reason for fleeing the country is not explicit, but it is implied that he was hounded by popular discontent over his corrupt administration of the courts and that he fled because of extended judicial persecution (*In Flaccum* 128–34). Philo describes a deliberately extended trial for treason (against Tiberius) which broke Lampo's health and a further trial over the seizure of Lampo's property in fulfilment of the liturgy of the gymnasiarch. Furthermore, he describes Lampo's career as clerk to the prefects and as a forger of documents. Isidoros is accused of manipulating the σύνοδοι καὶ κλῖναι (guilds and dining-clubs) and of being ὁ συμποσίαρχος, ὁ κλινάρχης, ὁ ταραξίπολις (leader of the drinking-club, the dining-club leader, the troubler of the city). He persuaded these clubs to demonstrate against Flaccus in the gymnasium, but Flaccus and the urban authorities clamped down on the demonstration and sought to arrest Isidoros when evidence emerged that he had instigated the disturbance. Isidoros then fled the city, presumably to take his case to Gaius (*In Flaccum* 135–45).

These events provide an appropriate context for the banning of *sunodoi* mentioned by Philo, but clearly also repeat a final breakdown in the relationship between Flaccus and Isidoros which would place the events towards the end of his tenure of office. One may perhaps postulate three stages in the relationship. A period of hostility between Flaccus and Isidoros and Lampo during which Lampo was persecuted and the *sunodoi* banned (when Flaccus was a good governor), a brief period of agreement during which the Jews were persecuted (the *sunodoi* reinstated and Lampo forgiven?), and then a complete breakdown of the relationship (after which action was taken against the *sunodoi*?). Yet, this seems overly complicated and compresses the chronology of events.[69] A more plausible narrative emerges if we assume that Philo is being somewhat creative. The hostility between Lampo and Isidoros and Flaccus appears to have been a long-established feature of his time in office and thus the Philonic assumption that they co-operated in the formulation of policy against the Jews seems somewhat unlikely. Nevertheless, Philo may have had good reason to associate Isidoros and Lampo (who were presumably influential figures after the disgrace of Flaccus) with anti-semitic activity and demagoguery, either because they contributed to the atmosphere which made such activities possible, or because of a wish to discredit their activities subsequent to the fall of Flaccus. Allowing for this, we may place the banning of the *sunodoi* and the exiles of Isidoros and Lampo before Agrippa's visit to the city. We then have a new sequence of events leading to Flaccus' fall. Disturbances in the gymnasium lead to the exile of Isidoros who flees to Rome. There, he joins forces with Lampo and they present their complaints to Gaius. Gaius decides to arrest Flaccus and he is summoned to the emperor to face his accusers. In the meantime, the riots against the Jews take place. This story would not suit Philo's purpose since it moves the Jews from centre stage, but would make Gaius' intervention more plausible since although Gaius was not renowned as being sympathetic to the Jews (Philo, *Legatio ad Gaium*), he was conscious of Alexandria's heritage and allegedly was so favourably inclined to the city that he considered switching his residence from Rome to Alexandria.[70]

This version of events provides a different political context for the riots of AD 38. Nevertheless, there is no reason to doubt Philo's assertion that Flaccus, who had enjoyed the support of Tiberius and Macro, found himself in a much weaker position after their deaths and that this political insecurity altered his approach to government. We can reconstruct a different narrative. Flaccus' style of government will have made him enemies and it looks as if rising tension within Alexandria resulted in a demonstration against Flaccus in the gymnasium which in turn encouraged Flaccus to take draconian action against the *sunodoi* and exile Isidoros. And then Agrippa visited the city. Philo rather passes over this, treating Flaccus' hostility as essentially disloyal, but Flaccus had a point. Agrippa came from the court of the new and possibly hostile emperor. He was a politically powerful client king visiting a politically nervous equestrian governor. His arrival, however it was intended, was a challenge to Flaccus' authority. Although Philo again emphasizes how discreetly Agrippa wished to be received, he clearly paraded through the city. When Karabas was dressed up, the Greeks chanted '*Marin*', the Aramaic for 'Lord' (*In Flaccum* 25–40). Unless the Greeks of the gymnasium had been practising their Aramaic, they must have been imitating the cries of the Jewish crowd that met Agrippa. We should, I think, envisage a large and noisy demonstration and a parade, the centrepiece of which was Agrippa himself, accompanied by a bodyguard decked out in gold and silver. This was not an unassuming entry. Flaccus was also forced to receive him and was probably faced with a riotous tumult acclaiming this man, whom he must rightly have seen as a political threat. This fear was justified since the Jewish leaders used the opportunity of Agrippa's visit to complain about the prefect and to entrust Agrippa with letters to be forwarded to Rome (*In Flaccum* 102–3).

This was the spark that turned the struggle to control Alexandria so violent. Flaccus had made every effort to control the city and had clearly won some of his political battles, but the changing political context had left him weaker and the Jewish demonstration had shown the ability of that community to take control of the city. Their brief moment of pride and control (confident in the political authority of their king) did not secure their position, for it merely encouraged the Greek community to exert their power against what they may have perceived as a Jewish threat. It remains an open question as to whether Flaccus acquiesced in the demands of the mob or actively encouraged them. He may have felt that he was too weak to control the crowds or have been hostile to the Jews (who had further weakened his authority) and seen the Greek-led disturbances as a way of gaining authority over them. Whatever the case, the Greeks drove the Jews from 'their city' and claimed the city as Greek, and Flaccus gave their actions legitimacy.

In AD 41 Gaius was assassinated, probably much to the relief of Jewish communities across the Mediterranean. It is probable that the death of Gaius sparked a fresh wave of violence in Alexandria. Whatever happened, the 'citizenship issue' was referred to Claudius. The text of the response is preserved in Josephus, *Ant.* XIX 280–5, the opening of which was quoted above. The text approaches the issue in a rather circumlocutory way, as was Claudius' style, and outlines the history of Roman preservation of Jewish rights in Alexandria before confirming the privileges of the Jews, and either allows or perhaps insists that they abide by their own customs.[71] He then calls on both parties to keep the peace. The second communication is preserved on a papyrus from Philadelphia in the Fayum and is a letter from Claudius to the Alexandrians (*P. Lond.* V 1912 = Bell 1924), the publication of which is dated to AD 41, just under eleven months after his accession to the throne. The letter is a response to embassies sent to him from Alexandria. The length of time between the letter and his accession would suggest that the first embassy had visited Rome to honour the emperor and had not been sent to make representations on the citizenship issue. It is to be regarded as an entirely separate statement from the edict. It opens by thanking the various ambassadors and by accepting honours and noting Alexandria's regard for Germanicus, Claudius' brother. Then honours are accepted, though an appointment of a high priest to Claudius is rejected. Citizenship rights are granted to the ephebes unless any can be shown to have had servile mothers. Arrangements for priests of the imperial cult and for the appointment of magistrates within the city are confirmed. The issue of the *boule* is deferred. Only then does Claudius turn to the violence between Jews and Greeks. In contrast to the rather plain condemnation of the Greek attack in the Josephus text, Claudius hedges his bets and refuses to condemn either side. But the language of the edict is significant. The Alexandrians were to behave in a kindly fashion towards the Jews 'who have for a long time lived in the same city'. The Jews were not to send separate embassies,[72] compete in the gymnasiarchs' games or games of the *Kosmetai*, but were to enjoy the fruits of living in ἀλλοτρία πόλει (a city belonging to others). They were also not to accept immigrants from Syria and this was reinforced by a threat to treat the Jews as a 'plague for the world' should they transgress. There is a notable violence in the language which is absent from the letter. Claudius confirms the rights of the Jews but also confirms that they are not citizens and that the city belongs to the Greeks. The tenor of the letter, though perhaps not the meaning, is rather different from the edict in Josephus.

The next violent outbreaks in Alexandria are to be associated with the Jewish war of 66–70. I have little to add to the standard accounts. The rhetoric of the violence appears to conform to that of the uprising under Gaius. The Greeks had met in the theatre where they were considering sending an embassy to Nero. Several Jews were identified in the crowd and attacked, whereupon the Jewish community rushed to their rescue and the Greeks were subsequently rescued by the Roman military (Josephus, *BJ* II 491–8; Alston 1995: 74–5).

At the end of the Jewish war, the internecine violence within the Jewish community apparently extended to Alexandria to where some of the Jews from Syria-Palestine had fled. These allegedly assassinated some members of the Jewish aristocracy within the city, who reacted by purging their community of the subversives (Josephus, *BJ* VII 420–5). The revolt *c.* 117 was more serious and appears to have had graver consequences. A revolt in Cyrenaica, probably sparked by messianic fervour, crossed the frontier into Egypt. The Roman troops sent against the rebels were defeated and, either in support of the invasion or as a response to anti-Jewish activity, some at least of the Jewish communities in Egypt appear to have joined the rebels, probably with disastrous results (Alston 1995: 75–6). The great synagogue in Alexandria appears to have been destroyed (*Jerusalem Talmud, Sukkah* V 55s in Kasher 1985: 350; Smallwood 1976: 399; Sly 1996: 43–4) and it is probable that the Jewish community was driven from the city at least temporarily.

Alexandria's history continued to be marked by turbulence during the second century, though we know very little about the various disturbances. Hadrian may have intervened to put an end to rioting over the location of an Apis bull and a prefect may have been killed during the reign of Antoninus Pius (Alston 1995: 77), but the sources give little detail.

The level of violence in first-century AD Alexandria demands some explanation. We must, however, exercise a certain amount of caution. First, although the outbreaks were frequent and the fighting fierce, violence continued to be a feature of Alexandrian life throughout the third, fourth and fifth centuries (Haas 1997) and of urban life in other large cities of the eastern Mediterranean, Antioch for instance. We may also compare Alexandria with other great urban centres, such as Rome and Constantinople. Most of our sources also emphasize the violence of Roman life, though in the imperial period this violence is comparatively low-level. This was in spite of the care many emperors took to entertain and provide for the masses, and the formidable military force they had at their disposal to police the city (Nippel 1995; Yavetz 1969). Before the Principate, urban violence had played a part in the destabilizing of the Roman Republic. Constantinople also faced warring factions, seemingly based around the circus (Cameron 1976). Occasional, large-scale violent events appear to have been common in ancient cities of the Roman period. Also, the quality of our source material for first-century AD Alexandria is unusual and violent Alexandrians became something of a *topos* of Classical literature (Barry 1993a; 1993b). This does not mean that their reputation was undeserved and one of the more famous attacks on Alexandrian violence, Dio Chrysostom, *Oratio* 32, does not even mention the Jewish–Greek conflict. Also, the ferocity of some of this violence appears to have been unusual. Claudius in his letter to the Alexandrians (*P. Lond.* V 1912) struggles to find appropriate language. He opts first for ταραχή (tumult, disorder, troubles) and then for the stronger στάσις (sedition, civil disorder), before lighting on πόλεμος (war).

It is very easy to assume that levels of urban violence are a good index of the proper functioning of a society. Yet, violence is one way of resolving political struggles and some societies tolerate more urban violence than others. Even among modern Western democracies, there are differing views concerning the legitimacy of urban political violence. France, for instance, has a much stronger tradition of popular radicalism and violence than Britain or the United States, especially in circumstances where a particular group feels it has no voice in mainstream politics. Violence can, however, also be used to suppress political debate. Elites in the ancient world frequently used force to prevent challenges to their authority from outside and within the elite. Nevertheless, violence was a crude and dangerous method of continuing political debate. It moved power to the streets and, potentially, to the masses. Perhaps for that reason, imperial Rome was hostile to demagoguery and, in the long term, there may have been a severe political price to pay for any politician who offended aristocratic sensibilities by resorting to street violence. In the imperial period, violence should be seen not as a breakdown of society, but as a failure of consensus, the achievement of which was one of the aims of government. Such an approach emphasizes political manipulation as a cause of ethnic violence and corresponds to Philo's presentation of the origins of the violence as lying in a political conspiracy led by disreputable politicians.

Nevertheless, 'theories of social collapse' remain prevalent and perhaps even predominant in popular modern discussion of ethnic violence. These tend to blame innate hostilities between groups which suddenly and largely unaccountably erupt into violence. Haas (1997: 10), rather depressingly, blames the 'distinctive communal consciousness separating various groups' and the competition between these groups for 'cultural hegemony' for violence in fourth- and fifth-century Alexandria and (p. 13) explains the violence of the first century AD as a pagan response to a Jewish threat (possibly backed by the Romans) to that pagan hegemony. Explicitly, the communal violence of Alexandria, especially from the fourth century onwards, is seen as an almost inevitable failure of fully multicultural cities to maintain peace without one group having an unchallengeable hegemony (p. 336).[73] This is similar to Gregory's (1979: 34) view that

> At the turn of the century [fourth–fifth], Judaism was still an important religion in the city, but the Jews also felt the power of the 'pope' of Egypt and they were expelled from the city. Thus the antagonisms that had rent Alexandrian society from the time of its foundation seemed resolved.

Such views are depressing partly because they suggest that cities cannot be fully multicultural and have peace, but must maintain a stable cultural hegemonial group which might allow ethnic minorities to exist. Second, they represent hostility between ethnic groups or groups with a 'communal consciousness' as inevitable. More worryingly, they, and I am sure this is unintentional on the part of the authors and pursues the logic of their arguments far further than they would wish, tend to shift blame for ethnic violence to the ethnic minority rather than to the perpetrators of violence. In other words, Alexandria has a Jewish problem rather than a racist problem and that problem is 'resolved' (surely an ironic usage) by Cyril's expulsion of the Jews, as it was by the destruction of the Jewish community in the Trajanic revolt.

Much of the violence of the first century was about political control in the city. Yet many different groups were competing for that power. Flaccus was in a difficult situation. He made enemies and some of these appear to have manipulated the *sunodoi* to demonstrate against him. If there were any underlying issues in this disturbance, they are not described in our sources. By acting as patron to *sunodoi* a political leader could garner political support. Such small groups could provide the necessary impetus to take control of the streets. Nevertheless, in the aristocratic world of the Roman empire, the most direct route to power was through the support of fellow aristocrats, many of whom will have feared the mob. Flaccus' response was to use aristocratic allies to suppress his enemies and abolish the *sunodoi* through which their power had been organized, and to exile his most prominent opponent, Isidoros. Yet, in the anti-semitic violence, it appears to have been this very group which returned to the attack.

It is probably not a coincidence that the violence again started in the gymnasium. The gymnasium contained various small cliques, educated together, who probably visited to exercise, bathe and talk business. In the absence of a mass assembly, it was only through groups such as these that individual opinions could find voice and sufficient support to become a crowd. The gymnasium then became the centre of an anti-semitic crowd voicing resentment against the semitic crowd that had so recently dominated the streets. It was this sub-section of the Greeks within the city that struck out and claimed control of the whole city by seizing the theatre. Flaccus, possibly because he saw this as an opportunity to ally himself with the politicians who had now seized the initiative, acquiesced in this seizure of power. Ethnic hostility was certainly an important part of this disturbance, but was not the only issue at stake. The riot was an assertion of power on behalf of a certain sector of the Greek community.

It may be that the triumph of this particular political group was rather short-lived. Flaccus established his power over the Jews within the city by sending soldiers into their houses, but we have no information as to whether he sought to reassert his authority over the gymnasial crowd and their leaders. Eventually, however, Flaccus' successors probably did defeat the popular leaders. The *Acta Alexandrinorum* dramatize the martyrdoms of Isidoros and Lampo, and although the text may be entirely fictitious, it is difficult to believe that these two did not fall from power. Instead, therefore, of seeing this as a primarily ethnic conflict, the riots of AD 38 should, I think, be seen in the context of political struggles to control Alexandria. The violence resulted not from a collapse of political structures which held Alexandria together, an 'intercommunal crisis', but from the ability of politicians to integrate the crowd and their political programmes and their willingness to lead that crowd into violence. The violence in Alexandria was very carefully orchestrated and controlled. It was not anarchy.

This argument switches attention to the relationship between the people and politicians and between political leaders and the government. Was Alexandria different from other cities in the constitution of these relationships? Frankly, I rely here on guesswork. Alexandria was a large city, probably with quite an unusual economic base. It seems to have had an important trading sector and perhaps also a significant manufacturing sector. This population may have been peculiarly sensitive to economic change and, unlike peasants and those dependent on income from land, they had little escape from the vagaries of the market. This may have encouraged political volatility. The hierarchical operation of guilds and the group organization of the gymnasium may also have meant that this population was well organized and in a position to transmit political discontents very quickly. Second, although there are no reliable estimates for the population of Alexandria, it was large and thus it was comparatively easy to mobilize a crowd. A crowd consisting of 10 per cent of adult males in a city of about 20,000 was probably around 500, whereas 500 men in Alexandria was probably less than 0.5 per cent of the male population. In addition, Alexandria had only a weak civic administration. The absence of a city council meant that there was no clearly defined urban leadership. Effectively, this reduced the ability of aristocratic elements to exert peer pressure which might restrain more populist elements from resorting to violence. We have already seen that Alexandria appears to have had at least some institutions which enabled popular feeling to be mobilized and that the absence of democratic institutions limited the areas in which those feelings could be voiced to the theatre and street violence. More speculatively, I wonder whether the violence in Alexandria might be associated with fierce competition and instability in the political elite. Alexandria had been showered with privileges by Augustus and his successors and it seems very likely that one of the aims of the elevation of Alexandria was to create a supportive elite within Egypt that would help secure and govern the province. This new administrative and political arrangement started to replace a system of government based on the royal court and although there may have been overlap, this process generated a new elite and possibly one that was shifting and unstable, and the absence of a *boule* deprived Alexandria of an institution that enhanced stability by providing a forum for previous holders of magistracies. Added to this, it seems very likely that the political elite in Alexandria was not drawn exclusively from one sector of the community. A Jewish leader could not, presumably, join the gymnasium or act as *kosmetes* or gymnasiarch, but could be a member of the Jewish *gerousia*. Families such as that of Philo himself were clearly well connected and their influence extended beyond the Jewish community. In exactly the same fashion as Greek political leaders, Jewish leaders could muster crowds, and when Agrippa visited, certain Jews, perhaps not the whole community, celebrated the success of their political leader, his gaining of imperial support and their vicarious power. Because of institutional and religious separation, it seems unlikely that any Jewish leader could secure sizeable support among the Greeks or any Greek leader amongst the Jews, and the ethnic mix in the city almost certainly contributed to the political instability in the city.

Acknowledging ethnic divisions is different from arguing for their pre-eminence in political conflict. Philo has an interest in representing the Jews as a single political group, and the anti-semites presumably had an interest in treating the Jews as a single faction. Yet, we have considerable evidence of communication across the ethnic divide in the pre-38 period. The rioting must have hardened political groupings and reduced cross-ethnic communication. Nevertheless, even after the events of 38–41, there is some reason to suggest that the politics of the city were not simply a matter of ethnic competition. Jews, for instance, went to the theatre in 66, presumably believing that they would be allowed to take part in the political debate, and it seems possible that the prefect Tiberius Julius Alexander, a former Jew and nephew of Philo, had at least some support from the Jewish community, which he tried to manipulate to bring an end to the rioting in AD 66. These events and the expulsion of the refugees from the Jewish war in Judaea and Galilee show that the Jewish community itself was politically divided. Although the Jews were probably marginalized after 38–41, their presence appears to have contributed to the political complexity and instability of the city, and it is that instability, rather than the mere presence of ethnic division, which, it seems to me, accounts for the violence of Alexandrian life from the Augustan period onwards.[74]

The second-century city: the Romanization of urban space

Architecture

Comparison between historical periods in Egypt is rendered difficult by the patterns of papyrological preservation. The first-century AD city, although well attested by Ptolemaic standards, is not as well attested as cities of the second and third centuries and impressionistic judgements may mislead as a result. Nevertheless, I start this section with a sweeping generalization. Although there is dramatic change in administrative structures in the 'long first century' of Roman rule in Egypt, the continuities in the organization of urban space appear notable. In the second century, in many places, urban topography catches up with administrative change and we see a dramatic Romanization of public architecture. The detail of this transformation is difficult to establish, partly because buildings may exist long before their first papyrological attestation, but the archaeological evidence comes into its own and provides a context in which we can understand the papyrological data. We start with a number of examples.

Athribis

Athribis, near the important modern town of Benha in the central oasis, was described by Jomard during the brief French occupation of Cairo from 1797 to 1801. The plate (figure 5.4; Description 1809, pl. V 27.3; Vernus 1978) shows a city with two main roads (in Roman terms, the *cardo* and *decumanus*) meeting at right-angles at what may have been the original centre of the city. The oldest part of the city appears to have been on the banks of the Nile (which ran to the east of the city). There is some evidence of Pharaonic development here in a cartouche of the ubiquitous Ramesses II (Rowe 1938). Nearby stone quays facilitated trade and perhaps also provided market space (by analogy with riverine markets at Elephantine and Thebes, see pp. 207–8 and Kemp 1989: 254). The majority of the town, however, dates from the Ptolemaic period to the seventh century.

There were major programmes of civic renovation in the Roman period. The area of the baths was developed under Claudius and Nero (probably) and then renovated under Trajan or Hadrian, before being further remodelled under Valens (Michalowski 1962b; el-Khashab 1949). A large head of Hadrian (Rowe 1938; Dabrowski 1962; cf. Kiss 1994) suggests some monumental construction under that emperor. The colonnades of the *cardo* and *decumanus*, and the major public buildings that probably followed their laying-out, appear to be mid-second century (Dabrowski 1962; Michalowski 1962a; Mysliwiec and Szymanska 1992). The excavations have also uncovered a Byzantine 'villa' and associated workshops (Mysliwiec and Szymanska 1992). In the west and north-west of the site, there is an area in which the surviving remains are mostly Ptolemaic, and although some pottery of the first century AD has been found, there are no traces of Roman construction. However, the upper layers of the site have been disturbed and there is evidence of Byzantine occupation (Mysliwiec 1992a; 1988). Other excavations, carried out in 1985, produced very different pictures (Mysliwiec and Herbich 1988). One uncovered a Ptolemaic building, probably of *c.* 250 BC, which had plastered walls and worked masonry. A large amount of Ptolemaic pottery was found, some of which was imported, and seventeen pieces of statuary were recovered. At some point the building burnt down and the site may have been reused in the Roman period as a dung heap. Another area produced coins of mainly fourth- to seventh-century AD date, though the architectural remains in the area are late Ptolemaic or early Roman. A further trench uncovered large numbers of coins dating from the first to the fourth century, a late Roman lamp and a terracotta head of a Roman empress. With this material, there was a deposit of mainly early Roman fine-ware pottery and some Ptolemaic material. Patterns of development and occupation appear to have been highly localized within the city (Mysliwiec 1995; Mysliwiec and Herbich 1988).[75]

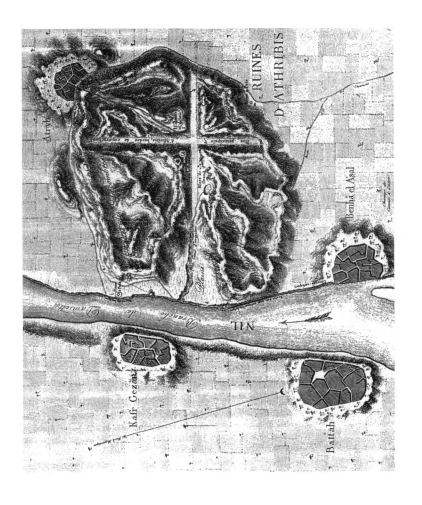

Figure 5.4 Athribis from the *Description d'Égypte*

Dabrowski (1962) argued that Roman building in the city amounted to a transformation in which 'l'ancien style pharaonique . . . fut abondonée'. The new city shifted attention away from the Pharaonic temples on its riverine eastern edge to the west where the *cardo* and *decumanus* met. This junction was later marked by a *tetrapylon* (a monumental gate), a feature attested at many other late Romano-Egyptian cities. This *tetrapylon* dates to 373–4 and was part of the renovation of the city (*SB* X 10697 = *OGIS* 722 = *SEG* XXIV 1194; *BL* VII, 200). Nevertheless, to contrast the thoroughly Romanized centre of the second century and the more traditional riverine area seems an overly simple reading of the topography of the city. The riverine area remained important and there is evidence of continuity of cultic activity.[76]

Hermopolis Magna

The topography of third-century Hermopolis is attested through a number of texts, most of them preserved as part of a very large archive dealing with business of the city council mainly from the 270s (Drew-Bear 1984). The most important text is the so-called repair papyrus (*CPH* = *Stud. Pal. Pap.* V 127v = *SB* X 10299 = *Stud. Pal. Pap.* XX 68), which gives details of repairs to be conducted on the colonnades of the city and on some public buildings. Extensive excavations conducted by the British Museum suggest that many of the buildings first attested in the third century were, in fact, second-century constructions and that the city was remodelled during the second century to present a more Romanized face to the outside world.

The basic topography of the city was very simple and long-established (see pp. 131–2). The city was divided into quarters, with a religious area to the north in which there were a number of temples, including the Great Hermaion which was either constructed or substantially remodelled in the early Ptolemaic period by Philip Arrhidaios and was dedicated to the baboon god, Thoth. Spectacular engravings of a portico of this temple were published in the *Description de l'Égypte* (Description 1809: IV, pls. 51–2), but the temple disappeared soon afterwards. Walls running at least 637.5 m east–west and 600 m north–south enclosed the temple (Roeder 1959: 26; Spencer 1989: 13). The wall was 20 m wide (Spencer et al. 1984: 30) and probably extremely high. It would have dominated the public space of the city. The road, known as Antinoe Street from an identification with a *plateia* attested in *CPH* = *Stud. Pal. Pap.* V 119 = *Sel. Pap.* II 357,[77] ran to the south of this wall and one presumes that this must have been a long-established route across the city (Kamal 1947). It connected the two gates identified in the repair papyrus as the Moon Gate and the Sun Gate. As in Alexandria, it seems that the Sun Gate was in the east while the Moon Gate was in the west.

The *Dromos* of Hermes, lined with statues of the baboon Thoth–Hermes, was the main north–south road and the intersection of the roads was marked a

Figure 5.5 The topography of Hermopolis (after Bailey 1991: pl. 1)

tetrastylon, four columns placed at the corners of the junction, which was dedicated in AD 176 (Baraize 1940; Bailey 1991: 29–31; Weigand 1928). Again this continued the topographic patterns established in the Pharaonic era. On the south-east corner of the crossroads was a major Ptolemaic sanctuary, the purpose of which is not clear (Wace et al. 1959: 4–10). The *spolia* from the site suggest that it was not redeveloped until the building of the main basilical church on the site in the late fourth or, more likely, fifth century. Roeder (1959: 115–16) identified it as an *agora*, but that identification is improbable. It was obviously a building whose importance survived the transition to the Roman period and an institution which could command such a prime site within the city.

Such continuities in the basic layout of the city do not, however, mask the fundamental changes. Architecturally, the centre of Hermopolis was remodelled in the mid-second century. Most notably, it seems that the great wall which demarcated the temple enclosure was cut down in places (Bailey 1991: 15; Spencer et al. 1984: 45). This opened up the area north of Antinoe Street. The British Museum excavations concentrated on the centre of the city, where they cleared sufficient material to suggest that a large piazza was built. One of the buildings surrounding that piazza was Ptolemaic, known as the 'bastion', and of uncertain purpose. Another was identified as the *komasterion* (see p. 215). This was an impressive building, constructed in Classical style, and was probably of the mid-second century. To the west of these was another temple, again constructed in straightforwardly Classical style and also of the mid-second century (Bailey 1991: 37–41). Such developments could, of course, considerably post-date the demolition of the wall, which cannot be dated archaeologically, though the wall's destruction cannot post-date these new buildings. In addition, this east–west avenue was graced by an Antinoeion (temple to Antinoos) and a Hadrianeion (temple to Hadrian), both likely to have been constructions of the mid-second century (*CPH* = *Stud. Pal. Pap.* V 127v = *SB* X 10299 = *Stud. Pal. Pap.* XX 68). The gymnasial baths were named after Hadrian, though one presumes that there was a set that pre-dated this emperor (*CPH* = *Stud. Pal. Pap.* V 66 + 67; 82; cf. *P. Brem.* 47 of AD 118).[78]

Historically, a mid-second-century restructuring of the city is extremely attractive. Hadrian took a great interest in the Hermopolite following the death of his beloved Antinoos in a mysterious boating accident. Hadrian's response was to develop Middle Egypt by the building of Antinoopolis, the development of which largely fell to the governors of his successor, Antoninus Pius. The new city of Antinoopolis retained strong links with Hermopolis, which it quickly surpassed in honours and in the legal status of its citizens (Schubert 1997). But these buildings suggest that Hermopolis also benefited from imperial patronage. By the third century, it seems that the major civic route across the city was east–west rather than north–south, a fundamental reorientation which directed traffic to and from the Nile (naturally), but also towards and away from Antinoopolis. The aping of Alexandria in the naming of the gates Sun and

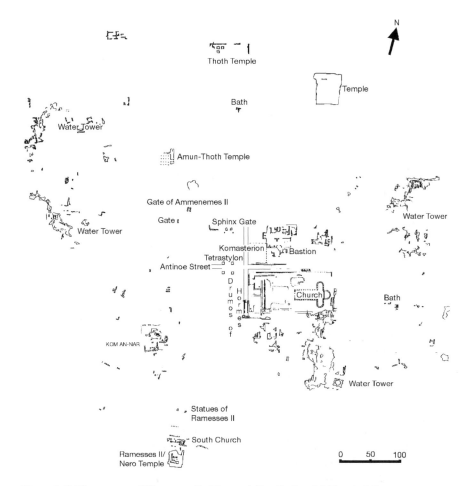

Figure 5.6 The centre of Hermopolis Magna (after Bailey 1991: pl. 23)

Moon seems significant as Hadrian is associated with remodelling the gates at Alexandria (see p. 157).

The Hadrianic and Antonine reshaping of the city was the culmination in a long process of urban development. To the north of the site was the Domitianic temple of Nehemet-'away, wife of Thoth (Snape 1989; Bailey et al. 1982: 5). To the south of Antinoe Street was another *plateia*, which was less grand but ran parallel to Antinoe Street (Roeder 1959: 109), of which no trace survived when the British Museum team started their investigations in the 1980s (Bailey 1991: 54). Again this is identified from a papyrological attestation (*CPH* = *Stud. Pal. Pap.* V 119 = *Sel. Pap.* II 357) as 'Domitian Street'.[79] There was a traditional temple in the south of the city which was reconstructed under Nero (Bailey 1991: 46–53; Roeder 1959: 27–8; Bailey et al. 1982: 3–4). *P. Amb.* II 64 of AD

241

103–7 attests the construction of a new set of baths and a *plateia*. The very considerable sums involved (16 talents (96,000 drachmas) for part of the work and possibly more than 420,000 drachmas for the whole project) suggest that this was a major construction.[80] It may be that this Trajanic construction dragged on into the reign of Hadrian and the baths are to be associated with those of Hadrian in the gymnasium (see above), though it is possible that the first half of the second century saw the construction or renovation of two major bath houses. The 'Baths of Augustus' are mentioned in *Pap. Agon.* 6 (= *P. Lond.* III, pp. 214, 1178 = W. *Chr.* 156). In the second century, the Kaisareion was used for meetings of officials (*P. Ryl.* II 77) and in the third century wills were opened in the Kaisareion (*P. Ryl.* II 109), suggesting a close but unsurprising association between the imperial cult and civic administration. There was also a Sebasteion in Hermopolis (*CPR* I 20 = *Stud. Pal. Pap.* XX 54).[81] These buildings cannot be closely dated.

Antinoopolis

The Description plan (1809: IV, pl. 53) of 'Antinoopolis of the New Hellenes' shows extensive remains. The site had an orthogonal city plan. The main entrance appears to have been through a monumental gateway with three arches (flanking arches *c.* 2.46 m, central arch *c.* 3.21 m wide). Above these there were what appear to be window niches, probably for the display of sculpture. These led onto a colonnaded avenue which ran east across the city. It crossed a north–south avenue the junction with which was marked by a *tetrastylon*, continued past a building identified as baths, before reaching another tetrastylon where the road is lost amid extensive debris of monumental buildings. The first north–south avenue was bordered by Doric colonnades which ran for most of the length of the city. Alongside this road were extensive remains of monumental architecture and some structures identified as houses. At the southern end of this avenue was a theatre, the portico of which was still standing in the late eighteenth century. To the north of the city, the avenue met another major east–west route, this time without colonnades, before again meeting a large building of uncertain purpose and a gate. At the intersection with the east–west avenue, there was another tetrastylon, this time dedicated to Alexander Severus. Away from these roads were great hills of Roman pottery, marble columns and other architectural debris. Further brick buildings and ruins lay outside the city walls to the north of the city. To the east, tucked under the ridge of hills leading into the desert, was a hippodrome.

Unfortunately, by the time relatively scientific excavation started at the site, much had been destroyed. Gayet's (1897; 1902) late nineteenth- and early twentieth-century excavations mainly concentrated on the *necropoleis* and on the remains of temples, as was the fashion of the time. He found extensive evidence of a New Kingdom site with temples carrying the cartouche of Ramesses II. The city had further deteriorated by the time of Johnson's visit

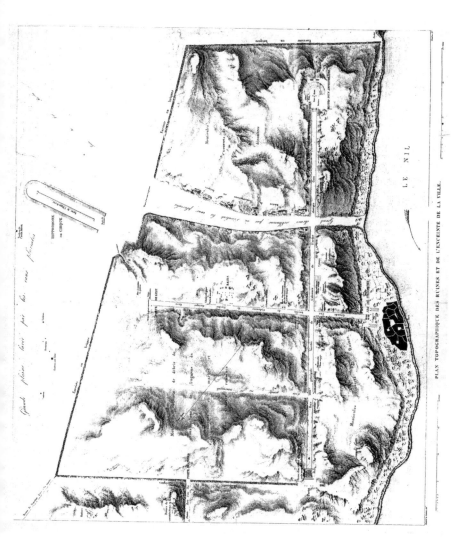

Figure 5.7 Antinoopolis from the *Description d'Égypte*

(1914) in 1913–14. Johnson's photographs suggest that few architectural features remained, except for the Ramassid temple excavated by Gayet. Italian excavations followed and these have uncovered much Byzantine material, but little of the monuments of the city (Donadoni 1939; 1974; Adriani 1939; Baldassare 1983).

The papyri attest a set of baths by a temple of Dionysios (*SB* XIV 11978, AD 187). There was also, as one would expect, a temple to Antinoos. Nothing is known of the architecture of this temple, but a petition of AD 207 was displayed there (*P. Oxy.* XVII 2131 = *Sel. Pap.* II 290). Such documentation was normally displayed in fora or in buildings relating to the imperial cult, though not normally in traditional Egyptian temples. A Kaisareion was also under construction at the site in 154 when four workmen were paid 34 drachmas for their labours (*SB* VIII 9904). The gymnasium must have been constructed fairly early in the development of the city, with related facilities for games and for bathing.

One is left, then, with an impression of a large city (Gayet's (1897) estimate is of an area of 1,500,000 m^2) which appears to have had major Classical elements, many of which were of the second century. Gayet (1897: 10; 17) concluded that that plan made the city appear as a purely Latin city, while the religious rites of the city conformed to Egyptian traditions. This seems a little cumbersome, but the overall impression of the archaeological fragments, supported by the papyri, is that, as one would expect, this was a city which displayed fine Classical monuments and a full range of Classical buildings. It thus conformed to the norms of a grand imperial city of the second century, but it also retained elements of its Egyptian precursor, a conclusion which is perhaps somewhat surprising given its overtly Hellenizing associations.

Other cities

Surprising as it may seem, the cities discussed above are among the best attested second-century settlements. For other cities we rely largely on scraps of information which tend to confirm the picture of second-century development. At Ptolemais Euergetis, for instance, a long second-century text deals with problems faced by the *bibliophulakes* (the record keepers), who were trying to find and store documents in a building which was in a state of considerable disrepair. Matters became so bad that copies of documents had to be obtained from Alexandria. The building was eventually demolished to make way for a new theatre constructed in 114–15 (*P. Fam. Tebt.* 15). A new theatre was also being built at Hibeh in 139 (*SB* XIV 11262) and another at Apollonospolis Heptakomias in 117–18 (*P. Alex. and Giss.* 43).

Oxyrhynchus saw the construction of bath houses, though it is difficult to work out quite how many.[82] *P. Oxy.* I 54 = W. *Chr.* 34 attests payments made to the managers of the baths of Hadrian[83] while *P. Oxy.* VI 896 = W. *Chr.* 48 = *Sel. Pap.* II 360 attests baths of Trajan [and] Hadrian in 316. *P. Giss.* I 50 of 259 associates 'Antonine and Trajanic baths' with the gymnasium.[84] The puzzle is almost completed with baths of Antoninianus attested in a supposedly second-century text (*P. Oxy.* XVII 2128 = *Sel. Pap.* II 407), and another set of 'Caesar's' baths appears in the third-century *P. Oxy.* XLIV 3185 and possibly in the early fourth-century *P. Oxy.* I 43v. This last set cannot be identified with the gymnasial baths in the south of the city, which implies that there were at least two sets of city baths in the second century (Krüger 1989).[85] By the early fourth century this number had grown to at least three (*P. Oxy.* I 43v), one in the north-west, another set in the south and a third set associated with the gymnasium. A fourth set is a private bath house which was transferred into civic ownership in the early third century (*P. Oxy.* XLIV 3173; 3176; L 3566).

Temples to Hadrian were built in various cities. The temple at Hermopolis has already been mentioned, but there were also temples at Bubastis (*P. Bub.* 1, p. 200), at Oxyrhynchus (*P. Merton* II 75; *P. Oxy.* VII 1045 (probably); VIII 1113; XLV 3251; LIV 3764; *SB* XVI 12629), where the temple was the scene of the public opening of wills and was also used as a prison or sanctuary in the fourth century (*P. Oxy.* XVII 2154), and probably at Memphis (*P. Ross. Georg.* II 21) and Ptolemais Euergetis (*P. Lund.* IV 9). At least one of the temples had associated dining facilities (*SB* XVI 12596). There was probably also a temple to Antinoos in Oxyrhynchus (*Pap. Agon.* 4; 9; *P. Oxy.* XVII 2132). Oxyrhynchus also had a Kapitoleion, dedicated to the Roman god Jupiter Capitolinus, which in the second century received new doors costing 2,500 drachmas (*P. Oxy.* XVII 2128 = *Sel. Pap.* II 407). The Kapitoleion in Ptolemais Euergetis is attested in accounts of AD 215, but its date of construction is not known.

The most notable feature of this brief survey of the public faces of the various cities of Roman Egypt is their uniformity. The second century appears to be a period of considerable investment in the urban infrastructure of the various cities. The goal of that investment appears to have been to provide the cities with the buildings common to contemporary Roman cities of the East, so that the cities of Egypt could make claims to a share in the dominant Mediterranean culture.

Rituals

Change was not limited to the architecture of the city. A second-century account from Oxyrhynchus details expenditure for a procession at the festival of the Nile for the priestly and 'religious' celebrants, payments to the mime, a Homericist, musicians, a dancer, *pankratistores* (fighters), 'competitors' and a boxer (*P. Oxy.* III 519 = W. *Chr.* 492 = *Sel. Pap.* II 402; see p. 195). Another extremely lacunose second-century account from Oxyrhynchus (*P. Oxy.* XVII 2127) notes expenditure on festivities in the theatre that cost 6,000 drachmas, on the procession of the *exegetes* (perhaps celebrating appointment) costing a further 6,000 drachmas, and uncosted sacrifices in the theatre. Aurelius Horion, an Alexandrian, petitioned the emperor in 199/200 to be allowed to establish a fund of 10,000 Attic drachmas (40,000 Egyptian drachmas) to provide prizes for the ephebic games to rival those on offer at Antinoopolis (*P. Oxy.* IV 705 = W. *Chr.* 153 = *CPJ* II 450).[86] Horion backs his request by stating that Oxyrhynchus showed exceptional loyalty to Rome and continued to celebrate its role in the defeat of the Jewish rebels in the revolt of *c.* 117. An account submitted by the manager of the public and sacred treasury of the city to the board of *kosmetai* attests payments for events at the hippodrome (*P. Ryl.* II 86). A payment of 600 drachmas by a gymnasiarch went to fund shows (*P. Oxy.* X 1333). A third-century text (*P. Oxy.* VII 1025 = W. *Chr.* 493 = *Sel. Pap.* II 359) is an invitation from a gymnasiarch, the *prytanis*, the *exegetes*, the chief priest and the *kosmetes* to an actor and a Homericist to celebrate the birthday of Kronous with them for the 'usual number of days'. Kronous was syncretized with Souchos, the crocodile god of the Fayum, and if this text in fact relates to celebrations in Ptolemais Euergetis (as is likely), this was probably a major public festival (Perpillou-Thomas 1993: 107–9). A fragmentary calendar of the second or third century (*P. Oxy.* XXXI 2553) attests a series of festivals and sacrifices in the period from the end of October to about 15 December. They include festivals of Zeus, for the deification of Antinoos, for the house of Britannicus, (sacrifices) in the temple of Tyche (Fortuna), in the Sarapeion, the birthday of Antinoos, and three days of games, for the victories of the Emperor Aurelius, sacrifices (?) in the Lageion (temple of the Ptolemaic ruler cult), two days of shows, sacrifices in the Sarapeion and an event in the Lageion, the day Hadrian entered the city, sacrifices by the gymnasiarch in the Sebasteion, and in another building, and another event in the Lageion, more games, the birthday of Venus, sacrifices in the Sebasteion, more games, sacrifices (?) in the Sarapeion, a ceremony of hair-cutting,[87] sacrifices (?) to the Nile, something at or to do with the temple of Herakles, and then an event in the temple of Apollo. There are other fragmentary calendars. *P. Oxy.* XVII 2127 of the second or third century mentions sacrifices in Tubi and Pachon in the theatre and includes another event at the theatre in the account. *P. Oxy.* XLV 3248 (third century) notes an event in the Sebasteion, possibly Capitoline Games, shows in the theatre, a festival day, and a meeting of the *boule*, over 8–9 days. *P. Oxy.* XLII 3072 mentions sacrifices in the theatre and in the Sebasteion.

BGU II 362 = W. *Chr.* 96 = *Sel. Pap.* II 340 of AD 215 is a set of accounts from the temple of Jupiter Capitolinus in Ptolemais Euergetis. The temple derived considerable income from property rented out and from long-term mortgages it issued at seemingly rather low rates of interest. The beneficiaries of this included a nomarch who was a councillor, a former chief-priest and councillor who had previously had charge of the temple finances, the daughter of a former *kosmetes*, a former *exegetes* of Alexandria, a woman whose status is unclear but who paid the interest on her mortgage through a former gymnasiarch, a man named Paas whose surety was a former chief priest and councillor whose son was acting *kosmetes*, an *agoranomos*, another *agoranomos* whose daughter paid on his behalf, the acting *exegetes*, yet another *agoranomos*, a former *exegetes*, and various people whose status is not known, including a minor and a large number of women, many of whom carry Roman names which might at this date reflect high status. The temple had a monthly procession but also celebrated the accession of the emperor, the Kalends (first day) of January, the tenth anniversary of a victory of Severus Alexander, a victory of the deified emperor Severus, and festivals for the safety of Severus Antoninus (Caracalla), for the raising and crowning of a statue to Severus Antoninus, for the visit of the prefect, for the visit of the procurator, for the victory and safety of Severus Antoninus, for the birthday of Severus Antoninus, for the victory and safety of Severus Antoninus, for the birthday of the deified Severus, for the proclamation of Julia Domna as mother of the camp, and for the birthday of Rome. Several additional festivals are lost in lacunae.

These festivities are additions to the Egyptian religious calendar and one presumes that the festivals of the traditional temples continued throughout this period as did the normal round of games and events associated with the gymnasium: events such as the *kosmetes'* games, the ephebic games and probably others. Magistrates were also crowned in civic ceremonies and some of the senior magistrates may have been obliged to provide a show or at least sacrifices to celebrate their elevation. Although the fragmentary calendars probably relate to the activities of civic or governmental officials and thus their association with the imperial cult and 'non-traditional events' comes as no surprise, local traditions were maintained and remained prominent, even in the temple of Jupiter Capitolinus in whose accounts there is a mysterious mention of some event or payment in connection with the great, great god Souchos. What impresses is the reorientation of ritual towards the spaces of a Classical city. In this context, Aurelius Horion's petition to establish prizes for the ephebic games appears as a celebration of the city's identity, an assertion of civic status in a traditionally Graeco-Roman form and a reinforcing of new traditions such as the memory of the honour that was granted to Oxyrhynchus by imperial visits (Hadrian's visit to Oxyrhynchus was still being celebrated at least two generations after the event) and the role of the Oxyrhynchites in the Jewish War of 115–17, more than eighty years earlier. Such ceremonies displayed a history that associated Oxyrhynchus with Rome.

Becoming Roman?

Greg Woolf (1998: 238–49) argues that 'Becoming Roman did not involve becoming more alike the other inhabitants of the empire, so much as participating in a cultural system structured by systematic differences that both sustained and were a product of Roman power' (p. 242; see also Alston 1996; Woolf 1994; Elsner 1992). The processes we see in second-century Egypt appear broadly to conform to this model. The urban elite incorporated Rome into the ritual life of the city and transformed the cityscape to give cities a more Classical aspect. The process was probably unevenly advanced in the different cities of Egypt, yet there is sufficient material from a range of sites to suggest that it was not confined to particular cities, and that it was far-reaching in its effects on the urban environment. Nevertheless, these developments coexist with traditional aspects of Egyptian urbanism. The traditional temples came under the control of the Hellenized elite of the cities, but that elite supported those temples, as can be seen from the building of the temple of Eseph at Herakleopolis and also from the temple of Sarapis at Luxor. Its dedication on Hadrian's birthday marks the integration of traditional and imperial elements (Golvin et al. 1981).

This process of integration (probably not completed for at least another century, if at all) can be paralleled in some literary texts on Egypt from the second century (Alston 1996). There are essentially two traditional portrayals of Egypt and Egyptians (Froidefond 1971). One emphasizes the irrational, ferocious, uncontrollably passionate peasants, devoted to their incomprehensible deities, rejecting civil authority and prone to extreme violence and banditry (Anderson 1988; Winkler 1980; Griffiths 1948; Alston 1999a; Henrichs 1972; Dio LXII 4; Achilles Tatius III 15; Sextus Empiricus III 24; Juvenal, *Satire XV*; Ammianus Marcellinus XXII 16. 23; Seneca, *Epistulae Morales* 51.3; Cicero *Tusc. Disp.* V 27.78; *De Nat. Deor.* I 29; 36; Diodorus Siculus I 83; Xenophon, *Ep.* III–V; Tacitus, *Hist.* I 11; Polybius XV 26–35; Propertius III 11; Eusebius, *HE* VI 40). The other is of an old culture of learning, religion and philosophy which goes back beyond even Greek civilization (Ammianus Marcellinus XXII 16. 2–22; Diodoros Siculus I; Seneca, *Quaestiones Naturales* VII 3; Nigidius Figulus, fr. 98; Plutarch, *De Iside et Osiride*). Juvenal, *Satire XV* and Plutarch, *De Iside et Osiride* appear to conform to these modes. Juvenal's is a brutal story of cannibalism and warfare between neighbouring towns contained within a vicious attack on Egypt and Egyptian religion while Plutarch, though also containing an account of intercommunal violence (379F–380C), is an allegorical study of the myth of Isis and Osiris and an exploration of Egyptian religion. Interpretation of Juvenal is extremely complex (Braund 1988; Anderson 1988), though it is generally agreed that the narrative is spoken in character. This technique may be used by the poet Juvenal to explore and comment on the attitudes expressed by the narrator Juvenal, in a manner very common in Latin poetry. The *Satire* dresses the account of cannibalism in mythic language, comparing the story of these sordid events to the epics of old, lamenting the degeneracy of mankind and of the Egyptians in particular, a nation compared unfavourably with Gauls and Britons. Throughout, Egyptian identity is defined through religion. The *Satire* ends by wondering what Pythagoras would have made of such events. This is a significant closure since Pythagoras was one of the Greek philosophers thought to have gained much from Egyptian learning, figuring in Plutarch's list in *De Iside et Osiride* (Griffiths 1970: 110) and Ammianus' similar list (XXII 16 21–2). The dramatic date of the cannibalism is 127 (described as 'recent'), just three years before Hadrian's visit. That visit probably added impetus to the contemporary fashion for Egyptian artefacts (Franceschini 1991). Egyptian religion had also long penetrated Italy, though it was not always regarded as respectable (Roullet 1972: 1–5; de Vos 1980;

Malaise 1972; Kater-Sibbes 1973). Juvenal was writing in a context in which the philosophical inheritance from Egypt was valued, Egyptian artefacts were imitated and Egyptian religion practised by the highest in Rome, and he presented that culture in the most unflattering light. However artificial the xenophobic disgust expressed in the *Satire*, I think we may conclude that the *Satire* demands that contemporaries evaluate the Egyptian contribution to Roman civilization.

Plutarch's treatise is a rather more staid attempt on the same theme. Clearly Plutarch knew quite a lot about Egyptian religion and was well advised, but the study, which follows Platonic allegorical methods, makes some extraordinary methodological leaps. An example of this is his derivation of Isis from οἶδα (I know) (351E–352A). Use of a Greek etymology for an Egyptian word is excused since words could move between languages (375E–F) (admittedly true, though a rather desperate argument) and meanings were the same whatever language was used (376A), an extraordinary point of view. Plutarch cites two Egyptian sources, Manetho and the Hermetic books, though he may have used others. By contrast, twenty-nine Greek sources are mentioned. The myth itself is described as an allegory in which reason (*logos*), Osiris, is dismembered by the disorderly Seth and restored by Isis. It is, therefore, not only rendered into Greek through translation but through the transposition of its interpretative context from Egyptian theology to Greek philosophy. Understandably, Plutarch finds the riotous religious enthusiasts on the streets of Egyptian cities rather remote from the true meaning of the myth.

Both Juvenal and Plutarch concern themselves with the assimilation of Egyptian culture into a Graeco-Roman religious milieu. Much is changed in that process, but much is also preserved in a way that seems directly analogous to the processes of change in the cities.

The third-century: cities in crisis?

It has been argued since antiquity that there was a sea-change in the fortunes of the Roman empire towards the end of the second century. Some of this is a result of narrowly political factors: the consensus that the emperors from Trajan to Marcus Aurelius appear to have generated runs into difficulty with Commodus, whose death sparked a series of civil wars ending with the victory of Septimius Severus (197). The historical tradition on the Severan dynasty is not quite so flattering as on earlier emperors and the death of Severus Alexander (235) inaugurated a period of imperial instability that lasted until the reign of Diocletian (284–305). This period has, however, been seen as one of a more general and pervasive crisis, marking a transition from the early Roman empire, the Principate, to a period of more autocratic rule, the Dominate, though the extent of that crisis has been questioned in recent years (Cameron 1993: 3–12). Some of the evidence for this general crisis has been drawn from the cities of Egypt (Lallemand 1964: 31–2; Parsons 1967; 1971; Thomas 1975; Skeat and

Wegener 1935). Egypt is a good province in which to assess the extent of the supposed crisis since the relative security of its frontiers (Alston 1995: 71–2) means that any socio-political disruption observable was likely to have been caused by internal imperial factors.

The third century opened with a gesture of confidence in the elites of the *metropoleis* of Roman Egypt. In AD 200, Septimius Severus granted councils to the cities and made those councils responsible for urban administration. The *strategoi* remained in place, but although they continued to have some oversight over urban matters, their activities appear to have concentrated on villages. This development has been studied at some length (Bowman 1971; Wegener 1948) and I have little to add here. The change in many ways formalized what had been emerging practice. The officials had met in boards and these boards could control the management of the city. Appointing councils simply brought these disparate boards together and provided a proper structure in which policy could be discussed and decided. Certain developments followed from this. First, a magisterial class of *bouleutai* was formed, probably from the gymnasial group. New magistrates were appointed to administer the *boule*, a *prytanis* to chair the meetings and a *hypomnematographos* to look after the records. The cities also developed new mechanisms for organizing the population. A tribal structure was imposed (see pp. 141–2) which further Hellenized the political structures of the city, though one may doubt whether this had any significant effect on the people.

The reason for this sudden change of policy is not clear, but then the rationale for denying the Egyptian cities councils is equally obscure. Tacitus associates the absence of magistrates with general lawlessness (*Hist.* I 11), and it may be that Augustus and his successors thought the *metropoleis* too disordered or that the civic (Classical) virtues of the municipal elite were not sufficiently developed to devolve power to them. Alexandria is, of course, a rather different case and here civil disorders may have encouraged the Romans to maintain direct rule, though Augustus turned to the Alexandrian elite to provide the *strategoi* to govern the nomes, which implies that there cannot have been any lack of faith in that particular group. Increasingly, however, it looks as though the political differential between Alexandrian and metropolitan elites was eroded. By the mid-second century, some *strategoi* were being appointed from among the metropolitan elite as well. Figure 5.8 shows that the number of *strategoi* with Roman names (a very crude measure of status) appears to decline in the second century while those gymnasiarchs with Roman names increase until the percentage meets in the latter half of the second century. Any relative decline in the status of the *strategoi* would have allowed the metropolitan elite greater political independence. The granting of councils to the *metropoleis* was an act of faith in and a recognition of the metropolitan elites' cultural assimilation.

Figures 5.9, 5.10.1 and 5.10.2 suggest that the foundation of the councils had very little effect on the pattern of attestation of officials and magistrates.[88] Although the number of attestations of *agoranomoi* increases disproportionately

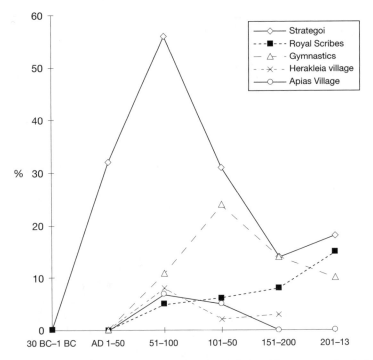

Note: The evidence of nomenclature is a very imperfect guide to status, but it is the only one available. Village populations taken from Hobson 1982; 1985b; 1986, gymnasiarchs from Sijpesteijn 1979, and *strategoi* and royal scribes from Bastianini and Whitehorne 1987

Figure 5.8 The status of *strategoi*, royal scribes, gymnasiarchs and two village populations on the evidence of the percentage of the 'population' with Roman names

in the early third century, the gymnasiarchy and the office of *exegetes* (the most prominently attested officials in the last years of the second century) continue to figure highly during the next half-century. They are joined by the *prytanis* after 240. The decline in the number of attestation of *agoranomoi* is comparatively steady after 250, but becomes notable after 270. The attestations of the office of *exegetes* remain remarkably steady from 150 to the decade ending 310 and then fall dramatically, while the gymnasiarchy (again quite steady in the number of attestations from 140) loses prominence in the decade after 310. The pattern of attestation of *kosmetai* is more irregular, but there does not appear to be any notable change until the decade ending in 290. It was the early fourth century, rather than the early third century, which saw dramatic changes in attestations of the magisterial body.

The council wielded considerable power within the city and by the second half of the century, and perhaps earlier, had some authority over the rest of the nome as well, though councillors were still supervised by the *strategos*. Some

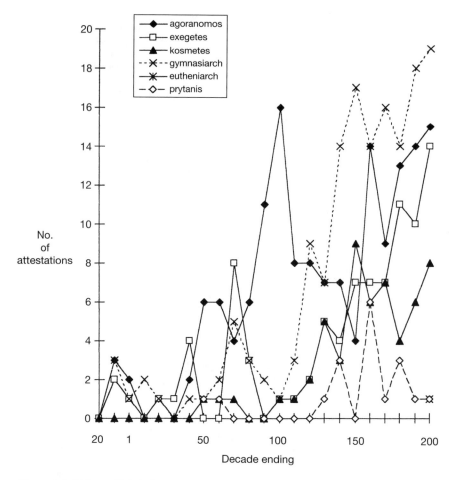

Figure 5.9 Urban officials from the decade ending 20 BC to the decade ending AD 200

responsibility for taxation was devolved to the councillors (Bowman 1971: 69–77) and the council appears to have been particularly important in meeting sudden and unexpected demands from the state, such as the provision of military supplies (*P. Oxy.* XII 1412; Bowman 1971: 78–82). The internal administration of the city, including financial administration, was also the responsibility of the council.

The establishing of councils may have increased competitive expenditure in cities. The petition of Aurelius Horion, discussed above, made on the eve of the foundation of the councils, makes it clear that Oxyrhynchus felt itself to be in competition with Antinoopolis and other cities for prestige. Favours granted to victors in games show a keenness to reward those who had brought distinction

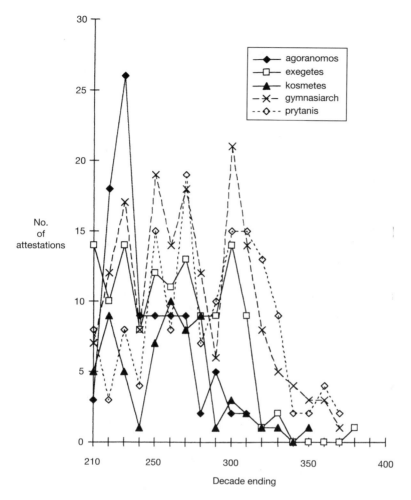

Figure 5.10.1 Major urban magistrates from the decade ending AD 210 to the decade ending AD 400

to the city (Bowman 1971: 84–7; *Stud. Pal. Pap.* V = *CPH* 74; 121; *P. Oxy.* XXVII 2475–7; XLIII 3116; cf. XXII 2338; *PSI* XII 1251; Drew-Bear 1988) which appears to have led to an inflation in the honours associated with games (Rigsby 1977). Benefactions continued to be made until at least the mid-third century when a petition to Appius Sabinus, the prefect, asking for permission to assign money to games, was granted on condition that the treasury's interest was safeguarded (*P. Oxy.* XVII 2132). Such confidence also appears in the building programmes of the cities, as far as they are known. In Hermopolis, for instance, the repair papyrus (*CPH* = *Stud. Pal. Pap.* V 127v = *SB* X 10299 = *Stud. Pal. Pap.* XX 6) details an extremely expensive (perhaps more than

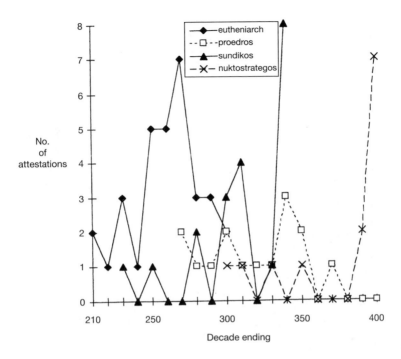

Figure 5.10.2 Minor urban magistrates from the decade ending AD 200 to the decade ending AD 400

1,203,385 drachmas) and large-scale programme of enhancement of the fabric of the city, though there is a suggestion that the council were repairing damage after a disturbance of some kind (Drew-Bear 1997). At the same time, the *boule* spent 15,000 drachmas on a new gate for the gymnasium (*Stud. Pal. Pap.* V = *CPH* 83; Orth 1983). The *stoa* of the gymnasium also appears to receive attention (*Stud. Pal. Pap.* V = *CPH* 94 = W. *Chr.* 194) at a price of 93,220 drachmas. Drew-Bear (1984) goes so far as to describe this as a 'veritable fever of construction'. Our texts do not attest activity on the same scale at Oxyrhynchus, but 18,000 drachmas were spent on the baths of Hadrian in 201 (*P. Oxy.* I 54),[89] and the guild of bronze workers charged 11,400 drachmas for a month's work repairing unnamed city baths at some point between 282 and 292 (*P. Laur.* IV 155; *BL* VIII, 167). Caesar's baths were also repaired (*P. Oxy.* XLIV 3195). There were repairs on a street running to the gymnasium gates in 283 (*P. Oxy.* I 55 = W. *Chr.* 196 = *Sel. Pap.* II 307) and the construction of what was probably a public building in which there was a room for exercises and a set of baths in 249–50 (*P. Oxy.* XII 1450). A third-century account of uncertain provenance (*P. Oxy.* XXXI 2581) details building on *stoai*, the gymnasium, a gatehouse and a *praetorium*. Much of this relates to repairs, but there was some new building in the third century, if only to accommodate the *boulai*. A bath house was built at Antinoopolis (*SB* XVIII 13174) in 258, though the amount spent on the baths cannot be read.[90]

The corn-dole archive from Oxyrhynchus suggests that the council had taken responsibility for feeding large numbers of people and that this was felt to be one of the most important areas of city administration (*P. Erl.* 18 [*BL* III, 52]; Wegener 1948; Carrié 1975). The registers record about 3,632 men receiving the dole in 271–2 (*P. Oxy.* XL 2928; 2929; see pp. 149–51), though this was not a new burden (see pp. 191–2).

The *boulai* do not appear to have had any new sources of income. The city was still reliant financially on the elite and since this group was the one with the most political power, councillors were also in a much better position to resist impositions. This was a considerable structural weakness in urban administration. There were various ways of spreading the financial burden. One was to reduce the amount of time any magistrate served so that costs and indeed temporal demands would be limited (see, for instance, *P. Oxy.* XLIV 3182; VI 981; *P. Oxy.* XII 1416). The disadvantage of this was that the distinction and honour were also reduced by their being made more common. Office might, therefore, be seen as more of a burden or tax than a privilege, thereby eroding the euergetistic spirit that had encouraged many to seek office (Mouritsen 1998). Another tactic was to spread the burden over a wider proportion of the population. In *c.* AD 250, the prefect Appius Sabinus ruled in a case between a group of villagers nominated to a liturgy and the city council of Ptolemais Euergetis (Skeat and Wegener 1935; *SB* V 7696). The villagers argued that they should not be forced to fulfil the liturgy since, as villagers, they were legally exempt. They quoted a ruling of the emperor Severus preventing villagers from performing urban liturgies. The counsel for the city responded ingeniously that the law was intended to protect the needs of the city (by maintaining exclusivity), but that now the situation had changed and the cities had need of the wealth and labour of the villagers as the cities could not fill their posts. The law should, therefore, be disregarded and the villagers appointed. Sabinus was unimpressed, since if the cities were poor, so were the villagers, and appears to give judgement for the villagers.[91]

The case demonstrates a reluctance to serve that can be replicated in numerous other instances. For example, *P. Oxy.* XLVI 3286 is a complaint about nomination to a gymnasiarchy. *Stud. Pal. Pap.* XX 54 (AD 250) is a notice of resignation of property by a man indignant that his son had been nominated to the office of *kosmetes*. The expenses of the office of *exegetes* also caused worry in c. AD 250 (*P. Leit.* 8 = *SB* VIII 10200). In AD 265, the contractor for the raising of water for the public baths resigned, having served for longer than the period for which he contracted since no other contractor could be found, and passed the duty back to the *exegetes* (*P. Oxy.* XXXI 2569). *P. Oxy.* XXXVI 2854 of AD 248 concerns a resignation of property by a man persuaded to take on the gymnasiarchy but who received the additional burden of the eutheniarchy. *P. Erl.* 18 (BL III, 52), also of 248, suggests that there were considerable difficulties with the food supply that year and that gymnasiarchs and eutheniarchs shared responsibilities. A much later (AD 289–90) letter to a *strategos* notes that eutheniarchs had not been appointed for a long time but were re-established by the prefect in 289–90 (*P. Oxy*. X 1252 [BL VII, 136]). The *prytanis*, whose job it was to recruit the new magistrates, could only find two of the three required and asked the *strategos* to apply some compulsion. A fragmentary account of a prefectural hearing (*P. Oxy*. XXXI 2612) of about the same date may result from the *prytanis*'s plea for help with the food supply. Even that most important office of *prytanis* appears to have been a burden from which some sought release. The *prytanis* of *P. Oxy*. X 1252 felt his resources stretched by his many duties, while the *prytanis* of an earlier account (*P. Oxy*. XII 1414 of AD 270–5), having made the announcement that he was intending to lay down his office, his health not being of the best, came under considerable pressure to withdraw his resignation. Such complaints are not solely third-century problems. *R. Ryl*. II 77 (discussed on p. 189) also demonstrates a reluctance to serve as *kosmetes*, though the particular nominee was willing to become *exegetes*. Nor was the problem limited to magisterial offices: *P. Oxy*. XII 1415 details attempts by someone nominated as public banker to withdraw from the office, pleading poverty and the disappearance of those chosen to conduct the food supplies to the soldiers. Such disappearances hampered administration throughout the Roman period.

It is not clear to me that such reluctance to serve amounts to a general loss of faith in metropolitan government or a decline in the public spirit of the urban aristocracy (*contra* Liebeschuetz 1996; Carrié 1976; Millar 1983; Garnsey 1974). A number of examples date from the years around AD 250 and there is some evidence to suggest that these were famine years in Egypt. The highest price for grain before the price rises of the 270s is 32 drachmas attested in *P. Brooklyn* 18, but the text (dated to after 215) cannot be closely dated. However, four prices of 20–24 drachmas per *artaba* are attested for the years 249–52, before prices dropped once more to the normal level of 12–16 drachmas (Rathbone 1997). In 246, the government arranged for compulsory purchase of corn (*P. Oxy*. XLII 3048), a measure clearly designed to alleviate famine. It would seem very likely that in common with many other peasant societies, Egyptians carried quite extensive stocks of food to see them through bad years (Husselman 1952; Gallant 1991: 94–8; Alston 1998), but the type of price surges and emergency measures put in place by the government suggest that either the stores had been eroded over the years (that is, the agricultural economy had insufficient spare capacity to insure against poor harvest) or that the crisis was prolonged and severe. In such circumstances, the role of eutheniarch might become rather challenging.[92]

There were other changes in the mid-third century. The urban office of *amphodogrammateus* (district scribe) was abolished in *c*. 245, to be replaced by the *phularchos* (see p. 141), and, perhaps more notably, the office of *dekaprotos* was introduced. This was part of a thorough reform of village administration which saw the introduction of komarchs, village chiefs (Thomas 1975; Turner 1936). The *dekaprotoi* were senior officials who had often already held the most important posts in the city, such as that of *exegetes* or *prytanis* (*P. Fay. Towns* 85; *P. Tebt.* II 368; *P. Flor.* I 26; *PSI* III 187; *P. Sakaon* 11; 12; 85; 86; *P. Select* 17). They took charge of taxation and management of farming throughout the nome and although the *boulai* appear to have had some authority in this area from their foundation, the direct control exercised by the *dekaprotoi* was an extension of the power and responsibilities of the bouleutic class, probably at the expense of the *strategoi*. Parsons (1967) represents the shift from *amphodogrammateus* to *phularchos* as a blow to the power of the same bouleutic class since he thinks that the new position was open to those not of the bouleutic order, but it is unclear to me whether this was a significant loss. All offices brought a certain responsibility and power, and the *phularchos* was responsible for person and property registration and for providing the lists of names of those qualified to perform other liturgies for the city. To a certain extent, however, this could be seen as a clerical position, with political authority resting with the magistrates, the *boule*, and the *strategos* who received and accepted nominations. On balance, therefore, it appears that the powers of the council increased in the mid-third-century reforms.

Nevertheless, the complaint of the town councils from elsewhere, given fullest voice in Libanius' orations (see, for example, *Orations* 47 and 48) of the mid- or late fourth century, was that their responsibilities were increasing while their power was decreasing. What combinations of factors could squeeze the bouleutic elites of Egypt? The power of this elite was based on both its political influence and its financial muscle. The only possible political threat to the elite could come from the Roman state, especially through the imposition of direct rule through appointed officials. This did not happen in the third century. A threat to their economic power might come from the state squeezing the elite for a higher percentage of the crops grown. Responsibility for taxation would, therefore, become a considerable burden. Opinion is currently divided as to whether such responsibilities eventually broke the back of the curial elite or were a source of power that enabled them to preserve their position into the sixth or possibly seventh century (see below and Delmaire 1996; Lepelley 1996; *contra* Liebeschuetz 1992). It seems unlikely that there was a significant increase in the burden of taxation in this period since although there was an increase in 'extraordinary monetary impositions' in the third century, inflationary price movements in the first and late second centuries had reduced the value of other coinage taxation. Taxes in kind, the main tax burden in Egypt, remained stable throughout the first three centuries AD and probably changed little even under Diocletian (Rowlandson 1996: 27–69).[93]

Another potentially important factor is the economy. Serious economic dislocation would affect the elite and prevent them from extracting the necessary surpluses from their estates to meet the costs of running the city. It is, however, notoriously difficult to reconstruct anything like a conventional economic history of the ancient world given the almost complete absence of plausible statistical information (Finley 1977; 1985a; 1985b). This does not, of course, prevent speculation. Rathbone (1996; 1997) has effectively demolished the idea that there was long-term and economically damaging inflation in Egypt connected with the gradual debasement of the coinage in the late second century and throughout the third century. Problems with the coinage are attested in the 270s, when there appears to have been a very sudden and dramatic tenfold increase in prices, and in 260 when the public bankers were reprimanded for not accepting certain specie (*P. Oxy.* XII 1411 = *Sel. Pap.* II 230). Rapid inflation or a loss of confidence in coin may have damaged the economic interests of those who relied on money rents, on specie saved, or, if the medium of exchange collapsed, on trade. Yet, it seems very unlikely that these factors were of great long-term importance. Most Oxyrhynchite leases on land were short-term: 55 per cent were for a single year and only 23 per cent were for four or more years. In addition, many rents were traditionally charged either in kind or cash, depending on the crop grown. There is no change in this pattern in the third century (Rowlandson 1996: 240–59; 327) when, if there had been a loss of faith in coin, we would expect a move to rents in kind. If any landowner lost in the hyper-inflation of the late third century, rents could have been rapidly adjusted to minimize damage.

Long-term, structural changes in the economy, to which the population might adapt, but which might have quite devastating effects, pose different problems of detection and there is rather more convincing evidence that the third century saw a significant economic down-turn. There were dramatic falls in population in the northern Fayum, though the relative absence of documentation from many of the marginal villages of the northern Fayum means that the transition from the seeming prosperity in the early third century to one of seeming decline (Bagnall 1985) is little understood. These troubles in the Fayum may have antecedents in the second century. In the late 160s Egypt was struck by a plague (Boak 1959; Gilliam 1961), which was a contributory factor in the depopulation of several villages in the Mendesian nome (Rathbone 1990) and in the Fayum was probably responsible for a 33 per cent drop in the population at Soknopaiou Nesos and a 40 per cent fall at Karanis.[94] Duncan-Jones (1996) argues that the effects of the plague were devastating. There is a possibility that the plague was responsible for a slight alteration in the age-structure of the Egyptian population after 170, suggesting that the disease, whatever it was, became endemic (Bagnall and Frier 1994: 173–7). 'Plagues' were common in Egypt (Casanova 1984a; 1984b; 1985; 1988), as in other pre-modern societies, and, in most cases, the population would be expected to recover quickly from such sudden shocks (Alston forthcoming). Recovery after the Antonine plague may have been slower. A register of house occupants from Oxyrhynchus from AD 235 suggests that about 50 per cent of houses were unoccupied (*P. Oslo.* III 111). A generation later, however, a far briefer report of occupancy of a single block of houses gives seventeen residences, of which only one was unoccupied.[95] Similarly, in the early fourth-century registers from Panopolis (*P. Berol Bork.*) fewer than 5 per cent of plots were unoccupied or derelict. The seemingly dire situation of 235 in Oxyrhynchus, if it was general, had been reversed by the early fourth century. House-occupancy rates are, of course, very different from population levels and a decline in the number of persons per house or a decline in the total area of housing might conceal population decline.

A sudden drop in population due to plague has very clear economic effects in non-irrigation agricultural economies. In the medium term, rents should fall as the pressure on land decreases and economic power shifts to the reduced peasant population. Prices and wages also fluctuate as marginal land goes out of production so reducing production costs, though costs of labour might increase and prices of manufactured goods rise. In an irrigation agricultural regime, the loss of manpower necessary to maintain the irrigation system may have been sufficient to offset any gains from the reduction in the pressure on land. Prices approximately doubled *c.* 170, which Rathbone (1996; 1997) interprets as being an effect of the plague, though the causal relationship is not obvious. Rents in wheat also rose dramatically in the middle and late second century whereas cash rents remained comparatively stable (Rowlandson 1996: 248–50), and again there does not seem to be an easy theoretical link to rapid demographic decline. Although the evidence is slight and confusing, it looks as though prolonged population decline may have had some deleterious economic effects.[96]

Such partial and gradual decline might help explain some of the evidence of elite discontent in the third century. Some may have found their resources eroded by an economic downturn, and particular crises, perhaps *c.* 250 and *c.* 272, may have been ruinous. Nevertheless, the story of the late second- and early third-century city is not of elites husbanding scarce resources but of competition between cities, the development of urban centres, the maintenance of grandiose public facilities, and the provision of doles for the urban population. This massive expenditure continued through the late third and early fourth centuries. The reluctance to serve in local magistrates seems to stem from the expenses imposed by the cities. If there was a problem, it was either over-reach on the part of the civic elite or the unfair distribution of the burden within the elite. Civic ambition could coexist with a period of declining general prosperity, since it only required a wealthy elite and not a wealthy population as a whole, and is not contradicted by evidence that suggests a willingness on the part of elites to tap the financial and labour resources of others within the city for civic functions. The cities may have had problems during the third century, but the century was not one of sustained crisis for the city or for the urban elites, but one of increasing power and confidence.

The Roman city: from the third into the fourth century

A number of texts from the late third and early fourth centuries provide us with insights into the topography of cities, especially Hermopolis Magna and Oxyrhynchus. This is, therefore, a convenient point at which to obtain something of a snapshot (with an exposure time of fifty years) of the developed cities of the Roman period.

Hermopolis Magna

Roeder's (1959) Hermopolis (excavated between 1929 and 1939) was a vast and ruinous site and even the huge resources that he had at his disposal were only sufficient to clear small areas in the centre.[97] He uncovered a series of substantial brick buildings which he associated with the water supply system.[98] Roeder excavated numerous 'public' buildings and identified these with structures known from the papyrological record (Roeder 1959: 28; 109–16), though the accuracy of these identifications is rather difficult to assess and many of the remains were inevitably unidentified (e.g. Roeder 1959: 97).

Wace, Megaw and Skeat (1959: 1–10) concentrated on a building to the south of the Great Tetrastylon in a prime site in the city. Its location was known as Kom el-Kenissa (the Kom of the Church) and, unsurprisingly, they identified the remains of a fifth-century basilical church, the cathedral of the city (see pp. 299–301). The building that pre-dated the church was an enclosure of possibly religious function dedicated by the settlers and cavalry of Ptolemy III. Surprisingly, it remained largely unaltered perhaps until the church was built. Similar continuities were found to the north of the Great Tetrastylon with the building known as the Bastion, excavated by the British Museum team (Bailey 1991: 28; see pp. 238–40). This plain hall of uncertain function is dated to the Ptolemaic period.

The most significant element of continuity, however, was the temple of Hermes–Thoth. The British Museum team excavated the courtyard of the temple, partly to date the end of occupancy (Spencer and Bailey 1982: 2–4; 11–35). There, they discovered a wall which closed off access to the temple and a rubbish dump on the temple side of the wall. The latest sherds in this dump were Islamic, but most were of fifth- or sixth-century date. The earliest dated form was African Red Slip Form 67 dating from 360–470. Although the bottom of the dump was not reached because of high ground-water levels, Bailey saw a connection between the formation of the dump and a closure of the temples by Theodosius in c. 391. The other closely datable material is lamps. Bailey observed that there were no frog lamps (a very common type from the second century onwards) at the fourth-century monastic site of Kellis in the Nile Delta, which suggested to him that frog lamps ceased to be used by 390 or even 360. There was a single frog lamp, of a crude type, in the temple forecourt excavations which Bailey dismissed as a residual.[99] The other lamps mainly date from the early fifth century. Since the bottom of the dump was not excavated and pottery forms and the frog lamp which could date before 390 were present, a slightly lower date for the dump seems possible, though it appears very unlikely that the dump could substantially pre-date *c.* 390, which is thus an effective *terminus ante quem* for the closure of the temple. This would seem to be contemporary with the build-up of rubbish on the *dromos* of Hermes outside the temple where, although some stray fragments are much earlier (third–fourth century), most fragments of African Red Slip and Egyptian Red Slip are Form 67 (AD 360–450) or later. It is difficult to push the effective end of the temple any earlier.

Hermes–Thoth was an important god in the Roman and late Roman period and was associated with a body of mystical and magical texts that became popular in the Greek and Roman world (Fowden 1993). Such interest should have meant that the cult was well placed to withstand the threats to paganism in the fourth century. The fourth-century archive of Theophanes emanates from a circle closely involved with the temple (*P. Ryl.* IV 616–51; *P. Herm.* 2–6; Moscadi 1970; Rees 1968) and tells us something of cult activity, though the archive cannot be closely dated.[100] We can, I think, assume that the temple continued to operate into the final third of the fourth century, though the cult had a long afterlife, as the continued circulation of Hermetic texts attests.[101]

South of the temple, by the Great Tetrastylon, the British Museum team excavated an Antonine temple (Bailey 1991: 37–40). The temple appears to have been robbed out in the mid- or late fourth century and demolished in the early fifth century when a new pavement was laid over the podium of the temple and wells cut in front of the podium. One of the wells contained a coin of AD 390 and some fifth-century pottery. It looks as if the temple may not have functioned beyond the mid-fourth century.

The papyri attest several elements of the topography of the city. The most famous text is the repair papyrus (*CPH* = *Stud. Pal. Pap.* V 127v = *SB* X 10299 = *Stud. Pal. Pap.* XX 6), attesting a sequence of buildings across the centre of Hermopolis. The text costs repairs to the *stoai* along Antinoe Street and sometimes deviates to consider other areas in need of refurbishment. I cannot produce a convincing plan of the site. It lists the Gate of the Moon, the Tetra-stylon of Athena, at least two private houses, the Antinoeion, the Hadrianeion, the *macellum* (market), the *stoa* to the *agora* (probably not on Antinoe Street), the Sarapeion, the Nilaion, the *komasterion*, the Nymphaion West and East, the Tuchaion, the Gate of the Sun, the first *tetrastylon*, the north and south *stoai*, the Apse, the Aphrodiseion, the Great Tetrastylon, the *stoa* of Athena and the Gate of the Moon. The city had several other major roads, including Domitian Street just to the south of Antinoe Street. *P. Vind. Sal.* 11 of AD 142 attests a number of avenues within the city, but the text is lacunose. There was also a Kaisareion by 192 (*P. Ryl.* II 77), a Sebasteion (*CPR* I 20), a gymnasium (*CPH* = *Stud. Pal.Pap.* V 82; 83; 94), Baths of Hadrian (*CPH* = *Stud. Pal. Pap.* V66; 82), a city treasury (*P. Flor.* I 47) and a mysterious covered area known as the *kamara* (*CPH* = *Stud. Pal. Pap.* V 119 = *Sel. Pap.* II 357). A women's baths is attested for the fifth century (*P. Flor.* III 384), though it is plausibly a much earlier construction. A temple of Thotoperios had some connection with the oil-workers' guild (*P. Ryl.* II 110). There was also a temple of Boubastis (*P. Ryl.* II 277). In the (late?) fourth century, Bishop Plousianos arbitrated disputes at the gates of the Catholic church (*P. Lips.* I 43 = M. *Chr.* 98). The basic topographical framework of the city was enhanced by colonnades along the main paved road. Any visitor entering the city would have found his or her line of sight directed along Antinoe Street towards the three *tetrastyla* whose columns must have risen considerably above the surrounding buildings, acting as 'spatial punctuation', marking the main intersections of the city. Proceeding further into the city, the visitor encountered various Classical-style public buildings and avenues, presumably also decked with *stoai* running north–south. This elongated civic centre culminated in the Great Tetrastylon, with the mysterious Ptolemaic structure to the south, the Roman *komasterion* to the north, the Bastion and the Antonine temple. Further to the north lay the temple area dominated by the temple of Hermes Trismegistos. The architecture appears to have been mainly Classical, though there were certainly Egyptian elements.

Considerable effort was expended in laying out a city that had elements of Classical urban morphology, driving long straight avenues through a possibly more disordered traditional Egyptian urban centre. Yet, instructions given to a letter-carrier setting out for Hermopolis (*P. Oxy.* XXXIV 2719) give a rather different impression. The letter-carrier was to enter the city through the Gate of the Moon and walk towards the granaries. He was then to take the first street on the left behind the baths and head to the west, go down and up some steps (presumably crossing a low-level road), turn right and pass the temple enclosure, before coming to a seven-storey house with a statue of Tyche (possibly) on the gatehouse, opposite a basket-weaver's, and there he is to ask. The instructions do not make obvious use of a grid-plan and suggest that even after such a tortuous journey, he had to rely on local knowledge. There is a contrast between the grandiose 'front' of the city with its Classical order and the rather freer 'back' with more alleys and passageways than avenues.

Oxyrhynchus

The best topographical information for Oxyrhynchus comes from the early fourth century. There are two major documents and a number of minor texts which combine to produce a deeply confusing picture of the city. *P. Oxy.* I 43 *verso* is undated, but the *recto* of the papyrus, a related text, is dated to 296, suggesting a date of *c.* 300 for the *verso*. The *verso* is a list of guards and their stations commencing from the north and moving anti-clockwise around the city, as detailed in table 5.3.

Table 5.3 P. Oxy. I 43 verso

Col. I

1. In the street of the house[ ]
   ]kue[
   near the gate
   (1 guard)
   houses in the street at the house[
   Thotos, oil worker.
2. In the street at the house of the fuller K[
   (1 guard)
3. In the street of the North Church
   (1 guard)
   houses at the stable of Aionia
4. and in the street of the house of the hayloft (?) in which there are rooms and a
   small well
   (1 guard)
   remaining near
5. and in the upper street of Seuthos
   (1 guard).
   staying in the same place
6. and in the street of the kitchen and the house of the priest Etsos (?)
   (1 guard)
   staying in the house of Amazonia, street of the Kaisareion
7. and in the street of the house[ ]Horion of Aniketos
   houses in the camp, street of the small well and [
8. and in the street of the house[ ] Theodoros of Olympios
   [ ]houses in the street

Col. II

9. and in the street of the house of Diogenes [
   (2? guards)
10. and in the street of the Sarapeion being[
    of the priest Thonion
11. and in the Sarapeion,
    (6 guards)
12. and in the Iseion
    (1 guard)
13. and in the street of the Iseion,
    (1 guard)
    remaining in the street to the house of Hierakion
14. and in the street to the house of Zoilos
    (1 guard)
    remaining near the house of Isidoros, knowing the district (?)
15. and in the Teumenoutis
    (1 guard)
16. and in the Shepherd street at the Machasantis
    (1 guard)
17. and in the street to the West gate of the three arches
    (1 guard)
18. and in the street of the [
    (1 guard)

Table 5.3 (continued)

Col. III
19. and towards the house of Ammonios, bean seller
     (1 guard)
20. and in the street of the Theatre,
     (1 guard)
21. and in the theatre,
     (3 guards)
22. and in the street of the warm baths
     (1 guard)
23. and in the street of the gate of Pesor where there is a vegetable market
     (1 guard)
24. and in the street to the street of Loupas

25. and in the street to the Kretikon (Cretan)
     (1 guard)
26. and in the street to the South Gate
     (1 guard)
27. and in the street to the South Church
     (1 guard)
     staying opposite the house of Epimachus, wax-maker (?)
28. and in the street to Apolloneion
     (1 guard)
29. and in the street to the (main?) baths and the canal of Krios
     (1 guard)
30. and in the street to the house of Matreos,
     (1 guard)
     remaining in the house of Parion, wine merchant
31. and in the street of the house of Aristo[ ]asis and the late Sarmatos
     (1 guard)
     staying near the house of Horion, former *sustates.*

Col. IV
32. and in the street to the Gate of Pses
     (1 guard)
     staying in the house of Scheirakos, near the Kapitoleion
33. and in the street to the Mutron
     (1 guard)
34. and in the street to the gymnasium
     (1 guard)
35. and in the gymnasium,
     (2 guards)
36. and in the street to the Tetrastylon of Thoeris
     (1 guard)
37. and in the street to the Thoereion
     (1 guard)
38. and in the Thoereion
     (7 guards)
39. and in the street to the new (or Caesar's) baths
     (1 guard)
40. and in the street to the house of Ok[
     (1 guard)

Col. V
41. and in the small Nilometer
    (1 guard)
42. and in the street of Phanios
    (1 guard)
43. and in the street of Apollonios the founder where there is a fruit-orchard

44. and in the street near the Apse of the house of Flavianos

45. and in the street of Psullos

The last three entries have no guards written in, which shows that the text is incomplete. But it seems unlikely that the topographical register lacks many entries.

The second text is a report to the *logistes* concerning areas of the city in need of restoration in AD 316 (*P. Oxy.* LXIV 4441), as in table 5.4.[102]

Reconstructing the city from these attestations is a matter of guesswork and very quickly any attempt makes one's head spin. Nevertheless, various assumptions listed in n. 104 are used to create figure 5.11, a schematic plan, the inaccuracies and wishfulness of which are obvious.[103] Krüger (1990), after extensive discussion, produced a schematic plan of Oxyrhynchus which did not take account of the then unpublished *P. Oxy.* LXIV 4441. I follow Krüger's plan in most aspects but would stress the considerable doubt about the exact location of buildings within the city.

In table 5.3, 25 entries cover the west of the city and one would expect that about 50 entries would cover the whole city. The Sarapeion is reached on entry 11, about 25 per cent of the way round the city. The Thoereion is reached at 38, about 75 per cent of the way round the city. It would be very attractive therefore to see the Thoereion and the Sarapeion at approximately the same latitude within the city. Yet, the gymnasium was in the south, with the Thoereion close by and probably someway south of the Sarapeion. Figure 5.11 leaves the north-east short of public buildings and clusters buildings near the Sarapeion and between the theatre, the gymnasium and the Thoereion in the central and southern sectors. The traditional temples of Sarapis and Thoeris still dominate the topography of the city, a continued importance reflected in the locating of multiple guards in the two temples. They were rivalled, though not equalled, by the gymnasium. The Sarapeion, with its cluster of associated religious buildings and market was a traditional focal point of the city, probably paralleled by the Thoereion. The new buildings of the Roman period appear to have been located with little account of this traditional bifocal topography, being dispersed, though the major development was towards the south of the city, around the gymnasium and the theatre. As in Hermopolis, it seems that wide avenues were cut through the topography of the city and one presumes that their colonnades drew visitors along the main streets and provided some unity to the urban plan.

Table 5.4 Areas of Oxyrhynchus in need of repair in AD 316

1. Northern *Stoa*.
   a. Wall at a bedchamber

2. West(?) *Stoa*
   a. From the doctor's house
   b. To a stable,
   c. To another house and an apse
   d. The schoolhouse
   e. The Apse to wall near a seller of vegetables.
   [   ]
   f. The Tuchaion
   g. The Achilleion
   h. The library/record house to Temgenouthis
   i. The *macellum*
   j. The place of announcements
   k. The place near [
   l. Opposite the temple [
   m. The places of the higher [
   n. The house of Thonios, hat-maker (?)

3. East *Stoa*
   a. [ ]
   b. House of Diogenes and Sarapion
   c. The place of Athenodoros
   d. The place of Didymos, fruitier
   e. [ ]
   f. The Hadrianeion
   g. Street opposite the public baths
   h. The beer-shop
   i. Opposite the temple of Demeter, the wall of the temple of Dionysios

4. South *Stoa*
   (The remaining two columns are mostly lost but a set of baths are mentioned.)

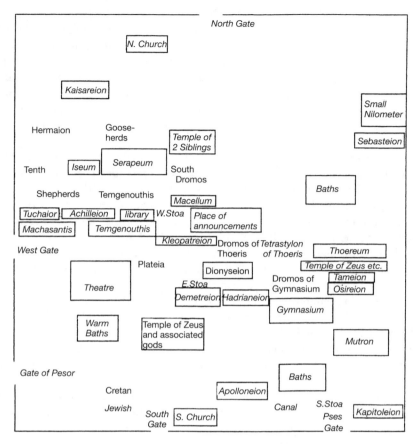

Note: Boxed entries are buildings. Italicized entries are topographical features and non-italicized entries are *amphoda*.

Figure 5.11 Diagrammatic guide to the topography of Oxyrhynchus

The archaeological record at Oxyrhynchus is extremely poor but provides some illustrative material. The first excavations were papyrus hunts and Grenfell and Hunt's archaeological publications were extremely brief. Grenfell's 1897 account mentioned a large and completely ruined 'temple' discernible only from the mound of stone chippings. He portrays a site with a number of very high mounds of rubbish on which the excavations concentrated so as to rescue as many papyri as possible. The architectural remains were mostly destroyed. Subsequent reports (Grenfell and Hunt 1904; 1905; 1906a; 1906b; 1907) trace the progress of the excavation across the site. Darbishire drew a sketch of the excavations, published in *P. Oxy.* L, but this, in fact, adds little of value. The photographs and notebooks of the excavations mention Byzantine coffins, a church uncovered in a clandestine dig conducted by locals, and various granite columns.

Subsequent visitors found the architectural remains little more inspiring. Petrie (1925: 12–14) paused only briefly at the site to clear part of the theatre.[104] He uncovered columns lining the street leading from the theatre towards the centre of the city and other fragments of colonnaded streets, one of which culminated in a pillar dedicated to the emperor Phokas (AD 602–10) and, further north, a fifth-century statue base. He also found a fragment of a second-century marble statue and some relief sculpture. He then abandoned the city itself and excavated in the necropolis area where he discovered a number of church-like tombs.[105]

Breccia led two visits to the site between 1928 and 1932 (Breccia 1932; 1934). The mounds still stood several feet high in places and broken columns rose from the debris. Breccia's team cleared a number of buildings, mostly private, and the photographs show houses (?) with paved courts and columns and bastions for supporting upper storeys. They also show barrel-vaulting (intact). Clearly, the extent of the remains overwhelmed the excavators and they were able to make little headway towards uncovering an obviously extremely confusing and late site. Breccia identified little public architecture but did rescue significant amounts of sculptural material including large numbers of funerary reliefs.[106] These are often of full-scale human figures. The style of these owes little to Egyptian traditions, though some of the figures carry items associated with traditional Egyptian religion (Kessler 1983). Clothing corresponds to Graeco-Roman norms. Such reliefs continued to appear on the antiquities market after 1945 and scholars tend to see parallels between them and Palmyrene sculpture of the second, third and fourth centuries AD (Schneider 1975; 1982; Kitzinger 1938; Kessler 1983; Parlasca 1978; Breccia 1934–7), which suggests that the elite displayed themselves using a sculptural language current throughout the eastern Mediterranean but into which they incorporated distinctive Egyptian elements.

A large number of literary papyri have been found at Oxyrhynchus. Of these, over 75 per cent were from the second and third century, as shown in figure 5.12 (Krüger 1990: 142–9). A more detailed breakdown of a sample of papyri from P. Oxy. shows that although Homer was by far the most popular single author, there was a tremendous diversity of second-century literary texts. The later literary material is less eclectic and Christian texts gradually achieve dominance.[107] Greek literature appears to have been widely disseminated in Roman Oxyrhynchus, which was, after all, a rather small and unimportant city, which suggests that a significant proportion of the population, in pre-modern terms, invested heavily in acquiring a Classical Greek education.[108] Greek culture was also disseminated through performance. Homericists were paid to perform in the theatre during festivals, but the number of dramatic texts preserved suggests that the theatre at Oxyrhynchus may have staged Greek tragedies, comedies and satyr plays.

The literary papyri, the iconographic material, the archaeology and what can be gleaned from the topography of the city suggest a heavily Hellenized city which preserved some of the traditional aspects of Egyptian religion.

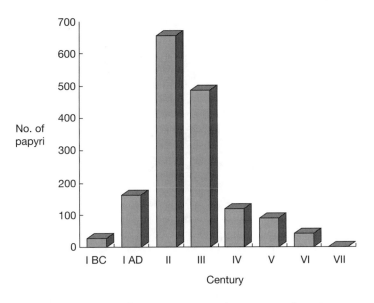

Figure 5.12 Literary papyri from Oxyrhynchus by century (after Krüger 1990: 150)

Ptolemais Euergetis

No other Egyptian cities are so well attested as Hermopolis and Oxyrhynchus. The topography of Ptolemais Euergetis, for instance, is mysterious. Archaeological exploration of the site has been somewhat desultory. Although Schweinfurth's map (published in Wilcken 1887) points to the survival of a large enclosure to the north of the site, various mounds which one presumes are the remains of ancient structures, and a substantial district of housing immediately south of the large enclosure, it was already obvious in 1887 that our understanding of the site would rely very heavily on the papyri (Wilcken 1887).[109] The best guide to the topography of the Roman city is a third-century papyrus (*BGU* IV 1087 + I 9 + XIII 2280) which lists those paying craft taxes in various streets in the city. Many of the street names are difficult to understand and, unlike those in other tax lists, do not appear in topographical order, as can be seen in table 5.5. There is some relationship between these streets and the *amphoda* (see pp. 135–6), but many new streets appear in this list. Some of these may be named from private houses (such as Theon), but others are named from public buildings: the gymnasium, Nymphaion, Theatre, Palation, the burial ground of sacred cattle, temples to Kleopatra, Ptolemy Lagus, the imperial cult, Pan, Tyche, Nemesis, Jupiter Capitolinus, and no doubt to others lurking in the text. It appears that many Ptolemaic temples were still important in the third century, but that they had been joined by a number of Roman buildings.

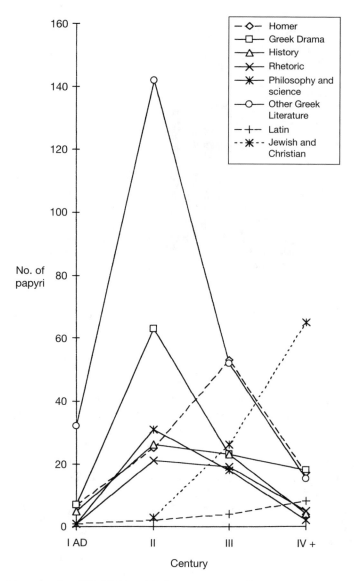

Note: Texts dated to I/II, II/III, or III/IV centuries have been excluded.

Figure 5.13 A sample of literary papyri from Oxyrhynchus by author and genre

A note on Alexandria

In chapter 4 (see pp. 162–5), I explored a single district of Alexandria and showed that the area was transformed in the fourth century. The seemingly opulent private houses were replaced by a large bath block, probably planned

Table 5.5 Groups of traders in sequences of streets in *BGU* IV 1087; I 9; XIII 2280

Streets in *BGU IV 1087*	Streets in *BGU I 9*	Streets in *BGU XIII 2280*
1. Gymnasium	1. Severion	1. Kapit(olei)on
Kleopatreion	Paneion	[ ]
2. House of Mikkalos	Typannon	Tympanon
Hermouthiathes	Lentil-shop	Nemsianon
Nymphaion	Muros	Muris
Theatre	Kaisareion	Severion
Palation	2. Loginon	Salt-sellers'
Sebasteion	Salt-sellers'	Severion
Mures	Phynikion	2. Syrian
3. Sanpallion	3. Nunpon	Kapit(olei)on
Akantheion	Nemesion	Alupis
Numphaion	Severion	Muris
(House of) Philoxenos	Tuchis (Tucheion?)	Palation
(House of) Theon	4 (?) Phremi	Gymnasium
4. Severon	Phremi	Muris
(House of) Theon	Muris	
Tharapias	5. Muris	
5. Near the Severion	[ ]	
Nupeion	Kapit(olei)on	
Palation	Nemesion	
(House of) Kylas	[ ]	
Gymnasium	Severion	
Typanon	Athena	
Old Parembole	Muron	
Remouthiakes	Kapit(olei)on	
Akation	Lageion	
Syrian	Phremi	
Alypos	6. Lycian	
Nupeion	Typanon	
Traton	Akation	
6. (?) Syrian	Nomachon	
Phremis	Hermoutiake	
Athena	7. (lacunose)	
Lageion	8. Severion	
Kapit(ol)eion	Salt-sellers'	
7. Tharapia		
Severion		
Paneion		
8. Boutapheion		
Trimoros (?)		
Artekos		
Sanpal (?)		
Syrian		
Mani( )		
Hermouthiakes		
9. Severion		

Numbers refer to the sequences of streets in a particular document.

in the early or mid-fourth century AD. A theatre or perhaps a *bouleuterion* was constructed in the same block in the early fourth century (probably). These buildings were not renovations but new constructions. The bath house was a grand construction, and may reflect imperial patronage. Such buildings were expressions of confidence in the city and its financial and political structures.[110]

Identity and urban change

The overwhelming impression of the previous sections has been of a relatively smooth transition from the temple-city of the first century to a more Classical city of the later period, a transition that can be paralleled across the Roman East and which gave rise to a cultural form identified as Hellenism (being mainly expressed through Greek, though often having local cultural peculiarities). Although the new cities of Egypt incorporated traditional elements, they were predominantly centres of Classical culture, as can be seen from the architectural developments, the prominence of Graeco-Roman institutions and religious and secular festivals, and in the evidence of the inculcation of a Greek literary culture. The undoubted success of Hellenism in absorbing local traditions (Bowersock 1990, with comments by Swain 1993), should not blind us to the fact that Hellenism was an elite culture, sponsored by the wealth of the gymnasial and bouleutic classes and which required a Greek literary education of those who would participate. Those who either did not wish to or could not share in the new culture were effectively silenced in the public sphere of the Roman city. Nevertheless, the old culture, through the traditional temples (absorbed as they had been into the culture of Hellenism), potentially provided a means by which the mass of the population could be integrated into this new urban culture, always assuming that the traditional temples continued to play the kinds of social roles I suggest for them in the first century. However, there is substantial evidence that in some places, the great Egyptian temples were in decline, a decline that some have dated to the mid-second century (Whitehorne 1980–1; Gilliam 1947; Evans 1961), though there is a better case for dating this decline to the end of the third century. Most notably, the great temple of Amun at Luxor cannot have been in use when Diocletian visited the site in AD 300 since he, a defender of pagan traditions, or his officers chose to construct a legionary camp in the ruins of the temple (el-Saghir et al. 1986). The temple at Hibis may have had a similar fate (Wagner 1987: 48). Fourth-century forts at Nag el'-Hagar, and El-Kab reused blocks from Roman or earlier temples (Alston 1995: 205–6). The absence of epigraphic material from the traditional temples suggests that from the mid-second century there was little new construction and the pace of renovation and construction of traditional temples had slowed from the early second century. Bagnall (1993: 267; cf. Bagnall 1988a) argues that 'it is difficult to avoid the conclusion that the temples of Egypt, along with their traditional scripts, personnel, influence, festivals, and wealth declined markedly in the third century'.

Dating decline is rather difficult, since often one is searching for evidence of absence. Changes in epigraphic habits are well documented throughout the Roman world, but the relationship of such changes to social and economic developments is less than clear. The archaeological record is a better guide, but here again one faces substantial problems, especially with older excavations of late Roman material.[111] For instance, Petrie dates the destruction of the temple at Herakleopolis to *c.* AD 250 (Petrie 1905: 17; 28) since there was a considerable accumulation of rubbish on top of the foundation stones, including pottery of the 'early fourth-century', which was then disturbed when the stone was robbed. Clearly, the stratigraphy was extremely complex, even if Petrie correctly dated the pottery.[112]

There is also evidence of continuity in pagan practice into the fourth century. The last known bull buried in the Bucheum at Hermonthis was interred in AD 295, whereas the coinage sequence continues until the end of the fourth century (Mond and Myers 1934: I, 23; 115–16; II, no. 19). Priests of Zeus and Hera responsible for carrying the busts of Nike and the emperors in Oxyrhynchus are attested in AD 322 (*P. Oxy.* LXI 4125) and 336 (*P. Oxy.* X 1265). Latjar (1991) published inscriptions from a guild of iron workers which show that they sacrificed annually at the temple of Deir el-Bahari and that this pilgrimage continued until at least 357 (*SB* XX 14508–11), though it is not clear that the temple continued to operate as late as this. The temple at Kellis in the Dakhleh oasis operated at least until the mid-fourth century (Hope et al. 1989). Similarly, the evidence cited above for traditional Egyptian temples in fourth-century Oxyrhynchus and Hermopolis suggests continuity beyond AD 300. Zucker (1956), in contrast to much that has been written later, argued that Egyptian temples were thriving in the early fourth century.

The growth of other institutions within the city and of other ways of displaying the city's status must have devalued the traditional temples and perhaps a draining of political attention from the temples gradually weakened their position. The decline of the traditional temples could, therefore, be related to the growth of the Romanized city. Nevertheless, the ability of Hellenism to incorporate traditional and local elements into its cultural framework means that the temples could only be accidental casualties rather than targets in a policy of cultural cleansing. Bagnall (1993: 267–8) attributes the decline to a slow starvation as funds were directed away from the temples during the financial problems of the late third century. Impecunity seems a possible explanation for the rather patchy process of decline. This cannot, however, be a complete answer. The municipal elites poured money into the fabric of their cities in the late third and early fourth centuries and cities such as Hermopolis and Oxyrhynchus must have had the resources necessary to maintain prestigious temples. Whatever the underlying cause, it was not until the fourth century that the social and cultural processes reflected in the changing role of the traditional temples become obvious in the failure of Hellenism to mobilize support for the traditional temples in the face of the Christian challenge.

Managing the Classical urban economy

The economy often integrates social groups into wider society since although neighbourhoods or cities may aim for an internal autarky, economic realities frequently force people into a wider world. In the first century AD, guilds acted both as significant communities for individual traders and as a way in which traders acted on the civic stage (see pp. 208–14) and they probably retained these functions into the fourth century.[113] The social power of guilds may be attested in a third-century marriage contract (P. Oxy. XLIX 3500) in which Aurelia Kyrilla, daughter of Isidoros and Sinthonis, gave herself in marriage to Aurelius Pasigonis. Both Kyrilla and Pasigonis were embalmers. The document is peculiar for several reasons. First, a woman appears to act as a member of a trade group and, second, that woman, Kyrilla, gave herself in marriage without the intervention of a legal guardian and without any mention of her right so to do. Embalming was a quasi-priestly task and intimate physical contact with the dead might be assumed to carry a ritual impurity that could have made Kyrilla and Pasigonis unattractive marriage prospects to those not in the profession. Embalmers may have been socially marginalized and thus unable to form 'normal' social relations outside the guild-group (Derda 1991). Such marginality might also account for Kyrilla's avoidance of social and legal niceties in contracting her marriage. Nevertheless, although all guilds probably developed from temple associations, guilds were neither endogamous nor hostile to new members who had no family link with the trade (P. Fouad 37; P. Oxy. VII 1035; Whitehorne 1990), nor all-encompassing social organizations which limited the social and political activities of their members.[114]

The number of guildsmen within cities cannot be estimated with confidence. From the available lists of persons, it appears that around 25 per cent of the male population were registered as traders (see pp. 334–7). This is quite a low figure, but it is not clear why a person uses a trade designation as part of his nomenclature. One would assume that there would have been a shifting population of unskilled or semi-skilled labour which is invisible in much of the documentation, and, if the structure of the guilds outlined on pp. 212–14 is correct, that there were many junior craftworkers in the workshops of the guildsmen. One of the most important areas of the pre-industrial economy was the production of cloth.[115] P. Oxy. Hels. 40 attests the export from the Oxyrhynchite of 1,956 pieces of finished cloth over a five-day period and van Minnen (1986) suggests that the annual cloth production (for export) of the Oxyrhynchite would be c. 100,000 pieces (unless export of cloth was seasonal). This supports his contention (van Minnen 1987) that about half the tradesmen of Oxyrhynchus were involved in cloth production.[116] However, in early fourth-century Panopolis, those involved in the cloth trade occupied only 8 per cent of residential plots. The much shorter P. Oxy. XLVI 3300 has two cloth-workers in twenty-four men, also 8 per cent. If this figure is applied to a city with an adult male population of c. 3,600, one ends up with about 290 cloth-workers in a total population of named traders of c. 900.

There were numerous urban guilds. An unprovenanced probably fourth-century tax list submitted to a *sustates* lists twenty-nine guilds including dyers, fullers, tarsic-weavers, bleachers, saddle-makers (?), box-makers (?), stone-workers, bakers, butchers, donkey-drivers, bean-sellers, bronzesmiths, glass-makers, fruitiers, sievers, ivory-workers and pot-sellers (*PUG* I 24). Coles (1987: 230–2) lists thirty-three guilds of Oxyrhynchus attested registering prices with the city authorities in the fourth century, though the list clearly does not represent the total number of guilds operating within the city.[117] Fikhman (1979) estimates there to be ninety different crafts attested at Oxyrhynchus. It is worth listing some to give an impression of the range: salt merchants (*P. Oxy.* LIV 3734; 3750), oil-workers (*P. Oxy.* LIV 3738), condiment-sellers (*P. Oxy.* LIV 3739), tavern-keepers (*P. Oxy.* LIV 3740), vetch-sellers (*P. Oxy.* LIV 3745), beekeepers (*P. Oxy.* LIV 3747), donkey-sellers (*P. Oxy.* LIV 3748), fish-sauce sellers (*P. Oxy.* LIV 3749), wool merchants (*P. Oxy.* LIV 3751), tow handlers (*P. Oxy.* LIV 3753), silversmiths, bakers, goldsmiths (*P. Oxy.* LIV 3773), linen merchants (*P. Oxy.* LIV 3765; 3776), perfumiers (and spice-merchants) (*P. Oxy.* LIV 3731), potters (*P. Oxy.* LIV 3767) and lentil-sellers. Guilds continued to operate into the sixth century and beyond (*CPR* XIV 32 (655); *P. Oxy.* LVIII 3933 (588); LIX 3987 *BL* X, 157 (532); *P. Cair. Masp.* III 67283 *BL* VIII, 74 (547); *SB* XVI 12282 (VIth century( ); *SB* XX 15134 (483) without obvious signs of any change in function.

The aforementioned price declarations were made through the monthly president (sometimes a collegial office) to the *logistes* and although prices rise notably over the period for which we have declarations, it is probable that this process restricted price movement and competition. Evidence of civic control of traders is common (Johnson and West 1949: 151–5). Such control aided the imposition of taxation and levies for military supplies (Jones 1960; *BGU* VII 1564 = *Sel. Pap.* II 395; *BGU* VII 1572 = *P. Phil.* 10; *P. Oxy.* XII 1414), enabled the authorities to find experts for particular tasks about the city (*P. Harr.* II 216), especially building work (*P. Oxy.* I 53; 84 = *W. Chr.* 197 = *Sel. Pap.* II 374; *P. Oxy.* XLIV 3195; LXIV 4441), and also allowed direct economic management.[118] In AD 327, an egg-seller declared on oath that he would sell eggs in public, not from home (*P. Oxy.* I 83 = *W. Chr.* 430 = *Sel. Pap.* II 331). In AD 275, an oil-seller swore to provide fine oil for the city from the workshop he held in the *agora* (*P. Oxy.* XII 1455). In AD 228 a fish-seller swore to provide fish for the city as long as the fishermen of the village of Monimou continued to supply him (*P. Oxy.* XLV 3244). A fruitier promised in 305/6 to continue to supply Hermopolis with fresh fruit (*P. Lond.* III, p. 115, 974 = *W. Chr.* 429). A vegetable-seller made repairs on 'the lord's property', which was his shop near Psou in Oxyrhynchus, and declared the expenses (presumably for refund) to a former chief priest and a former *hypomnematographos* (*P. Oxy.* XII 1461), though this may be a private transaction. The city itself controlled the *agora* and derived income from the renting of stalls in it (*CPH* = *Stud. Pal. Pap.* V 102). Presumably the *agora* was supervised by magistrates and a third-century itinerary for the *strategos* (*P. Oxy.* XLII 3072) attests time spent in the *agora*. However, the most dramatic intervention in the economy was in the supply of corn. From as early as 116, measures were taken to ensure the supply of bread (*P. Oxy.* XII 1454), and the building and equipping of bakeries by officials to provide 3,600 *artabai* per month is attested by 199 (*P. Oxy.* VI 908). By the middle of the third century Oxyrhynchus had a corn dole (*P. Oxy.* XL 2892–2940), but the near coincidence of the monthly provision of 3,632 *artabai* in the late third century and the 3,600 *artabai* per month of AD 199 suggests that at least some of the elements of provision visible in the third-century archive were already in place in 199. Antinoopolis may have had a corn dole from its foundation (*P. Oxy.* XL 2941; 2942). Hermopolis and Alexandria also had doles (*W. Chr.* 425; Eusebius, *HE* VII 21; Carrié 1975; Sharp 1998; Fikhman 1975a) and there were public bakeries in other cities (*P. Hib.* II 220; *P. Sakaon* 23; 25).

Figures for the corn dole at Oxyrhynchus were provided in chapter 4 (see pp. 149–51 and esp. n. 29). Of the three groups to whom the dole was provided at Oxyrhynchus, the citizens appear to have been selected by lot (see for example *P. Oxy.* XL 2894) at, presumably, some public ceremonial, while the *homologoi* (*P. Oxy.* XL 2912; cf. 2913) were admitted on obscure criteria related to their civic status, and the *remboi* qualified on account of liturgical service (*P. Oxy.* XL 2927; 2917; 2918; *P. Stras.* VI 616) (though one applicant may have been enrolled in the last group because he was not properly registered as a citizen, possibly because he was 'of weak mind' (*P. Oxy.* XL 2908)). All recipients appear to have been under an obligation to gather at a formal muster to receive their grain, at which a formulary, preserved as *P. Oxy.* XL 2927, was read out. The recipients also probably had to present tokens (*P. Oxy.* XL 2924; *SB* I 4514). Since the Oxyrhynchite registers show that the *numeri clausi* for the various groups were not reached, it seems likely that most adult male citizens were in receipt of the dole. The dole provided a public ceremonial at which the male citizens together with associated groups, presided over by their magistrates, received gifts effectively from the wealthy classes. The significance of the corn dole was guaranteed by its value. The feeding of the people on such a scale could not help but bring some unity to the population and differentiated the urban population from the villagers, who had no such support.

The urban economy was not a 'command-economy' in which the government attempted to determine all economic activity, but was a managed economy in which the civic authorities supervised economic transactions and intervened in the market. Prices were allowed to fluctuate.[119] Yet, by supporting guilds, providing grain and ensuring adequate supplies of other types of food, the cities emphasized the communality of the economic process. Individuals were not separate economic entities, but were tied to the wider civic culture through, in the first instance, guilds which integrated tradesmen into blocks and thereby reduced competition, and, second, through the dole or subsidized supplies of food which embraced a large section of the community. The investment of such effort and money in the food supply demonstrates a commitment on the part of the leaders of the city to their community as a whole.[120]

It is characteristic of managed economies that they operate alongside a 'hidden' economy, often exploited by sub-groups within society and liable to criminalization. Such economies do not produce paper records. Casual labour, the sale of domestically manufactured products and 'farm-gate' sales might all contribute to this hidden economy and keep individuals from the market and integrative institutions. Such activities must have formed part of the Roman economy (Wipszycka 1971; Beaucamp 1993) and one cannot but believe that the local exchange of goods and barter bypassed the market. Nevertheless, many people had an interest in limiting the hidden market. Those who had paid for their licences, joined guilds and undergone training will hardly have stayed mute if threatened by casual labour, and the guild structure gave a political authority to any who felt threatened by this hidden market. I guess that this *demi-monde* of hidden economic activity was not great and that most trade and craft production was integrated into the managed economy. The use of apprentices, casual labour and the labour of women and children also meant that far more people were involved in particular trades than joined guilds or used their profession as part of their identity in official documents. We can be confident that a substantial proportion of the population were integrated into the managed economy through trade and, of course, a far higher proportion were integrated through the dole. There is, perhaps unsurprisingly, no evidence of a major economic underclass in the cities. The managed economy of the Roman city was hierarchical and concentrated economic and political power on the elite. Yet, it was also inclusive and must have contributed considerably to the communality of civic life in the Roman period.

The struggle for the Roman city: the city in the fourth century

Institutions and administration: the Diocletianic reforms

The end of the third century brought a certain turbulence with the revolt of Domitius Domitianus and Diocletian's repression of that revolt and subsequent reorganization of Egypt and her frontiers (Jones 1983: 336; Lallemand 1964: 6–38). There were also various changes in urban administration. The eutheniarchy, reintroduced in 289/90 (*P. Oxy.* X 1252) did not survive long (*P. Stras.* VI 594; *M. Chr.* 171; *P. Oxy.* XII 1417 for probably later references). The *agoranomos* probably disappears around AD 300 (*P. Sakaon* 15 and *P. Köln* VII 316 of the early fourth century both attest former *agoranomoi*). Even the office of *exegetes* becomes far less prominent in our data after AD 310 (see figure 5.10.1), though the magistracy operated as late as AD 330, when it was sufficiently burdensome that a complaint was made about nomination to the

277

office (*P. Oxy.* XLVII 3350), and there is a single stray reference from the latter half of the century (*P. Lips.* 34).[121] Other magistracies survived longer. The two gymnasial positions, *kosmetes* and gymnasiarch, are attested markedly less frequently as the fourth century progresses, but it seems likely that the magistracies survived until *c.* 370. The *prytanis* similarly continued to operate throughout much of the fourth century. Nevertheless, such elements of continuity do not undermine the impression of dramatic change in the magistracies of the fourth century. A new poll tax was introduced in AD 295 (see pp. 145–6). Ten years earlier, the district notary, the *phylarch*, had been replaced by the *sustates*. In *c.* 302–10, the *dekaprotoi*, who were in charge of agricultural taxation in the nome, were replaced by *sitologoi* (see p. 146; Thomas 1971; 1975; Turner 1936). The old division of nomes into districts known as toparchies ended *c.* 307–8 and they were replaced by new units, known as *pagi*, administered by *praepositi pagi* (Thomas 1971). The office of *strategos* was also altered and was given a new title: *exactor* (Thomas 1959; 1960; 1989). Around 302, the office of *logistes* was introduced (see below; Rees 1953–4; *P. Oxy.* LIV, pp. 303–46; Sijpesteijn and Worp 1990). The *riparios* appears for the first time by the 340s (see below). The *sundikos*, a title attested occasionally in the third century, becomes prominent around AD 300 suggesting a reformation of the magistracy (*P. Stras.* VIII 789; *P. Oxy.* XXXIII 2665; 2673; XLIV 3187; *SB* XIV 11345; *M. Chr.* 196; Kramer 1990). The *ekdikos* first appears in 321 (*P. Kellis* I 21), though the reference may be anomalous,[122] and is generally attested after 330 (*P. Oxy.* LX 4082; XLIV 3195; 3127; *PSI* VII 767; *P. Oxy.* XII 1426; *P. Panop.* I 29; 30; Kramer 1990; Rees 1952). The *riparios, ekdikos* and *logistes*, together with the later pagarch, were to be the major officers of the late Roman and Byzantine city.

The most important new magistrates were the *logistes* and the *ekdikos*. The *logistes* is the Greek equivalent of the *curator civitatis*, a magistracy imposed on all cities in the empire. Technically, the *logistes* was an imperial appointee, but from very early in the development of the office, and perhaps from its very institution, the appointee tended to emerge from the city itself and the appointment be ratified by the imperial authorities (Liebeschuetz 1972: 168; Jones 1964: II, 726; Lallemand 1964: 113). The office had an overview of all aspects of urban administration (Lallemand 1964: 108–13; Rees 1953–4) including nomination to liturgy and magisterial office,[123] public order and legal disputes,[124] agricultural management and taxation,[125] urban finances,[126] food supply,[127] entertainment,[128] management of urban facilities,[129] prices,[130] and registration of pagan priests and supervision of religious institutions (including churches).[131] At least some of these activities had previously been the responsibility of the *strategos*, and the *logistes* would seem to be in a rather similar position to the *strategos* of the third century as both were imperial appointments. Yet the *logistes* and the new *exactores/strategoi* appear to have been drawn from the local bouleutic group so that these offices were part of and probably the senior posts in the local magisterial career structure.[132]

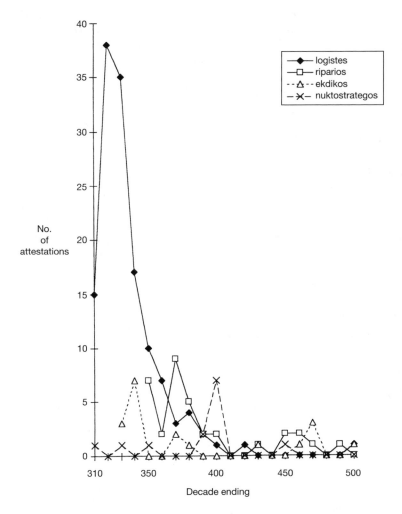

Figure 5.14 'New' fourth-century magistrates from the decade ending AD 310 to the decade ending AD 500

Such a wide-ranging remit meant that the *logistes* covered areas previously administered by the full range of municipal magistrates. The role of the *prytanis* at the head of the council would seem to be reduced, though he still chaired the meetings. Also, the office of *exegetes* was probably diminished, though such magistrates may have continued to fulfil some judicial functions (*P. Oxy.* LIV 3729 of AD 307 is a report from the public doctor to the *logistes* which went through the *exegetes*) and perhaps retained for a time the responsibility for the orphaned that generated many of the attestations of earlier centuries.

The increased role of *sundikoi* and *ekdikoi* may also have affected the position of the *exegetes*. The *sundikoi*, though attested in the third century, achieve prominence in the early fourth. Many of the earlier references attest the magistracy in the context of the council where one presumes they acted as judicial officers. Their role in hearing legal cases (*SB* XVI 12692), in preserving public order (especially in villages) (*P. Freib.* II 11; *P. Oxy.* VI 901(?); LIV 3769; LXIII 4366; *SB* XVIII 14056) and perhaps also supervising some tax-collecting (?) (*SB* XII 11038) is better attested after AD 330. A lacunose text from AD 314–25 (*P. Oxy.* LXIII 4363) associates the *sundikos* with the provision of the food supply. At about the time the *sundikoi* are attested in a wider role, the *ekdikoi* appear. It is not clear whether the duties of the *ekdikoi* were distinct from those of the *sundikoi*. *P. Oxy.* XLIV 3195, for instance, is a report from a public doctor sent to report on an incident at the village of Pela which seems to parallel the attested interest of the *sundikoi* in village violence (cf. *P. Oxy.* XII 1426). Nevertheless, after 339 'ekdikos' replaced 'sundikos' as the preferred title. This office is associated with the Latin *defensor civitatis* (Lallemand 1964: 114–18; Liebeschuetz 1972: 169; Schlumberger 1989; *P. Ross. Georg.* V 27) which, like the *logistes* / *curator civitatis*, was an imperial appointment, though, again, the magistrate was drawn from the local bouleutic class.

The *riparioi* were later introductions. The first attested *riparios* is probably Flavios Eulogios (*P. Oxy.* VI 897; XIX 2235; 2229; 2233; Bagnall 1993: 165; though see *P. Köln* V 234), who operated in the Oxyrhynchite between 346 and 350. The *riparioi* appear to have worked in pairs and were responsible for security (*P. Oxy.* VIII 1101; *PSI* I 47), which gave them a role in dispute-resolution (*P. Lond.* V 1650; *P. Oxf.* 6; *P. Oxy.* LX 4090) and in taxation (*P. Oxy.* XIX 2235; XLVIII 3393), as well as dealing with arrests (*P. Oxy.* VI 897; XIX 2229) and small- and large-scale outbreaks of violence (*P. Cair. Goodsp.* 15; *P. Lips.* I 37; *P. Mil.* II 45; *P. Oxy.* XIX 2233; *P. Rein.* II 92). This role appears to have extended the power of the bouleutic elite in that many of these tasks had previously been performed by district centurions (Roman military officials) (Alston 1995: 86–96). Intra-mural security had been the responsibility of the *nuktostrategos*. This latter official had operated since the second century, but was now subordinated to the *riparioi* (e.g. *P. Oxy.* VII 1033 = W. *Chr.* 476 = *Sel. Pap.* II 296). The *riparioi* probably had to employ their own assistants to carry out the various duties and a fifth-century *riparios*, who had stepped into a vacant position on the understanding that assistants would be provided, found himself in trouble when the promised support did not materialize (*P. Oxy.* VI 904). The *riparioi* were not only supposed to be able to use their own armed force, but also probably co-operated closely with local military officials (*P. Oxy.* I 54; VIII 1101; [XVI 1920; 2032; *Stud. Pal. Pap.* X 252 late references]) and demanded support from village liturgists responsible for security matters.

All the new posts were probably paid and part of the imperial administration and, therefore, it seems very likely that all the candidates for office had to be appointed by the imperial administration. Although it is tempting to view this as a concentration of power in the hands of the imperial bureaucracy, all the new posts appear to have been filled by locals and the candidates emerged from the local bouleutic order. These reforms represent an extension of the power of the local bouleutic group, which increased its control over the nome and reduced the external supervision of its activities. It also cut through the increasingly complicated and unsatisfactory magisterial system of the Roman city. By the late third century magisterial office had been a short-term burden inevitably shared among a significant proportion of the elite. The power of the magistrates was limited by these short periods of office and by the collegial nature of many of the posts. All power within the city flowed to the council, where the magisterial group operated as a collective. In the fourth-century system, the magistracies were held for extended periods and were limited in number. There can be little doubt that those who held these senior offices were powerful men within the community. The result was probably to strengthen the executive arm of municipal government at the expense of the council. The reforms, therefore, represent the concentration of authority in a smaller body within the bouleutic class.

It is not clear how these changes affected the day-to-day management of the city, though we have already noted a number of texts attesting the repair of cities in the early fourth century and there is nothing to suggest that the urban infrastructure went into decline (see also *Stud. Pal. Pap.* XX 230).

Christian triumph I: the pagan and Christian city

The victory of Constantine over his rival Licinius in 324 brought a nominally Christian emperor to the throne. Excepting the brief and extraordinary interlude that was the reign of Julian (361–3), Egypt was to be ruled by Christian emperors until the invasions of the seventh century. After nearly three centuries of intermittent persecution, Christians were almost certainly not a politically powerful minority, but, with the support of the imperial house, they were in a position to challenge the existing religious authorities and to engage in mass proselytizing. The fourth century was a transitional period between a pagan and a Christian empire and although pagans continued to be active long after the first decades of the fifth century, the battle for the religion of the empire was decided in this period. For much of this story we rely on literary sources, especially church historians and the hagiographic tradition. These religious writers can be counterbalanced by the obviously conservative narrative of Ammianus Marcellinus, who continued the traditions of Classical historiography. He, on the whole, tends to eschew the religious concerns that dominate ecclesiastical writings. These contrasts within the literary evidence reflect the historiographical problem of the fourth century: as is inevitable in periods of transition, there were elements of conservatism and our imperfect evidence reflects the old as well as the new. In addition, the ideological nature of the battle means that our literary sources could not feasibly attain objectivity (even if they had so wished) nor, and this is perhaps the most serious problem, could there be any general agreement as to the meaning of the events that shaped the century. For many Christians, the fourth century was animated by a divine spirit which worked through the Church, making history church history, while for many of the traditionalists (and not necessarily just pagans) the subject of history was very similar to what it had been three centuries earlier: the story of the interrelationship of the elite and the emperor and the relationships of the Roman state, as represented by that elite and emperor, with external powers. There is, therefore, no single 'true history' of the fourth century.

Roger Bagnall has argued that the Christian community of Egypt was at least 20 per cent of the population in *c.* AD 313, rising to more than 40 per cent by 324, formed the majority by 337, and achieved numerical dominance at more than 80 per cent of the population by the end of the century (Bagnall 1995: 85–9; 1993: 280–1; 1982; 1987; *contra* Wipszycka 1986; 1988). The method by which Bagnall reached these rather startling conclusions is simple. The fourth century sees the incorporation of names derived from biblical or other Christian traditions into the standard onomastic repertoire of Egypt. Bagnall argues that the rate of incorporation mirrors the rate of Christianization. Second, when one looks at sixth- and seventh-century material, in which everyone is Christian, one finds that just over 66 per cent of the population had obviously Christian names. Bagnall then uses a multiplier of 1.5 on the Christian names of the fourth century to estimate the percentage of Christians in the population. There are problems with this method, such as whether the multiplier is valid, what one does with names such as Theodoros, and how close the correlation between religion and nomenclature is at an individual level. Nevertheless, patterns of nomenclature in Egypt were conservative and highly localized in the third century but changed dramatically in the next century. Additionally, after a period of persecution, Christian institutions emerge early in the fourth-century documentary and official record (Judge and Pickering 1977; Griggs 1991: 23–7). At Oxyrhynchus, for instance, there were two churches by the early fourth century (*P. Oxy.* I 43v). A village church at Chysis in the Oxyrhynchite registered its property in 304 and Apphous, a church deacon, appears as early as 313–20 (*P. Oxy.* XXXIII 2673; *P. Oxy.* LV 3787 *BL* X, 155).[133]

The simplest way of explaining Christianity's triumph is to relate it to the patronage provided by the emperors. The developments in Egypt, however, seem too rapid to be a response to such a change in imperial attitude. Rather, it looks as if elements of paganism had already been eroded before Constantine and that the spectacular growth of Christianity in the fourth century took advantage of those difficulties. This turns attention to traditional temples and, indeed, to the Graeco-Roman temples of villages and cities. Bagnall's (1988a; 1993: 261–8) essays seek to bring coherence to the religious history of the period and explain the phenomenon of early conversion by deploying the deterioration of the traditional temples as a cause, rather than as a result of, Christianization.

As discussed above, the evidence for the third-century decline of traditional temples is not conclusive, nor is it easy to see why the traditional temples might have been in decline, especially if one rejects the old view of Romano-Greek hostility towards these temples. Earlier in this chapter I argue that by the early second century, if not before, there was a growing syncretism between Egyptian and Greek traditions. This process is associated with the Hellenism of a cultural movement known as the second sophistic which dominates much Greek literary cultural production from the second century (Bowersock 1969; 1990; Swain 1993; Fowden 1993; Walker and Cameron 1989; Brown 1992). The second sophistic was both archaizing and scholarly (Swain 1996; Spawforth and Walker 1985; 1986), producing texts that are both erudite and difficult and which even today fail to attract a great scholarly readership. Egypt produced several stars within this cultural firmament, a phenomenon which has caused some puzzlement. These writers included Ammonios Sakkas, Andronicos, Christodoros of Koptos, Claudian, Eudaimon, Harpokration, Helladios, Heraiskos, Horapollon, Hypatia, Kyros, Nonnos of Panopolis, Olympiodoros, Palladas, Pamprepius, Triphiodoros, and, perhaps most important, Plotinus (Cameron 1965; Chuvin 1986; 1991; Sheppard forthcoming; Cameron 1998: 691–6; Athanassiadi 1993; Ammianus Marcellinus XXII 16. 16–19). It was in this cultural context that pagan culture was most vigorously defended. Heraiskos, for instance, apparently was buried according to traditional Egyptian custom (Damascius, Athanassiadi 1993: Fr. 76). Inevitably, Christians identified this group as a threat and Bishop Cyril launched a lynch-mob against the philosopher Hypatia, a teacher of mathematical philosophy to the rich and powerful in the city (see below). Also, an alleged scandal involving the temple of Isis at Menouthis rocked pagan philosophers in the 480s and caused violent conflict with Christian groups (see below). Many of these intellectuals emerged from the Greek cultures of the cities of Roman and late Roman Egypt, and the cultural infrastructure which supported these scholars and poets was sustained by the urban elites, who were also responsible for supporting and maintaining traditional temples, new temples and other cultural institutions. Yet, the literary culture produced implies that what was valued (if the intellectuals shared the views of those who supported them) was an elitist and intellectual cultural production very different from the popular religion of the country.

There is no reason why a pagan 'high culture' could not coexist with a healthy pagan 'mass culture' and both groups might attend similar events and interpret those events in different ways. Plutarch's interpretation of Egyptian ritual and myth could hardly be shared by the majority of the population of Egypt (see pp. 248–9), but what did that matter? Such discrepant interpretations only become important when one interpretation or one group is excluded, as in Christian doctrinal disputes. Nevertheless, although the traditional temples were important in integrating the urban community, that function was already coming under threat during the second century as official activity tended to be located elsewhere in the city (see pp. 245–7).[134] This lack of religious unity and a single religious focus may have weakened pagan institutions when they came under Christian attack in the fourth and fifth centuries. More speculatively, the traditional temples' loss of centrality in the life of the city and in the self-presentation of the urban elite may not just have robbed the temples of the support of the most wealthy and influential, but also may have eroded their hold on the popular imagination.[135]

The Christianization of Egypt had an extraordinary corollary in the reinvention of native Egyptian literature in the Coptic script (Smith 1998) and what appears to be a rather determined rejection of Greek on the part of some of the early monastic leaders, who tended to make much of their rural origins (Athanasius, *Vita Antonii* 1; 72–80; Besa, *Life of Schenoute* 3–4; Palladius, *Lausiac History* 21.5).[136] This has traditionally been seen as some form of nationalistic reawakening (Davies 1951: 65; see also Athanassiadi 1993) or, more recently, a form of protest movement led by sub-elites against the dominant culture (Hopkins 1991), a view somewhat strengthened by the Coptic and Syriac use of 'Hellene' to mean pagan. Whatever one makes of this, the Coptic–Hellene opposition can only have had a brief life as the Syriac–Hellene equivalents did not last in the Levant. Cameron (1997) argues that 'the term "Syriac" describes a language, and does not convey any further implications about the meaning of "Syrian" as an ethnic term or about the extent of "Syria" as a geographical entity' and Griffiths (1997) shows that Greek continued to be the language of liturgy in 'Syriac' areas. The same sentiments could be expressed about 'Coptic', 'Egyptian' and 'Egypt' in later centuries and a Greek liturgy continued to be used in Egypt throughout the Byzantine period (Winlock and Crum 1926: I 254). The monastery of Epiphanius in Thebes was littered with inscriptions, many of which were excerpts from the writings of the religious leaders of Egypt from the previous three centuries. The texts were in both Greek and Coptic (MacCoull 1998). In the late fourth- or early fifth-century *Letter of Ammon* (Veilleux 1980–2: II, 71–109) Abba Theodore is depicted speaking to his monks in Egyptian using a system of simultaneous translation so that the Greeks could understand. Nevertheless, even if the dichotomy quickly fell apart, at one moment, the opposition between Coptic Christians and Hellenic pagans was real. The absence of a broad political strategy or a conservative ethnic manifesto in the Coptic literature of the period (as well as the absence of precursors and comparable movements in antiquity) makes a nationalistic movement unlikely. The opposition is fundamentally religious and it is to this that ethnic labels were attached, as were associations of city and village. The early success of Christianity in Egypt was in reaching the rural population, a population not obviously fluent in Greek, and a population potentially not integrated into the Hellenic civic culture of the *metropoleis*.

Hellenism had incorporated the traditional temples, but may then have both diluted the cultural focus on the temples and, perhaps by diminishing the role of temples in festivals, effectively weakened their role as popular institutions.

Since the paganism of the fourth-century elite was intellectual and philosophical and therefore less concentrated on temples (and thus was able to survive the end of the temples), the temples may have been under threat from both elite and popular disinterest. Such changes in intellectual atmosphere perhaps allow a more subtle and flexible account of the decline of pagan institutions. The closure of the temple at Luxor (an area which seems to see fairly rapid and early conversion) may be reconciled with continued practice at other sites. Continued elite interest in temples would allow their survival, but, as the interest of the elite in temples faded, partly as more converted, but partly due to changes in philosophy, the elite was not prepared to defend temples in the face of Christian and imperial hostility. The decline in paganism can be mirrored by a decline in the gymnasia, suggesting a complex realignment of social ideology. With the closure of the temples and the gymnasia, Hellenism as a mass cultural movement came to an end, as did the institutional infrastructure that had supported the Roman city. Pagan Hellenism became more and more the preserve of a narrow intellectual elite and Christianity triumphed as an integrating and genuinely popular social movement.

Christian triumph II: the ancient story

The process outlined above is one of structural change in Egyptian society, of gradual decline and a fading away of pagan institutions, and corresponds to the norms of modern historiography. Ancient historiography, by contrast, needs drama. The ancient story of the triumph of Christianity is more violent: riots, murder, the burning of temples and idols, sexual scandals, all make exciting reading. Yet, conversion at an individual level must, in the majority of cases, have been a slow process, the kind of event which does not make the 'headlines' of our narrative historians. Thousands of private transitions to Christianity would eventually have public effect with the Christianization of civic culture. If insufficient numbers were prepared to defend the old, then the new could slip in quietly. Only where there was a population minded and sufficiently numerous to confront the new, might we expect ancient literary attestations of the process of conversion. One of the places where Christianization is best attested is (inevitably) Alexandria, though here the record of communal disturbances is confused by the intra-Christian conflicts (especially those relating to the turbulent years in which the Patriarch Athanasius clashed with Melitians (a schismatic group) and Arians (a heretical group in Athanasius' eyes) and with various emperors and governors) which dominate many of the narratives. The sources are deeply committed. The ferocity of the theological divisions within the Church encouraged the portrayal of enemies in the worst possible light and a tendency to associate all dissident groups in their opposition to the one true path. It comes then as no surprise to find pagans and Jews in alliance with Arians. Such allegations permeate most of the narrative histories of this period, rendering them deeply untrustworthy.

Haas's (1997) study of late antique Alexandria makes redundant any extended recounting of events and it is sufficient to summarize the major conflicts in the city.

There were four major events in the pagan–Christian conflict in the city: the murder of George of Cappodocia, the destruction of the Sarapeion, the expulsion of the Jews and the murder of Hypatia. I recount these at some length to illustrate some of the problems.

George of Cappodocia had been installed as Arian bishop of the city with the support of the military and the emperor Constantius. Constantius had wanted to rid himself of the troublesome and argumentative Athanasius, who was theologically opposed to George and Constantius. Even with imperial and military support, George appears to have been driven out of the city in 358, though he returned later. On the death of Constantius and elevation of Julian, George's position was considerably weakened. Athanasius was no longer threatened by a theologically committed emperor and was free to return. The population rose against George and two associates, killed them, and processed their bodies around the city (George on a camel), before burning them. The *Historia Acephala* 6 attributes this to the citizens of Alexandria, but in such a context that it appears that Athanasius' supporters were responsible. Sozomen (*HE* IV 30) wrote that George was hated by both Athanasians and pagans, but more so by the pagans since he attacked their images and temples with the help of the governor Artemius. At *HE* V 7, he recounts that on the announcement of the death of Constantius, the pagans rose up and attacked George, throwing him into prison. The next day, they killed him and paraded and burnt his corpse. Sozomen admits that some claimed that this was the work of Athanasians. Prior to this event, George had found pagan idols while clearing a Mithraeum which had been granted to the Church. He then paraded them through the city and was attacked by enraged pagans who murdered many of those involved. Only later did they take this animosity further to kill George. Socrates (*HE* III 2) has the same story of the Mithraeum being given over to the Church by Constantius and George clearing it. Skulls found in the temple were displayed and then the pagans attacked the Christians, including George. Julian (*Ep.* 10) blames the pagans for the non-judicial murder of George on account of his earlier attack on a temple (in this case probably the Sarapeion). Ammianus Marcellinus (XXII 11), however, has a different sequence of events in which the Alexandrians were informed of the execution of Artemius, the governor who had installed George, then attacked the bishop and killed him. The ultimate cause of his downfall was a public statement, after visiting the court of Constantius, that he would attack the temple of the Genius, though, through fear of the absent Artemius, the Alexandrians restrained their assault.[137] The mob also killed Dracontius, *praepositus* at the mint, because he had overthrown an altar 'recently set-up' in the mint, and Diodoros, a *comes*, because he had cut the hair of some boys while engaged in building a church.

Table 5.6 Religious violence in Alexandria in the fourth and fifth centuries

Date	Event
c. 324–8	Conversion of the temple of Kronous.
339	Rioting against Athanasius.
341	Banning of sacrifices.
343	Return of Athanasius to Alexandria results in rioting.
c. 346	Conversion of the Caesareum.
351	Athanasius removed in rioting.
346–56	Decrees issued concerning the closure of temples.
356	Arian military forces storm Alexandria.
358	Rioting drives the bishop from the city.
361	Lynching of Bishop George the Cappodocian, Dracontius, praepositus of the mint, and Diodoros, comes, for their attacks on pagan monuments or for their Arianism. A Mithraeum or temple of the Genius of the city appears to have been under attack.
362	Pagan accused of eating a deacon.
369	Conversion of the temple of Mendes.
373	Lucius, Arian bishop of Alexandria, accused of attacking nuns.
377–80	Martyrdom of a certain Dorotheos at the hands of Arians.
385	Official closure of the temples.
391	Attack on the Sarapeion by the military with a Christian mob encouraged by Bishop Theophilos. Sarapeion becomes a monastic church.
c. 391	Destruction of the Tuchaion; destruction of the temple at Canopus and installation of a monastery. Purge of pagan temples and artefacts throughout Egypt.
392	Banning of sacrifices.
396	Abolition of pagan priesthoods.
397–8	Relics of John the Baptist transferred to Alexandria.
398–9	Rioting in Alexandria.
399	Imperial order to demolish rural temples.
407	Imperial order for the destruction of all urban temples.
412	Rioting at the election of Cyril.
c. 414	Expulsion of Jews from Alexandria.
415	Murder of Hypatia.
423–4	Rioting in Alexandria.
435–6	Theatre collapses during the festival of the Nile.
439–40	The martyr Euphemia transferred to Alexandria.
442–3	Rioting in Alexandria.
451	Deposition of Dioskoros and subsequent rioting.
452–3	Rioting in Alexandria over episcopal position.
457–8	Rioting in Alexandria led by Timothy the Cat. Murder of Bishop Proterius.
463–4	Elisha transferred to Alexandria.
476–7	Peter Mongus elected bishop and driven from the city and replaced by Timothy Wobble-Hat.
483–4	Peter Mongus drives John, successor of Timothy Wobble-Hat from the city.
c. 480	Violence between monks and followers of Horapollon results in the sack of the temple at Menouthis and a purge of pagans.

The second major incident was the storming of the Sarapeion by Roman soldiers, supported spiritually by Theophilos and legally by the emperor Theodosius. Coming together with the sacking of the temple of Marnas at Gaza and an attack on a synagogue at Callinicum, it marks the end of a phase of relative toleration and an increase in the militancy of bishops in the years around AD 400. Again, the story is confused, though the major discrepancies relate to the origins of the violence and, in most important details, our sources agree. Sozomen (*HE* VII 15) has a temple of Dionysus given over to Theophilos, who embarked on its conversion into a church and subjected the sacred material to public derision. The pagans then went to war, seizing the Sarapeion and using it as base from which to attack Christians. Imperial officials intervened but without success, and the wrath of Theodosius descended. He declared the dead Christians to be martyrs, pardoned the pagans (presumably in order to bring peace) and ordered the demolition of all pagan temples in Alexandria. The pagans fled and the Sarapeion became a church.[138] Rufinus (*HE* II 22–30), whose account is the fullest, has workmen chancing upon an underground temple (a Mithraeum?), which Theophilos then exploits to demonstrate the wickedness of the pagans, which resulted in rioting. Socrates (*HE* V 16–17) tells us that Theophilos extracted an order from Theodosius for the closure of all pagan temples and then began clearing a temple of Mithras and parading the spoils from the temple across the city, though the spark was a Christian assault on the Sarapeion. Eunapius (*Lives of the Philosophers* 470–2), the pagan philosopher, complains about a war with no enemy, suggesting that the attack had no prior pagan provocation and was a response to Theodosius' decree.

The third and fourth events are linked by our main source (Socrates, *HE* VII 13–15). Bishop Cyril found himself in conflict with the governor Orestes after a disturbance at the theatre. Then a night-alarm was raised concerning the burning of a church and the Christians rushed to save it. It was, however, a trap, since the Jews of the city were lying in wait and attacked the Christians, killing many, as became evident at daybreak. Cyril then led a pogrom against the Jews, excluding them from the city. Both Orestes and Cyril complained to the emperor. Orestes was subsequently set upon by a crowd of monks from the monasteries at Nitria (with which Cyril had strong links), who accused Orestes of being a pagan. Orestes was hit by a stone thrown by a certain Ammonios, but the citizenry attacked the monks, saving Orestes. Ammonios was promptly arrested and tortured to death. Cyril treated Ammonios as a martyr, changing his name because of its unfortunate pagan connotations. Next Hypatia was seized. She was the leading philosopher in the city and had a significant following among the elite, including (allegedly) Orestes. The mob took her to a church, stripped her, dismembered her and burnt her corpse. Damascius (Athanassiadi 1999 Fr. 43) blames Cyril's jealousy of her popularity.

Interpreting this violent history is problematic. The later events with Orestes and Cyril were obviously part of a political struggle within the city in which the patriarch challenged the authority of the governor. This was not a dispute over the religious nature of the city and it seems likely that the Jews and Hypatia were incidental victims. The story of the Jewish nocturnal massacre of Christians lacks credibility. What were the Jews hoping to gain? How was this Jewish conspiracy so effectively and quickly discovered by the patriarch? I suspect that the Jews were convenient scapegoats, allowing Cyril to mobilize his forces and slander Orestes in very much the same way as the monks were to accuse him of being an idolater. Hypatia also could hardly have been a cultural threat to the Christians (Dzielska 1995). She may have been prominent and courted by many of the great in the city, but there is no reason to see her at the centre of a militant pagan faction. Indeed, there is some reason to believe that her circle would not have been exclusively pagan: Orestes himself proclaimed his Christianity and her most prominent pupil, Synesius, later became a bishop. Her murder was probably intended to be an attack on Orestes, in that it removed one of his most influential supporters. Although Cyril may have clothed this dispute in the rhetoric of Christians against non-Christians, like the earlier anti-semitic violence in Alexandria, the disputes look more complicated. It is difficult to believe that the Alexandrians who intervened to save Orestes from the monks were non-Christian.

The attacks on the Sarapeion and on George raise difficulties mainly because of the confused stories concerning the preliminaries to the violence. Both the George tale and the sack of the Sarapeion have a clearance of a Mithraeum leading to abuse and rioting, which suggests that some details have been transferred. It is possible that the temple of the Genius (of the city), mentioned by Ammianus as George's next target, was in fact the temple of Sarapis, patron deity of the city, which would further confuse the stories. I would prefer to associate the story of the Mithraeum with the later events, partly because some our sources for those events are contemporary and one might have expected Ammianus, for instance, who misses out the Mithraeum episode in recounting the fall of George, and who was rather well informed, to have used it if he had known of the incident. In fact, although four of the major sources stress the role of pagan sentiment in the murder of George, only Socrates sees in it an immediate response to attacks on temples. George had won few friends in the city and it seems likely that this was an *ad hominem* attack, though the rhetoric of the day put the killings in a Christian theological or pagan–Christian context.

The comparative absence of pagan resistance, except in defence of the Sarapeion, is somewhat surprising. The Christian community took over pagan shrines prior to 391 without obvious difficulty, though such attacks probably caused resentment. Pagan religions tended to be led by members of the political elite who, one would have thought, were well positioned to oppose Christian mobs. Although the destruction of temples seems to represent a social and political triumph for bishops over an impotent elite, bishops did not enjoy a monopoly of political power in the city, witness Cyril's difficulties. One is drawn to the conclusion that the political elite watched over the dismantling of much of the infrastructure of traditional religion with relative equanimity. The introversion of religious scrutiny which was such a feature of Christian holy men, was paralleled by pagan concerns with the purity of soul and the relationship to divine spirit. Although that spirit could be recognized in icons and temples, it existed and could be accessed without the use of such images. The temples were useful but not necessary for the survival of paganism. The Sarapeion, however, may have had a special place in contemporary mystical conceptions. Damascius relates that Olympos, whom other sources mention as leading the defence of the Sarapeion in 391 (Athanassiadi 1999: Fr. 42), came to Alexandria from Cilicia to worship Sarapis. Eunapius (*Lives of the Philosophers* 470) discusses the philosopher Antoninus' prophesies of the doom of the temple and his subsequent withdrawal from the city as if they were a major blow to the philosophical community. It seems as though the pagan community centred itself around this temple and it was only this temple that they had to defend. Yet, even though the sack of the Sarapeion is represented as a symbolic end of paganism throughout Egypt by Christian and perhaps some pagan writers, the pagan community continued to function and the philosophical schools taught certainly into the 480s, probably little disturbed by the destruction of the temples. Zacharias Rhetor (1904) tells a scandalous and novelistic tale of conversion and conflict probably set in the 480s. A certain Paralios, who had come to Alexandria to study with the pagan Horapollon, began to have doubts. A miracle then occurred (coincidentally). A prominent childless pagan went to visit the Isis shrine at Menouthis outside Alexandria. There he had sexual relations with the statue of Isis in the hope that his wife would conceive. The couple, with a child born to her returned to Alexandria, thanking Isis for their good fortune. This confirmation of the power of Isis worried Paralios, who consulted a monastic leader, who advised him to discover (through a woman of good repute) whether the wife was lactating. When Paralios made his implicit accusation he was attacked by the students of Horapollon. Paralios turned to the monks for support, who enlisted the bishop, who organized the destruction of the sanctuary at Menouthis. Under interrogation, it was revealed that the child had been provided for the couple by the priestess of Isis. The willingness of the monks to move against the pagan community may be the result of other political factors, since in the late 480s several leading philosophers were caught up in a political intrigue and prosecuted (Damascius, Athanassiadi 1999: Fr. 117–20; 112–13; pp. 24–32). Nevertheless, the philosophical school functioned in Alexandria into the late sixth century and some of the sixth-century practitioners may have been pagan (Sheppard forthcoming).

The record of the Christianization of other areas of Egypt is sparse and even less trustworthy than that for Alexandria. One of the best stories is that of Macedonius. Having been appointed to govern the Upper Thebaid, Macedonius journeyed to Philae and discovered that it was a pagan city. On return to Alexandria, he suggested that Athanasius should do something about it and, in one of the more psychologically plausible stories about Athanasius, the esteemed archbishop immediately appointed Macedonius himself bishop of Syene. Macedonius returned to Upper Egypt, bluffed his way into the temple and decapitated the cult statue. Although the account lacks specifics, the atmosphere described is one of violence in which the vandalizing bishop was advised to lie low in case he was murdered (Paphnutius, *HM* 29–43).

Schenoute, the charismatic leader of the White monastery at Akmim (Panopolis) is also recorded as attacking pagan shrines as well as launching campaigns against prominent pagans, but whether these stories are more or less true than that of his sinking an island owned by a rapacious landlord or communing with various Old Testament prophets, the apostles or his saviour Himself is anybody's guess (Besa, *Life of Schenoute* 83–4; 125–7; 85–6; 91–7; 117–18; 123–4; 138; 146–7; 154–60). Besa's life shows that the urban Hellene was alive and well in reputation and the miracle stories attest what we know: that, gradually, the shrines of Egypt fell into disuse.[139]

Christians built many churches *de novo* but also converted many previously pagan sites. Two of the major temples of Alexandria, the Kaisareion and the Sarapeion, became churches. Literary sources also mention the conversion of the temple of Dionysos and that troublesome Mithraeum. The temple at Canopus became a monastic institution. At Hermopolis, the Ptolemaic structure to the south-east of the great tetrastylon became the principal church of the city and the presumed seat of the bishop. The south temple also ended its long life as a Christian church (Wace et al. 1959; Bailey 1991: 46–53).[140] At Talmis, the Augustan temple of Mandoulis was converted by the addition of several rooms (Grossmann 1991). At Thebes, a monastery, possibly that of Phoibammon, was placed before the great temple at Deir el-Bahari (Godlewski 1983; 1986; Winlock and Crum 1926: I 7–12; Winlock 1942; Latjar 1991). There may also have been a small monastic community in the Ramasseum (Winlock and Crum 1926: I 15), while at Jeme (Medinet Habu) the second court of the great temple was converted into a church and a small temple of the XVIIIth dynasty, which had continued in use in the Roman period, was also converted (Nelson and Hölscher 1931: 56; Wibber 1940; Doresse 1949). On the opposite bank of the river, at Karnak, the temple was Christianized by the use of crosses and this may have represented the conversion of the structure into a church (Lauffray et al. 1971; Coquin 1972). At Luxor the old temple had, as already noted, been turned into a fort. A church built close to a Roman-period temple of Sarapis may have been the first of five or more to be inserted into the fabric of the old temple (Golvin et al. 1981; Grossmann 1973; Kákosky 1995).[141]

Some of this recycling of the old temples may have been about continuity of religious space. Merely because the gods were defeated did not mean that they had no power and Christians continued to be on their guard. The Christianization of a structure drove the demonic from it and monastic occupations of important sites such as the Sarapeion or the temples at Menouthis or Canopus were about more than the seizure of a convenient building: they were part of a struggle on the divine plane in which Christian holy men led the community. It may also have been about continuity of place. The Sarapeion and the Caesareum in Alexandria and the site of the basilica in Hermopolis were topographically important. Christian builders were drawn to the sites as their pagan predecessors had been. It is more difficult to assess whether the places themselves retained a sacred and emotional hold. Did the local population continue to visit the Sarapeion after their conversion because they had done so in previous generations? Christianity showed a capacity to adopt elements of the pre-existing sacred topography in preserving pagan traditions of healing and prophecy in new Christian clothing. Frankfurter (1998; cf. Papaconstantinou 1994) collects many examples of this kind of continuity. Nevertheless, his argument that this represents a fundamental resistance to change is contentious. Frankfurter favours 'functionalist' interpretations of religious activity, derived mainly from nineteenth-century sociologists (in which what matters is what you do, not what you think you are doing), as against more subjective readings in which socio-political context and the views of the 'actors' take precedence.[142] I think the continuities worked slightly differently. Pagan shrines marked the topography of the city and topography acts as a mnemonic through which a city's culture can be remembered and transmitted. Fourth- and fifth-century Christianity was well practised at imposing its history on urban topography so that its stories infiltrated the city. Alexandria itself had few martyrs but the city's collection was improved through the translation of relics from elsewhere: John the Baptist, Euphemia and Elisha were entombed in new churches that provided centres of divine power, windows into another world and mnemonics for a Christian tradition. The old temple-churches preserved a memory of the victory of those brave bishops and Christians who had fought to extirpate paganism. Each time a Christian saw the church of the Sarapeion he or she could recall Theophilos and his supporters. The events of 391 were, then, significant, not only because of the ending of the institutions of paganism, but also, and perhaps more importantly, for the development of the Christian mythology and topography of the city and the creation of a new Christian civic identity.[143] This was the birth of the Byzantine city.

The Byzantine city: from c. AD 400 to the coming of the Arabs

Having moved through this chapter mostly by century, in this section I cover 250 years. This is a response to the nature of the period. The early fourth-century system of magistracies largely continued into the sixth century and beyond. We also see a consolidation of Christianity as the dominant cultural force within the city. The changes are more subtle and the workings of history seem rather slower in this period. Most pertinently, however, the unexplained dip in the numbers of preserved papyri from the fifth century means that we know little about the first half of this period. Of necessity, our understanding of the fifth century depends on information from the sixth and thus it makes sense to take the two centuries together.

The city of God

We do not have any equivalent to the topographical surveys of the late third and early fourth centuries which would allow the infiltration of the city by Christian institutions to be mapped, but the conversion of the urban topography is clear. When Rufinus visited Oxyrhynchus, probably in the 370s, he could describe a city filled with monks.

> Public temples (if there were any) or shrines of the ancient superstition were now the houses of monks and throughout the whole city, one sees many more monasteries than houses. There are in this city, which is large and strong and populous, twelve churches in which the public meetings of the people are held, exempting monasteries, in each house of which there is a prayer-room. But neither the gates themselves, nor the towers of the city, nor any corner at all is empty of monastic housing, and thus through all parts of the city, day and night, hymns and praise are offered to God, as if they have made the city one Church of God. For none is found there who is a heretic or pagan but all are Catholic, so that it makes no difference whether the bishop delivers his sermon on the square or in the church.
>
> (Rufinus, *HM* 5)

According to Rufinus, the population hung around the gates of the city waiting for visitors to whom they could extend their charity and the religious population of the nome numbered 20,000 virgins and 10,000 monks. This astonishing portrayal of a veritable city of God in the late fourth century is clearly subject to some rhetorical exaggeration. Rufinus was writing to bring the wonders of the monastic achievement to his compatriots in the West and the fervour of Oxyrhynchus was an ideal to emulate. Two elements are of great interest. The first is the extraordinarily high number of celibates in the nome. Of course, we have no figures for the population of the Oxyrhynchite in any ancient period, but calculations in chapter 6 (pp. 333–4) suggest that 150,000 would be a high estimate. Rufinus' estimate suggests that 50 per cent or more of the adult female population were celibates. The figure, however, is clearly intended to give the impression of 'a very large number' and the total number of celibates (30,000) is a figure often used for a 'large' city in Classical texts. More interesting is that a late fourth-century observer estimated that twice as many women embraced the celibate life as men. Rufinus' enumeration of churches, however, is less obviously fantastic. *P. Oxy.* I 43v attested two churches within the city and there is no reason to believe that there were not many more by the late fourth century. The mainly sixth- and seventh-century documentary evidence attests a considerable number of churches in Oxyrhynchus and the Oxyrhynchite, as listed in table 5.7.[144] Many of the churches are attested in the papers of the Apion family, who helped fund churches on their estates. The level of attestation suggests (unsurprisingly) that every significant centre of population had a church. The number of probably urban churches (42) is notable, especially when the comparative lack of material for Oxyrhynchus in this period is taken into account.

Attestations of monasteries in the Oxyrhynchite are comparatively rare and it is in most cases impossible to locate the institutions in village or city. The monastery 'called Kampos' is an exception, almost certainly being located within the city (*P. Wash. Univ.* I 46). The monastery of Kaisariou (*PSI* VII 791), if Oxyrhynchite, should be associated with the old Kaisareion, which was also a church. Some monasteries were identified by their associated village or location (Pela: *PSI* VIII 953; Senepta: *P. Oxy.* XVI 1912; Orous (edge of desert?): *P. Oxy.* XXVII 2480; Berku: *P. Oxy.* XVI 1913; Skutalitidos: *P. Col.* IX 303 reread by Papathomas 1999), but most were identified by their founder or leading light.[145] One may safely presume that the twenty-three monasteries attested are a far from complete roster (for the archaeological material see Coquin and Gascou 1991).

The churches of Hermopolis are mostly attested in Coptic material from the town, much of which is not fully published (Gascou 1994a and see also Coquin 1991).

Gascou (1994a) lists hospitals of Achilleus, Thoma, Ioannos of Germanus, Psanke, ama Kyra, Basileiou Antinoou, Basileiou Theologios, St Abba Leontios, and Christodoros Theodosios together with four hostels and a deaconate(?) within the Hermopolite.

At Ptolemais Euergetis we have churches of the Archangel Gabriel,[146] of St Thekla,[147] of St Theodoros,[148] of our Lady the Mother of God, the Virgin Mary,[149] of St Victor,[150] of St Peter,[151] of St George in *Parembole*,[152] of the Three Martyrs,[153] of St Iulios,[154] of St Stephanos,[155] of St Sansneus,[156] of Soter,[157] and the Great Church or the Holy Catholic Church,[158] and monasteries of Ptolemais,[159] of St Loukos,[160] of St Isi[ ],[161] of Abba Isak,[162] of Makarios,[163] of Nilopolis,[164] of the hamlet of Helia,[165] of Mikrou Psuon in the *proastion* of the city,[166] of Labla (similarly situated),[167] and of Andreas and Naaraos (which may in fact be single cells).[168] To these we can add the religious institutions which lent their names to administrative districts as in table 4.2 (pp. 135–6). These are St Apollo, St Dorotheos, St Leontiou, New Church, (monastery of the) Thebans, Hieron Signon (Holy Signs), and Mena(s). Although the number of attested churches does not match that for Oxyrhynchus, there is sufficient evidence here to allow us to postulate a similar wholesale Christianization of the topography of the city. The same pattern can be shown for Alexandria where the churches and monasteries are attested in the literary sources (Antonini 1940; Calderini 1935–66: s.v. Alexandria).

Table 5.7 Churches in the Oxyrhynchite[a]

Churches	Urban (Probable)	Urban (Possible)	Rural (Probable)	Rural (Possible)	Single reference
Alexander		*			*P. Oxy.* LVIII 3936
Anastasis		*			*P. Oxy.* XXVII 2478
Anniane	*				*P. Oxy.* XI 1357
Anta			*		*P. Oxy.* VI 1911
Apelle			*		*P. Oxy.* XVI 1911
Archangel		*			*P. Oxy.* XVIII 2195
Arour( )				*	*P. Oxy.* XVIII 2195
Aspida			*		*P. Oxy.* XVI 1832
Baptistery	*				*P. Oxy.* XI 1357
Bouko( )			*		*P. Wash. Univ.* II 101
Chenetorios			*		*P. Oxy.* XVI 1912
Chysis			*		*P. Oxy.* XXXIII 2673
St Epi[		*			*P. Oxy.* LXI 4132
St ama Er[	*				*Stud. Pal. Pap.* X 35
Erotos			*		*P. Oxy.* XVIII 2195
St. Euphemia	*				*P. Oxy.* XI 1357
Evangelist		*			*P. Oxy.* XI 1357
Euangelos			*		*P. Oxy.* XVIII 2195
St Gabriel	*				*P. Oxy.* XI 1357
St George also called Semeoneos		*			*P. Oxy.* XVI 1901
Herakleias			*		*P. Oxy.* XVI 1910
Father Hierakon	*				*P. Mert.* III 124
Jeremiah	*				*P. Oxy.* XI 1357
St John		*			*P. Oxy.* LVI 3862
Isiou Pagga			*		*P. Oxy.* LV 3804
St Iulianus	*				*P. Oxy.* XI 1357
St Iustus	*				*P. Oxy.* XI 1357
Kaisareion	*				*P. Mert.* I 41
Kissonos			*		*P. Oxy.* LV 3804
Kleon				*	*P. Oxy.* XVI 1912
Kollouthos		*			*P. Oxy.* XVI 1934
St Kosmas	*				*P. Oxy.* XI 1357
SS Kosma and Lamianos		*			*P. Oxy.* XVI 1955
Kotuleeiou			*		*P. Oxy.* XVI 1911
Limenias			*		*P. Oxy.* XVI 1910
Loukias			*		*P. Oxy.* LV 3804
martyrion	*				*P. Oxy.* XI 1357
Mary mother of Christ	*				*P. Oxy.* XI 1357
St Menas	*				*P. Oxy.* XI 1357
St Michael	*				*P. Oxy.* XI 1357
St Neilos		*			*P. Oxy.* XVI 1898
ktema of Nekontheos			*		*P. Oxy.* XVIII 2195
Nesos Leukadiou			*		*P. Oxy.* XVI 2024
North	*				*P. Oxy.* I 43v

Table 5.7 (continued)

Churches	Urban (Probable)	Urban (Possible)	Rural (Probable)	Rural (Possible)	Single reference
Notinou			*		P. Oxy. XVIII 2243
St Noup	*				P. Oxy. XI 1357
Pakiak			*		P. Oxy. LV 3804
St Pamouthios		*			P. Oxy. XVI 1917
St Paul	*				P. Oxy. XI 1357
Papsau			*		P. Oxy. XVI 1912
Pesla			*		P. Oxy. XVIII 2243
St Peter	*				P. Oxy. XI 1357
St Philoxenos	*				P. Oxy. XI 1357
St Phoibammon	*				P. Oxy. XI 1357
Piaa			*		P. Oxy. XVI 1912
Polemon			*		P. Oxy. XVIII 2243
Purgou			*		P. Oxy. XVI 2024
Samak[				*	P. Oxy. XVI 1912
St Serenos	*				P. Oxy. XI 1357
South	*				P. Oxy. XI 1357
Tarousebt			*		P. Oxy. LV 3804
Tarouthinos			*		P. Oxy. VI 1911
St The[	*				P. Oxy. XI 1357
St Theo[	*				P. Oxy. XI 1357
St Thekla	*				P. Oxy. XXII 2419
St Theodoros		*			P. Oxy. LVIII 3958
Theou				*	P. Oxy. XVI 1912
Thuesobtheos			*		P. Oxy. XVI 1912
ama Tittou					P. Oxy. XVI 2024
Trigeou			*		P. Oxy. XVI 1911
Valens			*		P. Oxy. XVI 1912
St Victor	*				P. Oxy. XI 1357
St Zach[	*				P. Oxy. XI 1357
Holy Father [	*				P. Oxy. XI 1357
Holy Saints		*			SB XVIII 14006
Abraham (?)		*			Stud. Pal. Pap. X 35

[a] It is difficult to know whether certain churches are urban or village. The rule of thumb employed is that churches identified by saint rather than by location are assumed to be urban but this may inflate the urban figures.

Perhaps the best attested community of the fifth to seventh century is that of Aphrodito. Although not a city, Aphrodito's Christianization may have been typical of the development of urban or other communities in this period.[169]

The pattern observable from the collections of references in tables 5.7–5.11 appears consistent between cities, though the exact balance between the numbers of monasteries and churches attested varies, as one might expect. Listing the material, however, may be misleading since we have no guarantee that all the various institutions coexisted or that institutions had prolonged lives.[170] Also, a community such as that of Apa Agenios may be closer to

Table 5.8 Churches in the Hermopolite[a]

Church	References
Church of the Agorai	*P. Sorb.* II 69; *SB* VI 9284
Holy Apostles	*P. Sorb.* II 69
Anastasias	*P. Stras.* V 470–8; *P. Flor.* I 73
Antinoos	*P. Sorb.* II 69
Archangel Michael	*P. Sorb.* II 69; *P. Bad.* II 30; *BM* MSS, 1110
Boou	*BM* MSS , 1077
The Catholic Church or the holy Church of God	*P. Lips* 43; *BGU* XII 2182; 2190; 2193; *P. Lond.* V 1776; 1782–84; 1832; *Stud. Pal. Pap.* III 271; 270; *P.Laur.* V 113; *SB* IV 7369
St Euphemia	*P. Sorb.* II 69
Church of the gate	*BM* MSS , 1077
Gabriel	*BM* MSS, 1110
George	*BM* MSS, 1110
Church of Herm( )	*BM* MSS , 1077
St Horouonchos	*P. Sorb.* II 69
St John	*P. Sorb.* II 69; *BM* MSS, 1110
St Kollouthos	*P. Sorb.* II 69; *BM* MSS, 1077; 1110
Kosmas	*BM* MSS, 1110
Kyros	*BM* MSS, 1110
Church of Holy Martyrs of Thuneis	*P. Sorb.* II 69
Church of Mary	*BM* MSS, 1077; 1110
Church of Mary at the place of Bik[	*P. Sorb.* II 69.
Menas	*BM* MSS, 1110
St Mercurius of the Boou	*Stud. Pal. Pap.* III 270; *BM* MSS, 1110
New Church	*P. Sorb.* II 69
Church of Noouis,	*BM* MSS , 1077
St Peripatos	*P. Sorb.* II 69
Phau	*P. Sorb.* II 69
Phbu (=Phoibammon)	*P. Sorb.* II 69
St Phoibammon	*P. Sorb.* II 69; *BM* MSS , 1077
St Phoibammon of the *agora*	*P. Herm.* 34
Church of the place of the *riparios*	*BM* MSS , 1077
St Sergos	*P. Sorb.* II 69
Church of the place of the shepherds	*BM* MSS , 1077
South Church	*P. Sorb.* II 69
St Stauros	*P. Sorb.* II 69
Church of the Three Saints/ Martyrs of the Sarapeion	*P. Sorb.* II 69; *BM* MSS, 1110
St Taurinos	*P. Sorb.* II 69
Thalmos	*P. Bad.* II 95
St Theodoros (at the Kaisareion or of the *agorai* or of the blue faction)	*P. Sorb.* II 69; *BM* MSS, 1110
Church of Thrake	*P. Sorb.* II 69
Victor	*BM* MSS, 1110

[a] *BM* = Greek and Coptic Documentary Manuscripts of the British Museum

Table 5.9 Monasteries in the Hermopolite[a]

Monastery	References
of Aithiopians	*P. Sorb.* II 69
Apa Anastasios	*P. Sorb.* II 69
Amon	*P. Sorb.* II 69; *P. Bad.* II 95
ama Anna	*BM* MSS , 1077; *P. Lond.* V 1758
Abba Antonios	*P. Sorb.* II 69
abba Aphouphos (Anouphos?)	*BM* MSS , 1077; *P. Sorb.* II 69
of Apollos	*BM* MSS, 1078; 1110; *P. Amst.* I 47; 48; *P. Anag.* I pg 171; 174; *P. Athens* 5; 8; 10; 19; *P. Lond.* V 1899; *SB* VI 9051; *P. Sorb.* II 69
of Banos	*CPR* IX 74
of the horos of Berku	*P. Oxy.* XVI 1913
Bourdon	*P. Sorb.* II 69
of the Brother	*BM* MSS , 1077
Apa Dorotheos	*P. Sorb.* II 69
Egos	*P. Sorb.* II 69
Erythreus	*P. Sorb.* II 69
Abba Ge	*P. Sorb.* II 69
sons of Germanus	*P. Sorb.* II 69
of the holy prize takers	*P. Ross. Georg.* V 42
abba Jakkob	*BM* MSS , 1077; *P. Sorb.* II 69
Apa Jeremios	*P. Sorb.* II 69
John of Germanus	*P. Sorb.* II 69
Klaudianos	*P. Sorb.* II 69
Abba Makarios	*P. Sorb.* II 69
Apa Makrobios	*P. Sorb.* II 69
Abba Martos	*P. Sorb.* II 69
Neos	*P. Sorb.* II 69
Pastios	*P. Sorb.* II 69
Peristeras	*P. Ant.* II 94
Porbeos	Gascou and MacCoull 1987; Gascou 1994a
Pruchtheos	*P. Oxy.* XVI 1913
Psobthis	*P. Sorb.* II 69
Rouinkoreis (?)	*P. Cair. Masp.* II 67168
of Sabinus	*PSI* XIII 1342
Salamit/Salamid	*P. Sorb.* II 69
sons of Salamit	*P. Sorb.* II 69
Sarapios	*P. Sorb.* II 69
St Severus	*P. Ryl* II 164
Sp[ ](	*P. Stras.* VIII 756
Taule	*P. Sorb.* II 69
Father Taurinus	Gascou 1994a
Tbnaupin	Gascou 1994a
Holy Virgins	*BM* MSS , 1077
Zoilos	*P. Stras.* VI 597

[a] *BM* = Greek and Coptic Documentary Manuscripts of the British Museum

Table 5.10 Churches in Aphrodito and area

Church	Selected references
Apa Anouphis	*P. Cair. Masp.* III 67289
Apollonos	*P. Flor.* III 297
Apostles	*P. Lond.* IV 1419; *P. Cair. Masp.* III 67283
Archangel	*P. Lond.* IV 1419
Apa Dios[a]	*SB* XX 14669–14471
of village of Euphrosyne	*P. Cair. Masp.* II 67150
Heragrapta[a]	*P. Lond.* IV 1460
Hermaios	*P. Flor.* III 297; *P. Cair. Masp.* III 67283
Herp[okra]tos[a]	*P. Lond.* IV 1460
John	*P. Lond.* IV 1419
Kollouthos	*P. Cair. Masp.* I 67058
Ama Maria/Theotokou	*P. Flor.* III 297; *P. Lond.* IV 1419; *P. Cair. Masp.* III 67283
Mark	*P. Lond.* IV 1419
Martha[a]	*P. Lond.* IV 1460
Apa Mena	*P. Cair. Masp.* III 67283
called Apa Mousaios	*P. Cair. Masp.* I 67097; 67296; III 67283; *P. Flor.* III 297
New Church	*P. Cair. Masp.* III 67307
Apa Onnophris	*P. Cair. Masp.* III 67289
Apa Pinoutis	*P. Cair. Masp.* III 67288; *P. Freer* 1 + 2
called Apa Pounis	*P. Cair. Masp.* I 67097; *P. Lond.* IV 1419
St Apa Promaios	*P. Cair. Masp.* III 67283
Prodromos and John the Baptist	*P. Cair. Masp.* III 67169
Apa Romanos	*P. Cair. Masp.* II 67139; III 67206; 67283; *P. Flor.* III 297
South Church	*P. Cair. Masp.* I 67088; 67206; 67118; *P. Freer* 1 + 2
Victor	*P. Lond.* IV 1419; *P. Cair. Masp.* III 67283

[a] It is unclear whether this reference is to a monastery or a church.

Antaiopolis than Aphrodito. Nevertheless, such concerns are hardly sufficient to undermine the impression given by the number of Christian institutions attested.

Even the most cursory survey demonstrates the variation in size of churches in the Byzantine period and this has obvious implications for the size of congregation (Grossmann 1980). At Hermopolis, for instance, the central basilica had a simple architectural plan: a wide nave and two narrow aisles.[171] The area of the church was about 1195 m^2 (Wace et al. 1959: 74) and was one of the larger churches in Egypt in this period. The South Church (Grossmann and Bailey 1994) had an internal area of about 680 m^2. This compares with a small church at Qasr Ibrim in Nubia which had an internal area of about 58 m^2, the cathedral at Qasr Ibrim with an internal area (in its major section) of *c.* 325 m^2 (Kjølbye-Biddle 1994) and the North-West Church at Pelusium, which was at least 80 m long and part of a complex that stretches at least

Table 5.11 Monasteries in Aphrodito and area

Monasteries	Selected references
Apa Agenios	*P. Cair. Masp.* I 67062; PSI VIII 933
Apollo	*P. Vat. Aphrod.* 13; *SB* VI 9144
Barbaros	*P. Lond.* IV 1413; 1414; 1416; 1419; 1433; 1434; 1442; 1552; *P. Ross. Georg.* IV 19; 20; W. *Chr.* 256
Abba Charisos	*P. Lond.* IV 1419
Apa Dios1	*SB* XX 14669–14471
Abba Enoch	*P. Cair. Masp.* I I 67234; 67242; *P. Lond.* IV 1419
Abba Entios	*P. Lond.* IV 1419
Genealiou	*P. Cair. Masp.* III 67288; *P. Hamb.* I 68
Heragrapta1	*P. Lond.* IV 1460
Abba Hermaos	*P. Lond.* IV 1413; 1414; 1416; 1419; 1433; 1434; 1442; 1445
Herp[okra]tos1	*P. Lond.* IV 1460
called Apa Ieremios	*P. Cair. Masp.* II 67151
Makrobios	*P. Lond.* IV 1674
Maria	*P. Lond.* IV 1413; 1414; 1416; 1419; 1432; 1433; 1434; 1436; 1445; *P. Ross. Georg.* IV 19; 20; *SB* I 5650
Martha1	*P. Lond.* IV 1460
Metanoias (Alexandreias)	*P. Cair. Masp.* III 67286; 67347; *P. Flor.* III 298; *P. Hamb.* III 232
called Kleopatras	*P. Cair. Masp.* I 67118
Oasiton	*P. Lond.* IV 1419
Peto	*P. Cair. Masp.* II 67138; 67139
Pobreos	*SB* XX 14669–14471
Poeinkoris	*P. Cair. Masp.* II 67168
Psempnouth	*P. Lond.* IV 1419
Apa Psentouses	*P. Mich.* XIII 667
Psinepois	*P. Cair. Masp.* I 67021
Apa Sabrios	*P. Cair. Masp.* I 67080
Apa Senouthis	*P. Cair. Masp.* III 67312; *P. Flor.* III 297; *P. Lond.* IV 1419; 1432; 1460
Smin/Zmin	*P. Cair. Masp.* I 67058; II 67170; 67171; *P. Flor.* III 297; *P. Lond.* IV 1486; 1690
Apa Sourous	*P. Cair. Masp.* I 67110; 67133; *P. Lond.* IV 1419; *P. Mich.* XIII 667
Pharoou	*P. Lond.* IV 1413; 1414; 1416; 1419; 1433; 1434; 1436; 1442; 1552; *P. Ross. Georg.* IV 19; 20; *SB* I 5651
Taurinos	*SB* I 5649
Taroou(t)	*P. Lond.* IV 1413; 1414; 1416; 1419; 1433; 1434; 1442; *P. Ross. Georg.* IV 19; 20
Terouthis	*SB* XX 14669–14471
Abba Zenobios	*P. Flor.* III 297; *P. Lond.* IV 1460

[a] It is unclear whether this reference is to a monastery or a church.

120 m (Grossmann and Hafiz 1998). All are dwarfed by the truly great churches of the period, such as Constantine's basilica in Jerusalem in which the two main elements had a combined area in excess of 2,500 m².

It appears that a moderately sized city might have had more than forty churches and thirty or more monasteries in its environs, along with various hostels and hospitals. When Rufinus visited Oxyrhynchus in the late fourth century, he was impressed by seeing Christianity wherever he turned; how much more pervasive would he have found Christianity a century later? Yet, the plurality of institutions is also a problem. The multiplicity of churches reflects in the first instance the complex historical process of the development of the Church within cities. Bishops never took over a *tabula rasa* and always had limited resources. The needs of bishops to monumentalize their religious achievements seem to have been pressing. Theophilos of Alexandria, for instance, 'remembered' a promise of Athanasius to build a church for John the Baptist at a derelict site and, on clearing the site, according to Eutychios (alias Said Ibn Batrik), *Annales* (PG 111, cols. 1025–6), Theophilos found a pavement inscribed with ΘΘΘ which he took to mean 'God', Theodosius (the emperor), Theophilos, and to be a sign of his fate to build on the spot. The necessary money was miraculously found under the pavement.[172] In one stroke, the bishop showed his historical connection to Athanasius, his political loyalty to the emperor, and that the blessing of God was on him and his projected church. He also glorified his name with a miracle by which the church and Theophilos could be remembered. Bishop Dioskoros' decision to turn the house of Cyril's family into a church appears to have been motivated by malice against a family that had dominated church politics in Alexandria for a considerable period and similarly killed two birds with a single stone (Theophanes Confessor, *Chronicle* AM 5939). If we add to such processes the Christianization of pagan shrines and the limits of available finance, the Christian topography of the city was inevitably generated piecemeal and the results consequently untidy.

Churches were invested with a religious authority that connected the Church to an altogether different geography. Miracles and saints established churches as windows into the divine through which God's power could be perceived. Such 'windows' were not merely local but shed light across the city. For instance, the oracle of Philoxenos at Oxyrhynchus must have drawn interested individuals from a broad catchment area (Papaconstantinou 1994) and the major churches almost certainly had a wide appeal. One may think of the churches as a network, all interconnected and drawing strength from each other; the nodes of the network stretching across the city and infiltrating the divine into the urban. In this, there is an incipient cultural unity: all the institutions are Christian and all are, theoretically at least, tied to the authority of the bishop. Yet, if the numerous centres of power across the city represent the completeness of Christianity's victory and the dominance of the Church, the organization also carried with it an innate capacity for fragmentation. Although one might argue that cities could hardly accommodate their Christian population in a single church, forty or more churches might seem excessive and, with their separate congregations and probably with a particular presiding priest, such a plurality would seem to devolve episcopalian authority and provide schismatic and heretical groups with an opportunity. Bishops were unable to exercise close control over the teaching in each of their churches and wresting control of a church from an opposed party could be very difficult. Heretical and schismatic groups could often survive by occupying churches marginal to the city. Indeed, it may have suited all parties if differences of opinion could be hidden by topographical separation.[173] The churches and monasteries represented a federation in which elements might prove intractable or effectively break away. The disputes that ripped apart the church in Alexandria from the fourth century onwards were maintained by this devolution of power. It was not enough simply to impose a bishop to ensure control of the Church, as emperor after emperor discovered. The ousted parties could survive and the local organization of churches gave them the means by which they could mobilize popular support against bishops, who were often forced to rely on troops.

It is against these centrifugal forces that bishops struggled, often unsuccessfully, to retain control and theological order. This attempt to control the local churches is reflected in *P. Oxy.* XI 1357 (Delehaye 1924; Papaconstantinou 1996), an early sixth-century calendar of places where the bishop of Oxyrhynchus was to officiate. The text covers 144 days and 55 festivals, though a lacuna of six lines suggests that there were 61 festivals over this period. There are probably 25 churches in the calendar, the most regularly attended of which were those of Saints Phoibammon and Philoxenos. If the proportion of festive days was maintained throughout the year, the bishop would attend about 154 days of festivals. Some of these missing festivals may have been held in churches already attested in our text, but since the bishop had attended no church more than nine times, and most churches once or twice in the 144 days, one must assume that there were several unattested churches due for visits. A reasonable (but very imprecise) estimate for churches to be visited during the year would be about 40. In addition, the *Canons of Athanasius* 68 (see below), suggest that the bishop should meet all his clergy at least three times a year.

The bishop was not just faced with a plethora of churches but also by monasteries (Barison 1938). The most famous form of monastic activity in early Christianity was hermitical, of the kind pioneered by St Antony, in which part of the experience appears to have been making a life on the desert margins, but it seems likely that this was always an extreme form of devotion and many monks found their solitude closer to urban areas (Judge 1977).[174] Under the influence of leaders such as Pachomius monasticism began a gradual and probably never complete metamorphosis into its coenobitic form.[175] Brakke (1995) shows how Athanasius sought to build links with individual monks and monastic communities in order to bolster his status and argues that this policy was generally successful. Athanasius' *Life of Antony* and his various treatises on monasticism established his credentials as a monastic leader, but his political problems meant that he was reliant on the support of the monks for his survival and in no position to exert institutional authority over the burgeoning Pachomian movement (*Life of Pachomius* (Bohairic), 28). Later bishops, such as Cyril, who was himself educated among the Nitrian monks (Evetts n.d.: s.v. Cyril), and Theophilos, used monks in their campaigns, but it would be a mistake to overemphasize their authority, which was moral as much as, and probably more than, institutional. Not all monks accepted the authority of the bishop, even the Alexandrian patriarch, and there are famous accounts of conflict between bishops and monks, sometimes at an individual level and sometimes institutional (Brakke 1995: 83; Socrates, *HE* VI 7; Sozomen, *HE* VIII 12–15). John Moschos (*Pratum Spirituale* 44) tells a tale of a monk residing on the outskirts of Antinoopolis. The elder had a wayward follower and after the follower's death, the elder was troubled. He saw, however, a vision of a river of fire into which people were thrust and in the middle of the fire was his former follower. Entering into conversation, the follower thanked the monk since his advice and support meant that he was only submerged in the flames to his neck and was allowed to support himself by standing on the head of a bishop.

In some places monks adopted what appears to have been a deliberately marginal place in the Egyptian city. At Ptolemais Euergetis we know of at least two monasteries in the *proastion* of the city, a suburban settlement. One of these sixth-century monasteries was Melitian. The monastery comes to our attention through a dispute over a cell owned at a Melitian monastery by a monk who had recently become orthodox (*P. Dublin* 32; 33 cf. *SB* I 5174; Husson 1967). This Melitian heterodoxy emerged during the great persecution of the third century and was one of the factors that destabilized Athanasius' patriarchy. So public a survival of a schismatic movement puts into question the ability of the bishops and of the see of Alexandria to suppress opposition.

At Alexandria, the monks of Nitria and those of Enaton played prominent roles in ecclesiastical politics. Timothy the Cat allegedly made use of the credulity of the monks by dressing up as an angel and, accompanied by a minion with a lamp, pretending to be a divine messenger sent to inform the monks that God was backing Timothy.[176] The equally scandalous tale of Paralios and the shrine at Menouthis involved the monks of Enaton in conflict with the Greek philosophers of the 480s and suggests that they contributed to the intellectual debates of Alexandria. We have already come across tales of Schenoute raiding the cities.

Many monastic institutions occupied the old sacred topography of the west bank at Thebes, with monasteries at Deir el Bahari (the temple of Hatchepsut) and the Ramasseum and dotted over the hills (Winlock and Crum 1926; Bachatly 1950; Wilfong 1989). Some of these advertised their presence by towers, which may have had practical purposes, but which also gave the monasteries a prominent place in a religiously powerful landscape marked by millennia of traditional worship (Montserrat and Meskell 1997).[177] The monasteries were centres of local power. Abba Epiphanius, whose monastery was excavated by Winlock and Crum, received letters asking him to intervene in matters of debt and other local disputes and possibly even to extract someone from jail (Winlock and Crum 1926: II text 271; 186; 176–7). The main local community with which the monastery had dealings was the village of Jeme (Medinat Habu), which was controlled by *lashane*, a headman. The monks were economically powerful, with some unquantifiable landholdings, but also with sufficient financial resources to act as moneylenders at Jeme (Winlock and Crum 1926: II text 84–5), and they also had religious authority, which meant that they were asked to intercede with the Divine (Winlock and Crum 1926: II text 199). Unsurprisingly, the *lashane* appears to have shown deference to the monks (Winlock and Crum 1926: II text 266). The monks had economic, political and cultural authority, and rented what appear to have been quite extensive tracts of land to villagers.

At Aphrodito, it is possible to judge the increasing power of the monasteries. Gascou and MacCoull (1987) published a long incomplete cadastral document from Aphrodito. The cadastre registers 1,070 *arourai* of grain land, of which 47 per cent was owned by the Church, and 81.5 arourai of other types of land, of which about 58 per cent was Church owned. Once this is further broken down, about 40 per cent of all grain land (85 per cent of Church holdings) and 57 per cent of other land (96 per cent of Church holdings) were owned by monasteries.[178] There is, of course, no guarantee that the remaining land in the village was apportioned in the same fashion as in this cadastre, nor that the prominence of monasteries at Aphrodito was paralleled elsewhere in Egypt. Yet in the eighth century, the monastery of St Jeremias at Saqqara was one of the biggest taxpayers in the Memphite (Gascou 1991). Such figures suggest that the monasteries came to wield considerable economic power.[179]

We know very little about how the monasteries managed their land. *P. Michael*. 41 is a sixth-century sale contract from Aphrodito. The Church sold land to a certain Apollos son of Joseph. What is interesting about this seemingly everyday transaction is the lack of detail. The size of the plot is not mentioned, no price is stated (which leads the editor to conclude that the land was given to free the Church from taxes), the harvest that is in the fields is granted to Apollos, and the buildings are not listed. The vagueness of this text is startling, especially when one compares it with the almost exactly contemporary *P. Michael*. 40, which follows traditional practice in delimiting the property by its neighbours. It is not clear, though, if this carelessness was typical. Churches used *oikonomoi* (stewards) to look after their financial interests and this might have insulated individual churches from priests of limited competence. At Aphrodito, the same priest, Joseph, acted as *oikonomos* for two different churches (*PSI* VIII 936; 937), which hints (though certainly does not prove) that individual churches took little interest in the business of managing their assets. Keenan (1980; 1984; 1985) argues that a certain remoteness from the everyday business of estate management was characteristic of the landlords of Aphrodito (secular and ecclesiastical), who tended to let their lands to powerful villagers, who would then sublet to others in the village, creating a kind of managerial class within the village.

The monasteries had powerful local friends, powerful links to local communities, and a certain spiritual authority. While not exactly independent of the bishop, the monasteries were at least partially autonomous. The priesthood may have been more closely controlled. However much the enthroned bishop may have wanted to adopt an autocratic position, his power was always limited. Bishops relied on a vast constituency of individual local agents with their own local power bases and faced the possibility that their community would fragment.

Nevertheless, the bishop was the leader of the Christian community and blessed and sanctified by the apostolic succession. He was guardian of the souls of his flock and such responsibility as well as the imminence of divine judgement in antiquity must have contributed significantly to his social power. Additionally, bishops disposed of considerable financial resources and had an official role in the administration and politics of the city. We can see something of their power in their interventions in what one might (possibly inaccurately) call secular society. John Moschos (*Pratum Spirituale* 207) tells a tale of an elite girl (and this is an important element: the degradation of the poor was somehow less important even for Christian writers) who was orphaned. She went out into her garden and found a man about to hang himself. She dissuaded him from this and gave him all her money so that he might escape from his debts. She was then herself afflicted by the twin evils of poverty and a lack of social protection and became a prostitute in order to feed herself. Her degradation led her to appeal for divine help, though the Church and her neighbours would not support an active prostitute. Angelic intervention ensued with the formerly suicidal bankrupt appearing and then several prominent men (who were all later to deny involvement) who took her to church and vouched for her soul. She was baptized and became a recipient of ecclesiastical charity. The bishop was asked to investigate how a prostitute came to be baptized and he accepted the girl back into the community as a recipient of divine charity. Another bishop, Apollinarius, wishing to help a proud but unfortunate youth whose trading endeavours had gone awry (*Pratum Spirituale* 193), ordered his *oikonomos* to forge a credit note in favour of the merchant against the Church which the *oikonomos* was to present to the man for a bribe. The bishop pretended to be unwilling to honour the debt, and the man refused to press, asking that the bishop pay only what he saw fit. He thus proved himself a loyal son of the Church and the bishop paid up the capital (without interest) and subsidized the merchant without patronizing him.

It is with the *Life of John the Almoner*, though, that we find spectacular evidence of the financial and social power of the bishop. The historicity of the account is extremely dubious given that not only is it hagiography and liable to the conventions of that genre, but that it was composed sometime after the fall of Alexandria, and it may be that the wealth of John became something of a mirage of an age lost with Persian and later Arab domination of the eastern Mediterranean. Nevertheless, the life informs us that John fixed the measures for the city by an ecclesiastical standard (*Life* 3), that he sat for two days each week before the church to resolve disputes (*Life* 5–6), that he strove against the corruption of *oikonomoi* who administered justice (*Life* 4), that he looked after the poor by establishing a register of 7,500 destitute people (*Life* 2), by visiting the Caesareum where the poor congregated (*Life* 27), and by supporting these people. His building work was extensive: hospitals and poor-houses (*Life* 6), hospitals where mothers could recover after childbirth (*Life* 7), and monasteries (*suppl.* 42). He supported refugees from the Persian wars (*Life* 6), supplying them with necessities from Church funds and accepting fleeing clergy into his church provided that they testify to their orthodoxy (*Life* 12), as well as using his cash to support Christians in Jerusalem (*Life* 9). He also bought himself a fragment of the True Cross (*Life* 11).[180] John was able to finance this activity through the extensive reserves of the Church (*suppl.* 45), but also through trade (*suppl.* 28), since the Church had a large fleet, and one presumes that the Church also had substantial estates, though these do not appear in the material. The fleet provides one of the more marvellous stories of the *supplement* (10) since John apparently sent a ship to Britain filled with corn which arrived in time to relieve a famine and returned laden with gold and tin. Obviously, Britain was chosen as the most remote and barbarous place that could be imagined, to emphasize the miraculous nature of John's knowledge, and it would be unwise to regard this as evidence of long-distance trading on the part of the Alexandrian patriarchy. The wealth of the Church, so obviously displayed, brought John into conflict with the political leadership of the city, who wished to use the Church's wealth for their own ends in what may have been a rather desperate period of the Persian conflict. John successfully resisted this pressure and was again in conflict with political leaders after his withdrawal from Alexandria to Cyprus when the Persians took the city. Isaac, whom John blamed for the loss of Alexandria, supposedly attempted to have him assassinated (*Life* 15; *suppl.* 12).

In Upper Egypt, in the late fourth century, Macedonius apparently arbitrated in disputes between Nubian non-Christians, finally solving the problem, which concerned a camel whose leg had been broken, by miraculously restoring the camel to full health, a miracle which appears to have led directly to a programme of mass conversion (Paphnutius, *HM* 44–52). His successor Abba Mark (who was apparently the son of the pagan high priest of the city) was renowned for his charitable works. Abba Aaron, who succeeded Abba Mark's brother, involved himself with fishermen by helping those who were having difficulty catching fish and were contracted to supply fish to a leading man and by bringing back to life the son of a fisherman who had drowned in a net (Paphnutius, *HM* 101; 119). He also intervened against a nobleman who refused to exercise mercy in his dealings with the poor (Paphnutius, *HM* 109–15).

The hagiography is, of course, instructional literature and the historicity of these stories cannot be established. The *Canons of Athanasius* provide more explicit instructions for bishops (Riedel and Crum 1904). Although mainly known from a late Arabic version, earlier Coptic fragments together with the Canons' emphasis on the Melitian schism and ignorance of the monophysite controversy suggest that they may genuinely have been authored by Athanasius. These instruct the bishop to give charity to the poor and the imprisoned (6), to be a 'father to the orphans and a father to the poor' (14; 65), to visit the sick (15; 47), to give alms each Sunday (16), to care for strangers (81), to care for the needs of the priests, the sick and the poor, in that order (82), and to look after widows, the sick and poor (84). He is also expected to show generosity in financial matters and be careful to give using a large measure and to take using a small (9).

Such activities can also be seen in the documentary material. Plousianos, bishop of Hermopolis, arbitrated in a dispute outside the gates of the basilica (presumably the central basilica) (*P. Lips.* I 43 = M. *Chr.* 98). The case involves a nun and the alleged theft of some Christian books. The bishop of Oxyrhynchus, Abba Theodoros, was asked to intervene in a family dispute between Aurelia Nonna and a monk, Alypios, who lived in a village. The dispute came to blows and Nonna looked for protection (*SB* IV 7449). In 663, Bishop Peter received notice of theft, though the early Arab period may have seen an enhancement in the role of the bishop as community leader (*P. Berl. Zill.* 8). In AD 710, for instance, the Arab administration made the bishop partially responsible for collecting a special tax or fine on the population of Aphrodito (*P. Lond.* IV 1345). In a sixth- or seventh-century case, a *comes* (acting through an agent) instructed a bishop to pressurize a *presbuteros* over a letter-carrier who had somehow offended (*P. Grenf.* II 93). Another case in which bishops intervened was a marital dispute for which we have the woman's complaint (*P. Oxy.* VI 903). The text opens *in medias res*. She appears to have deserted him, whereupon he seized her 'foster-daughters' and her slave and tortured them to gain an inventory of property taken from his house. After this seemingly ultimate breakdown in relations, 'bishops' intervened to restore the relationship and a formal contract was made. He continued to abuse her property and attempt to restrict her movements (allegedly getting rather upset when she went to church one Sabbath). There are several peculiarities about this case, the presence of foster-daughters being one, but this was obviously a high-status couple and as marriages could be major public events (see p. 89), divorce may also have convulsed a community. Here, apparently, more than one bishop intervened in order to patch up this prominent alliance and persuade an elite woman, who portrays herself as actively Christian, to return to an allegedly violent man, possibly against her better judgement. The common Christian distaste for divorce was probably making itself felt and a similar concern may have motivated the *presbuteroi* in the Aurelia Attiaena case, who kept together a couple after an abduction marriage and an apparent history of violence and adultery (*P. Oxy.* L 3581, see p. 91). In contrast to this later material, *P. Oxy.* XXII 2344 *BL* X, 148 of AD 351–2 seems to suggest that a bishop sought to escape from imposed duties of guardianship.

The Coptic material shows a similar involvement in 'secular' affairs. Bishop Pesunthius (Revillout 1900; 1902; 1914) is asked to intervene when a churchgoing couple demonstrate about the rape of their daughter (text no. 54). Disputes over marriages are brought to his attention, one of which resulted in violence (text no. 14; 15, 51). A son complained that he had been disinherited (text no. 48). A theft is reported (text no. 34) and a legal case explained (text no. 52). Most scandalously, a *lashane* (headman) is arrested in a sexually compromising situation (text no. 50). In a separate archive, Bishop Abraham announces that all those who divorce, draw up deeds of divorce, or receive the divorced into communion are excommunicated, unless the divorce was on grounds of adultery (Crum 1902: text 72). He also appointed a deacon to resolve a dispute (Crum 1902: text 69). A whole series of contracts from Medinet Habu were either written or witnessed by priests (Stefanski and Lichtheim 1952: nos. 58–61; 65–6; 73; 75).

The economic power of bishops is attested through rather less dramatic accounts. We see bishops involved in building and improving churches (eg. *I. Fayum* II 131 = *SB* I 1449; *I. Philae* 194; 195; 200; 202–4; 216). At Kom Ombo, the bishop organized the local population to cleanse and clear an area which had been used as a dung-heap, for the building of a hostel (*IGChEg* 561 = *SB* IV 7475 = *SEG* VIII 780; Gascou 1994b). In the early fourth century, Bishop Hierakonapollon moved grain belonging to the villagers of Karanis in his boat (*P. Col.* VII 160). Another fourth-century bishop, Theodoros, moved money in his boat (*P. Oxy.* XXXIV 2729). We see bishops paying for fodder (*P. Köln* III 152), for transport camels (*P. Oxy.* XVI 1871; cf. Crum 1902: text 221), paying an innkeeper (*Stud. Pal. Pap.* VIII 763), and receiving money for an oil works (*Stud. Pal. Pap.* VIII 963 *BL* I, 417). In AD 427, Bishop Peter of Oxyrhynchus was renting out an iron-smithy (*P. Oxy.* XVI 1965). Another text may locate a smithy in the environs of a church (*SEG* XVIII 720). Most of the attested financial dealings of the bishops, however, appear to have involved land and its management (*P. Köln* III 152; *P. Oxy.* XVI 1911; *P. Rain. Cent.* 126; *SB* VIII 9876; Crum 1902: texts 138; 140; 307; 206; 482).[181] Bishops were often involved in quite small transactions involving food (*P. Lond.* V 1803; *P. Oxy.* XVI 1848; *SB* XVI 12869), especially bread, and may have had close connections with bread-merchants and bakers (*SB* XII 10766; 10767; *Stud. Pal. Pap.* III 213–36; XX 253; *P. Brooklyn* 16). On occasion, a bishop might deal with large consignments of grain, wine or oil (*P. Cair. Masp.* II 67168 (wine); *P. Grenf.* I 63 (wine and grain); *SB* XII 10808. Some of this activity may have been to feed their households and their priests, but much, especially their involvement with bakers, may be as a result of charity, especially in the support of orphans, widows and the elderly (Wipszycka 1998; Martin 1998). We have a number of recommendations of poor people for receipt of charity (Crum 1902: texts 260; 262–3; 267–9; *P. Oxy.* XVI 1848). The charitable bishop of the hagiographies can be observed in the documentary material as well as in the literary material. Such generosity must have brought political power.

Christianity and its institutions pervaded the public life of the city. The Church was economically powerful, able to mobilize significant political support on the streets of cities and to integrate the population into its values and culture partly through the provision of charity. But the power of the Church was not concentrated on a single individual or institution. The bishop was very important. He had moral and administrative authority. He probably had significant wealth. Nevertheless, it was difficult for the bishop himself to impose his rule on all levels of the spatial matrix and other powers in the city and other communities were able to resist him. The Byzantine city may have been Christian, but it was not necessarily episcopalian.

Ruling the Byzantine city

The magisterial system established during the fourth century seems to have survived throughout the fifth and possibly much later. The office of *logistes* is attested into the seventh century (*P. Lond.* I, p. 217, 113. 7). In AD 553, Flavia Gabriela, a member of the prominent Apion family (see below), had titles derived from the offices of the *logistes*, *proedros* and *pater poleos* (*P. Oxy.* XXXVI 2780; Sijpesteijn 1987). A certain Samouel had the same combination of titles in 517 (*SB* XX 14964) and Flavius Apion had held the office of *pater* and *logistes* by AD 571 (*SB* XII 11079). Enoch, *riparios* and *logistes*, is attested in *P. Oxy.* LVIII 3949 of AD 610 when an assistant at the baths is mentioned.[182] The survival of an office, however, is not a guarantee that its role remained unchanged and it seems likely that new offices, such as that of the *pagarch* and *pater poleos*, diminished the power of the *logistes*.[183]

The office of *ekdikos* survived into the Arab period (*P. Apoll. Ano.* 46 of AD 703–15; cf. *CPR* XIV 17; *SB* I 4490 [*BL* VIII, 309]; 4694). The officials' function does not appear to have changed. They had some legal duties which meant that complaints about public order might be submitted to them (*PSI* VI 686; VIII 872) and were expected to protect the weak (*PSI* IX 1075). The *riparioi* are attested into the seventh century. In 655, Apphous, *riparios* of Ptolemais Euergetis, acted as intermediary between Duke John and the chair-makers of the city over some saddles (*CPR* XIV 32; cf. *SB* I 4666; *P. Ross. Georg.* III 23 [*BL* VIII, 290]; *P. Lond.* I, p. 218, 113.7).[184] Some sixth-century texts cover the traditional issues of violence and public order (e.g. *P. Cair. Masp.* I 67092–3; *SB* XX 15095 = *P. Cair. Preis.* 6; *P. Oxy.* XVI 1885) and security (*P. Cair. Masp.* III 67295), including a case of demonic possession (*P. Cair. Preis.* 2). The title may, however, be used promiscuously, perhaps to refer to village and estate officials as well as those whom we might term traditional *riparioi*.

The period sees the introduction of the pagarchate. The Diocletianic reforms introduced the division of the nomes into *pagi* (which replaced the old division into toparchies), controlled by *praepositi*. The pagarchate proper, however, was normally a post held by a single official who took the major role in the administration of the nome (Gascou 1972a). Some of the duties appear to have been financial (*BGU* I 304; 320; II 396; 403; *CPR* VIII 73; XIV 1; *SB* VIII 9750; VI 9577; W. *Chr.* 8), though it is difficult to separate private from public business. We have, for instance, two ambiguous texts about the rental of a workshop (*CPR* XIV 10; 11; cf. *SB* XVI 12481), though a request to rent land addressed to Flavius Apion is more obviously private business (*BGU* I 305). The village of Aphrodito clashed spectacularly with the *pagarch* Menas over taxes, though accusations about his general wickedness abounded (*P. Cair. Masp.* I 67002; 67005; 67019; III 67354; *P. Lond.* V 1677). The archive of Papas shows that it was the pagarch to whom the Arab emir turned to control the administration of the nomes in the eighth century (*P. Apoll. Ano* 7–22; 26–9; 32; 34; 37–42;45; 49; 50; 60; 67–8; 72; 79) and I presume that this reflects an Arab perception that the pagarchate was the crucial local power prior to 642.

Another new official was the *pater poleos* (the father of the city). Little is known of this office (Sijpesteijn 1987; Rouché 1979; Feissel 1987). In 553 the title was held by Flavia Gabriela (*P. Oxy.* XXXVI 2780) and in 584 by Flavia Theophania (*CPR* X 127), but other references are to male holders of the office: Flavius Apion (*SB* XII 11079 of 571), Flavius Phoibammon (*P. Oxy.* LXIII 4393), Samouel (*SB* XX 14964 of 517), Timotheos (*Stud. Pal. Pap.* III 176; *P. Ross. Georg.* III 46; 47 of the second quarter of the seventh century) and Kosma (*Stud. Pal. Pap.* III 67 of the seventh century). Timotheos appears to pay wages for work at the baths while a comparatively early text (*P. Mich.* XVIII 795 of the fifth or sixth century) concerns the distribution of oil at the city of Pelusium. Flavius Phoibammon was involved in a dispute over an inheritance and Theophania had an oath taken in her name. Feissel (1987) compares the office with other civic posts, such as that of the *logistes*, though Rouché (1979) argues that the *pater* was an honorific title, and this latter view appears to explain the Egyptian material.

The other official to gain prominence is the *proedros* (president). This post is attested in the fourth and sixth centuries. The comparatively uninformative attestations suggest that these officials supervised public works (*P. Göt.* I 7), taxation, and liturgies (*CPR* XVIIA 35; *P. Ross. Georg.* V 28; *ChLA* XLI 1195). The office appears to be associated with the council and, if this is the case, the survival of the *proedros* would suggest that the council continued to have a role until at least the mid-sixth century (*P. Oxy.* XXXVI 2780; *P. Flor.* III 293; *ChLA* XLI 1195; *SB* XII 11079; Worp 1999).

The above provides the bones of the administration of the Byzantine city, though, as bones go, these are extremely bare. The continuity in offices contrasts rather starkly with the number and quality of attestations of urban administration from the third and fourth centuries. We hear virtually nothing, for instance, of the council and its workings, and the *logistes* fades into obscurity. Although our sources cannot be described as silent, it is tempting to argue from their 'quietness' that the fourth-century administrative system had undergone radical change by the sixth century, one of the principal casualties of which was the council. Literary material places the fall of the councils *c.* AD 512, under

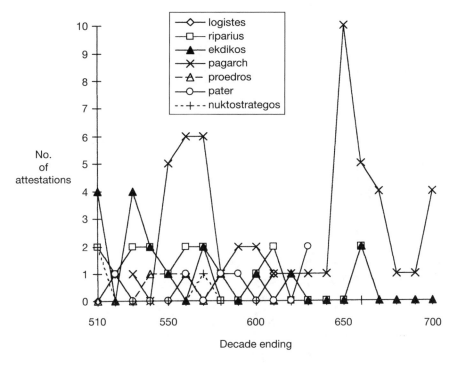

Figure 5.15 'New' fourth-century and later magistrates from the decade ending in
AD 510 to AD 700

the emperor Anastasius: the praetorian prefect Marinus supposedly appointed
vindices to supervise all aspects of urban life and thereby ended the power of
councils (Malalas XVI, p. 400; John Lydus, *De Mag.* I 28; III 46; 49; Delmaire
1996; Liebeschuetz 1996). Liebeschuetz (1973: 491–518) argues that the
imposition of the pagarchy may also be associated with Anastasius. Perhaps
the *pater poleos* was also created at the same time.[185] Nevertheless, *curiales*
(*bouleutai*) continued to exist in Egypt and elsewhere until the Arab invasions
(*SB* XX 14284; *P. Sorb.* II 69; Geremek 1990; Laniado 1997; Holum 1996;
Worp 1999; see also, for instance, Justinian, *Edict XIII* 12; 15; 25). By *Novella*
128, Justinian gave authority in financial matters and the right to appoint
the *pater poleos*, the providers of grain and others to a body made up of the
possessores, the *primates* and the bishop. A number of rulings empowered an
effective electoral assembly consisting of the bishop in conjunction with
possessores or others (e.g. *CJ* 1 4 17). As early as AD 409 the *defensores* (*ekdikoi*)
had to have their orthodoxy certified by the bishop and be chosen by the bishop,
clerici, *possessores* and the *bouleutai* (*CJ* I 55 8). The *possessores* and *primates* deserve
explanation. A *possessor* was someone who held a landed estate and here it must
surely mean the major landowners of an area. The *primates* are the leading men.

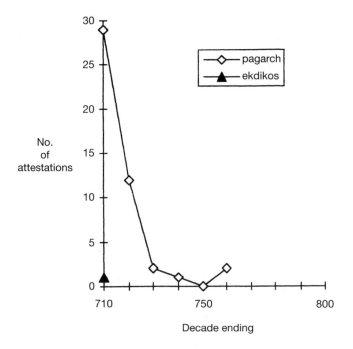

Figure 5.16 Eighth-century magistrates

Ammianus Marcellinus (XIV 7) talks of Gallus Caesar launching prosecutions that spared neither the *honorati* nor the *primates* of the city of Antioch. The *honorati* were those who had municipal honours, while the *primates* were leading figures who did not enjoy such honours. Men who had served in the imperial administration or in the army sought exemption from municipal services, though they were men of property and power. The Byzantine electing assembly was not necessarily a standing body, but its formation inevitably drew political power away from the council, though it is not necessarily the case that this local elite would exclude councillors. Indeed, the continued prominence of a *proedros*, and perhaps of the *logistes*, and the fact that these titles were held by those who held the title of *pater*, suggests that the councils retained some authority. Nevertheless, the impression of a change in the way power was manifested in society and of a consequent decline in the power and prestige of the councils is persuasive. The argument from relative silence is here a strong one.

Explaining the decline of councils is not straightforward. Libanius (*Oratio* XLVIII 3) claims that the Antiochene council underwent a 90 per cent reduction in membership during the fourth century.[186] Such a concentration of power might have been encouraged by the workings of the imperial administration, which by the fourth century provided a range of opportunities for the wealthy and well-connected which were sources of considerable prestige and probably profit and may have elevated certain families above the norm. Tracing this in the documentary material is, however, problematic.

There is no conclusive evidence that wealth was becoming more concentrated in Egyptian society, yet a reading of the first- and second-century papyri suggests that very few of the local elite accumulated the very large estates, such as those of Appianus (Rathbone 1991) and Claudia Isidora alias Apia, attested in the third century (Parassoglou 1978: 19). Bagnall (1992) shows that although landownership was spread across a considerable swathe of the urban community of mid-fourth-century Hermopolis (c. 20 per cent), 10 per cent of the land-owners (c. 2 per cent of the urban population) owned about 78 per cent of the land held by urban dwellers. I would estimate that this 2 per cent of the urban population owned about 23 per cent of the total productive land of the nome (see p. 333).[187] In the sixth century, the Apion family came to control huge tracts of land in the Oxyrhynchite and Arsinoite and probably elsewhere and although we cannot accurately assess the size of their estates, the Apions' wealth clearly dwarfed that of earlier elite families. Such snapshots point to (though certainly do not prove) a gradual concentration of wealth in the hands of a small elite, though small and medium-sized holdings remained common as late as the sixth century.

The Apion estate was heavily involved in the political life of the city. A long sixth-century account mentions wine or vinegar sent to the church of Papsas, the monastery of Abba Sarmatus, the house of Ama Bes, the church of St Serenos, the church of Abba Hierakon, the monastery of Pela, various guards (*boukellarioi*) on the estate, the church of St Euphemia, 139 guards of the house of the Apions for the festival of the Archangel Michael, guards for the festival of Anastasios, and the Blue faction (*PSI* VIII 953; see pp. 318–9 for further discussion of factions). *P. Oxy.* LVIII 3936 of AD 598 is a receipt for payment of the wages of a *presbuteros* of a probably urban church in the Oxyrhynchite issued to Flavius Strategius, one of the Apion family. *P. Oxy.* XVI 1898 of AD 587 is a receipt for a donation from the Apion family of 371 *artabai* of corn (enough to feed about thirty-one adults for a year) to the *nosokomion* (hospital) of Abba Helias near the church of Nilos. The receipt is, as is proper, issued by the *oikonomos* of the hospital, but this man was also a *notarios* (scribe or legal officer) of the house of the Apions. *P. Oxy.* LVIII 3958 of 614 appears to appoint a junior priest as rent collector in the city. In 595–6, a fruit-farmer declared on oath that he would farm land of Flavius Apion. The oath was administered by the *oikonomos* of the church of Anastasios (*P. Oxy.* XXVII 2478 *BL* V, 82). In 621, after the Apion estate had been taken over by the Persian invaders, an account of expenditure of wine (*P. Oxy.* LVIII 3960) notes that from 33,298 jars of wine 25 per cent was sent to the Church, 2 per cent went for the support of widows and orphans, and 22 per cent went to the Persians. A long set of accounts from the Apion estate (*P. Oxy.* LV 3804; see also *P. Oxy.* XVI 1911) lists payments to churches at Apele, Pakiak, Kissonos, Tarousebt, Trigiou, Ision Panga, Loukias, and the monastery of Abba Andreos. *P. Oxy.* XVI 1912 lists payments (almost certainly from the Apion estate) to churches of Papsau, Piaa, Kleon, God, Ouesobtheos, Chenetorios, Samakion, Valens, Holy Michael and a monastery. *P. Oxy.* XVI 1913 adds the monastery of Abba Apollo, the stable of the *velox cursus* (the official postal service), the monks of Pruchtheos and those of Berku. *P. Oxy.* XVI 1910 has payments to churches of Limenias, Herakleias, a *martyrion*, and the *xenodochion* (hostel) of Leonidos. *P. Oxy.* LIX 4003 notes the building of a church by the estate for the village of Tampemou and requests that the work is finished as a matter of urgency. The fact that the church was built of stone, which was expensive, rather than the virtually free mud-brick, suggests that this was a prestige building.

This material, heterogeneous though it is, shows links between estate and ecclesiastical administration at various levels. The Apions supported and funded churches where they held land, which presumably provided for the spiritual well-being of their peasantry, but they also funded activities within the city. Such euergetism continued long-established traditions of charitable donation that had their roots in the pre-Christian period, but the notable intimacy of the administration of the Church and of the estate erodes modern expectations of a separation of ecclesiastical, private and civic spheres. This is further exemplified by an agreement to rent a bakery consisting of a grindstone, three or four ovens, and two mills. There is little unusual about this apart from the fact that the owner, Serena, had inherited the bakery from the monk Kopreos and that the bakery was located within the monastery of Kopreos (probably the same Kopreos) (*P. Oxy.* XV 1890 = *Sel. Pap.* I 48). There is no suggestion that the baker renting the bakery was a monk or otherwise connected with the monastery and one presumes (which may be incorrect) that the bread would be marketed through normal, non-ecclesiastical outlets.

The beneficence of the Apions and other landowners was not, however, solely channelled through the Church. They supported circus factions (see below), for instance sending wine to the Blues (*P. Oxy.* XXVII 2480; Gascou 1976). They may have contributed to the running of the stables (cf. *P. Oxy.* I 152 = *Stud. Pal. Pap.* II 285). *P. Oxy.* XVI 2040 (see below) lists contributions to the running of the public new North Baths and for the baths at the village of Takona, which appear to be supported by a small group of leading families (cf. *PSI* IX 1061). It is to be presumed that other baths were also supported through the same process of donation.

The leading families also held political offices. In 556–79, Flavius Apion was *stratelates* and pagarch of the Fayumic nomes Theodosopolite and Arsinoite (*BGU* I 305; *CPR* XIV 10) where the Apions also had extensive estates. Flavius Strategius held the pagarchate of the same districts (*CPR* XIV 11; 9). Flavius Apion had the title *pater poleos* (*SB* XII 11079). The passing of this latter office to female members of the family suggests that their elevation above the normal urban elite was such that the city needed to incorporate the Apions into the administrative and honorific structures even when there was no available male family member. A parallel to this is Patrikia, who held the office of pagarch in

Antaiopolis *c.* AD 553 (*P. Lond.* V 1660). Her elevation would suggest that her family was predominant. The pagarchate was a real administrative office with significant duties which Patrikia appears to have delegated. Although the *pater poleos* did not obviously have duties, no office was purely honorary in the ancient world and such titles were granted in return for or in expectation of benefactions.

Quantifying the dominance of leading families is extremely difficult, but the aforementioned *P. Oxy.* XVI 2040 might provide a guide. This text attests the collection of 27 *nomismata* (the gold coinage of the period) for the public baths of the city. A relatively small number of families contributed, as shown in table 5.12.

The Apions also funded the baths at the village of Takona, which appears to be reckoned with this account and, if this payment is added, their contribution is raised to 30 per cent and those of others proportionately reduced.[188]

Hardy (1931, importantly modified by Gascou 1985) argued that the estate was so powerful that it took over state functions.[189] The appearance of magisterial and quasi-military figures within estates, such as the *riparios* of the house of Theon (*P. Oxy.* XVI 2039; cf. *P. Oxy.* XVI 1854) and the *riparioi* of the Apion household (*Stud. Pal. Pap.* III 86; *P. Oxy.* LVIII 3942), or perhaps the *boukellarioi* and *symmachoi* (armed men) (Schmitt 1994; e.g. *P. Oxy.* XVI 1903; 1904; 2045; 2046)[190] would seem to support this view. Nevertheless, one might argue that the titulature of these estate officials merely attests an importation of state vocabulary into estate management, though such a process could hardly be described as ideologically neutral.

The Apions were not the only power in Oxyrhynchus, nor indeed in other areas where they held estates, notably the Fayum. Although *P. Oxy.* XVI 2020, a list of taxes collected in grain, does not allow the kind of analysis conducted in table 5.12, it does list exactions from other major landowners: the imperial

Table 5.12 Funding of the north public baths of Byzantine Oxyrhynchus

Contributor	Amount in gold (nomismata and carats)	% of total
Apions	6 n. 19.75 c.	25
Church	3 n. 6.25 c.	12
house of Kometos	4 n. 8 c.	16
heirs of Ptolemaios	2 n. 19.25 c.	10
pagarchate	1 n. 10.5 c.	5
Iustus and brothers	2 n. 16 c.	10
pagarchate	1 n. 10.5 c.	5
heirs of Valerius, count	21.25 c.	3
Euphemia	1 n. 16.5 c.	6
heirs of Theodolos	1 n 14.25 c.	6
those from Eieme	1.75 c.	0
Total	27 n.	100

Source: P. Oxy. XVI 2040.

315

house, the Church, the heirs of Ptolemaios and the heirs of Iustus, the heirs of Theodoulos, Kometos, the heirs of Euphemia, the heirs of Paulos, the heirs of Patrikia, the heirs of Theodoros of Samouel, the wife of Letodoros and many others over at least three pages (one of which is lost). All those listed here contributed more than 100 *artabai* of grain from a total of nearly 16,000 and it takes little imagination to see this group as the survivors of the local aristocracy. Although the construction of the palatial house of the Apions may have had practical benefits in allowing the villa to spread without the necessity of large-scale urban restructuring, it also had a symbolic value in establishing a distance from the city, which was dominated by its Christian architecture. In spite of their administrative and financial power, the Apions had not taken over the city.

Elsewhere, the extensive archives from Aphrodito do not show a village dominated by a leading family. The most important institution was clearly the Church (see above). Several, or perhaps even many, of the landlords used intermediaries within the village to manage their affairs. This entailed a devolution of power to the village (Keenan 1980; 1984; 1985) and when the villagers fell out with the pagarch Menas, presumably the most powerful man in the district, they were able to challenge him (*P. Cair. Masp.* I 67002; *P. Lond.* V 1674; 1677; MacCoull 1988: 24–9). Similarly, in the material from Elephantine and Syene, the great landlords are notable by their relative absence.

Power did not shift decisively to any one group or individual in the Byzantine city but was concentrated in three different, but overlapping, areas. The first and most obvious area is that of the Church, whose authority was concentrated in the person of the bishop. The second is the new administrative positions, especially that of the pagarch. The third is a small number of leading, wealthy families. These powerful elements of Byzantine society were closely intertwined. The leading families served as pagarchs and supported the Church. This triad formed a much smaller group than the bouleutic elite of two centuries earlier. Nevertheless, the local aristocracy survived in numbers and retained some wealth and influence. There is continuity with the past. The pagarchy itself was a local office, through which men (and women?) with local power-bases exercised administrative control. Although, like the *logistes* of the fourth century, the office constitutionally could be seen as a way of taking power away from localities, effectively it consolidated local power so that nomes and cities continued to be governed by those with interests in the locality. The sixth century was very different from the fourth, but a local aristocracy (perhaps rather a different aristocracy) retained power.

Living in the Byzantine city: diversity and communality

To be a member of Byzantine urban society in the sixth century was, fundamentally, to be Christian. Christian iconography and Christian architecture dominate. In this new world, the old divisions of the city between Greek and Egyptian, pagan and Christian, which seemed so important during the fourth century, dissolved. This has implications. We have very little Coptic material from Oxyrhynchus, but Coptic was used extensively at Syene, Thebes and Hermopolis for documentary and literary purposes. Egyptian had once more entered the literate world from whence it had been exiled since the decline of hieroglyphics. People like Dioscoros in Aphrodito or Patermouthis in Syene were fluent in both languages and their written products, literary as well as documentary in the case of Dioscoros, show little sign of a preference for a particular language (MacCoull 1988), though Greek remained the language of administration. Such changes suggest a re-evaluation of the role of culture and a gradual abandoning of the division between the Hellene elite, participating in high culture, and the Egyptian majority.

Christianity, therefore, offered the possibility of a greater cultural integration of the urban population, but this does not imply that the Greek city, maintained as it had been by the cultural aspirations of the elite, thereby went into decline. In Syria and Asia Minor, the Classical order of the major streets was disrupted by encroachment from shops and houses into old public areas, and this narrowed streets, interrupted clear lines of access and vision, and broke up the visual and architectural unity of the major thoroughfares. The process has been described as an 'Islamicization' of cities, with a transfer from the organization of retailing by *agora* to that by *suq*, though I prefer the term 'multi-focal' to 'Islamic' for such categories (see p. 180; Kennedy 1985a; Claude 1969; Bouras 1981; Pentz 1992). Something of this process can be seen in Egypt (Saradi 1998). Flinders Petrie (1889: 59) showed that houses were built in front of the temple of Souchos at Ptolemais Euergetis, which must have disrupted the urban layout, and a similar situation is perhaps attested at Karnak, where the *dromos* of the temple was overlain with Coptic houses, though these developments are undatable and their association with traditional temples might suggest that the process was temple-colonization rather than the different issue of annexation of public land. Nevertheless, the central basilica at Hermopolis used columns to create a monumental gateway, which differs from Classical precursors but is in an essentially similar style. The pilgrimage centre at Abu Mina contained at least two large colonnaded squares which have been shown to have contained shops (Grossmann et al. 1997; Grossmann et al. 1994). These seem to be purpose-built market areas and although they differ from the old Classical *agorai* or *fora* since they had neither magisterial offices (though some may be found as the excavation progresses) nor temples, they are directly analogous in conception and layout. At Alexandria, the excavated area of Kom-el-Dikke (see pp. 189–90) shows the development of civic buildings within the framework of the old urban plan. The fourth-century baths and the sixth-century lecture rooms did not encroach on the old streets, though the small houses of the area did. At Marea, which was also connected with the pilgrimage route to the shrine of St Menas, the Church sits at the centre of a city in which orthogonally arranged roads were lined with columns and, behind the columns, shops (el-Fakhrani 1983).

At Oxyrhynchus, the Phokas pillar seems to align with an older street grid, suggesting perhaps a continuity through to the seventh century. This is embarrassingly weak material, but it shows some level of continuity.[191] Even where morphology changed fundamentally, the Church, through the reuse of Classical architectural elements or through the reuse of whole buildings, asserted a claim to be the heir of Classical culture. Christianity assimilated many of the cultural aspirations that had motivated the Greek elite in previous centuries (Brown 1992) and mainstays of Hellenism, not just architecture but rhetoric and learning, continued to be deployed to assert status in the new Christian context.

The Church was a powerful institution of social integration. Charity, dispute resolution, enforcement of social norms and agricultural activity extended the Church's influence outside the strictly religious sphere, so that its influence would be felt in most aspects of life and, it is easy to believe, by most people. The Church generated the cultural and spiritual unity of the Byzantine city. Nevertheless, the Church was also the greatest source of urban discord. The large number of ecclesiastical and other Christian institutions, especially monasteries, created diverse loci of spiritual power within the city. The bishop supervised a plethora of institutions and could deploy visitations, charismatic authority and institutional power to help overcome this fragmentation, but the disputatiousness of the late Roman and Byzantine Church and the survival of heretical movements, such as the Melitian monastery on the outskirts of Ptolemais Euergetis, suggests that the dominance of the orthodox did not extend to a monopoly on the spiritual lives of urban populations. Diversity within a Christian unity may be reflected elsewhere on the spatial scale. If I am correct in seeing a greater emphasis on privacy in houses and also correct in associating that with the bundle of changes in social attitudes we relate to Christian conversion, then we can see Christianity reaching into the homes of the ordinary Egyptians (see pp. 121–5). Yet, housing types also showed diversity in the seventh century and although one could hardly believe that the Classical-style houses at seventh-century Abu Mina could be occupied by pagans, such diversity surely represents social and cultural divisions. Similarly, the spread of Christian institutions may be related to the development of increasingly powerful neighbourhoods in the Byzantine city (see p. 176).

The other great social institution, sadly under-attested in our material, is the hippodrome. The circus was a powerful institution in the Byzantine city. Liebeschuetz (1996) argues that it took over from the council in providing some form of communal identity in the sixth-century city. Procopius provides us with a portrait of a rampaging urban mob, organized by the circus factions threatening to overthrow Justinian, until Theodora with the sense of theatre which makes ancient historiography such fun and seriously worries modern practitioners of the art, claimed the imperial robes would make a suitable winding sheet, thus stiffening the resolve of her imperial spouse (Cameron 1976; Procopius, De Bellis I 24). The factions relied on imperial or other aristocratic support to fund their stables, dancers and the extensive infrastructure needed for their competitions. The Apions lent their support to the Blues and one presumes that others supported the Greens. John of Nikiou tells us two seventh-century stories of the factions running amok. In the first, three brothers, aided by the son of one of them, launched an assault on the Blue faction, burning down bath houses and attacking at least two cities. They rose to such power that they were able to stop the supply of grain to Alexandria, but were eventually defeated by the army (97). The second story comes from the civil war between Phokas and Heraclius. Heraclius' general Niketas was besieged in Alexandria by Phokas' commander, Bonosos. Niketas broke the siege and routed Bonosos' army, eventually killing Bonosos. The Green faction then launched a fierce assault on the Blues (117).[192] John's stories find a parallel in a very fragmentary and possibly literary or epistolary account which appears to attest large-scale rioting in a hippodrome which demanded the intervention of the *comes* and *dux* of the region (Ioannidou 2000). John's portrayal of seventh-century Egypt is one of division and civil war in which loyalty to a particular faction was one of the fault-lines along which society could fracture.[193]

The Byzantine city shows a much greater level of cultural unity than cities of earlier periods, perhaps more than any Egyptian city since the arrival of the Greeks. The population appears to have shared many values and a common religion. It mattered little whether one was Greek or Copt. The city retained a certain amount of local independence and its importance as a political centre. The political elite was easily defined, narrow and powerful. Nevertheless, in spite of the communality of the Church and of the hippodrome, the city appears a more fragmented community than in previous centuries. Wherever one looks, at districts, at religion, at the hippodrome, one sees divisions, even within an essential ideological unity. The communality of the city that we see in the first-century temple-city and, rather differently, in the Roman city of the third and fourth centuries, breaks down in the Byzantine period. This seems to me to be an important shift in emphasis and a shift that would ultimately contribute to the end of ancient urbanism in Egypt.

Transformations and continuities: the meaning of change

Someone who fell asleep in Egypt in 30 BC and awoke in AD 620 would have far more chance of successfully operating in the new world than a similar sleeper waking in AD 2000 having drifted off in 1350. The crossroads at the gateway into the temple area of Hermopolis of the Pharaonic period was still the architectural centre of the city in the seventh century AD and was thus a focal point for nearly two millennia. The first- and seventh-century cities were dominated by religious institutions. The Byzantine city was ruled by a small and wealthy landed elite, as the Egyptian city had been since at least the late first century AD. Linguistically, the cities of Egypt were drifting towards the restoration of Egyptian as a major literary language by the seventh century. Economic life, though subject to fluctuation, can only have changed within various rather restrictive parameters imposed by technology and agricultural production. Nevertheless, such elements of what we might call structural continuity should not blind us to the changes in the Roman and Byzantine city. Much of what I have sketched above (though certainly not all) operates at the level of public culture and can be compared to rhetoric in both its power and the ease with which it could be subverted or ignored. The various transformations were attempts to alter the identity and nature of particular communities. Although reconstructing the rationales is not contentious, the success of those policies in generating fundamental changes is a more difficult issue.

Let us turn, momentarily, to the theory of urban design, especially as developed by the scholars of the post-colonial movement. The imposition of new spaces represents a new social and political hierarchy and different mechanisms of control and authority. The delineation of centres of power, of ranks and orders in occidental and Westernized societies made governing easier since responsible parties or institutions could be reached and identified. Peet argues that

> The control of space is an essential constituent of the disciplinary technology. In modernity . . . individuals are placed in a pre-ordered, disciplinary space, as for example with military hospitals or factories. Discipline "makes" individuals by this kind of distribution in space, by training, through hierarchical observation, normalizing judgement, examination, documentation, and the sciences.
>
> (Peet 1997: 74–5)

In this Peet follows lines in the thought of many others, Lefebvre, Foucault and Bourdieu to name three, who emphasis the role of spatial factors in social reproduction. Space in this context can be seen to act in two ways. First, perhaps more actively, it is an arena through which power can work and discipline subjects, as (most radically) in the space of the hospital or the prison. Second, and possibly more pervasively, space influences the formation of social relations, both being created by and creating society (see pp. 25–6). Thus, the imposition of colonial spatial patterns threatened a refashioning of social order.[194] The radical reshaping of a city literally altered the place of individuals in the world and can be seen as attempting to impose a different cosmology. Many such transformations are associated with colonialism, and in much of the modern literature on colonialism, the creation of new urbanisms is interpreted as part of a dichotomy of political power in which the powerful simply impose their values on the powerless (Crush 1994). Yet many of these changes in urban morphology were regarded by those imposing them as 'improvements' and it may be that some at least did actually improve the living conditions of the urban poor. Additionally, it is possible that the values of the developers were internalized by at least some within the colonized community. The politics of the remodelling of urban centres is as confused under colonialism as it was in the restructuring of cities in the modern West. Although in many cases the urban morphology was imposed by the politically powerful, the success of any newly generated morphology depended on the relative co-operation of the users of the city, partly because readings can be imposed on urban space that run counter to those intended by the authors of that space (Atkinson and Cosgrove 1998; Harvey 1979; Jacobs 1998). The influence of urban redevelopment on a population results from a political negotiation, normally between parties of unequal power (Nager 1997).

Most cities of the Roman empire adopted elements of Roman architecture. No one suggests that the new cities were all the work of the Roman government. The provincial authorities may have aided or guided local developments, but in many cases the initiatives were local. We cannot 'read' these cities as external impositions, but rather as manifestations of local power-structures and debates (in which the Roman state must have had a role). The tensions and negotiations were not necessarily between an imperialistic state and local, native society and its social structures, but were part of the communication of power within local societies and between local societies and the state. The rebuilding of the cities was part of a reidentification of their place and the place of their residents within the world. No longer was this a local world, but it now stretched beyond the boundaries of the city and nome to encompass Rome itself. If the elite had an interest in refashioning themselves and their city as somehow Roman and convincing others of their credentials to be part of the Roman system, it is less obvious that other groups in society were similarly inclined. Yet, the elite appear to have attempted to involve a large swathe of the community in the new cultural institutions. The driving of avenues through cities was a symbol of the power of the elite, but it was also an integrationist endeavour. The avenues produced visual communication through the city and possibly even eased physical communication. Theatres and corn doles brought people together and the adoption of the traditional temples as part of the elite's Graeco-Romano–Egyptian cultural framework greatly eased this process of building a new shared urban identity. This process was, however, always in tension with a desire on the part of the elite to assert their difference and it is my guess that this process of acculturation was never completely successful. Yet, even partial acculturation could have dramatic effects and I find it impossible to believe that after so many had adopted new values and when the architectural frame of the city had been so altered, that the changes were not manifested in every individual's view of their place in the world (their cosmology). Notably, we see a second transformation in seven centuries in which the explicit adoption of a new cosmology (Christianity) created a changed set of spatial relations and, in turn, generated new urban forms.

Arguing that the indisputable evidence of structural continuity between the first and seventh centuries AD means that the city was essentially unchanged is defensible only within an extreme Marxist or functionalist/structuralist ideology. Such approaches bring us no closer to what people thought they were about in antiquity and underplay the ideological forces which underpinned the workings of society (see pp. 35–9). For me, history is not just about materialism but about understanding our place in the world and about understanding how others developed and lived their cosmologies. Ideology is important now, as I believe it was important in antiquity. Understanding that ideology is a way of reaching their humanity and of making these historical individuals more than puppets dancing to a materialistic tune, unaware and unconscious of their own actions. Their city was not just about social functions (a place where there was religion, administration, etc.) but was also a place where identities were developed and played out and where people lived and thought. In this chapter I have traced the changes in the relations between individuals and their cities over almost seven centuries and shown how political and cultural changes affected 'the structures of everyday life'. By so doing, I hope to have demonstrated that the pre-industrial urban population of Egypt underwent as significant a change as one could imagine, not once, but twice.

6

THE CITY, REGION
AND WORLD

Introduction

Study of the region presents particular problems. Whereas with the house and city (and perhaps even the district or neighbourhood) boundaries are relatively clearly demarcated, such physical manifestations of boundaries are relatively unlikely with larger territorial divisions. Lines on a map may differentiate administrative territories (nomes), provinces or, indeed, empires, but such lines, like those drawn between colonial territories in the eighteenth and nineteenth centuries, need not have any particular emotive or practical force. Indeed, the ability and willingness of ancient and modern imperial states to redraw boundaries to suit changing administrative circumstances demonstrate the artificiality of such distinctions and it is only with the modern world, territorial nationalism, and the intense capitalistic exploitation of natural resources by nation states that such lines have come to be regarded as having almost spiritual significance. There are, however, ways of differentiating territories other than by polity. Economic systems bring people together. People move to trade, either from local villages to the city or from city to city. Outside the walls of ancient cities were farms and the exploitation of the land created a territory that formed part of the spatial context of the city. Institutions also had a territoriality, whether they be traditional temples, theatres, games (which may have drawn audiences from some distance) or Christian shrines. Institutional, economic and administrative networks connect settlements into systems and it is these systems on which this chapter concentrates. As a result, much of this chapter attempts to differentiate the role of the city within the system from those roles played by other settlements and, almost by accident, we deal with a further problem and one which, perhaps contentiously, this book has so far ignored: the definition of a city.[1]

All communities are imagined (Anderson 1991). Communities may have markers, such as walls, buildings, monuments, boundaries, institutions, rituals, but it is the imagination which gives meaning to these signifiers of community. Although it is comparatively easy to detail at an institutional level the fact of a relationship between urban communities and various other urban and non-urban communities, the provincial administration, Rome, and the empire, it is much more difficult to translate these structural elements into significant mental maps since it is the importance to individuals of those markers of community that is both crucial and indeterminate. To use a modern analogy, a citizen of Louisiana may have a rather different perception of her place in the world and her identity as an American in 2000 than a similarly located woman in 1850, in spite of the fact that both will have had experience of institutions that operated at state and federal level. Nevertheless, we can only gain knowledge of Egypt's imagined communities through the Egyptians' institutions, rituals and monuments, and it is precisely these social institutions which coexisted and interacted with the political and economic relationships to shape (and be shaped by) the intellectual construction of an individual's world.

Institutions and politics

Much here is familiar. The major traditional temples played a central role not just in the cities themselves but in mediating between cities and regions. This centrality operated at several levels. The guilds of Tebtunis appear to have met in the city temple (see pp. 208–12) and there is every reason to believe that other village guilds were also drawn into the city by such rituals. It is possible that festivals drew crowds to celebrate, trade, and do all the other things that happen when large numbers gather (Alston 1998; De Ligt 1993). Markets located near temples (see pp. 207–8) were probably frequented by traders and shoppers from the villages. Less mechanically, the temples also gave identity to the nomes. Egyptian deities went by many names and characters, especially divinities such as Isis and Osiris, but, within a nome, the village-by-village variations were on a theme. It was the crocodile who ruled the Fayum, appearing in various guises: Souchos at Ptolemais Euergetis, Sobek at Tebtunis, Soknopaios at Soknopaiou Nesos. Outside the Fayum, Amun (Thebes), Thoth (Hermopolis), Min (Panopolis) and Horus (Apollonospolis [Edfu]) ruled. The nomenclature of the local populations reflected local divinities and loyalties (Hobson 1989). As local accents in Coptic (Sahidic, Boharic, Akhmimic, etc.) associated later and probably earlier Egyptian-speakers with regions, so names identified local origins.

Although there does not appear to be an obvious institutional link between village temples and the great city temples, some of the more important village temples of the southern Fayum influenced temples of neighbouring villages. The best evidence comes from Narmouthis (Gallo 1992), from where temple personnel were sent to other villages to perform various rites. Such visits appear to have been regular and customary. The temple at Tebtunis supported a school of Demotic and a scriptorium where the old traditions could be preserved and transmitted. It seems likely that the school provided educated priests for a number of local temples (Tait 1992; see also *P. Tebt.* II, pp. 54–6). The large village temples at Tebtunis and Narmouthis (Vogliano 1936; 1937; 1938; Anti

1930; Bagnani 1934) functioned as institutional and religious central places for the region. Since the Arsinoite was a particularly large nome and Tebtunis and Narmouthis were on its southern fringes, rather remote from Ptolemais Euergetis, it may be that they were in some ways quasi-urban settlements and that their temples operated in ways analogous to the major traditional temples of the city. The argument is strengthened by *P. Merton* II 63, a letter of AD 57 from Herennia to her father Pompeius, a Roman veteran.[2] Herennia tells her father that they are asking for pious contributions (εὐσέβεια) to the temple of Souchos from all people, Romans, Alexandrians and settlers in the Arsinoite.[3] Pompeius had himself been billed, but Herennia had not paid since she expected Pompeius to arrive, though if she were to be asked again, she tells him that she will pay on his behalf. Obviously, the demand for money was contentious and operated in violation of the normal exemption from personal taxation (poll tax) enjoyed by Romans and Alexandrians and partial exemptions enjoyed by the settlers (*katoikoi*).[4] The temple appears to have been able to require contributions from across the Arsinoite.

Other urban institutions may not have had the same geographical reach. Urban gymnasia may have recruited some villagers in the early first century, but it appears to have been a requirement that 'those of the gymnasium' were registered within the city (see pp. 92–3) by the time the *epikrisis* documentation appears (c. AD 62), and perhaps from as early as AD 4/5. The Arsinoite gymnasium was probably rather more complicated. A mysterious group of 6,475 *katoikoi* operating in the Arsinoite were confirmed in their privileges by Nero (*SB* XII 11012; *OGIS* II 668 = *I. Fay.* III 147; Montevecchi 1970; Whitehorne 1982). These do not appear to have been an urban group but to have enjoyed privileges similar to those of the metropolites. It is unclear whether the 6,475 gained entry into the gymnasium or whether residence qualifications were waived, but I regard it as unlikely that the gymnasia normally recruited from outside the city.

The foundation of councils in AD 200 gave the cities a large measure of internal administrative independence, but the nome remained largely under the authority of the *strategos*. The power of the *strategos* was gradually eroded as town councils took over some responsibility for taxation and, very gradually, over the next two centuries, other administrative functions, such as security, were accumulated by the town councils and their representatives (see pp. 187–92; 250–5). Nevertheless, distinctions between city and country were maintained and perhaps even increased during the third century with villagers successfully resisting attempts to make them perform urban liturgies (see p. 255) and the corn dole powerfully supporting the urban population and distinguishing it from the villagers (see pp. 149–51). We cannot know whether the institutions of Hellenism, such as the theatre, attracted great crowds of villagers though Hellenic culture spread to some villages (van Minnen 1994; Youtie 1970; Lembke 1998). Nevertheless, I think it likely that the council and the institutions of the Roman city had fairly weak links with the villages.

The fifth and sixth centuries saw more change with the emergence of the pagarchy, of great estates in at least some nomes, and the bishop as a powerful figure. All these offered at least some opportunities for the further integration of city and region, but, as we have seen (pp. 293–309), the undoubted power of the bishop could be challenged and a tendency to fragment was inherent in early Christianity. Similarly, the new officials and the great estates may not have concentrated power and authority on the city so much as on the persons and families involved and, indeed, may have been detrimental to the city, making it less relevant to the population of the region.

Institutionally, the cities were at the administrative centre of a region in all periods, though I suspect that the importance of that centrality varied considerably over time, perhaps being at its peak in the late second, third and fourth centuries. Traditional temples provided the region with a symbolic and religious unity for at least the first two centuries AD. It does not seem to me obvious that other institutions took over that role in the later period.

Beyond the immediate region, analysis becomes more difficult. For political purposes in the Roman period, Egypt could be divided into territories under *epistrategoi*, Roman equestrian officials who deputized for the prefect. Thomas (1982) has gathered the information concerning the geographical regions which were supervised by the *epistrategoi* and concluded that there were more than two during most of the Roman period (before the Diocletianic reforms), with one operating in the Thebaid (Egypt above Hermopolis), one in the region I have been describing as Middle Egypt (Hermopolite to apex of the Delta), but possibly two in the Delta (East and West). The *epistrategoi* took responsibility for appointments to liturgies, though they appear to have acted on the recommendations of the *strategoi*, and probably deputized for the prefect in judicial and other roles. Nevertheless, the administrative regions supervised by them appear to have been a comparatively unimportant intermediate stage between the nome and the province. Political authority stemmed from Alexandria, in the first instance, and, second, from Rome. Contact with Alexandria was frequent since the *strategoi* of the first and early second centuries were Alexandrians. The prefect would also be represented by the army, especially centurions, though the army appears to have kept a low profile in urban settlements of the *chora* (Alston 1999b). As judicial, legal and administrative power was concentrated in the person of the prefect, Alexandria was the place to which those unable to win redress locally would travel.

The strength of the contacts between Alexandria and the *chora* and the extent to which the administrative elite of the cities saw Alexandria as part of their sphere of operation cannot be established with anything approaching certainty. All one can do is map the pattern of contacts as attested in the papyrological material. This I did in an experimental article (Alston 1998), for which I took a sample of papyri from Oxyrhynchus (using the *P. Oxy.* series, the papyri of which I assumed to have been found in the city itself) and noted attested locations, while discounting purely administrative documents (perhaps dubious in principle and certainly difficult in practice). This gave a map of communications with Oxyrhynchus (figure 6.1). Unsurprisingly, the people of Oxyrhynchus appear to have been in close contact with communities close to the Oxyrhynchite: Herakleopolis, Antinoopolis, Kynopolis and Ptolemais Euergetis figure highly. Communities slightly further afield, Ptolemais, Lykopolis, Memphis and Antaiopolis, are less often attested. Alexandria, however, was far more important to the Oxyrhynchites than any other city.

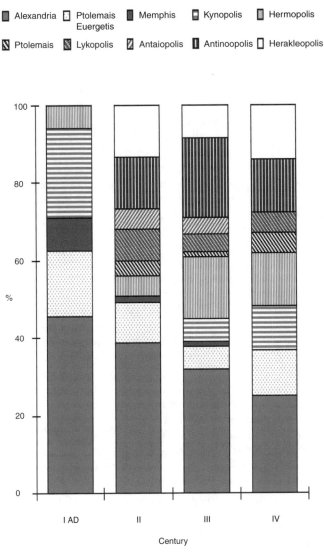

Figure 6.1 Attested connections with selected cities by century as a percentage of the connections with communities outside the Oxyrhynchite

Table 6.1 Connections to urban centres of the military and civilian populations of Karanis in the second century and all centuries as percentages

City	II c. military	II c. civilian	Total	All military	All civilian	Total
Alexandria	67	28	48	69	29	42
Antinoopolis		7	3		9	6
Koptos	7		3	6		2
Memphis		7	3		6	4
Ptolemais Euergetis		28	14		38	26
Herakleopolis		7	3		3	2
Outside Egypt	27	21	24	25	15	18

No other city provides an easy comparison, though we can use data from the village of Karanis in the Fayum as presented in table 6.1.[5] The figures can only be used impressionistically and, with a certain bravura, I take them to suggest that some residents of Oxyrhynchus were in frequent contact with Alexandria and with several other cities within Egypt, especially those of Middle Egypt, while residents of Karanis were in contact with a more restricted group of urban settlements, especially Alexandria, Ptolemais Euergetis and Antinoopolis. Nevertheless, even for those living in Oxyrhynchus, contact with communities outside Middle Egypt and the oases (for which Oxyrhynchus had administrative responsibilities) was comparatively rare, as was communication with communities outside Egypt. There are clearly zones of contact which differentiate and define regions covering several nomes. Such figures, however, provide no sense of the absolute volume of traffic between the various communities, though the very fact of communication establishes the means by which ideas, and political and cultural authority could be transmitted using, for instance, such simple technology as the book (Hopkins 1991). Much of Greek literary culture was available in Egyptian cities by the second century AD and possibly earlier (see pp. 268–9) and the expansion in the numbers of Christian literary texts in the fourth century suggests that books were important in the transmission of Christianity. The contributions of Egyptians to the culture of Hellenism from the third century onwards (see p. 283) demonstrated that at least some were able to achieve a notable fluency in this culture even in places as remote from the cultural centre of the Greek world as Panopolis and Thebes. The literary achievements of men such as Dioskoros of Aphrodito in being able to compose what was evidently passable Greek poetry in the sixth century while being no higher than a village scribe, even if modern critics tend to be a little sniffy about the literary merit of his work, do not seem exceptional (MacCoull 1988). Dioskoros may find an earlier parallel in a scribe of second-century Karanis (Youtie 1970; van Minnen 1994). The enjoyment of and participation in Greek literary culture was not limited to the highest echelons of Egyptian society. The value of literary texts to Christianity is shown by the creation of libraries in the coenobitic monasteries of the fourth and fifth centuries and the institutionalized teaching of literacy to monks.

Most urban settlements of the *chora* appear to have had entertainment facilities such as theatres and hippodromes by the second century AD, though a number of these buildings, such as the hippodrome at Oxyrhynchus, obviously pre-date Roman rule. Performances at the theatre included recitations by Homericists, mime, and athletics of various kinds (see pp. 244–5). In the sixth and seventh centuries, circus factions seem to have been widespread and important in at least some and possibly all major centres (see pp. 318–9). The visits of emperors were commemorated for decades and the visit of the prefect was a moment of communal celebration (*P. Oxy.* IV 705 = W. *Chr.* 153 = *CPJ* II 450). All these activities, locally based though many of them were, attest an active relationship between at least some in the cities of Roman and Byzantine Egypt and a world far beyond their city walls, a claim of belonging to a wider world of Greek culture that was manifested architecturally in the transformation of urban centres. I find it difficult to believe that when a resident of an Egyptian city listened to a recitation of Homer, either at home or in the theatre, he or she would not have been aware that Homer was a poet of the Mediterranean who was read by and familiar to thousands of people across the Roman empire. I do not think that we can see the importation of Greek culture in the Roman and Byzantine periods as a mere academic interest in the culture of the conquerors, in a foreign but important other, or as a recognition of technical superiority, but the only feasible explanation for the wholesale adoption of Greek and Roman cultural elements, and the enormous expense that this entailed, was to enable participation in the wider cultural world that was the Roman empire. It thus follows that some Egyptians saw themselves as part of this immense, imagined, imperial community.

Nowhere do we find that imagined community more clearly expressed than with Christianity (Fowden 1993). In theological terms, Christianity imposed a unified system in which all Christians were part of the same community, as Augustine famously and clearly outlines in the *City of God*. This may seem an extraordinary claim to anyone passingly familiar with heterodox and schismatic divisions of late Roman and Byzantine Christianity, many of which appear to have had specific local aspects, but whereas within pagan tradition no one would have been in the least interested in local diversity of religious practice, except as a curiosity, in Christianity, people fought each other in the streets over the correct interpretation of a single, if important, line of biblical text. For the first time, it mattered not just that you worshipped a divinity, but that what you were doing and what you believed were orthodox. Orthodoxy and heresy are largely Christian inventions and the immense energy poured into fighting the theological disputes of the fourth to the sixth centuries are eloquent testimony to the fundamental view that ancient Christianity was a unitary community, a view which was probably shared by most of the warring factions in the early Church. When Jerome (*Ep.* 107) celebrated the conversion of the Getae and other barbarian tribes threatening the metaphorical gates of Rome, he was proclaiming that they had joined the community of Christians that extended across and beyond the Roman empire.

Economy

Model settlement hierarchy

The technological level at which pre-industrial economies operated required that the majority of the population engaged in agricultural production and that most wealth was invested in land. By definition, pre-industrial economies show many common characteristics and variations are strictly limited. Nevertheless, a pre-industrial economy could operate within a settlement system comprised of a number of isolated farmsteads exploiting essentially similar agricultural resources and living in virtual autarky. This would be a non-hierarchized settlement system since the differences between settlements and the relationship (economic or political) between those settlements would be slight. At another level (this is not meant as an evolutionary model) some of the farmsteads might form small collectives such as hamlets or villages which would allow a certain amount of specialization and trade. A third system would have proto-urban or urban sites which might have regional administrative capacities and provide market facilities. Such sites draw surpluses from the villages sufficient to support a large population not directly engaged in agricultural labour and a greater level of specialization is possible, though centralization of craft and trade production may weaken village markets. A fourth system would centre on the great city, a city which maintained levels of specialization and political authority sufficient to draw surpluses from villages and cities over a very large area.

In the definition operating here an urban centre will have a population that differs both in size and type from those of settlements lower down in the settlement system (cf. De Ligt 1990). Any model must simplify and as soon as one applies it to a real society, its inadequacies become clear. Paper hierarchies do not easily reflect the levels of integration of a settlement system. A village may send agricultural goods to a city and thus be part of a settlement system, but it matters whether that village sends 2 per cent or 10 per cent or 30 per cent of its agricultural produce to the city and, of course, different villages may

Table 6.2 A model settlement hierarchy

Settlement	Nature of population	Population numbers	Market/political functions
Megalopolis	Mainly non-agricultural	Very large	Yes (for region and beyond)
Urban	Mixed agricultural/non-agricultural	Large	Yes (for region)
Proto-urban settlement	Mainly agricultural	Moderate	Some (for surrounding villages and hamlets)
Village	Mainly agricultural	Many households	Some (for surrounding hamlets)
Hamlet	Agricultural	Several households	No
Farmstead	Agricultural	Single household	No

330

despatch different proportions of their production. Also, some typically urban functions may be hived off. Reality was far more diverse than any model could adequately describe (Alston 1998), though the layering of systems in table 6.2 does, I hope, allow for variation.

Modelling Egyptian demographic and economic structures

Population figures

Estimates of the populations of various Roman-period Egyptian settlements rest on evidence of varying quality, though the evidence is rather better for Egypt than for any other province of the Roman empire.

In 199, six eutheniarchs from Oxyrhynchus contracted each to equip bakeries sufficient to process 20 *artabai* of grain a day, suggesting a daily production of 120 *artabai* and a monthly production of 3,600 *artabai* (*P. Oxy.* VI 908). Since the attested rate for the corn dole was 1 *artaba* per month, the number of recipients of the grain, whether as a dole or as subsidized supply, would be 3,600. This would suggest a total population of at least 11,901, while the corn dole archive of AD 270–2 (*P. Oxy.* XL 2928; 2929; see pp. 149–51 for an earlier discussion of these figures) suggests a minimum resultant population of 12,008. The best remaining figure derives from *Stud. Pal. Pap.* IV, pp. 58–83, a summary of the adult male population of one unknown *amphodon* of Ptolemais Euergetis and a detailed listing of the population of another district, Apolloniou Paremboles. Apolloniou Paremboles contained 179 adult males and the unknown *amphodon* had 385. Since there were about thirty-four *amphoda* in Ptolemais Euergetis (see pp. 135–6) in the Roman period, the population can be estimated at 27,891. If we were to treat the figure for the larger *amphodon* as unrepresentative, we could estimate a total population of 17,500. Conversely, a high estimate would be about 38,000.

Other figures for metropolitan populations are derived from the number of houses in the city. The estimated population per house of table 3.2 must be adjusted to take into account empty houses and, allowing 10 per cent for this, the multiple to be used to convert number of houses into population is 6.9 (still possibly a high figure). *P. Oslo.* III 111 lists fifty houses in the northern sector of the *amphodon* of Hermaion in Oxyrhynchus, suggesting 200 for the *amphodon* and, at 28–30 districts, about 5,500 houses for the city, giving a population of about 37,950, though in this instance we know that approximately 50 per cent of the houses were empty, suggesting a population close to 21,000. *Stud. Pal. Pap.* V 101 gives the number of houses in each of the four *amphoda* of Hermopolis, though the totals, 2,317 and 1,917 houses, are preserved for only two of the *amphoda*. Multiplied through, this gives a total population of 58,429. The second or twentieth *amphodon* of Thmouis had 178 houses (*PSI* III 230 *BL* VIII, 395) and, given that there were at least 20 *amphoda* at Thmouis (see p. 381 n 4), this suggests a total of 3,560 houses and 24,564 people. Thmouis was

Table 6.3 Estimated populations of Egyptian settlements[a]

Megalopolis	Source	Date (AD)	Estimated population
Alexandria	Delia 1991	various	c. 500,000

Metropolis	Document	Date (AD)	Estimated population
Hermopolis Magna	*Stud. Pal. Pap.* V 101	c. 175	58,429
Ptolemais Euergetis	*Stud. Pal. Pap.* IV, pp. 58–83	72/3	27,891
Thmouis	*PSI* III 230 BL VIII, 395	II c.	24,564
Oxyrhynchus	*P. Oslo.* III 111	235	21,000
Oxyrhynchus	*P. Oxy.* XL 2892–5	270–2	12,008
Oxyrhynchus	*P. Oxy.* VI 908	199	11,901
Apollonospolis Heptakomias	*Archiv* VI 427	116	8,784

Komai	Nome	Date (AD)	Estimated population
Narmouthis	Arsinoite	II c.	6,106
Karanis	Arsinoite	c. 150	3,316
Philadelphia	Arsinoite	48–9	2,848
Philadelphia	Arsinoite	50–1	2,637
Philadelphia	Arsinoite	32–3	2,502–2,851
Theadelphia	Arsinoite	mid-II c.	2,300
Karanis	Arsinoite	c. 172	1,907–2,135
Psenathre	Mendesian	131–2	928
Soknopaiou Nesos	Arsinoite	178	760
Soknopaiou Nesos	Arsinoite	179	520
Nemeo	Mendesian	159/60	436
Soknopaiou Nesos	Arsinoite	207–9	420
unknown village	Mendesian	159–60	372
Psenathre	Mendesian	159–60	247–59
Psen[ ]	Mendesian	159–60	163
Damastu	Mendesian	159–60	157
Psenokaia	Mendesian	159–60	79

[a] Estimates for *komai* are derived from Rathbone 1990 modified by using Bagnall and Frier's (1994: 103, n. 35) multiplier. Figures for Karanis are derived from Alston 1995: 121.

a twin city with Mendes, which had at least nine *amphoda* (*P. Thmouis* I 93), just 1.5 km north (Naville 1892–3), though its population cannot be estimated. *Archiv.* VI 427 = *P. Brem.* 21 + *P. Flor.* 333 registers 1,273 houses at Apollonospolis Heptakomias, which suggests a population of 8,784.

As is abundantly clear, the estimated populations are not likely to be accurate. The three estimates for Oxyrhynchus are sufficiently discrepant to cause worry and the method by which I have moved from number of houses (sometimes itself extrapolated from less than convincing material) to the total population is weak. We can, however, adjust the figures. The houses of Hermopolis are unlikely to have been evenly distributed across the four *amphoda* of the city and it seems probable that the estimate for the population of the city should be adjusted down, possibly substantially. Second, estimates of population per house may be based on unusually high occupation rates in the first century, which would again lead to a downward adjustment of figures for Hermopolis, Oxyrhynchus (235) and Apollonospolis Heptakomias. The Oxyrhynchus (235) figure of 21,000 is based on an extrapolation for part of a comparatively well-attested *amphodon*. It seems likely that the mechanical process of estimation significantly inflates the population figure. The corn-dole figures (Oxyrhynchus 270–2 and 199) may underestimate the city's population since we have no grounds for estimating the number of men who did not receive the dole. Nevertheless, although subject to significant error, such estimates provide orders of magnitude. Alexandria must have dwarfed all other settlements. Hermopolis and possibly Thmouis–Mendes were major centres of population. Ptolemais Euergetis probably also had a population comfortably in excess of 20,000, while Oxyrhynchus probably had a third-century population of *c.* 15,000. Apollonospolis Heptakomias seems rather small by comparison. We find two major categories of villages, one with populations of between *c.* 2,000 and *c.* 3,500 and another with populations of less than 1,000, though one could further subdivide the categories. Narmouthis stands out as an exception with a high population, though well under the estimate for the local city, Ptolemais Euergetis.

There are no reliable figures for the population of nomes as a whole and the best one can do is extrapolate population figures based on the productive capacity of the land. *SB* XIV 12208 registers 202,544 *arourai* of grain land in the Oxyrhynchite in the early fourth century (Bagnall and Worp 1980; Youtie 1978). There were other types of productive land on which fruit and vegetables and especially vines and olives were grown, but one can only guess at the proportion of land under such cultivation. Allowing for 5–10 per cent in this category, one ends up with a total for the nome of about 220,000 *arourai*. Bagnall (1992) and Bowman (1985) estimate that the Hermopolite was about 400,000 *arourai* while Rathbone (1990) estimates that the Arsinoite was 435,420 *arourai*. Rathbone (1990) estimates that 1.4 *arourai* could support one person while Bagnall (1992) goes for 1.66–2. This allows us to generate table 6.4.[6]

Wrigley (1987: 162–93) estimates that the proportion of the total population of England residing in cities (excluding London) reached 9.5 per cent *c.* 1750 but rose to 16.5 per cent by *c.* 1801 with the industrial revolution. Europe west of and including Germany saw the urban proportion of the population rise from 6.1 per cent in 1500 to 9.5 per cent in 1700 and to 10.6 per cent by 1800, though in the heavily urbanized north-western fringe the proportion reached 10.7 per cent by 1650 and 13.8 per cent by 1750. The population of the Netherlands had an urban element of 21 per cent by 1550 while the urban population of France only rose to 11.1 per cent by 1800. By comparison, the

Table 6.4 Estimated populations of nomes and cities

Nome	Area (*in* arourai)	Total nome population	City	Urban population	% urban population in nome
Arsinoite	435,420	212,000–311,000	Ptolemais Euergetis	27,891	9–13
Hermopolite	400,000	200,000–143,000	Hermopolis	40,000–58,429	20–41
Oxyrhynchite	220,000	110,000–157,142	Oxyrhynchus	15,000	10–14

figures for Middle Egypt are striking, suggesting a very high level of urbanism for a pre-industrial society. Like Mendes–Thmouis, there is some reason to treat Hermopolis as a twin city for Antinoopolis, which lay a little upstream on the opposite bank of the Nile and, one would have thought, might have been an effective competitor to the older city. Table 6.4 excludes Alexandria, which itself may have held about 10 per cent of the population of Egypt and influenced the settlement system of Middle Egypt. If the level of urbanization in Middle Egypt was replicated across the province, then we would be looking at a provincial urban population of around 20–25 per cent of the total (see also Rathbone 1990).

Occupational structure

Many of the statistics given in table 6.5 are untrustworthy. Starting at the top of the table, *P. Oslo.* III 144 lists contributors to a particular cult in Oxyrhynchus which may have attracted a disproportionate number of traders. *P. Oxy.* XLIV 3300 and *P. Oslo.* III 111 are very small samples of house owners or occupants and the latter especially may be weighted heavily towards the wealthier, property-owning segment of society. *P. Corn.* 23 is a puzzle since, in a village of moderate size, it would seem that weavers were around 10 per cent of the population. Additionally, it may be that the group of 248 of which the weavers comprise 88 are those paying the craft tax rather than the general population, which would suggest that traders and craftsmen numbered more than 25 per cent of the total village population. This figure, however, is not in keeping with the other statistics derived from Philadelphia and one might guess that the population attested is not that of the village, though it is not clear what alternative administrative unit would be plausible. The resident aliens of *P. Corn.* 22 may have owed their mobility to a lack of landed property which would automatically have encouraged them towards trade and craft production. *P. Col.* VII 230 is again weighted towards a certain economic group and although the calculation of a *poros* (income) necessary to perform a liturgic function was quite straightforward for a farmer who would have an easily distrainable amount of

Table 6.5 Percentage of tradesmen as a proportion of the total male population

Text	Provenance	Date[a]	No. of tradesmen	No. of men	Other information	Percentage tradesmen
P. Oslo. III 144	Oxyrhynchus	270–5	14	21	Contributors to a cult	66.7
P. Oxy. XLIV 3300	Oxyrhynchus	c. 270	10	24		41.7
P. Corn. 23	Philadelphia	I c.	88	248	Weavers only	35.4
P. Berol Bork	Panopolis	298–300	111	410		27.1
P. Corn. 22	Philadelphia	I c.	26	114	Resident aliens	22.8
P. Oslo. III 111	Oxyrhynchus	235	4	26	House owners and some residents	15.4
BGU IX 1898	Theadelphia	172	19	136	Tax receipts	14.0
SB XVI 12737	Philadelphia	30–1	13	94		13.8
SB I 5124	Tebtunis	192	46	337		13.6
SB XVI 12741	Philadelphia	35	6	86		8.8
P. Col. VII 230	Karanis	III c.	5	63	Men with poroi (incomes) of 700 or 800 drachmas	7.9
P. Oxy. XXIV 2412[b]	Herakleopolite nome	28–9	5	73		6.8
			10	143		7.0
SB XVI 12737–41	Philadelphia	30–35	31	510	Composite figure	6.1
P. Mich. IV 223–5	Karanis	172–5	41–43	c. 700		5.9 – 6.1
SB XVI 12740	Philadelphia	35	5	85		5.9
SB XIV 11715	Soknopaiou Nesos	207–9	8	135		5.9
P. Landlist.	Hermopolis	c. 350	24	409	Hermopolite landowners	5.9
Stud. Pal. Pap. IV, pp. 58–83	Ptolemais Euergetis	73	9	179	Potters and wool-carders only	5.0
P. Corn. 21	Philadelphia	23	16	360		4.4
P. Landlist.	Hermopolis	c. 350	17	398	Antinoite landowners	4.3
SB XVI 12738	Philadelphia	34	4	114		3.5
SB XVI 12739	Philadelphia	35–6	3	131		2.2

[a] All dates AD unless stated.
[b] The text lists taxpayers at a number of sites over several years. These taxpayers may simply be aggregated or one may attempt to use the fullest entry for each settlement. There is little reason to believe that the irregularities of the text affect the rate of attestation of tradesmen.

land, traders would be a much more difficult group to assess. *P. Landlist.* include only landowners and might be thought to under-represent traders within the cities.

In spite of these problems, there are patterns within this material. Figures for Philadelphia, Karanis, Soknopaiou Nesos, and various Herakleopolite villages group together at around 6 per cent. A further group of figures for Theadelphia, Tebtunis and one of the Oxyrhynchus group at *c.* 14 per cent, though the Oxyrhynchus figure may be an under-representation. By far the best urban sample is that from Panopolis at 27.1 per cent, but if we combine *P. Oxy.* XLVI 3300 and *P. Oslo.* III 111 (still not producing a realistic sample) one ends up with a composite figure of 28 per cent. These figures are counts of the number of males who added trade designations to their nomenclature in various tax lists, but it is evident that many who drew the majority of their income from crafts and trades may not have identified themselves in this way. One would assume that heads of workshops (as on guild-lists, see pp. 208–14) would be distinguished by profession and perhaps some of the more agricultural trades may not have had a workshop structure so that all practitioners registered as traders. We cannot know whether those working within someone else's workshop would be known by a trade designation and casual labour is presumably completely unattested, though some of this probably fell to women and children. It is tempting to double the figures to account for subordinate male labourers, but there are no grounds on which such an assessment can be made and all that can be established with confidence is that the occupational patterns of the urban population differed considerably from those of the rural population. Tebtunis and Theadelphia appear to have had occupational structures between urban and village norms.

Although the types of tradesmen attested in cities and villages are quite similar, some trades appear to be wholly or mainly metropolitan, such as the bleachers, the pitch-workers, the *oinemperoi* (a type of wine merchant, possibly selling a wide range of wines), the dyers, the linen weavers, the bakers, the silversmiths, the *entaphistai* (a group of necropolis workers), the glassmakers (though there are very few attestations of these craftsmen) and sailors. Predominantly non-metropolitan trades included oil workers, vegetable-sellers and donkey-drivers. Weavers are attested in all types of settlement, though they appear less regularly in cities.[7] The absence from smaller settlements of *oinemperoi* may be of only limited significance, especially since the differences between *oinopolai*, *oinopratai* and *oinemperoi* (all wine-sellers) are obscure, and *oinopolai* and *oinopratai* are attested for villages and cities. Nevertheless, the distribution of attestations suggests some socio-economic features of the different communities. The number of references to bakers in *metropoleis*, which is partly a result of official interest in their activities, may reflect a tendency of the metropolitan population to buy their bread, or receive it as dole, rather than bake it themselves, in contrast to the predominance of domestic production in more agricultural settlements. Clearly cloth was produced in all types of settlement, but the distribution of attestations of linen-weaving and cloth-finishing trades suggests that production and probably the sale of the higher qualities of cloth was concentrated in the *metropoleis*.

Retail and trade

There were retail facilities in villages. There was a market at Ptolemais Hormou, the Fayum port (*P. Petaus* 86). There were *agorai* at Alexandru Nesos (*BGU* XIII 2336; 2293; 2275) in the third century, at Philadelphia in the first century AD (*P. Athens*. 14; *P. Berl. Moeller* 4), at Theadelphia in the second century ('an Egyptian *agora*', whatever that means) (*BGU* IX 1898), at Tebtunis (*PSI* X 1098; *P. Lund* VI 6), and probably many other places (e.g. *P. Marm*. II 11). PSI V 459 of AD 72 is an application addressed to a metropolite to sell and measure wool at Karanis. The guild of gypsum and salt merchants at Tebtunis organized concessions to sell in neighbouring villages, suggesting village-retail facilities (*P. Mich*. V 247). Animals were traded at a market in the Upper Kynopolite (e.g. *P. Oxy*. XIV 1708; *P. Corn*. 13; *P. Berl. Leigh*. 21; Jördens 1995). *P. Fay. Towns* 93 = *W. Chr*. 317 = *Sel. Pap*. I 44) suggests that periodic markets associated with festivals (ἀγορῶν σὺν πανεγύρεσιν) might have been particularly valuable trading concessions. Nevertheless, much of the trade of the nome may have been concentrated in the cities. Livestock was sold in the *agora* at Ptolemais Euergetis in the early Roman period (*P. Amst*. I 41). Traders swore to provide eggs and oil in the market at Oxyrhynchus (*P. Oxy*. I 83 = *W. Chr*. 197 = *Sel. Pap*. II 331; XII 1455), where was also an *agora* of the shoemakers (*P. Oxy*. VII 1037), as well as an *agora* at the Sarapeion (*P. Köln*. V 228) and a vegetable market near the gate of Pesor (*P. Oxy*. I 43v). There is abundant evidence of markets in many cities (Palme 1989; see pp. 207–12 and Alston 1998) and of many other retail facilities, such as *macella* (*Stud. Pal. Pap*. V = *CPH* 127v = *Stud. Pal. Pap*. XX 68 = *SB* X 10299) and workshops. A fifth-century official letter laid down prices 'in the *agora* of each city', which suggests that the cities dominated retailing to the extent that it could be assumed that they controlled prices throughout the nome (*P. Oxy*. LI 3628).

The provision of retail facilities by the urban authorities probably aided the administration of trade and produced income from the rental of space to traders. It was easier to police the activities of traders if the space in which those traders operated could be controlled. The *agorai* of Egypt had officials and magistrates who could overlook the activities of the traders (see pp. 274–77 for a discussion of this). They could also tax them, as is evident from the list of market taxes found at Oxyrhynchus and the inscribed tax rates from Karnak (*SB* XVIII 13631; XVI 12695; Rea 1982; Bowman 1984; Wilcken 1906; Wagner 1972; *SB* XVIII 13315). The city probably derived income from these taxes and certainly drew income from the rental of space in the *agora* (*Stud. Pal. Pap*. V = *CPH* 102) and other places in the city, such as the *macellum* (if the city had one) and *ergasteria* located within the *stoai* which lined the city.[8] Excavations at the port city of Marea provide examples of shops constructed along a main road leading from the church and parallel to the harbour. These simple two-room structures had a narrow frontage opening onto the street and a small back-room, presumably for storage. Some of the shops appear to have sold wine (el-Fakhrani 1983) and I suspect that they would be described in the papyri as *ergasteria*. The units were obviously purpose-built and one would assume that the urban authorities derived income from the shops.

The cities of Roman Egypt had a powerful economic interest in concentrating retailing and trade within their walls. Elsewhere landowners sought authorization for holding markets on their estates (dominal markets) from the senate. L. Bellicus Sollers applied for this right but was opposed by the local city, Vicetia. The affair became a *cause célèbre* when it was pointed out to the counsel for the city that Sollers was a dangerous political rival, with the result that he failed to represent Vicetia, but still pocketed the fee. The subsequent scandal caused legislation on payment for legal representation (Pliny, *Ep.* V 4; 13). De Ligt (1993: 200–36 and virtually identically in 1995) argues convincingly that the town was afraid of losing revenue if peasants were attracted to Sollers' new market, but also suggests that they were also concerned about prices and food

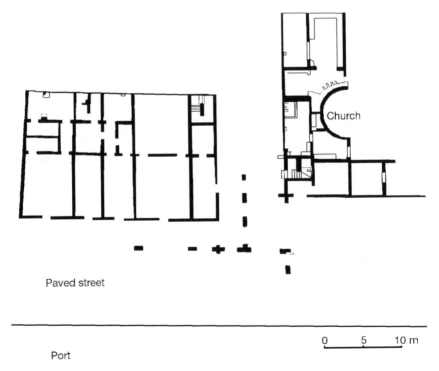

Paved street

Port

0   5   10 m

Figure 6.2 The centre of Marea (after el-Fakhrani 1983)

supply to the city. Most (all?) pre-industrial cities appear to have depended on a daily influx of smallholders from their territories to supplement other sources of supply or to provide the required fresh food. The council may have thought that Sollers' market would have drawn away this crucial supply, though it is unclear from where the prospective buyers would have come.[9] The prospect of inadequate supply of food was a continual source of worry for Roman cities and their plebs. Such problems were lessened if a city could control the marketing of food within its territory to ensure that food came through their market rather than being sold to merchants who might sell outside the immediate region or went to markets that supplied other urban centres. The cities thus had an interest in simplifying marketing structures to establish themselves as what might be called 'solar central places' (see figure 6.3.1) and opposing the development of more complex market systems (figure 6.3.2) in which peasants had considerably more choice of markets to patronize and strategies to use (de Neeve 1984).

Perhaps more telling than the opposition to Sollers' fair from Vicetia is the procedure necessary to gain the right to hold dominal markets (*ius nundinarum*). The emperor Claudius himself sought the permission of the consuls to hold markets on his estates (Suet. *Claud.* 12.2). The transferral of what might be thought a local matter to the consideration of the senate suggests that it was regarded as a matter of some importance. Shaw (1981) notes that the right to hold markets on large estates in Roman North Africa effectively reduced the interaction between estate workers and the outside world (*CIL* VIII 270 = 11451 = 23246). In a very similar way, early English industrialists tied their workers to the factory shop by paying them in tokens and thus effectively created a closed economy from which they benefited financially and which also considerably extended their power over their workforce. Would dominal markets have operated in a similar way, depriving peasants of opportunities to interact with local urban populations and effectively tying the workforce to the land? Also, if the buyers at the market were mainly merchants, they too might become tied to the political and economic power of the estate owner. The merchants who served Pliny's estates (*Ep.* VIII 2) were bailed out by the good senator partly so that he could depend on them to buy future harvests. Control of the market was a major political resource, which is presumably why the advocate who promised to represent Vicetia suddenly found himself intimidated into withdrawal. The senate might be expected to take an interest in such accretions of power irrespective of any damage to local cities that would result. Conversely, estate markets might be thought to reduce the political authority of the city and those who controlled the city irrespective of its economic effects. The city's political control of its territory would be undermined if those who worked the land never physically entered the world of the city. Political and economic structures operate in parallel and cities that established or maintained their position as solar central places should have been better able to establish their political and cultural centrality.

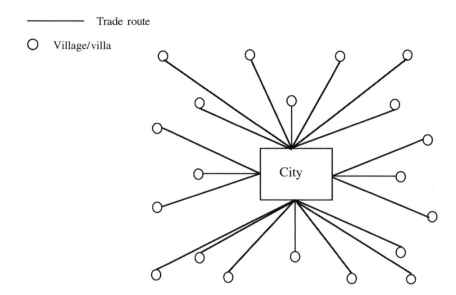

Figure 6.3.1 Solar central place

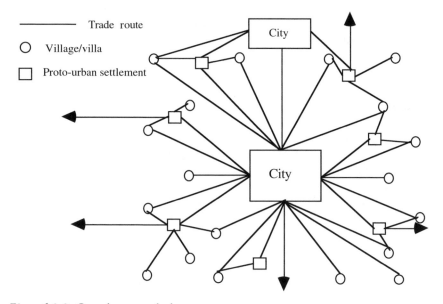

Figure 6.3.2 Complex central place system

In Egypt, urban trade networks appear to have extended beyond the boundaries of their nomes. Over 1,500 coins were uncovered at Oxyrhynchus dating from the Ptolemaic period to the seventh century, seemingly from stray finds (Milne 1922). The fourth-century coinage comes mainly from Eastern mints. Antioch, Alexandria (35 per cent), Nicomedia, Cyzicus and Constantinople account for 76 per cent of the coinage found. Rome (9 per cent), Aquileia, Arles, Trèves, Tarraco, Siscia and London account for 17 per cent. The coinage from outside Egypt presumably reached Oxyrhynchus through trade, though there are other possibilities.[10] The lamps from Antinoopolis (Donadoni 1974: 95), mainly of the third to fifth centuries, show typological similarities with lamps from across the eastern Mediterranean, notably from Asia Minor, Greece (though tracing origins is often problematic) and Africa, though there are a number of purely Egyptian types. The incomplete pottery report, by contrast, notes that the majority of reported finds of both fine ware and amphorae were of Egyptian origin (Donadoni 1974: 72–95). The lamps and pottery from Hermopolis (Spencer et al. 1984: 16–24) are not fully published, though a preliminary report on the pottery suggests that there was a small proportion of imported fine wares from Tunisia (28 per cent). Local potteries produced 27 per cent of fine ware, while Aswan ware (40 per cent) and Delta potteries (4 per cent) provided the rest. The Red Slip Ware shows a slightly different pattern. From the third to the eighth century, imported wares comprise 42 per cent of the attested examples, while local potteries produced 21 per cent and Aswan 29 per cent. A further 7 per cent came from an unknown Egyptian source.[11] The majority of the pottery came from Egyptian potteries, a pottery local to Hermopolis, potteries at Aswan and some wares from the Delta.

The excavations at Quseir al-Qadim on the Red Sea coast produced large amounts of non-Egyptian fine ware, mostly Eastern Sigillata A (c. 66 per cent), Eastern Sigillata B (10 per cent), Cypriot ware (10 per cent) and imitation Arretine, perhaps from Alexandria (10 per cent) (Whitcomb and Johnson 1982: 64–6). There are parallels between Quseir finds and Indian kitchen wares, and Nabataean wares also seem to have influenced the local pottery. The amphorae appear to have been a mixture of Egyptian, North African and Dressel 2–4 (Whitcomb and Johnson 1982: 67–9). The lamps are also informative. Of the 50 lamps analysed, 24 were imports (19 Italian), and 26 were Egyptian, a notably different pattern from that of other sites (Whitcomb and Johnson 1982: 243–4). A similar pattern emerges from the evidence from Alexandria. All the races of the world supposedly met and traded in Alexandria (Dio Chrysostom, *Oratio* 32. 36) and the archaeological remains show a general East Mediterranean mix but also that the city was part of the Egyptian trade network, trading especially with Lower Egypt. The pottery groups identified by Rodziewicz (1976) conform largely to the expected pattern. Of the imported wares, Group A is not commonly found in Egypt but was not present in great quantities at Alexandria. Groups C and D were again rare in the rest of Egypt, though common in the East Mediterranean. Only Group B had both a general

Mediterranean dispersal and was common throughout Egypt. There were also three common local wares which show different patterns of distribution between Lower and Upper Egypt, the Lower Egyptian forms being more common in Alexandria. The Alexandrian pattern may also be reflected at Marina el Alamein. The pottery shows extensive contacts overseas, with western pottery, mostly from Tunisia, but also from Gaul and Spain (though the extremely common Baetican oil amphorae are not attested) (Majcherek 1993). Nevertheless, this does not appear to be a 'Delta-pattern' since pottery found at the monastic site of Kellia, on the western fringes of the Delta, is mostly from Egyptian potteries, the two main sources being Abu Mina in the Delta and Aswan, though there are some imported amphorae and fine wares from Cilicia, Cyprus and Tunisia (Ballet 1988). The pottery may, however, have been untypical of secular Delta communities. The excavations at Tell Atrib in the Central Delta, not fully published, have produced a considerable amount of Roman fine ware (Mysliwiec and Herbich 1988).

All the cities of Egypt that can be assessed appear to have been connected to trade networks which brought coinage and pottery from as far afield as the western Mediterranean into Egypt, especially in the fourth century. The extent of involvement in these trade networks does, however, appear to vary between communities. Alexandria was more closely integrated into Mediterranean trade networks than the cities of the *chora* and it may be that an Alexandrian-type mix of trade goods spread across at least some of the Delta. Great hills of pottery have been found south of Lake Mareotis, an area known for its wine, and although these have not been excavated, it seems very likely that the pottery is to be related to the long-distance wine trade (Empereur 1986; Empereur and Picon 1986). Indeed, wine is one of the few products that we know had a regular trade between provinces, with non-Egyptian wine retailing in Egypt and Egyptian wines being exported until the sixth century at least (Rathbone 1983; Luzzatto 1996). In terms of markets, the cities appear to correspond more to the complex central place model of figure 6.3.2 than the solar central place model of figure 6.3.1.

Taxes and rents

In addition to trade, taxes and rents (the latter defined broadly to include profits derived from estates worked by paid agents) enabled surpluses to be extracted from farmers. In spite of the mass of evidence concerning taxation from Roman Egypt, there is virtually no information about the ultimate destination of that taxation. It is generally assumed, however, that in the Roman period, perhaps after local intermediaries had taken a cut, most tax went to the Roman government and not to city authorities. The Augustan *metropoleis* had few formal powers and were under the control of the *strategoi*. It seems to me unlikely that any tax-raising powers within the territory of the nome were delegated to the *metropoleis*, though matters may have been rather different within the city walls. After 200, more responsibilities fell to the councils, but probably without the redirection of significant taxation to the urban treasury. This leaves us with rents.

Fundamental to any understanding of rents must be an estimate of the area of land under metropolite control. We have some useful figures from *P. Landlist.* of *c.* AD 350 as analysed by Bagnall (1992) and Bowman (1985). Both agree that around 75,000 *arourai* were owned by metropolites. Bagnall calculates that an additional 2,200 *arourai* were owned by urban institutions or rented out to metropolites, but with the margins of error in these calculations, these holdings can be ignored. This leaves about 180,000 *arourai* controlled by villagers (total area taken from table 6.4). This amounts to a ratio of approximately 70 : 30 in the division of land between villagers and metropolites. Bagnall assumes that all the land in the *pagus* closest to the city, none of which is registered in *P. Landlist.*, would be owned by metropolites, though I see no reason to accept this. Clearly, an 'average rent' for land is a fairly arbitrary concept given the different qualities of land, the patterns of crop-rotation, and shifts in economic power between landlord and tenant (Rowlandson 1996: 247–52), but the best guess is that the landlord took about 66 per cent of the produce from which he or she paid public dues at about 1 *artaba* per *aroura* or 8–10 per cent of yield (Rowlandson 1996: 226–7; 37). Very roughly, this would suggest that landlords took home about 18 per cent of the total yield of the nome, perhaps less on non-grain crops. It follows, therefore, that *c.* 350, the proportion of the population that could be supported directly or indirectly by the landlords was 18 per cent of the total for the Hermopolite. Given that the percentage of urbanization of table 6.4 is likely to be high, it looks likely that the majority (though not all) of the population of fourth-century Hermopolis could be supported from the income of the landlords.

There are no similar figures for other nomes. *P. Oxy.* XLIV 3170 lists receipts for the *monoartabia* tax at Sinary in the Oxyrhynchite nome. The granary at Sinary appears to have been used as a collection point for taxes and it seems probable that all tax for the nome was collected there (a fairly sophisticated giro system was in operation so not all the grain had to be moved). The annual total for the urban account (early third century) was 12,020 *artabai*. The tax was charged at probably just over 1 *artaba* per *aroura* (Rowlandson 1996: 293; Wallace 1938: 13; 19) and allows an estimate for the total number of *arourai* of 11,234 or about 5.5 per cent of the total grain land of the nome. If we add 2,155 *artabai* from ousiac (estate) land (2,014 *arourai*), the total rises to about 6.5 per cent of grain land, suggesting that metropolites would receive about 4 per cent of the yield of Oxyrhynchite grain land in rent. This is, of course, a very low figure and one wonders whether significant areas of grain land owned by metropolites were not registered to pay tax in the metropolite account. In addition to this private land, public land could be managed and effectively owned by metropolites. *SB* XIV 12208 (Bagnall and Worp 1980) registers 38,857 *arourai* of public land in seed, or 19 per cent of the total for the nome.

If the public land was distributed in the same ratio between villagers and metropolites as private land (92 : 8), this would add 3,145 *arourai* to the landholdings of the metropolites. Yet, this latter assumption is too conservative. Rowlandson (1996: 97–101) argues convincingly that metropolites were able to use their financial muscle to outbid villagers for tenure of public land and that those charged with managing public assets probably had an interest in granting tenure of public land to those who could offer significant amounts of private land as security for the taxes. Given that those who managed such leases were probably easily persuaded by the politically influential metropolites, the situation would appear to conspire in favour of metropolite landowners. We have no material that would allow us to quantify the proportion of public land in the hands of metropolites, but I assume, for illustrative purposes, that they controlled 50 per cent of public land (19,428 *arourai*) in the early third century. The major difference between private and public land was the effective tax rate. It looks as though the rate on public land was about three times that on private land, though the land appears to have been sub-let at similar rates to private land. If we assume a similar return as on private land, this would mean that possibly another 4 per cent of the total product of the nome came through the city, giving a total of about 8 per cent for the early third century, which takes us much closer to the assumed population distribution between city and villages in the Oxyrhynchite.

For the Fayum, we depend on village land registers. *P. Cair. Isid.* 9 of 308–9 (as reconstructed by Bagnall 1992) suggests that 13.7 per cent of the land of Karanis was controlled by non-villagers. This is quite close to the overall figure for the Oxyrhynchite of 16.2 per cent, as imagined above. It is, however, evident that the distribution of metropolite landholdings throughout the nome was not even and Karanis, situated on the edge of the fertile zone of the Fayum and seemingly in increasing difficulty in the late third and early fourth centuries, may have had unusual patterns of metropolite investment.[12]

Although it seems that the urban populations of Hermopolis and Oxyrhynchus could not be supported by the income from metropolite landholdings alone and depended for some of their food on income from craft production or trade, income derived directly from the land could have fed the majority of the population.[13]

Change and development

Introduction

The picture that emerges from the above considerations is, essentially, a composite one. The margins for error in the calculations are very high and the primary evidence weak. Methodologically, it is very difficult to make a convincing case for 'borrowing' evidence for one city or nome and applying it to a different set of historical and topographical circumstances. The urban pattern of the fourth-century Hermopolite, for instance, must have been affected by the historically unusual development of nearby Antinoopolis. It is worth emphasizing the difference, given that we have already seen that there is evidence to suggest significant variations in economic structure between the various urban settlements of Egypt. It also seems improbable, given the evidence for social and political change presented in the previous chapters, that the economic structures of Egypt were unchanging. Yet, the paucity of our information and its quality means that establishing the dynamics of the urban economies of Roman Egypt is guesswork. We can, however, be relatively confident that the first three centuries AD saw an extension in the power and prosperity of the landed elite of the cities. I think it is also probable that the continued concentration of property in later centuries, and also in the Byzantine period, saw a narrowing of that elite. Nevertheless, remnants of earlier dominant patterns of landholding continued alongside later developments, so that, for instance, the smallholdings that dominated the first century AD can be found in the seventh century as the middling estates of the old metropolite elite continued to exist alongside those of the great houses of the fifth to seventh centuries.[14]

Finley (1977; 1985a; 1985b) argued that most Classical cities had essentially similar characteristics in that they depended for their economic existence mainly on surpluses extracted from their rural hinterlands through political or institutional means, rather than through exchange for goods and services. I think it likely that Egyptian cities conformed broadly to Finley's consumer city model but, although operating with a homogeneous category of the 'consumer city' seems relatively safe, the observable changes in Roman and Byzantine Egypt are not thereby explained. By making a few simple assumptions, the possibilities and problems become clearer. I am, however, searching for fine distinctions and slow developments in imperfect evidence, which renders comparative analysis over time deeply problematic.

The increased prosperity and prominence of the landed aristocracy after the early first century BC changed the nature of the urban market, perhaps encouraging the orientation towards the Mediterranean so evident in the culture of the Roman period. I assume that such developments would increase long-distance trade, generating the complex trading networks described above and increasing the opportunities for specialization in production and retailing. The growth in elite landholdings is very likely to be the result of opportunistic investment, either through loans or through direct purchase which eventually increased the elite's economic power. The elite was in a position to invest in land to improve its productive capabilities or to shift to more cash-productive crops and invest in technology by promoting better water-management systems. Although it is likely that investment was conservative (Kehoe 1997), as one might expect in an economy in which any growth must have been very slow, Rathbone (1991) shows that management strategies on at least one estate were sufficiently sophisticated to keep costs down and achieve economies of scale. This must have enabled investment and boosted profit. Many of the preconditions of industrialization appear to have been in place: comparatively flexible capital, long-distance trade networks, sophisticated retailing networks, large and hungry urban populations and, in Egypt, comparatively cheap, easy and safe communications, and proto-capitalistic (and possibly fully capitalistic) management strategies. Such factors suggest that we should consider the possibility of and probably expect economic growth in the Egyptian economy. Any such growth must have been limited since it is evident that there was no economic development in Egypt comparable with the industrial revolutions of the eighteenth and nineteenth centuries. Although it may seem a rather circuitous course on which I am about to embark, the explanation of this absence of economic revolution has significant implications for the nature of the city, though the story requires first an excursion into economic theory and then something of a suspension of disbelief as fragmentary evidence is used to support various elements of the thesis.

Development theory

In what follows I discuss three related concepts: economic growth, development and prosperity. The last is simply wealth and is the easiest to distinguish since it carries no implication of distribution. Economic growth and development are, however, more easily confused. In this context, development is used technically and perhaps unusually to refer to the alleviation of poverty. Economic growth means an increase in the production of society and carries no implications of reduction of poverty or of the distribution of that growth or even of an increase in production per capita.

Development economics is a difficult area of theory, made more problematic by pronouncements of ideologues and posturings of governments and non-governmental agencies that have turned the field into a political battleground, the main casualties of which have been the world's poor. Post-war theory was dominated largely by Keynesian economics which, in the West at least, held sway with comparatively little opposition. It was hoped to generate something akin to the economic revolutions that had brought prosperity and political dominance to the West in what was perhaps a ridiculously short period. Armed with Western knowledge and capital, developers, normally actively supported by newly decolonized governments, thought that the best way to generate economic development was to invest in cities. This was because it was believed that the rural population was under-productive and that there was surplus labour in the countryside. If that labour could be transferred to the towns, then it could be usefully employed in industrial activity. Meanwhile, the new workers would provide a market which the farmers could then supply at a handsome profit, allowing them to invest both in goods from the urban factories and in the improvement of agriculture, thus generating more prosperity, urbanization, industrial and agricultural growth in a virtuous circle. This policy was perceived to fail, especially in India, where the generated growth did not result in rural development (Leys 1996; Preston 1996; Sutton 1989).

Many explanations have been proffered for this perceived failure. Theorists of the New Right, especially the monetarist ideologues who came to control both Britain and the United States and, hence, the world's most important financial institutions, turned away from governmental intervention to rely upon the market to produce a solution. In this, they had some evidential support. Much of the new industry of the developing world was under-funded and unable to compete on the world market, with the result that tariff protection was necessary to preserve the industrial production on which the growing urban populations relied, though this meant the continuation of inefficient industries for which the country as a whole, consumers and taxpayers, ultimately paid the price. Also, the developing nations, anxious to avoid the deprivation of urban populations (from which revolutions might spring) that had followed in the wake of the industrial revolution in the West, sought to control agricultural prices and thus prevented profits rising in the countryside and agricultural investment. The virtuous circle of economic development was beaten out of shape by governmental intervention. By abolishing restrictive practices and tariffs and exposing the new industries to the harsh world of capitalistic competition, as well as the benefits of massive investment capital from the West, the road to prosperity, growth and development was assured. Free trade was and is proclaimed as the solution to the world's ills and the political triumph of the Right in the West means that this continues to be seen as the 'solution' (Corbridge 1989).

Yet, although economic growth has followed in many areas, as under the Keynesian regime, developmental goals have not been achieved. One should not be overly pessimistic about the developmental and economic achievements since decolonization. Some countries have seen massive increases in GDP and have closed the gap on the developed world. Literacy rates have risen. Infant mortality has fallen. Consumer goods have reached even the most deprived areas and undoubtedly improved the quality of life for millions. Nevertheless, although the numbers living in absolute poverty have fallen since 1950, they still remain high and the process of development is extremely uneven. Indeed, in many areas the late twentieth century has seen economic disaster, increased poverty and poverty-related mortality, and the destruction of communities, especially in rural areas. All this while urbanization has continued apace and the global market reaches to the most remote places of the world.

Some of this failure may be due to particular political and environmental circumstances, though the oft-repeated problems cannot be described as unusual. The developing world was at the forefront of the Cold War, the very name of the communist–capitalist conflict reflecting its Eurocentric bias. In the developing world, and indeed for American and Russian youth, the war was often very hot indeed. Communists and capitalists sought strong governments on whom they could rely and destabilized and supported aggression against inimicable regimes. The result was support for strongmen, kleptocrats, narrow oligarchies who ruled by violence and terror and lived off the immense financial and military resources deployed by the superpowers. The end of Soviet communism left Africa especially with a legacy of deeply objectionable regimes supported by huge armies and a series of bitter, violent conflicts that have torn so much of the continent apart. The more recent emphasis in developmental policy of supporting liberal and democratic regimes recognizes this legacy, but preaches despair in the face of the problems of nations such as Angola and Somalia.

Although such problems are political and may be seen as merely practical barriers that have prevented (perhaps only temporarily) the triumph of the theoretically supreme late-capitalist developmental strategy, many have seen the whole free-trade policy as misconceived since it exposes the most vulnerable to unbridled capitalism. The enormous financial power of many Western firms, often allied to the political power of Western governments who have manipulated aid to benefit their own local industries, has been used to exert political pressure on developing states to ensure, perhaps unfairly, favourable trading conditions. Huge surplus value has been extracted from workforces maintained in abject poverty, especially in industries such as textiles. Worse, the political leverage that has come with the massive debts on loans made by international monetary organizations, encouraged by the Western powers, has enabled a new generation of ideologues to demand fundamental reforms and reductions in state spending that have crippled the provision of social and infrastructural services while at the same time causing an enormous outflow of capital. Developing states are often forced to distort their economies in the search for hard-currency-generating economic sectors, such as tourism. The potential social or economic benefits of growth have not led to development but have tended to be monopolized by an educated, generally urban minority (Lipton 1977; 1982; Corbridge 1982) or even exported to the prosperous West. Free trade in agricultural produce and sometimes even food aid has damaged the economic viability of local agriculture and perhaps, together with increases in population, intensified the exploitation of agricultural resources without providing the necessary inputs to avoid environmental degradation. The result is that the very rapid urbanization has not generated rural prosperity nor led to the kind of developmental leaps envisaged. Instead, some cities appear to be gateway cities, oriented not so much to their rural hinterlands, but to global markets to which they are often peripheral. In such a system, urban growth does not generate markets which can be served by the rural population, nor does the rural population benefit notably from the produce of the city. Indeed, some areas, especially those affected by wars, have seen a notable decline in prosperity alongside rapid urbanization (Drakakis-Smith 1987). For this reason, some development economists have turned their attention away from *megalopoleis* to small towns (Baker and Pedersen 1992; Potter 1990; Unwin 1989), which are thought to be in a better position to provide facilities for local areas and develop functions which would integrate those areas and spread prosperity. In essence, however, it seems to me that the problem is one not of scale but of structure since even in small cities urban elites can monopolize resources and the benefits of economic growth (Potter 1990). Nevertheless, in spite of the fact that many developmental economists are turning their attention to small rural projects, it still seems likely that cities are a crucial element in the economic mix that generates and generated development and economic growth.

It has long been observed that central place theory, as developed in Germany and elsewhere by theorists such as Christaller (1996) and von Thünen (cf. Beaujeu-Garnier and Delobez 1979: 111–12) has been very good at modelling the interrelationship of an economic system and its central point or points. It has also long been acknowledged that the model is, to a greater or lesser extent, a fiction in that it assumes an even terrain and communications network. The descriptive success of central place theory, especially in relation to retailing, given these theoretical concerns, has been a matter of some surprise. Second, although central place theory appears to be quite good at looking at the spread of urban functions through a region, it seems less able to explain why an urban and subsequent regional system developed in the first instance. Perhaps as a result of these theoretical inadequacies and the difficulty of producing a mathematical model for urban location, 'pure' economists have tended to be shy of the spatial in their analyses, leaving such matters to the sub-fields of development economics, to sociology and to regional studies in its various forms. In a recent survey of economic thought in this area Krugman (1995) argues, if I understand the point correctly, that the crucial element missing from this analysis has been the modelling of how an urban centre is itself a market for the products of that urban centre. Traders and craftsmen remote from an urban centre would be at a disadvantage in competing for that market. This would tend to mean that industrial and trading activity would cluster and that cluster would increasingly act as a central place within the evolving settlement system. As traders concentrate, the potential market increases. One presumes that, theoretically, this would reach a balance with the development of sub-centres with lower transport costs to their particular sub-market, dealing with local needs and fully rural trading. Equilibrium would emerge without the concentration of all traders and craftsmen within the urban centre.

For the purposes of this analysis, we may presume that, very generally, the settlement system of Ptolemaic Egypt achieved equilibrium with a large number of urban centres extracting surpluses from the villages and acting as market centres, though in an economy which had many market outlets.[15] It seems very likely that the major dynamics in the structure of the economy of Roman Egypt in the first century of Roman rule were the slow rise of the landed aristocracy and the extraction of surplus by the Roman state. Although some of the surplus will have returned in payments for soldiers and perhaps in other subsidies, Rome almost certainly drained considerable resource from the Egyptian economy. This was most likely to affect those for whom the old

Ptolemaic state had provided an income, though I do not see that this can be traced in any evidence, and it would seem unlikely that it greatly affected the economy of Middle and Upper Egypt.

The emergence of a landed elite is, however, potentially more interesting since it probably led to a gradual concentration of wealth in urban centres, which would enhance the role of the urban market and perhaps further concentrate trade, thereby generating demographic growth in the cities and further enhancing the importance of the market. Although some of the needs of the new elite were almost certainly met by long-distance trade, it seems unlikely that this was ever sufficient to drain resources from the local economy, as it does in the modern developing world, and any ill-effects of complex trading patterns would be offset by the ability of traders and manufacturers to trade in more than one urban market. Moreover, as the elite became more powerful, its members appear to have taken measures to enhance the role of the city as a trading and market centre. We have already seen that the elite deployed considerable resources to ensure the adequate supply of food in the city and administered many trades, partly in order that those traders may be taxed. The provision of retail facilities must have aided trade and perhaps encouraged a concentration of trading activities within the *metropoleis*. Perhaps more significant was the provision of the doles. In a pre-industrial economy urban traders are one step removed from the main industry of food production and are thus more vulnerable to short-term fluctuations in food supply. For urban populations, starvation was always just around the corner (Garnsey 1988). To turn to full-time craft production was, therefore, a risk since one needed to guarantee an adequate income to provide for oneself and one's dependants in good times and bad, but the provision of a dole considerably reduced that risk since, in the last resort, at least some of the requirements of the family would be met by the city. Moreover, the provision of the dole effectively subsidized those residing in the city and must have allowed profit margins to be pared down if necessary and given an unfair advantage to urban traders over their rural competitors. Even if it was not designed primarily to support the very poor, it was a social security system that softened the blow of any economic disaster that befell a family.

Nevertheless, not only did the Egyptian economy not experience revolutionary development, it is even arguable that it did not achieve the complexities and development of sixteenth-century north-west Europe. We have, therefore, a similar problem to those facing modern development economists: explaining a lack of rapid progress: and we cannot rely on war, kleptocratic governments, or overly ambitious, state-driven economic strategies to solve the problem. Morley (1996) argues that the major differences between modern development and that of Italy of the Roman period were the severe limitations on production caused by a failure to invest in technology and limitations on agricultural investment, so that although Rome 'became a driving force in the development of the Italian economy . . . , this process could not continue indefinitely . . . [since t]he chief constraint on development . . . was . . . the limits set on surplus production' (p. 185). He also claims that

> [t]he main difference between the Roman Empire and the capitalist world-economy . . . lies in the different levels of demand in pre-industrial and industrial systems . . . In the modern world the underdevelopment of the periphery ensures the supply of cheap raw materials and a market for manufactured goods. Rome . . . had little reason to prevent areas of its hinterland from developing as they wished.
>
> (Morley 1996: 158)

The argument is complex, but Morley seems to suggest that it is the economic relationship with the hinterland that is (also) crucial since economic growth at the core depended on the underdevelopment of that hinterland so that it could provide the raw materials to the benefit of the core and act as a market for finished goods.[16]

Morley's theory has close links with dependency theory. This argues that the periphery of the capitalistic world was maintained in underdevelopment in order to provide raw materials for core areas (Frank 1969). Few would claim that the temporal conjunction of the development of European colonial empires and industrialization was coincidental and Wallerstein (1974, but more explicitly 1979: 24–35), in developing dependency theory for his 'world-systems theory', argues that capitalism created a global division of labour and that much conventional Marxist analysis fails since it refuses to analyse on a world scale, sticking instead to national boundaries.[17] The problem with such models is not that they are necessarily ineffective or, indeed, wrong (capitalism was clearly a global issue from the seventeenth century and it seems both useful to think of the ramifications of economic 'cores' on 'peripheries' and foolish to discount the impact of empire on European, especially British, capitalistic development), but that they are counter-intuitive. As Massey (1991b) argues, the local still 'feels' more important to the person in the street, and away from international businessmen, and jet-setting academics and politicians, local exploitation and economic competition seem far more immediate. If one can still feel this today in a developed Western society, while writing on an American computer, while sitting on a Korean chair and at a Swedish desk, how much less apparent would globalization have been twenty or a hundred years ago?[18] The problem is not the globalization of capitalism, but the degree to which this was effective and integrated disparate local economic systems. A second problem lies in the overly simple representation of core–periphery (industrial England versus under-developed Africa for instance), when one can find 'peripheral' areas geo-graphically close or even within core *metropoleis* in Britain and complex, powerful, business communities forming local 'cores' in India.

Although core–periphery models and dependency theory have obvious benefits in the analysis of colonialism and modern capitalism (I have doubts as to its contemporary application), I am not sure that it can easily be applied to the Roman situation. Obviously, the Roman empire was a world-system in Wallerstein's scheme. Rome extracted a surplus from across the empire and, through military and other expenditure, influenced the economies of provinces through which some elements of a common imperial material culture were spread. Nevertheless, within Egypt, and in spite of the evidence for quite important regional economic activity, it appears likely that it was social relations within the local area (the nome), the region (the immediate network of cities) and the province that were most important in generating economic and class structures. Second, we face an issue of agency. A whole series of modern institutions can be accused of reinforcing 'third-world' dependency, from the large multinational corporations that use political muscle so that governments and labour organizations cannot increase the wages of their workforces or secure environmental protection, to 'first-world' governments that manipulate world economic policy, and international agencies such as the IMF and World Bank which have often rather particular ideological agendas. None of these agencies was at work in the Roman world and there is no evidence that Rome ever had anything as grand as an economic policy. It is unlikely that Romans could have maintained an area in underdevelopment, even if they had had an understanding of what that might mean. Even viewing the Romans as unintentionally generating a periphery through high taxation seems a little far-fetched since it seems rather unlikely that taxation was the major dynamic of Roman economic development.[19]

Rome, as an imperial centre, drew on rural surpluses through its political authority. This meant that the economic effects of the metropolis were spread across the entire empire (creating a world-system). Morley (1996), however, shows convincingly that the economic impact of Rome transformed the immediate hinterland of the city. The obvious model to which one can compare Rome (and one which Morley uses) is early modern London. Although Rome's population probably topped 1,000,000 while the population of seventeenth-century London was only about 500,000 (about 9 per cent of the total population of England and Wales), the very rapid growth of London (figure 6.4) and of other urban centres had dramatic economic effects on the economy of England.[20] The years 1680–1740 saw an increase in large commercial estates as smaller landowners were pushed out (Mathias 1983: 25; 50). Increased commercialization saw a transformation in agriculture in which 'a vast extension of the cultivated area took place and previously cultivated land became farmed more intensively' (Mathias 1983: 57). Even those small farmers who were able to resist the encroachment of capitalistic landlords survived and found prosperity by integrating with the market and following 'progressive' farming techniques (Large 1990). In spite of the very rapid urbanization of England (not just through London), Britain remained a net and increasingly important exporter of corn until the decade 1770–9, and not until after the catastrophes of the Napoleonic wars did grain imports rise to more than 5 per cent of total consumption (Mathias 1983: 64–5). As early as the 1500s the London market was having an increasing effect on the agriculture of Essex (Poos 1991: 41). The profits to be made from supplying London and other new urban centres encouraged rural investment, generating the virtuous circle of urban and rural prosperity so sought by modern developmental economists. This was also achieved in Roman Italy. Ancient economic attitudes, so denigrated by modern critics of the ancient economy and elite, find marked parallels in the English early modern period. Although great profits could be made in trade and industry, security was to be found in the land. Italian investment was directed at supplying urban markets. Rome acted, in the modern parlance, as a growth pole in the local economic system.

Yet, I think there is a further crucial difference. The precondition for urban growth in England was rural prosperity. The unsurprising increase in per capita rural wealth that followed the shedding of population in the Black Death probably resulted in increasing demand for manufactured goods which generated relative urban demographic growth. For complex and little understood reasons, in the aftermath of the plague population dynamics were restructured towards low nuptuality and slow population growth in the countryside (Poos 1991: 71–109). Even with the commercialization of farming,

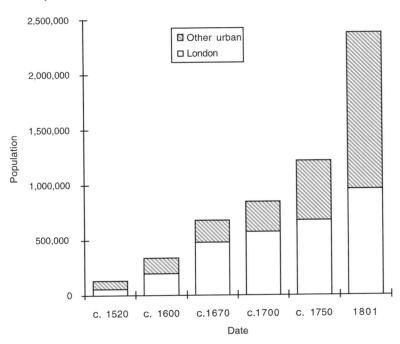

Figure 6.4.1 Estimated urban population of England 1520–1801 (after Wrigley 1987: 162)

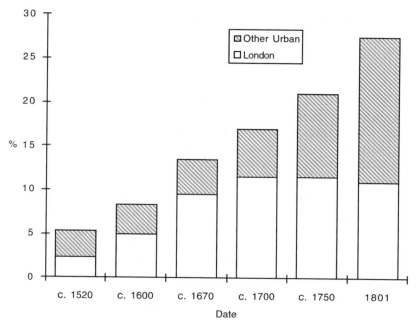

Figure 6.4.2 Estimated urban population of England as a percentage of total English population 1520–1801 (after Wrigley 1987: 162)

it seems likely that demand for labour remained high in competition with urban labour markets, and relative rural prosperity and development were maintained. Rural development appears to have generated economic growth which, in turn, sustained the development trajectory. The political structures of Rome, however, allowed the prosperity generated by the city and empire to be concentrated in the hands of a narrow urban elite. The contrast with Rome is marked since at least some of the demand for produce was met through taxation and slavery provided an institutional means by which the workers could be maintained in poverty. Also low intensity farming, such as ranching, with its low labour costs and limited investment needs but highly commercial product, may have been more financially attractive than high-investment, labour-intensive farming.[21] It seems likely that a high proportion of the surplus generated by agricultural production was retained by the landed elite so that rural development did not necessarily follow from the prosperity generated by the Roman market.

A transforming economy?

At first sight, Egypt's basic economic structures were similar to those of early eighteenth-century Britain. Alexandria, with probably about 10 per cent of the total population, was integrated into international trade networks and probably supported significant trade and manufacturing sectors, though all the evidence is anecdotal (e.g. Dio Chrysostom, *Oratio* XXXII. 36). Although Alexandria enjoyed political dominance, it is not clear that this was used to extract a surplus for the support of the city. As in eighteenth-century England, Egyptian urbanism appears to have depended on economic rather than political exploitation of the cities' rural hinterlands. I think, therefore, we are entitled to wonder whether the urbanization of Egypt can be related to a general transformation of the economic system and settlement pattern as occurred in England in the seventeenth century.

The concentration of papyri attesting settlements in the Oxyrhynchite allows us to trace first and last dates of attestation and therefore probable periods of occupation. This is obviously methodologically questionable since first and last dates of attestation need not correlate closely with dates of occupation (though the density of references is such that this is not a particular worry) and bare attestation tells us little about the nature of occupation, particularly in the case

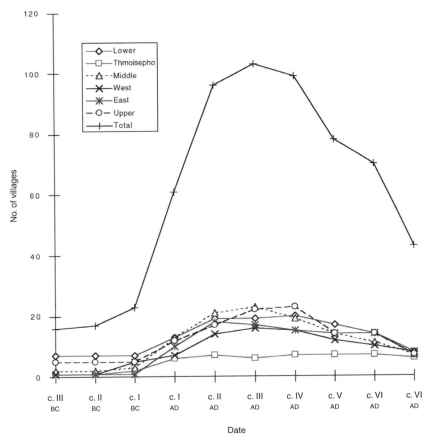

Figure 6.5 Probably occupied villages of known toparchy by century

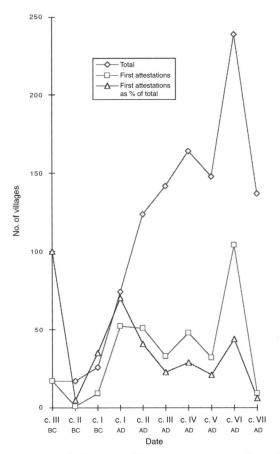

Figure 6.6 Total attested villages and first attestations of villages by century

of sites which are only known as monastic centres in the later period. The problem is somewhat worsened by the variety of ancient terminology deployed to identify settlements and inconsistency of usage of that terminology. In the analysis below, a cautious approach is used and the smallest level of settlement (the *epoikion* – farmstead/hamlet) is excluded, though if '*kome*' (village) is ever used of the settlement, the site is counted. Also, several toponyms are used for more than one site. In such cases, late non-specific uses of the name are treated as attesting all the sites known by such a name. The results are not significantly distorted by this practice. The material is collated in figures 6.5 and 6.6.

Figure 6.5 reflects what one might call the Ptolemaic and early Roman settlement system. The rise in the number of villages mirrors the rise in the number of papyri from the first century and it seems very likely that the vast majority of the villages are attested by the end of the second century. Thus, judging from figure 6.5, the number of villages stabilizes between the second and the fourth centuries. After the fourth century, the number of attested villages falls dramatically. The villages of figure 6.5 are a particular non-random sample and if we compare that sample with figure 6.6, an extraordinary pattern appears. As with figure 6.5, we may presume that the increase in all attested villages in figure 6.6 during the first and second centuries is a result of the pattern of preservation of papyri at Oxyrhynchus, but the curve for total number of villages continues to rise into the sixth century. This is peculiar, but I do not think that it is a statistical anomaly. The percentage of new attestations falls during the third century (though it is still perhaps surprisingly high), which would suggest that the roster of attested villages was almost complete.[22] Yet, although one would expect the percentage of new attestations to continue to fall (perhaps to negligible levels by the fifth century), it rises in the fourth century, is maintained at a high level in the fifth century in spite of a dearth of papyri, and then rises dramatically during the sixth century. I can see no easy explanation for this other than a dramatic rise in the number of villages in the fourth and later centuries set against a pattern of decline in some traditional villages.

Other nomes, such as the Herakleopolite (Falivene 1998) or Hermopolite (Drew-Bear 1979), do not have an even enough chronological distribution of papyri to allow such analysis. Nevertheless, the Oxyrhynchite material does

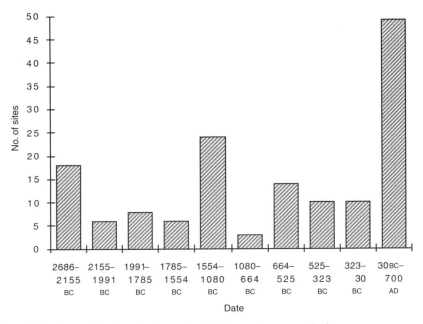

Figure 6.7 Occupation density by period in the north-eastern Delta

not stand alone. A survey of the fringes of the Eastern Delta suggests not only continued occupation of the region in the late Roman period, but a far more intense exploitation of the area (van den Brink 1987), see figure 6.7.[23] A survey at Buto (Ballet and von der Way 1993), in the north central Delta uncovered no evidence of occupation of koms surrounding the main city-site before the 'High Empire' and continuous occupation until the eighth or ninth century. The pottery from Thmouis, also in the Central Delta (Hansen 1965; cf. Hansen 1967), suggests that the site reached its maximum occupation in the period 450–650. Thirty-five topographically linked suburban sites at Pelusium produced material from the fourth century BC to the seventh century AD, most of of which appear to be of early Roman origins. The expansion of settlement is linked to a major programme of land drainage, probably in the third or fourth century (Jaritz et al. 1996). Cosson's (1935) survey of the Marea region depicts an area with few Pharaonic or Ptolemaic remains in comparison with Roman and late Roman structures.[24] This evidence must be set alongside the gradual depopulation of various Mendesian villages over the middle third of the second century and dramatic evidence of population decline in the Fayum in the same period (Rathbone 1990; Bagnall and Frier 1994: 173–7; Duncan-Jones 1996; *P. Thmouis* I), decline probably continuing in the third century and beyond (Bagnall 1978; 1985; Pollard 1998).

This trajectory of settlement development can be mirrored in other provinces, especially Syria and Africa. Tate (1992: 170–85) suggests that there was a period of expansion in rural settlement in North Syria from 270 to 450 which was increasingly vigorous after 330. There was a period of stagnation from the sixth century and then a steady decline. The region surveyed is harsh. Considerable effort and money must have been invested in the development of the small and mostly fairly poor villages that dotted the landscape. After the abandonment of many of the villages by the early eighth century, it was not until the late twentieth century that significant centres of population once more developed within the region. This pattern, with some chronological variations, can be observed throughout much of the Near East (see Foss 1995 for a survey), but the most spectacular evidence is the greening of the desert fringes achieved throughout much of North Africa. Dietz et al. (1995: II 773–86) show that the number of occupied sites in the semi-desert or desert of the Segermes valley in Tunisia rose from 7 in the period from AD 1–50 to 26 (250–300) to 59 (400–50) to 83 (500–50) before declining to 12 (600–50) and 3 (650–700). Barker and Mattingly (1996) argue for a rather more complex pattern of settlement change and development and are very careful to distinguish between the various types of sites that appear in the valleys. Clearly, however, the number of settlements increased rapidly in the Roman imperial period and the intensified exploitation of this extremely harsh landscape was made possible by a very high level of investment and skilled water-management. The ample evidence of olive oil manufacture suggests that the production of the area was directed towards urban markets and I strongly suspect that the financial investments in this territory were capitalistic in their desire to meet the demands of urban centres.[25]

The evidence from Egypt is mixed, with some signs of decay of older settlements from the fourth century, but also quite widespread evidence of economic growth which seems rather similar to Syrian and African patterns of change. Settlement patterns appear to be in flux and the most obvious source of change on this scale is an economy changing to meet the demands of the urban populations.

The most detailed records of farming from Egypt in this period come from estate managements, most notably the Heroninus archive from the third-century Fayum (Rathbone 1991) and the Apion archive from the fifth- and sixth-century Oxyrhynchite (Gascou 1985), though these can be supplemented by many smaller estate archives (Kehoe 1992; Parassoglou 1978) and the far more disparate dossier of material collected by Rowlandson (1996) for land-leasing. Estate management strategies remain, however, a much disputed area. The debate turns on the level of 'rationality' of the estate management, which, in this case, has the technical and very restricted meaning of 'profit maximization' (Kehoe 1988; 1992; 1993a; 1993b; Rathbone 1991; 1994). Nevertheless, there is considerable common ground between the protagonists and, since the sophistication and complexity of some of the attested management systems is now clear, disagreement is restricted to exactly how efficient or conservative management strategies were. The Appianus estate certainly worked to deploy its resources effectively and appears to have invested in technology, such as water-management systems.[26] This interest in either supporting or improving irrigation appears also in the Apion archives in the sixth century (P. Oxy. XIX 2244; Tacoma 1998). Although we cannot know whether the attested improvements were marginal, the accumulation of land and the evidence of active and well-resourced management point to a commercialization of large estate farming directed towards supplying the urban populations. We thus appear to be seeing the virtuous circle of urban growth encouraging structural development of agriculture and generating increasing prosperity. This is the London pattern.

Nevertheless, there were clear limits on growth. By the third century, Egypt had a powerful urban elite that deployed very considerable resources in improving the status of the city. Many of these improvements were architectural or ceremonial, but some, such as the corn doles, brought material benefits to the urban population. This not only gave the less wealthy in the city a material advantage over any potential village competition, but also increased the distinction between urban and rural. This had disastrous implications. First, the concentration of wealth would tend to mean that the most fruitful opportunities for the lower classes would come from the provision of services for the wealthy rather than catering for a mass urban or rural market. The heavily administered market of the Roman city (pp. 274–7) probably limited the opportunities of small farmers to profit from the supply of foodstuffs to the urban market. Economic growth could not depend on powerful village demand and would not produce extensive rural development. Consequently, the most serious brake on development and economic growth was the relative poverty of 80 per cent of the total population.

In summary, I think that the Roman and later Roman periods saw the emergence of a landed aristocracy, and the interrelationship of that landed aristocracy with the rural hinterland of cities encouraged an adjustment of the settlement patterns and probably significant economic growth. The prosperity of the Roman and late Roman economic system was poured into the towns and the estates of the urban elite. At the same time, that urban elite sought to differentiate itself from the villagers and to assert and defend urban status. The concentration of wealth in the hands of the elite did not encourage the growth of mass markets and the social boundaries between city and village were reinforced by the 'administered economy' of the Roman city. Thereby, at the very point at which the economic integration of village and city became closer, the cultural and institutional boundaries between city and village became more prominent. Nevertheless, although economic and political structures encouraged the urban elite to look beyond the nome to other cities and urban systems, the cultural boundaries between villages and the city of the elite may have been rather less obvious in the markets and among the less prosperous, who themselves probably had only limited access to the Greek culture of the landed and wealthy. The demands of the urban populations must have influenced the economic lives of the vast majority of Egyptians and those demands were almost certainly most strongly felt within local systems. It was the relationship between local cities and their hinterlands that were most important for the majority of the population and it would be the local settlement systems that might benefit from urban growth. If the cities truly acted as 'growth-poles' within settlement systems, then one would expect at least part of the cultural system and wealth of the cities to 'trickle down' to the villages. Nevertheless, the limits of growth flow from one of the fundamental aspects of the economic structure of antiquity and indeed of so very many modern developing nations: gross inequalities of wealth.

There is a danger in dismissing any historic economic and political development if it falls short of the revolutionary changes we have seen in the last three centuries. 'Revolution' seems inappropriate for what we can see in Egypt, but it is obvious that the influence of the cities spread far beyond the city walls and affected cultural and settlement patterns in the villages throughout Middle Egypt and no doubt elsewhere. Cities and villages developed and functioned as part of the same system and were perhaps much more closely (but not perfectly) integrated in the fourth century than in the first century AD.

The end of the Roman and Byzantine city in Egypt

All great historical boundaries are artificial. Few events are sufficiently cataclysmic to so destroy a society that virtually all elements of the earlier social system are swept away. Perhaps only the Spanish conquests in South America can merit such importance. Yet, although it is currently fashionable and reasonable to discuss the conventional boundaries between antiquity and the Middle Ages by using words such as 'transition' or 'transformation', avoiding the finality of 'end', events of the seventh and eighth centuries in the East appear sufficiently calamitous to justify the usage. Byzantium survived the onslaughts of Slavs, Avars, Arabs and Turks until 1453 and Christianity hung on in various communities of Egypt and Syria until the modern era, surviving even the crusades. Nevertheless, the cultural values and the economic and social system that had supported the cities of Roman and Byzantine Egypt gave way at some point between the sixth and the ninth centuries and, as can be seen from the survey below, the cities themselves declined and were sometimes virtually abandoned. The Byzantine urban system, with its roots in the earlier Roman and late Roman cities, was replaced by a different urban system, often focused on different urban centres, and structured in rather different ways.

Alexandria was a vibrant city in the third to fifth centuries and literary depictions stress its grandeur (Fraser 1951; Heinen 1991; Eutychius, *Annales* (PG 111, col. 1107); *Expositio Totius Mundi et Gentium* 34–7), but the early seventh century saw four sieges of the city, by the Persians, the forces of Phokas, and the Arabs (twice), and Christian attempts to recapture the city may also have caused damage (Borkowski 1981: 14–40; Haas 1997: 338–51; Eutychius, *Annales* (PG 111, cols. 1062; 1106–7; 1112; 1149)). Leontius' *Life of John the Almoner* is one of the last major Byzantine sources for the city and depicts the Church using its very considerable wealth against an increasingly tumultuous political background, though the creative elements of Leontius' hagiographic art are such that much of the tone and detail of the *Life* may have been interpolated into the tradition (Magdalino 1999). The Kom el-Dikke excavations (Rodziewicz 1982; 1983; 1991) suggest that the heating system for the baths, which had been repaired in the mid-fifth century, was abandoned in the early seventh century, probably soon after AD 618 and before the Arab invasions (see p. 163). The meeting rooms in the same block of the city were probably destroyed in the early seventh century and the site was reused in the early eighth century by a large courtyard house with animal troughs and perhaps some small shops (Kiss 1992b). The theatre, judging from the inscriptions, continued in use into the seventh century and may still have been an important building in the early Arab period (Borkowski 1981). Large sections of the site were reused as an Arabic burial ground from the eighth to the thirteenth century (Kiss 1992a), which was probably on the outskirts of the built-up area (suggesting considerable reduction in the size of the city). The pottery shows Mediterranean influence up until the mid-seventh century, after which the pottery is nearly all

Egyptian ware (Rodziewicz, 1976; Majcherek 1992). Although the seventh century does not see the end of occupation of Alexandria, it seems likely that there was both a significant decline in public facilities and probably a reduction in the area occupied.[27]

Marea, which may have effectively been a satellite community to Alexandria, shows a similar pattern. The fourth-century development of the city appears to be related to the large church and the association of the site with the pilgrimage route to the shrine of St Menas can hardly be coincidental (el-Fakhrani 1983; Rodziewicz 1983; 1988). The absence of Islamic glazed wares on the site suggests that it ceased to be occupied or extensively used in the seventh century. The shrine of St Menas at Abu Mina appears to have developed at the end of the fourth century. At the start of the fifth, a small church was built to house the shrine. This was developed in the early fifth century into a small basilical church before a Justinianic expansion saw the building of perhaps the largest basilical church in Egypt. This church and most of the rest of the community were destroyed by the Persians in 619 (see Altheim-Stiehl 1991; 1992 for the dating of the Persian war). When the population returned, possibly only in the eighth century, a much smaller basilica was built (probably in 744–68) and the rigorous urban plan of the early seventh-century city was lost (Grossmann 1989; 1998; for further details of the excavation of the settlement see Grossmann 1982; 1995; Grossmann et al. 1997; Grossmann and Kosciuk 1991; 1992; Grossmann et al. 1994; Grossmann et al. 1984).

The prosperity of Abu Mina may well have generated rural development. A village 1.5 km west of Abu Mina shows considerable evidence of both commercial development and prosperity. The publication is preliminary (Negm 1998) and the excavation appears to be incomplete, but the archaeologists have uncovered several private houses with painted walls and some painted floors, a large number of wine presses, a small number of shops, storerooms, water reservoirs and a church. The occupation of the site appears to have commenced in the fifth century and lasted into the eighth.

In the central Delta, suburban sites at Buto developed in the late Roman period and show continuous occupation until the eighth or ninth centuries when they were deserted (Ballet and von der Way 1993). Thmouis, also in the central Delta, reached its maximum occupation in the period 450–650 (Hansen 1967; Ammianus Marcellinus XXII 16. 6). The city is thought to have been in ruins in the early Arab period and the attestation of a bishop of Thmouis in 744 (disappeared again by 1086) is not considered significant (Meulenaere and MacKay 1976; see also Holz et al. 1980; Hansen 1965).[28] Very little of the material from Athribis appears to date from after the fifth century, though publication is piecemeal (see pp. 236–8; Mysliwiec 1992a; 1992b; 1992c; Mysliwiec and Rageb 1992) and numismatic material suggests that the site continued to be occupied into the eighth century (Ruszczyc 1992; Kryzanowska 1995).

At Pelusium, on the extreme eastern fringe of the Delta, there is substantial evidence for Arab occupation of the main urban site, but of thirty-five suburban sites only one contained Islamic material and the mid-sixth century saw systematic destruction (Jaritz et al. 1996).[29]

Excavations at Marina el-Alamein, west of Alexandria, uncovered a number of quite spacious houses displaying some signs of luxury. The houses are not closely dated but were still occupied in the sixth century. There are, however, no traces of Arab occupation (Marina el-Alamein 1991; Medeksza 1998).

Babylon–Fustat was developed in the early Roman period as the location of a major Roman garrison and it remained an important military centre, whose fall to the Arab invaders was a crucial defeat for the Byzantines (Butler 1978; see also Sheehan 1996). The city became a focal point for the Arab government and probably a significant centre of population as early as 700, perhaps thriving off the development of the military and administrative centre of nearby Cairo, with which Fustat eventually merged (Scanlon 1984; 1994). By contrast, the excavations at Hermopolis Magna have produced a great deal of Roman pottery, but few Islamic wares (Spencer and Bailey 1982: 11; Spencer et al. 1984: 16–24), while locally produced amphorae circulated until at least the late sixth century. It seems likely that the site was largely deserted in the early Islamic period (Spencer and Bailey 1982: 16; Spencer et al. 1984: Appendix III; Roeder 1931–2: 122; Bailey 1991: 59). Nearby Antinoopolis, certainly an important Coptic centre, is probably a better candidate for continuity as the regional administrative capital (Donadoni 1974: 72–95).

Further up the Nile, the settlements on the West Bank at Thebes have a very clear terminus of 810–20, probably connected with a tax revolt (Wilfong 1989). Syene–Elephantine appears to have been densely settled until at least the seventh century. The papyri showed shared occupation of houses and sales of parts of houses (Farber and Porten 1986; Clackson 1995; Porten 1996: D20–E3; Husson 1990; *P. Lond.* V 1722; 1724; 1733; *P. Monac.* 8; 9; 11; 12; 13; 14) and the site retained a garrison probably until the fall of Egypt to the Persians or possibly until the Arab invasions (Jaritz and Rodziewicz 1994). The houses on Elephantine (see pp. 116–18) continued to be occupied until at least 780 and possibly into the early ninth century (Grossmann 1980; Gempeler 1992).

This brief catalogue produces a pattern that is rather familiar to students of the sixth, seventh and eighth centuries since a similarly ragged pattern of decline and abandonment can be perceived in the archaeological material from Syria, Jordan and Israel. There, urban sites show some continuity beyond the Arab invasions, but from the seventh century to the early ninth, the process of demographic retreat is marked (Alston forthcoming, with references).

Explaining this decline is a major historical problem, but there is no shortage of causes, with famine, pestilence and war being three of the four possible horsemen of this apocalypse. Although the seventh century saw extended periods of warfare throughout the Byzantine East, which certainly affected Abu Mina and Alexandria, it seems very unlikely that the damage was by itself enough to lead to the long-term decline of a particular site. Catastrophes (warfare, earthquakes, plagues, famines) were comparatively common features of ancient life, and, in normal circumstances, populations and cities recovered, though sometimes this may have taken some time. The situation was rather different if political or military authorities had an interest in destroying a site, such as Corinth after the Roman conquest in the second century BC or Carthage after the third Punic war, but there is no evidence that the Arabs or the Persians were particularly hostile to urban centres. Indeed, it served little purpose for them to rule a wasteland.

'Plague' (the Greek equivalent for which is used in ancient texts to describe any widespread epidemic producing high mortality) may normally also be seen as a similarly short-term demographic blip, but in 542 the Byzantine empire was subject to a devastating outbreak of bubonic plague (John of Ephesus IV 29; Procopius, *Wars*, II 22-3). Bubonic plague appears to have been a demographic event of an altogether different order from other plagues and the attacks were repeated over more than a century. There is a chronic lack of data for the sixth–eighth-century plagues (Conrad 1981; 1994) and one can only gain insight into the probable demographic effects by comparison with fourteenth-century and sixteenth-century outbreaks. The historian is, however, faced with substantial problems. Estimated death rates for the fourteenth-century plague vary wildly and are often very different from those for the far better-attested later outbreaks. However, judging from the latter statistics, one might expect that general and severe plague visitations removed around 20 per cent of the Egyptian population (Alston forthcoming).[30] Repeated shocks by which 20 per cent of the population was killed would surely be too much for any population to make up and would inevitably lead to rapid decline. Nevertheless, there is reason to believe that after the first outbreak (probably the most devastating), the plague did not affect every community (Slack 1985: 113–19). Changes in the geographical range of the disease would have dramatic effects on total mortality, as is demonstrated by the hypothetical calculations in figure 6.8, which show that by adopting different assumptions concerning the spread of the disease, estimated mortality can vary between 25 per cent and about 5 per cent of total population.

Plague (*pestis pestis*) is transmitted in two forms, pneumonic (transmitted through airborne infection) and bubonic (transmitted through blood). Pneumonic plague produces higher fatality rates, though if the infection becomes septicaemic (which can result from either transmission), it kills extraordinarily quickly. The bubonic plague appears to be by far the most common form and is the way in which plague is recognized from ancient and medieval descriptions. The biological characteristics of the disease seem to change little and its very virulence meant that too few survived infection for antibodies to protect the next generation.[31] The main factor that could change was the physical process of transmission. Plague needs fleas to be transmitted and these fleas (very temperature-sensitive) only move with rats and humans, though they can be preserved in cloth for some time. Unsurprisingly, then, plague follows trade routes, but if plague disrupts the economy, then the absence

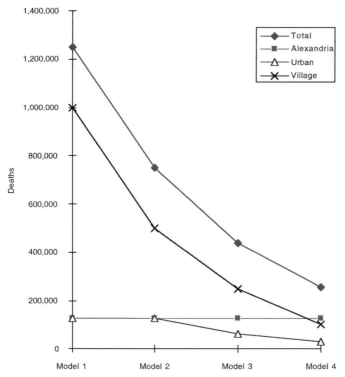

Model Population: 5,000,000 of whom 500,000 are in Alexandria, 500,000 in other urban settlements, 4,000,000 in villages.
All models assume 25% mortality in all settlements visited by plague.
Model 1: Plague visits all settlements.
Model 2: Plague visits Alexandria, all urban settlements and 50% of village settlements.
Model 3: Plague visits Alexandria, 50% of all urban settlements and 25% of villages.
Model 4: Plague visits Alexandria, 25% of all urban settlements and 10% of villages.

Figure 6.8 Mortality of a model Egyptian population in four different hypothetical plague visitations

of trade will limit the spread of the disease, which is (from figure 6.8) the most important variable in assessing plague's demographic impact. It seems likely that the disease is, in fact, self-limiting.

The comparative evidence for the effect of plague on social systems is inconclusive. The best evidence for demographics in the fourteenth century comes from Tuscany. This shows that the population of rural Pistoia fell from a high in 1244 of *c.* 31,220 to a low in 1404 of 8,989. A survey of 1344, three years before the plague reached Italy, shows the population at 23,964. Sixty years later, the population had fallen to 38 per cent of its pre-plague level and to 29 per cent of its thirteenth-century high (Herlihy 1965; 1967). In England, Slack (1985: 118–21; 129–32; 151; cf. Wrigley 1987: 162) guesses that the plague killed 658,000 between 1570 and 1670. In spite of this, the population of Exeter rose by perhaps as much as 50 per cent in the seventy years after 1570, the population of Bristol nearly doubled in the 150 years after 1547, and that of Norwich, which had five severe outbreaks of plague, rose from under 17,000 in 1579 to probably over 20,000 in 1640. Most dramatic are the estimates for the increase in the population of London during the plague years. From 85,000 in 1563, the population rose to 459,000 in 1665. The population of the country as a whole probably doubled in this period. In neither fourteenth-century Tuscany nor sixteenth- and seventeenth-century England does plague appear to have altered the direction of demographic change. In rural Tuscany the population was already in decline before the plague visitation, while in England the plague struck in a context of a rising population and does not appear to have undermined that demographic development. Some communities in England were in decline during the sixteenth and seventeenth centuries and it seems likely that their relative decline was worsened by plague. Nevertheless, the plague may have encouraged the relocation of population and perhaps concomitant economic changes that laid the foundations for the spectacular economic and demographic growth of Britain in the sixteenth and seventeenth centuries. In Tuscany, it may have similarly speeded up demographic and economic changes leading to a rapid fall in population. By shaking a society, plague encourages more rapid change and there is little reason to believe that its effects would have been any different in the sixth, seventh and eighth centuries AD.

Conclusions

The Roman and late Roman settlement system was based on cities. These cities generated a certain prosperity which supported and was supported by the perception of the difference of the city from the surrounding countryside. That special status of the city was eroded in the Byzantine period. Christianity valued the city only to the extent that it was the residence of the bishop, and we have seen how the bishops' authority was, in many ways, limited. Developed Christianity had alternative centres of authority and wealth in the monasteries, mainly located outside cities. The citizens were reintegrated with the villagers, now all Christians together, and the boundary between urban and rural ceased to have much meaning. The location of the house of the Apions outside Oxyrhynchus may also be significant, demonstrating that the politically powerful no longer required residences within the city. Although the pagarchs may be seen as local officials, there is no obvious sense in which they were urban officials. Political and religious power and wealth were being displayed and articulated in new ways in the sixth century and these rendered the cities less distinctive and special within the settlement systems.

Many cities appear to remain vibrant communities into the sixth century and beyond and a demographic shift is not convincingly observable in the

366

material until the seventh century. The structural changes that were undermining the late antique cities were subtle, perhaps slower in effect than those that generated the increased prosperity of the cities in the Roman period, and may even in the short term have had beneficial economic effects in encouraging investment and perhaps even exporting more wealth from the cities to the villages. Nevertheless, the distribution of wealth probably remained very unequal. With the city probably becoming increasingly irrelevant to the most powerful within the settlement system, I suspect that, very gradually, the prosperity of the urban markets was undermined and the shocks of the sixth and seventh centuries, including the inevitable disruption that followed the Arab invasions and the changed political and trading relations that resulted, further destabilized the cities. Any investment probably did not sufficiently increase the prosperity of the farmers and the farm-workers to the extent that they were able to become a vibrant market capable of compensating for the decline in the cities. Rather, the economic integration of villages and city that had generated growth probably ensured that the villages were not immune from urban decline and that the fate of the whole settlement system rested on the prosperity of its central places, the cities. To survive, villages which were partially economically dependent on the city had to return to a non-commercialized, non-urbanocentric farming and to adjust to a new world, with perhaps more localized political and economic structures, in which the cities perhaps played a less pivotal role.

The decline of the ancient city is, therefore, intimately related to a change in culture, one which undermined the carefully constructed sense of difference that had been integral to the Roman and early Byzantine city. The city's claim on the identity of individuals was eroded. If to be a member of an early Byzantine community was to be Christian, then primary identity lay with the Church, and possibly the Byzantine state, but not local cities.[32] Egyptian Christian identity could survive without local urban communities as it has throughout the Islamic period. Nevertheless, the end of the Byzantine city in Egypt was not the end of urbanism in the country. Egypt maintained its continuous urban history with the emergence of a new settlement pattern and a new form of urbanism with a different cultural and political orientation. The population of Egypt, the villages and the cities had to adjust to a new world. Cairo–Fustat rapidly replaced Alexandria as the primary urban centre in Egypt (Kubiak 1982; Kubiak and Scanlon 1989). The cities of the new Islamic urbanism were centres of religion and culture, centres which looked out to fellow urban *metropoleis* throughout the Arab world. Islam, with new forms of social organization, came to challenge Christianity. The city and Egypt itself was once more transformed, but this is a story beyond what skill and knowledge I have, and a book, unlike a city, must have an end.

NOTES

2 CITIES AND SPACE

1 Rather desultory excavations from 1719 gathered pace towards the middle of the century (Mau 1899: 26–7).

2 The process of removal of the obscene to make texts more palatable was not solely confined to Classics. When reading *Macbeth* for my pre-university examinations, I was a little puzzled that the Porter's speech, which I had been told was a brilliant piece of drama, changing the mood and building tension before the crucial discovery of the body of the slain king, lasted a mere four lines and was horrified that I was expected to write a 45-minute essay on this seemingly pointless episode. Like most translations, such processes elided the difference between the foreign text and the receiving culture and helped naturalize the Classics. It became easier to explain the (invisible) obscenity as a display by the writer of behaviour worthy of admonition (which it evidently was not) or, when influenced by anthropology, evidence of (residual) primitivism and simplicity which our more sophisticated age would rather not discuss, rather like the vulgarities of Shakespeare.

3 Bernal's recent attempt (1987) to reconstruct a vast conspiracy among eighteenth-century Classicists, who, affected by the racism of the period, down-played or ignored the Egyptian influence on Greek culture, has been heavily criticized, not because Classicists in the nineteenth and twentieth centuries did not make racist assumptions and allow such assumptions to influence their work, but because it ignores the complexity of the nineteenth-century reception of the ancient world and the multiplicity of responses to the Classical tradition (Palter 1996; Norton 1996; Jenkyns 1996).

4 Taplin (1989: 1–33) argues that the Greeks with their religion, social structures and sexual attitudes are very distant from us but at once seem to speak to us so directly, while Beard and Henderson (1995) argue that it is this place of Classics within modern culture that makes it different and more important for Westerners than studying the societies of the Indus valley or the Benin. Earlier generations felt that the connection between modernism and the Classics was more direct and Mackail (1925: 3–4) argued that 'classics are . . . at once the roots and soil out of which the modern world has grown, and from which . . . it draws life through a thousand fibres' and (p. 219)

> [from Graeco-Roman civilization], as a matter not of argumentative theory but of plain historical fact, we derive our institutions, our ways of

life, our methods of thinking and acting . . . In our world . . . nothing moves that is not derived from Greece, nothing stands that is not derived from Rome.

Compare Livingstone 1916. This feeling of connection lies behind the furore over the African contribution to Hellenic culture. Bernal (1987; 1991) brought the theories of an African origin for Classical culture from the fringes of academia to serious critical attention. The debate concerned the status of historical facts and the nature of academic discourse (Jenkyns 1996; Lefkowitz and Rogers 1996). Yet, in Lefkowitz's response (1996), one of the fundamental premises of the argument was not challenged: that the heritage of Classical culture is linked in a peculiarly direct way with modern civilization.

5 After the demise of the East India Company, it was thought that the British empire's officials were less corrupt than their ancient equivalents (Cromer 1910: 50). The financial relationship between the colonies and the mother country was rather different from that between the provinces and Rome and whereas the influence of the empire on Rome was great, several writers deny rather oddly that the empire had much effect on British domestic politics (Cromer 1910: 41–5; Bryce 1914: 71). Also the nature of the territories and the pattern of acculturation of the conquered peoples was very different (Cromer 1910: 73–91).

6 There is a huge bibliography on the consumer model, see Whittaker 1993; 1990; Jongman 1988; Engels 1990; Morley 1996; 1997; Parkins 1997; Andreau 1987–9; Bruhns 1985.

7 Finley and the Braudelians prefer to speak through the narrative of their histories. The invisibility of its historiographic theory is such that historians who follow a Braudelian line sometimes deny that their approach involves any general historical theoretical position (Bagnall 1995).

8 Laurence (1997) has recently surveyed images of ancient urbanism in modern historiography, pointing to the prevalence of dystopic visions of ancient Rome which he associates with modern urban concerns.

9 Mumford 1991: 174–5, argues that the Greek city was

> neither too small nor too big, neither too rich nor too poor, it kept the human personality from being dwarfed by its own collective products, whilst fully utilising all the urban agents of co-operation and communion. Never had any city, no matter how big, harboured and fostered such a multitude of creative personalities as were drawn together in Athens for about a century. That is the most important fact about it; but if we lacked the written documents, the stones of Athens would not tell the story.

Cf. p. 198.

10 Clearly Rome could not have attained the standards of sanitation of many modern cities and this has sociological and medical implications. But a text such as Juvenal, *Satire III*, which inspires much of the dystopic literature on Rome, sits happily within a genre noted for hyperbole and uses the city as a symbol of social chaos and moral decline (Edwards 1996: 126–7). It thus no more deserves to be taken as an accurate description of social conditions than the reflections of country life in the pastoral of the Augustan age.

11 The colonnades that crossed so many of the provincial cities of the Roman empire are architecturally simple, but not easy to understand: are they just symbols of *Romanitas* or in hiding the spaces behind the columns and in emphasizing the line of the street, do they perform a more complex spatial function which should tell us something fundamental about the city? In the face of such problems, Segal 1997 falls back on aesthetic value.

12 History has been an ideological battleground for social theorists, though much of that history has contained a strong spatial element, considering issues within specific spatial frames or being extremely conscious of the flows of peoples and goods, as with the *Annales* school. Disciplinary divisions seem to be more an effect of institutional preferences than deeper ideological dichotomies, and geography and history have responded to and influenced new thinking about the world in similar ways. I do not deny the differences between geographical and historical approaches, only these seem less important than ideological fissures which run through disciplines.

13 Soja (1989: 1) argues that history has had a privileged relationship with social theory but that history is being replaced by spatial analysis, though such an adversarial projection of sociological debate seems somewhat extreme.

14 The Tom Van Sant and The Geosphere Project (1990) satellite map of the world has to be projected onto a flat surface and in so doing chooses a particular projection with the ideological consequences inherent in that choice. Equally notably, the world depicted is a world without weather.

15 Benko argues that the rise of post-modernism is a feature of an intellectual crisis on the left relating to the failure of the Marxist regimes of Eastern Europe and elsewhere, and a similar sense of the failure of the modern project on the right arising from the 'crisis' of capitalism in the 1970s and early 1980s.

16 Architects sometimes worry about the activities of bees, especially their abilities to transmit complex spatial messages through dance, and to build; cf. Mumford 1991: 11; 14; Virgil, *Georgics* IV; *Aeneid* XII 587–92.

17 Morris (1987: 32–3) argues that funeral rituals are important in establishing the continuation of social bonds even after the death of socially significant individuals.

18 It is arguable that this investment in building has now been broken or is in danger of being broken in the West. The advent of telecommunications and information technology, the fragmentation of communities, the decline of large industrial employers all erode the sense of spatiality. One may talk of a 'virtual office', 'home pages', and 'hyperspace', of an existence which has only the most marginal material spatiality. Location is of only minor importance in this technology and the ability of the *world wide* web to elide topography is startling. Perhaps, then, we need to invest less in our building, if our being can be transmitted by electrons.

19 Smith (1993) argues that landscapes attract partly because of a sense that they have escaped the flux of time and achieved completeness. People are moved by mountains, deserts, forests, wildernesses that render the human insignificant and in which the religious might see the hand of their maker: there is a poetic in the immense which is often lost if the human intervenes. It is a poetic that also lies in the human archaic, the sense that 'medieval towns' have slipped through the destructiveness of the modern, and thus establish a place in the world in which values and identity can reside.

20 One of the more puzzling factors in sociological debates is the prevalence of spatial metaphors such as 'sexual orientation' which may ultimately be related to 'real' geographical practice.

21 Lipietz (1997) uses the metaphor of weaving to describe social formation through individual agency: the individual threads are constrained to follow similar patterns which form a describable whole. This may be a little too ordered a metaphor of society since weaving is a consciously productive activity and the threads do not simply come together of their own accord.

22 Mitchell's (1988: 26–8) description of the way in which the Western viewers disguised their identity in Egypt by covering themselves in cloth and wearing dark glasses suggests that contemporary ideological representations of objectivity had a physical manifestation.

23 These criticisms are a little unfair. Pratt 1992 emphasizes the variety of reactions to the newly acquired empires among the geographers and scientists she studies and Driver 1992 is ultimately sympathetic to the methodology deployed by Said and others. It may be argued (Alston 1996; Cormack 1994) that a necessary first step in understanding imperialism is to assess the imperialist agenda rather than decentring imperialism, making it an issue of the provinces rather than of the imperialistic state.

3 HOUSES

1 Papyrologists show a tremendous capacity to generate typologies. Such listing is a considerable aid in editing texts and extremely useful for historical work, see, for example, Rowlandson 1996.

2 Recent excavations at the military sites of the Eastern Desert and at the village of Kellis on the edge of the Dakhleh Oasis in the Western Desert have also produced large numbers of papyri with an adequate archaeological context.

3 The authorities cited here all make extensive use of ethnographic or literary material in their interpretation of the spatiality of the particular houses.

4 When archaeologists write about the social structure of houses, they tend to import anthropological and ethnographic material.

5 As Nevett (1997: 282) puts it, 'a dialectical relationship exists between social and spatial behaviour'.

6 The excavations reflect a pre-1945 scientific methodology. See Maehler 1983; Alston 1995: 118–42.

7 Much of the following analysis is based on the maps in Husselman 1979.

8 These are comparable with the figures for Ptolemaic house areas in Nowicka 1969: 115. The 29 houses listed have a median area of 68 m^2 and a mean area of 86 m^2.

9 The figure for the area of the Dura Europos houses refers to the planned housing rather than the much smaller and irregular houses of other quarters which might be as small as 56 m^2 in individual cases.

10 Even in the example given, house C168, it seems possible that the main living quarters were grouped to one side of the large yard.

11 There are problems with this analysis in that the upper storeys of Karanis houses are not planned or preserved. In the middle-class housing especially, access from outside is frequently complicated by points of access which are only rarely used.

12 One may object that a single point of access to the upstairs makes such clustering more likely, but although one set of stairs saves space, there is no technical reason why there should not be external access to upstairs and in some periods middle-class British housing has made use of two staircases to the upper storeys. In any

case, rooms might be arranged according to a linear plan rather than a clustered plan.

13 Romano-Egyptian houses have been excavated elsewhere in Egypt and reports published, notably from the Fayum (Boak 1935; Rubensohn 1905a) and from Edfu in Upper Egypt, though the state of preservation of the houses from the latter site was insufficient to allow the archaeologists to reconstruct much of the ground plan. The other Fayumic houses appear to be similar to those from Karanis. Fragments of more Hellenized housing have been uncovered near Alexandria (see p. 108) and see p. 102 for some examples of fourth-century houses which probably differ little from the housing of earlier centuries.

14 Husson's (1983a) lexicon of architectural terminology in the papyri is an indispensable guide throughout this section.

15 On towers see Preisigke 1919; Grimal 1939; Nowicka 1972; Husson 1983a: 248–51; Rostem 1962.

16 Figures for the number of village houses by storey excluding houses from Tebtunis have been given here since Tebtunis appears to conform closely to the urban pattern. On the status of Tebtunis, see Alston and Alston 1997 and pp. 324–5.

17 *SB* XX 14681 is a report of a burglary of a house in Bakchias. The thieves gained access through the αὐλή.

18 The distribution of attestations of house prices and numbers of storeys of houses between villages and cities suggests that an evenly distributed feature should be attested 20–30 per cent more often in villages than in cities.

19 Mention of a μέσαυλη (a central courtyard) in a papyrus of AD 540 (*SB* IV 7340) suggests that the distinction between the αὐλή and αἴθριον was sometimes blurred.

20 See also the obscure usage of *P. Lond.* VII 1974 (254 BC).

21 As in other Mediterranean countries, modern Egypt shows a certain vertical zoning with the more wealthy families living towards the top of apartment blocks. Towers appear quite commonly in other arid regions (Negev 1980; see also Grimal 1939; Jones 1973 for agricultural towers). These are not to be confused with the frequently attested watchtowers which had a military or policing purpose: Alston 1995: 81–2; Alt 1920; Meyer 1920.

22 I have found thirteen references to this feature dating from the first three centuries AD, while there are about twenty-three attestations from the next four centuries, a preponderance of attestations being from villages in the early period and from urban sites in the later period. The significance of this distribution is not obvious.

23 There is no guarantee that the housing stock attested in the sale documents is representative, but the processes by which houses reached the market are not easily established.

24 Urban prices: First century: *P. Oxy.* XXXIV 2720; I 99; II 334; II 331 = *SB* XVI 12391; II 333; *PSI* IX 1183 = *CPL* 170.
    Second century: *P. Oxy.* III 577; 513 = W. *Chr.* 183 = *Sel. Pap.* I 77; *SB* XX 14199; *P. Strasb.* I 34; *CPR* I 223; *BGU* XI 2092; *Stud. Pal. Pap.* XX 12; *P. Dublin* 10.
    Third century: *P. Oxy.* XIV 1634; X 1276; X 1284; XIX 2236; XIV 1701; VI 980; *P. Palau Ribs* 11 = *SB* XVI 12537; *P. Lond.* III, p. 154, 1164 c, e, f, k; III 1158; III 1298; *P. Lips* I 3 = M. *Chr.* 172; *Stud. Pal. Pap.* V 119 IV = *Sel. Pap.* II 357; XX 72 = *CPR* I 9; *P. Hamb.* I 14.

Village prices: First century: *P. Vindob. Salomons* 4; *P. Mich.* V 235; X 583; *BGU* XV 2476; XI 2095–2100; *P. Ryl.* II 107; *P. Lond.* II, p. 184, 289 (*BL* I 261); *P. Strasb.* IV 208 (with *BGU* I 184); *PSI* XIII 1319; 1320; *P. Fay.* 100 = *Sel. Pap.* I 177; *P. Oxy.* XLI 2972; *Stud. Pal. Pap.* XXII 23 (*BL* IX, 351); *P. Louvre* I 10.
Second century: *SB* XVI 12957; X 10571; XX 14974; *BGU* I 350; I 282; VII 1643; *P. Hamb.* I 97; *Stud. Pal. Pap.* XX 10 = *CPR* I 5; *CPR* I 11; *P. Lond.* II, p. 211, 334 = *Sel. Pap.* I 76; *P. Tebt.* II 323 = *M. Chr.* 208; II 580; *P. Fay. Towns* 31 = *M. Chr.* 201; *P. Mich.* VI 427; 428; *P. Vind. Tand.* 26; *P. Ryl.* II 162; *P. Amh.* II 97 (*BL* IX, 97); *P. Petaus* 10; 14; *P. Oxy.* IV 719; *P. Oxy.* LII 3691.
Third century: *P. Hamb.* I 15; *BGU* II 667; *P. Gen.* I 44 = *M. Chr.* 215; *CPR* I 3; I 147; *P. Oxy.* XIV 1699.
See also Alston 1997a; Gendy 1990; Drexhage 1991; Montevecchi 1941.

25 The flimsy nature of the data explains the differences between the data here presented and those in Alston (1997a) and Alston and Alston (1997). I have taken a slightly more robust attitude to incomplete or otherwise difficult texts. A small number of additional texts have been included and a number of errors have been corrected by new readings. The conclusions are not thereby substantially altered. One could deploy more complex statistical measures to smooth the data but the scatter graph (figure 3.9) is perhaps the clearest guide.

26 Since this study depends on relative prices, inflation is not a significant analytical problem.

27 Caesar (*De Bell. Alex.* I 18), besieged in Alexandria by the forces of King Ptolemy, found that the buildings (possibly houses) were so closely packed that the continuous line of their towers could be used as fortifications.

28 Interestingly, the pattern for urban prices is paralleled for village prices and one must presume that the explanation is similar, though from figure 3.11, the development in villages appears to be a century earlier. I would not, however, see the chronological difference as necessarily being significant given the uneven distribution of data from second-century villages and the aforementioned paucity of data. The median/mean comparison of the 150-year periods suggest no differential development between cities and villages.

29 Sale of fraction of house: *P. Oxy.* XXIV 2720 (1/12); I 99 (1/2); XLI 2972 (1/2); II 331 (= *SB* XVI 12391) (2/3; 1/3); 335 (1/6); III 577 (2/3); LII 3691 (1/8); IV 719 (1/2); XIV 1648 (1/4); X 1276 (1/2); 1284 (1/2); XIV 1701 (1/2); XIV 1703 (1/3); *SB* I 5247 (1/5); *P. Ryl.* II 107; (1/2; 1/4); 161 (1/4); 160a (2/5); 160d (2/7); 162 (1/2); 289 (1/4); *P. Mich.* II 123 (1/3; 1/2; 1/10; 1/2; V 245 (with *Enchoria* 13 (1985), p. 67) (1/2); 253 (1/2 of 2 rooms); 257 (1/4); 235 (1/2); 269–71 (1/2); 276 (1/14); 288–9 (fraction); 296 (1/2); 299 (1/2); 304 (1/2); VI 427 (1/2); X 583 (1/3; 1/9); *PSI* III 151 (1/3); VIII 907 (1/2); 908 (2/3); 910 (1/4); 912 (2/5); 913 (*P. Mich.* V 298) (1/5); 914 (= *P. Mich.* V 307) (2/5); 915 (1/2); XIII 1320 (1/2); *P. Vind. Tand.* 25 (1/10); 26 (1/3); *P. Tebt.* II 350 (1/2); 580 (1/4); *P. Strasb.* I 31 (1/2; share; 1/8; 1/4); IV 208 (1/9); V 585 (1/2?; 5/18); *BGU* I 243 (3/4?); 350 (1/3); VII 1643 (1/3); XI 2095 (1/2); *P. Fay. Towns* 31 (1/5); 100 (1/2); *CPR* I 3 (1/3); 11 (1/4); 187 (1/4); 191 (1 room); 223 (1/9; 1/36); *P. Hamb.* I 97 (1/2); 14 (2/3); 15 (2/15); *P. Lond.* II, p. 110, 297b (1/2); II, p. 211, 334 (1/42); III, p. 151, 1158 (1/3); III, p. 152, 1298 (1/3); III, p. 154, 1164c (1/2); 1164d (1/3); 1164e (1/3; 1/4); 1164f (1/2); 1164k (1/3); *Stud. Pal. Pap.* XX 10 (1/2); *P. Amh.* II 97 (1/2); *P. Bingen* 105 (1/4); *P. Petaus* 14 (1/3; 2/3); 15 (1/3; 1/5); *P. Gen.* I 44 (9/16); *P. Corn.* 12 (5/12); *P. Louvre* I 10 (1/8).
Sale of whole house: *P. Mich.* II 123 (9 sales); III 191 & 192; V 249; 277; 293;

294; 300; VI 428; *P. Oxy.* II 334; III 513; XIV 1696; 1698; 1699; 1634; 1700; 1701; XII 1475; VI 980; *SB* I 5246; X 10571; XII 11233; XIV 11895 (= *BGU* III 854); *CE* 121 (1986), p. 104; *P. Strasb.* I 31; 34; IV 602; *PSI* III 909; 911; *BGU* II 667; III 748; XV 2476; *P. Ryl.* II 160b; 160c; 310; *CPR* I 120; *P. Tebt.* II 323; *Stud. Pal. Pap.* XX 12; 72; *P. Petaus* 13; *P. Gen.* I 44; *P. Flor.* I 47(?); *P. Lips.* 3; *P. Louvre* I 9.

Sale of indeterminate portion: *P. Oxy.* II 333; *P. Tebt.* II 351; *PSI* XIII 1319; *P. Louvre* I 8. For house rentals see Müller 1985: 142, n. 1; 145, n. 2; Sijpesteijn 1995; *SB* XVI 13005; 12583.

30 This may have been to provide space to expand their existing properties or (and perhaps more likely) to install family members or dependants in neighbouring residences.

31 Males became liable for poll tax in their fourteenth year.

32 Bagnall and Frier (1994: 103, n. 35) suggest a ratio of poll tax payers to population of 1:2.909. There are considerable difficulties in accepting Bagnall and Frier's model population, as the authors themselves frequently stress, but their model is the most sophisticated and plausible reconstruction of the demographics of the province and I use their figures extensively throughout this chapter.

33 Given the fragmentary nature of many of the returns, these figures can only be an estimate.

34 Bagnall and Frier (1994: 13) state that declarations were probably by household, but their distinction is between a household which contained lodgers and a family and they do not adopt a terminological distinction between houseful and household. The returns analysed by Bagnall et al. 1997 are by household.

35 Although there is no obvious distinction in the language of the text that would allow us to decide whether we were dealing with households or housefuls, the fact that one unit is headed by a woman, Kyrilla, suggests that the text is organized by house not household.

36 Village families showed a greater tendency to form households with complex family structures: 51 per cent of urban 'households' were constructed around a conjugal family (26 per cent of 'households' being formed based on families with more complex structures) compared with only 37 per cent of rural 'households' (33 per cent having families with complex structures). When these different family structures are analysed, both conjugal and extended families in cities tend be slightly larger than their village equivalents.

37 The data are drawn from the catalogue of returns in Bagnall and Frier (1994: 181–312) using only complete entries of 'households'. I have taken a conservative view of the data.

38 The urban medians also fluctuate, even for the best-represented periods (everything being relative). The village pattern is more stable, probably reflecting the greater quantity of the surviving returns, but even here there are fluctuations, with medians falling in the mid-second century and rising in the late second and third centuries.

39 We might expect that conjugal family would be comparatively stable in size across long periods provided that marriage patterns did not change. Birth control was exercised through the formation of conjugal units rather than within the conjugal relationship. Wrigley (1987: 223) points to the crucial role of nuptiality by arguing that 'in seeking to understand the remarkable pace at which English population grew in the eighteenth century, we should look to nuptiality as the principal immediate reason for the acceleration that occurred'. Family size was

mainly limited by controlling marriage and not by wider economic and social factors in the first instance.

40 An unstable population with a high intrinsic growth rate which suffers occasional catastrophic population declines may be rather difficult to differentiate from a more stable population simply by examining the age-structure of the population. Population growth might paradoxically produce an age-profile that would suggest lower life expectancy than was, in fact, the case (cf. Herlihy 1967).

41 This position represents something of a retreat from that taken up by Alston 1997a.

42 One may argue that if relations living in the same house formed separate households, this should be seen as a more potent statement of their relationship than any assumptions based upon genealogical connections.

43 In Latin and Greek, the words for house, *domus* and οἶκος, carried the same implications of household and family that in modern English are attached to aristocratic 'houses' such as the House of Windsor.

44 The methodology used to calculate houseful and household size is dependent on Hobson's article.

45 The statistical analysis was performed by my brother Robert D. Alston to whom I once more give thanks.

46 A loose kin-based unit such as the *consorteria* of medieval Italy would not be detectable on the basis of nomenclature. Even the topographical unity of *consorteria* territories was comparatively vague, though, of course, their social existence was symbolized by the towers that dominated so many North Italian cities.

47 Priestly compounds are the exception that proves the rule since they represent a religiously divided, coherent group within Egyptian society whose distinctiveness can be represented in the spatial patterns of that society.

48 Compare Girouard's (1978: 242) remarks on the sudden revival of Classical and crenallated frontages in the country house of the early nineteenth century, which he sees as a response to the social uncertainties engendered by the French Revolution and related political radicalism.

49 See the discussion of divisions other than that between public and private within the household in George 1997a.

50 See Montserrat et al. 1994: 44–7.

51 Ovid, *Ars. Am.* I 229–52; 565–630 recommends dinner as a moment to pick up a girl.

52 Rental: *SB* X 10278; *P. Fam. Tebt.* 31 (AD 144); *P. Oxy.* VIII 1128 (AD 173); *BGU* I 253 *BL* I, 99 (AD 244–9); *P. Panop.* I 13 = *SB* XIII 10980 (with ἐξέδρα; AD 339); *P. Oxy.* XLIV 3203 (AD 400); *P. Oxy.* XVI 1957 (AD 430); *P. Oxy.* VIII 1129 (AD 449); *P. Yale* I 71 (AD 456); *PSI* III 175 (462). The rental periods were normally for one or two years and there is no evidence for rental for a specific party, though this may have happened in the temple dining rooms.
Sale: *CPR* I 95 (with other property?; 3rd cent.); *P. Münch.* 84 (AD 211); *SB* XII 11225 (with house; AD 425–50); *P. Oxy.* XX 2270 *BL* VIII, 256 (5–6th cent.).
Other attestations: *P. Ryl.* II 233 = *Sel. Pap.* I 123 *BL* III, 161 (dining room for estate workers?; AD 118); *Pap. Choix* 7 (AD 136); *P. Brem.* I 15 = *CPJ* II 446 (2nd cent.); *P. Oxy.* I 76 (AD 179); *P. Fuad I Univ.* 25 (2nd or 3rd cent.); *P. Oxy.* LXI 4120 (AD 287); *P. Flor.* I 5 (3rd cent.); *P. Oxy.* VIII 1159 (3rd cent.); *P. Oxy.* XXXVI 2784 (3rd cent.); *PSI* VI 698 *BL* VIII, 400.

53 Patermouthis archive: *P. Lond.* V 1722; 1723; 1724; 1733; 1734; *P. Münch.* I 8;

9; 11;12. Other sixth- or seventh-century references: *P. Oxy.* L 3600; *SB* I 5112; VI 8987; 8988; *P. Harr.* II 238.

54 See *SB* XVIII 13320 = *P. Mich.* XIII 665 for a house named Pselch.

55 Wills, especially Roman wills, appear to have been opened in the main agora or forum of the local city.

56 See pp. 92–3 for a discussion of these status groups.

57 The evidence of Roman social patterns also seems unsettling. The influential and quite recent view that family structures tended, in normal circumstances, to be nuclear in the imperial period has come under pressure and an increased consciousness of the complexity of social relations within households (including slaves, freed and perhaps others) and families and issues of individual and family identity threatens to break down traditional conceptions of family structure (D. Martin 1996 (with bibliography given there); Hope 1997; Saller and Shaw 1984; Saller 1984; 1994: 74–101). The patterns of public donations within municipalities have also raised issues of the relationship of individual and family to the wider community (van Bremen 1996; F. Martin 1996a; 1996b).

58 There are various forms in which access to public space might be limited and different ways in which the boundary could be placed. See Ardener 1993.

59 Walker and Bierbrier 1997: no. 11; 15; 16; 17; 18; 19; 33; 34; 35; 37; 38; 39; 40; 41; 42; 49; 50; 51; 52; 53; 76; 77; 86; 89; 90; 91; 92; 93; 96; 99; 101; 103; 104; 106; 108; 111; 122; 180; 181. Of the women depicted in the mummy portraits only an elderly woman, no. 79, is shown without jewellery. Walker and Bierbrier (1997: 162–76) discuss the jewellery found in Petrie's excavations at Hawara. For the statues from Oxyrhynchus see Schneider 1982: 34; 37; 38; 39.

60 One can compare this with the rather later *SB* VI 9107, which records the sending of 10 ducks to add to the wedding feast of George, a comes (count) of the Byzantine period. See Bell 1950.

61 This seems more plausible an interpretation of Tryphon's dealings with his second wife than Whitehorne's (1984) suggestion that he was reluctant to commit following his bruising break-up with his previous wife. For Tryphon see also Biscottini 1966 and Brewster 1927.

62 A comparatively relaxed attitude is suggested by Pharaonic wisdom literature, which seems to suggest that physical attraction was a major motivating factor in marriages and that girls consulted their mothers as to the suitability of partners rather than relying on the business sense of their fathers (Depla 1994).

63 Schneider 1975 notes that the care lavished on the depiction of jewellery in the grave-reliefs contrasts with the crudity with which feet and hands are treated.

64 In an age when infanticide was socially acceptable, the unwanted could have been exposed or, through a ritual exposure and recovery, adopted as a slave and hence would not be entitled to inherit.

65 The common ancient definition of adultery is rather different from the modern usage. For the ancients, adultery was a married woman having sex with someone who was not her husband and the male adulterer was the participant in that sexual act. A married man who had sex with a slave or an unmarried woman was not, in the common ancient sense, an adulterer.

66 See, for instance, *P. Ant.* I 36, a complaint about an anti-social individual (Antinoos) which mentions adultery in a fragmentary line at the end of the text.

67 The reading here is difficult, only the first two letters of γάμον (marriage) being clear.

68 In an earlier period Attiaena should have been given some protection by a guardian and should still have been protected if she was under twenty-five. By the fourth century, however, the institution of guardianship was in decline (Arjava 1996: 112–23). Given that Constantine had issued terrible threats against those who took part in such 'abduction marriages' (possibly repealed by this date: *C. Th*. IX 24; Evans Grubbs 1989; 1995; Arjava 1996: 37–41), Attiaena's inability to bring him to justice might suggest that there were layers of complexity to this case that are not made obvious in this petition.

69 See Pestman 1961 on the capability of women in Egyptian law.

70 Goody 1983: 29 argues that there was a considerable emphasis on virginity with young brides in early Europe but that attitudes towards the sexual activity of older women were probably very different. The social logic of this is not entirely clear, but does offer a possible parallel with and explanation for the Egyptian material.

71 For the importance of the gymnasial group, see pp. 86–7.

72 Such emotional investment in houses may be unusual. For the Roman elite, for instance, houses were both an economic and a social investment and there was a certain reluctance to sell property they had inherited from their parents. Yet, the Roman aristocrat moved, built new houses and constructed new spaces which were invested with religious and social power. The family gods were transferred from one residence to the next. The Tiswana had family spirits residing in their courtyards so that the house was connected with the past and also, since time gets confused in religious contexts, the house embodied the future: what would survive to the next generation. There was a cycle of emotional investment. Yet the Tiswana could also change residence, after elaborate religious ceremonies (Werner 1985).

73 Those wishing to break into a house brought an axe with them. See, for example, *P. Oxy* LX 4082.

74 When the religious bubble that sustained el-Amarna burst and the bureaucrats and the powerful moved away, they took their lintels and doorposts with them.

75 Patlagean 1977: 118–28 argues that the popularity of endogamous marriage from the fourth century reflected social uncertainties.

76 Scheidel 1996: 1–38 argues that such inbreeding will have had a genetically significant effect.

77 The nature of royal sibling marriages is not attested. It is impossible to know whether the royals involved had a 'normal' attitude to incestuous relations which they were able to overcome, and Roman emperors' alleged incestuous unions are also problematic. The ancient historian does not have access to the secrets of royal marriage beds.

78 There is a huge scholarly industry devoted to Philo. Radice (1983) lists 1,095 items published on Philo between 1937 and 1982.

79 The *Legatio ad Gaium* and the *In Flaccum* (an account of the persecution of the Jews under the prefect Flaccus), being justificatory texts concerning the pogroms of AD 38, provide good examples of this 'dual audience'. At first, they would seem to be addressed to a predominantly gentile audience, to explain the wickedness of Flaccus and Gaius in allowing and encouraging the mistreatment of the Jews. Yet Philo's demonstration that the Jews were ultimately protected and avenged by God is a primarily theological argument which could bolster Jewish resistance to the gentile threat. Compare Eusebius, *HE*, which shows the triumph of the Church over its persecutors, and Lactantius, *De Mortibus Persecutorum* (*On the*

Deaths of the Persecutors), for similarly intentioned works. Another possibility lies in the discipline of Philo's chosen genre. Philo wrote within a Greek philosophical tradition which made assumptions of shared knowledge of Greek customs but often gave ethnographic details about other cultures. Very much as Procopius, the Byzantine historian, felt obliged to explain elements of Christian practice which must have been known to his audience because they were foreign to the historiographic tradition in which he placed himself, it seems to me possible that Philo wrote within a Greek tradition to which these Jewish elements were foreign and thus required explanation, even if most of his audience already had a working knowledge of Judaism.

80 David Noy suggested to me that Philo's whole description is an idealized *topos*, but one derived from fifth-century Athenian domestic arrangements rather than Jewish literature. This is certainly attractive in that there are obvious parallels with Athenian arrangements, though it seems to me more likely that Philo's depiction of the house reflects similar, though not identical, ideological concerns.

81 The Egyptian emphasis on the continuity of the needs of life in death (which meant in the Pharaonic period representations of goods and sometimes artefacts necessary to maintain the deceased in the style which he or she had been used to in life) increases the likelihood that tombs would have had some resemblance to houses. The layout of these tombs seems very similar to Greek-style houses attested elsewhere. For the mix of Greek and Egyptian cultures in the tombs see the beautiful example from Kom el Shoqafa published by Guimier-Sorbets (1999), which contains two decorative schemes, one of Isis and Osiris and the other of Persephone, both of which centre on resurrection.

82 In the *In Flaccum*, this claim is made in order to demonstrate the extent of the violation that occurred when Flaccus ordered troops to search the Jewish houses for weapons and thus the maidens of the household, who would have blushed at the gaze of the closest male relatives, were displayed before the eyes of the Roman soldiery. There was no similar rhetorical device in the *De Specialibus Legibus*.

83 See Sly 1990 on Philo's treatment of women generally and pp. 195–8 on Alexandrian women.

84 The whole passage in the *De Specialibus Legibus* is problematic and not merely because of the evident contradictions. The destination of the travelling woman is the temple, of which there were only two in the Jewish world, one at Jerusalem and one at Leontopolis. The *De Specialibus Legibus* are, as one would expect, not topographically specific and I suspect the temple was chosen here simply as an example of a place to which the ideal Jewish woman would be travelling.

85 Baker 1998 argues that the house is used consistently as an image of female genitalia, so that the husband's mastery of the house and the 'housing' of the women become images of sexual intercourse.

86 There is a considerable problem in establishing the status of small bath houses. There were public bath houses in Egypt in the pre-Roman period and these continued to function after the conquest, their management contracted out to entrepreneurs (see *P. Mich.* V 312). One of the managers of the baths was a Tiberius Claudius Barbillus, who may be identical with the prominent Alexandrian who led an embassy to Claudius in AD 41 and who is perhaps further to be identified with the prefect of Egypt of AD 55. I see no way of distinguishing between small public baths and private baths from the fragmentary archaeological record. See el-Khashab 1949; Youtie 1949; Wasif 1979; Nielson 1990: no. 279–85.

87 As more houses are excavated from Italy, the diversity over time and place of Roman housing becomes more striking, see George 1997b; Wallace-Hadrill 1997; Bruno and Scott 1993.

88 Smith (1997) argues that changes in villa structure relate to a development in property transmission and ownership that affected family structures. This change may be seen as tangential to Roman cultural influence.

89 The problematic link between identity and housing has been the subject of some recent debate, with Nevett (1995) suggesting that the essential similarities in Greek housing across the Classical Greek world show a sense of Greek identity, while Grahame (1998) argues that divergences between house-types at Pompeii suggest that ethnicity was not a feature of Pompeian culture.

90 The houses at Akhmim are not discussed here since the archaeological remains are so fragmentary that I can make little sense of those that have been published (MacNally and Schrunk 1993).

91 For the documentary material see *P. Kellis* I. For the archaeology of the site see Hope 1987; 1988; 1995; Hope et al. 1989.

92 Many of the fragments of the Kellis texts were dispersed across a single house, though often the texts were in adjacent rooms. The portions of *P. Kellis* 3, however, were found in houses 1 and 3.

93 For an earlier 'villa' see Mysliwiec 1988.

94 Προαστίον is a word used for an extramural or suburban development which is sometimes associated with monastic establishments (Husson 1967).

95 See in addition to the texts listed *PSI* III 193.

96 For the Persian invasion see Altheim-Stiehl 1991 and 1992.

97 For the dating of documents in the archive see Farber and Porten 1986. For Coptic documents in the archive see Clackson 1995. For English translations of all texts, see Porten 1996.

98 *SB* VI 8987 (AD 644–5) attests the sale of a συμπόσιον near a small αἴθριον in the street of Dr Abraham in Oxyrhynchus. *SB* VI 8988 (AD 647, Apollonospolis Magna) concerns a small συμπόσιον above the gate and a small room off the αἴθριον.

99 See also *P. Lond.* III, p. 267, 1023 (Hermopolis, V–VIth cent.) and *P. Oxy.* XLVII 3355 (Oxyrhynchus, AD 535), which attest a sequence of αυλή, well, αἴθριον and δῶμα (main house) (cf. *SB* XII 11225).

100 There are now many publications on the Kom el-Dikke site and related work. The main publication used in this section is M. Rodziewicz 1984 but see also M. Rodziewicz 1976; 1982; 1988; 1991; E. Rodziewicz 1978; Lichocka 1992; Majcherek 1992; Kolataj 1992; Tkaczow 1993. These are summarized in Haas 1997: 189–206.

101 Workshops seem to have been situated along the arcaded streets and may be attested in the excavations at Marea (el-Fakhrani 1983). Similar architectural forms, normally interpreted as shops, are attested across the Roman empire.

102 An intriguing possible parallel comes from the recently discovered Petra papyri which describe houses (οἶκοι) grouped around a court: Koenen 1996. Safrai 1976 describes a similar arrangement in Palestinian-Jewish houses.

103 The continued occupation of the fort after the Arab invasions suggests the integration of military and civilian elements (Dunscombe Colt 1962).

104 There is considerable debate as to whether small local units continued to operate in the late sixth and early seventh centuries. See Harper 1995 and Parker 1986: 149–52.

105 A considerable number of Coptic and Greek papyri from Jeme made their way to the antiquities market. See Wilfong 1989; 1990. For the 'cleared' remains of late Roman houses at Karnak see Chevrier 1939 and Lauffray 1971. A similar clearance was conducted at the temple of Hatschepsout at Deir el-Bahari (Godlewski 1983).

106 Husson's (1990) argument for chronological continuity also implies an absence of significant regional architectural variation.

107 See also Fathy and Grossmann 1994.

108 See Gascou 1985 for a discussion of the private and public role of the Apion estate.

109 At Kom el-Dikke, the community had a different avenue of integration in their shared trade. Christianity is so dominant in the literary and historical tradition that it is tempting to see it as the only cultural force (Beaujard 1996).

110 This is not, of course, a new observation. Herlihy (1985: v–vi) argues that the ancient world had a distinctive asymmetrical household system, which means that households in different sectors of society had very different patterns of organization. He also argues that even in the medieval period, it was only through the extreme pressure of the Church that household structures were gradually regularized and later changed. Saller (1997) argues that 'in practical terms, propertied Romans did not normally rely on kin for daily support and services in so far as they utilized slaves, freedmen and other dependants'. The *domus* (household) was a very significant social unit for the Roman aristocrat and kin played a correspondingly less significant role. Saller does not argue that kin ties did not exist or were unimportant, but that the normal Roman emphasis was on the *domus* as a key social structure rather than the kin, though he acknowledges that this might not have been the case in 'prehistoric' Roman society (by which he means, I think, society before the second century BC). Such insights offer a challenge to the historian of the family to evaluate the significance and strength of the most basic social ties. Simply because families existed, we should not assume that the way people lived in those families remotely resembled our experience (see also Demos 1972). Moreover, Saller has driven a wedge between linguistic and legal descriptions of the family and actual social behaviour. In so doing, he has disturbed the clarity of structuralist approaches (which used such material to develop social rules) and stressed the confusion and variety that was social practice. The corollary of this must be that any description of the family and household must be imperfect since it can never grasp the totality of experience.

4 STREETS, DISTRICTS AND NEIGHBOURHOODS

1 There are many examples that one could choose from modern literature. Westwood and Williams (1997) look to the novels of Salman Rushdie and his depiction of Bombay, and one could add London and other cities, where the fantastic and realistic are intertwined often disturbingly. But the tradition goes back much further and one could cite Joyce's *Ulysses*, a portrait of Dublin no less dislocated or imagined that Rushdie's worlds.

2 Haverfield, in his characteristically cautious way, while commending the Greek and especially the Roman model of town planning to the Town Planners' Conference, noted that the problems that modern planners face were so much more extreme and possibly insoluble because the urban communities they planned for were far larger than those of the Roman empire.

3 Apart from the rather peculiar context of the Memphite temple of Sarapis and associated structures, our knowledge of the Ptolemaic city is extremely sketchy. See Thompson 1988.

4 Thmouis: Second *amphodon*, third district: *P. Thmouis* I 91; 144–5; *PSI* III 230 *BL* VIII, 395.
Fourth *amphodon*: *P. Thmouis* I 160.
Sixth *amphodon*, first district: *P. Thmouis* I 142.
Seventh *amphodon*: *PSI* III 230.
Eighth *amphodon*, first district: *PSI* III 231.
Eleventh *amphodon*: *P. Thmouis* I 119; 160.
Twentieth *amphodon*: *PSI* III 231; 230 *BL* VIII, 395.
Twentieth *amphodon*, first district: *P. Thmouis* I 119.
Unknown *amphoda*: *P. Thmouis* I 146; *PSI* I 107.
Mendes: Second *amphodon*: *P. Thmouis*. I 133.
Seventh *amphodon*: *P. Thmouis* I 92.
Ninth *amphodon*: *P. Thmouis* I 93.
Unknown *amphodon*: *P. Thmouis* I 92.

5 *Stud. Pal. Pap.* XIII, p. 8; 9; *SB* VIII 9745; *O. Edfou* I 70; 78; 82–7; 104–5; 110–11; 115–17; 151–2; 279; 282; 296. Most of these documents are receipts of similar date and were probably deposited as a result of the violence surrounding the Jewish revolt of *c*. AD 117.

6 For other *amphoda*, see *P. Rain. Cent.* 59; *P. Stras.* IV 195; *C. Pap. Gr.* II 1 79.

7 Little is known of Panopolis (Kuhlmann 1983; Al-Masri 1983; Sauneron 1952) since the site of the city appears to have been largely robbed out in the medieval period.

8 Roeder's plan suggests that the wall enclosed an area approximately 637.5 m by more than 1,000 m, but it is unclear what evidence Roeder had for such a long wall. Spencer was only able to detect about 600 m of north–south wall.

9 In Polis East, there was the street of the mat- (or possibly basket-) makers (*P. Flor.* I 13), a basket-makers' street (*P. Flor.* I 47), a street of the temple of Asklepios (*P. Vind. Sal.* 12), and a street of Αλ.μω[..]ς (*SB* VIII 9931). In Phrourion West there was an Asynkretion Street (Ασυγκρητιου) (*P. Cair. Goodsp.* 13), a Jewish street (*P. Amh.* II 98) and a street of Pakouk (*P. Lond.* V 1768). In Phrourion East, there was an Aphaiseos Street (Αφαισεως).

10 For the literary tradition concerning Thebes see Bataille 1951

11 Daris 1981 and Wessely 1902 for earlier discussions of the districts of Ptolemais Euergetis. References to administrative units are listed here.
Alopolion: *P. Fay.* 23 (II. cent); *BGU* III 820 (192/3); *BGU* I 9 = *BGU* IV 1087 = W. *Chr.* 293 (276); *Stud. Pal. Pap.* XX 127 (487); *PSI* IX 1058 (V/VI); *Stud. Pal. Pap.* X 125 (V–VI cent.); *Stud. Pal. Pap.* III 127 (VI).
Ammoniou: Wessely (1902: 18) (105) (see Daris 1981); *SB* I 5808 (124); *BGU* I 55 (175); *BGU* I 89 (163 *BL* I, 17); *BGU* II 493 (II).
Apolloniou Hierakou: *SB* XIV 11270 (96–8); [*P. Lond.* III, p. 26, 1119a (105) *BL* IV, 44, X, 103 (or Paremboles]; *P. Mich.* IX 533 (137); *P. Corn.* I 16 = *SB* XX 14303 (146–7); *P. Tebt.* II 321 (147); *BGU* XV 2471 (158); *CPR* I 246 (162); *BGU* I 55 (175); *P. Fay.* 27 (175) *BL* I, 129; *SB* XVI 13070 (187); *P. Ryl.* II 106 (188); *BGU* I 118 (189); *BGU* XIII 2225 (189); *SB* VI 9618 (192) *BL* VI, 156; *P. Vind. Sal.* 5 (192); *BGU* II 494 (II); *Stud. Pal. Pap.* XX 21 = M. *Chr.* 151 (214); *P. Gen.* I 43 (226); *SB* XVI 13071 (222–35); *P. Vind. Sal.* 14 (242); *BGU* IV 1069 (243–4); *SB* VI 9080 (254–68); *SB* XIV 12173 (IV).

Apolloniou Paremboles: *Stud. Pal. Pap.* IV pp. 58 f. (72–3); [*P. Lond.* III, p. 26, 1119a (105) *BL* IV, 44, X, 103 (or Paremboles]; *P. Mich.* IX 533 (137); *P. Ryl.* II 330 (130); *P. Mich.* XV 695 (143); *P. Corn.* I 16 = *SB* XX 14303 (146–7); *BGU* I 79 (175–6); *SB* XVI 12288 (175–8); *P. Gen.* I 18 (187) *BL* I, 159; *BGU* I 116 (189); *P. Wisc.* II 41 (189); *BGU* II 493 (II); *P. Berl. Leigh.* II 42 (II); *P. Flor.* I 24 = M. *Chr.* 187 (II); *P. Ross. Georg.* V 17 (211); *BGU* II 362 (215); *BGU* II 667 (221–2); *P. Prag.* I 18 = *SB* I 4299 (245); *SB* XX 14584 (253); *P. Laur.* II 24 = *SB* XVI 12498 (III); *P. Prag.* I 14 (III); *SB* XVI 12497 (III); *P. Cair. Isid.* 103 = *SB* V 7675 (313).

Arabon: *P. Warren* 2 (72); *P. Harris* I 70 = *SB* XVIII 13324 (77) *BL* VIII, 147, IX , 301; *P. Merton* III 131 (I–II); *BGU* III 832 (113); *P. Fouad* 15 (119); *P. Grenf.* II 49 (141) *BL* I, 188; *SB* XVI 13008 (144); *SB* XVI 13009 (144); *BGU* I 254 (160); *P. Hamb.* I 15 (209); *P. Lund* VI 10 = *SB* VI 9359 (400).

Bithunon allon topon: *P. Lond.* II, p. 244, 371 (I); *P. Oxf.* 10 (98–117); *SB* VI 9639 (104–5); *P. Med.* 35 (108); *P. Wisc.* II 54 (116); *CPR* VI 1 (125); *P. Ryl.* II 103 = *Sel. Pap.* II 314 (134); *CPR* V 2 (134–6); *Stud. Pal. Pap.* XX 5 (136 cf. *CPR* I 25); *PSI* VIII 921 (143/4); *P. Lond.* II, p. 218, 308 (145); [*P. Stras.* III 240 (147)]; *P. Gen.* I 19 (147–8) *BL* I 160; *Stud. Pal. Pap.* XXII 31 = *SB* XVI 13072 (155); *BGU* XIII 2230 (159–60); *P. Strasb.* VI 547 (161–9); [*BGU* XIII 2224 (175)?]; *P. Mich* XV 697 (177); *BGU* I 115 = *W. Chr.* 203 (187–8); *PSI* IV 314 (195); *BGU* II 510 (II); *BGU* III 907 (II); *P. Berl. Leigh.* II 42 (II); *P. Ross. Georg.* II 36 f (II); *P. Grenf.* II 62 (211); *Stud. Pal. Pap.* XX 31 (230); *Stud. Pal. Pap.* II, p. 32 (257–8); *SB* XVIII 13305 (271); *BGU* II 373 (298); *P. Sakaon* 60 (306); *SB* XVI 12889 (309); *P. Mich.* IX 574 (IV).

Bithunon Isionos (topon): *PSI* Congr. XV 15 (80); *Stud. Pal. Pap.* XXII 86 (86); *P. Fay.* 31 = M. *Chr.* 201 (129); *BGU* I 111 (138–9); *P. Prag.* I 40 (141); *PSI* VIII 921 (143–4); [*P. Stras.* III 240 (147)?]; *BGU* II 468 (151); *SB* XII 10806 (153); *P. Flor.* I 97 (155); [*P. Stras.* V 302 (155)?]; *BGU* XIII 2230 (159–60); [*BGU* XIII 2224 (175)?]; *BGU* I 128 (188); *BGU* I 115 = *W. Chr.* 203 (187–8); *BGU* I 116 (189); *BGU* I 118 (189); *P. Fay.* 23 (II); *P. Ross. Georg.* II 35 (II); *BGU* II 496 (II); *P. Stras.* V 324 (c.200); *BGU* XI 2086 (235); *BGU* I 253 (244–9) *BL* I, 99; *P. Cair. Isid.* 80 = *SB* VI 9267 (296); *P. Cair. Isid* 81 (297); *SB* VI 9069 (III); *P. Sakaon* 59 (305); *SB* XVI 12889 (309); *Stud. Pal. Pap.* XX 139 (531); *SB* VIII 9755 (VI); *Stud. Pal. Pap.* XX 219 (604); *P. Prag.* I 49 (628); *SB* XVI 12481 (668); *Stud. Pal. Pap.* III 355 (VII–VIII).

Boubasteiou (Mikrou Boubasteiou): *BGU* I 118 (189); *P.Ross. Georg.* II 36 (II); *BGU* III 820 (II); *P. Fay.* 23 (II); *BGU* XI 2086 (235); *P. Corn.* 20 (302).

Boutapheion: *P. Stras.* VIII 706 (122–3); *SB* I 5808 (124); *CPR* I 206 (117–36); *CPR* I 223 (117–36); *P. Lond.* II, p. 150, 299 = *W. Chr.* 204 (128); *P. Ryl.* II 279 = *SB* XVIII 13956 (138–61); *P. Grenf.* II 49 (141) *BL* I, 188; *P. Ryl.* II 360 (160); *P. Ross. Georg.* II 35 (II); *BGU* I 9 = *BGU* IV 1087 = *W. Chr.* 293 (276); *BGU* XI 2034 (II–III).

Gymnasiou: [*BGU* XI 2099 (83)]; *P. Merton* II 67 (130); *P. Mil. Vogl.* III 145 (142) *BL* VII, 120, IX, 168; *SB* XX 14303 = *P. Corn.* I 16 (146–7); *P. Oslo.* III 132 (147–56); *BGU* II 619 (155); *P. Heid.* III 239 (164); *P. Fay.* 108 (171); *PSI* X 1105 (173); *BGU* I 123 (173–4); *P. Mich.* XII 628 = *SB* XII 10923 (183); *BGU* I 115 = *W. Chr.* 203 (187–8); [*BGU* I 138 (187–8) *BL* X, 13); *SB* XIV 11355 (188–9); *BGU* I 116 (189); *SB* XIV 11268 (189); *BGU* XI 2120 (II); *P. IFAO* I 27 (II); *Stud. Pal. Pap.* XX 12 (II–III); *BGU* III 989 = M. *Chr.* 989 (226); *SB* XX 14584 (253); *P. Turner* 37 (270); *BGU* I 9 = *BGU* IV 1087 = W.

Chr. 293 (276); *P. Thead.* 54 (299); *P. Laur.* II 24 = *SB* XVI 12498 (III); *P. Prag.* I 14 (III); *SB* XVI 12497 (III); *P. Sakaon* 2 = *ChLA* XLI 1205 (300); *P. Sakaon* 3 = *ChLA* XLI 1206 (300); *P. Lond.* I, p. 211, 113 5(b) (543).

Demetriou [Probably not an *amphodon*]: *BGU* II 573; 601; VII 1623.

Dionysiou topon: *SB* X 10759 (35) *BL* X, 205; *P. Heid.* II 219 = *SB* VI 9539 (100); *P. Oxf.* 8 (104–5); *P. Fay.* 98 (123); *CPR* I 223 (117–36); *PSI* IX 1064 = *Sel. Pap.* II 310 (129); *BGU* I 355 (140–1); *PSI* VIII 921 (143–4); *BGU* III 891 (144); *P. Meyer* 9 (147); *P. Ryl.* II 88 (156); *PSI* III 189 (157–61); *SB* XX 14111 (160–1); *P. Ryl.* II 111 (161); *P. Fay.* 283 (166–7); *P. Vind. Worp* 5 (169); *P. Fay.* 280 (174); *BGU* XIII 2224 (175); *SB* XIV 11642 (178); *SB* XVI 13067 (175–88); *P. Prag.* I 63 (180); [*BGU* I 138 (187–8) *BL* X, 13]; *SB* XIV 11268 (189); *P. Vind. Sal.* 5 (192); *P. Warren* 6 (198–9); *BGU* XI 2034 (II–III); *P. Stras.* IV 192 (207); *P. Hamb.* I 14 (209–10); *CPR* I 21 = *Stud. Pal. Pap.* XX 31 (230); *SB* I 4299 (245); *P. Sakaon* 59 (305); [*BGU* III 838 (578): Dionysiou not Dionysiou Topon].

Helleniou: [*SB* XIV 11269 (I)]; *BGU* I 133 (144–5); *BGU* VII 1581 (147); *P. Gen.* I 19 (147–8) *BL* I 160; *SB* XIV 11603 (157–9); *BGU* I 18 = W. *Chr.* 398 = *Sel. Pap.* II 342 (169) *P. Fay.* 108 (171); *BGU* I 55 (175) *BL* I, 12–13; *P. Ups. Frid* 8 (150–200); [*BGU* II 508 (II)]; *BGU* II 570 (II); *BGU* VII 1677 (II); *SB* V 8263 (II); *P. Flor.* I 19 (209); *BGU* I 144 (III).

Hermiouthakes: *SB* VI 9639 (104–5); *P. Lond.* III, p. 25, 1119a = *CPJ* II 430 (105) *BL* IV, 44; *PSI* VIII 921 (143–4); *P. Fay.* 28 (150–1); *P. Ryl.* II 111a (c. 161); *BGU* IV 1016 (166); *BGU* IV 1046 = W. *Chr.* 265 (166–7) *BL* VI, 14; *P. Ups. Frid* 8 (150–200); *P. Stras.* IV 238 (177–8); *P. Vind. Sijp.* 12 (184); *PSI* IV 314 (195); *BGU* III 971 (195–6); *P. Berl. Leigh.* II 42B (II); *P. Flor.* I, p. 49, n.3 (II); *P. Hamb.* I 14 (209–10); *BGU* XI 2086 (235); *BGU* I 9 = *BGU* IV 1087 = W. *Chr.* 293 = *BGU* XIII 2280 (276); *P. Flor.* III 376 (III); *P. Sakaon* 67 (321) *BL* VIII, 302; *Stud. Pal. Pap.* X 125 (V–VI).

Therapeias: *P. Stras.* VI 502 = *SB* XVI 12686 (67–9); *P. Col.* VIII 213 (84–105); *SB* XVIII 13233 (102); *P. Hawara* 323 = *Archiv* 5 (1913), 389 (102); *BGU* II 562 = W. *Chr.* 220 (after 103–4); *P. Merton* I 15 = *P. Wisc.* II 80 (114); *P. Fam. Tebt.* 23 (123); *P. Hawara* 308 = *Archiv.* 5 (1913), 393 (131); *SB* XVI 13240 (131); *SB* XII 10842 (133); *P. Tebt.* II 329 (139); *SB* XVI 13006 (144); *SB* XVI 13007 (144); *P. Mil. Vogl.* II 56 (152–3); *Stud. Pal. Pap.* XXII 31 = *SB* XVI 13072 (155); *P. Erl.* 22 (160–1); *P. Flor.* I 67 (161–9); *P. Mil. Vogl.* III 132 = *SB* VI 9313 (165) *BL* VII, 119; *P. Mil Vogl.* III 133 = *SB* VI 9380 (165); *P. Ups. Frid* 8 (150–200); *BGU* I 138 (187–8); *P. Stras.* IV 189 (192); *SB* I 5170 (II); *P. Flor.* I, p. 49, n. 3 (II); *BGU* I 217 (II–III); *P. Fam. Tebt.* 48 (202–3); *P. Stras.* V 378 (215); *BGU* I 9 = *BGU* IV 1087 = W. *Chr.* 293 = *BGU* XIII 2280 (276); *P. Sakaon* 60 (306).

Thesmophoriou: *BGU* II 581 = M. *Chr.* 354 (133); *PSI* VIII 921 (143–4); *SB* XVI 13008 (144); *P. Stras.* VI 509 (138–61); *CPR* I 31 (153) *BL* I, 117–8, VIII, 97; *P. Berl Leigh.* I 17 (161); *SB* X 10219 (161); *P. Ups. Frid* 8 (150–200); *P. Brooklyn* I 8 = *SB* VIII 9740 (177); *P. Fay.* 52 (194); *P. Fay.* 335 (II); *PSI* III 221 (II); *P. Ross. Georg.* II 35 (II); *BGU* I 125 (II–III); *BGU* II 362 (215); *BGU* XI 2086 (235); *SB* XX 14584 (253); *P. Prag.* I 14 (III); *SB* XVI 12497 (III).

[**Thrakon:** The presence of this *amphodon* depends on dubious readings in *BGU* I 138; *P. Mich.* IX 552.]

Hieras Pules: *P. Lond.* II, p. 111, 297b (119); *SB* VIII 9768 = *P. Fay.* 355 (122); *P. Fay.* 98 (123); *P. Lond.* II, p. 206, 298 = M. *Chr.* 332 (124); *PSI* IX

1064 = *Sel. Pap.* II 310 (129); *P. Corn.* I 16 = *SB* XX 14303 (146–7); *P. Wisc.* I 18 (146–7); *BGU* III 702 = M. *Chr.* 333 (151); PSAA 35 (153–4); *P. Flor.* I 67 (161–9); *BGU* I 126 (187–8); *P. Mich.* XV 756 (193); *P. Berl. Leigh.* II 42 B (II); *P. Ryl.* II 398 (II–III); *P. Gen.* I 78 (II–III) *BL* I, 167; *P. Diog.* 11 & 12 (213); *SB* XVI 13242 (212–17); *SB* I 4299 (245); *P. Grenf.* II 79 (III); *P. Hawara* 399 = *Archiv* 5 (1913), 394 (III); *PSI* X 1127 (III); *P. Corn.* 20 (302).

Isiou Dromou: *P. Mil. Vogl.* II 106 (134); *P. Diog.* 24 (138–61); *P. Gen.* I 33 = W. *Chr.* 211 (155) *BL* III, 63; *BGU* XV 2471 (158); *BGU* XIII 2230 (159–60); *SB* VI 9555 (162–74); *P. Heid.* IV 302 (177–8); *P. Fay.* 50 (182); *BGU* III 734 (230/1–234/5) *BL* X, 16.

Kilikon: *SB* V 7955 (95); *PSAA* 43r (131–2); *P. Ryl.* II 103 = *Sel. Pap.* II 314 (134); *PSI* VIII 921 (143–4); *P. Stras.* VI 509 (138–61); *Stud. Pal. Pap.* XXII 170 (145); *P. Meyer* 3 (148); *P. Ryl.* II 98a = *Sel. Pap.* II 351 (154–5); *BGU* XIII 2230 (159–60); *P. Ups. Frid* 8 (150–200); *BGU* III 919 (II); *CPR* I 196 (II) *BL* VII, 43; *P. Ross. Georg.* II 35 (II); *BGU* I 217 (II–III); *P. Lond.* II, p. 215, 348 = M. *Chr.* 197 (205); *SB* VI 9049 = *SB* XVI 12557 (222–35).

Kopronos: *BGU* III 890 (II).

Linupheion: *P. Coll. Youtie* I 24 (121–2); *BGU* I 110 (138–9); *BGU* I 137 (146–7); *BGU* I 122 (146–8); *P. Tebt.* II 321 (147); *SB* VI 9554c (147); *P. Fay.* 281 (162–3) *BL* I 455, VII 49; *BGU* I 324 = W. *Chr.* 219 (166–7); *P. Ryl.* II 104 (167); *P. Fay.* 59 (178); *SB* XII 10954 (181); *SB* XII 10955 (188) *BL* IX 16; *BGU* II 504 (II); *BGU* VII 1642 (II); *BGU* XIII 2226 (203); *P. Fay.* 90 (234); *SB* XIV 11386 (288).

Lykion: *P. Rein.* I 42 (I–II); *BGU* III 982 (108); *BGU* XIII 2220 (133) *BL* X, 25; *P. Tebt.* II 566 = *SB* XX 14163 (133); *P. Fay.* 96 = W. *Chr.* 313 (143) *BL* VI, 37; *P. Vind. Sijp.* 25 (188–9); *BGU* II 503 (II); *BGU* I 94 (289) *BL* I, 18–19; *P. Lond.* I, p. 211, 113.5(b) (543).

Lusaniou Topon: *P. Med.* 38 (108) *BL* VIII, 206; *BGU* III 742 (117–36); *P. Bas.* 4 (141); *P. Hawara* 401 (161–9); *P. Stras.* I 122 (161–9); *P. Stras.* IV 204 (161–9); *P. Ryl.* II 175 (168); *P. Fay.* 30 = W. *Chr.* 214 (171) *BL* VIII, 122; *P. Berl. Leigh* II 42 B (II); *Stud. Pal. Pap.* XX 30 (230).

Makedonon: *BGU* III 981 (79); *BGU* IV 1065 (97); *P. Lond.* III, p. 181. 1177 = W. *Chr.* 193 = *Sel. Pap.* II 406 (113); *P. Ross. Georg.* II 18 (140); *P. Tebt.* I 175 (140); *SB* XVI 13008 (144); *SB* XVI 13009 (144); *P. Meyer* 9 (147); *P. Erl.* 22 (160–1); *P. Berl. Leigh.* I 17 (161); *SB* X 10723 (161); *P. Tebt.* II 318 = M. *Chr.* 218 (166); *SB* XVI 12983 (167–9); *P. Mil. Vogl.* II 63 (169–70); *P. Princ.* II 45 (174); *P. Fay.* 27 (175) *BL* I 129; *P. Stras.* V 371 (178); *BGU* I 118 (188–9) *BL* I 21; *P. Ross. Georg.* V 54 (II); *BGU* II 505 (II); *P. Flor.* I 25 (II); *CPR* I 218 (II); *P. Fay.* 23 (II); *Stud. Pal. Pap.* XX 12 (II–III); *P. Lond.* II, p. 215, 348 = M. *Chr.* 197 (205); *PSI* XI 1126 (III); *P. Fouad* 42 (III) *BL* VII 56; *P. Flor.* I 24 =M. *Chr.* 187 (III) *BL* III, 55; *P. Rain. Cent* 84 (315); *SB* I 5333 (Byzantine); *SB* I 5220 (?).

Mendesiou: *SB* X 10294 (161).

Moereos: *P. Harr.* I 70 = *SB* XVIII 13324 (77) *BL* VIII, 147, IX 301; *SB* XIV 11634 (89–90) *BL* X, 301; *P. Mich.* XV 693 (104–5) *BL* X, 210; *SB* XVI 13010 (144); *P. Corn.* I 16 = *SB* XX 14303 (146–7); *P. Vind. Tand.* 20 (146–7); *P. Tebt.* II 321 (147); *P. Oxy.* XLVII 3338 (150); *BGU* XIII 2230 (159–60); *BGU* I 57 (160–1); *P. Ryl.* II 111a (161); *P. Berl. Leigh.* I 17 (161); *P. Ryl.* II 363 (165); *P. Vind. Worp* 5 (169); *P. Ryl.* II 364 (171); *BGU* IX 1898 (172); [*P. Lond.* II, p. 69, 170 (175)]; *P. Aberd.* 56 (176); *SB* XVI 12888 (175–8); *P. Fay.* 279 (182); *P. Flor.* I 42 (183); *P. Ryl.* II 348 (181–9); *BGU* I 115 = W. *Chr.* 203

(187–8); *P. Vind. Sijp.* 25 (188–9); *SB* XIV 11355 (188–9); *P. Tebt.* II 322 = *Sel. Pap.* II 313 (189); *P. Hamb.* III 203 (189); *Stud. Pal. Pap.* XX 15 = *CPR* I 27 = M. *Chr.* 189 (190); *P. Frieb.* 10 = *SB* III 6293 (195–6); *P. Bodl.* I 12 (II); *CPR* I 197 (II); *P. Fay.* 354 (II); *P. Ross. Georg.* V 54 (II); *SB* I 5170 (II); *P. Mich.* XV 702 (199–201); *P. Hamb.* I 55 (241); *BGU* IV 1069 (243–4); *P. Flor.* I 5 (243–4) *BL* IX, 83; W. *Chr.* 125 (250); *Stud. Pal. Pap.* II, p. 32 (257–8); *P. Turner* 37 (270); *BGU* I 9 = *BGU* IV 1087 = W. *Chr.* 293 = *BGU* XIII 2280 (276); *P. Cair. Isid.* 93 (282); *BGU* II 572 (III); *BGU* IV 1071 (III); *BGU* VII 1623 (III); *P. Grenf.* II 79 (III); *PSI* X 1126 (III); *P. Corn.* 20 (303) *BL* VIII, 90; *P. Sakaon* 59 (305); *P. Würzb.* 17 (454); *SB* I 4821 (465) *BL* VIII, 316; *P. Bodl.* I 36 (542/547); *Stud. Pal. Pap.* III 164 = *Stud. Pal. Pap.* XX 198 (635) *BL* VIII, 316.

[**Nemesiou**: Not an *amphodon*: *P. Laur.* II 24 = *SB* XVI 12498; *BGU* XI 2052; *BGU* I 9 = *BGU* IV 1087 = W. *Chr.* 293 = *BGU* XIII 2280].

Plateias: *P. Hawara* 303 (109); *CPR* I 24 = *Stud. Pal. Pap.* XX 5 = M. *Chr.* 288 (136); *P. Ryl.* II 362 (162); *BGU* XIII 2224 (175); *BGU* I 132 (II); *BGU* II 494 (II); *CPR* I 26 (II) *BL* I, 114–6; [*CPR* I 164, *BL* I 120].

Sekneptuneiou: *P. Med.* 57 (73–4) *BL* VIII, 207; *BGU* XI 2017 (88); *P. Rein* I 42 (I–II) *BL* I, 386; *PSI* IX 1062 (104–5); *P. Ryl.* II 103 (134); *PSI* VIII 922 (180–92); *BGU* II 571 (II) *BL* I, 53–4; *BGU* XIII 2363 (II); *PSI* VII 776 (II–III); *Stud. Pal. Pap.* XX 12 (II–III) *BL* X, 269; *Stud. Pal. Pap.* II, p. 32 (257–8) *BL* I, 407; M. *Chr.* 215 (259).

Syriakes: *SB* XIV 11634 (89–90) *BL* X, 210; *P. Mil. Congr.* XIV, p. 22, (96–8); *PSI* X 1159 (post 132–3); *P. Ross. Georg.* II 18 (140); *P. Princ.* II 43 (141); *PSI* X 1141 (141); *PSAA* 27 = *SB* V 8256 (150); *PSI* X 1142 (154–5); *SB* XII 10890 (156); *P. Mich.* XV 696 (162); *P. Berl. Leigh* I 18 (163); *P. Merton* III 105 (164); *P. Coll. Youtie* I 27 (165); *P. Tebt.* II 318 = M. *Chr.* 218 (166); *SB* XIV 11355 (188–9); *P. Tebt.* II 322 = *Sel. Pap.* II 313 (189); *SB* VI 9625 (192); *P. Tebt.* II 397 = M. *Chr.* 321 (198); *SB* XII 10956 (198); *SB* XII 10952 (II); *P. Berl. Leigh.* 42 A (II); *P. Tebt.* II 351 (II); *P. Fam. Tebt.* 48 (202–3); *SB* XII 11150 (202–3); *SB* XX 14584 (253); *BGU* I 9 = *BGU* IV 1087 = W. *Chr.* 293 = *BGU* XIII 2280 (276); *CPR* I 191 (III) *BL* X, 46; *P. Stras.* I 9 (352) *BL* III, 230.

Tameion = Katotero: *PSI* VIII 918 (38–9); *P. Mich.* V 276 (47); *Stud. Pal. Pap.* XX 1 (83–4); *P. Grenf.* II 43 (92); *P. Heid.* IV 298 (104–5); *P. Lond.* III, p. 25, 1119a = *CPJ* II 430 (105); *SB* V 7870 (107–8); *SB* XII 10887 (119–38); *P. Fam. Tebt.* 22 (122); *P. Fam. Tebt.* 23 (123); *P. Princ.* III 124 (130–1); *PSAA* 43r (131–2); *P. Fam. Tebt.* 28 (133); *SB* XII 10786 (133); *SB* XII 10787 (133); *P. Ross. Georg.* II 18 (140); *P. Tebt.* II 389 = M. *Chr.* 173 = *Sel. Pap.* I 70 (141); *P. Grenf.* II 49 (141) *BL* I, 188; *P. Grenf.* II 51 (143); *BGU* III 697 = W. *Chr.* 321 = *Sel. Pap.* II 370 (140); *P. Mil. Vogl.* III 132 = *SB* VI 9313 (165); *P. Mil. Vogl.* III 133 = *SB* VI 9380 (2) (165); *P. Mil. Vogl.* III 134 = *SB* VI 9380 (3) (165); *P. Mil. Vogl.* III 135 = *SB* VI 9380 (4) (165); *CPR* I 14 (166); *P. Lond.* II, p. 210, 332 (166); *Stud. Pal. Pap.* XXII 172 (166); *P. Mil. Vogl.* VI 273 (168); *BGU* I 18 = W. *Chr.* 398 = *Sel. Pap.* II 342 (169); *P. Mil. Vogl.* III 138 = *SB* VI 9380 (8) (169); *P. Mil. Vogl.* III 139 = *SB* VI 9380 (10) (169); *SB* XII 10953 (172); *SB* VI 9625 (177–92); *BGU* III 907 (180–92); *BGU* I 115 = W. *Chr.* 203 (187–8); *P. Tebt.* II 320 (188–9); *P. Fam. Tebt.* 44 (188–9); *P. Tebt.* II 322 (189); *SB* XX 14166 (189); *P. Mich.* XV 698 (192); *P. Tebt.* II 397 = M. *Chr.* 321 (198); *SB* XII 10796 (c.198); *P. Ross. Georg.* II 35 (II); *BGU* II 540 (II); *P.*

Lond. III, p. 147, 1179 (II); *PSI* III 195v (II); *P. Fam. Tebt.* 48 (202–3); [*CPR* I 21 = *Stud. Pal. Pap.* XX 31 (230)]; *P. Flor.* I 5 (243–4); *SB* XX 14584 (253); *P. Turner* 37 (270); *P. Laur.* II 24 = *SB* XVI 12498 (III); *SB* XVI 12497 (III); *CPR* VII 51 (629) *BL* VIII, 113.

Phanesiou: *P. Tebt.* II 483 = *SB* XVIII 13786 (94); *CPR* I 187 (I–II); *SB* XVI 12728 (116); *CPR* I 206 (117–36); *P. Gen.* I 19 (147–8) *BL* I 160; *P. Lond.* II, p. 189, 314 = W. *Chr.* 356 = M. *Chr.* 149 (149); *BGU* III 907 (180–92); *P. Berl. Leigh* II 42 B (II)

Phremei: *PSI* VIII 905 = *P. Mich.* V 252 (25–6); *BGU* III 748 (62); *CPR* I 179 (I–II); *PSI* VIII 875 (I–II); *PSI* IX 1062 (104–5); *Stud. Pal. Pap.* XXII 76 (105) *BL* X, 274; *BGU* I 117 (98–117); *BGU* XI 2093 (125); *PSI* X 1159 (post 132–3); *P. Harris* II 180 (134); *BGU* I 193 = M. *Chr.* 268 (136); *P. Harris* II 181 (136); *P. Harris* II 182 (137); *P. Harris* II 183 (139); *P. Harris* II 184 (140); *P. Ross. Georg.* II 18 (140); *P. Bas.* 4 (141); *P. Harris* II 185 (141); *P. Harris* II 186 (143); *P. Lond.* III, p. 32, 909 (b) (143–4); *SB* XVI 13005 (144); *SB* XVI 13011 (144); *P. Harris* II 187 (144); *P. Harris* II 188 (145); *P. Harris* II 189 (146); *P. Lond.* III, p. 33, 912(a) (149) *BL* I, 274; *CPR* I 15 (149); *P. Oxf.* 11 (151); *SB* X 10565 (155); *SB* XX 14111 (160–1); *SB* X 10281 = *BGU* XIII 2217 (161) *BL* VII, 100; *BGU* II 629v (c.161); *P. Hawara* 401 (161–9); *P. Stras.* IV 204 (161–9); *P. Lond.* II, p. 221, 336 = M. *Chr.* 174 (167); *P. Vind. Worp* 5 (169); *P. Aberd.* 56 (176); *CPR* I 29 = M. *Chr.* 335 (184); *P. Petaus* 123 (184); *BGU* I 243 = M. *Chr.* 216 (186); *BGU* I 129 (187–8); *BGU* I 117 (189); *CPR* I 174 (190–1); *SB* VI 9618 (192); *P. Fay.* 23 (II); *CPR* I 196 (II); *P. Berl. Leigh.* II 42 A, B (II); *CPR* I 145 (II–III); *BGU* XI 2092 (203); *BGU* I 9 = *BGU* IV 1087 = W. *Chr.* 293 = *BGU* XIII 2280 (276); *P. Mich.* IX 542 (III); *P. Cair. Isid.* 73 (314); *P. Cair. Isid.* 122 = *SB* VI 9175 (314/315); *P. Col.* VII 185 (319); *P. Col.* VII 158 (344); *SB* VI 9311 = *P. Oslo.* II 38 = *P. Merton* I 37 (373)

Chenoboskion Heteron: *P. Harris* I 70 = *SB* XVIII 13324 (77) *BL* VIII, 147, IX, 301; *P. Mich.* IX 541 (c. 72); *SB* XIV 12105 (129); *P. Oslo.* II 39 = *SB* XVIII 13313 (146); *P. Vind. Tand.* 20 (146–7); *P. Fay.* 93 = W. *Chr.* 317 = *Sel. Pap.* I 44 (161); *P. Stras.* IV 201 (162); *P. Petaus* 125 (165); *BGU* I 123 (173–4) *BL* X, 12; *BGU* I 138 (187–8); *P. Fouad* 42 (III) *BL* VII, 56; *P. Alex.* 33 (591–602) *BL* VIII, 3 [perhaps Chenoboskion Proton].

Chenoboskion Proton: *BGU* XI 2032 (113); *BGU* I 137 (131–2); *P. Lond.* II, p. 67, 208 (138); *P. Lond.* II, p. 195, 303 = M. *Chr.* 160 (142); *CPR* VI 2 (144); *P. Meyer* 9 (147); *BGU* VII 1582 (149); *BGU* XIII 2230 (159–60); *BGU* II 493 (II); *P. Corn.* 20 (303), *BL* VIII, 90; *P. Alex.* 33 (591–602) *BL* VIII, 3 [perhaps Chenoboskion Heteron].

Horionos Hierakou: *BGU* I 109 (121) *BL* I, 20–1; *P. Lond.* III, p. 108, 906 = W. *Chr.* 318 (128); *BGU* XI 2092 (140); *P. Ross. Georg.* II 18 (140); *BGU* I 353 (140–1); *BGU* XIII 2333 (143–4); *Stud. Pal. Pap.* XXII 27 (155); *Stud. Pal. Pap.* XXII 29 = *SB* XVIII 13866 (155) *BL* VIII, 480; *BGU* I 123 (173–4); *P. Petaus* 123 (184); *P. Laur.* III 66 (188–9); *SB* XX 14328 = *BGU* I 182 (II); *BGU* III 907 (II); *P. Ross. Georg.* II 35 (II).

Byzantine Districts:

Hagiou Apollo omou: Byzantine: *SB* I 5127.

Hagiou Biktor: Byzantine: *SB* I 5127; 5128; VI–VII cent.: *Stud. Pal. Pap.* III 606 = *Stud. Pal. Pap.* XX 158; VII cent.: *Stud. Pal. Pap.* III 675; 667; 698; VIII 719; 723; 727; 728; 729; 737 = *P. Grenf.* I 69.

Hagiou Dorotheou: Byzantine: *SB* I 5127.

Hagiou Dorotheou omou: Byzantine: *SB* I 5127.

Hagias Thekles: Byzantine: *SB* I 4890; 5127; VI cent.: *Stud. Pal. Pap.* VIII 762; VII cent.: *Stud. Pal. Pap.* VIII 717.

Hagiou Theodorou: Byzantine: *SB* I 5127; 5128. VI–VII cent.: *Stud. Pal. Pap.* III 660; 671; 681; VIII 702; 706; 722; VII cent.: *Stud. Pal. Pap.* VIII 740 = *P. Lond.* I, p. 221, 116a = W. *Chr.* 286 *BL* V, 49 ; VIII cent.: *Stud. Pal. Pap.* VIII 766 = *Stud. Pal. Pap.* XX 188; Byzantine–Arabic: *Stud. Pal. Pap.* VIII 716 = *BGU* II 738.

Hagiou Theodorou omou: Byzantine: *SB* I 5127.

Hagiou Theotokou: Byzantine: *SB* I 5127; VII cent.: *Stud. Pal. Pap.* III 685; VIII 712 = *Stud. Pal. Pap.* XX 175; *Stud. Pal. Pap.* VIII 744; Arabic: *Stud. Pal. Pap.* VIII 738 = *BGU* II 676.

Hagiou Theotokou omou: Byzantine: *SB* I 5127.

Hagiou Leontiou: Byzantine: *SB* I 4890.

Hagion Marturon: Byzantine: *SB* I 4890; *SB* I 5127.

Hagiou Petrou: Byzantine: *SB* I 5128.

Hagiou Sansneou: Byzantine: *SB* I 5127; 5128; 5131; VI–VII cent.: *Stud. Pal. Pap.* III 661; VII cent.: *Stud. Pal. Pap.* VIII 707; 710.

Ale: VI cent.: *Stud. Pal. Pap.* III 621; 641; 647; 648; VII cent.: *Stud. Pal. Pap.* III 699.

Alupiou: *SB* I 4748 (605); *Stud. Pal. Pap.* XX 220 (618); *SB* I 4483 (636) *BL* VI, 132; V cent.: *P. Grenf.* II 83; VI cent.: *Stud. Pal. Pap.* III 385; VI–VII cent.: *Stud. Pal. Pap.* III 83.

Aperotos: *CPR* VIII 61 (546); *CPR* X 128 (586); *P. Alex.* 35 (618) *BL* V, 4; *CPR* XIV 16 (675); VII cent.: *Stud. Pal. Pap.* III 695; *SB* VIII 9760; VII–VIII cent.: *Stud. Pal. Pap.* X 71; VIII 735; Byzantine: *SB* I 5128.

Apollo/Apolloniou: Byzantine: *SB* I 4890; 5127; 5128; VII cent.: *Stud. Pal. Pap.* VIII 701.

Basil[ ]: *SB* I 4481 = *SB* XVIII 14001 (486).

Georg: Byzantine: *SB* I 4890.

Gunaikiou: *CPR* X 29 (536–7); [*SB* I 4858 = *SB* XVI 12701 (601) *BL* VII, 185, VIII, 385].

Ekklesias Kanon: *P. Ross. Georg.* V 31 (503); *P. Lond.* I, p. 211, 113 5(b) (543); *CPR* XIV 10 (556–79).

Heliou: Byzantine: *SB* I 4890.

epoikou Theatrou: Byzantine: *SB* I 5128.

Thebaion: *P. Sakaon* 60 (306).

Theonos: *SB* VI 9456 (594) *BL* VII, 209.

Hieron Signon: Byzantine: *SB* I 4787.

Katotero = Tameion: *SB* XVI 12497 (200–50); *BGU* I 3 (605); *P. Lond.* I, p. 212, 113.6 (a) (612) *BL* I, 238, VIII, 173; *P. Heid.* VII 404 (630); *Stud. Pal. Pap.* III 324 (672) *BL* VII, 256, VIII, 439; *Stud. Pal. Pap.* VIII 724 (681); Byzantine: *SB* I 5127; 5128; VI cent.: *Stud. Pal. Pap.* III 71; 108; VII cent.: *Stud. Pal. Pap.* VIII 736; 756 = *SB* I 5132; VII–VIII cent. : *Stud. Pal. Pap.* X 6;

Kleopatriou: Probably not an *amphodon* in the first four centuries AD: *SB* IV 7465 (44); *P. Lond.* III, p. 181, 1177 = W. *Chr.* 193 (113); *BGU* II 445 (148–9); *BGU* I 9 = *BGU* IV 1087 = W. *Chr.* 293 = *BGU* XIII 2280 (276); *Stud. Pal. Pap.* XX 240 (622) *BL* VII, 240; VI cent.: *CPR* X 41; XIV 7; VI–VII cent.: *Stud. Pal. Pap.* XX 173 = *Stud. Pal. Pap.* III 651; *Stud. Pal. Pap.* III 652; 653; 654; 655; 656; VII–VIII cent.: *Stud. Pal. Pap.* X 6; Byzantine: *SB* I 5128.

Megales Ekklesias: Byzantine: *SB* I 5127; VI–VII cent.: *SB* I 5133 = *Stud. Pal. Pap.* VIII 741; *Stud. Pal. Pap.* III 657; 670; 680; 700; VIII 703; 741; 753; VII cent.: *Stud. Pal. Pap.* III 613; VIII 742; 746; 749; 750; Arabic: *BGU* II 677 = *Stud. Pal. Pap.* III 615; *BGU* III 750; *BGU* II 681 = *Stud. Pal. Pap.* VIII 715.

Megales Ekklesias omou: Byzantine: *SB* I 5127.

Mena: Byzantine: *SB* I 4890.

Mikres Laures: *P. Ross. Georg.* III 57 (VII–VIII).

Numphaiou: Byzantine: *SB* I 5680 = *Stud. Pal. Pap.* III 115; VI–VII cent.: *Stud. Pal. Pap.* III 26.

Olump/Olumpias Lauras/Olumpiou Theatrou: Byzantine: *SB* I 4721; 4834; 4890; VI–VII cent.: *Stud. Pal. Pap.* III 334; Arabic: *SB* I 4664.

Paremboles: *SB* XIV 12195 (608); *SB* I 4488 (635); VI–VII cent.: *Stud. Pal. Pap.* III 239; 413; VII cent.: *P. Prag.* I 73; 76; *Stud. Pal. Pap.* III 128 = *P. Grenf.* I 68; *Stud. Pal. Pap.* III 658; 659; 662; 663 = *Stud. Pal. Pap.* VIII 755; 664; 668; 673; 674; 682; 683; 686; 687; 689; 693; 696; 697; VIII 704; 705; 709; 718; 721; 730; 747; 748; 751; 752; *Stud. Pal. Pap.* XX 209 (610) *BL* II.2, 165, VIII, 471; Byzantine: *SB* I 4791; 5127; *BGU* II 679 = *Stud. Pal. Pap.* VIII 714; Arabic: *BGU* III 739 = *Stud. Pal. Pap.* VIII 713; *Stud. Pal. Pap.* VIII 731; 733.

Paremboles ton andr[ ]: *CPR* XIV 13.

Perseas: *SB* I 4753 (523) *BL* VIII, 314; *BGU* II 631 (531); *CPR* X 27 (533); VII cent.: *Stud. Pal. Pap.* VIII 720; III 694; 665; 672; Byzantine: *SB* I 4890; 5127; 5128.

Pioo[ ]: Byzantine: *Stud. Pal. Pap.* X 216.

Proklou: *Stud. Pal. Pap.* XX 135 = *SB* XVIII 13860 (511).

Tetrapulou: Byzantine: *SB* I 5825 = *Stud. Pal. Pap.* III 114.

Tripolou: VI cent.: *Stud. Pal. Pap.* III 661; VII cent.: *Stud. Pal. Pap.* VIII 711; 1081.

Psappalliou: *BGU* I 305 (556); *CPR* XIV 11 (578); *Stud. Pal. Pap.* XX 243 (633/648) *BL* VIII, 474; Byzantine: *SB* I 4903; 4899.

Xerou Akanthiou: *P. Rain. Cent.* 100 (452).

12   The identification of Dromou Thoeridos with Kmelos comes from *P. Oxy.* III 478. Data in the table derived from Krüger (1990: 82–8) which replaces Rink (1924) with the additions of *P. Oxy.* LXIV 4440 (various); *P. Oxy. inv.* 91 B 173/c(b) (Anamphodarchon: Temgenouthis); *P. Oxy.* LV 3796, LXIV 4438, *SB* XX 14288 (Dromou Gymnasiou); *C. Pap. Gr.* II 1 26, *P. Oxy.* LXIII 4357; *SB* XX 14288 (Dromou Thoeridos); including *PSI* 67–9, which attest a laura Sarapidos; *P. Merton* II 76, *C. Pap. Gr.* II 1 44; *PSI* V 450 (Hermaiou); *P. Col.* VIII 231 and *C. Pap. Gr.* II 1 82 (Hippeon Paremboles); *C. Pap. Gr.* II 1 15, 51, *SB* XX 14285 (Lukion Paremboles); *P. Oxy.* LXI 4120 (Kretikou); *P. Fouad* 30, *P. Oxy.* XVIII 2186, XXXVIII 2858, XL 2900, *PSI* V 457 (Metroiou); *P. Oxy.* LIV 3750; *C. Pap. Gr.* II 1. 71; 81 (Pammenous Paradeisou); *P. Oxy.* LXV 4479 (Plateias); *P. Heid.* IV 330, *P. Oxy.* LXV 4489 (Poimenikes); *P. Oxy.* XLIV 3183; *P. Oxy.* LXV 4478, and possibly *P. Oxy.* VII 1129 (Temgenoutheos); *P. Oxy.* LVIII 3916 (Chenoboskon) and possibly *PSI* III 175 (Thoeriou Thenepmoi) and excluding *P. Oxy.* XII 1550 (Dromou Gymnasiou); the speculative restoration of Sijpesteijn (1983) *PSI* VIII 871 (Hippeon Paremboles); *P. Oxy.* XL 2913, 2930, LI 3639 (Lukion Paremboles); *P. Oxy.* 3077 (Poimenikes); substituting *P. Oxy.* XL 2915 for 2925 (Murobalanou). See also the problematic districts in *P. Oxy.* LX 4079 and 4080.

13 *'Amphodon'* was read in *P. Ashm.* I 25 = *SB* XIV 11413 of 71 BC, but *BL* VIII, 13 reads (far more probably) ἀμφό(τερου) (Jouguet 1911: 65).

14 Rathbone (1993) and Bagnall and Frier (1994: 2–4) argue that the undated census return, *P. Oxy.* II 254, comes from AD 19.

15 The register of residents in *Stud. Pal. Pap.* IV, pp. 58–83 lists changes since the first year of Nero's reign, suggesting that the original register was created before 54/5, perhaps 51/2 (*SB* XII 11012). Nero wrote to confirm the privileges of the 6,475, a special status group within Ptolemais Euergetis, perhaps synonymous with the gymnasial group elsewhere. It is possible that there was a later general registration and improbable that the late Claudian or early Neronian registration was the first.

16 The word could be used with other synonyms of street or road, such as the *Laura Dromou Thoeridou* (the street of the avenue/processional way of Thoeris); (*P. Oxy.* II 284) or the *Laura Dromou Sarapidos* (the street of the avenue/processional way of Sarapis); (*P. Oxy.* XXXVIII 2837), and it would seem likely that it also carried the meaning 'district'.

17 One could argue that *P. Oxy.* II 257 perhaps reflects some recollection on the part of the family of the ancestor's district of residence. *P. Oxy.* IV 711, however, seems more difficult to explain away, though I have failed to find a satisfactory variant on επ[. . .]φ[υλ]ων in the lacuna, pointing to tribal organization. I suspect that the reference is to Alexandria and not a *metropolis*.

18 By 46 BC, the number of recipients of the dole had apparently risen to 320,000, though Rickman 1980: 176 is a little suspicious of the figure. Caesar reduced the number of recipients to 150,000. This was accomplished by a population survey (Suet. *Div. Jul.* 41.3): *Recensum populi nec more nec loco solito, sed vicatim per dominos insularum egit* (He held a census of the people not in the usual custom or by place, but by street, through the owners of the *insulae*).

19 Augustus' distributions to the Roman plebs reached 250,000–320,000, though the recipients of the grain dole numbered nearer 200,000. From 18 BC, Augustus appears to have given supplementary grants to 100,000 or more people, perhaps meeting 50 per cent of the bill for grain distributions in years of shortfall (*Res Gestae* 15; 18; Dio, LV 26).

20 Dio and Dionysius of Halicarnassus agree on the correct Greek term for a *vicus*: στενωπός.

21 The association of these areas in Rome with the imperial cult might suggest a link between these district units elsewhere and the *Augustales*, the rather problematic organization of priests of the imperial cult. The *Augustales* were often of comparatively low social status, overwhelmingly freedmen, as were many of the known *vicomagistri*. See Jongman 1988: 292–307; Robinson 1992: 12; Fishwick 1987–92: II. 1, 609–10; Liebeschuetz 1979: 70–1; Ostrow 1990.

22 This may be the origin of some of the mysterious numbers in Hermopolite applications for gymnasial status, which probably refer to a numerical filing system within the *amphodal* rolls (*P. Amh.* II 75; *P. Ryl.* II 102).

23 This discounts *PSI* I 86 reread in *BL* III, 220 and VIII, 392.

24 The *amphodogrammateus* is sometimes associated in title with the *komogrammateus*, suggesting that no clear distinction operated between village and district scribe (*PSI* VII 796; *BGU* II 659 *BL* I, 59 VII, 14; cf *P. Giss. Univ.* VI 52). Borkowski and Hagedorn (1975) view the *amphodokomogrammateus* as specific and different from either the *komogrammateus* or the *amphodogrammateus*.

25 The text establishes the area to be policed by the city-guards by describing the

boundaries of the areas rather than making reference to already known topographic units, such as *amphoda*.

26 At first sight, one might think that we could use the data in tables 4.2 and 4.3 to estimate the relative size of the various *amphoda*, but such a procedure seems unwise. First, the assumption that numbers of attestations will loosely relate to numbers of people ignores the idiosyncrasies of the preservation and discovery of papyrus. The texts concerning Ptolemais Euergetis are overwhelmingly from the Fayum villages and would, if anything, only tell us about the level of interaction between the various villages and the *metropolis*. The formation of the *metropolis* in the Arsinoite may also have been rather unusual in that there was a large body of 'Greek' settlers in the nome, recognized as the 6,475 (Montevecchi 1975). It seems that they were assimilated into the metropolite population and may have been registered in the *amphoda*, though it is not clear how (or if) this was done. The texts from Oxyrhynchus were mainly found at the city itself, but even in a single site, papyri tend to be found in clumps, often where they were dumped and where the environmental conditions allowed their preservation. Although, judging from the photographs of the excavation, Grenfell and Hunt worked systematically to clear the site, Petrie's (1925) later discoveries and Derbishire's 1908 map of the excavations, published in *P. Oxy.* L, suggests a rather uneven coverage of the site which, after all, has probably been continuously occupied since antiquity (Grenfell and Hunt 1906a; 1906b; Grenfell 1897).

27 The issue of the ideal size of a neighbourhood is nearly as insoluble as the ideal length of a piece of string, but studies of social networks in the United States suggest that although the total number of people within a network may be very large, 2,700 in New York, the core of that network is likely to be smaller, around 400. The people of New York appear to be particularly gregarious and average network size in the United States is 1,526, with Florida at 1,700 and Mexico City, by comparison, a mere 600. Obviously such networks depend on a host of culturally specific as well as technological factors, but they do provide an indication of the possible size of neighbourhood communities (Davies and Herbert 1993: 69).

28 The 3,000 were the main body of adult male citizens. The *homologoi* were the 'agreed'. The category is obscure, though it seems likely that these were residents of other cities to whom the Oxyrhynchites extended this privilege, perhaps by individual agreement of by mutual inter-urban arrangement. The *remboi*, the remainder, appear to have been granted the privilege following the performance of some service for the city.

29 A further problem lies in the summary total in *P. Oxy.* XL 2929 of 3,75[.]. This figure is at least 118 more than the total of the categories in table 4.4, about which there is only limited doubt. The total is, however, within reach of the *numeri clausi* of 3,000 + 100 + the *remboi* at 653, though there may be a slight difference in the date of texts *P. Oxy.* XL 2928 and 2929. The significant obstacle to this is Rea's reading of *P. Oxy.* XL 2908 iii, which is an application from Aurelius Sarapidos on behalf of his foster-brother to be registered 'among the men receiving the 9[00] artabas of dole'. This group looks to be the *remboi* and the text may, therefore, be used to suggest a *numerus clausus* of 900 which the *remboi* of the 270s numbered only 73 per cent (the 3,000 were only 3 per cent short of the *numerus clausus*). Unless, therefore, the 3,75 . . was calculated using two *numeri clausi* and the real figure for the *remboi*, an unusual but not

unthinkable calculation, the number is puzzling and it may be (though I regard this as unlikely) that there is yet another small group of recipients receiving the dole of which we know nothing.

30 Excluding from the corn dole those over 63, an age at which men seem to have been able to join the *gerousia*, would have only a marginal effect on the calculation of the total population, raising it by about 700. Though *SB* VIII 9901 suggests that entry into the *gerousia* might have been at the very early age of 58, which would so change the multiple to raise the total population. See also *P. Oxy.* XLIII 3099, 3100; *SB* VIII 10075; *PSI* XII 1240.

31 Interestingly, a priest of Sarapis is also attested in Hippodromou.

32 *P. Oxy.* IV 711 may provide a further attestation of Alexandrian *amphoda*.

33 The legal separation of Jews from other settlers does not seem in doubt, see Jos. *Ant.* XII 8; *Contra Ap.* II 35–7; Philo, *In Flaccum* 80; Jos. *BJ* VII 412; Kasher 1985; Alston 1997b; Delia 1991: 27. The issue appears rather to have been whether the legal separation of the Jewish *politeuma* meant that the Jews were not Alexandrians. About this there appears to be as little agreement now as there was in antiquity.

34 Many of the texts do not mention the district of residence and so it is difficult to locate the various Jews attested in the early Roman papyri. We know of a house owned by a certain Aristonikos in Delta and a Sarapion of Aristeios. A freedwoman Antonia, acting with her guardian C. Iulius Felix, were engaged in renting a house in the same quarter (*BGU* IV 1115; 1116). C. Iulius Philius and Agathokles also had dealings over a workshop and a woodshop in the Delta (*BGU* IV 1151 = *CPJ* II 143). None of these texts appear to involve Jews, though of course Jewish identity might be hidden behind a Greek or Roman name. See also Horbury and Noy 1992: xiii–xvi; inscription 1–4; 6–8; 10; Fraser 1972: 32–4.

35 The gradual segregation of the Jewish community in Alexandria may have been paralleled in other cities in the same way that the eventual destruction of the community in Alexandria in 116–17 can be associated with the disappearance of Jewish communities in Oxyrhynchus and Apollonospolis Magna (*CPJ* II, pp. 108–77; *P. Oxy.* III 500 = *CPJ* II 448; *P. Oxy.* IV 705 = *CPJ* II 450; *P. Oxy.* IX 1189 = *CPJ* II 445).

36 Strabo actually describes the palaces as comprising a quarter or even a third of the *peribolos*. The normal meaning would be 'circuit', but this seems an inappropriate translation here. Since the word could mean 'enclosure' or the precincts of a temple, I prefer 'area' as a translation. Strabo may, nonetheless, have used the word because of its religious connotations.

37 The largest palace appears to have been in Brucheion, but the Ptolemies also had residences outside the main city, on the promontory called Lochias, probably an ideal site for a summer palace, fanned by the sea breezes. It seems likely that the current archaeological exploration of the harbour at Alexandria will reveal more Ptolemaic palaces (Goddio 1998).

38 Possibly Antinoos or Antoninos Pandotos.

39 The confusion between the baths of Trajan or Gratian rests on divergent manuscript readings. Three manuscripts read variously Τραιανόν, Τραγιανόν and Τρατιανόν.

40 The interpretation given here relies heavily on accepting the arguments as to the spatial arrangement of the houses given in chapter 3 (see pp. 112–6).

41 In eleventh-century Florence, the towers were often shared installations owned by companies, the members of which might have interests in several towers.

42 Even with all the urban change in Liverpool from 1939, elements of that pattern can still be seen today.

43 One would assume that the circulation of the so-called *Acta Alexandrinorum* (a series of novelistic martyr acts in which prominent Alexandrians are persecuted and killed by the Roman authorities and which sometimes blend anti-semitism into their narratives) in Middle Egypt attests an interest in Alexandrian matters and perhaps shared anti-semitic attitudes.

44 Nomenclature ceases to be a good guide to ethnic status by the end of the second century BC, and the emergence of a broad 'Greek' law suggests that settlers' separate identities were being merged. It seems likely that these identities were no more than a legal fiction, existing merely in name, by the later Ptolemaic period (Goudriaan 1992; Clarysse 1998; 1995; 1992; 1985b; Bagnall 1988b; Peremans 1981; 1970).

45 Clearly there were substantial extant remains when Roeder and his team excavated at the site between 1929 and 1939, and although the excavations were on a major scale, it seems very likely that much remained uncovered or unreported. One would assume that the water-management system was substantially greater than that detailed in the report.

46 The location of pumps may have been important in community formation in nineteenth-century England. One of the earliest and most famous works of medical geography traced the importance of water-supply in an outbreak of cholera in nineteenth-century London (Snow 1949, 2nd edn 1855). See also www.ph.ucla.edu/ epi/snow.html for material on Snow.

47 The illegitimacy of the children is regarded as a ploy by Gemella and Sokrates so that the twins inherit the citizenship status of their mother rather than that of Sokrates. The benefit of Roman citizenship would have to be balanced against the loss of inheritance rights that would follow from their technical illegitimacy.

48 There is, of course, no guarantee that any social pattern observable in a particular period will have been a feature of other periods in the history of the city in Egypt. For instance, the pattern observable at Panopolis is not necessarily one that can be applied to the first-century city. Indeed, the Augustan invention of a gymnasial elite and the subsequent evolution of that elite into a bouleutic order suggests a process of development.

49 Finley's reductionism is more persuasive since it recognizes and works from the economic and socio-cultural similarities of many political and social systems of the Greek and Roman worlds.

50 Sjoberg's model has found some support in the primary evidence (see Langton 1975), and may be defended as an 'ideal type' which one would not expect to correspond directly to any reality, but, as ever with this methodology, defining the moment when such characterizations cease to be 'broadly true' is problematic.

51 Simms (1992) notes that the absence of a sense of a history in the morphology of a town can be extremely disorientating, presumably because the processes of community creation are not attested in the architecture and thus one gets no sense of the community that inhabits a particular area.

52 See Singerman's 1995 study of the importance of neighbourhoods as political organizations in modern Cairo.

53 Interestingly, it seems that most Egyptian houses of the period did not have harems as such. Harems were Turkish and not popular outside the elite.

54 One wonders whether the decline of the factory system and the post-Fordist

industrialism of recent decades marks the end of an unusual historical period in which major capitalistic concerns were interested in the provision of topographically concentrated housing for their workforces. This has allowed the re-emergence of a more inchoate and negotiable pattern of residential and locational differentiation across cities.

5 THE CITY

1 One can compare this with the ideas of European imperialists about conquered societies as outlined in Said 1978 and Ranger 1983.

2 Alexandrian status was regarded as being intermediate between Egyptian and Roman by Trajan, his legal advisers, Pliny, who was himself an experienced lawyer, and Josephus (Pliny, *Ep.* X 6; 7; cf. Jos. *Contra Apion* II 38–42; Delia 1991: 39–42; Wolff 1976: 239–51; Sherwin-White 1973: 390–2; Segrè 1940; 1944; Bell 1942; 1944).

3 The rhetoric of the new settlement, emphasizing that Greek identity was to be a claim for privileged status, placed many of the Fayum villagers in an anomalous position since the Fayum had been an area of heavy 'Greek' settlement. Some kind of official compromise emerged with a rather mysterious group known as the 6,475 *katoikoi* (settlers) who appear by the middle of the first century claiming privileges similar to those of metropolites (Montevecchi 1970; 1982; Whitehorne 1982; Bowman and Rathbone 1992; *SB* XII 11012; *I. Fay.* III 147 = *OGIS* II 668).

4 A tentative reading of this text (*BL* V, 77) led to the suggestion that the *exegetes* supervised the baths, see Bagnall 1993: 58, with support from *P. Oxy.* XXXI 2569. Further examination of the papyrus led to the reading being withdrawn (*BL* VII, 131). I suggest that the association with baths in *P. Oxy.* XXXI 2569 results from the financial management of the city rather than the baths *per se*.

5 A similar roster of taxes found in the *dromos* of the temple at Karnak makes no mention of the tax-collecting authority (Wagner 1972).

6 The absence of the *prytanis* from this list of magistrates might suggest that the text belonged to the second rather than the third century.

7 The traditional temples may have provided some income for the urban administration.

8 This compares astonishingly closely to the funds left by Pliny the Younger for the baths at Comum. He provided 300,000 HS (each equivalent to an Egyptian drachma) for furnishing the baths and a fund of 200,000 for their upkeep, which should have provided an income of approximately 12,000 HS per year. Though these sums are dwarfed by the 3,518,000 HS the citizens of Nicomedia spent on two aqueducts, neither of which worked, and the 10,000,000 HS spent on the theatre at Nicaea which was subsiding (Pliny, *Ep.* X 37; 39; *CIL* V 5262).

9 Assuming a 6 per cent annual return, this would provide prizes to the value of 2,400 Egyptian drachmas per year.

10 Memphis is a special case, having been the most important city in Egypt for centuries, but Thompson's outline can probably be applied to most other urban centres of the late Ptolemaic period.

11 Augustan poetry is complex and allusive, which makes deriving information about social and political attitudes from such texts extremely difficult. Propertius III 11; IV 6; Virgil, *Aen.* VIII 675–713; and Horace, *Odes* I 37 take an overtly hostile line which echoes Cicero, *Tusc. Disp.* V 27 78; *De Nat. Deor.* I

29; 36; III 16; *De Repub.* III 14, whose religious views may have been shaped in part by his dislike of Cleopatra, while Tibullus I 3 and I 7 honour Isis and Osiris. For Augustan hostility, see Suet. *Aug.* 18 and 93, Dio LI 16 and Thompson 1990. Although Augustus used an Egyptianizing symbol on his seal (a sphinx) (Suet. *Aug.* 50; Dio LI 3), this could be interpreted as alluding to his Egyptian triumph, though Dio suggests that it was already in use before 30 BC. See Wyke 1992 and Etman 1992 on Augustan poetic Cleopatras.

12 The root of Syene, *swnw*, which was preserved in Coptic and in 'Aswan', means 'market', presumably referring to the frontier trade between Nubians and Egyptians (Kees 1931).

13 Syene had a substantial garrison (Alston 1995: 27–36), which might explain the extensive building in the region. Although it is possible that the local *strategos* supervised 'the Ombite, the land around Elephantine and Philae and about Thebes and the Hermonthite' (*SB* V 7922), it seems more likely that 'the land about Elephantine and Philae' was administered with the Ombite (*SB* V 7927; 7951) and that Elephantine was the centre of the *strategos*'s activity (Wilcken 1894).

14 The Romans imposed their own system of public–private categories of land on the complex Ptolemaic categorization, though much of the Ptolemaic system survived as subdivisions of those essential Roman categories. Temple land, not being in any sense private, became a form of public land.

15 The *idios logos* was the 'holder of the private account'. This was a Ptolemaic office which continued into the Roman period, but was then held by Roman equestrian officials. The office was equivalent to a procuratorship as instituted elsewhere in the empire.

16 There appear to have been two forms of declaration. One was a list of personnel connected with the temple and the other was a list of property deposited within the temple. See Grassi 1973 on the latter type.

17 Our main text of the *Gnomon* (*BGU* V 1210) dates from the mid-second century, though it appears that versions of the *Gnomon* had been in circulation since the reign of Augustus, presumably periodically reissued to remind the nome administrators of governmental regulation and practice. It is, in most cases, impossible to date any specific provision.

18 The inscription is partially restored.

19 *Pax* (peace) and *Concordia* (harmony) are imperial attributes often given a divine personification.

20 Upper Egypt appears to have been more conservative than other areas and was certainly less Hellenized than the Fayum or the Oxyrhynchite, but there is no straightforward inverse correlation between Hellenization and traditional temple-building. For instance, Gayet (1897: 17) argued that the major rituals at Antinoopolis of the New Hellenes (to give it its full title), which one might expect to have been one of the most Hellenized centres in the Nile valley, 'conformed to the tradition of the country'.

21 For the Coptic cathedral see Wace et al. 1959; Wace 1945; Kamal 1947; Baraize 1940; Baranski 1989. For an early epigraphic survey of the hieroglyphs, see Effendi Chabân 1907.

22 For more on Athribis, see pp. 236–8.

23 Interestingly, the patterns of building attested do not correlate with the state money supply judging from the dated money issues. Indeed, there appears to have been very little state minting of coins, silver or bronze, until the 50s. There

were, however, quite high numbers of bronze coins minted in the later first century. See Bland 1996.

24 For the 'public market' see *SB* XX 14110 (VIth century). For an *agora* near the *logisterion* (accounts house), see *P. Oxy.* XLII 3074 (IIIrd century). For the vegetable market, see *P. Oxy.* I 43 verso. For the shoemakers' *agora* see *P. Oxy.* VII 1037 (AD 444).

25 Apart from Flinders Petrie (1889), the archaeological record for the site is extremely poor. See pp. 269–70.

26 Since all emperors carried the epithet Augustus this is of no help in dating the *agora*.

27 For banks not associated with the temple of Sarapis see *P. Oxy.* II 288 = Biscottini 1966: no. 9; *P. Oxy.* II 308 = Biscottini 1966: no. 25.

28 It is unclear whether this is a syncretic name for a temple of Thoeris or was a Greek temple (Quaegebeur et al. 1985).

29 There were also banks in Phremei district (*P. Bas.* 4; *BGU* I 93 = M. *Chr.* 268; *BGU* I 281; *CPR* I 15; *SB* X 10565; *P. Stras.* 204; *P. Lond.* II, p. 221, 336 = M. *Chr.* 174; *Stud. Pal. Pap.* XXII 76), in Phanesiou district (*P. Tebt.* II 483), in the Tameion district (*PSI* VIII 918; *Stud. Pal. Pap.* XX 1; XXII 172; *SB* XII 10786; 10787; 10887; *P. Tebt.* II 51 = M. *Chr.* 173; *P. Tebt.* II 51; *BGU* III 697 = W. *Chr.* 321; *CPR* I 14; *P. Lond.* II, p. 210, 332; III, p. 147, 1179), on the *plateia* of the gymnasium (*BGU* IV 1016), on the *plateia* (*P. Hawara* 303), in the Makedonian quarter (*BGU* III 981; IV 1065), the Holy Gate district (*P. Lond.* II 298 = M. *Chr.* 332). See also *BGU* XI 2052, *P. Tebt.* III 700; *P. Merton* II 67.

30 'Temple granaries' for the payment of tax are attested in Thebes (*O. Theb.* 44; 46; 55; 117 (at a village); *O. Wilbour* 44–48; *O. Theb.* D19) and other examples are listed in Clarysse 1985a. Rather confusingly, the main measure at Hermopolis appears to have been the Athenian measure which has been interpreted as the measure of the temple of Athena, but Clarysse argues that this was rather the 'Athenian unit of measure', which is the best reading of the Greek and makes sense of several rather problematic references. See, for example, *P. Bad.* II 18 (AD 61/2); *P. Bad.* II 38 (AD 105); *P. Ryl.* II 168 (AD 120); *PSI* VII 788 (AD 125); *P. Stras.* I 76 (AD 128); *P. Stras.* I 77 (II/III centuries); *BGU* XI 2125 (II/III centuries); *BGU* XI 2048 (AD 217); *P. Stras.* I 2 (AD 217); *P. Stras.* I 10 (AD 268); *P. Lips.* 18 (III/IV centuries); *P. Lips.* 19 (AD 319/20); *P. Lips.* 20 (AD 381); *BGU* XII 2157 (AD 483); *CPR* V 16 (AD 486); *P. Flor.* I 94 (AD 491); *BGU* XII 2194 (VI century); *BGU* XII 2181 (AD 508). Nevertheless, Athena was a major figure within the topography of the city with a tetrastylon named after her which appears to have been relatively close to the city granaries (*P. Oxy.* XXXIV 2719), which one would assume to be a logical location for the city measure. There is, however, no attestation of the temple, apart from a few explicit mentions in the context of the measure which, if Clarysse is right, are scribal errors. One wonders whether there remains a case for a topographical relationship between a temple of Athena and the measure of Athenian units. For the association of Athena and Thoeris see Quaegebeur et al. 1985.

31 In addition to the material cited here, *IGRR* I 1117 = *I. Fay.* III 212 = *SB* I 984 + 2035 is a rather mysterious inscription, without provenance, dating from AD 3 in which the pastry-cooks of the Arsinoite honoured their president.

32 These are fascinating sums. Many tax payments in Roman Egypt were renderable in the major high-value coin in circulation, the tetradrachm. As the

difference between these two payments was 4 drachmas, it suggests that there is but a single taxation unit between the two groups and that the taxation unit is charged at 4 drachmas. In this case there would be 273 units of fullers and 272 units of dyers. Any interpretation must be speculative, but the numbers may have corresponded to the numbers in the guild at the time the tariff was created. If this was the case, it would suggest that not only did these traders act as a unit across the nome in this dispute but that they were also organized into a nome-wide guild.

33 Trajan refused Pliny permission to establish a fire brigade in Nicomedia because it might become a forum for political discontent (Pliny. *Ep.* X 33–4). One of the issues that led to the persecution of the Christians seems to have been their collegial status (Pliny, *Ep.* X 96–7). Clubs were banned by Flaccus in Alexandria (Philo, *In Flaccum* 1; Milne 1925; see pp. 227–8).

34 For the history of these 'corporations' in the West see Waltzing 1895; Hermansen 1982: 56–9; and Patterson 1992b, 1994. It is sometimes assumed that a large building on the Forum at Pompeii, built by Eumachia, was associated with the fullers (*CIL* X 810–15).

35 For the syncretism of Athena Thoeris see Quaegebeur et al. 1985.

36 The editor interprets this text in the light of a connection between Thoeris and the fish cult which gave Oxyrhynchus its name and which is otherwise very poorly attested in the documentary record (it appears more frequently in the iconographic material). The connection is tenuous, but possible.

37 For more fishing in this area see *PSI* VIII 901 = *Sel. Pap.* II 329. There may be some connection between collection of the tax on fishing and temple sales taxes in *PSI* III 160.

38 A much later text, *P. Oxy.* XII 1414, records a dispute between weavers and the council of Oxyrhynchus over the price to be paid for linen cloths. The account could be read as suggesting that the temple controlled payments to the linen-weavers, but Bowman (1971: 70–4) argues that 'sacred' [account] was that of the imperial treasury, not a temple.

39 In the early third century, the temple of Jupiter Capitolinus at Ptolemais Euergetis (*BGU* II 362 = *W. Chr.* 96 = *Sel. Pap.* II 340) derived income from a village bath house. This was, however, a Roman temple and it is unclear to what extent its pattern of income can be extrapolated.

40 Tebtunis, as a village, provides a rather different context from the cities of the Roman period, but I do not see why the structures of guilds in the cities would be markedly different.

41 See Scheidel (1996: 53–91). The technique used here is extremely simple. The number of priests or guildsmen for the five years around each age group has been aggregated. This also somewhat offsets the effect of age-rounding, which is a notable feature of the documentation.

42 The texts were declarations of property sent to central authorities. They would, therefore, probably only declare the senior priests who enjoyed tax-exempt status (Gilliam 1947).

43 The guild age-structure is a snapshot of the population from the middle of the first century and may be distorted by some perfectly normal demographic event (plague for instance). Nevertheless, the figures are sufficiently odd that it is tempting to look for an institutional explanation.

44 It is not clear what *kline* means in this context. The word in Classical Greek means 'couch' but here must mean either 'dining-room' or 'feast'. I favour 'feast'.

45 The other hostess attested is Thermouthis, who invites people to her house for the wedding of her daughter (*P. Oxy.* XII 1579).

46 The one group which appears to have been excluded from the *klinai* of the temple were the senior priests, the *prophetai*, though the junior priests, the *pastophoroi*, were allowed to attend (*BGU* V 1012, ch. 88). Their exclusion has no obvious explanation.

47 There is rather more evidence for processions from the second century, though the political and institutional context of these was rather different (see pp. 245–7).

48 Great ceremonials were occasions on which the political relationship and power structures within a community could be displayed and reinforced, but were also potential flashpoints when the license of holidays could be transformed into rebellion. See Le Roy Ladurie 1980.

49 Ptolemais Euergetis is less well attested than Oxyrhynchus, but we know of temples of Souchos (*BGU* III 748; *SB* X 10281 = *BGU* XIII 2217; cf. *BGU* II 489; *CPR* I 206(?), a temple of Thoeris (*I. Fayum* I 2 = *SB* I 1567), a temple of Bubastis (*I. Fayum* I 23 = *SB* I 4625; *P. Enteux* 78; *BGU* XI 2086), and a Sarapeion (*I. Fayum* I 27 = *SB* I 5802), and one guesses that there were several other traditional temples.

50 See Perpillou-Thomas 1993: 29–60 for a calendar of all known religious festivals of the Ptolemaic and Roman periods

51 Aphthonius, *Progymasmata* p. 48 (Spengel 1854), discusses the akropolis of Alexandria and says that it rivals Athens. Alexandria is largely flat, but the ground does rise very gently to a slight hill on top of which was the Sarapeion. One presumes, then, that this was akropolis of Aphthonius, though one should not discount the possibility of invention.

52 It seems unlikely, however, that the Sarapeion had grown in relative size and grandeur in the period from Strabo to when Achilles Tatius and the others were writing. The dating of Achilles Tatius is a complex and difficult problem, but he was probably writing in either the first or early second century (see Alston 1999a). Ammianus Marcellinus was writing in the late fourth century. The *Expositio* is probably also fourth century. Aphthonius' dating is uncertain.

53 The archaeological record of the site is impossibly confused. Rowe (1946) suggested that the site was extensively remodelled under Hadrian (see also Rowe 1942; Tkaczow 1993: 68–70). Hadrian's involvement with the Sarapeion is largely speculation (HA, *Hadrian* 12; Dio, LXIX 8 1a; Alston 1995: 75–7). Hadrian visited the city in *c*. 130 and discussed important matters with philosophers, defeating them in debate (HA, *Hadrian* 20.2), and perhaps associating himself with new gates for the city (Achilles Tatius V 1; John Malalas XI 280; John of Nikiou, *Chronicle* 74; *P. Lond.* V = *P. Jews* 1914). The Sarapeion does not figure in the narratives of Philo or Josephus, while Philo does discuss the gymnasium, *agora* and theatre. There are good reasons for this since Philo was unlikely to complain about Jews being excluded from the Sarapeion, and it was a common complaint about monotheists that they failed to participate in the rituals to assuage the city gods and could not, therefore, be considered part of the urban community (Jos. *C. Ap.* II 65–7).

54 Cleopatra was confirmed as Queen of Egypt and granted many of the old Ptolemaic lands, Cyprus, Libya and Coele Syria, and was to rule with her son by Caesar, Kaisarion. Antony recognized Caesar's son, which must have had political implications, though these are not easy to understand. He may have been threatening Octavian's (Caesar's adopted son) position as heir to Caesar's political

and, indeed, financial legacy, though such a threat had no basis in law and I cannot reconstruct how a Roman would have viewed Kaisarion's moral claim. Perhaps more likely, Kaisarion was a reminder that Caesar himself had been where Antony now was. Of Antony's sons with Cleopatra, Alexander was granted Armenia, Media and Parthia, while Ptolemy received Phoenicia, Syria and Cilicia. Cleopatra received her honours dressed as Isis and declared herself the New Isis. Alexander wore Median dress while Ptolemy was dressed as a Macedonian.

55 Confusingly, a petition for exemption from poll tax from a certain Helenos, a Jew of Alexandria, may state that he had been educated in a gymnasium, though the restoration is very dubious (*BGU* IV 1140 = *CPJ* II 151; Kasher 1985: 204, n. 59).

56 The strictness with which Alexandrian citizenship was defended is illustrated by a legal dispute involving a soldier and his children (Alston 1995: 55–6; *P. Cattoui* = M. *Chr.* 372 = *FIRA*² III 19). Since soldiers were not allowed to contract legal marriages, any children they had while in service were illegitimate and technically they could not acknowledge them as their children. They were, therefore, fatherless. Thus, the children could not have an Alexandrian father and mother and were not eligible for Alexandrian citizenship. This ruling was particularly harsh since if the higher status of Roman citizenship had been in question, the children's status would have followed that of their mother. See also Pliny, *Ep.* X 5; 6; 7; 10.

57 Josephus also mentions decrees of Caesar, Augustus (*C. Ap.* II 61–2; *Ant.* XIX 283–4, cf. Philo, *In Flaccum* 74), Alexander the Great (*C. Ap.* II 37; 42; *BJ* II 487) and Ptolemy I Lagus (*C. Ap.* II 37), as well as the treatment of the Jews by the Ptolemies (*C. Ap.* II 44–60), to try and demonstrate Jewish equality.

58 An understanding of Jewish–Greek relations in the Ptolemaic period partly depends on one's view of the extraordinary story told in 3 Maccabees. The story is of Ptolemy Philopater (222–205 BC) who, after the battle of Raphia (217 BC), turned against the Jews and, after a process of exclusion, registration and colonization (in which Alexandrian citizenship was an issue), decided to kill all the Jews by having them trampled by elephants. After the normal three attempts at this, when he first fell asleep and failed to wake at the appointed time and at a second attempt was struck by temporary amnesia, and on the third day watched as the elephants, who had been fed drugs and alcohol, turned tail and fled (trampling Ptolemy's army), he repented and granted the Jews many honours. This highly literary and faintly ludicrous story is paralleled by Josephus (*C. Ap.* II 53–6), who says that Ptolemy IX Euergetes II Physkon in *c.* 146 BC bound and stripped the Jews of the city and attempted to get drunken elephants to trample them, but the elephants turned and trampled Ptolemy's forces, thereby persuading him to grant the Jews privileges. Neither tale is immediately credible, though obviously reliant on a common source, and the difference of opinion as to the date of the events does not lead to confidence as to their likely historicity. The date of the author of 3 Maccabees is not known and elements of the story may reflect much later concerns.

59 The slight documentary evidence for Alexandria in the early first century attests separate Jewish institutions, such as an *archeion* where documents could be stored, but the contracts involving Jews do not appear to differ significantly from those involving Greeks and Egyptians. The Jewish community does not appear to have been topographically segregated. See also Balconi 1985; Schubart 1913.

60 This association of gymnasial membership and citizenship may be paralleled at Athens. Augustus visited Athens in the winter of 21–20 BC and had some difficulty with the Athenian population. His stay coincides with changes in a long-established epigraphic sequence of ephebic lists which, prior to Augustus' reign, contained many boys who were non-Athenians but later seems to have been restricted to Athenian boys (Bowersock 1964; 1987; Geagen 1979; Benjamin and Raubitschek 1959; Davies 1977; Hoff 1989). Schmalz (1996) argues that Augustus reformed the *ephebeia*, presumably rooting out non-Athenians, and may have made the performance of the ephebate tantamount to citizenship. Making access to Athenian citizenship more difficult probably had financial implications for the Athenian state, but the justification for this was almost certainly in terms of a restoration of Athens' historical identity, very much as Augustus allowed and probably encouraged the Spartans to bask in their historical glory (Cartledge and Spawforth 1989: 97–101). In a similar way, the emphasis on the gymnasium in Alexandria could be represented as a restoration of the city of Alexander. *P. Oxy.* 2177 = Musurillo 1954: X is a probably fictional account of a hearing before the emperor at which Athenian ambassadors speak for Alexandria, much to the consternation of the emperor. The excuse given is that Athenian and Alexandrian law were very similar in their *philanthropia*.

61 See Tac. *Ann.* II 53–62 for Germanicus' Eastern tour.

62 Germanicus' behaviour conformed to a pattern manifested throughout his tour of the East. Germanicus assumed his command at Nikopolis in Greece in AD 18, a year in which he was consul. Nikopolis had been built by Augustus to commemorate his great victory at nearby Actium and since Germanicus was the closest surviving male blood relative of Augustus, the grandson of Mark Antony and the husband of Augustus' granddaughter Agrippina, and in many ways the 'natural successor' to Augustus, he could hardly have chosen a more auspicious or historic place to enter the East. His next stop was Athens where great play was made on Athens' historic greatness. The mutual compliments flowed so lavishly that Piso, who was hostile to Germanicus and whom Tiberius had appointed as governor of Syria, felt compelled to be rude to the Athenians in an effort to remind them of their subservient status. After Athens, Germanicus sailed to the Black Sea and stopped off at Troy to explore the supposed origins of his family and the Roman race. The tour proclaimed Germanicus' credentials as an educated Roman, well-versed in the culture and history of Greece. In Alexandria, he was at home.

63 This raises the issue, central to much Philonic scholarship, as to how the culture of Alexandria influenced Philo's thought and whether Philonic theology may be classified as 'Alexandrian' and therefore different from what was happening in Palestine and other areas. Huzar (1988) argues that Alexandria does not play a large part in Philo's writings while Sly (1996) struggles valiantly to write about 'Philo's Alexandria' in spite of the fact that the Philonic corpus, with the exception of the *In Flaccum* and the *Legatio ad Gaium* is almost without explicit reference to the city. The influence of Alexandria is to be seen in the culture through which Philo writes rather than in the detail and the anecdote. Yet, these cultural influences are much more difficult to tease out convincingly from the theological discourses.

64 Alston (1996) comments on literary aspects of the work.

65 The Greek here is obscure but the murderers are described as being like 'mime actors', (θεατρικοῖς μίμοις).

66 Philo speaks of φίλοι καὶ συγγενεῖς (friends and relatives) being persecuted in *In Flaccum* 72 while in *In Flaccum* 64 some Jews approach the same category or categories of sympathizers for aid in gaining food. These people were evidently not restricted to Delta and presumably had not been recognized as Jews during the rioting. The 'friends' are relatively unproblematic, merely demonstrating that social relationships crossed the ethnic divide, but the 'relatives' are difficult to understand, suggesting perhaps marriage and religious conversion between communities. One can only speculate what such activities would mean for citizenship status. Alternatively, one could interpret συγγενής more freely. The word was bestowed as a title under the Ptolemies, presumably representing a fictional family relationship with the royal house. This would, however, render the word redundant, as it is a synonym for 'friend'.

67 The presence of a woman here is slightly surprising. Aphrodisia was a comparatively common name in Roman Egypt, but its divine etymology might suggest that there is a sexual sub-plot.

68 See also Musurillo 1954: VIII (= *P. Oxy.* X 1242) and IX.

69 Sherwin White (1972) found the chronology impossible and decided that Philo's story of a conspiracy between Flaccus and these leaders was a fabrication.

70 As with much that is written about Gaius, it is difficult to know how seriously one should take these rumours (Suet. *Gaius* 49.2), but, if Suetonius (*Gaius* 19; 52; cf. Dio LIX 17) is to be believed, Gaius made considerable use of the Alexander myth, posing as the new Alexander. The threat to shift the capital to Alexandria may be seen in the context of his (mischievous?) attempts to restore the reputation of M. Antony. The Alexandrians had also been particularly impressed by Gaius' father, Germanicus.

71 There is a textual problem here.

72 If the substance of the embassy concerned citizenship, this is a ridiculous ruling. If, however, this was a congratulatory embassy following Claudius' accession, the admonition is understandable.

73 Haas (1997: 336), concludes his study:

> We are becoming painfully aware at the close of the twentieth century that age-old enmities are not easily resolved, and the clumsy intervention of an outside authority [Rome] can fan the flames of these hatreds or even cause the warring factions to unite against the outsider.

74 This view is, I think, rather similar to that of Purcell (1999), whose study of the crowd in Rome also criticizes the approach of Haas (1997).

75 The shifts in occupation seem similar to, though less dramatic than, patterns at Naukratis (Coulson 1988; 1996) and most Roman buildings at Athribis had Ptolemaic structures beneath them (Michalowski 1962a; 1962b).

76 Although Athribis is traditionally associated with Khentekhtai, whose aspects were a crocodile or, more popularly, a hawk, there appears to have been a strong local association with Aphrodite, a popular goddess throughout the Delta (Mysliwiec 1992b).

77 The secondary and archaeological literature on the site tend to translate *plateia* by 'street'. This seems to me to be slightly inappropriate since the Greek πλατεῖα carries an implication of width and is to be distinguished from other words for street used in the papyri which appear to mean rather more minor and narrow routes. 'Street' is preserved as a translation here.

78 There were women's baths by 116 (*P. Brem.* 23).

79 This text contains a request to rent a collapsed house and dung-heap bordered to the north by Antinoe Street and on the south by Domitian Street.

80 Three *plateiai* may be mentioned in a text from AD 149 (*P. Vind. Sal.* 11), but the readings are very dubious.

81 It is not certain how or whether these structures relate to each other or to the cult of Severus Alexander attested in *P. Bad.* 89.

82 One *amphodon* was known as the Murobalanion and this presumably relates to a Ptolemaic bath house.

83 *P. Oxy.* XLIII 3088 *BL* IX, 200 of AD 128 attests the construction of baths, which one would naturally associate with Hadrian.

84 That set of baths replaced an earlier set: a second-century text talks of the old baths of the gymnasium (*P. Oxy.* XVII 2127), which would be a rather surprising description of baths built under Hadrian or even Trajan. See Meyer (1997) for the association of baths and the gymnasium.

85 A reference to the 'larger' baths has been reread: *P. Oxy.* III 473 = *W. Chr.* 33 *BL* VIII, 235.

86 Assuming a 6 per cent annual return, this would provide prizes to the value of 2,400 Egyptian drachmas per year.

87 This was a *rite de passage* associated with male puberty. See *P. Oxy.* XLIX 3463.

88 Of course, variations in level of attestation depend on many factors, only one of which is the relative importance of the office. For instance, the rise in attestation of most magistrates in the late third century is an effect of the preservation of council archives from Oxyrhynchus and Hermopolis from this period.

89 See *P. Oxy* I 53 and VI 896 = *W. Chr.* 48 = *Sel. Pap.* II 360 for repairs to the baths in 316.

90 The amount is likely to be substantial. The figure given is for .8 talents, 3 . . . drachmas. Earlier the text mentions payments for the provision of water and chaff (for heating) for the baths of the praetorium amounting to 71 talents, 2,400 drachmas (428,400 drachmas). This looks to be about twenty times the second-century costs for the provision of water, a rise which cannot easily be attributed to inflation. Rathbone (1996) dates the great price inflation to the 270s. See also Rathbone 1997.

91 A further third-century text (*P. Oxy.* XLII 3064) appears to suggest that villagers had been registered in the city for liturgies and that this was disputed, but the text is lacunose.

92 *P. Oxy.* X 1252 tells us that the office of eutheniarch was in abeyance for a considerable period before 289–90. Rather oddly, figure 5.9.2 does not show any notable reduction in the attestations of the office (which could be attested through former holders) through the late third century. The office does not seem to survive the Diocletianic reforms, so its restoration in the 290s was probably very short-lived.

93 Perhaps the major possible extension of taxes of kind was the provision of the military *annona* (taxes in kind to supply the troops), but the impact of this imposition is much debated (see Alston 1995: 110–12 with bibliography cited there).

94 Hobson 1984a; Alston 1995: 121; Boak 1955; Rathbone 1990, but see *contra* these views van Minnen (1994), who proposes a very much higher population for the village in the 170s.

95 *P. Oxy.* XLVI 3300 is on the back of XLVI 3294, which is dated to 271–2. That text is a blank nomination to liturgical office from the *phularchos*. It would seem

very likely that the register of houses also came from the office of the *phularchos* and probably dates to soon after 271–2.

96   Evidence from Africa and Syria, the provinces one would expect to be most similar in development to Egypt, suggest that the third century was a period of temporary 'retrenchment'. See Dietz et al. 1995: II, 773–86; Therbert 1983; Barker and Mattingly 1996; Tate 1992: 170–1.

97   Earlier investigators were probably faced with substantially more material than Roeder but their work tended to concentrate on discovering documents rather than on the archaeology of the site (Rubensohn 1905b; 1906; Clédat 1908; Chabân 1907). Gabra (1941) worked on the necropolis.

98   Four substantial water towers were identified (Roeder 1959: 124–5), of which Roeder measured one as having a capacity of 120 m³ and another of 8.635 m³. Another (p. 33) had an associated canal and water conduits spread across the city (p. 123). Many baths were identified, though Bailey (1991: 54) expresses some doubt about the identification and some will have been private (pp. 23; 130–2). This compares closely to the water distribution system at Ptolemais Euergetis known from *P. Lond.* III, pp. 180–90, 1177 (see pp. 174–5). Oxyrhynchus may also have had a similarly complex system (Krüger 1989).

99   Style provides a guide to the date of manufacture, but archaeologists normally see material as it was deposited and residuals, items which had an unusually long life before deposit, can easily confuse chronologies.

100 See especially *P. Herm.* 3; 2.

101 Snape (1989) shows that the Domitianic temple in the north of the site was demolished by the sixth century, while the south temple (rebuilt under Nero) had a much longer life since it was converted into a church (Bailey 1991: 53).

102 The city council appears to have commissioned extensive repairs to the city in 316. Apart from the *stoai*, this same papyrus mentions repairs at the *palation* (residence for important visitors) and at the baths. See also *P. Oxy.* VI 896.

103 The neighbouring temples of Dionysios and Demeter (3i in table 5.4) are attested in a return of temple property (*P. Oxy.* XII 1449) of the early third century. This is a joint return from the priests of Zeus, Hera, Atargatis, Kore (Persephone), Dionysios, Apollo and Neotera. The temple of Dionysios was in the Dromos of the Thoeris *amphodon*. The temple of Demeter was north of a temple of Zeus, Hera, Atargatis and Kore located in the Plateia *amphodon*. Other temples of these gods were located in the *Dromos* of the Gymnasium and Knights' Camp *amphoda*. The Plateia *amphodon* is associated with the theatre (20 in table 5.3) (*PSI* IX 1040; XIII 1331). It seems very likely that the *plateia* was to the east or south of the theatre. *P. Erl.* 76 locates a house on the eastern edge of the *plateia* (though the text is lacunose), while *PSI* XII 1240 locates a residence in the south of Plateia *amphodon*. If the theatre was to the east of the *plateia*, it would be on top of this house and if it was to the south, then the better direction would be 'near the theatre'. Therefore, it would seem likely that the theatre bordered the north or the west of the *plateia*. Since the temple of Dionysios was opposite the temple of Demeter and the temple of Thoeris (36 in table 5.3), from which the *Dromos* of Thoeris ran, must be in the east and centre of the city, and the theatre in the west and south of the city, I think the only plausible restoration is to suggest that the *Dromos* of Thoeris ran west from the temple and met the *plateia* near the centre of the city at the temples of Demeter and Dionysios. The listing in *P. Oxy.* LXIV 4441 for the East Stoa should, therefore, end towards the centre of the city. *P. Oxy.* XII 1449 also lists the

temple of Neotera in association with the temple of Apollo (28 in table 5.3) as being in the south and east of the city. Temgenouthis, a religious structure of some kind, was in the west of the city (15 in table 5.3). It also gave its name to an *amphodon* which we know from *P. Oxy.* I 99 lay near the Shepherds' *amphodon*. Both of these were close to the temple of Sarapis (*P. Oxy.* II 316). The location of the West Stoa is unclear. Although table 5.4, 2a–h, connects it to Temgenouthis, *SB* XX 14110, of the sixth century, puts the West Stoa west of the *agora*, and if the sixth-century *agora* was still located at the Sarapeion, then the stoa and its buildings may have to be squeezed between the Sarapeion and the city wall. One of the other buildings known is the Temple of the Two Siblings in the Murabalanion *amphodon* (*P. Oxy* II 254). This temple might be associated with Kastor and Pollux, but the text in which the temple is attested is a registration of residence by a priest of Isis who is living within the temple. We are also told that the temple was by the Sarapeion. Its precise location is a matter of guesswork.

104 Revel Coles suggested to me that the theatre cleared by Petrie is to be identified with 'the temple' described by Grenfell.

105 Petrie's notebooks (unpubl.) add little beyond some sketches on tombs and inscriptions and a note on Coptic ostraka.

106 Padró et al. (1996) reports on three years of campaigns at Oxyrhynchus. Few new architectural fragments were uncovered, though the excavators found considerable Saitic remains to the north of the Graeco-Roman city.

107 Papyrologists have tended to place a higher value on publishing literary texts and texts of known Classical authors than on documentary material. It is very likely that this, and the interest in early Christianity, has influenced the data collected in figures 5.11 and 5.12.

108 Notably, Latin does not appear to have been read or written to any significant degree in Oxyrhynchus, or indeed elsewhere in Egypt.

109 The modern growth of Medinet el-Fayum caused considerable damage to the archaeological remains by the early 1880s. Much of the stone was robbed to make the new city. Petrie's (1889) publication suggests that there had been further encroachment and adds little beyond mention of a colonnade around the temple and that a piazza in front of the temple was used as a rubbish tip in the late Roman period. Habachi (1937; 1955; Engelbach 1935) led excavations of a mound which produced Pharaonic material and Manfredi's (1978) team, in a brief stay at the site, discovered remains of an aqueduct, baths and buildings dated without confidence to the Ptolemaic period. Yacoub (1968) also excavated a bath house. Hussain (1983) showed that there are still substantial remains. See also Erman 1886 and Bernand 1975 for reports of early excavations and visits to the site. Casarico (1987a; 1987b) collected the papyrological material for the Ptolemaic city, which amounts to little more than a list of temples, but does point out that the city underwent a change of name from Crocodilopolis to Ptolemais Euergetis *c.* 116–115 BC and that the latter name continued in use until about AD 348, supplemented by 'city of the Arsinoites' in normal usage (see also Oates 1975).

110 The Alexandrian development can be compared with the building of a small second theatre-arena at Pelusium, probably again of fourth-century date (Jaritz et al. 1996: 121–2).

111 The stratigraphic dating adopted by the excavators at Karanis, for instance, has come under considerable scrutiny (Grande 1985; Alston 1995; Montserrat

1996b; Pollard 1998) and the consensus appears to be that the archaeologists compressed the chronology of the site. It is no longer safe to follow them in concluding that the north temple at Karanis had collapsed by the mid-third century (Husselman 1979: 9; Boak 1933: 16). Even if one accepted the traditional dating, the south temple, which paralleled its northern partner, appears to have had a much longer history (Boak 1933: 22).

112 Petrie (1905: 28) dated house L, 'a large and important mansion', to *c.* 500 on the basis of architectural style, and this house reused mid- or late second-century temple blocks in its basement. Petrie was working before the birth of scientific archaeology and often under extreme pressure (his excavations at Herakleopolis led to a dramatic altercation with those holding contracts to remove the sebakh). Without epigraphic or numismatic evidence, it would be naive to build much on his datings.

113 Although Fikhman (1994) points out correctly that guilds changed in purpose and function over the centuries and that applying material from the first century to the guilds of the fourth century is dangerous, the guilds appear markedly conservative (Latjar 1991). Carrié (1999) argues that the guilds continued to perform complex social functions in the late Roman and Byzantine periods.

114 *P. Ryl.* IV 654 is a fourth-century legal dispute in which builders tried and failed to force the son of a builder into his father's profession. Their motivation and legal argument are obscure (free-market logic would suggest that he was competition). It is possible that the son was thought liable for some dues to the guild or for a share in their craft tax (Fikhman 1981). *P. Oslo.* III 144 lists contributors to a fund for the 'holy victors'. The contributors include a carpet-weaver, a dyer, a bronze-smith, a baker, a perfume-seller, a silver-smith, an oil-seller, an oil-worker, a carpenter, a wine-seller, an embroiderer, a labourer, and a purple-trader. Not all the contributors were tradesmen.

115 Weaving was not a mainly urban trade. An unscientific survey of 176 references to weavers produced 121 rural references and 55 urban references (of which 28 were from the first century). The ostraka from the Theban area were excluded from this survey because of the difficulty in identifying urban and rural tax-payments.

116 Van Minnen works with high estimates for the total population of Oxyrhynchus (30,000) and of the proportion involved in crafts and trades to produce a figure of around 6,000 for those involved in the cloth trade. These were divided into many different groups, coarse-cloth-weavers, linen-weavers, linen-sellers, dyers, bleachers, fullers, wool-merchants, embroiderers, carders and spinners, and specialist weavers, who probably produced cloth of a particular grade or type or who worked on a particular type of loom (Wipszycka 1965; Jones 1960). Fikhman (1976; 1979) opts for a total population of 15,000–25,000 with a flourishing industrial element. For guilds see also Fikhman 1965; 1981; 1994.

117 See *P. Oxy.* LI 3624–6; 3628; LIV 3731–73; LX 4081; *P. Harris* I 73; *PSI* I 85; III 202; *SB* XVI 12648; *SB* XVIII 13631 (AD 239–43). For lists of crafts see Fikhman 1965: 24–34; 122–7 (*non vidi*).

118 For the involvement of government in the supply of food see Sharp 1998.

119 The fourth-century declarations of prices themselves show rising prices. *P. Brooklyn* 18 is a third-century complaint from the agent of a certain Apollonia that his employer had been demanding a price of 32 drachmas per *artaba* for grain rather than the customary price.

120 The fact that provision in the mid-third century extended beyond the citizens to

those residents who appear not to have had citizenship status, shows that the community was considered to extend to all residents and eroded the special status of metropolite citizenship. This concern for the provision of food continued after the Diocletianic reforms when the duties appear to fall to the *logistes* (see n. 127 below).

121 There was no appreciable fall in the number of papyri attesting civic business in the early fourth century, which would explain the declining numbers of attestation of *exegetai*.

122 *P. Kellis* I 21 is a petition το ἐ]κδίκῳ χώρας (*ekdikos* of the countryside). This particular office is not attested elsewhere.

123 *P. Ant.* I 31; *P. Harr.* II 216; *P. Oxy.* VI 900 = W. *Chr.* 437; *P. Oxy.* VIII 1116 = W. *Chr.* 403; *P. Oxy.* XII 1426; XLV 3249; XLVII 3350; LX 4078–83; *PSI* X 1108.

124 *P. Ant.* I 36; *P. Lips.* I 40: *P. Münch.* III 619; *P. Oxy.* I 52; XVIII 2187; 2235; XLIII 3126; XLVI 3311; LIV 3758; LX 4122; *P. Ryl.* IV 654; *P. Sakaon* 40.

125 *P. Cair. Isid.* 79; *P. Oxy.* I 87 = W. *Chr.* 446 = *Sel. Pap.* II 374; *P. Oxy.* XVII 2106 = *Sel. Pap.* II 227 [BL III 141; VII 144, VIII 253]; *PSI* IV 285; *SB* XVIII 13260.

126 *P. Erl.* 105; *P. Oxy.* XXXIII 2666; 2667; XLIV 3193.

127 *P. Harr.* II 211; *P. Oxy.* I 83 = W. *Chr.* 430 = *Sel. Pap.* II 331 [BL IX, 178, X, 135].

128 *P. Oxy.* I 42.

129 *P. Oxy.* I 53; 84 = W. *Chr.* 197 = *Sel. Pap.* II 374; *P. Oxy.* VI 892 = W. *Chr.* 49; *P. Oxy.* VI 896 = W. *Chr.* 48 = *Sel. Pap.* II 360; *P. Oxy.* VIII 1104 [BL VII]; XLV 3265.

130 *P. Oxy.* LI 3624–5; LIV 3728–60; 3765–76; *SB* XVI 12628; 12648.

131 *PSI* V 454; *P. Oxy.* X 1265; XXXIII 2673.

132 Flavius Paeanius was *strategos* in 351 (*P. Oxy.* LX 4089; 4091) and *logistes* in 336 (*P. Oxy.* X 1265; 1303). Flavius Iulianus was *strategos* in 345 having been *sundikos* and *logistes* (*P. Oxy.* LX 4086), and was to become *riparius* in 352 (*P. Oxy.* LX 4090).

133 The Panopolite registers (*P. Berol. Bork*) of the very early fourth century attest at least six deacons and a church.

134 A series of cases of AD 325 were heard before the *logistes* at the Kapitoleion, logisterion (record-house), the Hadrianeion, the Kapitoleion, and the gymnasium (*P. Oxy.* LIV 3758). Similar texts of the same year locate hearings at the Kapitoleion (*P. Oxy.* LIV 3757) and the temple of Kore (*P. Oxy.* LIV 3759) and a slightly later hearing was held at the Hadrianeion (*P. Oxy.* LIV 3767). Another case before the *logistes* (*P. Harris* II 160) was also heard at the Hadrianeion (Coles 1980), which was also the location of a hearing in the 320s (*P. Oxy.* LIV 3764). Liturgists presented themselves at the same place in 326 (*P. Oxy.* XLV 3249). A fourth-century text complains about a breach of procedure in that a report of a sale of public land was not published at the Kapitoleion (*SB* VIII 9883), which also appears to have been where wills were opened in third-century Oxyrhynchus (*P. Laur.* I 4). At Ptolemais Euergetis, the Hadrianeion and the Augustan Agora appear to have been the main centres for official activity (*BGU* I 361; 326 = M. *Chr.* 316 = *Sel. Pap.* I 85; *P. Amh.* II 80). At Antinoopolis, official documents were posted at temple of Antinoos (see p. 244).

135 It seems likely that the third-century Egyptian was as religious as his or her

ancestors and the evidence of private religious activity is abundant if, unfortunately, mostly undatable (Dunand 1979; Frankfurter 1998).

136 Some of the early monks were learned, see Rufinus, *HM* 137–8; 144–56.

137 Artemius had been transferred to Rome, where he faced problems (perhaps because of his militant Christianity), but nothing that Ammianus felt worth recording (Amm. Marc. XVII 11 5).

138 Socrates (*HE* V 16–17) continues with the pagans fleeing and Theophilos, assisted by troops, destroying the Sarapeion and dismantling the icons. Theodoret (*HE* V 22) discusses the destruction of cult statues but fails to mention the associated violence. See Schwartz 1966 for an attempt to reconcile the conflicting accounts and a list of other important sources.

139 Trombley (1994: II 210–20) argues that Schenoute's activities suggest that the struggle between Christians and pagans continued long after Schenoute's death in 466. See Frankfurter 1998: 68–70; 265–6; 282–4 for further stories of monks and pagans in conflict over temples and images in the fifth century.

140 The Holy Church of God of Hermopolis acted through an elder of the Ἁγιου Μερ(κουριου) βωου in the sixth century (*Stud. Pal. Pap.* III 270). This may be the Church of the Altar of St Mercurius, a known Coptic saint (Orlandi and Camaioni 1976), or be linked to Hermes (Mercury) and located in the old temple. This latter suggestion, however, verges on the fanciful.

141 For an overview of Christian Thebes see Krause 1979–82.

142 This mirrors debates concerning structuralist, Marxist, post-structuralist and other post-modern theories of society discussed on pp. 35–9.

143 For similar readings of developments elsewhere in the Roman world see Brown 1981; Van Dam 1985; 1993; MacLynn 1994; Markus 1990; Wharton 1995.

144 For an earlier list see Antonini 1940 and for a survey of Christianity at Oxyrhynchus see Modena 1936–7; 1938–9.

145 Abba Andreos: *P. Oxy.* I 146; 147; XVI 1911; LV 3804; *SB* XVIII 14061; 14062; 14063; Abba Apollos: *P. Oxy.* XVI 1913; Demetrios: *PSI* VII 791; Abba Hermelogos: *P. Oxy.* XXVII 2480; Abba Hermes: *P. Oxy.* XXVII 2480; Abba Hierax: *P. Oxy.* LI 3640, LXII 4397, *PSI* VII 791; Homoousion; *P. Oxy.* XVI 1952; Abba Jeremios: *P. Oxy.* XXVII 2480; Abba Kopreus: *P. Oxy.* XVI 1890; Lamason: *PSI* VII 791; Musaios: *P. Oxy.* XVI 2920; Pamous: *P. Oxy.* XXVII 2480; Papsenios: *PSI* VII 791; Philoxenos: *PSI* VII 791; St Phoibammon: *P. Oxy.* LV 3805; Abba Saraous: *P. Oxy.* XXXIII 3150; Abba Sarmatos: *PSI* VIII 953

146 *P. Rain. Cent.* 145.

147 *P. Prag.* I 74.

148 *P. Prag.* I 75; *Stud. Pal. Pap.* XX 198; X 168; III 164; *SB* I 5129.

149 *Stud. Pal. Pap.* XX 243; X 216.

150 *Stud. Pal. Pap.* X 168; *P. Lond.* I, p. 220, 113; *BGU* I 311.

151 *SB* I 4758; *Stud. Pal. Pap.* VIII 724.

152 *Stud. Pal. Pap.* III 126; 128; 239; *P. Grenf.* I 68.

153 *Stud. Pal. Pap.* III 126; VIII 881; *P. Lond.* I, pp. 220, 113.

154 *SB* I 5134; *Stud. Pal. Pap.* VIII 743.

155 *P. Flor.* III 336.

156 *SB* I 5128.

157 *SB* I 5129.

158 *P. Prag.* I 52; 77; *Stud. Pal. Pap.* III 324; *SB* I 4839; 4891; 4898; 4936; 5129; 5313; 5691; XVI 12943; *P. Col.* VIII 244; *P. Dublin.* 30; 34.

159 *CPR* XX 8.

160 *Stud. Pal. Pap.* III 321.

161 *Stud. Pal. Pap.* III 603.

162 *Stud. Pal. Pap.* VIII 854; *P. Dublin* 29.

163 *Stud. Pal. Pap.* X 60.

164 *Stud. Pal. Pap.* VIII 906.

165 *Stud. Pal. Pap.* VIII 1286.

166 *P. Dublin* 32; 33. For *proastion* see p. 375 n. 95.

167 *P. Dublin* 32; 33; 34; McGing 1990.

168 *P. Dublin* 32.

169 For village churches see *P. Bad.* 94 and Rémondon (1972). We face a difficulty with Aphrodito since the community enjoyed urban status for at least some of its history and even after its absorption into the Antaiopolite nome, it defended vigorously elements of autonomy (mainly in matters of taxation) that it retained.

170 At Aphrodito a series of eighth-century registers list monasteries of Pharoou, Taroou, Hermaos, Maria and Babarou many times and seemingly in sequence, but do not attest other Christian institutions, which might lead historians to believe that these institutions had lapsed, but for *P. Lond.* IV 1419, which shows much greater levels of continuity into the eighth century.

171 The central basilica at Hermopolis was a major structure, with monumental entrances to the north (a rather grander entrance) and west, marked by columns and stairs which would have elevated the bishop above the street and provided an impressive facade. Basilicas were not always equipped with great frontages and even at Hermopolis, the basilical area was rather untidy, with many associated buildings cluttering lines of sight to the basilica itself. With theatres and amphitheatres one of the major aims was to get people close to the action, but this was not a principal feature of the basilica design (which in terms of 'stage' and 'actors' was very similar in function). The basilical structure provided the officiants with a narrow line of sight to the audience which allowed priests and bishops to talk to all the congregation directly. The direct relationship of the audience with the events 'staged' in the basilica may have enhanced the sense of a community headed by the bishop. The enclosure of basilicas meant that to enter was to make a transition from a secular outside to a sacred inside, but by so doing one separates the internal community of the congregation and the external, more varied and much larger community of the city.

172 See also John of Nikiou, *Chronicle* 83 (ed. H. Zotenberg); Orlandi c.1967: II 1–69; Evetts (n.d.): II, Theophilos.

173 Under the patriarchy of Theodosius I (535–67), the patriarch quarrelled with Justinian, Justinian closed the churches to impose his own bishop, Paul, but the 'orthodox' built their own church at 'the Pillars of the Sarapeum' and a church of Kosmas and Damian (Evetts (n.d.): II, Theodosius I). Meier (1995) and Haas (1997: 271; cf. MacLynn 1994) separately argue that bishops had difficulty controlling the fringes of their cities, which meant that dissident groups could gather in these areas.

174 See John Moschos, *Pratum Spirituale* 194, on a dispute between an urban monk and one from the community at Sketis.

175 Wipszycka (1994) has argued that urban monasticism was a form of internal colonization of abandoned areas which were a kind of urban desert.

176 Wipszycka (1994), quoting Theodoros Anagnostes, *EH* (ed. G.Ch. Hansen)

(Berlin, 1971), p. 104, sees no reason to take this story seriously, though it must suggest an expectation of monkish involvement in ecclesiastical politics.

177 Winlock and Crum (1926: I 32–3) argue that the tower at the monastery of Epiphanius was also for defence. Godlewski's (1986: 30–3) excavation of what appears to have been a very similar monastery at Deir el-Bahari also uncovered a tower on the south side of the monastic site and so in its most prominent position. This tower had large windows. Towers were common aspects of domestic and agricultural architecture and were used to store agricultural produce or to provide a lighter, cooler environment, but such structures were not just functional.

178 If Apa Dios is taken as a monastic foundation, then the figures for monastic land are 42 per cent of all grain land (89 per cent of Church holdings) and 59 per cent of other land (98 per cent of Church holdings).

179 Gascou (1991) has a more conservative view based on the Oxyrhynchite and Hermopolite tax lists, which do not appear to register monasteries among the wealthier individuals or institutions within the nome, concluding that 'it does not look as if the wealth of the monasteries . . . had developed to the extent of the patriarchate, the imperial crown, the various bishops' churches or the lay dignitaries, such as the Apions'.

180 See also Eutychius (PG 111, col. 1084) on John's gifts to Jerusalem.

181 See Wipszycka 1972 for a survey of the economic activities of the Church. The Hermopolis lists of landowners of the mid-fourth century (Bagnall 1992; Bowman 1985; *P. Landl.*) contain references to four bishops: Ammonianos (47.25 *arourai*), Arion (25 *arourai*), Makarios (8 *arourai*) and Dios (c. 494 *arourai*). It seems very likely that the land registered to bishops in the Hermopolite was private land and not part of Church property. Two estates owned by sons of bishops are attested in the Oxyrhynchite (*P. Oxy.* LV 3804; cf XVI 1911) and an unprovenanced text attests a boat belonging to a bishop's son (*P. Harr.* I 94).

182 The grammar of this letter is confusing, and although the editor assumed that the assistant was Enoch and remarked at the rather odd combination of offices, it is possible that the bath-attendant and the magistrate were different people.

183 The office was still an honour in the late sixth century. Governors of Sicily were expected to ratify the appointment of *curatores* after AD 537 (Justinian, *Novellae* 75), though it is not clear whether this ruling was of any significance in Egypt.

184 Apphous is also probably attested in *SB* I 4666 of AD 659. The Dukedom survived the Arab conquest but was already divested of its military role by the late Byzantine period (Grohmann 1957).

185 These developments, it has been argued, were the culmination in a long decline of the councillors (Liebeschuetz 1996; Whittow 1990; Bowman 1971: 126).

186 See Petit 1955: 82–90. The emergence of a core body of councillors is discussed by Garnsey (1974) and Mouritsen (1998).

187 Landownership (although the most important form of wealth), is not directly correlated to wealth since wealth could be generated through trades and crafts. A weaver's skill is not an easily measurable asset, but is a form of wealth. The distribution of wealth across the city would be far more equal than the distribution of land.

188 The baths at Takona were included possibly because of the location of the circus stables. *P. Oxy.* XVI 2040 should not be compared with the tax list *P. Oxy.* XVI 2020, in which the contribution by the Apions appears far less significant.

Gascou (1972b) argues that the Apions act only as intermediaries responsible for the tax collected in the latter text and the totals of grain collected, extremely large though they are, do not relate to the size of landholdings. The contributions of the Apions to the *fiscus* were, as can be seen in *P. Oxy.* XVI 1918, extremely large.

189 The difference between Gascou and Hardy rests on diametrically opposed assumptions as to whether the 'feudal' elements of the system would bring power to the local lords or to the state that imposed those lords. Both depend on readings of Byzantine history external to the archive, seeing the period either as one of the decay of the ancient world and thus the ancient state, or as one of the gradual centralization of power in the hands of the emperor, a view that can be traced back to Procopius, *Anecdota*. I would suggest that the obvious ability of the Byzantine state to mobilize significant resources in the sixth and seventh centuries should incline us towards Gascou's version.

190 Schmitt (1994) argues that *bucellarioi* were real soldiers who were associated with officers and who served as their personal guard. This would account for their close involvement with estates. Although these men do appear to be part of the official army, their integration into estate management is not so clear.

191 Unfortunately, the nature of such accretions (normally quite flimsy extensions around existing architectural features) means that they would be difficult to detect and the distaste of early archaeologists for late Roman and Byzantine material means that any visible accretions may have been cleared without being reported.

192 Epigraphic material from Alexandria attests the activity of the circus factions (Borkowski 1981), and it is clear that the factions operated throughout Egypt. One of the few illustrated papyri, a sixth-century text from Antinoopolis, depicts members of the circus factions (Gasiorowski 1931). The Alexandrian material is paralleled at Aphrodisias (Roueché 1989; 1993).

193 One of the problems of evaluating John of Nikiou is that other sources do not discuss the factions' role in the traumas of the seventh century, but, following the general late antique literary preference, emphasize religion. For instance, the *Chronicon Pascale*, p. 699, tells us that Heraclius had the patriarch of Alexandria killed on seizing the city.

194 This is not just modern theory. The remodelling of cities, from Hausmann's demolition of Paris, to the slum clearances in British industrial cities in the third quarter of the twentieth century, to the great colonial enterprises of the nineteenth century were explicitly designed to produce new societies. Perhaps more damagingly, the imposition of new or foreign spatial patterns on a society may considerably disrupt existing modes of socialization and the formation of social relationships without imposing new structures (Shields 1997; Katz 1991).

6 THE CITY, REGION AND WORLD

1 I wish to avoid reductionist analyses of urbanism, such as that of Sjoberg (1960), which frequently degenerate into a discussion of categories and typologies. Category analyses should provide a base for further analysis of particular urban forms, but there is no agreement about what should be in the list (a literate culture, for instance, often figures without qualification). De Ligt (1990)

suggests that towns may be defined by differences in population and occupational structure: 'a settlement should not be defined as a town when its population is much below 2,000, nor when over 50 per cent of its inhabitants are engaged in agricultural production'. Marshall (1989: 4) notes that the United States operates a formal lower threshold for an urban settlement of 2,500 people while Canada uses 1,000. Levi (1989: 34) offers six criteria to which a settlement should conform before it can be classed as a city: (1) single topographic unit; (2) number of inhabitants above a certain number (1,000); (3) labour and social differentiation; (4) variety of workshops by type and volume; (5) manner of life; (6) central point in respect to a territory. Hodges (1989: 20–5) summarizes various criteria offered for defining a town. To cut through this morass, I argue that a city should be a densely occupied centre of population. Ancient settlements called cities by modern scholars have vast ranges of population from a few hundred to a few hundred thousand. Where should the line be drawn and, given the absence of good figures for population, how can one judge when a settlement (and settlement is not always easy to define) is a city? The very fact that agreement cannot be reached on the characteristics of the urban in ancient or modern societies confirms that 'city' is a shifting category and has no absolute definition, being only meaningful in the context of a particular settlement system. It cannot, therefore, be defined until the settlement system as a whole is considered.

2   D.W. Rathbone and I hope to complete a study of this archive.

3   *Stud. Pal. Pap.* XXII 183 from Soknopaiou Nesos lists similar contributions to the temple.

4   The *katoikoi* seem to have made some claim for a Greek identity, probably as Ptolemaic military colonists within the Fayum and hence an alternative ethnic reading is possible in that these 'non-Egyptian' groups are listed because of the expectation that they would not be asked to contribute to a traditional Egyptian temple.

5   This village had a strong military presence (Alston 1995: 117–42), which undoubtedly distorts the pattern of attestation. The numbers involved are also very small (total n. for second century = 29; total n. for all centuries = 50).

6   The figures for the Oxyrhynchite seem plausible. If we assume 150 villages within the nome (see figures 6.5–6.6) this would suggest an average population per village of *c.* 900, which is lower than the mean figures for village population derived from table 6.3 (1,200–1,400) though substantially higher than the median figure for village size. See also Rathbone 1990.

7   Most references to weavers in *metropoleis* are from the first century AD.

8   *P. Oxy.* XVII 2109 = *Sel. Pap.* II 356 of AD 261 publishes a request to rent an *ergasterion* in the stoa near the Kapitoleion of Oxyrhynchus. *P. Oxy.* XVI 1966 of AD 505 attests an *ergasterion* with two rooms in the *stoa* of the *amphodon* of Pses in the same city. *P. Merton* II 76 of 181 is a rental of an *ergasterion* and associated buildings in a *stoa* in the *amphodon* of Heroon also in Oxyrhynchus. *P. Turner* I 37 attests *ergasteria* facing the *plateia* (square/avenue) at Ptolemais Euergetis (cf. *P. Ross. Georg.* III 38 = *CPJ* III 511 *BL* IX, 226; *P. Oxy.* X 1323; Hickey 1996; *P. Oxy.* XII 1461).

9   De Ligt (1993: 200–36; 1995) argues that the influx of peasants prevented middlemen raising their margins on foodstuffs in the urban market since they could be undercut by the peasants.

10 Duncan-Jones (1994: 176) suggests that most money moved through the

military in the late second century AD and it may be that money was imported to pay soldiers. I think it is difficult to reconcile the economic model proposed by Duncan-Jones with the rather more outwardly oriented and integrated economic networks postulated here and in Alston 1998. The Oxyrhynchite coin-finds can be compared with other fourth-century Egyptian hoards, mostly from   the Fayum (Milne 1920). The various finds are composed of 41.4–54.7 per cent of Alexandrian coins while Western coins contribute 8.8 per cent (all Rome), 7.3 per cent (various mints), 2.8 per cent and 8.62 per cent (7.4 per cent from Rome) of the total (Lallemand 1966; Milne 1920).

11   See also the discussion of amphorae and the identification of a Hermopolite type in Spencer and Bailey 1982: 16; Spencer et al. 1983: Appendix III.

12   See Bagnall 1978 and 1985 on Karanis. The uneven distribution of metropolite property in the Hermopolite is more complex and I hope to publish on this in a study of the settlement pattern of the Oxyrhynchite. Essentially, the argument is based on a comparison of tax payments by villages in *P. Oxy.* XIV 1659 with *P. Oxy.* X 1285 and XXIV 2422. Since I have found no one who argues that the distribution of metropolite landholdings would be even, it seems otiose to make much of a counter-case here, but one would assume that topographical irregularities, patterns of investment, and historical accident, such as the location of Ptolemaic land settlements, would create diversity. I think it is also to be expected that those communities located closer to the city might be more attractive investments.

13   We know nothing of agricultural production within the city or about the export of surplus to Alexandria.

14   One should perhaps think in terms of 'hegemonic modes of economic exploitation' as suggested by Wickham 1984.

15   This model oversimplifies since the Ptolemaic period saw significant investment in developing new lands and, of course, in the growth of Alexandria. Nevertheless, it seems unlikely that the economy was undergoing significant structural change by the late Ptolemaic period.

16   The thesis concerning limits set on surplus production would seem to depend on arguments concerning economic rationalism (see p. 359). This debate turns on a precise and narrow definition of economic rationality: that all 'rational' agents seek to maximize their profit. This makes two questionable assumptions. First, any social investment is not in the economic best interests of the investor in the long term (which automatically assumes that the economy is not closely embedded in a social world). Second, the answer to the economic problems of the Roman world was the generation of increased surplus for the already extremely wealthy economic elite.

17   This has obvious similarities with Lefebvre's (1991) conception of the globalization of spatial division at the opening of the twentieth century. See also Slater (1992) on post-modernism.

18   'Capitalism in one country' has been unfeasible in Britain for a century or more, a lesson my grandfather had absorbed. As a Lancashire cotton weaver, he went to see Gandhi when the Indian leader toured Britain to explain his policy of economic resistance to British imperialism, a policy that threatened to destroy my grandfather's trade.

19 Hopkins (1980b) argues that the imposition of monetary taxation by Rome stimulated economic growth since it forced farmers to produce for the market so that they could meet the tax burden. This increased specialization and efficiency within agriculture generated prosperity while the resulting trade led to the foundation of market-centres. In Egypt, monetary taxation, though significantly increased by Rome, had existed for centuries and taxes in kind were probably a greater burden. It seems likely that the net effect of taxation would be detrimental to the Egyptian economy, depriving it of resources, though its net effect was probably not great.

20 See the broadly similar estimates in Slack 1985: 151.

21 This is an artificial calculation, but if we assume that aristocratic farmers do not need to generate a return on capital tied up in land (i.e. the value of the land did not figure in their economic calculations), then they needed only to make a return on short-term investment so that doubling investment means that the land needs to work twice as hard. In which case, low investment strategies may be a sensible option. Columella, *De Re Rustica* III 3 is an ancient and rather problematic attempt to calculate returns from a high investment strategy and he makes clear that one of the concerns of farmers is the initial outlay.

Table 6.6 Hypothetical returns on agricultural investment

Value of farm	Annual investment	Required return on farm	Required return on annual investment	Total required return	Return as % of annual investment	Return as % of value of land
100,000	10,000	6,000	10,600	16,600	166	16.6
100,000	5,000	6,000	5,300	11,300	226	11.3
100,000	10,000	0	10,600	10,600	106	10.6
100,000	5,000	0	5,300	5,300	106	5.3

22 An obvious assumption would be that references from the second and third centuries attest only large taxpaying villages. Nevertheless, I do not see why the fourth-century evidence (where the change starts to become visible) should be any different in its pattern of attestations.

23 The broad periods used to classify the various sites present considerable methodological difficulties since a shifting population might occupy several sites only briefly within a particular period.

24 Obviously, there are some doubts about Cosson's classifications.

25 I imply nothing about the ethnic identities of the farmers.

26 There is some debate as to whether the increased evidence of water-wheels, probably saqiyas, represents greater investment in water-management or is simply a function of the level of attestation of the great estates in the fifth and sixth centuries. A parallel debate concerns the efficiency with which labour was organized to maintain the canals, the evidence being greater for the earlier period (Sijpesteijn 1964; Bonneau 1970; Morelli 1999).

27 Haas (1997: 338–51) uses Arabic sources that show Alexandria to have been an important centre until the eighth or ninth century, though probably in the context of a population decline. Fraser (1981) argues for a rapid seventh-century depopulation.

28 I think this is somewhat counter-intuitive and it seems to me likely, even if a population cannot be detected archaeologically, that there remained a small congregation for a bishop to supervise at Thmouis.

29 This desertion is linked to hydrological changes that resulted from the increased exploitation of the area. The success of the aforementioned drainage scheme led to an increase in saline building land but a decrease in agricultural land. The area was completely desiccated in the early sixth century. Purely local factors explain this decline.

30 Fourteenth-century documentary sources can be used to generate 'rates of disappearance' following plague outbreaks of 76 per cent or *c.* 50 per cent for France (Gottfried 1983: 49–64) and 19–80 per cent (perhaps averaging at 35–45 per cent) for England (Goldberg 1996; Hatcher 1977: 20–5). This might suggest that 20 per cent mortality was a low estimate, though the socio-economic disruption that tends to follow severe outbreaks of plague probably meant that disappearance rates were higher than mortality rates. See Champion 1993; 1995 and Slack 1985: 101–51 for sixteenth-century death rates, though note the scepticism of Twigg 1993.

31 Horrox (1994: 7–8) and Dols (1977: 156) suggest that the biological characteristics may have changed in that the plague infected common domestic animals, not just rats and humans. Twigg (1993) is, however, sceptical and argues that 'plague' was a multi-epidemic event so that the described animal deaths could be related to a different epidemic (or just be a function of the mass hysteria that followed the outbreak of plague). Landers (1993) shows just how improbable and inexact many of the diagnoses were in the late seventeenth and eighteenth centuries, high mortality again seemingly resulting from multi-epidemic events. One is reminded that the Greeks and Romans used blanket terminology to describe 'plague' / 'disease'.

32 The problem with the identification between the Byzantine state and Christianity explored by Fowden (1993) is that this is essentially a top-down view. It was a way in which the emperors liked their rule to be portrayed and which inevitably suited others playing political games, such as bishops. In the villages and neighbourhoods of Egypt, however, the primary representatives of the new order were the local churches and these repeatedly proved their ability to survive without imperial support and to withstand official hostility. The identification of the Byzantine state with Christianity may have been powerful in Constantinople but was rather less convincing in Oxyrhynchus.

BIBLIOGRAPHY

Abu Lughod, J.L. (1971) *Cairo: 1001 Years of the City Victorious*, Princeton.

Adriani, A. (1939) 'Scavi della missione dell'Istituto Papirologico Fiorentino ad Antinoe', *ASAE* 39: 659–63.

Alcock, A. (2000) 'Women cobblers in a 4th cent. Egyptian oasis', *Archiv* 46: 50.

Allam, S. (1981) 'Quelques aspects du mariage dans l'Égypte ancienne', *JEA* 67: 116–35.

—— (1990) 'Note sur le mariage par deux contrats dans l'Égypte gréco-romaine', *CE* 129: 323–33.

Allison, P.M. (1997a) 'Artefact distribution and spatial function in Pompeian houses', in B. Rawson and P. Weaver (eds) *The Roman Family in Italy: Status, Sentiment, Space*, Canberra and Oxford: 321–54.

—— (1997b) 'Roman households: an archaeological perspective', in H.M. Parkins (ed.) *Roman Urbanism: Beyond the Consumer City*, London and New York: 112–46.

Al-Masri, Y.S.S. (1983) 'Preliminary report on the excavations in Akhmim by the Egyptian antiquities organization', *ASAE* 69: 7–13.

Al Sayyad, N. (1992) 'The Islamic city', in N. Al Sayyad (ed.) *Forms of Dominance: On the Architecture and Urbanism of the Colonial Enterprise*, Berkeley: 27–43.

Alston, R. (1995) *Soldier and Society in Roman Egypt: A Social History*, London and New York.

—— (1996) 'Conquest by text: Juvenal and Plutarch on Egypt', in J. Webster and N. Cooper (eds) *Roman Imperialism: Post-Colonial Perspectives* (Leicester Archaeology Monographs, 3), Leicester: 99–109.

—— (1997a) 'Houses and households in Roman Egypt', in R. Laurence and A. Wallace-Hadrill (eds) *Domestic Space in the Roman World: Pompeii and Beyond* (*JRA* Suppl., 22), Portsmouth, RI: 25–39.

—— (1997b) 'Philo's *In Flaccum*: Ethnicity and social space in Roman Alexandria', *Greece and Rome* 44: 165–75.

—— (1997c) 'Ritual and power in the Romano-Egyptian city', in H.M. Parkins (ed.) *Roman Urbanism: Beyond the Consumer City*, London and New York: 147–72.

—— (1998) 'Trade and the city in Roman Egypt', in H. Parkins and C. Smith (eds) *Trade, Traders and the Ancient City*, London and New York: 168–202.

—— (1999a) 'The revolt of the Boukoloi: Geography, history and myth', in K. Hopwood (ed.) *Organised Crime in Antiquity*, London: 129–53.

—— (1999b) 'The ties that bind: soldiers and societies', in A. Goldsworthy and I. Haynes (eds) *The Roman Army as Community* (*JRA* Suppl., 34), Portsmouth, RI: 175–95.

—— (forthcoming) 'Urban population in Late Roman Egypt and the end of the ancient world', in W. Scheidel (ed.) *Debating Roman Demography*, Leiden, Cologne and Boston, 161–204.

Alston, R. and R.D. Alston (1997) 'Urbanism and the urban community in Roman Egypt', *JEA* 83: 199–216.

Alt, A. (1920) 'Noch einmal ΠΥΡΓΟΣ "Wirtschaftsgebäude"', *Hermes* 55: 334–6.

Altheim-Stiehl, R. (1991) 'Wurde Alexandreia im Juni 619n. Chr. durch die Perser erobert? Bemerkungen zur zeitlichen Bestimmung der sāsānidischen Besetzung Ägyptens unter Chosrau II Parwez', *Tyche* 6: 3–16.

—— (1992) 'The Sasanians in Egypt – some evidence of historical interest', *BSAC* 31: 87–96

Amelotti, M. (1966) *Il testamento romano attraverso le prassi documentale. I. Le forme classiche di testamento*, Florence.

Anderson, B. (1991) *Imagined Communities*, London and New York.

Anderson, K. (1998) 'Sites of difference: Beyond a cultural politics of race polarity', in R. Fincher and J.M. Jacobs (eds) *Cities of Difference*, New York and London: 201–25.

Anderson, M. (1972) 'Household structure and the industrial revolution: mid-nineteenth-century Preston in comparative perspective', in P. Laslett (ed.) *Household and Family in Past Time*, London: 215–35.

Anderson, W.S. (1988) 'Juvenal Satire XV: Cannibals and culture', in A.J. Boyle (ed.) *The Imperial Muse: Ramus Essays in the Roman Literature of the Empire: To Juvenal through Ovid*, Berwick: 203–14.

Andreau, J. (1987–9) 'La cité antique et la vie économique', *Opus* 6–8: 175–85.

Anti, C. (1930) 'Gli scavi della missione archeologia Italiano a Umm el Breighât (Tebtunis)', *Aegyptus* 11: 389–91.

Antonini, L. (1940) 'La chiese cristiane nell' Egitto dal IV al IX secolo secondo i documenti dei papiri greci', *Aegyptus* 20: 129–208.

Anus, P. and Sa'ad, R. (1971), 'Habitations de prêtres dans le temple d' Amon de Karnak', *Kêmi* 21: 217–38.

Arafa, D. (1995) 'Fresh investigations into the tombs of the Ptolemaic period in Alexandria', in N. Bonacasa, C. Naro, E. Chiara Porlale and A Tullio (eds) *Alessandria e il Mondo Ellenistico-Romano: I Centenario del Museo Greco-Romano: Atti del II Congresso Internazionale Italo-Egiziano*, Rome: 119–23.

Arnaoutoglou, I. (1995) 'Marital disputes in Greco-Roman Egypt', *JJP* 25: 11–28.

Archer, L.J. (1990) *Her Price is Beyond Rubies: The Jewish Woman in Graeco-Roman Palestine* (*Journal for the Study of the Old Testament* Suppl., 60), Sheffield.

Ardener, S. (1993) 'Ground rules and social maps for women. An introduction', in S. Ardener (ed.) *Women and Space: Ground Rules and Social Maps*, Oxford: 11–34.

Arjava, A. (1996) *Women and Law in Late Antquity*, Oxford.

Athanassiadi, P. (1993) 'Persecution and response in late paganism: The evidence of Damascius', *JHS* 113: 1–29.

—— (1999) *Damascius: The Philosophical History*, Athens.

Atkinson, D. and Cosgrove, D. (1998) 'Urban rhetoric and embodied identities: City, nation, and empire in the Vittorio Emanuele II Monument in Rome, 1870–1945', *AAAG* 88: 28–49.

Bachatly, C. (1950) 'Thebes – "le Monastère de Phoibammon"', *CE* 25: 167–9.

Bachelard, G. (1994) *The Poetics of Space* (trans. M. Jolas), Boston, Mass.

Badian, E. (1972), *Publicans and Sinners: Private Enterprise in the Service of the Roman Republic*, Dunedin.

Bagnall, R.S. (1978) 'Property-holdings of liturgists in fourth-century Karanis', *BASP* 15: 9–16.

—— (1982) 'Religious conversion and onomastic change in early Byzantine Egypt', *BASP* 19: 105–24.

—— (1985) 'Agricultural productivity and taxation in fourth-century Egypt', *TAPA* 115: 289–308.

—— (1987) 'Conversion and onomastics: A reply', *ZPE* 69: 243–50.

—— (1988a) 'Combat ou vide: christianisme et paganisme dans l'Égypte romaine tardive', *Ktema* 13: 285–96.

—— (1988b) 'Greeks and Egyptians: Ethnicity, status and culture', in *Cleopatra's Egypt: Age of the Ptolemies*, Brooklyn: 21–7.

—— (1991) 'The beginnings of the Roman census in Egypt', *GRBS* 32: 255–65.

—— (1992) 'Landholding in late Roman Egypt: The distribution of wealth', *JRS* 82: 128–49.

—— (1993) *Egypt in Late Antiquity*, Princeton.

—— (1995) *Reading Papyri, Writing Ancient History*, London, New York.

Bagnall, R.S. and Frier, B.W. (1994) *The Demography of Roman Egypt*, Cambridge.

Bagnall, R.S., Frier, B.W., and Rutherford, I.C. (1997) *The Census Register P. Oxy. 984: The Reverse of Pindar's Paeans* (Papyrologica Bruxellensia, 29), Brussels.

Bagnall, R.S. and Worp, K.A. (1980) 'Grain land in the Oxyrhynchite nome', *ZPE* 37: 263–4.

Bagnani, G. (1934) 'Gli scavi di Tebtunis', *Aegyptus* 14: 1–13.

Baigent, E. (1988) 'Economy and society in eighteenth century English Towns', in D. Denecke and G. Shaw (eds) *Urban Historical Geography: Recent Progress in Britain and Germany*, Cambridge: 109–24.

Bailey, D.M. et al. (1982) *British Museum Expedition to Middle Egypt: Ashmunein (1980)*, London.

—— (1986) 'The procession-house of the Great Hermaion at Hermopolis Magna', in M. Henig and A. King (eds) *Pagan Gods and Shrines of the Roman Empire*, Oxford: 231–7.

—— (1991) *Excavations at El-Ashmunein IV: Hermopolis Magna: Buildings of the Roman Period*, London.

Baker, C.M. (1998) '"Ordering the House": On the domestication of Jewish bodies', in M. Wyke (ed.) *Parchments of Gender: Deciphering the Bodies of Antiquity*, Oxford: 221–42.

Baker, J. and Pedersen, P.O. (1992) 'Introduction', in J. Baker and P.O. Pedersen (eds) *The Rural–Urban Interface in Africa: Expansion and Adaptation*, Uppsala: 11–28.

Balconi, C. (1985) 'Alessandria nell' età augustea: aspetti di vita', in *Egitto e Storia Antica: Atti del Convegno Turino 8/9 vi –23/24 xi 1984*, Milan: 181–96.

Baldassare, I. (1983) 'Antinoe–Necropoli meridionale (Saggi 1978)', *ASAE* 69: 157–66.

Ballet, P. (1988), 'La ceramique des Kellia: Nouvelles orientations de recherches', in E.C.M. van den Brink (ed.) *The Archaeology of the Nile Delta, Egypt: Problems and Priorities*, Amsterdam: 297–312.

Ballet, P. and von der Way, T. (1993) 'Exploration archéologique de Bouto et de sa région (époques romaine et byzantine)', *MDAIK* 49: 1–22.

Balty, J.C. (1989) 'Apamée au VIe siècle. Témoignages archéologiques de la richesse d'une ville', in *Hommes et richesses dans l'Empire byzantine I: IVe–VIIe siècle*, Paris: 79–86.

Baraize, E. (1940) 'L'"agora" d'Hermoupolis', *ASAE* 40: 741–5.

Baranski, M. (1989) *Reports from Ashmunein: Polish–Egyptian Archaeological and Preservation Mission at El-Ashmunein*, Warsaw.

—— (1996) 'The archaeological setting of the great basilical church at el-Ashmunein', in D.M. Bailey (ed.) *Archaeological Research in Roman Egypt* (*JRA* Suppl., 19), Ann Arbor: 98–106.

Barison, P. (1938) 'Ricerche sui monasteri dell' Egitto bizantino ed arabo secondo i documenti dei papiri greci', *Aegyptus* 18: 29–148.

Barker, D.C. (1997) 'The place of residence of the divorced wife in Roman Egypt', in *Akten des 21 internationalen Papyrologenkongresses, Berlin 13–19.8.1995*, Leipzig and Stuttgart: 59–66.

Barker, G. and Mattingly, D. (1996) *Farming the Desert: The UNESCO Libyan Valleys Survey*, Paris, Tripoli and London.

Barnes, T.J. and Duncan, J.S. (1992a) 'Afterword', in T.J. Barnes and J.S. Duncan (eds) *Writing Worlds: Discourse, Text and Metaphor in the Representation of Landscape*, London and New York: 248–53.

—— and —— (1992b) 'Introduction: Writing Worlds', in T.J. Barnes and J.S. Duncan (eds) *Writing Worlds: Discourse, Text and Metaphor in the Representation of Landscape*, London and New York: 1–17.

Barraclough, R. (1984) 'Philo's politics: Roman rule and Hellenistic Judaism', *ANRW* II 21.1: 417–553.

Barry, W.D. (1993a) 'Aristocrats, orators and the "Mob": Dio Chrysostom and the world of the Alexandrians', *Historia* 42: 82–103.

—— (1993b) 'The crowd of Ptolemaic Alexandria and the riot of 203 BC', *EMC/CV* 37: 415–31.

Barth, F. (1969) *Ethnic Groups and Boundaries*, Oslo.

Barzano, A. (1988) 'Tiberio Guilio Alessandro, Prefetto d'Egitto (66/70)' *ANRW* II 10.1: 518–80.

Bastianini, G. (1985) 'Le instituzione pubbliche nell' Egitto romano', in *Egitto e Società Antica. Atti del Convegno Turino 8/9 vi – 23/24 xi 1984*, Milan: 197–209.

—— and J.E.G. Whitehorne (1987) *Strategi and Royal Scribes of Roman Egypt. Chronological List and Index* (Papyrologica Florentina, 15), Florence.

Bataille, A. (1951) 'Thèbes gréco-romaine', *CE* 26: 325–53.

Beard, M. and Henderson, J. (1995) *Classics: A Very Short Introduction*, Oxford and New York.

Beaucamp J. (1990) *Le statut de la femme à Byzance (4e–7e siècle) I: Le droit imperial* (*Travaux et Mémoires*, monographies, 5), Paris.

—— (1992) *Le statut de la femme à Byzance (4e–7e siècle) II: Les pratiques sociales* (*Travaux et Mémoires*, monographies, 6), Paris.

—— (1993) 'Organisation domestique et rôles sexuels: les papyrus byzantins', *DOP* 47: 185–94.

Beaujard, B. (1996) 'L'évêque dans la cité en Gaule aux Ve et VIe siècles', in C. Lepelley (ed.) *La fin de la cité antique et le début de la cité médiévale de la fin du IIIe siècle à l'avènement de Charlemagne*, Bari: 127–45.

Beaujeu-Garnier, J. and Delobez, A. (1979) *Geography of Marketing*, London and New York.

Belkin, S. (1940) *Philo and the Oral Law: The Philonic Interpretation of Biblical Law in Relation to Palestinian Halakah*, Cambridge, Mass.

Bell, H.I. (1924) *Jews and Christians in Egypt: The Jewish Troubles in Alexandria and the Athanasian Controversy*, London.

—— (1933) 'Diplomata Antoninoitica', *Aegyptus* 13: 514–28.

—— (1940) 'Antinoopolis: A Hadrianic foundation in Egypt', *JRS* 30: 133–47.

—— (1941) 'Anti-semitism in Alexandria', *JRS* 31: 1–13.

—— (1942) 'P. Giss. 40 and the *Constitutio Antoniniana*', *JEA* 28: 39–49.

—— (1944) 'A reply to the foregoing', *JEA* 30: 72–3.

—— (1950) 'Two private letters of the Byzantine period', in *Coptic Studies in Honor of Walter Ewing Crum*, Boston: 251–4.

Benbon, M. (1988) 'Epistemological assumptions in the study of racial differentiation', in J. Rex and D. Mason (eds) *Theories of Race and Ethnic Relations*, Cambridge: 42–63.

Benjamin, A. and Raubitschek, A.E. (1959) 'Arae Augusti', *Hesperia* 28: 65–85.

Benko, G. (1997) 'Introduction: Modernity, post-modernity and the social sciences', in G. Benko and U. Strohmayer (eds) *Space and Social Theory: Interpreting Modernity and Postmodernity*, Oxford: 1–44.

Bentley, G.C. (1987) 'Ethnicity and practice', *CSSH* 29: 24–55.

Bergmann, B. (1991) 'Painted perspectives of a villa visit: Landscape as a status metaphor', in E.K. Gazda (ed.) *Roman Art in the Private Sphere: New Perspectives on the Architecture and Decor of the Domus, Villa and Insula*, Ann Arbor: 49–70.

Bernal, M. (1987), *Black Athena: The Afroasiatic Roots of Classical Civilization I*, London.

—— (1991), *Black Athena: The Afroasiatic Roots of Classical Civilization II*, London.

Bernand, É. (1975) *Recueil des inscriptions grecques du Fayoum I*, Leiden.

Berquist, J.L. (1988) 'Controlling daughters' bodies in Sirach', in M. Wyke (ed.) *Parchments of Gender: Deciphering the Bodies of Antiquity*, Oxford: 95–120.

Bilde, P., Engberg-Pedersen, T., Hannestad, L., and Zahle, J. (eds) (1992) *Ethnicity in Hellenistic Egypt* (Studies in Hellenistic Civilization, 3), Aarhus.

Bingen, J. (1955), 'Anses d'amphores de Crocodilopolis–Arsinoé', *CE* 30: 130–3.

Birnbaum, E. (1996) *The Place of Judaism in Philo's Thought: Israel, Jews and Proselytes* (Brown Judaic Studies, 290), Atlanta.

Biscottini, M.V. (1966) 'L'archivio di Tryphon, tessitore di Oxyrhynchos', *Aegyptus* 46: 60–90, 186–292.

Blanchard-Lemée, M. (1975) *Maisons à mosaïques du quartier central de Djemila (Cuicul)*, Paris.

Bland, R. (1996) 'The Roman coinage of Alexandria, 30 BC–AD 296: Interplay between Roman and local designs', in D.M. Bailey (ed.) *Archaeological Research in Roman Egypt* (*JRA* Suppl., 19), Ann Arbor: 113–27.

Boak, A.E.R. (1933) *Karanis: The Temples, the Coin Hoardes, Botanical and Zoological Reports, Seasons 1924–1931*, Ann Arbor.

—— (1935) *Soknopaiou Nesos: The University of Michigan Excavations at Dime in 1931–32*, Ann Arbor.

—— (1937) 'The organisation of gilds in Greco-Roman Egypt', *TAPA* 68: 212–20.

—— (1955) 'The population of Roman and Byzantine Karanis', *Historia* 4: 157–62.

—— (1959) 'Egypt and the plague under Marcus Aurelius', *Historia* 8: 248–50.

Boak, A.E.R. and Peterson, E.E. (1931) *Karanis: Topographical and Architectural Reports of Excavations during the Seasons 1924–1928*, Ann Arbor.

Boak, A.E.R. and Youtie, H.C. (1960) *The Archive of Aurelius Isidorus*, Ann Arbor.

Boardman, J., Griffin, J. and Murray, O. (eds) (1986) *The Oxford History of the Classical World*, Oxford, New York.

Boatwright, M.T. (1987) *Hadrian and the City of Rome*, Princeton.

Bodel, J. (1997) 'Monumental villas and villa monuments', *JRA* 10: 5–35.

Boëthius, A. and Ward-Perkins, J.B. (1970) *Etruscan and Roman Architecture*, Harmondsworth.

Bonneau, D. (1970) 'L'administration de l'irrigation dans les grands domaines en

Égypte au VI siècle de n.è.', *Proceedings of the XIIth International Congress of Papyrology (Ann Arbor 1968)*, Toronto: 45–62.

Borkowski, Z. (1981) *Inscriptions des factions à Alexandrie*, Warsaw.

Borkowski, Z. and Hagedorn, D. (1975) 'ΑΜΦΟΔΟΚΟΜΟΓΡΑΜΜΑΤΕΥΣ: zur Verwaltung der Dörfer Ägyptens in 3 Jh.n.Chr.', *Le Monde Grec: Hommages à Cl. Preaux*, Brussels: 775–83.

Bouras, C. (1981) 'City and village: Urban design and architecture', *Jahrbuch der Österreichischen Byzantinisik* 31: 611–53.

Bourdieu, P. (1977) *Outline of a Theory of Practice*, Cambridge.

—— (1990) *The Logic of Practice*, Cambridge.

Bowersock, G.W. (1964) 'Augustus on Aegina', *CQ* 14: 120–1.

—— (1969) *Greek Sophists in the Roman Empire*, Oxford.

—— (1987) 'The mechanics of subversion in the Roman provinces', in A. Giovanni (ed.) *Oppositions et résistances à l'Empire d'Auguste à Trajan* (Entretiens Hardt, 33), Geneva: 291–320.

—— (1990) *Hellenism in Late Antiquity*, Cambridge.

—— (1997) 'Polytheism and monotheism in Arabia and the three Palestines', *DOP* 51: 1–10.

Bowman, A.K. (1971) *The Town Councils of Roman Egypt* (American Society of Papyrologists, 11), Toronto.

—— (1984) 'Two notes: II Market taxes at Oxyrhynchus', *BASP* 21: 33–8.

—— (1985) 'Landholding in the Hermopolite nome in the fourth century AD', *JRS* 75: 137–63.

—— (1992) 'Public buildings in Roman Egypt', *JRA* 5: 495–503.

Bowman, A.K. and Rathbone, D.W. (1992) 'Cities and administration in Roman Egypt', *JRS* 82: 107–27.

Brakke, D. (1995) *Athanasius and the Politics of Asceticism*, Oxford.

Braudel, F. (1972) *The Mediterranean and the Mediterranean World in the Age of Philip II* (trans S. Reynolds), London.

—— (1981) *The Structures of Everyday Life: The Limits of the Possible* (trans. S. Reynolds), London.

—— (1982) *The Wheels of Commerce* (trans. S. Reynolds), London.

Braund, S.H. (1988) *Beyond Anger*, Cambridge.

—— (1984) *The Perspective of the World* (trans. S. Reynolds), London.

Breccia, E. (1922) *Alexandrea ad Aegyptum*, Bergamo.

—— (1932) 'Fouilles à Oxyrhynchos et à Tebtunis. 1928–1930', *Le Musée Gréco-Romain 1925–1931*, Bergamo: 60–3.

—— (1934) 'Fouilles d'Oxyrhynchos' *Le Musée Gréco-Romain 1931–1932*, Bergamo: 36–47.

—— (1934–7) 'Un "Cronos Mitriaco" ad Oxyrhynchos', *Mélanges Maspero II: Orient Grec, Romain et Byzantine*, Cairo: 257–64

Brenk, F.E. (1992) 'Antony-Osiris, Cleopatra-Isis. The end of Plutarch's *Antony*', in P.A. Stadtler (ed.) *Plutarch and the Historical Tradition*, London: 159–82.

Bresciani, E., Foraboschi, D., and Pernigotti, I. (1978) *Assuan*, Pisa.

Brewster, E.H. (1927) 'A weaver of Oxyrhynchus: Sketch of a humble life', *TAPhA* 58: 132–54.

Brödner, E. (1989) *Wohnen in der Antike*, Darmstadt.

Brothers, A.J. (1996) 'Urban housing', in I.M. Barton (ed.) *Roman Domestic Buildings* (Exeter Studies in History), Exeter: 33–63.

Brown, P. (1971) 'The rise and function of the holy man in late antiquity', *JRS* 61:

80–101, reprinted in P. Brown (1982) *Society and the Holy in Late Antiquity*, Berkeley, Los Angeles: 103–52.

—— (1981) *The Cult of the Saints: Its Rise and Function in Latin Christianity*, London.

—— (1988) *The Body and Society: Men, Women and Sexual Renunciation in Early Christianity*, London, Boston.

—— (1992) *Power and Persuasion in Late Antiquity: Towards a Christian Empire*, Madison.

Bruhns, H. (1985) 'De Werner Sombart à Max Weber et Moses I. Finley: La typologie de la ville antique et la question de la ville de consommation', in P. Leveau (ed.) *L'origine des richesses dépensées dans la ville antique: Actes du colloque organisé à Aix-en-Provence par l'UER d' histoires les 11 et 12 Mai 1984*, Aix-en-Provence: 255–73.

Bruneau, P. (1970) *Exploration archéologique de Délos XXVII. L'Îlot de la Maison des Comédiens*, Paris.

Bruneau, P. and Ducat, J. (1983) *Guide de Délos*, Paris.

Bruno, V.J. and Scott, R.T. (1993) *Cosa IV: The Houses*, Philadelphia.

Brunt, P.A. (1965) 'The Equites in the Late Republic', in *Deuxième Conférence internationale d'histoire economique I: Trade and Politics in the Ancient World*, Paris: 17–49.

—— (1975) 'Did imperial Rome disarm her subjects?', *Phoenix* 29: 260–70, reprinted in P.A. Brunt (1990) *Roman Imperial Themes*, Oxford: 215–54.

Bruyère, B., Manteuffel, J., Michalowski, K., and Saint Faire Garnet, T. (1937) *Fouilles Franco-Polonaises. Rapports I: Tell Edfou 1937*, Cairo.

Bryce, J. (1914) *The Ancient Roman Empire and the British Empire in India: The Diffusion of Roman and English Law Throughout the World: Two Historical Studies*, Oxford.

Burgess, E.W., McKenzie, R.D., and Park, R.E (1925) *The City*, Chicago.

Burkhalter, F. (1992) 'Le gymnase d'Alexandrie: centre administratif de la province romaine d'Égypte', *BCH* 116: 345–73.

Butler, A.J. (1978) *The Arab Conquest of Egypt and the Last Thirty Years of Byzantine Rule* (2nd edn), Oxford.

Calderini, A. (1935–66) *Dizionario dei nomi geografici e topografici dell' Egitto-Romano*, Cairo.

—— (1938) 'Censimento topografico delle banche dell' Egitto greco-romano', *Aegyptus* 18: 244–78.

Cameron, Al. (1965) 'Wandering poets: A literary movement in Byzantine Egypt', *Historia* 14: 470–509.

—— (1976) *Circus Factions: Blues and Greens at Rome and Byzantium*, Oxford.

Cameron, Av. (1989) 'Introduction', in Av. Cameron (ed.) *History as Text*, London: 1–10.

—— (1993) *The Later Roman Empire*, London.

—— (1997) 'Hellenism and the emergence of Islam', *Dialogos* 4: 4–18.

—— (1998) 'Education and literary culture', in A. Cameron and P. Garnsey (eds) *The Cambridge Ancient History XIII: The Late Roman Empire, A.D. 337–425*, Cambridge: 665–707.

Cannadine, D. (1982) 'Residential differentiation in nineteenth-century towns from shapes on the ground to shapes in society', in J.H. Johnson and C.G. Pooley (eds) *The Structure of Nineteenth Century Cities*, London: 235–52.

Carcopino, J. (1941) *Daily Life in Ancient Rome: The People and the City at the Height of the Empire* (trans. E.O. Lorimer), London.

Carr, E.H. (1961) *What is History?* London.

Carrié, J.M. (1975) 'Les distributions alimentaires dans les cités de l'empire romain tardif', *MEFRA* 87: 995–1101.

—— (1976) 'Patronage et propriété militaires au IVe s.: Objet rhétorique et objet réel du discours sur le patronage de Libanius', *BCH* 100: 159–76.

—— (1999) 'Économie et société de l'Égypte Romano-Byzantine (IVe–VIIe siècle) à propos de quelques publications récentes', *An. Tard* 7: 331–52.

Cartledge, P. and Spawforth, A. (1989) *Hellenistic and Roman Sparta: A Tale of Two Cities*, London, New York.

Casanova, G. (1984a) 'Epidemie e Fame in Egitto', *Aegyptus* 64: 163–201.

—— (1984b) 'La peste nella documentazione greca d'Egitto', *Atti del XVII Congresso internazionale di Papirologia*, Naples: III, 949–56.

—— (1985) 'Le epigrafi di Terenouthis e la peste', *YCS* 28: 145–54.

—— (1988) 'Altre testimonianze sulla peste in Egitto', *Aegyptus* 68: 93–7.

Casarico, L. (1987a) 'Crocodilopolis–Ptolemais Euergetis in epoca tolemaica', *Aegyptus* 67: 127–59.

—— (1987b) 'Per la storia di un toponimo: Ptolemais Euergetis–Arsinoitōn polis', *Aegyptus* 67: 161–70.

Castrén, P. (1975) *Ordo Populusque Pompeianus: Polity and Society in Roman Pompeii*, Rome.

Cerny, J. (1954) 'Consanguineous marriages in Pharaonic Egypt', *JEA* 40: 23–9.

—— (1957) 'A note on the ancient Egyptian family', *Studi in Onore di Aristide Calderini e Roberto Paribeni*, Milan: II, 51–5.

Chabân, M. Effendi (1907) 'Fouilles à Achmounéîn', *ASAE* 8: 211–23.

—— (1910) 'Monuments recueilles pendant mes inspections', *ASAE* 10: 28–30.

Chalon, G. (1964) *L'Édit de Tiberius Julius Alexander*, Olten.

Chamonard, J. (1922) *Exploration archéologique de Délos VIII: La Quartier du Theatre*, Paris.

Champion, J.A.I. (1993) 'Epidemics and the built environment in 1665', in J.A.I. Champion (ed.) *Epidemic Disease in London* (Centre for Metropolitan History, Working Papers Series, 1), London: 35–52.

—— (1995) *London's Dreaded Visitation: The Social Geography of the Great Plague in 1665* (Historical Geography Research Series, 31), London.

Chantraine, P. (1964) 'Grec ΑΙΘΠΙΟΝ', *Rech. de Pap.* 3: 7–15.

Chevrier, H. (1939), 'Rapport sur les travaux de Karnak (1938–1939)', *ASAE* 39: 553–602.

Christaller, W. (1966) *Central Places in Southern Germany* (trans. C.W. Bask) (Englewood Cliffs, NJ).

Chuvin, P. (1986) 'Nonnos de Panopolis, Païen ou Chrétien', *BAGB*: 387–96.

—— (1991) *Mythologie et géographie dionysiaques. Recherches sur l'œuvre de Nonnos de Panopolis*, Clermont-Ferrand.

Clackson, S.J. (1995) 'Four Coptic papyri from the Patermouthis archive in the British Library', *BASP* 32: 97–116.

Clarke, J.R. (1991), *The Houses of Roman Italy 100 BC–AD 250: Ritual, Space and Decoration*, Berkeley, Los Angeles, Oxford.

Clarysse, W. (1979) 'Egyptian estate holders in the Ptolemaic period', in E. Lipinski (ed.) *State and Temple Economy in the Ancient Near East: Proceedings of the International Conference Organised by the Katholieke Universiteit Leuven from the 10th to the 14th April 1978*, Leuven: II, 731–43.

—— (1985a) 'The Athenian measure at Hermupolis', *ZPE* 60: 232–6.

—— (1985b) 'Greeks and Egyptians in the Ptolemaic army and administration', *Aegyptus* 65: 57–66.

—— (1992) 'Some Greeks in Egypt', in Janet. H. Johnson (ed.) *Life in a Multicultural*

Society: Egypt from Cambysses to Constantine and Beyond (Studies in Ancient and Oriental Civilization, 51) Chicago: 51–6.

—— (1995) 'Greeks in Ptolemaic Thebes', in S.P. Vleeming (ed.) *Hundred-Gated Thebes: Acts of a Colloquium on Thebes and the Theban Area in the Graeco-Roman Period* (Pap. Lugd. Bat., 27), Leiden, New York, Cologne: 1–19.

—— (1998) 'Ethnic diversity and dialect among the Greeks of Hellenistic Egypt', in A.M.F.W. Verhoogt and S.P. Vleeming (eds) *The Two Faces of Graeco-Roman Egypt: Greek and Demotic and Greek Demotic Texts and Studies presented to P.W. Pestman* (Pap. Lugd. Bat., 30), Leiden, New York, Cologne: 1–13.

Claude, D. (1969) *Die byzantinische Stadt im 6. Jahrhundert* (Byzantinisches Archiv, 13), Munich.

Clédat, J. (1908) 'Notes d'archéologie Copte', *ASAE* 9: 213–30.

Coles, R. (1980) '*P. Harr.* 73 and 160 revised', *ZPE* 37: 229–37.

—— (1987) 'Appendix II: The guilds of Oxyrhynchus', in *P. Oxy. LIV*: 230–2.

Conrad, L. (1981) 'The Plague in the Early Medieval Near East' (Princeton, Ph.D. thesis).

—— (1994) 'Epidemic disease in central Syria in the late sixth century: some new insights from the verse of Hassan ibn Thabit', *BMGS* 18: 12–58.

Cooper, B.M. (1997) 'Gender, movement and history: social and spatial transformation in 20th century Maradi, Niger', *Environment and Planning D: Society and Space* 15: 195–221.

Coquin, R.G. (1972) 'La christianisation des temples de Karnak', *BIFAO* 72: 169–78.

—— (1991) 'Monasteries of the Middle Sa 'id', *The Coptic Encyclopedia*, New York: V, 1654–5.

—— and Gascou, J. (1991) 'Monasteries of the Lower Sa 'id', *The Coptic Encyclopedia*, New York: V, 1652–3.

Corbridge, S. (1982) 'Urban bias, rural bias, and industrialization: an appraisal of the work of Michael Lipton and Terry Byres', in J. Harriss (ed.) *Rural Development: Theories of Peasant Economy and Agrarian Change*, London and New York: 94–116.

—— (1989) 'Urban–rural relations and the counter-revolution in development theory and policy', in R.B. Potter and T. Unwin (eds) *The Geography of Urban– Rural Interaction in Developing Countries*, London, New York: 233–56.

Cormack, L.B. (1994) 'The fashioning of empire: Geography and the state in Elizabethan England', in A. Godlewska and N. Smith (eds) *Geography and Empire*, Oxford, Cambridge, Mass.: 15–30.

Cosgrove, D. (1988) 'The geometry of landscape: Practical and speculative arts in sixteenth-century Venetian lands', in D. Cosgrove and S. Daniels (eds) *The Iconography of Landscape*, Cambridge: 254–76.

Cosgrove, D. and Domosh, M. (1993) 'Author and authority: Writing the new cultural geography', in J. Duncan and D. Ley (eds) *Place/ Culture/ Representation*, London, New York: 25–38.

Cosson, A. de (1935) *Mareotis*, London.

Coulson, W.D.E. (1988) 'The Naukratis survey', in E.C.M. van den Brink (ed.) *The Archaeology of the Nile Delta: Problems and Priorities*, Amsterdam: 259–63.

—— (ed.) (1996) *Ancient Naukratis II: The Survey of Naukratis and Environs: Part 1: The Survey at Naukratis*, Oxford.

Coulson, W.D.E. and Leonard, A. jr (1981) *Cities of the Delta I: Naukratis* (ARCE 4), Malibu.

Cracco Ruggini, L. (1976) 'La vita associativa nella città dell' Oriente greco: tradizioni locali e influenze romane', in D.M. Pippidi (ed.) *Assimilation et résistance à la culture gréco-romaine dans le monde ancien: Travaux du VIe congrès international d'études classiques*, Paris: 463–91.

Crawford, M.H. (1995) 'Roman towns and their charters: Legislation and experience', in B. Cunliffe and S. Keay (eds) *Social Complexity and the Development of Towns in Iberia: From the Copper Age to the Second Century AD* (*PBA*, 86), Oxford: 421–30.

Criscuolo, L. (1985) 'Le instituzioni pubbliche nell' Egitto Tolemaico', in *Egitto e Società antica. Atti del Convegno Turino 8/9 vi – 23/24 xi 1984*, Milan: 133–45.

Cromer, Earl of (1910) *Ancient and Modern Imperialism*, Oxford.

Crum, W.E. (1902) *Coptic Ostraca*, London.

Crush, J. (1994) 'Post-colonialism, de-colonization, and geography', in A. Godlewska and N. Smith (eds) *Geography and Empire*, Oxford, Cambridge, Mass.: 333–50.

Dabrowski, L. (1962) 'La topographie d'Athribis à l'époque romaine', *ASAE* 57: 19–31.

Daniels, S. (1988) 'The political iconography of woodland in later Georgian England', in D. Cosgrove and S. Daniels (eds) *The Iconography of Landscape*, Cambridge: 43–82.

Daniels, S. and Cosgrove, D. (1988) 'Introduction: Iconography and landscape', in D. Cosgrove and S. Daniels (eds) *The Iconography of Landscape*, Cambridge: 1–10.

Daniels, S. and Cosgrove, D. (1993) 'Spectacle and text: Landscape metaphors in cultural geography', in J. Duncan and D. Ley (eds) *Place/ Culture/ Representation*, London, New York: 57–77.

Daris, S. (1981) 'I quartieri di Arsinoe in età romana', *Aegyptus* 61: 143–54.

D'Arms, J.H. (1991) 'Slaves at a Roman Convivia', in W.J. Slater (ed.) *Dining in a Classical Context*, Ann Arbor: 171–83.

Darwall-Smith, R.H. (1996) *Emperors and Architecture: A Study of Flavian Rome*, Brussels.

Davidoff, L., L'Esperance, J., and Newby, H. (1977) 'Landscape with figures: Home and community in English society', in J. Mitchell and A. Oakley (eds) *The Rights and Wrongs of Women* (Harmondsworth), reprinted in S. Daniels and R. Lee (eds) (1996) *Exploring Cultural Geography*, London, New York: 263–81.

Davies, J.K. (1977) 'Athenian citizenship: The descent group and the alternatives', *CJ* 73: 105–21.

Davies, S. (1951) *Race-relations in Ancient Egypt: Greek, Egyptian, Hebrew and Roman*, London.

Davies, W.K. and Herbert, D.T. (1993) *Communities within Cities: An Urban Social Geography*, London.

Davis, M. (1992) *City of Quartz: Excavating the Future in Los Angeles*, London (first published 1990).

Davis, N. de Garis (1929) 'The town house in ancient Egypt', *Metropolitan Museum Studies* 1: 233–55.

Dear, M. (1997) 'Postmodern bloodlines', in G. Benko and U. Strohmayer (eds) *Space and Social Theory: Interpreting Modernity and Postmodernity*, Oxford: 49–71.

Deckers, J.G. (1973) 'Die Wandmalerei des tetrarchischen Lagerheiligtums im Ammon-Tempel von Luxor', *Röm. Quartalschrift*. 68: 1–34.

—— (1979) 'Die Wandmalerei im Kaiserkultraum von Luxor', *JDAI* 94: 600–52.

Delehaye, H. (1924) 'Le calendrier d'Oxyrhynque pour l'année 535–536', *Anal. Boll.* 42: 83–99.

Delia, D. (1988) 'The population of Roman Alexandria', *TAPA* 118: 273–93.

—— (1991) *Alexandrian Citizenship during the Roman Principate*, Atlanta.

De Ligt, L. (1990) 'Demand, supply, distribution: The Roman peasantry between town and countryside: rural monetization and peasant demand', *MBAH* 9: 24–56.

—— (1993) *Fairs and Markets in the Roman Empire: Economic and Social Aspects of Periodic Trade in a Pre-industrial Society*, Amsterdam.

—— (1995), 'The Nundinae of L. Bellicius Sollers', *De Agricultura: Essays in Honour of P.W. de Neeve*, Amsterdam: 238–62.

Delmaire, R. (1996) 'Cités et fiscialité au Bas-Empire. À propos du rôle des curiales dans la levée des impots', in C. Lepelley (ed.) *La fin de la cité antique et le début de la cité médiévale de la fin du IIIe siècle à l'avènement de Charlemagne*, Bari: 59–70.

Demos, J. (1972) 'Demography and psychology in the historical study of family life: A personal report', in P. Laslett (ed.) *Household and Family in Past Time*, London: 561–9.

Denecke, D. (1988) 'Social status and place of residence in pre-industrial German towns: Recent studies in social topography', in D. Denecke and G. Shaw (eds) *Urban Historical Geography: Recent Progress in Britain and Germany*, Cambridge: 125–40.

Depla, A. (1994) 'Women in ancient Egyptian Wisdom literature', in L. Archer, S. Fischler and M. Wyke (eds) *Women in Ancient Societies: An Illusion of the Night*, Basingstoke: 24–52.

Derda, T. (1991) 'Necropolis workers in Graeco-Roman Egypt in the light of the Greek papyri', *JJP* 21: 13–36.

Description (1809) *Description de l'Égypte ou recueil des observations et des recherches qui ont été faites en Égypte pendant l'expédition de l'armée Française* (Paris).

Deutsche, R. (1991) 'Boys Town', *Environment and Planning D: Society and Space* 9: 5–30.

de Vos, M. (1980) *L' Egittomania in pitture e mosaici Romano-Campani della prima età imperiale*, Leiden.

De Wit, C. (1960) 'Les inscriptions du temple de Domitièn à Assouan', *CE* 35: 108–19

Dietz, S., Sebai, L.L., and Hassen, H.B. (1995) *Africa Proconsularis: Regional Studies in the Segermes Valley of Northern Tunisia*, Copenhagen.

Dols, M.W. (1977) *The Black Death in the Middle East*, Princeton.

Donadoni, S. (1939) 'Rapporto preliminare degli scavi della missione Fiorentina nel Tempio di Ramessese II ad Antinoe', *ASAE* 39: 665–77.

—— (1974) *Antinoe (1965–1968): Missione Archeologica in Egitto dell' Università di Roma*, Rome.

Donley-Reid, L.W. (1990) 'A structuring-structure: The Swahili house', in S. Kent (ed.) *Domestic Architecture and the Use of Space*, Cambridge: 114–26.

Doresse, J. (1949) 'Monastères coptes aux environs d'Armant en Thébaide', *Anal. Boll.* 67: 327–49.

Dorren, G. (1998) 'Communities within the community: aspects of neighbourhood in seventeenth-century Haarlem', *Urban History* 25: 173–88.

Dover, K. (1976) 'Expurgation of Greek literature', in W. den Boer (ed.) *Les études classiques aux xixe et xxe siècles: leur place dans l'histoire des idées*, Geneva: 55–82.

Drakakis-Smith, D. (1987) *The Third World City*, London, New York.

Drew-Bear, M. (1979) *Le nome Hermopolite: Toponymes et sites* (American Society of Papyrologists, 21), Atlanta.

—— (1984) 'Les archives du conseil municipal Hermoupolis Magna', *Atti del XVII Congresso internazionale di Papirologia*, Naples: III, 807–13.

—— (1988) 'Les athlètes d'Hermoupolis Magna et leur ville au 3e siècle', *Proceedings of the XVIII International Congress of Papyrology. Athens 25–31 May 1986*, Athens: II, 229–35.

—— (1997) 'Guerre civile et grands travaux à Hermoupolis Magna sous Gallien', *Akten des 21. internationalen Papyrologenkongresses, Berlin, 13–19.8.1995*, Stuttgart, Leipzig: 237–43.

Drexhage, H.J. (1982) 'Beitrag zum Binnenhandel im römischen Ägypten aufgrund der Torzullquittungen und Zollhausabrechnungen des Faiyum', *MBAH* 1: 61–84.

—— (1991) *Preise, Mieten/Pachten, Kosten und Löhne im römischen Ägypten bis zum Regierungsantritt Diokletians* (Vorarbeiten zu einer Wirtschaftsgeschichte des römischen Ägypten, 1), St Katharinen.

Driver, F. (1992) 'Geography's empire: Histories of geographical knowledge', *Environment and Planning D: Society and Space* 10: 23–40, reprinted in S. Daniels and R. Lee (eds) (1996) *Exploring Cultural Geography*, London, New York: 340–59.

Dudley, D. (1967) *Urbs Roma: A Source Book of Classical Texts on the City and its Monuments*, London.

Dunand, F. (1979) *Religion populaire en Égypte romaine*, Leiden.

Dunbabin, K.M.D. (1996) 'Convivial spaces: Dining and entertainment in the Roman villa', *JRA* 9: 66–80.

Duncan, J.S. (1981) 'From container of women to status symbol: The impact of social structure on the meaning of the house', in J.S. Duncan (ed.) *Housing and Identity: Cross-Cultural Perspectives*, London: 36–59.

Duncan-Jones, R.P. (1974) *The Economy of the Roman Empire: Quantitative Studies*, Cambridge.

—— (1994) *Money and Government in the Roman Empire*, Cambridge.

—— (1996) 'The impact of the Antonine plague', *JRA* 9: 108–36.

Dunscombe Colt, H. (1962) *Excavations at Nessana I*, London.

Dwyer, E. (1991) 'The Pompeian Atrium house in theory and in practice', in E.K. Gazda (ed.) *Roman Art in the Private Sphere: New Perspectives on the Architecture and Decor of the Domus, Villa and Insula*, Ann Arbor: 25–48.

Dzielska, M. (1995) *Hypatia of Alexandria*, Cambridge.

Eck, W. (1997) 'Rome and the outside world: Senatorial families and the world they lived in', in B. Rawson and P. Weaver (eds) *The Roman Family in Italy: Status, Sentiment, Space*, Canberra, Oxford: 73–99.

Edgar, M.C. (1907), 'Notes from the Delta', *ASAE* 8: 154–9.

Edwards, C. (1996) *Writing Rome: Textual Approaches to the Ancient City*, Baltimore, London.

Ehrenberg, V. and Jones, A.H.M. (1949) *Documents Illustrating the Reigns of Augustus and Tiberius*, Oxford.

Ellis, S.P. (1988) 'The end of the Roman house', *AJA* 92: 565–76.

—— (1991) 'Power, architecture, and decor: How the late Roman aristocrat appeared to his guests', in E.K. Gazda (ed.) *Roman Art in the Private Sphere: New Perspectives on the Architecture and Decor of the Domus, Villa and Insula*, Ann Arbor: 117–34.

—— (1997) 'Late-antique dining: Architecture, furnishings and behaviour', in R. Laurence and A. Wallace-Hadrill (eds) *Domestic Space in the Roman World: Pompeii and Beyond* (*JRA* Suppl., 22), Portsmouth, RI: 41–51.

el Abbadi, M. (1988) 'The grain supply of Alexandria and its population in Byzantine times', *Proceedings of the XVIIIth International Congress of Papyrology, Athens 25–31 May 1986*, Athens: II, 317–23.

el-Fakhrani, F. (1983) 'Recent excavations at Marea in Egypt', in G. Grimm, H. Heinen and E. Winter (eds) *Das römisch–byzantinische Ägypten: Akten des internationalen Symposions 26–30 September 1978 in Trier*, Mainz: 175–86.

el-Khashab, Abd. el. M. (1949) *Ptolemaic and Roman Baths at Kôm el Ahmar* (*ASAE* Suppl., 10), Cairo.

el-Messiri, S. (1977) 'The changing role and function of the Futuwwa in the social structure of Cairo', in E. Gellner and J. Waterbury (eds) *Patrons and Clients in Mediterranean Societies*, London: 239–53.

el-Mosallamy, A.H. (1997) 'The evolution of the position of the woman in Ancient

Egypt', *Akten des 21. internationalen Papyrologenkongresses, Berlin 13–19.8.1995*, Leipzig, Stuttgart: 251–72.

el-Nassery, S.A.A., Wagner, G. and Castel, G. (1976) 'Un grand bain gréco-romain à Karanis', *BIFAO* 76: 231–75.

el-Saghir, M., Golvin, J.C., Reddé, M., Hagazy, El-S., Wagner, G. (1986) *Le camp romain de Louqsor* (IFAO Memoires, 83), Cairo.

Elsner, J. (1992) 'Pausanias: A Greek pilgrim in the Roman world', *P&P* 135: 3–29.

Elsner, J. and Masters, J. (1994) *Reflections of Nero: Culture, History and Representation*, London.

Elton, G.R. (1967) *The Practice of History*, Sydney.

Empereur, J.-Y. (1986) 'Un atelier de Dressel 2–4 en Égypte au IIIe siècle de notre ère', in J.-Y. Empereur and Y. Garlan (eds) *Recherches sur les amphores grecques: Actes du colloque international organisé par le Centre National de la Recherche Scientifique, l'Université de Rennes II et l'École Française d'Athènes* (*BCH* Suppl., 13), Athens: 599–608.

Empereur, J.-Y. and Picon, M. (1986) 'A la recherche des fours d'amphores', in J.-Y. Empereur and Y. Garlan (eds) *Recherches sur les amphores grecques: Actes du colloque international organisé par le Centre National de la Recherche Scientifique, l'Université de Rennes II et l'École Française d'Athènes* (*BCH* Suppl., 13), Athens: 104–26.

Engelbach, R. (1921) 'Small temple of Domitian at Assuan', *ASAE* 21: 195–6.

—— (1935) 'Statuette-group, from Kîmân Fâris, of Sebekhotpe and his womenfolk', *ASAE* 35: 203–5.

Engels, D. (1990) *Roman Corinth*, Chicago.

Engels, F. (1971) *The Condition of the Working Class in England in 1844*, Oxford.

Erman, A. (1886) 'Herkunft der Faijum papyrus', *Hermes* 21: 585–9.

Etman, A. (1992) Cleopatra and Egypt in the Augustan Poetry', in *Roma e l'Egitto nell' antichità Classica: Atti del Congresso internazionale Italo-Egiziano*, Rome: 161–75.

Evans, J.A.S. (1961) 'A social and economic history of an Egyptian temple in the Greco-Roman period', *YCS* 17: 143–283.

Evans, R. (1997) *In Defence of History*, London.

Evans Grubbs, J. (1989) 'Abduction marriage in antiquity: A law of Constantine (CTh ix 24 1) and its social context', *JRS* 79: 59–83.

—— (1995) *Law and Family in Late Antiquity: The Emperor Constantine's Marriage Legislation*, Oxford.

Eyre, C. (1984) 'Crime and adultery in ancient Egypt', *JEA* 70: 92–105.

Evetts, B. (ed.) (n.d.) *History of the Patriarchs of the Coptic Church of Alexandria* (Patrologia Orientalis, 4).

Fabbro, M. del (1982) 'Note a papiri ossirinchiti', *Studia Papyrologica* 21: 15–22.

Fakhouri, H. (1985) 'An ethnographic survey of a Cairene neighbourhood: The Darb el-Ahmar', *JARCE* 22: 119–27.

Falivene, M. R. (1998) *The Herakleopolite Nome: A Catalogue of the Toponyms with Introduction and Commentary* (American Society of Papyrologists, 37), Atlanta.

Farber, J. J. and Porten, B. (1986) 'The Patermouthis archive: A third look', *BASP* 23: 81–97.

Fathy, S.F. and Grossmann, P. (1994) 'Early Christian ruins at Kom al-Namrud', *BSAC* 33: 69–78.

Favro, D. (1995), *The Urban Image of Augustan Rome*, Cambridge.

Feissel, D. (1987) 'Nouvelles données sur l'institution du πατήρ τῆς πόλεως, in G. Dagron and D. Feissel (eds) *Inscriptions de Cilicie* (*Travaux et Mémoires* monographies, 4), Paris: 215–20.

Feucht, E. (1997) 'Women', in S. Donadoni (ed.) *The Egyptians*, Chicago, London: 315–46.

Fikhman, I.F. (1965) *Egipet na rubezhe dvukh epokh*, Moscow.

—— (1975a) 'The corn dole in the cities of Roman Egypt (*P.Oxy.* XL)', *VDI* 134: 60–70.

—— (1975b) 'Quelques données sur la genèse de la grande propriété foncière à Oxyrhynchus', in *Le Monde Grec: Hommages à Cl. Préaux*, Brussels: 784–90.

—— (1976) *Oksirinkh: Gorod papirusov*, Moscow.

—— (1979) 'Die spätantike ägyptische Stadt Oxyrhynchos', *Das Altertum* 25: 177–82.

—— (1981) 'Sur l'attache professionelle dans l'Égypte romaine', in *Scritti in onore di Orsolina Montevecchi*, Bologna: 149–54.

—— (1994) 'Sur quelques aspects socio-économique de l'activité des corporations professionelles de l'Égypte byzantine', *ZPE* 103: 19–40.

Finley, M.I. (1977) 'The ancient city from Fustel de Coulanges to Max Weber and beyond', *CSSH* 19: 305–27, reprinted in M.I. Finley (1981) *Economy and Society in Ancient Greece* (ed. B.D. Shaw and R.P. Saller), Harmondsworth.

—— (1981) *Economy and Society in Ancient Greece* (ed. B.D. Shaw and R.P. Saller), Harmondsworth.

—— (1985a) *The Ancient Economy*, London.

—— (1985b) *Ancient History: Evidence and Models*, London.

Fisher, N. (1998) 'Gymnasia and the democratic virtues of leisure', in P. Cartledge, P. Millett and S. von Reden (eds) *Kosmos: Essays in Order, Conflict and Community in Classical Athens*, Cambridge: 84–104.

Fishwick, D. (1984 [1990]) 'The temple of Caesar at Alexandria', *AJAH* 9: 131–4.

—— (1987 [1995]) 'The Caesareum at Alexandria again', *AJAH* 12: 62–75.

—— (1987–92) *The Imperial Cult in the Latin West*, Leiden and New York.

Fontani, E. (1995) *Ricerche sulla ginnasiarchia nelle città della provincia d'Asia*, Florence.

Foss, C. (1995) 'The Near Eastern countryside in late antiquity: a review article', in *The Roman and Byzantine Near East: Some Recent Archaeological Research* (*JRA* suppl., 14), Ann Arbor: 213–34.

Foss, P. (1997) 'Watchful *lares*: Roman household organization and the rituals of cooking and dining', in R. Laurence and A. Wallace-Hadrill (eds) *Domestic Space in the Roman World: Pompeii and Beyond* (*JRA* Suppl., 22), Portsmouth, RI: 197–218.

Fowden, G. (1982) 'The pagan holy man in late antique society', *JHS* 102: 33–59.

—— (1986) *The Egyptian Hermes: A Historical Approach to the Late Pagan Mind*, Princeton.

—— (1993) *Empire to Commonwealth: Consequences of Monotheism in Late Antiquity*, Princeton.

Franceschini, M. de (1991) *Villa Adriana. Mosaici, Pavimenti, Edifici*, Rome.

Frank, A.G. (1969) *Capitalism and Underdevelopment in Latin America*, New York.

Frankfurter, D. (1998) *Religion in Roman Egypt: Assimilation and Resistance*, Princeton.

Fraser, P.M. (1951) 'A Syriac *Notitia Urbis Alexandrinae*', *JEA* 37: 103–8.

—— (1972) *Ptolemaic Alexandria*, Oxford.

—— (1981) 'Alexandria from Mohammed Ali to Gamal Abdal Nassar', in N. Hinske (ed.) *Alexandrien: Kulturbegegnungen dreier Jahrtausende im Schmelztiegel einer mediterranen Großstadt*, Mainz: 63–74.

Freeman, P. (1996) 'British imperialism and the Roman Empire', in J. Webster and N. Cooper (eds) *Roman Imperialism: Post-Colonial Perspectives* (Leicester Archaeology Monographs, 3), Leicester: 19–34.

—— (1997) 'Mommsen to Haverfield: The orgins of studies of Romanization in late

19th-c. Britain', in D.J. Mattingly (ed.) *Dialogues in Roman Imperialism: Power, Discourse and Discrepant Experience in the Roman Empire* (*JRA* Suppl., 23), Portsmouth, RI: 27–50.

Froidefond, C. (1971) *Le mirage égyptien dans la littérature grecque d'Homére à Aristote*, Orphys.

Fustel de Coulanges, N.D. (1980) *The Ancient City* (1st edn 1864), Baltimore, London.

Gabra, S. (1941) *Université Fouad Ier rapport sur les fouilles d'Hermoupolis Ouest (Touna el-Gebel)*, Cairo.

Gagos, T., Koenen, L., and McNellan, B.E. (1992), 'A first century archive from Oxyrhynchus or Oxyrhynchite loan contracts and Egyptian marriage', in Janet. H. Johnson (ed.) *Life in a Multicultural Society: Egypt from Cambysses to Constantine and Beyond* (Studies in Ancient and Oriental Civilization, 51), Chicago: 181–205.

Gallant, T.W. (1991) *Risk and Survival in Ancient Greece: Reconstructing the Rural Domestic Economy*, Cambridge.

Gallo, P. (1992) 'The wandering personnel of the temple of Narmuthis in the Faiyum and some toponyms of the meris of Polemon', in Janet. H. Johnson (ed.) *Life in a Multicultural Society: Egypt from Cambysses to Constantine and Beyond* (Studies in Ancient and Oriental Civilization, 51), Chicago: 119–31.

Gardner, E.A. (1888) *Naukratis II*, London.

Gardner, I.M.F. and Lieu, S.N.C. (1996) 'From Narmouthis (Medinet Madi) to Kellis (Ismant El-Kharab): Manichaean documents from Roman Egypt', *JRS* 86: 146–69.

Garnsey, P. (1974) 'Aspects of the decline of the urban aristocracy in the empire', *ANRW* II 1: 229–52, reprinted in P. Garnsey (1998) *Cities, Peasants and Food in Classical Antiquity*, ed. W. Scheidel, Cambridge: 3–27.

—— (1988) *Famine and Food Supply in the Graeco-Roman World: Responses to Risk and Crisis*, Cambridge.

Gascou, J. (1972a) La détention collégiale de l'autorité pagarchique dans l'Égypte byzantine', *Byzantion* 42: 60–72.

—— (1972b) 'Notes critiques sur quelques papyrus des Ve et VIe siècles', *CE* 47: 243–53.

—— (1976) 'Les institutions de l'hippodrome en Égypte byzantine', *BIFAO* 76: 185–212.

—— (1985) 'Les grand domaines, la cité et l'état en Égypte byzantine (Recherches d'histoire agraire, fiscale et administrative)', *Travaux et Memoires* 9: 1–90.

—— (1991) 'Monasteries, economic activities of', *The Coptic Encyclopedia*, New York: V, 1639–45.

—— (1994a) *Un codex fiscal Hermopolite (P. Sorb. II 69)*, Atlanta.

—— (1994b) 'Deux inscriptions byzantines de Haute-Égypte (réédition de I. Thèbes-Syene 196 r° et v°)', *Travaux et Memoires* 12: 323–42.

Gascou, J. and MacCoull, L.S.B. (1987) 'Le cadastre d'Aphrodito', *Travaux et Memoires* 10: 103–58.

Gascou, J. and Worp, K.A. (1982) 'Problèmes de documentation Apollonopolite', *ZPE* 49: 83–95.

Gasiorowski, S.J. (1931) 'A fragment of a Greek illustrated papyrus from Antinoë', *JEA* 17: 1–9.

Gayet, A. (1897) *L'exploration des ruines d'Antinoë et la découverte d'un temple de Ramsès II enclos dans l'enceinte de la ville d'Hadrien* (Annales du Musée Guimet, 26.3), Paris.

—— (1902) *L'exploration des nécropoles gréco-byzantines d'Antinöe et les sarcophages de tombes pharaoniques de la ville antique*, Paris.

Gazda, E.K. (1978) *Guardians of the Nile: Sculptures from Karanis*, Ann Arbor.

—— (1983) *Karanis: An Egyptian Town in Roman Times*, Ann Arbor.

Geagen, D.J. (1979) 'The third hoplite generalship of Antipatros of Phyla', *AJP* 100: 59–68.

Geertz, C. (1973) *The Interpretation of Cultures*, New York.

Gellner, E. (1983) *Nations and Nationalism*, Oxford.

Gempeler, R.D. (1992) *Elephantine X. Die Keramik römischer bis früh05arabischer Zeit*, Mainz.

Gendy, I. A. el A. (1990) 'Economic aspects of houses and housing in Roman Egypt' (unpubl. Ph.D. thesis, University of London).

George, M. (1997a) 'Repopulating the Roman house', in B. Rawson and P. Weaver (eds) *The Roman Family in Italy: Status, Sentiment, Space*, Canberra and Oxford: 299–319.

—— (1997b) *The Roman Domestic Architecture of Northern Italy* (*BAR* International Series, 670), Oxford.

Geraci, G. (1983) *Genesi della provincia romana d'Egitto*, Bologna.

Geremek, H. (1990) 'Sur la question des Boulai dans les villes Égyptiennes aux Ve–VIIe siècles', *JJP* 20: 47–54.

Giddens, A. (1979) *Central Problems in Social Theory*, London.

—— (1984) *The Constitution of Society*, Berkeley.

Gilliam, E.H. (1947) 'The archive of the temple of Soknobraisis at Bacchias', *YCS* 10: 181–282.

Gilliam, J.F. (1961) 'The plague under Marcus Aurelius', *AJP* 82: 225–51.

Girouard, M. (1978) *Life in the English Country House: A Social and Architectural History*, London and New Haven.

Glare, P. (1993) 'The temples of Egypt: The impact of Rome' (Univ. of Cambridge, Ph.D. thesis).

Glazer, N. and Moynihan, D.P. (eds) (1975) *Ethnicity: Theory and Experience*, Cambridge, Mass.

Goddio, F. (1998) *Alexandria: The Submerged Royal Quarters*, London.

Godlewska, A. and Smith, N. (ed.) (1994) *Geography and Empire*, Oxford and Cambridge, Mass.

Godlewski, W. (1983) 'Monastère Nord ou Monastère St Phoibammon', *ÉT* 12: 93–8.

—— (1986) *Deir el-Bahari V: Le monastère de St Phoibammon*, Warsaw.

Goitein, S.D. (1969) 'Cairo: An Islamic city in the light of the Geniza documents', in I.M. Lapidus (ed.) *Middle Eastern Cities: A Symposium on Ancient, Islamic, and Contemporary Middle Eastern Urbanism*, Berkeley and Los Angeles: 80–95.

Goldberg, J. (1996) 'Introduction', in W.M. Ormrod and P.G. Lindley (eds) *The Black Death in England*, Stamford: 1–15.

Golvin J.-C. et al. (1981) 'Le petit Serapieion romain de Louqsor', *BIFAO* 81: 115–48.

González, J. (1986) 'The Lex Irnitania: A new copy of the Flavian municipal law', *JRS* 76: 147–250.

Goodenough, E.R. (1962) *An Introduction to Philo Judaeus*, Oxford.

Goody, J. (1983) *The Development of the Family and Marriage in Europe*, Cambridge.

Gottfried, R.S. (1983) *The Black Death: Natural and Human Disaster in Medieval Europe*, New York.

Goudriaan, K. (1988) *Ethnicity in Ptolemaic Egypt* (Dutch Monographs on Ancient History and Archaeology, 5), Amsterdam.

—— (1992) 'Ethnical strategies in Graeco-Roman Egypt', in P. Bilde, T. Engberg-Pedersen, L. Hannestad and J. Zahle (eds) *Ethnicity in Hellenistic Egypt* (Studies in Hellenistic Civilization, 3), Aarhus: 74–99.

Grahame, M. (1997) 'Public and private in the Roman house: Investigating the social order of the Casa del Fauno', in R. Laurence and A. Wallace-Hadrill (eds) *Domestic Space in the Roman World: Pompeii and Beyond* (*JRA* Suppl., 22), Portsmouth, RI: 137–64.

—— (1998) 'Material culture and Roman identity: The spatial layout of Pompeian houses and the problem of ethnicity', in R. Laurence and J. Berry (eds) *Cultural Identity in the Roman Empire*, London and New York: 156–78.

Gramsci, A. (1971), *Selections from Prison Notebooks* (ed. and trans. Q. Hoare and G.N. Smith), London.

Grande, C. (1985) review of L.A. Shier (1978), *Karanis: Terracotta Lamps from Karanis, Egypt: Excavations of the University of Michigan*, Ann Arbor, *JRS* 75: 284.

Grant, M. (1991) *A Short History of Classical Civilization*, London.

Grassi, T. (1973) *Le liste templari nell' Egitto Greco-Romano secondo i papiri*, Milan.

Gregory, D. (1994) *Geographical Imaginations*, Cambridge, Mass. and Oxford.

Gregory, T.E. (1979) *Vox Populi: Popular Opinion in the Religious Controversies of the Fifth century AD*, Columbus, Oh.

Grenfell, B.P. (1897) 'Oxyrhynchus and its papyri', *Egypt Exploration Fund: Archaeological Report 1896–1997*, London: 1–12.

Grenfell, B.P and Hunt, A.S. (1904) 'Oxyrhynchus and its papyri', *Egypt Exploration Fund: Archaeological Report 1903–1904*, London: 14–17.

—— and —— (1905) 'Oxyrhynchus and its papyri', *Egypt Exploration Fund: Archaeological Report 1904–1905*, London: 13–17.

—— and —— (1906a) 'Englische Ausgraben in Hibeh und Oxyrhynchos', *Archiv* 3: 139–40.

—— and —— (1906b) 'Oxyrhynchus and its papyri', *Egypt Exploration Fund: Archaeological Report 1905–1906*, London: 8–16.

—— and —— (1907) 'Oxyrhynchus and its papyri', *Egypt Exploration Fund: Archaeological Report 1906–1907*, London: 8–11.

Grenier, J.C. (1989) *Les titulatures des empereurs romains dans les documents en langue Égyptienne* (Papyrologica Bruxellensia, 22), Brussels.

—— (1997) 'La religion traditionelle: temples et clergés', in *Égypte Romaine: l'autre Égypte: catalogue de l' exhibition Marseille*, Marseilles: 175–7.

Greven, P.J. (1972) 'The average size of families and households in the province of Massachusetts in 1764 and in the United States in 1790: An overview', in P. Laslett (ed.) *Household and Family in Past Time*, London: 545–60.

Griffin, J. (1986) 'Introduction', in J. Boardman, J. Griffin and O. Murray (eds) *The Oxford History of the Classical World*, Oxford and New York: 1–13.

Griffiths J.G. (1948) 'Human sacrifice in Egypt: the Classical evidence', *ASAE* 48: 409–23.

—— (1970) *Plutarch's 'De Iside et Osiride'*, Cardiff.

Griffiths, S.H. (1997) 'From Aramaic to Arabic: The languages of the monasteries of Palestine in the Byzantine and early Islamic periods', *DOP* 51: 11–31.

Griggs, C.W. (1991) *Early Egyptian Christianity from its Origins to 451 CE*, Leiden.

Grimal, P. (1939) 'Les maisons à tours hellenistiques et romaines', *MEFRA* 56: 28–59.

Grohmann, A. (1957) 'Greek papyri of the early Islamic period in the collection of Archduke Rainer', *Études de Papyrologie* 8: 5–40.

Grossmann, P. (1973) 'Eine vergessene frühchristliche Kirche beim Luxor-Tempel', *MDAIK* 29: 167–81.

—— (1980) *Elephantine II: Kirche und spätantike Hausenlagen im Chnumtempelhof. Beschreibung und typologische Untersuchung*, Mainz.

—— (1982) 'Abu Mina: Zehnter vorläufiger Bericht. Kampagnen 1980 und 1981', *MDAIK* 38: 131–54.

—— (1989) *Abû Mînâ I: Die Gruftkirche und die Gruft* (DAIK Archäologische Veröffentlichungen, 44), Mainz.

—— (1991) 'Christliche Einbauten im Tempel des Mandulis von Kalabsa', *MDAIK* 47: 143–50.

—— (1995) 'Report on the excavations at Abu Mina in Spring 1994', *BSAC* 34: 149–59.

—— (1998) 'The Pilgrimage centre of Abû Mînâ', in D. Frankfurter (ed.) *Pilgrimage and Holy Space in Late Antique Egypt*, Leiden, Boston and Cologne: 281–302.

Grossmann, P., Arnold, F., and Kosciuk, J. (1997) 'Report on the excavations at Abu Mina in Spring 1995', *BSAC* 36: 83–98.

Grossmann, P. and Bailey, D.M. (1994) 'The South Church at Hermopolis Magna (Ashmunein): A preliminary account', in K. Painter (ed.) *'Churches built in Ancient Times': Recent Studies in Early Christian Archaeology*, London: 49–71.

Grossmann, P. and Hafiz, M. (1998) 'Results of the 1995/96 excavations in the North-West Church of Pelusium (Farama-West)', *MDAIK* 54: 177–82.

Grossmann, P. and Kosciuk, J. (1991) 'Report on the excavations at Abu Mina in Autumn 1989', *BSAC* 30: 65–75.

Grossmann, P. and Kosciuk, J. (1992) 'Report on the excavations at Abu Mina in Autumn 1990', *BSAC* 31: 31–41.

Grossmann, P., Kosciuk, J., Negm, M. Abd.-Aziz and Uricher, C. (1994) 'Report on the excavations at Abu Mina in Spring 1993', *BSAC* 33: 91–104.

Grossmann, P., Kosciuk, J., Severin, G., and Severin, H.-G. (1984) 'Abu Mina: Elfter vorläufiger Bericht. Kampagnen 1982 und 1983', *MDAIK* 40: 123–51.

Guimier-Sorbets, A.M. (1999) 'The function of funerary iconography in Roman Alexandria: An original form of bilingual iconography in the necropolis of Kom el Shoqafa', in R.F. Doiter and E.M. Moormann (eds) *Proceedings of the XVth International Congress of Classical Archaeology, Amsterdam, July 12–17, 1998*, Amsterdam: 180–2.

Gutbob, A. (1995) *Kôm Ombo I*, Cairo.

Haas, C. (1997) *Alexandria in Late Antiquity: Topography and Social Conflict*, Baltimore and London.

Haatvedt, R.A. and Peterson, E.E. (1964) *Coins from Karanis: The University of Michigan Excavations 1924–1935*, Ann Arbor.

Habachi, L. (1937) 'Une vaste salle d'Amenemhat III à Kiman-Farès (Fayoum)', *ASAE* 37: 85–95.

—— (1955) 'A strange monument of the Ptolemaic period from Crocodilopolis', *JEA* 41: 106–11.

Haldon, J. (1990) *Byzantium and the Seventh Century: The Transformation of a Culture*, Cambridge.

Hall, J.M. (1997) *Ethnic Identity in Greek Antiquity*, Cambridge.

Hall, P. (1998) *Cities in Civilization*, London.

Hammel, E.A. (1972) 'The zadruga as process', in P. Laslett (ed.) *Household and Family in Past Time*, London: 335–73.

Hansen, D.P. (1965) 'Mendes 1964', *JARCE* 4: 31–7.

Hansen, D.P. et al. (1967) 'Mendes 1965 and 1966', *JARCE* 6: 1–52.

Hanson, A.E. (1980) 'Juliopolis, Nicopolis, and the Roman camp', *ZPE* 37: 249–54.

—— (1992) 'Egyptians, Greeks, Romans, *Arabas* and *Ioudaioi* in the first century AD tax archive from Philadelphia: P. Mich. inv. 880 recto and *P. Princ.* III 152 revised', in Janet. H. Johnson (ed.) *Life in a Multicultural Society: Egypt from Cambysses to Constantine and Beyond* (Studies in Ancient and Oriental Civilization, 51), Chicago: 133–45.

—— (1994) 'Topographical arrangement of tax documents in the Philadelphia tax archive', in A. Bülow-Jacobsen (ed.) *Proceedings of the XXth International Congress of Papyrologists, Copenhagen, 23–29 August, 1992*, Copenhagen: 210–18.

Harden, D.B. (1936) *Roman Glass from Karanis found by the University of Michigan Expedition in Egypt, 1924–29*, Ann Arbor.

Hardy, E.G. (1912) *Three Spanish Charters*, Oxford.

Hardy, E.R. (1931) *The Large Estates of Byzantine Egypt*, New York.

Harley, J.B. (1988) 'Maps, knowledge and power', in D. Cosgrove and S. Daniels (eds) *The Iconography of Landscape*, Cambridge: 277–312.

—— (1992) 'Deconstructing the map', in T.J. Barnes and J.S. Duncan (eds) *Writing Worlds: Discourse, Text and Metaphor in the Representation of Landscape*, London, New York: 231–47.

Harper, R.P. (1995) *Upper Zohar: An Early Byzantine Fort in Palaestina Tertia: Final Report of Excavations in 1985–1986*, Oxford.

Harries, J. (1994) *Sidonius Apollinarius and the Fall of Rome, AD 407–485*, Oxford.

Harvey, D. (1973) *Social Justice and the City*, London.

—— (1979) 'Monument and myth', *Annals of the Association of American Geographers* 69: 362–81.

—— (1990) 'Between space and time: Reflections on the geographical imagination', *Annals of the Association of American Geographers* 80: 418–34, reprinted in T. Barnes and D. Gregory (eds) (1997) *Reading Human Geography: The Poetics and Politics of Inquiry*, London: 257–79.

—— (1991) *The Condition of Postmodernism: An Enquiry into the Origins of Cultural Change*, Cambridge and Oxford.

—— (1995) 'Geographical knowledge in the eye of power: Reflections of Derek Gregory's *Geographical Imaginations*', *Annals of the Association of American Geographers* 85: 160–4.

Harvey, D. and A.J. Scott (1989) 'The practice of human geography: Theory and empirical specificity in the transition from Fordism to flexible accumulation', in B. MacMillan (ed.) *Remodelling Geography*, Oxford, reprinted in T. Barnes and D. Gregory (eds) (1997) *Reading Human Geography: The Poetics and Politics of Inquiry*, London: 92–8.

Hasebroek, J. (1922) 'Nochmals ΠΡΓΟΣ "Wirtschaftsgebäude"', *Hermes* 57: 621–3.

Hatcher, J. (1977) *Plague, Population and the English Economy 1348–1530*, London and Basingstoke.

Haverfield, F. (1910) 'Town planning in the Roman world', *Transactions of the Town Planning Conference, Oct., 1910*: 123–32.

—— (1912) *The Romanization of Roman Britain*, Oxford.

—— (1913) *Ancient Town Planning*, Oxford.

—— (1916) *Some Roman Conceptions of Empire* (Occasional Publications of the Classical Association, 4), Cambridge.

—— (1923) *The Romanization of Roman Britain*, Oxford.

—— (1924) *The Roman Occupation of Britain*, Oxford.

Hayami, A. and Uchida, N. (1972) 'Size of household in a Japanese county throughout the Tokugawa era', in P. Laslett (ed.) *Household and Family in Past Time*, London: 473–515.

Heinen, H. (1991) 'Alexandria in late antiquity', in A.S. Atiya (ed.) *The Coptic Encyclopedia*, New York, Toronto, Oxford, Singapore and Sydney: I 95–102

Heidegger, M. (1993) *Basic Writings from Being and Time (1927) to the Task of Thinking (1964)* (ed. D.F. Krell), London.

Helin, É. (1972) 'Size of households before the industrial revolution: The case of Liège in 1801', in P. Laslett (ed.) *Household and Family in Past Time*, London: 319–34.

Henrichs, A. (1972) *Die Phoinikika des Lollianos*, Bonn.

Herbert, D.T. and Johnson, R.J. (1976) 'An introduction: Spatial processes and forms', in D.T. Herbert and R.J. Johnson (eds) *Social Areas in Cities I: Spatial Processes and Form*, London: 1–4.

Herlihy, D. (1965) 'Population, plague and social change in rural Pistoia, 1201–1430', *EHR* 18: 225–44, reprinted in D. Herlihy (1980) *Cities and Society in Medieval Italy*, London: II.

—— (1967) *Medieval and Renaissance Pistoia: The Social History of an Italian Town*, New Haven and London.

—— (1970) 'The Tuscan town in the quattrocento: a demographic profile', *Medievalia et Humanistica* 1: 81–109, reprinted in D. Herlihy (1980) *Cities and Society in Medieval Italy*, London: IV.

—— (1973) 'The population of Verona in the first century of Venetian rule', in J.R. Hale (ed.) *Renaissance Venice*, London: 91–200, reprinted in D. Herlihy (1980) *Cities and Society in Medieval Italy*, London: X.

—— (1985) *Medieval Households*, London and Cambridge, Mass.

Hermansen, G. (1982) *Ostia: Aspects of Roman City Life*, Edmonton.

Hickey, T.M. (1996) 'P. Oxy. X 1323 descr. A receipt for an Orbiopôleion', *ZPE* 113: 227–9.

Hillier, B. and Hanson, J. (1984) *The Social Logic of Space*, Cambridge, New York and Melbourne.

Hingley, R. (1996) 'The "legacy" of Rome: The rise, decline, and fall of the theory of Romanization', in J. Webster and N. Cooper (eds) *Roman Imperialism: Post-Colonial Perspectives* (Leicester Archaeology Monographs, 3), Leicester: 35–48.

Hobson, D.W. (1982) 'The village of Apias in the Arsinoite nome', *Aegyptus* 62: 80–123.

—— (1983) 'Women as property owners in Roman Egypt', *TAPA* 113: 311–21.

—— (1984a) 'P. Vindob. gr. 24951 + 24556: New evidence for tax exempt status in Roman Egypt', *Atti del XVII Congresso internazionale di Papirologia*, Naples: 847–64.

—— (1984b) 'The role of women in the economic life of Roman Egypt: A case study from first century Tebtunis', *Echos du Monde Classique/Classical Views* 28: 373–90.

—— (1985a) 'House and household in Roman Egypt', *YCS* 28: 211–29.

—— (1985b) 'The village of Herakleia in the Arsinoite nome', *BASP* 22: 101–15.

—— (1986) 'The inhabitants of Herakleia', *BASP* 23: 99–123.

—— (1989) 'Naming practices in Roman Egypt', *BASP* 26: 157–74.

Hodder, I. (1992) *Theory and Practice in Archaeology*, London.

—— (1994) 'Architecture and meaning: The example of Neolithic houses and tombs', in M. P. Pearson and C. Richards (eds) *Architecture and Order: Approaches to Social Space*, London and New York: 73–86.

Hodges, R. (1989) *Dark Age Economics: The Origins of Towns and Trade AD 600–1000*, London.

—— (1998) 'Henri Pirenne and the question of demand in the sixth century', in R. Hodges and W. Bowden (eds) *The Sixth Century: Production, Distribution and Demand*, Leiden, Boston and Cologne: 2–14.

Hoepfner, W. and Schwandner, E.L. (1986) *Haus und Stadt im klassischen Griechenland* (Wohnen in der klassischen Polis, 1), Munich.

Hoff, M. (1989) 'Civil disobedience and unrest in Augustan Athens', *Hesperia* 58: 267–76

Hogarth, D.G. (1898–9) 'Excavations at Naukratis', *ABSA* 5: 26–97.

—— (1905) 'Naukratis, 1903' *JHS* 25: 105–36.

Holum, K.G. (1996) 'The survival of the Bouleutic class of Caesarea in late antiquity', in A. Raban and K.G. Holum (eds) *Caesarea Maritima: A Retrospective of Two Millennia*, Leiden, Cologne and New York: 615–27.

Hölscher, T. (1991) 'The city of Athens: Space, symbol, structure', in A. Mohlo, K. Raaflaub and J. Emlin (eds) *City States in Classical Antiquity and Medieval Italy*, Ann Arbor: 355–80.

Hölscher, U. (1932) *Excavations at Ancient Thebes 1930/31* (Oriental Institute of the University of Chicago, Communications, 15), Chicago.

Hölscher, U. and Wilson, J.A. (1930), *Medinet Habu Studies 1928/29* (Oriental Institute of the University of Chicago, Communications, 7), Chicago.

Holz, R.K., Hall, E.S., and Bothmer, B.V. (1980) *Mendes I*, Cairo.

Hope, C.A. (1987) 'The Dakleh Oasis Project: Ismant el-Kharab 1988–1990', *Journal of the Society for the Study of Egyptian Antiquities* 17: 157–75.

—— (1988) 'Three seasons of excavations at Ismant el-Gharab in Dakhleh Oasis', *Mediterranean Archaeology* 1: 160–78.

—— (1995) Ismant el-Kharab (ancient Kellis) in the Dakhleh Oasis, Egypt', *Mediterranean Archaeology* 8: 138–43.

Hope, C.A., Kaper, O.E., Brown, G.E., and Patten, S.F. (1989) 'Dakleh Oasis Project: Ismant el-Kharab 1991–92', *Journal of the Society for the Study of Egyptian Antiquities* 19: 1–26.

Hope, V. (1997) 'A roof over the dead: Communal tombs and family structure', in R. Laurence and A. Wallace-Hadrill (eds) *Domestic Space in the Roman World: Pompeii and Beyond* (JRA Suppl., 22), Portsmouth, RI: 69–88.

Hopkins, K. (1980a) 'Brother–sister marriage in Roman Egypt', *CSSH* 22: 303–54.

—— (1980b) 'Taxes and trade in the Roman empire, 200 BC–AD 400', *JRS* 70: 101–25.

—— (1991) 'Conquest by book', in *Literacy in the Roman World* (JRA Suppl., 3), Ann Arbor: 133–57.

Horbury, W. and Noy, D. (1992) *Jewish Inscriptions of Graeco-Roman Egypt*, Cambridge.

Horrox, R. (1994) *The Black Death* (Manchester Medieval Sources), Manchester and New York.

Housman, A.E. (1969) *The Confines of Criticism: The Cambridge Inaugural 1911*, London.

Hughes, D.O. (1978) 'Urban growth and family structure in Medieval Genoa', in P. Abrams and E.A. Wrigley (eds) *Towns in Societies*, Cambridge: 105–30.

Hughes-Hallett, L. (1990) *Cleopatra: Histories, Dreams and Distortions*, London.

Huss, W. (1992) 'Some thoughts on the subject "state" and "church" in Ptolemaic Egypt', in Janet H. Johnson (ed.) *Life in a Multicultural Society: Egypt from Cambysses to Constantine and Beyond* (Studies in Ancient and Oriental Civilization, 51), Chicago: 159–63.

Hussain, A. Gonda (1983) 'Magnetic prospecting for archaeology in Kom Oshim and Kiman Faris, Fayum, Egypt', *ZÄS* 110: 136–51.

Husselman, E.M. (1952) 'The granaries of Karanis', *TAPA* 83: 56–73.

—— (1979) *Karanis: Excavations of the University of Michigan in Egypt 1928–1935: Topography and Architecture*, Ann Arbor.

Husson, G. (1967) 'Recherches sur les sens du mot ΠΡΟΑΣΤΙΟΝ dans le grec d'Égypte', *Recherches de Papyrologie* 4: 187–202.

—— (1976) 'La maison privée à Oxyrhynchos aux trois premiers siècles de notre ère' *Ktema* 1: 5–27.

—— (1981) 'Traditions pharaoniques attestées dans l'architecture domestique de l'Égypte grecque, romaine et byzantine', *Proceedings of the XVI International Congress of Papyrology*, Chico: 519–26.

—— (1983a) *Oikia: Le vocabulaire de la maison privée en Égypte d'après les papyrus grecs*, Paris.

—— (1983b) 'Un sens méconnu de ΘΥΡΙΣ et de *fenestra*', *JJP* 19: 155–62.

—— (1990) 'Houses in Syene in the Patermouthis archive', *BASP* 27: 123–37.

Huzar, E.G. (1988) 'Alexandria ad Aegyptum in the Julio-Claudian age', *ANRW* II 10: 619–68.

Ilan, T. (1995) *Jewish Women in Greco-Roman Palestine: An Inquiry into Image and Status*, Tübingen.

Ioannidou, G. (2000), 'P. Berol. 25706: Riot in the Hippodrome', *Archiv* 46: 51–61.

Iversen, E. (1965) 'The date of the so-called inscription of Caligula on the Vatican obelisk', *JEA* 51: 149–54.

Jacobs, J.M. (1998) 'Staging difference: Aestheticization and the politics of difference in contemporary cities', in R. Fincher and J.M. Jacobs (eds) *Cities of Difference*, New York and London: 252–78.

Jameson, M.H. (1990) 'Domestic space and the city state', in S. Kent (ed.) *Domestic Architecture and the Use of Space*, Cambridge: 92–113.

Janssen, J.J. (1979) 'The rôle of the temple in the Egyptian economy during the New Kingdom', in E. Lipinski (ed.) *State and Temple Economy in the Ancient Near East: Proceedings of the International Conference organised by the Katholieke Universiteit Leuven from the 10th to the 14th April 1978*, Leuven: II, 505–15.

Jaritz, H. (1975) 'Untersuchungen zum "Tempel des Domitian" in Assuan', *MDAIK* 31: 237–57.

—— (1980) *Elephantine III: Die Terassen vor den Tempeln des Chnum und der Satet*, Mainz.

Jaritz, H., Favre, S., Nogara, G. and Rodziewicz, M. (1996) *Pelusium: Prospection archéologique et topographique de la région de Tell el-Kanais 1993 et 1994*, Stuttgart.

Jaritz, H. and Rodziewicz, M. (1994) 'Syene: Review of the urban remains and its pottery', *MDAIK* 50: 115–41.

Jenkyns, R. (1980) *The Victorians and Ancient Greece*, Oxford.

—— (1996) 'Bernal and the nineteenth century', in M.R. Lefkowitz and G.M. Rogers (eds) *Black Athena Revisted*, Chapel Hill and London: 411–20.

Johnson, A.C. (1936) *Roman Egypt to the Reign of Diocletian*, Baltimore.

Johnson, A.C. and West, L.C. (1949) *Byzantine Egypt: Economic Studies*, Princeton.

Johnson, B. (1981) *Pottery from Karanis: Excavations of the University of Michigan*, Ann Arbor.

Johnson, J. de M. (1914) 'Antinöe and its papyri: Excavations by the Graeco-Roman branch, 1913–14', *JEA* 1: 168–81.

Jones, A.H.M. (1938) 'The election of metropolitan magistrates in Egypt', *JEA* 24: 65–72.

—— (1960) 'The cloth industry under the Roman empire', *EHR* 13: 183–92, reprinted in A.H.M. Jones (1974) *The Roman Economy*, Oxford: 350–64.

—— (1964) *The Later Roman Empire 284–602: A Social, Economic and Administrative Survey*, Oxford.

—— (1983) *The Cities of the Eastern Roman Provinces* (2nd edn), Amsterdam.

Jones, C.P. (1973) 'The date of Dio of Prusa's Alexandrian oration', *Historia* 22: 302–39.

Jones, J. (1973) 'An Attic country house below the cave of Pan at Vari', *ABSA* 68: 355–452.

Jones, W.F. (1999) *The Associations of Classical Athens: The Response to Democracy*, New York and Oxford.

Jongman, W. (1988) *The Economy and Society of Pompeii* (Dutch Monographs on Ancient History and Archaeology, 4), Amsterdam.

Jördens, A. (1995) 'Sozialstrukturen im Arbeitstierhandel des kaiserzeitlichen Ägypten', *Tyche* 10: 37–100.

Jouguet, P. (1901) 'Rapport sur les fouilles de Médinet-Mâdi et Médinet-Ghôran', *BCH* 25: 380–411.

—— (1911) *La vie municipale dans l'Égypte romaine*, Paris.

—— (1917) 'Sur les métropoles Égyptiennes à la fin du IIe siècle après J.C. d'après les papyrus Rylands', *REG* 30: 294–328.

Judge, E.A (1977) 'The earliest use of monachus for "monk" (P. Coll. Youtie 77) and the origins of monasticism', *JbAC* 20: 72–89.

Judge, E.A and Pickering, S.R. (1977) 'Papyrus documentation of Church and community in Egypt to the mid-fourth century', *JbAC* 20: 42–71.

Junge, F. (1987) *Elephantine XI: Funde und Bauteile*, Mainz.

Kákosky, L. (1989) 'Germanicus in Theben', *Acta Antiqua Hung.* 32: 129–36.

—— (1995) 'Probleme der Religion im römerzeitlichen Ägypten', *ANRW* II 18.5: 2894–3049.

Kalavrezou-Maxeiner, I. (1975) 'The imperial chamber at Luxor', *DOP* 29: 225–51.

Kamal, M. (1947), 'Excavations of the antiquities department (1942) in the so-called "agora" of Hermopolis (Ashmunein)', *ASAE* 46: 289–95.

Kaper, O.E. (1998) 'Temple building in the Egyptian deserts during the Roman period', in O.E. Kaper (ed.) *Life on the Fringe: Living in the Southern Egyptian Deserts during the Roman and Early Byzantine Periods*, Leiden: 139–58.

Kasher, A. (1985) *The Jews in Hellenistic and Roman Egypt: The Struggle for Equal Rights*, Tübingen.

Kater-Sibbes, G.J.F. (1973) *A Preliminary Catalogue of Sarapis Monuments*, Leiden.

Katz, S. (1991) 'Sow what you know: The struggle for social reproduction in rural Sudan', *Annals of the Association of American Geographers* 81: 488–514, reprinted in S. Daniels and R. Lee (eds) (1996) *Exploring Cultural Geography*, London and New York: 44–61.

Keenan, J.G. (1980) 'Aurelius Phoibammon, son of Triadelphus: A Byzantine Egyptian land entrepreneur', *BASP* 17: 145–54.

—— (1984) 'The Aphrodite papyri and village life in Byzantine Egypt', *BSAC* 26: 51–63.

—— (1985) 'Notes on absentee landlordism at Aphrodito', *BASP* 22: 137–69.

Kees, H. (1931) 'Syene' *PW* IV A: q.v.

—— (1934) 'Thebai (Ägypten)', *PW* V A.2: q.v.

Kehoe, D.P. (1988) *The Economics of Agriculture on Roman Imperial Estates in North Africa* (Hypomnemata, 89), Göttingen.

—— (1992) *Management and Investment on Estates in Roman Egypt during the Early Empire* (Papyrologische Texte und Abhandlungen, 40), Bonn.

—— (1993a) 'Economic rationalism in Roman agriculture', *JRA* 6: 475–84.

—— (1993b) 'Investment in estates by upper-class landowners in early imperial Italy: The case of Pliny the Younger', *De Agricultura: Essays in Honour of P.W. de Neeve*, Amsterdam: 214–37.

—— (1997) *Investment, Profit, and Tenancy: The Jurists and the Roman Agrarian Economy*, Ann Arbor.

Kemp, B.J. (1971) 'Fortified towns in Nubia', in P.J. Ucko, R. Tringham and G.W Dimbleby (eds) *Man, Settlement and Urbanism*, London: 651–80.

—— (1989) *Ancient Egypt: Anatomy of a Civilization*, London and New York.

Kendrick, P.M. (1986) *Excavations at Sabratha 1948–1951*, London.

Kennedy, H. (1985a) 'From *Polis* to *Madina*: Urban change in late antique and early Islamic Syria', *P&P* 106: 3–27.

—— (1985b), 'The last century of Byzantine Syria: A re-interpretation', *Byz. Forsch.* 10: 141–83.

Kessler, D. (1983) 'Zwei Grabstelen mit Oxyrhynchosfischen', *Die Welt des Orients* 14: 176–88.

Kiss, Z. (1992a) 'Alexandrie 1986', *ET* 16: 337–43.

—— (1992b) 'Alexandrie 1987', *ET* 16: 345–51.

—— (1992c) 'Remarques sur la datation et les fonctions de l'edifice theâtral à Kôm el-Dikke', in S. Jakobielski and J. Karkowski (eds) *Fifty Years of Polish Excavations in Egypt and the Near East: Acts of the Symposium at the Warsaw University, 1986*, Warsaw: 171–8.

—— (1994) 'Un portrait romain d'Athribis', *BIFAO* 94: 303–9.

Kitto, H.D.F. (1951) *The Greeks*, Harmondsworth.

Kitzinger, E. (1938) 'Notes on early Coptic sculpture', *Archaeologia* 87: 181–215.

Kjølbye-Biddle, B. (1994) 'The small early church in Nubia with reference to the church on the point at Qasr Ibrim', in K. Painter (ed.) *'Churches built in Ancient Times': Recent Studies in Early Christian Archaeology*, London: 17–47.

Knights, C. (1994) 'The spatiality of the Roman domestic setting: An interpretation of symbolic content', in M. P. Pearson and C. Richards (eds) *Architecture and Order: Approaches to Social Space*, London and New York: 113–46.

Kock, E.L. (1948) *Die Kosmeet in Egipte*, Leiden.

Koenen, L. (1967) 'Eine Einladung zur Kline des Sarapis (P. Colon. inv. 2555)', *ZPE* 1: 121–6.

—— (1996) 'The carbonized archive from Petra', *JRA* 9: 177–86.

Kolataj, W. (1992) *Alexandrie VI; Imperial Baths at Kom el-Dikke*, Warsaw.

Kortenbeutel, H. (1937) 'Γυμνάσιον und βουλή. Eine ptolemäische Inschrift', *Archiv* 12: 44–53.

Kramer, B. (1990) 'Liste der Syndikoi, Ekdikoi und Defensores in den Papyri Ägyptens', in M. Capasso, G.M. Savorelli and R. Pintaudi (eds) *Miscellanea Papyrologica in occasione del bicentenario dell' edizione della Charta Borgiana* (Papyrologica Florentina, 19), Florence: 305–29.

Krause, M. (1979–82) 'Das christliche Theben: neuene Arbeiten und funde', *BSAC* 24: 21–33.

Kraut, S. (1984) 'Seven Heidelberg papyri concerning the office of exgetes', *ZPE* 55: 167–90.

Krüger, J. (1989) 'Badeanlagen von Oxyrhynchus: Eine historisch-terminologische Untersuchung', *Tyche* 4: 109–18.

—— (1990) *Oxyrhynchos in der Kaiserzeit: Studien zur Topographie und Literaturrezeption*, Bern, Frankfurt, New York and Paris.

Krugman, P. (1995) *Development, Geography and Economic Theory*, Cambridge and London.

Kryzanowska, A. (1995) 'Observations sur la circulation monétaire en Égypte', *ET* 17: 79–84.

Kubiak, W. (1982) *Al Fustat: Its Foundation and Early Development*, Warsaw.

Kubiak, W. and Scanlon, G.T. (1989) *Fustat Expedition: Final Report II: Fustat C* (ARCE, 11), Winona Lake.

Kuhlmann, K.P. (1983) *Materialien zur Archäologie und Geschichte des Raumes von Achmim* (DAIK Sondenschrift, 11), Mainz.

Kühn, E. (1913) *Antinoopolis: Ein Beitrag zur Geschichte des Hellenismus im römischen Ägypten. Gründung und Verfassung*, Göttingen.

Kus, S. and Raharijana, V. (1990) 'Domestic space and the tenacity of tradition among some Betsileo of Madagascar', in S. Kent (ed.) *Domestic Architecture and the Use of Space*, Cambridge: 24–42.

Lallemand, J. (1964) *L'administration civile de l'Égypte de l'avènement de Dioclétien à la creation du diocèse (284–382)* (Memoires de l'académie royale de Belgique: Classe des lettres, 57.2), Brussels.

—— (1966) 'Trésor de monnaies romaines en bronze découvert en Égypte: Constant à Constance Galle', *CE* 41: 380–94.

Lamprakos, M. (1992) 'Le Corbusier and Algiers: The Plan Obus and colonial urbanism', in N. Al Sayyad (ed.) *Forms of Dominance: On the Architecture and Urbanism of the Colonial Enterprise*, Berkeley: 183–210.

Landers, J. (1993) *Death and the Metropolis: Studies in the Demographic History of London 1670–1830* (Cambridge Studies in Population, Economy and Society in Past Time, 20), Cambridge.

Langton, J. (1975) 'Residential patterns in pre-industrial cities: Some case studies from seventeenth-century Britain', *Transactions of the Institute of British Geographers* 65: 1–27.

Laniado, A. (1997) 'Βουλευταί et πολιτευόμενοι', *CE* 72: 130–44.

Lansing, C. (1991) *The Florentine Magnates: Lineage and Faction in a Medieval Commune*, Princeton.

Lapidus, I.M. (1969) 'Muslim cities and Islamic societies', in I.M. Lapidus (ed.) *Middle Eastern Cities: A Symposium on Ancient, Islamic, and Contemporary Middle Eastern Urbanism*, Berkeley and Los Angeles: 47–79.

—— (1984) *Muslim Cities in the Later Middle Ages*, Cambridge.

Large, P. (1990) 'Rural society and agricultural change: Ombersley 1580–1700', in J. Chartres and D. Hey (eds) *English Rural Society, 1500–1800: Essays in Honour of Joan Thirsk*, Cambridge: 105–37.

Laskowska-Kusztal, E. (1984) *Deir el-Bahari III. Le sanctuaire ptolémaique de Deir el-Bahari*, Warsaw.

Laslett, P. (1972) 'Mean household size in England since the sixteenth century', in P. Laslett (ed.) *Household and Family in Past Time*, London: 125–58.

Latjar, A. (1991) 'Proskynema inscriptions of a corporation of iron-workers from Hermonthis in the temple of Hatshepsut in Deir el-Bahari: New evidence for pagan cults in Egypt in the fourth century AD', *JJP* 21: 53–70.

Lauffray, J. (1971) 'Abords occidentaux du premier pylône de Karnak: Le dromos, la tribune et les aménagements portuaires', *Kêmi* 21: 77–144.

Lauffray, J., Sa'ad, R. and Sauneron, S. (1971) 'Rapport sur les travaux de Karnak, Activités du "Centre Franco-Égyptien des temples de Karnak" (Campagne de travaux 1969–70)', *Kêmi* 21: 53–76.

Laurence, R. (1997) 'Writing the Roman metropolis', in H.M. Parkins (ed.) *Roman Urbanism: Beyond the Consumer City*, London and New York: 1–20.

—— (1994) *Roman Pompeii: Space and Society*, London, New York.

Laurence, R. and Smith, C. (1995–6) 'Ritual, time and power in ancient Rome', *Accordia Research Papers* 6: 133–51.

Laurence, R. and Wallace-Hadrill, A. (1997) (eds) *Domestic Space in the Roman World: Pompeii and Beyond* (*JRA* Suppl., 22), Portsmouth, RI.

Lawrence, R.J. (1990) 'Public collective and private space: A study of urban housing in Switzerland', in S. Kent (ed.) *Domestic Architecture and the Use of Space*, Cambridge: 73–88.

Leach, E. (1997) 'Oecus on Ibycus: Investigating the vocabulary of the Roman house', in S.E. Bon and R. Jones (eds) *Sequence and Space in Pompeii*, Oxford: 50–72.

Le Corbusier (1970) *Towards a New Architecture* (trans. F. Etchells), London.

—— (1971) *The City of Tomorrow and its Planning*, London.

LeGates, R.T. and Stout, F. (eds) (1996) *The City Reader*, London and New York.

Lee, T.R. (1976) 'Cities in the mind', in D.T. Herbert and R.J. Johnson (eds) *Social Areas in Cities II: Spatial Perspectives on Problems and Policies*, London: 159–87.

Lefebvre, H. (1991) *The Production of Space* (trans. D. Nicholson-Smith), Oxford and Cambridge.

Lefkowitz, M.R. (1996) *Not Out of Africa: How Afrocentrism Became an Excuse to Teach Myth as History*, New York.

Lefkowitz, M.R. and Rogers, G.M. (eds) (1996) *Black Athena Revisited*, Chapel Hill and London.

Lembke, K. (1998) 'Private representations in Roman times: The statues from Dimah/Fayyum', in N. Bonacasa, M.C. Naro, E.C. Portale and A. Tullio (eds), *L'Egitto in Italio dall' Antichità al Medioevo*, Rome: 289–95

Lepelley, C. (1996) 'Le survie de l'idée de cité republicaine en Italie au début du VIe siècle dans un édit d'Athalric rédigé par Cassiodore (*Variae* IX 2)', in C. Lepelley (ed.) *La fin de la cité antique et le début de la cité médiévale de la fin du IIIe siècle à l'avènement de Charlemagne*, Bari: 71–83.

Le Roy Ladurie, E. (1980) *Carnival: A People's Uprising at Romans 1579–1580*, London.

Lesko, B.S. (1994) 'Rank, roles, and rights', in B.S. Lesko (ed.) *Pharaoh's Workers: The Villagers of Deir el Medina*, Ithaca and London: 15–39.

Lesquier, J. (1918) *L'armée romaine d'Égypte d'Auguste à Dioclétien*, Cairo.

Levi, M.A. (1989) *La città antica: morfologia e biografia della aggregazione urbana nell' antichità*, Rome.

Lewis, N. (1983) 'The metropolitan gymnasiarchy, heritable and saleable (a reexamination of CPR VII 4)' *ZPE* 51: 85–91.

—— (1981) 'Notationes legentis', *BASP* 18: 73–81.

Ley, D. (1983) *A Social Geography of the City*, New York, Cambridge, Philadelphia, London, Mexico City, San Paolo and Sydney.

—— (1989) 'Coherence and limits to theory in human geography', in A. Kobayshi and S. Mackenzie (eds) *Remaking Human Geography*, Boston and London, reprinted in T. Barnes and D. Gregory (eds) (1997) *Reading Human Geography: The Poetics and Politics of Inquiry*, London: 98–111.

Leys, C. (1996) *The Rise and Fall of Development Theory*, Nairobi, Bloomington, Indianapolis and Oxford.

Lichocka, B. (1992) 'Une trouvaille des monnaies Alexandrines du Haut Empire dans la maison H à Kôm el-Dikke (Alexandrie)', *ET* 17: 112–15.

Lichtheim, M. (1955) *Demotic Ostraka from Medinet Habu*, Chicago.

Lidov, J.B. (1968) 'Tribal cycles in Oxyrhynchus', *TAPA* 99: 259–63.

Liebeschuetz, J.H.G.W. (1972) *Antioch: City and Imperial Administration in the Later Roman Empire*, Oxford.

—— (1973) 'The origins of the office of the pagarch', *Byzantinische Zeitschrift* 66: 38–46, reprinted in J.H.G.W. Liebeschuetz (1990) *From Diocletian to the Arab Conquest: Change in the Late Roman Empire*, Aldershot: XVII.

—— (1974) 'The pagarchy: City and imperial administration in Byzantine Egypt', *JJP* 18, 163–8: reprinted in J.H.G.W. Liebeschuetz (1990) *From Diocletian to the Arab Conquest: Change in the Late Roman Empire*, Aldershot: XVIII.

—— (1979) *Continuity and Change in Roman Religion*, Oxford.

—— (1992) 'The end of the ancient city', in J. Rich (ed.) *The City in Late Antiquity*, London and New York: 1–49.

—— (1996) 'Administration and politics in the cities of the fifth and sixth centuries with special reference to the circus factions', in C. Lepelley (ed.) *La fin de la cité antique et le début de la cité médiévale de la fin du IIIe siècle à l'avènement de Charlemagne*, Bari: 161–82.

Ling, R. (1990) 'A stranger in town: Finding the way in an ancient city', *Greece and Rome* 37: 203–14.

Lipietz, A. (1997) 'Warp, woof and regulation: A tool for the social sciences', in G. Benko and U. Strohmayer (eds) *Space and Social Theory: Interpreting Modernity and Postmodernity*, Oxford: 250–84.

Lipton, M. (1977) *Why Poor People Stay Poor: A Study in Urban Bias in World Development*, London.

—— (1982) 'Why poor people stay poor', in J. Harriss (ed.) *Rural Development: Theories of Peasant Economy and Agrarian Change*, London and New York: 66–81.

Litinas, N. (1997) 'Market places in Graeco-Roman Egypt: The use of the word ἀγορά in the papyri', *Akten des 21. internationalen Papyrologenkongresses, Berlin 13–19.8.1995*, Leipzig and Stuttgart: 601–6.

Livingstone, R.W. (1916) *A Defence of Classical Education*, London.

Llewelyn, S. (1994a) 'The εἰς (τὴν) οἰκίαν formula and the delivery of letters to third persons or to their property', *ZPE* 101: 71–8.

—— (1994b) 'The function of the ΣΗΜΑΣΙΑ texts, P. Oxy. XXXIV 2719 and SB XVI 12550', *ZPE* 104: 230–2.

Lloyd, J.A. (1979) *Excavations at Sidi Khrebish, Benghazi (Berenice) I* (*Libya Antiqua* Suppl., 5), Tripoli.

Luckhard, F. (1914) *Das Privathaus im ptolemäischen und römischen Ägypten*, Giessen.

Lukaszewicz, A. (1984) 'Nouveaux textes documentaires d'Alexandrie', *Atti del XVII congresso internazionale di Papirologia*, Naples: III, 879–84.

—— (1986) *Les édifices publiques dans les villes de l'Égypte romaine: Problèmes administratifs et financiers*, Warsaw.

—— (1989) 'Alexandrie sous les Sévères et l'historiographie', in L. Criscuolo and G. Geraci (eds) *Egitto e storia antica dell' ellenismo all' età araba*, Bologna: 491–6.

—— (1990) 'Fragmenta Alexandrina I: Some inscriptions from the Roman baths at Kom el-Dikke', *ZPE* 82: 133–6.

Luzzatto, M.J. (1996) 'P. Vat. gr. 52: Transporto di vino dall' Egitto a Constantinopoli nel VII sec. d.C.', *ZPE* 114: 153–6.

MacCoull, L.S.B. (1988) *Dioscorus of Aphrodito: His Work and his World*, Berkeley, Los Angeles and London.

—— (1998) 'Prophethood, texts and artifacts: The monastery of Epiphanius', *GRBS* 39: 307–24.

MacDonald, G. (1924) 'Biographical notice', in F. Haverfield, *The Roman Occupation of Britain*, Oxford: 15–38.

Mackail, J.W. (1925) *Classical Studies*, London.

MacLynn, N.B. (1994) *Ambrose of Milan: Church and Court in a Christian Capital*, Berkeley.

MacNally, S. and Schrunk, I.D. (1993) *Excavations in Akhmim, Egypt: Continuity and Change in City Life from Late Antiquity to the Present: First Report*, Oxford.

McGing, B.C. (1990) 'Melitian monks at Labla', *Tyche* 5: 67–94.

McKay, A.G. (1975) *Houses, Villas and Palaces in the Roman World*, London.

Maehler, H. (1983) 'Häuser und ihre Bewohner im Fayûm in der Kaiserzeit', in G. Grimm, H. Heinen and E. Winter (eds) *Das römisch–byzantinisch Ägypten. Akten des internationalen Symposions 26.–30. September 1978 in Trier*, Mainz: 119–37.

Magdalino, P. (1999) ' "What we have heard in the Lives of the saints we have seen with our own eyes": The holy man as literary text in tenth-century Constantinople', in J. Howard-Johnston and P.A. Hayward (eds) *The Cult of the Saints in Late Antiquity and the Middle Ages: Essays on the Contribution of Peter Brown*, Oxford: 83–112.

Magi, F. (1963) 'Le inscrizione recentemente scoperte sull' obelisco vaticano', *Studi Romani* 11: 50–6.

Majcherek, G. (1992) 'The late Roman ceramics from sector "G" (Alexandria 1986–1987)', *ET* 16: 81–117.

—— (1995) 'Notes on Alexandrian habitat: Roman and Byzantine houses from Kom el-Dikke', *Topoi* 5: 133–50.

—— (1999) 'Kom el-Dikke, excavations, 1997/98', *Polish Archaeology in the Mediterranean: Reports (1998)*, Warsaw: 29–39.

Majcherek, J. (1993) 'Roman amphorae from Marina el-Alamein', *MDAIK* 49: 215–20.

Malaise, M. (1972) *Les conditions de pénétration et de diffusion des cultes Égyptiens en Italie*, Leiden.

Manfredi, M. (1965) 'Scavi in Egitto', *Atene e Roma* 10: 93–5.

—— (1978) 'Ricerche papirologiche in Egitto (1964–1975)', *Quaderni de 'La ricerca scientifica'* 100: 291–310.

—— (1984) 'Notizie sugli scavi recenti ad Antinoe', *Atti de XVII congresso internazionale di Papirologia*, Naples: I 85–96.

Manniche, L. (1987) *Sexual Life in Ancient Egypt*, London.

Marina el Alamein (1991) *Marina el Alamein: Archaeological Background and Conservation Problems. The Polish–Egyptian Preservation Mission at Marina 1988: The Polish Excavation Mission at Marina 1987–1989, I*, Warsaw.

Markus, R.A. (1990) *The End of Ancient Christianity*, Cambridge.

Marrou, H.I. (1948) *Histoire de l'éducation dans l'antiquité*, Paris.

Marshall, J.U. (1989) *The Structure of Urban Systems*, Toronto.

Martin, A. (1998) 'L'image de l'évêque à travers les "Canons d'Athanase": Devoirs et réalités', in E. Rebillard and C. Sotinel (eds) *L'évêque dans la cité du IVe au Ve siècle: Image et autorité*, Paris and Rome: 59–70.

Martin, D.B. (1996) 'The construction of the ancient family: Methodological considerations', *JRS* 86: 40–60.

Martin, F. (1996a) 'The award of civic honorific statues in Roman imperial Italy, c. 31 BC–AD 500' (unpubl. University of London thesis).

—— (1996b) 'The importance of honorific statues: A case study', *BICS* 41: 53–7.

Massey, D. (1991a) 'Flexible sexism', *Environment and Planning D: Society and Space* 9: 31–57.

—— (1991b) 'A global sense of place', *Marxism Today* (June): 24–9, reprinted in T. Barnes and D. Gregory (eds) (1997) *Reading Human Geography: The Poetics and Politics of Inquiry*, London: 315–23.

Mathias, P. (1983) *The First Industrial Nation: An Economic History of Britain 1700–1914*, London and New York.

Mattingly, D.J. (1996) 'From one colonialism to another: Imperialism and the Maghreb', in J. Webster and N. Cooper (eds) *Roman Imperialism: Post-Colonial Perspectives* (Leicester Archaeology Monographs, 3), Leicester: 49–69.

—— (1997a) (ed.) *Dialogues in Roman Imperialism: Power, Discourse and Discrepant Experience in the Roman Empire* (*JRA* Suppl., 23), Portsmouth, RI.

—— (1997b) 'Dialogues of power and experience in the Roman Empire', in D.J. Mattingly (ed.) *Dialogues in Roman Imperialism: Power, Discourse and Discrepant Experience in the Roman Empire* (*JRA* Suppl., 23), Portsmouth, RI: 7–24.

Mau, A. (1899) *Pompeii: Its Life and Art* (trans. F.W. Kelsey), New York and London.

Medeksza, S. (1998) 'Marina el Alamein: Conservation work, 1998', *Polish Archaeology in the Mediterranean 10: Reports 1998*: 51–62.

Meier, H.O. (1995) 'The topography of heresy and dissent in late-fourth-century Rome', *Historia* 44: 232–49.

Mendelson, A. (1986) *Philo's Jewish Identity* (Brown Judaic Studies, 161), Atlanta.

Mertens, P. (1958) *Les services de l'état civil et le contrôle de la population à Oxyrhynchus au IIIe siècle de notre ère* (Mem. Acad. Royale de Belgique, 53.2), Brussels.

Meulenaere, H. de and MacKay, P.J. (1976) *Mendes II*, Warminster.

Meyer, B. (1997) '"Gymnase" et "thermes" dans l'Égypte romaine et byzantine', *Akten des 21. internationalen Papyrologenkongresses, Berlin 13–19.8.1995*, Leipzig and Stuttgart: 691–5.

Meyer E. (1920) 'ΠΥΡΓΟΣ "Wirtschaftsgebäude"', *Hermes* 55: 100–2.

Meyer, K.E. (1999) 'Axial peristyle houses in the Western Empire', *JRA* 12: 101–21.

Michalowski, K. (1962a) 'Les fouilles polonaises à Tell Atrib (1957–1959)', *ASAE* 57: 49–66.

—— (1962b) 'Fouilles polonaises à Tell Atrib en 1960', *ASAE* 57: 67–77.

Millar, F. (1983) 'Empire and city, Augustus to Julian: Obligations, excuses and status', *JRS* 73: 76–96.

Milne, J.G. (1920) 'Two Roman hoards of coins from Egypt', *JRS* 10: 169–84.

—— (1922) 'The coins from Oxyrhynchus', *JEA* 8: 158–63.

—— (1925) 'The *kline* of Sarapis', *JEA* 11: 6–9.

—— (1935) 'Report on coins found at Tebtunis in 1900', *JEA* 21: 210–16.

Mitchell, T. (1988) *Colonising Egypt*, Cambridge.

Modena, L.G. (1936–7) 'Il Christianesimo ad Ossirinco secondo i papiri', *BSAA* 9: 254–69.

—— (1938–9) 'Il Christianesimo ad Ossirinco: papiri letterari e cultura religiosa', *BSAA* 10: 293–310.

Momigliano, A. (1947) 'The first political commentary on Tacitus', *JRS* 37: 91–101, reprinted in A. Momigliano (1977) *Essays in Ancient and Modern Historiography*, Oxford: 205–29.

—— (1950) 'Ancient history and the antiquarian', *Journal of the Warburg and Courtauld Institutes* 13: 285–315, reprinted in A. Momigliano (1966) *Studies in Historiography*, London: 1–39.

Mond, R. and Myers, O.H. (1934) *The Bucheum*, London.

—— and —— (1940) *Temples of Armant: A Preliminary Survey*, London.

Mondésert, C. (1999) 'Philo of Alexandria', in W. Horbury, W.D. Davis and J. Sturdy (eds) *The Cambridge History of Judaism*, Cambridge: 877–900.

Montevecchi, O. (1935) 'Ricerche di sociologia nei documenti dell' Egitto greco-romano I: I testamenti', *Aegyptus* 15: 67–121.

—— (1941) 'Ricerche di sociologia nei documenti dell' Egitto greco-romano III: I contratti di compra-vendita', *Aegyptus* 21: 93–151.

—— (1970) 'Nerone a una polis e ai 6475', *Aegyptus* 50: 5–33.

—— (1973) *La Papirologia*, Turin.

—— (1975) 'L'epikrisis dei greco-egizi', *Proceedings of the XIV International Congress of Papyrologists*, Oxford: 227–32.

—— (1982) 'Il significato dell'età Neroniana secondo i papiri greci d'Egitto', *Neronia 1977*: 41–54.

—— (1988) 'L'amministrazione dell'Egitto sotto i Giulio-Claudi', *ANRW* II 10.1: 412–71.

—— (1998) 'La provenienza di P. Oxy 984', *Aegyptus* 78: 49–76.

Montserrat, D. (1990), 'P. Lond. inv. 3078 reappraised', *JEA* 76: 206–7.

—— (1992) 'The Kline of Anubis', *JEA* 78: 301–7.

—— (1996a) *Sex and Society in Graeco-Roman Egypt*, London, New York.

—— (1996b) '"No papyrus and no portraits": Hogarth, Grenfell and the first season in the Fayum, 1895–6', *BASP* 33: 133–76.

Montserrat, D., Fantoni, G. and Robinson, P. (1994) 'Varia Descripta Oxyrhynchita', *BASP* 31: 11–80.

Montserrat, D. and Meskell, L. (1997) 'Mortuary archaeology and religious landscape at Graeco-Roman Deir el-Medina', *JEA* 83: 179–97.

Morelli, F. (1999) '"Nuovi" documenti per la storia dell'irrigazione nell'Egitto bizantino. SB XVI 12377, P. Bad. IV 93, SPP X 295–299 e altri', *ZPE* 126: 195–201.

Moretti, L. (1977) 'La scuola, il ginnasio e l'efebia', in *Storia e civiltà dei Greci*, Milan: V 469–90.

Morley, N. (1996) *Metropolis and Hinterland: The City of Rome and the Italian Economy 200 BC–AD 200*, Cambridge.

—— (1997) 'Cities in context: Urban systems in Roman Italy', in H.M. Parkins (ed.) *Roman Urbanism: Beyond the Consumer City*, London and New York: 42–58.

Morris, I. (1987) *Burial and Ancient Society*, Cambridge.

Moscadi, A. (1970) 'Le lettere dell'archivio di Teofane', *Aegyptus* 50: 88–154.

Mouritsen, H. (1988) *Elections, Magistrates and Municipal Elite: Studies in Pompeian Epigraphy* (Analecta Romana Instituti Danici, Suppl., 15), Rome.

—— (1998) 'The album from Canusium and the town councils of Roman Italy', *Chiron* 28: 229–54.

Müller, H. (1985) *Untersuchungen zur Μισθωσις von Gebäuden im Recht der gräko-ägyptischen Papyri*, Cologne, Bonn, Berlin and Munich.

Mumford, L. (1991 [1961]) *The City in History: Its Origins, its Transformations and its Prospects*, Harmondsworth.

Murray, O. (1990) 'Cities of reason', in O. Murray and S. Price (eds) *The Greek City: From Homer to Alexander*, Oxford: 1–25.

Murray, O. and Price, S. (eds) (1990) *The Greek City: From Homer to Alexander*, Oxford.

Musurillo, H. (1954) *The Acts of the Pagan Martyrs: Acta Alexandrinorum*, Oxford.

—— (1961) *Acta Alexandrinorum*, Leipzig.

Myers, G. (1994) 'From "Stinkibar" to "The Island Metropolis": The geography of British hegemony in Zanzibar', in A. Godlewska and N. Smith (eds) *Geography and Empire*, Oxford and Cambridge, Mass.: 212–27.

Mysliwiec, K. (1988) 'Remains of a Ptolemaic villa at Athribis', *MDAIK* 44: 183–97.

—— (1992a) 'Excavations at Tell Atrib in 1985', *ET* 16: 383–91.

—— (1992b) 'Polish–Egyptian excavations at Tell Atrib in 1991', *Polish Archaeology in the Mediterranean III Reports 1991*, Warsaw: 24–8.

—— (1992c) 'Some ancient Egyptian aspects of Hellenistic cults at Athribis', in S. Jakobielski and J. Karkowski (eds) *50 Years of Polish Archaeology in Egypt and the Near East (Acts of the Symposium at the Warsaw University, 1986)*, Warsaw: 290–5.

—— (1995) 'L'habitat d'Athribis à la lumière des fouilles récentes', *Topoi* 5: 119–31.

Mysliwiec, K. and Herbich, T. (1988) 'Polish archaeological activities at Tell Atrib in 1985', in E.C.M. van den Brink (ed.) *The Archaeology of the Nile Delta, Egypt: Problems and Priorities*, Amsterdam: 177–203.

Mysliwiec, K. and Rageb, M.A.H. (1992) 'Fouilles polono-égyptiennes à Tell Atrib en 1986–1990', *ET* 16: 393–416.

Mysliwiec, K. and Szymanska, H. (1992) 'Les terres cuites de Tell Atrib', *CE* 67: 112–32.

Nager, R. (1997) 'The making of Hindu communal organisations, places and identities in post-colonial Dar es Salaam', *Environment and Planning D: Society and Space* 15: 707–30.

Nakane, C. (1972) 'An interpretation of the size and structure of the household in Japan over three centuries', in P. Laslett (ed.) *Household and Family in Past Time*, London: 517–43.

Naville, E. (1892–3) 'Excavations. Prof. Naville's work of the winter 1892', *EEF Archaeological Report 1892–1893*, London: 1–8.

—— (1894) *Ahnas el Medinah (Heracleopolis Magna) with Chapters on Mendes, the Nome of Thoth and Leontopolis*, London.

Neeve, P.W. de (1984) *Peasants in Peril: Location and Economy in Italy in the Second Century BC*, Amsterdam.

Negev, A. (1980) 'House and city planning in the ancient Negev and the provincia Arabia', in G. Golany (ed.) *Housing in Arid Lands: Design and Planning*, London: 3–32.

Negm, A.A. Mohamed (1998) 'An ancient village discovered near Abu-Mina (5th–8th cent. AD)', in N. Bonacasa, M.C. Naro, E.C. Portale and A. Tullio (eds) *L'Egitto in Italio dall' antichità al medioevo*, Rome: 307–12.

Nelson, C.A. (1979) *Status Declarations in Roman Egypt* (American Society of Papyrologists, 19), Amsterdam.

Nelson, H.H. and Hölscher, U. (1929) *Medinet Habu 1924–28* (Oriental Institute of the University of Chicago, Communications, 5), Chicago.

—— and —— (1931) *Medinet Habu Reports* (Oriental Institute of the University of Chicago, Communications, 10), Chicago.

Nevett, L. (1994) 'Separation or seclusion? Towards an archaeological approach to investigating women in the Greek household in the fifth to third centuries BC', in M. P. Pearson and C. Richards (eds) *Architecture and Order: Approaches to Social Space*, London and New York: 98–112.

—— (1995) 'The organisation of space in Classical and Hellenistic houses from mainland Greece and the western colonies', in N. Spencer (ed.) *Time, Tradition and Society in Greek Archaeology: Bridging the Great Divide*, London and New York: 89–108.

—— (1997) 'Perceptions of domestic space in Roman Italy', in B. Rawson and P. Weaver (eds) *The Roman Family in Italy: Status, Sentiment, Space*, Canberra and Oxford: 282–98.

—— (1999) *House and Society in the Ancient Greek World*, Cambridge.

Nicolet, C. (1991) *Space, Geography and Politics in the Early Roman Empire*, Ann Arbor.

Niebling, G. (1956) 'Laribus Augustis magistri primi. Der Beginn des Compitalkultus der Lares und des Genius Augusti', *Historia* 5: 303–31.

Nielson, I. (1990) *'Thermae et Balnea': The Architecture and Cultural History of Roman Public Baths*, Aarhus.

Nippel, W. (1995) *Public Order in Ancient Rome*, Cambridge.

Nock, A.D. (1952) 'The Roman army and the Roman religious year', *HThR* 45: 186–252, reprinted in A.D. Nock (1972) *Essays on Religion and the Ancient World*, Oxford: II 736–90.

Norton, R.E. (1996) 'The tyranny of Germany over Greece: Bernal, Herder and the German appropriation of Greece', in M.R. Lefkowitz and G.M. Rogers (eds) *Black Athena Revisited*, Chapel Hill and London: 403–10.

Nowicka, M. (1969) *La maison privée dans l'Égypte ptolémaïque*, Warsaw.

—— (1972) 'A propos des tours- πύργοι dans les papyrus grecs', *Archeologia* 21: 53–62.

—— (1973) 'A propos d'oikia ΔΙΠΥΡΓΙΑ dans le monde grec', *Archaeologia Polonia* 14: 175–8.

Oates, J.F. (1975) 'Ptolemais Euergetis and the city of the Arsinoites', *BASP* 12: 113–20.

Orlandi, T. (c. 1967) *Storia della chiesa di Alessandria: Testo Copto, traduzione e commento*, Milan, Varese.

Orlandi, T. and Camaioni, S. di Giuseppe (1976) *Passione e miracoli di S. Mercurio*, Milan.

Orth, W. (1983) 'Zum Gymnasium im römerzeitlichen Ägypten', in H. Heinen (ed.) *Althistorische Studien. Hermann Bengtson* (Historia Einzelschriften, 40), 223–32.

Østergård, U. (1992) 'What is national and ethnic identity?', in P. Bilde, T. Engberg-Pedersen, L. Hannestad and J. Zahle (eds) *Ethnicity in Hellenistic Egypt* (Studies in Hellenistic Civilization, 3), Aarhus: 16–38.

Ostrow, S.E. (1990) 'The Augustales in the Augustan System', in M. Toher and K. Raaflaub (eds) *Between Republic and Empire: Interpretations of Augustus and his Principate*, Berkeley, Los Angeles and Oxford: 364–79.

Otto, E. (1952) *Topographie des thebanischen Gaues* (Untersuchungen zur Geschichte und Altertumskunde Aegyptens, 16), Berlin.

Otto, W. (1905) *Priester und Tempel im hellenistischen Ägypten*, Leipzig and Berlin.

Owens, E.J. (1991) *The City in the Greek and Roman World*, London and New York.

Padró, J. et al. (1996) 'Excavacions arqueològiques a Oxirrinc (El Bahnasa, Egipte)', *Tribuna d'Arqueologia, 1994–1995*, Barcelona: 161–73.

Palme, B. (1989) 'Zu den Unterabteilungen des Quartieres Ἀγοράι in Theben', *Tyche* 4: 125–9.

Palter, R. (1996) 'Eighteenth-century historiography in Black Athena', in M.R. Lefkowitz and G.M. Rogers (eds) *Black Athena Revisited*, Chapel Hill and London: 349–402.

Papaconstantinou, A. (1994) 'Oracles chrétiens dans l'Égypte byzantines: Le témoignage des papyrus', *ZPE* 104: 281–6.

—— (1996) 'La liturgie stationnale à Oyrhynchos dans la première moitié du 6e siècle: Réédition et commentaire du P.Oxy. XI 1357', *REB* 54: 135–59.

Papathomas, A. (1999) 'ΜΟΝΑΣΤΗΡΙΟΝ ΕΠΟΙΚΙΟΥ ΣΚΥΤΑΛΙΔΟΣ: Ein neues Kloster in Oxyrhynchites', *ZPE* 128: 167–8.

Parassoglou, G.M. (1978) *Imperial Estates in Roman Egypt* (American Studies in Papyrology, 18), Amsterdam.

—— (1987) 'Request for help', in S. Janeras (ed.) *Miscellània Papirològica Ramon Roca-Puig*, Barcelona: 242–58.

Parker, S.T. (1986) *Romans and Saracens: A History of the Arabian Frontier*, Winona Lake.

Parkins, H.M. (1997) 'The consumer city domesticated?', in H.M. Parkins (ed.) *Roman Urbanism: Beyond the Consumer City*, London and New York: 83–111.

Parlasca, K. (1978) 'Der Übergang von der spätrömischen zur frühkoptischen Kunst im Licht der Grabreliefs von Oxyrhynchos', *Enchoria* 8 (Sonderband): 115–20.

Parlebas, J. (1977) 'Les Égyptiens et la ville d'après les sources littéraires et archéologiques', *Ktema* 2: 49–57.

Parsons, P.J. (1967) 'Philippus Arabs and Egypt', *JRS* 57: 134–41.

—— (1971) 'The wells of Hibis', *JEA* 57: 165–80.

Parsons, T. (1975) 'Some theoretical considerations of the nature and trends of change of ethnicity', in N. Glazer and D.P. Moynihan (eds) *Ethnicity: Theory and Experience*, Cambridge, Mass.: 53–83.

Patlagean, E. (1976) 'Dans le miroir, à travers le miroir: un siècle de déclin du monde antique', in W. den Boer (ed.) *Les études classiques aux xixe et xxe siècles: Leur place dans l'histoire des idées*, Geneva: 209–40.

—— (1977) *Pauvreté économique et pauvreté sociale à Byzance: 4e–7e siècles*, La Haye and Paris.

Patterson, J.R. (1992a) 'The city of Rome: From republic to empire', *JRS* 82: 186–215.

—— (1992b) 'Patronage, *collegia* and burial in imperial Rome', in S. Bassett (ed.) *Death in Towns: Urban Responses to the Dying and the Dead*, Leicester and New York: 15–27.

—— (1994) 'The collegia and the transformation of the towns of Italy in the second century AD', in *L'Italie d'Auguste à Dioclétien: Actes du colloque internationale organisé par l'École française à Rome*, Rome: 227–38.

Patterson, O. (1975) 'Context and choice in ethnic allegiance: A theoretical framework and Caribbean case study', in N. Glazer and D.P. Moynihan (eds) *Ethnicity: Theory and Experience*, Cambridge, Mass.: 305–49.

Pearson, M.P. and Richards, C. (1994) 'Architecture and order: Spatial representation and archaeology', in M.P. Pearson and C. Richards (eds) *Architecture and Order: Approaches to Social Space*, London and New York: 38–72.

Peet, R. (1997) 'Social theory, postmodernism, and the critique of development', in G. Benko and U. Strohmayer (eds) *Space and Social Theory: Interpreting Modernity and Postmodernity*, Oxford: 72–87.

Pélékides, C. (1962) *Histoire de l'éphébie Attique des origines à 31 av. J.C.*, Paris.

Pensabene, P. (1998) 'Il ruolo urbanistico delle vie colonnate nell'impianto delle città egiziane di età imperiale', in N. Bonacasa, M.C. Naro, E.C. Portale and A. Tullio (eds) *L'Egitto in Italia dall'antichità ad medioevo*, Rome: 325–58.

Pentz, P. (1992) *The Invisible Conquest: The Ontogenesis of Sixth- and Seventh-Century Syria*, Copenhagen.

Percival, J. (1976) *The Roman Villa: An Historical Introduction*, London and New York.

—— (1996) 'Houses in the country', in I.M. Barton (ed.) *Roman Domestic Buildings* (Exeter Studies in History), Exeter: 65–90.

Peremans, W. (1970) 'Sur l'identification des Égyptiens et des étrangers dans l'Égypte des Lagides', *Ancient Society* 1: 25–38.

—— (1981) 'Les mariages mixtes dans l'Égypte des Lagides', *Scritti in onore di Orsolina Montevecchi*, Bologna: 273–81.

Perpillou-Thomas, F. (1993) *Fêtes d'Égypte ptolémaïque et romaine d'après la documentation papyrologique grecque* (Studia Hellenistica, 31), Louvain.

Perring, D. (1991) 'Spatial organisation and social change in Roman towns', in J. Rich and A. Wallace-Hadrill (eds) *City and Country in the Ancient World*, London and New York: 273–93.

Pesando, F. (1989) *La Casa dei Greci*, Milan.

Pestman, P.W. (1961) *Marriage and Matrimonial Property in Ancient Egypt* (Pap. Lugd. Bat., 9), Leiden.

—— (1985) 'Le manuel de droit Égyptien de Hermoupolis: Les passages transmis en démotique et en grec', in P.W. Pestman (ed.) *Textes et Études de papyrologie grecque, démotique et copte* (Pap. Lugd. Bat., 23), Leiden: 116–43.

Petit, P. (1955) *Libanius et la vie municipale à Antioche au IVe siècle après J.-C.*, Paris.

Petrie, W.M. Flinders (1886) *Naukratis I: 1884–5*, London.

—— (1889) *Hawara, Biahmu and Arsinoe*, London.

—— (1905) *Ehnasya 1904*, London.

—— (1908) *Athribis*, London.

—— (1925) *Tombs of the Courtiers and Oxyrhynkhos*, London.

—— (unpubl.) 'Notebooks: 76: Oxyrhynchos' (Petrie Museum).

Plaumann, G. (1910) *Ptolemais in Oberägypten. Ein Beitrag zur Geschichte des Hellenismus in Ägypten*, Leipzig.

Pollard, N. (1998) 'The chronology and economic condition of late Roman Karanis: An archaeological reassessment', *JARCE* 35: 147–62.

Pomeroy, S.B. (1984) *Women in Hellenistic Egypt from Alexander to Cleopatra*, New York.

Pooley, C.G. (1982) 'Choice and constraint in the nineteenth-century city: A basis for residential differentiation', in J.H. Johnson and C.G. Pooley (eds) *The Structure of Nineteenth Century Cities*, London: 199–233.

Poos, L.R. (1991) *A Rural Society after the Black Death: Essex 1350–1525*, Cambridge.

Porten, B. (1996) *The Elephantine Papyri in English: Three Millennia of Cross-cultural Continuity and Change*, Leiden, New York and Cologne.

Potter, R.B. (1990) 'Cities, convergence, divergence and third world development', in R.B. Potter and A.T. Salau (eds) *Cities and Development in the Third World*, London: 1–11.

Potts, A. (1994) *Flesh and the Ideal: Winckelmann and the Origins of the History of Art*, New Haven and London.

Pratt, G. (1998) 'Grids of difference: Place and identity formation', in R. Fincher and J.M. Jacobs (eds) *Cities of Difference*, New York and London: 26–48.

Pratt, M.L. (1992) *Imperial Eyes: Travel Writing and Transculturation*, London.

Preisigke, F. (1919) 'Die Begriffe ΠΥΡΓΟΣ und ΣΤΕΓΗ bei der Hausenlage', *Hermes* 54: 423–32.

Preston, P.W. (1996) *Development Theory: An Introduction*, Oxford and Cambridge, Mass.

Pruneti, P. (1981) *I centri abitati dell' Ossirichite: Repertorio toponomastico* (Papyrologica Florentina, 9), Florence.

Purcell, N. (1999) 'The populace of Rome in late antiquity: Problems of classification and historical description', in W.V. Harris (ed.) *The Transformations of Urbs Roma in Late Antiquity* (*JRA* Suppl., 33), Portsmouth, RI: 135–61.

Quaegebeur, J. (1979) 'Documents égyptiens et rôle économique de clergé en Égypte hellenistique', in E. Lipinski (ed.) *State and Temple Economy in the Ancient Near East: Proceedings of the International Conference organised by the Katholieke Universiteit Leuven from the 10th to the 14th April 1978*, Leuven: II, 707–29.

—— (1981) 'Demotic and Greek ostraca excavated at El-Kab', *Proceedings of the XVI International Congress of Papyrology*, Chico: 527–36.

—— (1992) 'Greco-Egyptian double names as a feature of a bi-cultural society: The case of Ψοσνεῦς ὁ καὶ Τριάδελφος', in Janet. H. Johnson (ed.) *Life in a Multicultural Society: Egypt from Cambysses to Constantine and Beyond* (Studies in Ancient and Oriental Civilization, 51), Chicago: 265–72.

Quaegebeur, J., Clarysse, W. and Van Maele, B. (1985) 'Athena, Neith and Thoeris in Greek documents', *ZPE* 60: 217–32.

Quartermaine, L. (1995) '"Slouching towards Rome": Mussolini's imperial vision', in T. Cornell and K. Lomas (eds) *Urban Society in Roman Italy*, London: 203–15.

Radice, R. (1983) *Filone di Alessandria: Bibliografia generale 1937–1982* (Elenchos, 8), Milan.

Ranger, T. (1983) 'The invention of tradition in colonial Africa', in E. Hobsbawm and T. Ranger (eds) *The Invention of Tradition*, Cambridge: 211–62.

Rapoport, A. (1969) *House Form and Culture*, Englewood Cliffs.

—— (1981) 'Identity and environment: A cross-cultural perspective', in J.S. Duncan (ed.) *Housing and Identity: Cross-Cultural Perspectives*, London: 6–35.

Raschke, M.G. (1974) 'The office of the agoranomos in Ptolemaic and Roman Egypt', *Akten internationalen Papyrologenkongresses 13, Marburg/Lahn, 2.–6. August 1971*, Munich, 349–56.

—— (1978) 'New studies in Roman commerce with the East', *ANRW* II 9.2: 605–1363.

Rathbone, D.W. (1983) 'Italian wines in Roman Egypt', *Opus* 2: 81–98.

—— (1990) 'Villages, land and population in Graeco-Roman Egypt', *PCPhS* 36: 103–42.

—— (1991) *Economic Rationalism and Rural Society in Third-Century Egypt: The Heroninus Archive and the Appianus Estate*, Cambridge.

—— (1993) 'Egypt, Augustus and Roman taxation', *Cahiers G. Glotz* 4: 81–112.

—— (1994) 'More (or less?) economic rationalism in Roman Agriculture', *JRA* 7: 432–6.

—— (1996) 'Monetisation, not price-inflation, in third-century AD Egypt?', in C.E. King and D.G. Wigg (eds) *Coin Finds and Coin Use in the Roman World: The Thirteenth Oxford Symposium on Coinage and Monetary History* (Studien zu Fundmünzen der Antike, 10), Berlin: 321–39.

—— (1997) 'Prices and price formation in Roman Egypt', in J. Andreau, P. Briant and R. Descat (eds) *Économie antique: Prix et formation des prix dans les économies antiques*, Saint Bertrand de Comminges: 183–244.

Rea, J.R. (1982) '*P. Lond.* inv. 1562 verso: market taxes in Oxyrhynchus', *ZPE* 46: 191–209.

Rees, B.R. (1952) 'The defensor civitatis in Egypt', *JJP* 6: 73–102.

—— (1953–4) 'The curator civitatis in Egypt', *JJP* 7–8: 83–105.

—— (1968) 'Theophanes of Hermopolis Magna', *Bulletin of the John Rylands Library* 51: 164–83.

Reggiani, C.K. (1984) 'I rapporti tra l'impero romano e il mondo ebraico al tempo di Caligola secondo la "Legatio ad Gaium" di Filone Alessandrino', *ANRW* II 21.1: 554–86.

Rémondon, R. (1952) 'L'Égypte et la suprême résistance au Christianisme (Ve–VIIe siècles)', *BIFAO* 51: 63–87.

—— (1972) 'L'Église dans la société Égyptienne à l'époque byzantine', *CE* 47: 254–77.

Revillout, E. (1900) 'Textes coptes: Extraits de la correspondance de St Pésunthius évêque de Coptos et de plusieurs documents analogues (juridiques et économiques)', *Revue Égyptologique* 9: 133–77.

—— (1902) 'Textes coptes: Extraits de la correspondance de St Pésunthius évêque de Coptos et de plusieurs documents analogues (juridiques et économiques)', *Revue Égyptologique* 10: 34–47.

—— (1914) 'Textes coptes: extraits de la correspondance de St Pésunthius évêque de

Coptos et de plusieurs documents analogues (juridiques et économiques)', *Revue Égyptologique* 14: 22–32.

Reynolds, J. (1971) 'Roman inscriptions 1966–1970', *JRS* 61: 136–52.

Rheinhold, M. (1984) *Classica Americana: The Greek and Roman Heritage in the United States*, Detroit.

Richard, C.J. (1994) *The Founders and the Classics: Greece, Rome and the American Enlightenment*, Cambridge, Mass. and London.

Rickman, G. (1980) *The Corn Supply of Ancient Rome*, Oxford.

Riedel, W. and Crum, W.E. (1904) *The Canons of Athanasius of Alexandria*, London and Oxford.

Riggsby, A. (1997) '"Public" and "private" in Roman culture: The case of the cubiculum', *JRA* 10: 36–56.

Rigsby, K.J. (1977) 'Sacred ephebic games at Oxyrhynchus', *CE* 62: 147–55.

—— (1978) 'An ephebic inscription from Egypt', *GRBS* 19: 239–49.

Rink, H. (1924) *Strassen- und Viertelnamen von Oxyrhynchos*, Giessen.

Roberts, R. (1971) *The Classic Slum: Salford Life in the First Quarter of this Century*, Manchester.

Robinson, D.M. (1946) *Excavations at Olynthus XII: Domestic and Public Architecture*, Baltimore.

Robinson, D.M. and Graham, J.W. (1938), *Excavations at Olynthus VIII: The Hellenic House*, Baltimore.

Robinson, O.F. (1992) *Ancient Rome: City Planning and Administration*, London and New York.

Rodziewicz, E. (1978) 'Reliefs figurés en os des fouilles à Kôm el-Dikke', *ET* 10: 317–36.

Rodziewicz, M. (1976) *La céramique romaine tardive d' Alexandrie (Alexandrie I)* , Warsaw.

—— (1982) 'Graeco-Islamic elements at Kom el-Dikke in the light of new discoveries: Remarks on early medieval Alexandria', *Graeco-Arabica* 1: 35–49.

—— (1983) 'Alexandria and the district of Mareotis', *Graeco-Arabica* 2: 199–216.

—— (1984) *Alexandrie III: Les habitations romaines tardives d' Alexandrie à la lumière des fouilles polonaises à Kôm el-Dikke*, Warsaw.

—— (1988) 'Remarks on the domestic and monastic architecture in Alexandria and surroundings', in E.C.M. van den Brink (ed.) *The Archaeology of the Nile Delta: Problems and Priorities*, Amsterdam: 267–76.

—— (1991) 'Archaeological evidence of Byzantine architecture in Alexandria', *Graeco-Arabica* 4: 287–97.

Roeder, G. (1931–2) *Vorläufliger Bericht über die Ausgrabungen in Hermopolis 1929–1932*, Vienna.

—— (1959) *Hermopolis 1929–1939. Ausgraben der deutschen Hermopolis-Expedition in Hermopolis, ober-Ägypten*, Hildesheim.

Rogers, G.M. (1991) *The Sacred Identity of Ephesus*, London and New York.

Rose, G. (1993) *Feminist Geography: The Limits of Geographical Knowledge*, Cambridge and Oxford.

Rossiter, J. (1991) 'Convivium and villa in late antiquity', in W.J. Slater (ed.) *Dining in a Classical Context*, Ann Arbor: 199–214.

Rostem O.R. (1962) 'Modern granaries as relics of an ancient building' *ASAE* 57: 99–105.

Rouché C. (1979) 'A new inscription from Aphrodisias and the title πατήρ τῆς πόλεως, *GRBS* 20: 173–85.

—— (1989) *Aphrodisias in Late Antiquity: The Late Roman and Byzantine Inscriptions*

Including Texts from the Excavations at Aphrodisias Conducted by Kenan T. Erim (*JRS* Monographs, 5), London.

—— (1993) *Performers and Partisans at Aphrodisias in the Roman and Late Roman Periods: A Study Based on Inscriptions from the Current Excavations at Aphrodisias in Caria* (*JRS* Monographs, 6), London.

Roueché, M. (1990) 'The definition of a philosopher and a new fragment of Stephanus the philosopher', *Jahrbuch der Österreichischen Byzantinistik* 40: 107–28.

Rouillard, G. (1928) *L'administration civile de l'Égypte byzantine*, Paris.

Roullet, A. (1972) *The Egyptian and Egyptianizing Monuments of Imperial Rome*, Leiden.

Routledge, P. (1994) 'Backstreets, barricades and blackouts: Urban terrains of resistance in Nepal', *Environment and Planning D: Society and Space* 12: 559–78.

Rowe, A. (1938) 'Short report on the excavations of the institute of archaeology, Liverpool, at Athribis', *ASAE* 38: 523–32.

—— (1942) 'Short report on excavations of the Graeco-Roman museum made during the season 1942 at Pompey's pillar', *BSAA* 35: 124–42.

—— (1946) *Discovery of the Famous Temple and Enclosure of Serapis at Alexandria* (*ASAE* Suppl., 2), Cairo.

Rowland, R.J., Jr (1976) 'The "very poor" and the grain dole at Rome and Oxyrhynchus', *ZPE* 21: 69–72.

Rowlandson, J. (1996) *Landowners and Tenants in Roman Egypt: The Social Relations of Agriculture in the Oxyrhynchite nome* (Oxford Classical Monographs), Oxford.

—— (1998) *Women and Society in Greek and Roman Egypt: A Sourcebook*, Cambridge.

Rubensohn, O. (1905a) 'Aus griechisch-römischen Häusern des Fayum', *JDAI* 20: 1–25.

—— (1905b) 'Griechische-römische Funde in Ägypten', *Archäologischer Anzeiger Beiblatt zum JDAI* 20: 65–70.

—— (1906) 'Aegypten', *Archäologischer Anzeiger Beiblatt zum JDAI* 21: 124–43.

Rule, J. (1992) *The Vital Century: England's Developing Economy 1714–1815*, London and New York.

Runia, D.T. (1990) 'Philo, Alexandrian and Jew', in D.T. Runia, *Exegesis and Philosophy: Studies on Philo of Alexandria*, Aldershot: 1–18.

Ruszczyc, B. (1992) 'Tell Atrib, Kôm Sidi Youssef 1983', *ET* 16: 421–3.

Sadek, A.I. (1987) *Popular Religion in Egypt during the New Kingdom*, Hildesheim.

Safrai, S. (1976) 'Home and family', in S. Safrai and M. Stern (eds) *The Jewish People in the First Century*, Assen: II, 730–5.

Said, E.W. (1978) *Orientalism*, London.

—— (1993) *Culture and Imperialism*, London.

Ste Croix, G.E.M. de (1981) *The Class Struggle in the Ancient Greek World*, London.

Saller, R.P. (1984) 'Familia, domus, and the Roman conception of the family', *Phoenix* 38: 336–55.

—— (1994) *Patriarchy, Property and Death in the Roman Family*, Cambridge.

—— (1997) 'Roman kinship: Structure and sentiment', in B. Rawson and P. Weaver (eds) *The Roman Family in Italy: Status, Sentiment, Space*, Canberra and Oxford: 7–34.

Saller, R.P. and Shaw, B.D. (1984) 'Tombstones and Roman family relations in the Principate: Civilians, soldiers and slaves', *JRS* 74: 124–56.

San Nicolo, M. (1972) *Ägyptisches Vereinswesen zur Zeit der Ptolemäer und Römer: I: Die Vereinsarten; II: Vereinswesen und Vereinsrecht* (Münchener Beiträge zur Papyrusforschung und antiken Rechtsgeschichte, II. 1; II. 2), Munich.

Saradi, H. (1998) 'Privitization and sub-division of urban properties in the early Byzantine centuries: Social and cultural implication', *BASP* 35: 17–43.

Sauneron, S. (1952) 'Le temple d'Akhmîm décrit par Ibn Jobair', *BIFAO* 51: 123–35.

Sawyer, P. (1986) 'Early fairs and markets in England and Scandanavia', in B.L. Anderson and A.J.H. Latham (eds) *The Market in History: Papers presented at a Symposium at St George's House Windsor Castle held 9–13 September 1984*, London: 59–77.

Sayce, A.H. (1886) 'Some Roman inscriptions at Assuân', *PSBA* 18: 107–9.

—— (1908) 'Recent discoveries in Egypt', *PSBA* 30: 72–4.

Scanlon, G.T. (1984) 'Fustat expedition: Preliminary report, 1978', *JARCE* 21: 1–38.

—— (1994) 'Al-Fustāt: The riddle of the earliest settlement', in G.R.D. King and A. Cameron (eds) *The Byzantine and Early Islamic Near East II: Land Use and Settlement Patterns* (Studies in Late Antquity and Early Islam, I), Princeton: 171–9.

Schama, S. (1995) *Landscape and Memory*, London.

Scheidel, W. (1995) 'Incest revisited: Three notes on the demography of sibling marriage in Roman Egypt', *BASP* 32: 143–55.

—— (1996) *Measuring Sex, Age and Death in the Roman Empire: Explorations in Ancient Demography* (*JRA* Suppl., 21), Ann Arbor.

Schiffer, M. (1985) 'Is there a Pompeii premise?', *Journal of Anthropological Research* 41: 18–41.

Schiller, A.A. (1953) 'A family archive from Jeme', *Studi in onore di Vincenzo Arangio-Ruiz*, Naples: IV, 327–53.

Schlumberger, J.A. (1989) '*Potentes* and *Potentia* in the social thought of late antiquity', in F.M. Clover and R.S. Humphries (eds) *Tradition and Innovation in Late Antiquity*, Madison and London: 89–104.

Schmalz, G.C.R. (1996) 'Athens, Augustus and the settlement of 21 BC', *GRBS* 37: 381–98.

Schmitt, O. (1994) 'Die Buccellarii: Eine Studie zum militärischen Gefolgschaftswesen in der Spätantike', *Tyche* 9: 147–74.

Schneider, H.D. (1975) 'Four Romano-Egyptian tomb-reliefs from el-Behnasa, Egypt', *Bulletin Antieke Beschaving* 50: 9–12.

—— (1982) *Beelden van Behnasa: Egyptische kunst uit de Romeinse Keizertijd 1e–3e eeuw na Chr.*, Zutphen.

Schubart, W. (1913) 'Alexandrinische Urkunden aus der Zeit des Augustus', *Archiv* 5: 35–131.

Schubert, P. (1990) *Les archives de Marcus Lucretius Diogenes*, Bonn.

—— (1997) 'Antinoopolis: pragmatisme ou passion', *CE* 72: 119–27.

Schwartz, J. (1966) 'La fin du Sérapéum d'Alexandrie', in *Essays in Honor of C. Bradford Welles*, New Haven: 97–111.

—— (1975) *L. Domitius Domitianus (Étude numismatique et papyrologique)* (Papyrologica Bruxellensia, 12), Brussels.

Scobie, A. (1986) 'Slums, sanitation, and mortality in the Roman World', *Klio* 68: 399–433.

Scott, S. (1997) 'The power of images in the late-Roman house', in R. Laurence and A. Wallace-Hadrill (eds) *Domestic Space in the Roman World: Pompeii and Beyond* (*JRA* Suppl., 22), Portsmouth, RI: 53–67.

Segal, A. (1997) *From Function to Monument: Urban Landscapes of Roman Palestine, Syria and Provincial Arabia* (Oxbow Monograph, 66), Oxford.

Segrè, A. (1940) 'Note sull'editto di Caracalla', *Rend. Pont. Acc.* 16: 181–214.

—— (1944) 'A reply to H.I. Bell: *P. Giss.* 40 and the Constitutio Antoniniana', *JEA* 30: 69–72.

Sharp, M. (1998) 'The food supply in Roman Egypt' (D.Phil. thesis, University of Oxford).

Shaw, B.D. (1981) 'Rural markets in North Africa and the political economy of the Roman Empire', *Antiquités Africaines* 17: 37–83, reprinted in B.D. Shaw (1995) *Rulers, Nomads and Christians in Roman North Africa*, Aldershot: I.

—— (1992) 'Explaining incest: Brother–sister marriage in Graeco-Roman Egypt', *Man* 27: 267–99.

Sheehan, P. (1996) 'The Roman fortress of Babylon in Old Cairo', in D.M. Bailey (ed.) *Archaeological Research in Roman Egypt: The Proceedings of the Seventeenth Classical Colloquium of the Department of Greek and Roman Antiquities, British Museum (JRA* Suppl., 19), Ann Arbor: 95–7.

Sheppard, A.D. (forthcoming) 'Philosophy and philosophical schools', *CAH* XIV².

Sherwin-White, A.N. (1966) *The Letters of Pliny: A Historical and Social Commentary*, Oxford.

—— (1972) 'Philo and Avillus Flaccus: A conundrum', *Latomus* 31: 820–8.

—— (1973) *The Roman Citizenship*, Oxford.

Shields, R. (1997) 'Spatial stress and resistance: social meanings of spatialization', in G. Benko and U. Strohmayer (eds) *Space and Social Theory: Interpreting Modernity and Postmodernity*, Oxford: 186–202.

Shier, L.A. (1978) *Karanis: Terracotta Lamps from Karanis, Egypt: Excavations of the University of Michigan*, Ann Arbor.

Shurmer-Smith, P. and Hannam, K. (1994) *Worlds of Desire: A Cultural Geography*, London, New York, Melbourne and Auckland.

Shweinfurth, G. (1887) 'Zur Topografie der Ruinenstätte des alten Schet (Krokodilopolis-Arsinoe)', *Zeitschrift der Gesellschaft für allgemeine Erdkunde* 22: 54–79; 87–8.

Sibley, B. (1992) 'Outsiders in society and space', in K. Anderson and F. Gale (eds) *Inventing Places: Studies in Cultural Geography*, Melbourne, reprinted in S. Daniels and R. Lee (eds) (1996) *Exploring Cultural Geography*, London and New York: 281–98.

Sijpesteijn, P.J. (1964) *Penthemeros Certificates in Graeco-Roman Egypt* (Pap. Lugd. Bat., 12), Leiden.

—— (1976) 'Some remarks on the epicrisis of οἱ ἀπὸ γυμνασίου in Oxyrhynchus', *BASP* 13: 181–90.

—— (1979) *Nouvelle liste des gymnasiarques des métropoles de l'Égypte romaine* (Studia Amstelodamensia ad epigraphicam ius antiquum et papyrologicam pertinentia, 28), Zutphen.

—— (1983) 'PSI VIII 871: A note', *Studia Papyrologia* 22: 159.

—— (1987) 'The title πατὴρ (τῆς) πόλεως and the papyri', *Tyche* 2: 171–4.

—— (1995) 'Receipts from the Michigan Papyrus collection', *ZPE* 109: 87–109.

Sijpesteijn, P.J. and Worp, K. (1990) 'Three London Papyri', in M. Capasso, G.M. Savorelli and R. Pintaudi (eds) *Miscellanea Papyrologica in occasione del bicentenario dell' edizione della Charta Borgiana* (Papyrologica Florentina, 19), Florence: 507–20.

Simisatonius, A.P. (ed.) (1972) *Expositio Totius Mundi et Gentium*, London.

Simms, A. (1992) 'The early origins and morphological inheritance of European towns', in J.W.R. Whitehead and P. J. Larkham (eds) *Urban Landscapes: International Perspectives*, London and New York: 23–42.

Singerman (1995) *Avenues of Participation: Family, Politics and Networks in Urban Quarters of Cairo*, Princeton.

Sjoberg, G. (1960) *The Pre-industrial City: Past and Present*, New York.

Skeat, T.C. (1975) 'Another dinner invitation from Oxyrhynchus (P. Lond. inv. 3078)', *JEA* 61: 251–4.

Skeat, T.C. and Wegener, E.P. (1935) 'A trial before the Prefect of Egypt Appius Sabinus, c. AD 250', *JEA* 21: 224–47.

Slack, P. (1985) *The Impact of Plague in Tudor and Stuart England*, Oxford.

—— (1988) *Poverty and Policy in Tudor and Stuart England*, London.

Slater, D. (1992) 'On the borders of social theory: Learning from other regions', *Environment and Planning D: Society and Space* 10: 307–27, reprinted in T. Barnes and D. Gregory (eds) (1997) *Reading Human Geography: The Poetics and Politics of Inquiry*, London: 48–69.

Sly, D.I. (1990) *Philo's Perception of Women* (Brown Judaic Studies, 209), Atlanta.

—— (1996) *Philo's Alexandria*, London and New York.

Small, A.M. and Buck, R.J. (1994) *The Excavations of San Giovanni di Ruoti: I: The Villas and their Environment*, Toronto, Buffalo and London.

Smallwood, E.M. (1967) *Documents Illustrating the Principates of Gaius, Claudius and Nero*, Cambridge.

—— (1976) *The Jews under Roman Rule: From Pompey to Diocletian*, Leiden.

Smith, A.D. (1981) *The Ethnic Revival*, Cambridge.

—— (1986) *The Ethnic Origin of Nations*, Oxford.

Smith, H.S. (1971) 'Society and settlement in ancient Egypt', in P.J. Ucko, R. Tringham and G.W. Dimbleby (eds) *Man, Settlement and Urbanism*, London: 705–19.

Smith, J. (1993) 'The lie that blinds: destabilizing the text of landscape', in J. Duncan and D. Ley (eds) *Place/ Culture/ Representation*, London and New York: 78–92.

Smith, J.T. (1997) *Roman Villas: A Study in Social Structures*, London and New York.

Smith, M. (1998) 'Coptic literature, 337–425', *CAH* XIII^2: 720–35.

Smith, N. (1996) 'After Tompkins Square Park: degentrification and the revanchist city', in A.D. King (ed.) *Re-presenting the City: Ethnicity, Capital and Culture in the Twenty-first Century Metropolis*, Basingstoke and London: 93–107.

Snape, S.N. (1989) *British Museum Expedition to Middle Egypt: A Temple of Domitian at el-Asmunein* (British Museum Occasional Paper, 68), London.

Snow, J. (1949, 2nd edn 1855) *On the Mode of Communication of Cholera*, London.

Soja, E.W. (1989) *Postmodern Geographies: The Reassertion of Space in Critical Social Theory*, London and New York.

Spawforth, A.J. and Walker, S. (1985) 'The world of the Panhellenion I. Athens and Eleusis', *JRS* 75: 78–104.

—— and —— (1986) 'The world of the Panhellenion II. Three Dorian cities', *JRS* 76: 88–105.

Spencer, A.J. (1983) *Excavations at El-Ashmunein I. The Topography of the Site*, London.

—— (1989) *Exacavations at El-Ashmunein II. The Temple Area*, London.

Spencer, A.J. and Bailey, D.M. (1982) *British Museum Expedition to Middle Egypt: Ashmunein 1981*, London.

Spencer, A.J. and Bailey, D.M. (1985) *British Museum Expedition to Middle Egypt: Ashmunein (1984)*, London.

Spencer, A.J., Bailey, D.M. and Burnett, A. (1983) *British Museum Expedition to Middle Egypt: Ashmunein (1982)*, London.

Spencer, A.J., Bailey, D.M. and Davies, V.W. (1984) *British Museum Expedition to Middle Egypt: Ashmunein (1983)*, London.

Spengel, L. (ed.) (1854) *Rhetores Graeci*, Leipzig.

Spitzl, T. (1984) *Lex Municipii Malacitani*, Munich.

Spiegelberg, W. (1904) *Die demotische Denkmäler*, Leipzig.

Stambaugh, J.E. (1988) *The Ancient Roman City*, Baltimore and London.

Staveley, E.S. (1956) 'The constitution of the Roman Republic 1940–1954', *Historia* 5: 74–122.

—— (1972) *Greek and Roman Voting and Elections*, London.

Stead, M. (1984) 'A model to facilitate the study of temple administration in Graeco-Roman Egypt', *Atti del XVII Congresso internazionale di Pairologia*, Naples: III, 1045–52.

Stead, P. (1980) 'Essays in traditional and vernacular architecture in arid zones', in G. Golany (ed.) *Housing in Arid Lands: Design and Planning*, London: 33–44.

Stefanski, E. and Lichtheim, M. (1952) *Coptic Ostraca from Medinet Habu*, Chicago.

Stock, B. (1993) 'Reading, community and a sense of place', in J. Duncan and D. Ley (eds) *Place/Culture/Representation*, London and New York: 314–28.

Strassi Zaccaria, S. (1991) 'Prosopografia e incarichi amministrativi a Karanis nel II sec. d.C. Proposte interpretative', *ZPE* 85: 245–62.

Strocka, V.M. (1977) *Forschungen in Ephesos VIII/1: Die Wandermalerei der Hanghäuser in Ephesos*, Vienna.

Sutton, K. (1989) 'The role of urban bias in perpetuating rural–urban and regional disparities in the Maghreb', in R.B. Potter and T. Unwin (eds) *The Geography of Urban–Rural Interaction in Developing Countries*, London and New York: 68–108.

Swain, S. (1993) 'Hellenism in the East', *JRA* 6: 461–6.

—— (1996) *Hellenism and Empire: Language, Classicism and Power in the Greek World* AD 50–250, Oxford.

Swarney, P.R. (1970) *The Ptolemaic and Roman Idios Logos* (American Society of Papyrologists, 8), Toronto.

Swiderek, A. (1957–8) 'Deux papyrus de la Sorbonne relatifs à des travaux effectués dans des temples de l'Heracléopolite', *JJP* 11–12: 59–91.

Tacoma, L. (1998) 'Replacement parts for an irrigation machine of the divine house at Oxyrhynchus: P. Columbia inv. 83 October 12 AD 549(?)', *ZPE* 126: 195–201.

Tait, W.J. (1992) 'Demotic literature and Egyptian society', in Janet. H. Johnson (ed.) *Life in a Multicultural Society: Egypt from Cambysses to Constantine and Beyond* (Studies in Ancient and Oriental Civilization, 51), Chicago: 303–10.

Taplin, O. (1989) *Greek Fire*, London.

Tate, G. (1992) *Les campagnes de la Syrie du Nord du IIe au VIIe siècle: Un example d'expansion démographique et économique à la fin de l'antiquité*, Paris.

Taubenschlag, R. (1927) 'Das Recht auf εἴσοδος und εἴξοδος in den Papyri', *Archiv.* 8: 25–33.

Taylor, L.R. (1966) *Roman Voting Assemblies*, Ann Arbor.

Therbert, Y. (1983) 'L'evolution urbaine dans les provinces orientales de l'Afrique romaine tardive', *Opus* 2: 99–131.

—— (1987) 'Private life and domestic architecture in Roman Africa', in P. Veyne (ed.) *A History of Private Life I: From Pagan Rome to Byzantium*, Cambridge, Mass. and London: 313–409.

Thomas, J.D. (1959) 'The office of the exactor in Egypt', *CE* 34: 124–40.

—— (1960) 'The strategus in fourth century Egypt', *CE* 35: 262–70.

—— (1971) 'The disappearance of the Dekaprotoi in Egypt', *BASP* 11: 60–8.

—— (1975) 'The introduction of Dekaprotoi and comarchs into Egypt in the third century AD', *ZPE* 19: 111–19.

—— (1982) *The Epistrategos in Ptolemaic and Roman Egypt: The Roman Epistrategos* (Pap. Colon., 6), Cologne.

—— (1989) 'Exactores in the papyri and in the legal codes', in L. Criscuolo and G. Geraci (eds) *Egitto e storia antica dall' ellenismo all'età araba*, Bologna: 683–91.

Thompson Crawford, D.J. (1984) 'The Idumaeans of Memphis and the Ptolemaic *Politeumata*', *Atti del XVII Congresso internazionale di Papirologia*, Naples: III, 1069–75.

Thompson, D.J. (1988) *Memphis under the Ptolemies*, Princeton.

—— (1990) 'The high priests of Memphis under Ptolemaic rule', in M. Beard and J. North (eds) *Pagan Priests*, London: 95–116.

Thompson, E.P. (1978) 'The poverty of theory or an orrery of errors', in E.P. Thompson, *The Poverty of Theory and Other Essays*, London: 193–397.

Tibiletti, G. (1979) *Le lettere private nei papiri greci del III e IV secolo d.C: Tra paganesimo e cristianesimo*, Milan.

Tietze, C. (1985) 'Amarna. Analyse der Wohnhäuser und soziale Struktur der Stadtbewohner', *ZÄS* 112: 48–84.

Till, W.C. (1939) 'Eine Verkaufsurkunde aus Dschême', *BSAC* 5: 43–59.

Timm, C. (1984–92) *Das christlich-koptische Ägypten in arabischer Zeit*, Wiesbaden.

Timms, D.W.G. (1976) 'Social bases to social areas', in D.T. Herbert and R.J. Johnson (eds) *Social Areas in Cities I: Spatial Processes and Form*, London: 19–39.

Tkaczow, B. (1993) *The Topography of Ancient Alexandria: An Archaeological Map* (Travaux du centre d'archéologie mediterranéenne de l'Acadamie Polonaise des Sciences, 32), Warsaw.

Tomlinson, R.A. (1992) *From Mycenae to Constantinople: The Evolution of the Ancient City*, London and New York.

Tosh, J. (1991) 'Domesticity and manliness in the Victorian middle class: The family of Edward White Benson', in M. Roper and J. Tosh (eds) *Manful Assertions: Masculinities in Britain since 1900*, London and New York: 44–73.

Toulan, N.A. (1980) 'Climatic considerations in the design of urban housing in Egypt', in G. Golany (ed.) *Housing in Arid Lands: Design and Planning*, London: 74–84.

Treggiari, S. (1998) 'House and forum: Cicero between "public" and "private"', *TAPA* 128: 1–23.

—— (1999) 'The upper class house as symbol and focus of emotion in Cicero', *JRA* 12: 33–56.

Trombley, F. (1994) *Hellenic Religion and Christianization c. 370–529*, Leiden.

Trümper, M. (1998) *Wohnen in Delos: Eine baugeschichtliche Untersuchung zum Wandel der Wohnkultur in hellenistischer Zeit* (Internationale Archäologie, 46), Rahden.

Turner, E.G. (1936) 'Egypt and the Roman empire: The ΔΕΚΑΠΡΩΤΟΙ', *JEA* 22: 7–19.

—— (1954) 'Tiberius Julius Alexander', *JRS* 44: 54–64.

—— (1975) 'Roman Oxyrhynchus', *HSCP* 79: 1–24.

Twigg, G. (1993) 'Plague in London: Spatial and temporal aspects', in J.A.I. Champion (ed.) *Epidemic Disease in London* (Centre for Metropolitan History, Working Papers Series, 1), London: 1–17.

Unwin, T. (1989) 'Urban–rural interaction in developing countries: A theoretical perspective', in R.B. Potter and T. Unwin (eds) *The Geography of Urban–Rural Interaction in Developing Countries*, London and New York: 11–32.

van Aken, A.R.A. (1949) 'Late Roman domestic architecture', *Mnemosyne* 2: 242–51.

van Berchem, D. (1939) *Les distributions de blé et d'argent à la plèbe romaine sous l'empire*, Geneva.

van Bremen, R. (1996) *The Limits of Participation: Women and Civic Life in the Greek East in the Hellenistic and Roman Periods*, Amsterdam.

Van Dam, R. (1985) *Leadership and Community in Late Antique Gaul*, Berkeley.

—— (1993) *Saints and their Miracles in Late Antique Gaul*, Princeton.

van den Brink, E.C.M. (1987) 'A geo-archaeological survey in the north-eastern Nile Delta, Egypt: The first two seasons, a preliminary report', *MDAIK* 43: 7–24.

Vandoni, M. (1964) *Feste pubbliche e private nei documenti greci*, Milan.

Vandorpe, K. (1995) 'City of many a gate, harbour for many a rebel: Historical and topographical outline of Greco-Roman Thebes', in S.P. Vleeming (ed.) *Hundred-Gated Thebes: Acts of a Colloquium on Thebes and the Theban Area in the Graeco-Roman Period* (Pap. Lugd. Bat., 27), Leiden, New York and Cologne: 203–39.

van Groningen, B.A. (1924) *Le gymnasiarque des métropoles de l'Égypte romaine*, Paris.

van Landuyt, K. (1995) 'The Soter family: Geneology and onomastics', in S.P. Vleeming (ed.) *Hundred-Gated Thebes: Acts of a Colloquium on Thebes and the Theban Area in the Graeco-Roman Period* (Pap. Lugd. Bat., 27), Leiden, New York and Cologne: 69–82.

van Minnen, P. (1986) 'The volume of the Oxyrhynchite textile trade', *MBAH* 5: 88–95.

—— (1987) 'Urban craftsmen in Roman Egypt', *MBAH* 6: 31–88.

—— (1991) 'Appendix: The systates', in F.A.J. Hoogendijk and P. van Minnen, *Papyri, Ostraca, Parchments and Waxed Tablets in the Leiden Papyrological Institute* (Pap. Lugd. Bat., 25), Leiden, New York, Cologne and Copenhagen: 275–83.

—— (1994) 'House to house enquiries: An interdisciplinary approach to Roman Karanis', *ZPE* 100: 227–51.

—— (1997) 'Patronage in fourth-century Egypt: A note on P. Ross. Georg. III 8', *JJP* 27: 67–73.

van Nijf, O.M. (1997) *The Civic World of Professional Associations in the Roman East* (Dutch Monographs on Ancient History and Archaeology, 17), Amsterdam.

Van Sant, T. and The Geosphere Project (1990) *The Earth from Space: A Satellite View of the World*, Ontario.

van 't Dack, E. (1992) 'L'armée de terre Lagide: Reflet d'un monde multiculturel?', in Janet H. Johnson (ed.) *Life in a Multicultural Society: Egypt from Cambysses to Constantine and Beyond* (Studies in Ancient and Oriental Civilization, 51), Chicago: 327–41.

Varaille, A. (1943) *Karnak I*, Cairo.

Veilleux, A. (ed.) (1980–2) *Pachomian Koinonia: The Lives, Rules and Other Writings of St Pachomius and his Disciples*, Kalamazoo.

Vergote, J. (1957–8) 'Appendice: Note sur ΕΣΗΦ, *JJP* 11–12: 93–6.

Vernus, P. (1978) *Athribis: Textes et documents relatifs à la geographie, aux cultes, et à l'histoire d'une ville du delta egyptien à l'époque pharaonique*, Cairo.

Vogliano, A. (ed.) (1936) *Primo rapporto degli scavi condotti dalla missione archeologica d'Egitto della R. Università di Milano nella zona di Madinet Madi (Campagna inverno e primavera 1935: XIII)*, Milan.

—— (ed.) (1937) *Secondo rapporto degli scavi condotti dalla missione archeologica d'Egitto della R. Università di Milano nella zona di Madinet Madi (Campagna inverno e primavera 1936: XIV)*, Milan.

—— (1938) 'Rapporto preliminare della IVa campagna di scavo a Madînet Mâdi', *ASAE* 38: 533–49.

—— (1939) 'Medinet Madi: Fouilles de l'Université Royale de Milan', *CE* 14: 87–9.

—— (1942) *Un Impressa archeologica Milanese ai Margini orientale del Deserto Libico*, Milan.

von Reden, S. (1995) *Exchange in Ancient Greece*, London.

Wace, A.J.B. (1945) 'Hermopolis Magna', *JHS* 65: 109.

Wace A.J.B., Megaw, A.H.S. and Skeat, T.C. (1959) *Hermopolis Magna, Ashmunein: The*

Ptolemaic Sanctuary and the Basilica (Alexandria University, Faculty of Arts Publications, 8), Alexandria.

Wagner, G. (1971) 'Inscriptions grecques du temple de Karnak I', *BIFAO* 70: 1–38.

—— (1972) 'Inscriptions grecques du dromos de Karnak II', *BIFAO* 71: 161–79.

—— (1987) *Les oasis d'Égypte à l'époque grecque, romaine et byzantine d'après les documents grecs* (Recherches de papyro logie et d'épigraphie grecques), Cairo.

Wagner, G., Leblanc, C., Lecuyot, G. and Loyrette, A.-M. (1990) 'Documents grecs découverts dans la vallée des Reines', *BIFAO* 90: 365–80.

Walker, S. (1983) 'Women and housing in Classical Greece: The archaeological evidence', in A. Cameron and A. Kuhrt (eds) *Images of Women in Antiquity*, London: 81–91.

Walker, S. and Bierbrier, M. (1997) *Ancient Faces: Mummy Portraits from Roman Egypt*, London.

Walker, S. and Cameron, A. (eds) (1989) *The Greek Renaissance in the Roman Empire* (*BICS* Suppl., 55), London.

Wall, R. (1972) 'Mean household size in England from printed sources', in P. Laslett (ed.) *Household and Family in Past Time*, London: 159–203.

Wallace, S.L. (1938) *Taxation in Egypt from Augustus to Diocletian*, Princeton.

Wallace-Hadrill, A. (1988) 'The social structure of the Roman house', *PBSR* 56: 43–97.

—— (1991) 'Elites and trade in the Roman town', in J. Rich and A. Wallace-Hadrill (eds) *City and Country in the Ancient World*, London and New York: 241–72.

—— (1993) *Augustan Rome*, London.

—— (1994) *Houses and Society in Pompeii and Herculaneum*, Princeton.

—— (1997) 'Rethinking the Roman atrium house', in R. Laurence and A. Wallace-Hadrill (eds) *Domestic Space in the Roman World: Pompeii and Beyond* (*JRA* Suppl., 22), Portsmouth, RI: 219–40.

Wallerstein, I. (1974) *The Modern World-System I: Capitalist Agriculture and the Origins of the European World-Economy in the Sixteenth Century*, New York, San Francisco and London.

—— (1979) *The Capitalist World Economy*, Cambridge and Paris.

Waltzing, J.-P. (1895) *Étude historique sur les corporations professionelles chez les romains*, Louvain.

Wasif, F.M. (1979) 'A Graeco-Roman bath at Tell Sersena', *ASAE* 63: 177–82.

Webster, J. (1996) 'Roman imperialism and the "post imperial age"', in J. Webster and N. Cooper (eds) *Roman Imperialism: Post-Colonial Perspectives* (Leicester Archaeology Monographs, 3), Leicester: 1–17.

Wegener, E.P. (1938) 'Notes on the φυλαί of the metropolis', *Actes du Ve Congrès international du Papyrologie*, Brussels: 512–20.

—— (1948) 'The Βουλή and the nomination to the ἀρχαί in the μητροπόλεις of Roman Egypt', *Mnemosyne* 15–42; 115–32; 297–326; reprinted in P.W. Pestman (ed.) (1985) *Textes et études de papyrologie grecque, démotique et copte* (Pap. Lugd. Bat., 23), Leiden: 62–114.

Weigand, E. (1928) 'Propylon und Bogentor in der östlichen Reichkunst ausgehend vom Mithridatistor', *Wiener Jahrbuch für Kunstgeschichte* 5: 71–114.

Werner, C.M. (1985) 'Temporal aspects of homes', in I. Altman and C.M. Werner (eds) *Home Environments* (Human Behaviour and Environment. Advances in Theory and Research, 8), New York: 1–32.

Wessely, C. (1902) 'Die Stadt Arsinoe (Krokodilopolis) in griechischer Zeit', *Sitzungsberichte der kaiserlichen Akadamie der Wissenschaften in Wien. Philosophisch-historische Classe* 145: IV.

Westwood, S. and Williams, J. (1997) 'Imagining cities', in S. Westwood and J. Williams (eds) *Imagining Cities: Scripts, Signs, Memory*, London and New York: 1–16..

Wharton, A.J. (1995) *Refiguring the Post Classical City: Dura Europos, Jerash, Jerusalem and Ravenna*, Cambridge.

Whitcomb, D.S. and Johnson, J.H. (1982) *Quseir al-Qadim: Preliminary Report* (ARCE, 7), Malibu.

Whitehorne, J.E.G. (1979) 'Sex and society in Graeco-Roman Egypt', *Actes du XVe Congrès international de Papyrologie*, Brussels: IV, 240–6.

—— (1980–1) 'New light on temple and state in Roman Egypt', *Journal of Religious History* 11: 218–26.

—— (1981) 'The role of the strategia in administrative continuity in Roman Egypt', *Proceedings of the XVI International Congress of Papyrology*, Ann Arbor: 419–28.

—— (1982) 'The ephebate and the gymnasial class in Roman Egypt', *BASP* 19: 171–84.

—— (1984) 'Tryphon's second marriage (P.Oxy. II 267)', *Atti del XVIII Congresso internazionale di Papirologia*, Naples: III, 1267–74.

—— (1988) 'Recent research on the strategi of Roman Egypt (to 1985)', *ANRW* II 10.1: 598–617.

—— (1990) 'Soldiers and veterans in the local economy of first century Oxyrhynchus', in M. Capasso, G.M. Savorelli and R. Pintaudi (eds) *Miscellanea Papyrologica in occasione del bicentenario dell'edizione della Charta Borgiana* (Papyrologica Florentina, 19), Florence: 543–67.

—— (1995) 'The pagan cults of Roman Oxyrhynchus', *ANRW* II 18.5: 3050–91.

Whitelaw, T.M. (1994) 'Order without architecture: Functional, social and symbolic dimensions in hunter-gatherer settlement organization', in M.P. Pearson and C. Richards (eds) *Architecture and Order: Approaches to Social Space*, London and New York: 217–43.

Whittaker, C.R. (1993) 'Do theories of the ancient city matter?', in C.R. Whittaker, *Land, City and Trade in the Roman Empire*, Aldershot: IX, reprinted in T. Cornell and K. Lomas (eds) (1995) *Urban Society in Roman Italy*, London: 9–26.

—— (1990) 'The consumer city revisited: the *vicus* and the city', *JRA* 3: 110–18, reprinted in C.R. Whittaker (1993) *Land, City and Trade in the Roman Empire*, Aldershot: VIII.

Whittow, M. (1990) 'Ruling the late Roman and early Byzantine city: A continuous history', *P&P* 129: 3–29.

Wibber, D.W. (1940) 'The Coptic frescoes of Saint Menas at Medinet Habu', *Art Bulletin* 32: 86–103.

Wickham, C. (1984) 'The other transition: From the ancient world to feudalism', *P&P* 113: 3–36, reprinted in C. Wickham (1994) *Land and Power: Studies in Italian and European Social History, 400–1200*, London: 7–42.

Wiegand, T. and Schrader, H. (1904) *Priene. Ergebnisse der Ausgrabungen und Untersuchungen in den Jahren 1895–1898*, Berlin.

Wilcken, U. (1887) 'Zusätze zu dem Aufsatz: Zur Topographie der Ruinenstätte des alten Schet (Krokodilopolis–Arsinoë)', *Zeitschrift der Gesellschaft für allgemeine Erdkunde* 22: 79–86.

—— (1894) 'Ὑπομνηματισμοί', *Philologus* 53: 80–126.

—— (1899) *Griechische Ostraka*, Berlin.

—— (1906) 'Ein ΝΟΜΟC ΤΕΛΩΝΙΚΟC aus der Kaiserzeit', *Archiv* 3: 185–200.

Wilfong, T.G. (1989) 'Western Thebes in the seventh and eighth centuries: A bibliographic survey of Jême and its surroundings', *BASP* 26: 89–145.

—— (1990) 'The archive of a family of money lenders from Jême', *BASP* 27: 169–81.

Wilk, R.R. (1990) 'The built environment and consumer decisions', in S. Kent (ed.) *Domestic Architecture and the Use of Space*, Cambridge: 34–42.

Williams, R. (1973) *The Country and the City*, London.

Wilson, K.L. (1982) *Cities of the Delta II. Mendes. Preliminary Report on the 1979 and 1980 Seasons* (ARCE, 5), Malibu.

Wilson, L.M. (1953) *Ancient Textiles from Egypt in the University of Michigan Collection*, Ann Arbor.

Winlock, H.E. (1942) *Excavations at Deir el Bahri 1911–1931*, New York.

Winlock, H.E. and Crum, W.E. (1926) *The Monastery of Epiphanius at Thebes*, New York.

Wipszycka, E. (1965) *L'industrie textile dans l'Égypte romaine*, Warsaw.

—— (1971) 'Les impôts professionnels et la structure de l'industrie dans l'Égypte romaine. A propos de la κοπὴ τριχός', *JJP* 16–17: 117–30.

—— (1972) *Les ressources et les activités économiques des églises en Égypte du IVe au VIIIe siècle* (Papyrologica Bruxellensia, 10), Brussels.

—— (1986) 'La valeur de l'onomastique pour l'histoire de la Christianisation de l'Égypte: a propos d'une étude de R.S. Bagnall', *ZPE* 62: 173–81.

—— (1988) 'La Christianisation de l'Égypte aux IVe–VIe siècles. Aspects sociaux et ethniques', *Aegyptus* 68: 119–65.

—— (1994) 'Le monachisme Égyptien et les villes', *Travaux et Mémoires* 12: 1–44.

—— (1998) 'L'attività caritativa dei vescovi egiziani', in E. Rebillard and C. Sotinel (eds) *L'évêque dans la cité du IVe au Ve siècle: Image et autorité*, Paris and Rome: 71–80.

Winkler, J. (1980) 'Lollianus and the desperadoes', *JHS* 100: 155–81.

Wolff, H.J. (1976) *Die Constitutio Antoniniana und Papyrus Gissensis 40 I*, Cologne.

Wood, D. (1993) *The Power of Maps*, London.

Woolf, G.D. (1994) 'Becoming Roman, staying Greek: Culture, identity and the civilizing process in the Roman East', *PCPhS* 40: 116–43.

—— (1998) *Becoming Roman: The Origins of Provincial Civilization in Gaul*, Cambridge.

Worp, K.A. (1999) '*Bouleutai* and *Politeuomenoi* in Later Byzantine Egypt again', *CÉ* 74: 124–32.

Wrigley, E.A. (1987) *People, Cities and Wealth: The Transformation of Traditional Society*, Oxford and New York.

Wyke, M. (1992) 'Augustan Cleopatras: Female power and poetic authority', in A. Powell (ed.) *Roman Poetry and Propaganda in the Age of Augustus*, London: 98–140.

Yacoub, F. (1968) 'A private bath discovered at Kîmân Fâris, Fayum', *ASAE* 60: 55–6.

Yardley, J.C. (1991) 'The symposium in Roman Elegy', in W.J. Slater (ed.) *Dining in a Classical Context*, Ann Arbor: 149–55.

Yavetz, Z. (1958) 'The living conditions of the urban plebs in Republican Rome', *Latomus* 17: 500–17.

—— (1969) *Plebs and Princeps*, Oxford.

Yelvington, K. (1991) 'Ethnicity as practice? A comment on Bentley', *CSSH* 33: 158–68.

Yinger, J.M. (1986) 'Intersecting strands in the theorisation of race and ethnic relations', in J. Rex and D. Mason (eds) *Theories of Race and Ethnic Relations*, Cambridge: 20–41.

Youtie, H.C. (1948) 'The *Kline* of Sarapis', *HThR* 41: 9–29.

—— (1949) 'Records of a Roman bath in Upper Egypt', *AJA* 53: 268–70, reprinted in H.C. Youtie (1973) *Scriptiunculae II*, Amsterdam: 990–2.

—— (1970) 'Callimachus in the tax rolls', *Proceedings of the XIIth International Congress of Papyrology*, Toronto: 545–51, reprinted in H.C. Youtie (1973) *Scriptiunculae II*, Amsterdam: 1035–41.

—— (1975) 'ΑΠΑΤΟΡΕΣ: Law vs custom in Roman Egypt', in *Le Monde Grec: Hommages à Cl. Preaux*, Brussels: 723–40, reprinted in H.C. Youtie (1981) *Scriptiunculae Posteriores*, Bonn: I, 17–34.

—— (1978) 'P. Mich. inv. 335 verso: A summary register of wheat land', *ZPE* 32: 237–40, reprinted in H.C. Youtie (1982) *Scriptiunculae Posteriores*, Bonn: II, 501–4.

Zacharias Rhetor (1904) *Sévère Patriarche d'Antioche 512–518: Textes Syriaques publiées, traduits et annotées* (ed. M.A. Kugener), Paris.

Zahrnt, M. (1988) 'Antinoopolis in Ägypten: Die hadrianische Gründung und ihre Privilegien in der neueren Forschung', *ANRW* II 10.1: 669–706.

Zanker, P. (1988) *The Power of Images in the Age of Augustus*, Ann Arbor.

Zauzich, K.-T. (1983) 'Demotische Texte römischer Zeit', in G. Grimm, H. Heinen and E. Winter (eds) *Das römisch-byzantinisch Ägypten. Akten des internationalen Symposions 26.–30. September 1978 in Trier*, Mainz: 77–80.

Zingale, L. Migliardi (1991) *I Testamenti romani nei papiri e nelle tavolette d'Egitto: Silloge di documenti dal I al IV seculo d.C.*, Turin.

—— (1997) *I Testamenti romani nei papiri e nelle tavolette d'Egitto: Silloge di documenti dal I al IV secolo d.C.*, Turin.

—— (1956) 'Priester und Tempel in Ägypten in den Zeiten nach der decianischen Christenverfolgung', *Akten des VIII internationalen Kongresses für Papyrologie, Wien 1955*, Vienna: 167–74.

Zucker, F. (1961) 'Verfahrensweisen in der Einführung gewisser Einrichtungen des Augustus in Ägypten', *RIDA* 8: 155–64.

INDEX LOCORUM

INDEX

283, 328–9; language 99–100,
202–3, 272, 283–4, 317, 328
Gregory of Tours 123
guilds 169, 208–14, 262, 273–7, 324,
336
gymnasiarch 62, 175, 188, 190, 191,
192, 194, 278
gymnasium 61, 142, 187, 189–90, 191,
195, 240, 244–5, 247, 254, 261,
269, 285, 399 n. 60; of Alexandria
219–21, 223–4, 228–9, 233; 'those
from the gymnasium' 2, 86–7, 92–3,
138–9, 146, 154–5, 325

Haarlem 182
Hadrian, emperor 160, 236, 240–2,
248, 397 n. 53; cult of 82, 191, 245,
261, 405 n. 134
Harvey, D. 32, 35
Hausmann 182
Haverfield, Francis 8, 13–14
headman, village 112, 304, 308
Hebrew 99
Heidegger, M. 33, 34
Heraclius, emperor 319
Herakleopolis 202–3, 248, 273
Herculaneum 6, 48, 53, 129
Herennia 88, 325
Hermetic corpus 249, 261
Hermonthis 198, 273
Hermopolis Magna 70, 73, 84, 111,
131–2, 143, 148, 190, 195, 207,
238–42, 253–4, 260–2, 275; baths
of 240, 242, 261; churches at 203,
240, 260, 262, 291, 294, 299–301,
317, 394 n. 21; desertion of 363;
excavations of 131–2, 174, 202–3,
260–1, 341, 363; food supply of 192,
276; gates of 132, 238, 261;
Kaisareion at 242, 261; *komasterion* in
215, 240; population of 331–3;
Sebasteion at 242, 261; *stoai* 254,
261–2; temples of 174, 202–3,
260–1; territory of 313, 333;
tetrastyla of 240, 260
Hibeh 244
Hibis 272
Hierakonapollon, bishop 308

Hillier, B. and Hanson, J. 21–2, 25–6,
33, 48
hippodrome 142, 195, 242
history, invention of 23, 33; *see also*
theory; historiographic
Horapollon 290
hospitals 294, 306, 313
housefuls 69–75, 77, 94–5
households 69–75, 93
houses (*see also* architecture, domestic
and particular sites) 14–15, 20, 30,
33, 44–127; Alexandrian 57, 100,
112–16, 121; descriptions of 58–9;
Greek 79–80; and immigrant
communities 51–2, 103; industrial
English 17–19, 34; Jewish 100–2,
224; Kabyle 16–17, 21, 48, 50–1; at
Karanis 52–8, 65–7, 93–4; medieval
79; middle-class, English 53, 55–6;
Moghul 103; Neolithic 33–4; niches
in 58, 67, 93; ownership of 69, 72;
Pharaonic 85, 94; prices 63–7; rental
of 84, 111–12; residence in 69–76,
115–16; Roman 14–16, 19–20,
48–9, 78–9, 94, 103; sale of 58,
68–9, 84, 86, 93; as scene of
socialization 50–1; topographical
concentration of 69
Hypatia 283, 288–9
hypomnematographos 188, 192, 250

icons 109, 115
idios logos 199–200 see *Gnomon of the idios
logos*
imperialism 7–8, 27–9
individualism 122–3
industrial revolution 4
inflation 258
inheritance 67
intertextuality 29
Ischyrion 82
Isidoros 225–8, 233
Isis 192, 198, 200, 215, 248–9, 283,
290
Islam 115, 180–1

Jeme 85, 104, 119–20, 121, 124, 134,
176, 291, 304, 308